Liberty and Justice

THE MODERN CONSTITUTION:
AMERICAN CONSTITUTIONAL DEVELOPMENT
SINCE 1865

Volume II

Edited by JAMES MORTON SMITH
CORNELL UNIVERSITY

and PAUL L. MURPHY
UNIVERSITY OF MINNESOTA

NEW YORK ALFRED A. KNOPF

THIS IS A BORZOI BOOK,
PUBLISHED BY ALFRED A. KNOPF, INC.

 Distributed by Random House, Inc. Published simultaneously in Toronto, Canada, by Random House of Canada Limited.

FIRST EDITION, *published 1958*

REVISED EDITION, VOLUME I, *published 1965*

REVISED EDITION, VOLUME II, *published 1968*

Reprinted Three Times
Fifth Printing, March 1973

Library of Congress Catalog Card Number: 65-6677

Manufactured in the United States of America, by H. Wolff Book Manufacturing Company, New York, New York.

This edition is Volume II of LIBERTY AND JUSTICE: *A Historical Record of American Constitutional Development,* published in one volume.

PREFACE

IN ANY ANALYSIS of the American tradition the theme of constitutional government is a central feature. Although no one would argue today that the history of the United States from colonial times to the present can be wholly understood in terms of its constitutional record, few would deny that a study of the evolution of our constitutional system gets as close to the mainstream of American development as any single historical approach. The mighty torrent of constitutional history is a blending of the troubled waters of political turmoil, the steady current of economic change, the swirling eddies of social tension, and the allegedly placid pools of intellectual ferment. To integrate constitutional evolution with these aspects of America's democratic development, therefore, we have stressed materials of broad historical significance above those of purely legal importance.

A study of the role of the Constitution in American society must deal not only with the shaping and interpretation of that historic document, but also with it as symbol and instrument. Today it is venerated for its age, its success, and its source of authority. Now the oldest written constitution in the world, it has survived the tumultuous twists that have characterized human affairs in America; it remains today, as it was when it was adopted, a vital instrument of government.

There is no doubt that the American doctrine of a written constitution owes much to English and European theorists, but it owes much more to colonial experience. James Madison, the "Father of the Constitution," observed during its formative period that although Americans had "paid a decent regard to the opinions of former times and other nations," they had not allowed "a blind veneration for antiquity, for custom, or for names, to overrule the suggestions of their own good sense, the knowledge of their own situations, and the lessons of their own experience." Although space limitations are partly responsible, it is chiefly the pragmatic nature of American constitutionalism and culture—the concentration on experience rather than logic, on practice rather than theory—which explains our emphasis on practical problems throughout the book.

From the standpoint of the history of ideas, it is probably true that few, if any, of the "self-evident" principles of the American Revolution, and perhaps of the American experience, were wholly new. The basic concept of popular government, which has since evolved into democracy; the principle of equality; the doctrine of limited government; the principle of federalism—all these had long histories as concepts. The peculiar contribution of the Founding Fathers was that they translated theory into practice, actualizing the doctrines by putting them to the acid test of experience in what Carl Becker has called "an experiment in democracy." Starting with the fundamental proposition of popular sovereignty—that government rests on the consent of the governed—they institutionalized this revolutionary concept by perfecting constitutional conventions, both state and federal.

By prescribing governmental limits with a written constitution, with built-in checks and balances, and with an additional bill of rights insisted upon by the rank and file, they broke with the monolithic concept of governmental sovereignty and actualized the principle of limited government—"a government of laws and not of men," as John Adams phrased it in the Massachusetts Constitution of 1780. At the same time, they divided the indivisible; by splitting sovereignty, they established a workable federal system.

In this second of two volumes delineating the constitutional development of the United States, we have sought to place in historical perspective the gradual adaptation of the eighteenth-century constitution to the needs and demands of the new post-Civil War industrial nation which emerged in the late nineteenth century and grew to a world power in the twentieth. Although such a reorientation of the original document has required use of the admendment process thirteen times in the years since 1865, the principal changes in interpretation, focus, and emphasis have been far more the result of Congressional and executive action and judicial readaptation.

This volume, like the first, has an interesting internal continuity. While the former emphasized the origin of constitutional government in the United States and its withstanding of the greatest internal challenge in our history—secession and civil war—the second begins with the constitutional attempts to grant full citizenship and all its rights to the freed Negro and ends with the Supreme Court and Congress returning to the completion of that process in the late 1950's and early 1960's. In between, we have sought to show why such a process took a hundred years; how emphasis upon economic factors and social and psychological ones, particularly healing the wounds of the war, effectively deflected it as a major focus for Americans; how Progressivism necessitated a new jurisprudence with a new emphasis upon public needs above personal and property rights; how the New Deal ushered in a new era of constitutionally-sanctioned "big government"; and how the challenge of war and cold war forced Americans, including those on the Supreme Court, to reassess the primary importance of revitalizing the eighteenth- and early nineteenth-century ideals of the Founding Fathers of liberty, equality, and a functioning democratic process.

As in Volume One, we have sought to illuminate these developments through a wide variety of source material, including statutes, reports, letters, interviews, and public manifestoes. To broaden the scope of the book we have condensed the introductory essays sharply and edited the documents as economically as possible. The diversified coverage will give the student some idea of the range of constitutional history and will demonstrate concretely the degree to which constitutional history is the history of the struggle of the American people with social, economic, political, religious, and diplomatic problems and challenges, encapsulated in and projected through the legal process. It will also allow the instructor to stress whatever aspects he desires.

The chronological and topical organization is designed to supply a framework of historical continuity and perspective, to help make comprehensible the transformation of the United States from an agrarian republic into a highly industrialized urban democracy, from a minor nation to a major world power. The documents in this book and its companion volume covering the period prior to 1869 were chosen to illustrate the integral role of constitutional evolution in these fundamental alterations of the American political, economic, and social order. In a sense, the documentary materials that follow systematize and symbolize the historical record not only of American constitutional development but also of the evolution of American society and politics.

However, we feel the materials also have broader implications. The ability of Americans to adapt traditional and, in some instances, ancient forms to the pressing and ever-changing needs of the dynamic modern world is an encouraging study of the practicality and pragmatism of a nation's people committed to the vitality and correctness of the republican principle and convinced of its ability to function effectively regardless of the magnitude of the challenges confronting it. The ability of Americans to transmit the wisdom of the ages, as their forefathers had done, and to bring it to bear constructively on new and unprecedented problems, should once again demonstrate the importance of a vital link with the past in combination with a sensitive and practical appreciation of the needs of the present and the challenges of the future.

This book is designed primarily for classroom use and reflects our belief in the modern applicability of the Jeffersonian doctrine that the diffusion of knowledge among the people is the only sure foundation "for the preservation of freedom and happiness," and that in the minds of youth, stretched by the experience of dealing with ideas and their varied application, the United States and other nations have their greatest natural resource.

Finally, it is impossible to estimate the extent of the valuable contribution which students have made to this revision—both as sounding-boards for the ideas and contentions set forth in the documents, and as critical analysts of their structure, content, and implications. They have inspired us to take a deeper and more profound look at the makers of American constitutionalism, particularly its judicial expounders, thus bringing about a renewed and more sophisticated learning process —as valuable and important to the professor as any he experiences.

October 21, 1966

JAMES MORTON SMITH *and* PAUL L. MURPHY
Ithaca, New York — *Minneapolis, Minnesota*

CONTENTS

Liberty and Justice

THE MODERN CONSTITUTION:

AMERICAN CONSTITUTIONAL DEVELOPMENT

SINCE 1865

CHAPTER XIII

Reconstruction

LIKE the issues of the Civil War, those of Reconstruction were extremely complex, involving social and economic tensions, political and psychological pressures. Similarly, postwar politicians dealt with these problems as they had in the prewar period, translating sectional antagonisms into constitutional controversies. The basic constitutional problem was to determine whether the seceded states were ever out of the Union. The South, by resorting to secession, had clearly indicated its belief in the voluntary nature of a loosely organized confederacy of sovereign states. The Northern wartime position denied the legality of secession, maintaining that the nation was an indestructible union of indestructible states. Projecting these Northern premises into the postwar period, the logical conclusion was that the Southern states were never out of the Union and thus continued to possess all the normal rights and privileges of statehood.

With the end of hostilities, constitutional expediency led to a hasty exchange of sectional wartime logic. Southern secessionists grasped the Northern view, denying that the Union had been dissolved despite their four-year struggle to secure that end. The North, triumphant in its efforts to preserve the American nation, virtually accepted secessionist principles in its desire to prove that the Southern states had forfeited their rights by leaving the federal Union. Only Lincoln was consistent in his constitutional views. Having argued from the beginning that secession was impossible, he avoided the theoretical and vindictive aspects of this thorny problem and, maintaining his Inaugural position that the Union was perpetual, advocated a direct restoration of the seceded states. In a proclamation of December 8, 1863, he formulated the Presidential plan of reconstruction. This magnanimous policy of "malice toward none, with charity for all" he reiterated in his second Inaugural Address (No. 112). Greatly concerned with reconciliation and reconstruction, Lincoln, in what proved to be his last public speech, rejected constitutional theorizing on the status of the Southern states as "a merely pernicious abstraction"; the pragmatic problem was "to again get them into their proper practical relation" (No. 113).

Presidential plans met congressional opposition from the outset. Radical Republicans, whether subscribing to the "conquered province" or "state suicide" theories, argued that rebellion converted the Confederate states into unorganized territory subject to congressional authority. The Wade-Davis Bill of 1864 actualized this concept, but Lincoln's pocket veto temporarily defeated the congressional attempt to wrest the reconstruction process from the President. Not to be denied the last word, defiant men issued the Wade-Davis Manifesto (No. 114), asserting "that the authority of Congress is paramount," and warning Lincoln to "confine himself to his executive duties . . . and leave political reorganization to Congress."

The assassination of Lincoln raised the hopes of Radicals that Andrew Johnson would endorse congressional control of reconstruction. When a congressional committee called on the new President, Senator Wade expressed their faith in him, declaring, "By the gods, there will be no trouble now in running the government." Harmony did not materialize, however, for Johnson adopted substantially the Lincolnian program. Moreover, subsequent actions of the Presidentially reconstructed states played into the hands of the Radicals. The North was especially aroused by the election of prominent ex-Confederates to high governmental offices and the adoption of "Black Codes" (No. 115), which represented the Southern solution to "the Negro problem." The congressional solution was embodied in the Freedman's Bureau Bill which Johnson vetoed in February, 1866.

Open war between the President and Congress ensued. Initial victory was Johnson's, for the Radicals failed to override his veto of the Freedmen's Bill. But Congress regained the initiative in March by passing the Civil Rights Act, a detailed measure designed to protect the freedman from legislative discrimination such as the Black Codes. Vetoed by President Johnson as an unwarrantable stride "toward centralization and the concentration of all legislative powers in the national government" (No. 116), it was quickly re-enacted, signaling the triumph of Congress. This *fait accompli* was formalized two months later in the report of a joint congressional committee on Reconstruction (No. 117). Asserting the supremacy of Congress over the President in outlining a reconstruction program, the report denied the right of representation to the Presidentially reconstructed Confederate states. The committee, fearful of the constitutionality of the Civil Rights Act, also rephrased that measure as the Fourteenth Amendment (No. 118A). One of the most important amendments ever added to the Constitution, it was remarkably inclusive in dealing with the various aspects of the Southern question. Ironically, Congress, while insisting that the Southern states were out of the Union, nevertheless required that they ratify this amendment. Since the citizenship clause of the Amendment was later interpreted by the Supreme Court as a protection of corporate wealth, the intentions of the framers, as revealed in the speech of Representative Thaddeus Stevens (No. 118B), are of more than historical significance.

With the overwhelming victory of the Radicals in the election of 1866, Congress's assertion of complete authority over Reconstruction challenged the principle of the separation of powers. Outraged by Johnson's consistent vetoes, Congress attempted to reduce the President to a figurehead, curbing his power to appoint new Supreme Court Justices, restricting, in the Command of the Army Act, his authority as commander in chief, and subordinating to Senate control his power to remove executive appointees. Johnson's veto of the Tenure of Office Act (No. 119) typified his cogent constitutional objections. After Congress overrode his veto, Johnson decided to test the constitutionality of the measure and dismissed Secretary of War Stanton, who had earlier assisted in drafting the veto message. Alleging violation of the Tenure of Office Act, the House impeached President Johnson for "high crimes and misdemeanors." Chief Justice Salmon P. Chase, a Lincoln appointee, presided over the Senate trial, but despite his insistence on fair legal procedure, the Radicals battered down legal obstacles. The Radical position on the nature of impeachable offenses is set forth by Senator Henry Wilson (No. 120A), later Vice-President under General Grant. Several Republicans resisted party pressure for conviction, and joined with Senator Grimes in his opposition to the "doctrine of the omnipotence of Congress" (No. 120B). By the narrow margin of one vote the President escaped conviction. Senator Lyman Trumbull, who bolted the Radicals, defended Johnson's position and observed that if the Chief Executive were removed for insufficient cause "no future President will be safe who happens to differ with a majority of the House and two thirds of the Senate on any measure deemed by them important, particularly if of a political character."

The congressional majority also attempted to subject the Supreme Court to its will. The Milligan decision of 1866 (Chapter XII) stood as a tacit challenge to the Radical program of military reconstruction instituted in 1867, and in the same year judicial invalidation of discriminatory legislation against ex-Confederates (The Test Oath Cases, No. 121) set off a bitter attack by the Radicals. Aware of its precarious position, the Court avoided the basic issue of the constitutionality of the Military Reconstruction Acts, refusing to enjoin President Johnson's enforcement on the ground that political processes were not subject to judicial restraint (*Mississippi v. Johnson,* No. 122). This temporarily mollified the Radicals, but when the Court agreed in February, 1868, to consider *Ex parte* McCardle, a case challenging by implication the legality of the Congressional program, the Radicals promptly deprived it of jurisdiction. In the only other important decision involving Reconstruction, the Court in *Texas v White* (Chapter XII), although accepting Lincoln's position on the indestructibility of the Union, acquiesced in Congress's authority to reconstruct the states.

The Presidential Plan

112. *Lincoln, Second Inaugural Address, March 4, 1865*

Richardson, ed., *Messages and Papers of the Presidents*, VI, 276-7.

At this second appearing to take the oath of the presidential office there is less occasion for an extended address than there was at the first. Then a statement somewhat in detail of a course to be pursued seemed fitting and proper. Now, at the expiration of four years, during which public declarations have been constantly called forth on every point and phase of the great contest which still absorbs the attention and engrosses the energies of the nation, little that is new could be presented. The progress of our arms, upon which all else chiefly depends, is as well known to the public as to myself, and it is, I trust, reasonably satisfactory and encouraging to all. With high hope for the future, no prediction in regard to it is ventured.

On the occasion corresponding to this four years ago all thoughts were anxiously directed to an impending civil war. All dreaded it, all sought to avert it. While the inaugural address was being delivered from this place, devoted altogether to *saving* the Union without war, insurgent agents were in the city seeking to *destroy* it without war—seeking to dissolve the Union and divide effects by negotiation. Both parties deprecated war, but one of them would *make* war rather than let the nation survive, and the other would *accept* war rather than let it perish, and the war came.

One-eighth of the whole population was colored slaves, not distributed generally over the Union, but localized in the southern part of it. These slaves constituted a peculiar and powerful interest. All knew that this interest was somehow the cause of the war. To strengthen, perpetuate, and extend this interest was the object for which the insurgents would rend the Union even by war, while the Government claimed no right to do more than to restrict the territorial enlargement of it. Neither party expected for the war the magnitude or the duration which it has already attained. Neither anticipated that the *cause* of the conflict might cease with or even before the conflict itself should cease. Each looked for an easier triumph, and a result less fundamental and astounding. Both read the same Bible and pray to the same God, and each invokes His aid against the other. It may seem strange that any men should dare to ask a just God's assistance in wringing their bread from the sweat of other men's faces, but let us judge not, that we be not judged. The prayers of both could not be answered. That of neither has been answered fully. The Almighty has His own purposes. "Woe unto the world because of offenses; for it must needs be that offenses come, but woe to that man by whom the offense cometh." If we shall suppose that American slavery is one of those offenses which, in the providence of God, must needs come, but which, having continued through His appointed time, He now wills to remove, and that He gives to both North and South this terrible war as the woe due to those by whom the offense came, shall we discern therein any departure from those divine attributes which the believers in a living God always ascribe to Him? Fondly do we hope, fervently do we pray, that this mighty scourge of war may speedily pass away. Yet, if God wills that it continue until all the wealth piled by the bondsman's two hundred and fifty years of unrequited toil shall be sunk, and until every drop of blood drawn with the lash shall be paid by another drawn with the sword, as was said three thousand years ago, so still it must be said, "The judgments of the Lord are true and righteous altogether."

With malice toward none, with charity for all, with firmness in the right as God gives us to see the right, let us strive on to finish the work we are in, to bind up the nation's wounds, to care for him who shall have borne the battle and for his widow and his orphan, to do all which may achieve and cherish a just and lasting peace among ourselves and with all nations.

113. *Lincoln, Speech on Reconciliation and Reconstruction, April 11, 1865*

John G. Nicolay and John Hay, eds., *Complete Works of Abraham Lincoln* (New York, 1894), II, 672.

We all agree that the seceded States, so called, are out of their proper practical relation with the Union, and that the sole object of the Government, civil and military, in regard to those States is to again get them into that proper practical relation. I believe that it is not only possible, but in fact easier, to do this without deciding or even considering whether these States have ever been out of the Union, than with it. Finding themselves safely at home, it would be utterly immaterial whether they had ever been abroad. Let us all join in doing the acts necessary to restore the proper practical relations between these States and the Union, and each forever after innocently indulge his own opinion whether in doing the acts he brought the States from without into the Union, or only gave them proper assistance, they never having been out of it. . . .

Congressional Opposition to Presidential Reconstruction

114. *The Wade-Davis Manifesto, August 5, 1864*

Edward McPherson, ed., *The Political History of the United States During the Great Rebellion* (4th ed., Washington, 1882), 332.

The President, by preventing this bill from becoming a law, holds the electoral votes of the rebel States at the dictation of his personal ambition. If those votes turn the balance in his favor, is it to be supposed that his competitor, defeated by such means, will acquiesce? If the rebel majority assert their supremacy in those States, and send votes which elect an enemy of the Government, will we not repel his claims? And is not that civil war for the Presidency inaugurated by the votes of rebel States?

Seriously impressed with these dangers,

Congress, *"the proper constituted authority,"* formally declared that there are no State governments in the rebel States, and provided for their erection at a proper time; and both the Senate and the House of Representatives rejected the Senators and Representatives chosen under the authority of what the President calls the free constitution and government of Arkansas. The President's proclamation *"holds for naught"* this judgment, and discards the authority of the Supreme Court, and strides headlong toward the anarchy his proclamation of the 8th of December inaugurated. If electors for President be allowed to be chosen in either of those States, a sinister light will be cast on the motives which induced the President to "hold for naught" the will of Congress rather than his government in Louisiana and Arkansas. That judgment of Congress which the President defies was the exercise of an authority exclusively vested in Congress by the Constitution to determine what is the established government in a State, and in its own nature and by the highest judicial authority binding on all other departments of the Government. . . .

A more studied outrage on the legislative authority of the people has never been perpetrated. Congress passed a bill; the President refused to approve it, and then by proclamation puts as much of it in force as he sees fit, and proposes to execute those parts by officers unknown to the laws of the United States and not subject to the confirmation of the Senate! The bill directed the appointment of Provisional Governors by and with the advice and consent of the Senate. The President, after defeating the law, proposes to appoint without law, and without the advice and consent of the Senate, *Military* Governors for the rebel States! He has already exercised this dictatorial usurpation in Louisiana, and he defeated the bill to prevent its limitation. . . .

The President has greatly presumed on the forbearance which the supporters of his Administration have so long practiced, in view of the arduous conflict in which we are engaged, and the reckless ferocity of our political opponents. But he must understand that our support is of a cause and not of a man; that the authority of Congress is paramount and must be respected; that the whole body of the Union men of Congress will not submit to be impeached by him of rash and unconstitutional legislation; and if he wishes our support, he must confine himself to his executive duties—to obey and execute, not make the laws—to suppress by arms armed rebellion, and leave political reorganization to Congress. If the supporters of the Government fail to insist on this, they become responsible for the usurpations which they fail to rebuke, and are justly liable to the indignation of the people whose rights and security, committed to their keeping, they sacrifice. Let them consider the remedy for these usurpations, and, having found it, fearlessly execute it.

115. *The Presidentially Reconstructed States Enact "Black Codes"*

Acts of the Session of 1865-1866 of the General Assembly of Alabama (Montgomery, 1866), 119-21.

SECTION 1. . . . That the commissioners' court of any county in this State may purchase, rent, or provide such lands, buildings and other property as may be necessary for a poor-house, or house of correction for any such county, and may appoint suitable officers for the management thereof, and make all necessary by-laws, rules and regulations for the government of the inmates thereof, and cause the same to be enforced; but in no case shall the punishment inflicted exceed hard labor, either in or out of said house; the use of chain-gangs, putting in stocks, if necessary, to prevent escapes; such reasonable correction as a parent may inflict upon a stubborn, refractory child; and solitary confinement for not longer than one week, on bread and water; and may cause to be hired out such as are vagrants, to work in chain-gangs or otherwise, for the length of time for which they are sentenced; and the proceeds of such hiring must be paid into the county treasury, for the benefits of the helpless in said poor-house, or house of correction.

SEC. 2. . . . That the following persons are vagrants in addition to those already declared to be vagrants by law, or that may hereafter be so declared by law; a stubborn or refractory servant; a laborer or servant who loiters away his time, or refuses to comply with any contract for a term of service, without just cause; and such person may be sent to the house of correction in the county in which such offense is committed; and for want of such house of correction, the common jail of the county may be used for that purpose.

SEC. 3. . . . That when a vagrant is found, any justice of the peace of the county must, upon complaint made upon oath, or on his own knowledge, issue his warrant to the sheriff or any constable of the county, to bring such person before him; and if, upon examination and hearing of testimony, it appears to the justice, that such person is a vagrant, he shall assess a fine of fifty dollars and costs against such vagrant; and in default of payment, he must commit such vagrant to the house of correction; or if no such house, to the common jail of the county, for a term not exceeding six months, and until such fine, costs and charges are paid, or such party is otherwise discharged by law; *Provided,* That when committed to jail under this section, the commissioners' court may cause him to be hired out in like manner as in section one of this act.

SEC. 4. . . . That when any person shall be convicted of vagrancy, as provided for in this act, the justice of the peace, before whom such conviction is had, may, at his discretion, either commit such person to jail, to the house of correction, or hire such person to any person who will hire the same, for a period not longer than six months, for cash, giving three days' notice of the time and place of hiring; and the proceeds of such hiring, after paying all costs and charges, shall be paid into the county treasury for the benefit of the helpless in the poor-house.

SEC. 5. . . . That all fines received by any justice of the peace under the provisions of this act, shall be paid into the county treasury for the purposes as set forth in section one of this act.

SEC. 6. . . . That it shall be the duty of the justice of the peace to settle with the county treasurer at least once a month, for all fines received by him under this act, and for a wilful default so to do, he shall be guilty of a misdemeanor; and upon conviction in any court having jurisdiction, shall be fined in double the amount so received or collected by him, and all costs of suit.

SEC. 7. . . . That the court of county commissioners of each county shall have full and complete control of the public works and public highways therein, and shall make all contracts in relation thereto; and shall have power to appoint a superintendent of said public works and highways, under such rules and regulations as said court shall determine; and any justice of the peace trying any cause under this act, on conviction, shall have power to sentence such vagrant to work on said public works and highways, under the supervision of such superintendent, for not more than forty days.

116. *President Johnson's Veto of the Civil Rights Act, March 27, 1866*

Richardson, ed., *Messages and Papers of the Presidents,* VI, 405-13.

I regret that the bill, which has passed both Houses of Congress . . . contains provisions which I can not approve consistently with my sense of duty to the whole people and my obligations to the Constitution. . . .

By the first section of the bill all persons born in the United States and not subject to any foreign power . . . are declared to be citizens of the United States. . . . It does not purport to give these classes of persons any status as citizens of States, except that which may result from their status as citizens of the United States. The power to confer the right of State citizenship is just as exclusively with the several States as the power to confer the right of Federal citizenship is with Congress.

The right of Federal citizenship thus to be conferred on the several excepted races before mentioned is now for the first time proposed to be given by law. If, as is claimed by many, all persons who are native born already are, by virtue of the Constitution, citizens of the United States, the passage of the pending bill can not be necessary to make them such. If, on the other hand, such persons are not citizens, as may be assumed from the proposed legislation to make them such, the grave question presents itself whether, when eleven of the thirty-six States are unrepresented in Congress at the present time, it is sound policy to make our entire colored population and all other excepted classes citizens of the United States. Four millions of them have just emerged from slavery into freedom. . . . It may also be asked whether it is necessary that they should be declared citizens in order that they may be secured in the enjoyment of the civil rights proposed to be conferred by the bill. Those rights are, by Federal as well as State laws, secured to all domiciled aliens and foreigners, even before the completion of the process of naturalization; and it may safely be assumed that the same enactments are sufficient to give like protection and benefits to those for whom this bill provides special legislation. Besides, the policy of the Government from its origin to the present time seems to have been that persons who are strangers to and unfamiliar with our institutions and our laws should pass through a certain probation, at the end of which, before attaining the coveted prize, they must give evidence of their fitness to receive and to exercise the rights of citizens as contemplated by the Constitution of the United States. The bill in effect proposes a discrimination against large numbers of intelligent, worthy, and patriotic foreigners, and in favor of the negro, to whom, after long years of bondage, the avenues to freedom and intelligence have just now been suddenly opened. . . .

The first section of the bill also contains an enumeration of the rights to be enjoyed by these classes so made citizens "in every State and Territory in the United States." These rights are "to make and enforce contracts; to sue, be parties, and give evidence; to inherit, purchase, lease, sell, hold, and convey real and personal property," and to have "full and equal benefit of all laws and proceedings for the security of person and property as is enjoyed by white citizens." So, too, they are made subject to the same punishment, pains, and penalties in common with white citizens, and to none other. Thus a perfect equality of the white and colored races is attempted to be fixed by Federal law in every State of the Union over the vast field of State jurisdiction covered by these enumerated rights. In no one of these can any State ever exercise any power of discrimination between the different races. . . .

The object of the second section of the bill is to afford discriminating protection to colored persons in the full enjoyment of all the rights secured to them by the preceding section. . . .

This provision of the bill seems to be unnecessary, as adequate judicial remedies could be adopted to secure the desired end without invading the immunities of legislators, always important to be preserved in the interest of public liberty; without assailing the independence of the judiciary, always essential to the preservation of individual rights; and without impairing the efficiency of ministerial officers, always necessary for the maintenance of public peace and order. The remedy proposed by this section seems to be in this respect not only anomalous, but unconstitutional; for the Constitution guarantees nothing with certainty if it does not insure to the several States the right of making and executing laws in regard to all matters arising within their jurisdiction, subject only to the restriction that in cases of conflict with the Constitution and constitutional laws of the United States the latter should be held to be the supreme law of the land. . . .

In all our history, in all our experience as a people living under Federal and State law, no such system as that contemplated by the details of this bill has ever before been proposed or adopted. They establish for the security of the colored race safeguards which go infinitely beyond any that the General Government has ever provided for the white race. In fact, the distinction of race and color is by the bill made to operate in favor of the colored and against the white race. They interfere with the municipal legislation of the States, with the relations existing exclusively between a State and its citizens, or between inhabitants of the same State—an absorption and assumption of power by the General Government which, if acquiesced in, must sap and destroy our federative system of limited powers and break down the barriers which preserve the rights of the States. It is another step, or rather stride, toward centralization and the concentration of all legislative powers in the National Government. The tendency of the bill must be to resuscitate the spirit of rebellion and to arrest the progress of those influences which are more closely drawing around the States the bonds of union and peace. . . .

117. *Congress Presents a Plan of Radical Reconstruction, June 18, 1866*

Report of the Joint Committee on Reconstruction, 39th Cong., 1st Sess. (1866), xiii-xxi *passim.*

Your committee came to the consideration of the subject referred to them with the most anxious desire to ascertain what was the condition of the people of the States recently in insurrection, and what, if anything, was necessary to be done before restoring them to the full enjoyment of all their original privileges. It was undeniable that the war into which they had plunged the country had materially changed their relations to the people of the loyal States. Slavery had been abolished by constitutional amendment. A large proportion of the population had become, instead of mere chattels, free men and citizens. Through all the past struggle these had remained true and loyal, and had, in large numbers, fought on the side of the Union. It was impossible to abandon them, without securing them their rights as free men and citizens. The whole civilized world would have cried out against such base ingratitude, and the bare idea is offensive to all right-thinking men. Hence it became important to inquire what could be done to secure their rights, civil and political. It was evident to your committee that adequate security could only be found in appropriate constitutional provisions. By an original provision of the Constitution, representation is based on the whole number of free persons in each State, and three-fifths of all other persons. When all became free, representation for all necessarily follows. As a consequence the inevitable effect of the rebellion would be to increase the political power of the insurrectionary States, whenever they should be allowed to resume their positions as States of the Union. As representation is by the Constitution based upon population, your committee did not think it advisable to recommend a change of that basis. The increase of representation necessarily resulting from the abolition of slavery was considered the most important element in the questions arising out of the changed condition of affairs, and the necessity for some fundamental action in this regard seemed imperative. It appeared to your committee that the rights of these persons by whom the basis of representation had been thus increased should be recognized by the general government. While slaves they were not considered as having any rights, civil or political. It did not seem just or proper that all the political advantages derived from their becoming free should be confined to their former masters, who had fought against the Union, and withheld from themselves, who had always been loyal. Slavery, by building up a ruling and dominant class, had produced a spirit of oligarchy adverse to republican institutions, which finally inaugurated civil war. The tendency of continuing the domination of such a class, by leaving it in the exclusive possession of political power, would be to encourage the same spirit, and lead to a similar result. Doubts were entertained whether Congress had power, even under the amended Constitution, to prescribe the qualifications of voters in a State, or could act directly on the subject. It was doubtful, in the opinion of your committee, whether the States would consent to surrender a power they had always exercised, and to which they were attached. As the best if not the only method of surmounting the difficulty, and as eminently just and proper in itself, your committee came to the conclusion that political power should be possessed in all the States exactly in proportion as the right of suffrage should be granted, without distinction of color or race. This it was thought would leave the whole question with the people of each State, holding out to all the advantage of increased political power as an inducement to allow all to participate in its exercise. Such a provision would be in its nature gentle and persuasive, and would lead, it was hoped, at no distant day, to an equal participation of all, without distinction, in all the rights and privileges of citizenship, thus affording a full and adequate protection to all classes of citizens, since all would have, through the ballot-box, the power of self-protection. . . .

The conclusion of your committee therefore is, that the so-called Confederate States are not, at present, entitled to representation in the Congress of the United States; that, before allowing such representation, adequate security for future peace and safety should be required; that this can only be found in such changes of the organic law as shall determine the civil rights and privileges of all citizens in all parts of the republic, shall place representation on an equitable basis, shall fix a stigma upon treason, and protect the loyal people against future claims for the expenses incurred in support of rebellion and for manumitted slaves, together with an express grant of power in Congress to enforce those provisions. To this end they offer a joint resolution for amending the Constitution of the United States, and the two several bills designed to carry the same into effect, before referred to. . .

118. *Congress Restricts State Infringements of Civil Rights*

A. THE FOURTEENTH AMENDMENT

Proposed June 16, 1866; adopted July 28, 1868.

SECTION 1. All persons born or naturalized in the United States, and subject to the jurisdiction thereof, are citizens of the United States and of the State wherein they reside. No State shall make or enforce any law which shall abridge the privileges or immunities of citizens of the United States; nor shall any State deprive any person of life, liberty, or property, without due process of law; nor deny to any person within its jurisdiction the equal protection of the laws.

SECTION 2. Representatives shall be apportioned among the several States according to their respective numbers, counting the whole number of persons in each State, excluding Indians not taxed. But when the right to vote at any election for the choice of electors for President and Vice-President of the United States, Representatives in Congress, the executive and judicial officers of a State, or the members of the legislature thereof, is denied to any of the male inhabitants of such State, being twenty-one years of age, and citizens of the United States, or in any way abridged, except for participation in rebellion, or other crime, the basis of representation therein shall be reduced in the proportion which the number of such male citizens shall bear to the whole number of male citizens twenty-one years of age in such State.

SECTION 3. No person shall be a Senator or Representative in Congress, or elector of President and Vice-President, or hold any office, civil or military, under the United States or under any State, who, having previously taken an oath as a member of Congress, or as an officer of the United States, or as a member of any State legislature, or as an executive or judicial officer of any State, to support the Constitution of the United States, shall have engaged in insurrection or rebellion against the same, or given aid or comfort to the enemies thereof. But Congress may, by a vote of two-thirds of each house, remove such disability.

SECTION 4. The validity of the public debt of the United States, authorized by law, including debts incurred for payment of pensions and bounties for services in suppressing insurrection or rebellion, shall not be questioned. But neither the United States nor any State shall assume or pay any debt or obligation incurred in aid of insurrection or rebellion against the United States, or any claim for the loss or emancipation of any slave; but all such debts, obligations, and claims shall be held illegal and void.

SECTION 5. The Congress shall have power to enforce, by appropriate legislation, the provisions of this article.

B. THE FOURTEENTH AMENDMENT: "THE FINAL TRIUMPH OF THE RIGHTS OF MAN"

Thaddeus Stevens, May 8, 1866, *Congressional Globe*, 39th Cong., 1st Sess., XXXVI, Pt. 3, 2459-60.

This proposition is not all that the committee desired. It falls far short of my wishes, but it fulfills my hopes. I believe it is all that can be obtained in the present state of public opinion. . . .

I can hardly believe that any person can

be found who will not admit that every one of these propositions [in the first section] is just. They are all asserted, in some form or other, in our DECLARATION or organic law. But the Constitution limits only the action of Congress, and is not a limitation on the States. This amendment supplies that defect, and allows Congress to correct the unjust legislation of the States, so far that the law which operates upon one man shall operate *equally* upon all. Whatever law punishes a white man for a crime shall punish the black man precisely in the same way and to the same degree. Whatever law protects the white man shall afford "equal" protection to the black man. Whatever means of redress is afforded to one shall be afforded to all. Whatever law allows the white man to testify in court shall allow the man of color to do the same. These are great advantages over their present codes. Now different degrees of punishment are inflicted, not on account of the magnitude of the crime, but according to the color of the skin. Now color disqualifies a man from testifying in courts, or being tried in the same way as white men. I need not enumerate these partial and oppressive laws. Unless the Constitution should restrain them, those States will all, I fear, keep up this discrimination, and crush to death the hated freedmen. . . .

The second section I consider the most important in the article. It fixes the basis of representation in Congress. If any State shall exclude any of her adult male citizens from the elective franchise, or abridge that right, she shall forfeit her right to representation in the same proportion. The effect of this provision will be either to compel the States to grant universal suffrage or so to shear them of their power as to keep them forever in a hopeless minority in the national Government, both legislative and executive. If they do not enfranchise the freedmen, it would give to the rebel States but thirty-seven Representatives. Thus shorn of their power, they would soon become restive. Southern pride would not long brook a hopeless minority. True, it will take two, three, possibly five years before they conquer their prejudices sufficiently to allow their late slaves to become their equals at the polls. That short delay would not be injurious. In the mean time the freedmen would become more enlightened, and more fit to discharge the high duties of their new condition. In that time, too, the loyal Congress could mature their laws and so amend the Constitution as to secure the rights of every human being, and render disunion impossible. . . .

The third section may encounter more difference of opinion here. Among the people I believe it will be the most popular of all the provisions; it prohibits rebels from voting for members of Congress and electors of President until 1870. My only objection to it is that it is too lenient. . . . I would be glad to see it extended to 1876, and to include all State and municipal as well as national elections. In my judgment we do not sufficiently protect the loyal men of the rebel States from the vindictive persecutions of their victorious rebel neighbors. Still I will move no amendment, nor vote for any, lest the whole fabric should tumble to pieces.

I need say nothing of the fourth section, for none dare object to it who is not himself a rebel. To the friend of justice, the friend of the Union, of the perpetuity of liberty, and the final triumph of the rights of man and their extension to every human being, let me say, sacrifice as we have done your peculiar views, and instead of vainly insisting upon the instantaneous operation of all that is right accept what is possible, and "all these things shall be added unto you."

Constitutional Challenges to Congressional Reconstruction

119. *President Johnson Vetoes the Tenure of Office Act, March 2, 1867*

Richardson, ed., *Messages and Papers of the Presidents,* VI, 492-7.

I have carefully examined the bill "to regulate the tenure of certain civil offices." . . . In effect the bill provides that the President shall not remove from their places any of the civil officers whose terms of service are not limited by law without the advice and consent of the Senate of the United States. The bill in this respect conflicts, in my judgment, with the Constitution of the United States. The question, as Congress is well aware, is by no means a new one. That the power of removal is constitutionally vested in the President of the United States is a principle which has been not more distinctly declared by judicial authority and judicial commentators than it has been uniformly practiced upon by the legislative and executive departments of the Government. . . .

The question has often been raised in subsequent times of high excitement, and the practice of the Government has, nevertheless, conformed in all cases to the decision thus early made.

The question was revived during the Administration of President Jackson, who made . . . a very large number of removals, which were made an occasion of close and rigorous scrutiny and remonstrance. The subject was long and earnestly debated in the Senate, and the early construction of the Constitution was, nevertheless, freely accepted as binding and conclusive upon Congress.

The question came before the Supreme Court in January, 1839, *ex parte* Hennen. It was declared . . . that the power of removal from office was a subject much disputed, and upon which a great diversity of opinion was entertained in the early history of the Government. This related, however, to the power of the President to remove officers appointed with the concurrence of the Senate, and the great question was whether the removal was to be by the President alone or with the concurrence of the Senate, both constituting the appointing power. No one denied the power of the President and Senate jointly to remove where the tenure of the office was not fixed by the Constitution, which was a full recognition of the principle that the power of removal was incident to the power of appointment; but it was very early adopted as a practical construction of the Constitution that this power was vested in the President alone. . . .

Thus has the important question presented by this bill been settled, in the language of the late Daniel Webster . . . by construction, settled by precedent, settled by the practice of the Government, and settled by statute. . . .

120. *The Impeachment of President Johnson*

A. THE RADICAL INDICTMENT

Speech by Senator Henry Wilson, 1868, *Proceedings in the Trial of Andrew Johnson, President of the United States, before the United States Senate . . .* (Washington, 1868), 952-3.

High misdemeanors may or may not be violations of the laws. High misdemeanors may, in my judgment, be misbehavior in office detrimental to the interests of the nation, dangerous to the rights of the people, or dishonoring to the government. I entertain the conviction that the framers of the Constitution intended to impose the high duty upon the House of Representatives to arraign the Chief Magistrate for such misbehavior in office as injured, dishonored, or endangered the nation, and to impose upon the Senate the duty of trying, convicting, and removing the Chief Magistrate proved guilty of such misbehavior. Believing this to be the intention of the framers of the Constitution and its true meaning; believing that the power should be exercised whenever the security of the country and the liberties of the people imperatively demand it; and believing by the evidence adduced to prove the charges of violating the Constitution and the tenure-of-office act, and by the confessed and justified acts of the President, that he is guilty of high misdemeanors, I unhesitatingly vote for his conviction and removal from his high office.

The President is charged by the House of Representatives with violating the Constitution and the tenure-of-office act in removing Mr. Stanton from the office of Secretary of War, and in appointing Adjutant General Thomas Secretary of War *ad interim*. The removal of Mr. Stanton and the appointment of Adjutant General Thomas, and the violation of the tenure-of-office act, if Mr. Stanton be within that act, stand confessed and justified in the answer of the President to the charges of the House of Representatives. The answer of the President, without any other evidence, is to my mind conclusive evidence of his guilt. Upon his answer, confessions, assumptions, and justifications I have no hesitation in recording my vote of "guilty." The assumptions of power put forth by the President in his defense cannot but startle and alarm all men who would maintain the just powers of all branches of the Government. Had the President inadvertently violated the Constitution and the laws; had he pleaded in justification misconstruction of the Constitution and the laws, I might have hesitated to vote for his conviction. But he claims the right to remove civil officers and appoint others *ad interim* during the session of the Senate. If that claim of power is admitted by a vote of acquittal, the President can remove during the session of the Senate tens of thousands of civil officers with their millions of compensation, and appoint his own creatures to fill their places without the advice and consent of the Senate, and thus nullify that provision of the Constitution that empowers the Senate to give its advice and consent to appointments.

Not content with this assumption of power, the President claims the right to pronounce a law of Congress unconstitutional, to refuse to execute it, although he is sworn to do so, and to openly violate it with a view of testing its constitutionality in the courts, although no means may exist for months or years to come, to test the constitutionality of the law so violated in the judicial tribunals of the country.

The President claims and has exercised the right to declare Congress an unconstitutional body, incapable of enacting laws or of proposing amendments to the Constitution; to hold the laws in abeyance; to refuse to execute them, and to defiantly violate them in order to test their constitutionality. These are the positions assumed by Andrew Johnson. These assumptions, if admitted, radically change the character of our Government. If they are sustained by a verdict of acquittal, the President ceases to be the servant of the law, and becomes the master of the people; and a law-non-executing power, a law-defying power, a law-breaking power is created within the Government. Instead of an Executive bound to the faithful execution of the laws of Congress, the nation has an Executive bound only to execute the laws according to his own caprices, whims, and sovereign pleasure. Never can I assent, by a vote of acquittal, to executive assumptions so unconstitutional, so subversive of the Government, so revolutionary in their scope and tendency. These assumptions will introduce into our constitutional system, into our government of nicely adjusted parts, derangement, disorganization, and anarchy. . . .

B. "I AM NO CONVERT TO ANY DOCTRINE OF THE OMNIPOTENCE OF CONGRESS."

Senator James W. Grimes, *Trial of Andrew Johnson*, 871-6.

It is clear to my mind that the *proviso* does not include, and was not intended to include, Mr. Stanton's case. It is not possible to apply to his case the language of the proviso unless we suppose it to have been intended to legislate him out of office; a conclusion, I consider, wholly inadmissible. He was appointed by President Lincoln during his first term of office. He cannot hereafter go out of office at the end of the term of the President by whom he was appointed. That term was ended before the law was passed. The proviso, therefore, cannot have been intended to make a rule for his case; and it is shown that it was not intended. This was plainly declared in debate by the conference committee, both in the Senate and in the House of Representatives, when the proviso was introduced and its effect explained. The meaning and effect of the *proviso* were then explained and understood to be that the only tenure of the Secretaries provided for by this law was a tenure to end with the term of service of the President by whom they were appointed, and as this new tenure could not include Mr. Stanton's case, it was here explicitly declared that it did not include it. . . .

I come now to the question of intent. Admitting that the President had no power under the law to issue the order to remove Mr. Stanton and appoint General Thomas Secretary for the Department of War *ad interim*, did he issue those orders with a manifest *intent* to violate the laws and "the Constitution of the United States," as charged in the articles, or did he issue them, as he says he did, with a view to have the constitutionality of the tenure-of-office act judicially decided?

It is apparent to my mind that the President thoroughly believed the tenure-of-office act to be unconstitutional and void. He was so advised by every member of his cabinet when the bill was presented to him for his approval in February, 1867 . . . including the Attorney General, whose duty it is made by law to give legal advice to him, including the Secretary for the Department of War, also an eminent lawyer and an Attorney General of the United States under a former administration. . . . The question [is] whether Mr. Stanton's case is included in the provisions of that act. If it was not, as I think it clearly was not, then the question of intent is not in issue, for he did no unlawful act. If it was included, then I ask whether, in view of those facts, the President's *guilty intent* to do an unlawful act "shines with such a clear and certain light" as to justify, to require us to pronounce him guilty of a high constitutional crime or misdemeanor? . . .

It is not denied, I think, that the constitutional validity of this law could not be tested before the courts unless a case was made and presented to them. No such case could be made unless the President made a removal. That act of his would necessarily be the basis on which the case would rest. He is sworn to " preserve, protect, and defend the Constitution of the United States." He must *defend* it against all encroachments, from whatever quarter. A question arose between the legislative and executive departments as to their relative powers in the matter of removals and appointments to office. That question was, Does the Constitution confer on the President the power which the tenure-of-office act seeks to take away? It was a question manifestly of construction and interpretation. The Constitution has provided a common arbiter in such cases of controversy—the Supreme Court of the United States. Before that tribunal can take jurisdiction a removal must be made. The President attempted to give the court jurisdiction in that way. For doing so he is impeached, and for the reason, as the Managers say, that—

> He has no authority under the Constitution, or by any law, to enter into any schemes or plans for the purpose of testing the validity of the laws of the country, either judicially or otherwise.

If this be true, then if the two Houses of Congress should pass by a two-thirds vote over the President's veto an act depriving the President of the right to exercise the pardoning power, and he should exercise that power nevertheless, or if he should exercise it only in a single case for the purpose of testing the constitutionality of the law, he would be guilty of a high crime and misdemeanor and impeachable accordingly. The Managers' theory establishes at once the complete supremacy of Congress over the other branches of government. I can give my assent to no such doctrine.

This was a *punitive* statute. It was directed against the President alone. It interfered with the prerogatives of his department as recognized from the foundation of the Government. It wrested from him powers which, according to the legislative and judicial construction of 80 years, had been bestowed upon him by the Constitution itself. In my opinion it was not only proper, but it was his duty to cause the disputed question to be determined in the manner and by the tribunal established for such purposes. This Government can only be preserved and the liberty of the people maintained by preserving intact the co-ordinate branches of it—legislative, executive, judicial—alike. I am no convert to any doctrine of the omnipotence of Congress. . . .

121. *The Test Oath Cases: Bills of Attainder and Ex Post Facto Laws*

Ex parte Garland, 4 Wallace 333 (1867).

FIELD, J.: . . . The petitioner . . . now produces his pardon, and asks permission to continue to practise as an attorney and counsellor of the court without taking the oath required by the act of January 24, 1865, and the rule of the court, which he is unable to take, by reason of the offices he held under the Confederate government. He rests his application principally upon two grounds:

1st. That the act of January 24th, 1865, so far as it affects his status in the court, is unconstitutional and void; and,

2d. That, if the act be constitutional, he is released from compliance with its provisions by the pardon of the President. . . .

The statute is directed against parties who have offended in any of the particulars embraced by these clauses. And its object is to exclude them from the profession of the law, or at least from its practice in the courts of the United States. As the oath prescribed cannot be taken by these parties, the act, as against them, operates as a legislative decree of perpetual exclusion. And exclusion from any of the professions or any of the ordinary avocations of life for past conduct can be regarded in no other light than as punishment for such conduct. The exaction of the oath is the mode provided for ascertaining the parties upon whom the act is intended to operate, and instead of lessening, increases its objectionable character. All enactments of this kind partake of the nature of bills of pains and penalties, and are subject to the constitutional inhibition against the passage of bills of attainder, under which general designation they are included.

In the exclusion which the statute adjudges it imposes a punishment for some of the acts specified which were not punishable at the time they were committed; and for other of the acts it adds a new punishment to that before prescribed, and it is thus brought within the further inhibition of the Constitution against the passage of an *ex post facto* law. . . .

The legislature may undoubtedly prescribe qualifications for the office, to which he must conform, as it may, where it has exclusive jurisdiction, prescribe qualifications for the pursuit of any of the ordinary avocations of life. The question, in this case, is not as to the power of Congress to prescribe qualifications, but whether that power has been exercised as a means for the infliction of punishment, against the prohibition of the Constitution. That this result cannot be effected indirectly by a State under the form of creating qualifications we have held in the case of *Cummings v. The State of Missouri,* and the reasoning by which that conclusion was reached applies equally to similar action on the part of Congress.

This view is strengthened by a consideration of the effect of the pardon produced by the petitioner, and the nature of the pardoning power of the President.

The Constitution provides that the President "shall have power to grant reprieves and pardons for offenses against the United States, except in cases of impeachment."

The power thus conferred is unlimited, with the exception stated. It extends to every offense known to the law, and may be exercised at any time after its commission, either before legal proceedings are taken, or during their pendency, or after conviction and judgment. This power of the President is not subject to legislative control. Congress can neither limit the effect of his pardon, nor exclude from its exercise any class of offenders. The benign prerogative of mercy reposed in him cannot be fettered by any legislative restrictions.

Such being the case, the inquiry arises as to the effect and operation of a pardon, and on this point all the authorities concur. A pardon reaches both the punishment prescribed for the offense and the guilt of the offender; and when the pardon is full, it releases the punishment and blots out of existence the guilt, so that in the eye of the law the offender is as innocent as if he had never committed the offense. If granted before conviction, it prevents any of the penalties and disabilities consequent upon conviction from attaching; if granted after conviction, it removes the penalties and disabilities, and restores him to all his civil rights; it makes him, as it were, a new man, and gives him a new credit and capacity. . . .

The pardon produced by the petitioner is a full pardon "for all offences by him committed, arising from participation, direct or implied, in the Rebellion," and is subject to certain conditions which have been complied with. The effect of this pardon is to relieve the petitioner from all penalties and disabilities attached to the offence of treason, committed by his participation in the Rebellion. So far as that offence is concerned, he is thus placed beyond the reach of punishment of any kind. But to exclude him, by reason of that offence, from continuing in the enjoyment of a previously acquired right, is to enforce a punishment for that offence notwithstanding the pardon. If such exclusion can be effected by the exaction of an expurgatory oath covering the offence, the pardon may be avoided, and that accomplished indirectly which cannot be reached by direct legislation. It is not within the constitutional power of Congress to inflict punishment beyond the reach of executive clemency. From the petitioner, therefore, the oath required by the act of January 24th, 1865, could not be exacted, even if that act were not subject to any other objection than the one thus stated.

It follows, from the views expressed, that the prayer of the petitioner must be granted.

122. *The Court Sidesteps the Reconstruction Issue*

Mississippi v. Johnson, 4 Wallace 475 (1867).

CHASE, C.J.: A motion was made, some days since, in behalf of the State of Mississippi, for leave to file a bill in the name of the State, praying this court perpetually to enjoin and restrain Andrew Johnson, President of the United States, and E. O. C. Ord, general commanding in the District of Mississippi and Arkansas, from executing, or in any manner carrying out, certain acts of Congress therein named.

The acts referred to are those of March 2d and March 23d, 1867, commonly known as the Reconstruction Acts. . . .

The single point which requires consideration is this: Can the President be restrained by injunction from carrying into effect an act of Congress alleged to be unconstitutional? . . .

By the first of these acts he is required to assign generals to command in the several military districts, and to detail sufficient military force to enable such officers to discharge their duties under the law. By the supplementary act, other duties are imposed on the several commanding generals, and these duties must necessarily be performed under the supervision of the President as commander-in-chief. The duty thus imposed on the President is in no just sense ministerial. It is purely executive and political.

An attempt on the part of the judicial department of the government to enforce the performance of such duties by the President might be justly characterized, in the language of Chief Justice Marshall, as "an absurd and excessive extravagance."

It is true that in the instance before us the interposition of the court is not sought to enforce action by the Executive under constitutional legislation, but to restrain such action under legislation alleged to be unconstitutional. But we are unable to perceive that this circumstance takes the case out of the general principles which forbid judicial interference with the exercise of Executive discretion.

It was admitted in the argument that the application now made to us is without a precedent; and this is of much weight against it. . . .

The fact that no such application was ever before made in any case indicates the general judgment of the profession that no such application should be entertained.

It will hardly be contended that Congress [*sic*] can interpose, in any case, to restrain the enactment of an unconstitutional law; and yet how can the right to judicial interposition to prevent such an enactment, when the purpose is evident and the execution of that purpose certain, be distinguished, in principle, from the right to such interposition against the execution of such a law by the President?

The Congress is the legislative department of the government; the President is the executive department. Neither can be restrained in its action by the judicial department; though the acts of both, when performed, are, in proper cases, subject to its cognizance.

The impropriety of such interference will be clearly seen upon consideration of its possible consequences.

Suppose the bill filed and the injunction prayed for allowed. If the President refuse obedience, it is needless to observe that the court is without power to enforce its process. If, on the other hand, the President complies with the order of the court and refuses to execute the acts of Congress, is it not clear that a collision may occur between the executive and legislative departments of the government? May not the House of Representatives impeach the President for such refusal? And in that case could this court interfere, in behalf of the President, thus endangered by compliance with its mandate, and restrain by injunction the Senate of the United States from sitting as a court of impeachment? Would the strange spectacle be offered to the public world of an attempt by this court to arrest proceedings in that court?

These questions answer themselves. . . .

It has been suggested that the bill contains a prayer that, if the relief sought cannot be had against Andrew Johnson, as President, it may be granted against Andrew Johnson as a citizen of Tennessee. But it is plain that relief as against the execution of an act of Congress by Andrew Johnson, is relief against its execution by the President. A bill praying an injunction against the execution of an act of Congress by the incumbent of the presidential office cannot be received, whether it describes him as President or as a citizen of a State.

The motion for leave to file the bill is therefore denied.

CHAPTER XIV

Aftermath of Reconstruction

THE Reconstruction Amendments—the Thirteenth, Fourteenth, and Fifteenth—involved the first formal changes in the text of the Constitution for over sixty years, comprising the only alterations made between 1804 and 1913. They necessitated far-reaching readjustments not only in constitutional doctrine but also in social organization, government-business relations, political representation, and definition of suffrage requirements.

The Slaughterhouse Cases (No. 123) were the first judicial pronouncements on the Fourteenth Amendment. These cases had nothing to do with the rights of freedmen but arose over the protest of the Butchers' Benevolent Association of New Orleans against a Louisiana act granting a monopoly of the slaughterhouse business to a favored firm. The ousted butchers challenged the law as a violation of the privileges and immunities clause of the new Amendment. By a majority of 5 to 4, the Court upheld the state enactment. The majority distinguished between state and national citizenship, placing the great bulk of civil rights under the protection of the state governments. Only the rights and privileges of federal citizenship are protected by the Fourteenth Amendment and these the Court defined narrowly. Giving the due process and equal protection clauses of the Amendment only cursory attention, the majority did not consider them limitations on the economic regulatory powers of the state, holding that the equal protection guarantee applied solely to state laws that discriminated against Negroes. By this restrictive interpretation, the majority failed to carry out the nationalistic revolution in the American constitutional system which the Radical framers of the

Amendment intended, and permanently devitalized the privileges and immunities clause as a federal protection against state encroachments. The due process and equal protection clauses, however, have since emerged as vital concepts; indeed, they have been responsible for more adjudication than any other constitutional provision.

In the Slaughterhouse Cases Justice Miller stated that the pervading purpose of the equal protection clause was to remedy the evil caused by state laws that "discriminated with gross injustice and hardship" against "the newly emancipated negroes"; it was "clearly a provision for that race and that emergency." Congress, which had drafted the Fourteenth Amendment to validate the Civil Rights Act of 1866, now enacted a Second Civil Rights Act (No. 124) in their attempt to guarantee civil and legal equality to Negroes. Unlike the earlier measure, which protected the voting rights and legal status of Negroes from state discrimination, this final all-out effort of the Radicals to establish civil equality was frustrated by the Court in the Civil Rights Cases (No. 125). These cases grew out of discriminations by individuals who refused equal accommodations to Negroes in public inns, conveyances, and theatres. In emasculating the Radical legislation, the Court held that "it would be running the slavery argument into the ground to make it apply to every act of discrimination which a person may see fit to make as to the guests he will entertain, or as to the people he will take into his coach or cab or car." Moreover, Justice Bradley stated, "individual invasion of individual rights is not the subject-matter of the amendment," which was prohibitory solely upon the states; wrongful acts of individuals, unsupported by state authority ". . . could not impair the civil rights protected by the Constitution against state aggression." The Court's ruling that these were social rather than civil rights, Harlan argued in his dissent, was "entirely too narrow and artificial," and sacrificed the spirit of the Civil War amendments "by a subtle and ingenious verbal criticism." He viewed the rights as "legal" rather than "social," contending that the majority decision would sanctify the continuation of discrimination with the full acquiescence of the state. "We shall enter upon an era of constitutional law," the former Kentucky Unionist predicted, "when the rights of freedom and American citizenship cannot receive from the nation that efficient protection which heretofore was unhesitatingly accorded to slavery and the rights of the master."

This prediction proved true. In the settlement of the Disputed Election of 1876, Northern Republicans agreed to jettison Radical policies in the South in return for Southern support of Hayes over Tilden. The effect of this compromise was to return control of race relations to the states, which then evolved less crude devices than the Black Codes to prevent Negro equality. The most generally accepted fomula was the "separate but equal" doctrine which gave the states an acceptable legal principle for compulsory segregation of the races. In *Plessy v. Ferguson*, thirteen years after the Court had sanctioned discrimination by individuals, it approved separation of the races by state action. Justice Henry B. Brown agreed that the object of the Fourteenth Amendment "was undoubtedly to enforce the absolute equality of the two races before the law, but in the nature of things it could not have been intended to abolish distinctions based on color, or to enforce social, as distinguished from political equality, or a commingling of the two races upon terms unsatisfactory to either (No. 126)." Although Brown denied that "enforced separation of the two races stamps the colored race with a badge of inferiority," Justice Harlan, in the only dissent, countered with the argument that "the arbitrary separation of citizens, on the basis of race, while they are on a public highway, is a badge of servitude wholly inconsistent with the Constitution" (No. 127). Insisting that the Constitution is "color-blind," he denounced the "thin disguise of 'equal' accommodations" for passengers in railroad coaches—a disguise which "will not mislead anyone, nor atone for the wrong this day done." Three years later, the Court inferred that the "equality" of separate educational accommodations in the states need not be exactly "equal"; indeed, the case of *Cumming v. County Board of Education* (1899) ruled that a Georgia county did not deny equal protection to colored children by failing to provide them with a high school, although it maintained a high school for white students.

Just as the Fourteenth Amendment prompted the freedman to strive for political equality, so it sparked an unexpected movement by women to gain long-denied legal and political equality. In *Minor v. Happersett* (No. 128), however, the Court denied the argument of women that the right to vote was a privilege or immunity of citizenship guaranteed against state infringement by the Fourteenth Amendment.

Another undefined term in that all-important amendment presented the court with difficulties. In the clause prohibiting state deprivation of "life, liberty, or property without due process of law," did the word "liberty" include the guarantees of the federal Bill of Rights? Prior to the adoption of the Fourteenth Amendment, the Court had ruled that the first ten amendments were not limitations upon the states (*Barron v. Baltimore*, Chapter IV). Without specifically saying so, the Slaughterhouse Cases ruled that the Fourteenth Amendment did not alter the Barron doctrine. In *Hurtado v. California* (No. 129), the Court held that the due process clause of the Fourteenth Amendment did not require a grand jury indictment in a state court, even though the Bill of Rights requires one in federal courts. In subsequent cases, the Court ruled that the amendment did not incorporate other liberties of the Bill of Rights as procedural guarantees which the states cannot violate. Thus, just as the Court cut down the meaning of equal protection and privileges and immunities, so did it vitiate the due process clause as a protection of civil liberties against state encroachment.

There was one important exception to this early erosion of the guarantees in the Fourteenth Amendment. Whereas the Supreme Court was unwilling to probe behind state assertions to determine whether separate facilities for Negroes were really "equal," in another instance of racial discrimination (*Yick Wo v. Hopkins*, 1886), it went behind a San Francisco ordinance to examine its actual administration. The local regulation required every laundryman to obtain a permit, unless his business was conducted in a brick or stone building. In administering this measure, city supervisors consistently discriminated against Chinese laundrymen, and thus, the Court ruled, violated the equal protection clause of the Fourteenth Amendment.

A Chinese also figured in another fundamental interpretation of the Fourteenth Amendment. Although the original Constitution recognized citizenship of the United States, it was not until the addition of the Fourteenth Amendment that this citizenship was specifically defined in terms of birth in the United States and subjection to its jurisdiction. As Representative Thaddeus Stevens cogently pointed out (Chapter XIII), this provision was designed to confer citizenship on the freedman, but as time went by the applicability of its provisions to other races raised problems. In the 1880's and 1890's, Congress complicated the issue by barring Chinese and other Asiatics from naturalization. Were native-born children of these disqualified aliens entitled to citizenship? In the Wong Kim Ark Case (No. 130), the definitive ruling on citizenship, the Court ruled that they were.

The last of the Civil War Amendments was the Fifteenth (No. 131). Military Reconstruction of the South was based on the Radical concept that the freedmen should vote, assuming, of course that they would vote Republican. When Southern whites organized the Ku Klux Klan and other secret societies to destroy Radical political power and re-establish white supremacy, the Republicans retaliated with the Fifteenth Amendment and a series of anti-Klan Enforcement Acts designed to protect the electoral and civil rights of the Negro. As in its interpretation of the Fourteenth Amendment, the Supreme Court also narrowly construed the Fifteenth Amendment. In *U.S. v. Reese* (No. 132A), two election inspectors in a Kentucky election were indicted for violating the Enforcement Act by refusing to receive the vote of a Negro. The Court noted that the Amendment did not give anyone a positive right to vote; it simply stated that persons could not be denied the right because of race, color, or previous condition of servitude. The "appropriate legislation" that the Amendment authorized Congress to pass was limited to these specific discriminations. Therefore, the sections of the Enforcement Act which attempted to prevent other kinds of discrimination exceeded Congress's authority and were unconstitutional.

In the same year, the Court dismissed the charge against Louisianans who had, by fraud, violence, and murder, denied Negroes the right to vote, holding that the allegations did not show that the denial had been based on race or color. "We may suspect," the Court concluded laconically, "that race was the cause of the hostility; but it is not so averred" (*U.S. v. Cruikshank*, 1876). Despite the severe judicial limitations on the guarantees of the Fifteenth Amendment, some provisions of the Enforcement Acts were upheld. In *Ex parte* Yarbrough (No. 132B), Justice Miller sustained the conviction of Georgia Klansmen who used physical violence to deprive a Negro of his right to vote for a member of Congress. The Court stated that the right to vote for federal officers is a right of United States citizenship "and Congress has the power to enforce that right."

Civil Rights Under the Fourteenth Amendment

RADICAL RECONSTRUCTION RECONSTRUED

123. *The Supreme Court Interprets the Fourteenth Amendment Narrowly*

The Slaughterhouse Cases, 16 Wallace 36 (1873).

MILLER, J.: . . . No one can fail to be impressed with the one pervading purpose found in . . . [the Thirteenth, Fourteenth, and Fifteenth Amendments], lying at the foundation of each, and without which none of them would have been even suggested; we mean the freedom of the slave race, the security and firm establishment of that freedom, and the protection of the newly-made freeman and citizen from the oppressions of those who had formerly exercised unlimited dominion over him. It is true that only the Fifteenth Amendment, in terms, mentions the negro by speaking of his color and his slavery. But it is just as true that each of the other articles was addressed to the grievances of that race, and designed to remedy them as the Fifteenth. . . .

In any fair and just construction of any section or phrase of these amendments, it is necessary to look to the purpose which we have said was the pervading spirit of them all, the evil which they were designed to remedy, and the process of continued addition to the Constitution, until that purpose was supposed to be accomplished, as far as constitutional law can accomplish it.

The first section of the fourteenth article, to which our attention is more specially invited, opens with a definition of citizenship—not only citizenship of the United States, but citizenship of the States. No such definition was previously found in the Constitution, nor had any attempt been made to define it by act of Congress. . . . It had been said by eminent judges that no man was a citizen of the United States, except as he was a citizen of one of the States composing the Union. Those, therefore, who had been born and resided always in the District of Columbia or in the Territories, though within the United States, were not citizens. Whether this proposition was sound or not had never been judicially decided. But it had been held by this court, in the celebrated Dred Scott Case, only a few years before the outbreak of the civil war, that a man of African descent, whether a slave or not, could not be a citizen of a State or of the United States. This decision, while it met the condemnation of some of the ablest statesmen and constitutional lawyers of the country, had never been overruled; and if it was to be accepted as a constitutional limitation of the right of citizenship, then all the negro race who had recently been made freemen, were still, not only not citizens, but were incapable of becoming so by anything short of an amendment to the Constitution.

To remove this difficulty primarily, and to establish a clear and comprehensive definition of citizenship . . . , the first clause of the first section was framed. . . .

It is quite clear, then, that there is a citizenship of the United States, and a citizenship of a State, which are distinct from each other, and which depend upon different characteristics or circumstances in the individual.

We think this distinction and its explicit recognition in this amendment of great weight in this argument, because the next paragraph of this same section, which is the one mainly relied on by the plaintiffs in error, speaks only of privileges and immunities of citizens of the United States, and does not speak of those of citizens of the several States. . . .

It is a little remarkable, if this clause was intended as a protection to the citizen of a State against the legislative power of his own State, that the word citizen of the State should be left out when it is so carefully used, and used in contradistinction to citizens of the United States, in the very sentence which precedes it. It is too clear for argument that the change in phraseology was adopted understandingly and with a purpose.

Of the privileges and immunities of the citizen of the United States, and of the privileges and immunities of the citizen of the State, . . . only the former . . . are placed by this clause under the protection of the federal Constitution. . . .

If, then, there is a difference between the privileges and immunities belonging to a citizen of the United States as such, and those belonging to the citizen of the State as such, the latter must rest for their security and protection where they have heretofore rested; for they are not embraced by this paragraph of the amendment.

The first occurrence of the words "privileges and immunities" in our constitutional history, is to be found in the fourth of the Articles of the old Confederation. . . .

In the Constitution of the United States, which superseded the Articles of Confederation, the corresponding provision is found in section two of the fourth article, in the following words: "The citizens of each State shall be entitled to all the privileges and immunities of citizens of the several States." . . .

The constitutional provision . . . did not create those rights, which it called privileges and immunities of citizens of the States. It threw around them in that clause no security for the citizens of the State in which they were claimed or exercised. Nor did it profess to control the power of the state governments over the rights of its own citizens.

Its sole purpose was to declare to the several States, that whatever those rights, as you grant or establish them to your own citizens, or as you limit or qualify, or impose restrictions on their exercise, the same, neither more nor less, shall be the measure of the rights of citizens of other States within your jurisdiction. . . . But with the exception of . . . a few . . . restrictions, the entire domain of the privileges and immunities of citizens of the States, as above defined, lay within the constitutional and legislative power of the States. . . . Was it the purpose of the Fourteenth Amendment, by the simple declaration that no State should make or enforce any law which shall abridge the privileges and immunities of citizens of the United States, to transfer the security and protection of all the civil rights which we have mentioned, from the States to the federal government? And where it is declared that Congress shall have the power to enforce that article, was it intended to bring within the power of Congress the entire domain of civil rights heretofore belonging exclusively to the States?

All this and more must follow, if the proposition of the plaintiffs in error be sound. For not only are these rights subject to the control of Congress whenever in its discretion any of them are supposed to be abridged by state legislation, but that body may also pass laws in advance, limiting and restricting the exercise of legislative power by the States, in their most ordinary and usual functions, as in its judgment it may think proper on all such subjects. And still further, such a construction followed by the reversal of the judgments of the Supreme Court of

Louisiana in these cases, would constitute this court a perpetual censor upon all legislation of the States, on the civil rights of their own citizens, with authority to nullify such as it did not approve as consistent with those rights, as they existed at the time of the adoption of this amendment. The argument, we admit, is not always the most conclusive which is drawn from the consequences urged against the adoption of a particular construction of an instrument. But when, as in the case before us, these consequences are so serious, so far-reaching and pervading, so great a departure from the structure and spirit of our institutions; when the effect is to fetter and degrade the state governments by subjecting them to the control of Congress, in the exercise of powers heretofore universally conceded to them of the most ordinary and fundamental character; when in fact it radically changes the whole theory of the relations of the state and federal governments to each other and of both these governments to the people; the argument has a force that is irresistible, in the absence of language which expresses such a purpose too clearly to admit of doubt.

We are convinced that no such results were intended by the Congress which proposed these amendments, nor by the legislatures of the States which ratified them. . . . We are of opinion that the rights claimed by these plaintiffs in error, if they have any existence, are not privileges and immunities of citizens of the United States within the meaning of the clause of the Fourteenth Amendment under consideration. . . .

The argument has not been much pressed in these cases that the defendant's charter deprives the plaintiffs of their property without due process of law, or that it denies to them the equal protection of the law. The first of these paragraphs has been in the Constitution since the adoption of the Fifth Amendment, as a restraint upon the federal power. It is also to be found in some form of expression in the constitutions of nearly all the States, as a restraint upon the power of the States. This law, then, has practically been the same as it now is during the existence of the government, except so far as the present amendment may place the restraining power over the States in this matter in the hands of the federal government. . . .

In the light of the history of these amendments, and the pervading purpose of them, which we have already discussed, it is not difficult to give a meaning to this [equal protection] clause. The existence of laws in the States where the newly emancipated negroes resided, which discriminated with gross injustice and hardship against them as a class, was the evil to be remedied by this clause, and by it such laws are forbidden.

If, however, the States did not conform their laws to its requirements, then by the fifth section of the article of amendment Congress was authorized to enforce it by suitable legislation. We doubt very much whether any action of a State not directed by way of discrimination against the negroes as a class, or on account of their race, will ever be held to come within the purview of this provision. It is so clearly a provision for that race and that emergency, that a strong case would be necessary for its application to any other. But as it is a State that is to be dealt with, and not alone the validity of its laws, we may safely leave that matter until Congress shall have exercised its power, or some case of state oppression, by denial of equal justice in its courts, shall have claimed a decision at our hands. We find no such case in the one before us. . . .

124. *The Second Civil Rights Act, March 1, 1875*

U. S. Stat. at L., XVIII, Part 3, 335-7.

Whereas it is essential to just government we recognize the equality of all men before the law, and hold that it is the duty of government in its dealings with the people to mete out equal and exact justice to all, of whatever nativity, race, color, or persuasion, religious or political; and it being the appropriate object of legislation to enact great fundamental principles into law: Therefore,

Be it enacted . . . That all persons within the jurisdiction of the United States shall be entitled to the full and equal enjoyment of the accommodations, advantages, facilities, and privileges of inns, public conveyances on land or water, theaters, and other places of public amusement; subject only to the conditions and limitations established by law, and applicable alike to citizens of every race and color, regardless of any previous condition of servitude.

SEC. 2. That any person who shall violate the foregoing section by denying to any citizen, except for reasons by law applicable to citizens of every race and color, and regardless of any previous condition of servitude, the full enjoyment of any of the accommodations, advantages, facilities, or privileges in said section enumerated, or by aiding or inciting such denial, shall, for every such offense, forfeit and pay the sum of five hundred dollars to the person aggrieved thereby, . . . and shall also, for every such offense, be deemed guilty of a misdemeanor, and, upon conviction thereof, shall be fined not less than five hundred nor more than one thousand dollars, or shall be imprisoned not less than thirty days nor more than one year. . . .

SEC. 3. That the district and circuit courts of the United States shall have, exclusively of the courts of the several States, cognizance of all crimes and offenses against, and violations of, the provisions of this act. . . .

SEC. 4. That no citizen possessing all other qualifications which are or may be prescribed by law shall be disqualified for service as grand or petit juror in any court of the United States, or of any State, on account of race, color, or previous condition of servitude; and any officer or other person charged with any duty in the selection or summoning of jurors who shall exclude or fail to summon any citizen for the cause aforesaid shall, on conviction thereof, be deemed guilty of a misdemeanor, and be fined not more than five thousand dollars.

SEC. 5. That all cases arising under the provisions of this act . . . shall be reviewable by the Supreme Court of the United States, without regard to the sum in controversy. . . .

125. *Discrimination by Private Individuals*

The Civil Rights Cases, 109 U.S. 3 (1883).

BRADLEY, J.: . . . It is obvious that the primary and important question in all the cases is the constitutionality of the [Second Civil Rights] law: for if the law is unconstitutional none of the prosecutions can stand.

The sections of the law referred to . . . [are paragraphs 2 and 3 of the preceding selection].

The essence of the law is, not to declare broadly that all persons shall be entitled to the full and equal enjoyment of the accommodations, advantages, facilities, and privileges of inns, public conveyances, and theatres; but that such enjoyment shall not be subject to any conditions applicable only to citizens of a particular race or color, or who had been in a previous condition of servitude. . . . The second section makes it a penal offense in any person to deny to any citizen of any race or color, regardless of previous servitude, any of the accommodations or privileges mentioned in the first section.

Has Congress constitutional power to make such a law? Of course, no one will contend that the power to pass it was contained in the Constitution before the adoption of the last three amendments. The power is sought, first, in the Fourteenth Amendment. . . .

It is state action of a particular character that is prohibited [by the Fourteenth Amendment]. Individual invasion of individual rights is not the subject-matter of the amendment. It has a deeper and broader scope. It nullifies and makes void all state legislation, and state action of every kind, which impairs the privileges and immunities of citizens of the United States, or which injures them in life, liberty, or property without due process of law, or which denies to any of them the equal protection of the laws. It not only does this, but, in order that the national will, thus declared, may not be a mere brutum fulmen, the last section of the amendment invests Congress with power to enforce it by appropriate legislation. To enforce what? To enforce the prohibition. To adopt appropriate legislation for correcting the effects of such prohibited state law and state acts, and thus to render them effectually null, void, and innocuous. This is the legislative power conferred upon Congress, and this is the whole of it. It does not invest Congress with power to legislate upon subjects which are within the domain of state legislation; but to provide modes of relief against state legislation, or state action, of the kind referred to. It does not authorize Congress to create a code of municipal law for the regulation of private rights; but to provide modes of redress against the operation of state laws, and the action of state officers, executive or judicial, when these are subversive of the fundamental rights specified in the amendment. Positive rights and privileges are undoubtedly secured by the Fourteenth Amendment; but they are secured by way of prohibition against state laws and state proceedings affecting those rights and privileges, and by power given to Congress to legislate for the purpose of carrying such prohibition into effect; and such legislation must necessarily be predicated upon such supposed state laws or state proceedings, and be directed to the correction of their operation and effect. . . .

In this connection it is proper to state that civil rights, such as are guaranteed by the Constitution against state aggression, cannot be impaired by the wrongful acts of individuals, unsupported by state authority in the shape of laws, customs, or judicial or executive proceedings. The wrongful act of an individual, unsupported by any such authority, is simply a private wrong, or a crime of that individual, an invasion of the rights of the injured party, it is true, whether they affect his person, his property, or his reputation; but if not sanctioned in some way by the state, or not done under state authority, his rights remain in full force, and may presumably be vindicated by resort to the laws of the state for redress. . . .

If the principles of interpretation which we have laid down are correct, . . . it is clear that the law in question cannot be sustained by any grant of legislative power made to Congress by the Fourteenth Amendment. That amendment prohibits the states from denying to any person the equal protection of the laws, and declares that Congress shall have power to enforce, by appropriate legislation, the provisions of the amendment. The law in question, without any reference to adverse state legislation on the subject, declares that all persons shall be entitled to equal accommodations and privileges of inns, public conveyances, and places of public amusement, and imposes a penalty upon any individual who shall deny to any citizen such equal accommodations and privileges. This is not corrective legislation; it is primary and direct; it takes immediate and absolute possession of the subject of the right of admission to inns, public conveyances, and places of amusement. It supersedes and displaces state legislation on the same subject, or only allows it permissive force. It ignores such legislation, and assumes that the matter is one that belongs to the domain of national regulation. Whether it would not have been a more effective protection of the rights of citizens to have clothed Congress with plenary power over the whole subject, is not now the question. What we have to decide is, whether such plenary power has been conferred upon Congress by the Fourteenth Amendment, and, in our judgment, it has not. . . .

But the power of Congress to adopt direct and primary, as distinguished from corrective legislation, on the subject in hand, is sought in the second place, from the Thirteenth Amendment, which abolishes slavery. . . .

It is true that slavery cannot exist without law any more than property in lands and goods can exist without law, and therefore the Thirteenth Amendment may be regarded as nullifying all state laws which establish or uphold slavery. But it has a reflex character also, establishing and decreeing universal civil and political freedom throughout the United States; and it is assumed that the power in Congress to enforce the articles by appropriate legislation, clothes Congress with power to pass all laws necessary and proper for abolishing all badges and incidents of slavery in the United States; and upon this assumption it is claimed that this is sufficient authority for declaring by law that all persons shall have equal accommodations and privileges in all inns, public conveyances, and places of public amusement; the argument being that the denial of such equal accommodations and privileges is in itself a subjection to a species of servitude within the meaning of the amendment. Conceding the major proposition to be true, that Congress has a right to enact all necessary and proper laws for the obliteration and prevention of slavery with all its badges and incidents, is the minor proposition also true, that the denial to any person of admission to the accommodations and privileges of an inn, a public conveyance, or a theatre, does subject that person to any form of servitude, or tend to fasten upon him any badge of slavery? If it does not, then power to pass the law is not found in the Thirteenth Amendment. . . .

But is there any similarity between such servitudes and a denial by the owner of an inn, a public conveyance, or a theatre, of its accommodations and privileges to an individual, even though the denial be founded on the race or color of that individual? Where does any slavery or servitude, or badge of either, arise from such an act of denial? Whether it might not be a denial of a right which, if sanctioned by the state law, would be obnoxious to the prohibitions of the Fourteenth Amendment, is another question. But what has it to do with the question of slavery? . . .

The long existence of African slavery in this country gave us very distinct notions of what it was, and what were its necessary incidents. Compulsory service of the slave for the benefit of the master, restraint of his movements except by the master's will, disability to hold property, to make contracts, to have a standing in court, to be a witness against a white person, and such like burdens and incapacities were the inseparable incidents of the institution. . . . Can the act of a mere individual, the owner of the inn, the public conveyance, or place of amusement, refusing the accommodation, be justly regarded as imposing any badge of slavery or servitude upon the applicant, or only as inflicting an ordinary civil injury, properly cognizable by the laws of the State, and presumably subject to redress by those laws until the contrary appears?

After giving to these questions all the consideration which their importance demands, we are forced to the conclusion that such an act of refusal has nothing to do with slavery or involuntary servitude, and that if it is violative of any right of the party, his redress is to be sought under the laws of the State; or, if those laws are adverse to his rights and do not protect him, his remedy will be found in the corrective legislation which Congress has adopted, or may adopt, for counteracting the effect of state laws, or state action, prohibited by the Fourteenth Amendment. It would be running the slavery argument into the ground to make it apply to every act of discrimination which a person may see fit to make as to the guests he will entertain, or as to the people he will take into his coach or cab or car, or admit to his concert or theatre, or deal with in other matters of intercourse or business. . . .

On the whole we are of the opinion that no countenance of authority for the passage of the law in question can be found in either the Thirteenth or Fourteenth Amendment of the Constitution. . . .

THE ORIGINS OF THE "SEPARATE BUT EQUAL" DOCTRINE

126. *The Court Upholds Jim Crow Laws*

Plessy v. Ferguson, 163 U.S. 537 (1896).

BROWN, J.: . . . This case turns upon the Constitutionality of an act of . . . Louisiana, passed in 1890, providing for separate railway carriages for the white and colored races. . . .

The constitutionality of this act is attacked upon the ground that it conflicts both with the Thirteenth Amendment of the Constitution, abolishing slavery, and the Fourteenth Amendment, which prohibits certain restrictive legislation on the part of the States.

1. That it does not conflict with the Thirteenth Amendment, which abolished slavery and involuntary servitude, except as a punishment for crime, is too clear for argument. Slavery implies involuntary servitude—a state of bondage; the ownership of mankind as a chattel, or at least the control of the labor and services of one man for the benefit of another, and the absence of a legal right to the disposal of his own person, property, and services. . . .

A statute which implies merely a legal distinction between the white and colored races—a distinction which is founded in the color of the two races, and which must always exist so long as white men are distinguished from the other race by color—has no tendency to destroy the legal equality of the two races, or re-establish a state of involuntary servitude. Indeed, we do not understand that the Thirteenth Amendment is strenuously relied upon by the plaintiff in error in this connection. . . .

2. . . . The object of the amendment was undoubtedly to enforce the absolute equality of the two races before the law, but in the nature of things it could not have been intended to abolish distinctions based upon color, or to enforce social, as distinguished from political, equality, or a commingling of the two races upon terms unsatisfactory to either. Laws permitting, and even requiring, their separation in places where they are liable to be brought into contact do not necessarily imply the inferiority of either race to the other, and have been generally, if not universally, recognized as within the competency of

the state legislatures in the exercise of their police power. The most common instance of this is connected with the establishment of separate schools for white and colored children, which has been held to be a valid exercise of the legislative power even by courts of States where the political rights of the colored race have been longest and most earnestly enforced. . . .

So far, then, as a conflict with the Fourteenth Amendment is concerned, the case reduces itself to the question whether the statute of Louisiana is a reasonable regulation, and with respect to this there must necessarily be a large discretion on the part of the legislature. In determining the question of reasonableness it is at liberty to act with reference to the established usages, customs, and traditions of the people, and with a view to the promotion of their comfort, and the preservation of the public peace and good order. Gauged by this standard, we cannot say that a law which authorizes or even requires the separation of the two races in public conveyances is unreasonable or more obnoxious to the Fourteen Amendment than the acts of Congress requiring separate schools for colored children in the District of Columbia, the constitutionality of which does not seem to have been questioned, or the corresponding acts of state legislatures.

We consider the underlying fallacy of the plaintiff's argument to consist in the assumption that the enforced separation of the two races stamps the colored race with a badge of inferiority. If this be so, it is not by reason of anything found in the act, but solely because the colored race chooses to put that construction upon it. The argument necessarily assumes that if, as has been more than once the case, and is not unlikely to be so again, the colored race should become the dominant power in the state legislature, and should enact a law in precisely similar terms, it would thereby relegate the white race to an inferior position. We imagine that the white race, at least, would not acquiesce in this assumption. The argument also assumes that social prejudices may be overcome by legislation and that equal rights cannot be secured to the Negro except by an enforced commingling of the two races. We cannot accept this proposition. If the two races are to meet upon terms of social equality, it must be the result of natural affinities, a mutual appreciation of each other's merits, and a voluntary consent of individuals. . . . Legislation is powerless to eradicate racial instincts or to abolish distinctions based upon physical differences, and the attempt to do so can only result in accentuating the difficulties of the present situation. If the civil and political rights of both races be equal, one cannot be inferior to the other civilly or politically. If one race be inferior to the other socially, the Constitution of the United States cannot put them upon the same plane.

127. *Justice Harlan: "Our Constitution is color-blind."*

Plessy v. Ferguson, 163 U.S. 537 (1896).

HARLAN, J., dissenting: . . . In respect of civil rights, common to all citizens, the Constitution of the United States does not, I think, permit any public authority to know the race of those entitled to be protected in the enjoyment of such rights. Every true man has pride of race, and under appropriate circumstances when the rights of others, his equals before the law, are not to be affected, it is his privilege to express such pride and to take such action based upon it as to him seems proper. But I deny that any legislative body or judicial tribunal may have regard to the race of citizens when the civil rights of those citizens are involved. Indeed, such legislation, as that here in question, is inconsistent not only with that equality of rights which pertains to citizenship, National and State, but with the personal liberty enjoyed by everyone within the United States. . . .

It is one thing for railroad carriers to furnish, or to be required by law to furnish, equal accommodations for all whom they are under a legal duty to carry. It is quite another thing for government to forbid citizens of the white and black races from traveling in the same public conveyance, and to punish officers of railroad companies for permitting persons of the two races to occupy the same passenger coach. If a State can prescribe, as a rule of civil conduct, that whites and blacks shall not travel as passengers in the same railroad coach, why may it not so regulate the use of the streets of its cities and towns as to compel white citizens to keep on one side of a street and black citizens to keep on the other? Why may it not, upon like grounds, punish whites and blacks who ride together in streetcars or in open vehicles on a public road or street? Why may it not require sheriffs to assign whites to one side of a courtroom and blacks to the other? And why may it not also prohibit the commingling of the two races in the galleries of legislative halls or in public assemblages convened for the consideration of the political questions of the day? Further, if this statute of Louisiana is consistent with the personal liberty of citizens, why may not the State require the separation in railroad coaches of native and naturalized citizens of the United States, or of Protestants and Roman Catholics?

The answer given at the argument to these questions was that regulations of the kind they suggest would be unreasonable and could not, therefore, stand before the law. Is it meant that the determination of questions of legislative power depends upon the inquiry whether the statute whose validity is questioned is, in the judgment of the courts, a reasonable one, taking all the circumstances into consideration? A statute may be unreasonable merely because a sound public policy forbade its enactment. But I do not understand that the courts have anything to do with the policy or expediency of legislation. . . .

The white race deems itself to be the dominant race in this country. And so it is, in prestige, in achievements, in education, in wealth, and in power. So, I doubt not, it will continue to be for all time, if it remains true to its great heritage and holds fast to the principles of constitutional liberty. But in view of the Constitution, in the eye of the law, there is in this country no superior, dominant, ruling class of citizens. There is no caste here. Our Constitution is color-blind and neither knows nor tolerates classes among citizens. In respect of civil rights, all citizens are equal before the law. The humblest is the peer of the most powerful. The law regards man as man and takes no account of his surroundings or of his color when his civil rights as guaranteed by the supreme law of the land are involved. It is, therefore, to be regretted that this high tribunal, the final expositor of the fundamental law of the land, has reached the conclusion that it is competent for a State to regulate the enjoyment by citizens of their civil rights solely upon the basis of race. . . .

The sure guarantee of the peace and security of each race is the clear, distinct, unconditional recognition by our governments, National and State, of every right that inheres in civil freedom, and of the equality before the law of all the citizens of the United States without regard to race. State enactments, regulating the enjoyment of civil rights, upon the basis of race, and cunningly devised to defeat legitimate results of the war, under the pretense of recognizing equality of rights, can have no other result than to render permanent peace impossible, and to keep alive a conflict of races, the continuance of which must do harm to all concerned. . . .

The arbitrary separation of citizens, on

the basis of race, while they are on a public highway, is a badge of servitude wholly inconsistent with the civil freedom and the equality before the law established by the Constitution. It cannot be justified upon any legal grounds.

If evils will result from the commingling of the two races upon public highways established for the benefit of all, they will be infinitely less than those that will surely come from state legislation regulating the enjoyment of civil rights upon the basis of race. We boast of the freedom enjoyed by our people above all other peoples. But it is difficult to reconcile that boast with a state of the law which, practically, puts the brand of servitude and degradation upon a large class of our fellow-citizens, our equals before the law. The thin disguise of "equal" accommodations for passengers in railroad coaches will not mislead anyone, nor atone for the wrong this day done. . . .

I am of opinion that the statute of Louisiana is inconsistent with the personal liberty of citizens, white and black, in that State, and hostile to both the spirit and letter of the Constitution of the United States. If laws of like character should be enacted in the several States of the Union, the effect would be in the highest degree mischievous. . . . Such a system is inconsistent with the guarantee given by the Constitution to each state of a republican form of government, and may be stricken down by congressional action, or by the courts in the discharge of their solemn duty to maintain the supreme law of the land, anything in the constitution or laws of any state to the contrary notwithstanding.

PRIVILEGES AND IMMUNITIES OF FEDERAL CITIZENSHIP

128. *Suffrage Is Not One of the Privileges and Immunities of Citizenship*

Minor v. Happersett, 21 Wallace 162 (1875).

WAITE, C.J.: . . . The argument is, that as a woman, born or naturalized in the United States and subject to the jurisdiction thereof, is a citizen of the United States and of the State in which she resides, she has the right of suffrage as one of the privileges and immunities of her citizenship, which the State cannot by its laws or constitution abridge.

There is no doubt that women may be citizens. . . . Sex has never been made one of the elements of citizenship in the United States. In this respect men have never had an advantage over women. The same laws precisely apply to both. The Fourteenth Amendment did not affect the citizenship of women any more than it did of men. In this particular, therefore, the rights of Mrs. Minor do not depend upon the amendment. She has always been a citizen from her birth, and entitled to all the privileges and immunities of citizenship. . . .

If the right of suffrage is one of the necessary privileges of a citizen of the United States, then the constitution and laws of Missouri confining it to men are in violation of the Constitution of the United States, as amended, and consequently void. The direct question is, therefore, presented whether all citizens are necessarily voters.

The Constitution does not define the privileges and immunities of citizens. For that definition we must look elsewhere. In this case we need not determine what they are, but only whether suffrage is necessarily one of them.

It certainly is nowhere made so in express terms. The United States has no voters in the States of its own creation. The elective officers of the United States are all elected directly or indirectly by state voters. . . .

The amendment did not add to the privileges and immunities of a citizen. It simply furnished an additional guaranty for the protection of such as he already had. No new voters were necessarily made by it. Indirectly it may have had that effect, because it may have increased the number of citizens entitled to suffrage under the constitution and laws of the States, but it operates for this purpose, if at all, through the States and the state laws, and not directly upon the citizen.

It is clear therefore, we think, that the Constitution has not added the right of suffrage to the privileges and immunities of citizenship as they existed at the time it was adopted. This makes it proper to inquire whether suffrage was coextensive with the citizenship of the States at the time of its adoption. If it was, then it may with force be argued that suffrage was one of the rights which belonged to citizenship, and in the enjoyment of which every citizen must be protected. But if it was not, the contrary may with propriety be assumed.

When the Federal Constitution was adopted, all the States, with the exception of Rhode Island and Connecticut, had constitutions of their own. . . . Upon an examination of these constitutions we find that in no State were all citizens permitted to vote. . . .

In this condition of the law in respect to suffrage in the several States it cannot for a moment be doubted that if it had been intended to make all citizens of the United States voters, the framers of the Constitution would not have left it to implication. . . . In all, save perhaps New Jersey, this right was only bestowed upon men and not upon all of them. . . . Women were excluded from suffrage in nearly all the States by the express provision of their constitutions and laws. . . .

No new State has ever been admitted to the Union which has conferred the right of suffrage upon women, and this has never been considered a valid objection to her admission. On the contrary, . . . the right of suffrage was withdrawn from women as early as 1807 in the State of New Jersey, without any attempt to obtain the interference of the United States to prevent it. . . .

Besides this, citizenship has not in all cases been made a condition precedent to the enjoyment of the right of suffrage. Thus, in Missouri, persons of foreign birth, who have declared their intention to become citizens of the United States, may under certain conditions vote. The same provision is to be found in the constitutions of Alabama, Arkansas, Florida, Georgia, Indiana, Kansas, Minnesota, and Texas.

Certainly if the courts can consider any question settled, this is one. For nearly ninety years the people have acted upon the idea that the Constitution, when it conferred citizenship, did not necessarily confer the right of suffrage. If uniform practice long continued can settle the construction of so important an instrument as the Constitution of the United States confessedly is, most certainly it has been done here. Our province is to decide what the law is, not to declare what it should be. . . . No argument as to woman's need of suffrage can be considered. We can only act upon her rights as they exist. It is not for us to look at the hardship of withholding. Our duty is at an end if we find it is within the power of a State to withhold.

Being unanimously of the opinion that the Constitution of the United States does not confer the right of suffrage upon any one, and that the constitutions and laws of the several States which commit that important trust to men alone are not necessarily void, we affirm the judgment.

PROCEDURAL RIGHTS IN THE STATES UNDER THE FOURTEENTH AMENDMENT

129. *Grand Jury Indictment Is Not Necessary to Justice in the States*

Hurtado v. California, 110 U.S. 516 (1884).

MATTHEWS, J.: . . . The proposition of law we are asked to affirm is that an indictment or presentment by a grand jury, as known to the common law of England, is essential to that "due process of law," when applied to prosecutions for felonies, which is secured and guaranteed by this provision of the Constitution of the United States, and which accordingly it is forbidden to the States respectively to dispense with in the administration of criminal law. . . .

It is maintained on behalf of the plaintiff in error that the phrase "due process of law" is equivalent to "law of the land," as found in the 29th chapter of Magna Charta; that by immemorial usage it has acquired a fixed, definite, and technical meaning; that it refers to and includes, not only the general principles of public liberty and private right, which lie at the foundation of all free government, but the very institutions which, venerable by time and custom, have been tried by experience and found fit and necessary for the preservation of those principles, and which, having been the birthright and inheritance of every English subject, crossed the Atlantic with the colonists and were transplanted and established in the fundamental laws of the State; that, having been originally introduced into the Constitution of the United States as a limitation upon the powers of the government, brought into being by that instrument, it has now been added as an additional security to the individual against oppression by the States themselves; that one of these institutions is that of the grand jury, an indictment or presentment by which against the accused in cases of alleged felonies is an essential part of due process of law, in order that he may not be harassed or destroyed by prosecutions founded only upon private malice or popular fury. . . .

A critical examination and comparison of the text and context will show that it . . . was not intended to assert that an indictment or presentment of a grand jury was essential to the idea of due process of law in the prosecution and punishment of crimes, but was only mentioned as an example and illustration of due process of law as it actually existed in cases in which it was customarily used. . . .

The Constitution of the United States was ordained . . . by descendants of Englishmen, who inherited the traditions of English law and history; but it was made for an undefined and expanding future, and for a people gathered and to be gathered from many nations and of many tongues. And while we take just pride in the principles and institutions of the common law, we are not to forget that in lands where other systems of jurisprudence prevail, the ideas and processes of civil justice are also not unknown. Due process of law, in spite of the absolutism of continental governments, is not alien to that code which survived the Roman Empire as the foundation of modern civilization in Europe. . . . There is nothing in Magna Charta, rightly construed as a broad charter of public right and law, which ought to exclude the best ideas of all systems and of every age; and as it was the characteristic principle of the common law to draw its inspiration from every fountain of justice, we are not to assume that the sources of its supply have been exhausted. On the contrary, we should expect that the new and various experiences of our own situation and system will mould and shape it into new and not less useful forms. . . .

In this country written constitutions were deemed essential to protect the rights and liberties of the people against the encroachments of power delegated to their governments, and the provisions of Magna Charta were incorporated into Bills of Rights. They were limitations upon all the powers of government, legislative as well as executive and judicial.

It necessarily happened, therefore, that as these broad and general maxims of liberty and justice held in our system a different place and performed a different function from their position and office in English constitutional history and law, they would receive and justify a corresponding and more comprehensive interpretation. Applied in England only as guards against executive usurpation and tyranny, here they have become bulwarks also against arbitrary legislation; but, in that application, as it would be incongruous to measure and restrict them by the ancient customary English law, they must be held to guarantee not particular forms of procedure, but the very substance of individual rights to life, liberty, and property. . . .

We are to construe this phrase in the Fourteenth Amendment by the *usus loquendi* of the Constitution itself. The same words are contained in the Fifth Amendment. That article makes specific and express provision for perpetuating the institution of the grand jury, so far as relates to prosecutions for the more aggravated crimes under the laws of the United States. It declares that:

"No person shall be held to answer for a capital or otherwise infamous crime, unless on a presentment or indictment of a grand jury, except in cases arising in the land or naval forces, or in the militia when in actual service in time of war or public danger; nor shall any person be subject for the same offence to be twice put in jeopardy of life or limb; nor shall he be compelled in any criminal case to be witness against himself." [It then immediately adds]: "Nor be deprived of life, liberty, or property, without due process of law."

According to a recognized canon of interpretation, especially applicable to formal and solemn instruments of constitutional law, we are forbidden to assume, without clear reason to the contrary, that any part of this most important amendment is superfluous. The natural and obvious inference is, that in the sense of the Constitution "due process of law" was not meant or intended to include, *ex vi termini,* the institution and procedure of a grand jury in any case. The conclusion is equally irresistible, that when the same phrase was employed in the Fourteenth Amendment to restrain the action of the States, it was used in the same sense and with no greater extent; and that if in the adoption of that amendment it had been part of its purpose to perpetuate the institution of the grand jury in all the States, it would have embodied, as did the Fifth Amendment, express declarations to that effect. Due process of law in the latter refers to that law of the land which derives its authority from the legislative powers conferred upon Congress by the Constitution of the United States, exercised within the limits therein prescribed, and interpreted according to the principles of the common law. In the Fourteenth Amendment, by parity of reason, it refers to that law of the land in each State, which derives its authority from the inherent and reserved powers of the State, exerted within the limits of those fundamental principles of liberty and justice which lie at the base of all our civil and political institutions, and the greatest security for which resides in the right of the people to make their own laws, and alter them at their pleasure.

Definition of American Citizenship

130. *Birth constitutes "a sufficient and complete right to citizenship."*

U.S. v. Wong Kim Ark, 169 U.S. 649 (1898).

GRAY, J.: . . . The Constitution of the United States, as originally adopted, uses the words "citizen of the United States," and "natural-born citizen of the United States." By the original Constitution, every Representative in Congress is required to have been "seven years a citizen of the United States," and every Senator to have been "nine years a citizen of the United States"; and "no person except a natural-born citizen, or a citizen of the United States at the time of the adoption of this Constitution, shall be eligible to the office of President." The Fourteenth Article of Amendment, besides declaring that "all persons born or naturalized in the United States, and subject to the jurisdiction thereof, are citizens of the United States and of the State wherein they reside," also declares that "no State shall make or enforce any law which shall abridge the privileges or immunities of citizens of the United States; nor shall any State deprive any person of life, liberty, or property, without due process of law; nor deny to any person within its jurisdiction the equal protection of the laws." And the Fifteenth Article of Amendment declares that "the right of citizens of the United States to vote shall not be denied or abridged by the United States, or by any State, on account of race, color, or previous condition of servitude."

The Constitution nowhere defines the meaning of these words, either by way of inclusion or of exclusion, except in so far as this is done by the affirmative declaration that "all persons born or naturalized in the United States, and subject to the jurisdiction thereof, are citizens of the United States." In this, as in other respects, it must be interpreted in the light of the common law, the principles and history of which were familiarly known to the framers of the Constitution. . . .

The fundamental principle of the common law with regard to English nationality was birth within the allegiance—also called "ligealty," "obedience," "faith," or "power," of the King. The principle embraced all persons born within the King's allegiance, and subject to his protection. Such allegiance and protection were mutual . . . and were not restricted to natural-born subjects and naturalized subjects, or to those who had taken an oath of allegiance; but were predicable of aliens in amity, so long as they were within the kingdom. Children, born in England, of such aliens, were therefore natural-born subjects. But the children, born within the realm, of foreign ambassadors, or the children of alien enemies, born during and within their hostile occupation of part of the King's dominions, were not natural-born subjects, because not born within the allegiance, the obedience, or the power, or, as would be said at this day, within the jurisdiction, of the King. . . .

The real object of the Fourteenth Amendment of the Constitution, in qualifying the words "all persons born in the United States," by the addition, "and subject to the jurisdiction thereof," would appear to have been to exclude, by the fewest and fittest words (besides children of members of the Indian tribes, standing in a peculiar relation to the national government, unknown to the common law), the two classes of cases—children born of alien enemies in hostile occupation, and children of diplomatic representatives of a foreign state—both of which, as has already been shown, by the law of England and by our own law, from the time of the first settlement of the English colonies in America, had been recognized exceptions to the fundamental rule of citizenship by birth within the country. . . .

The foregoing considerations and authorities irresistibly lead us to these conclusions: The Fourteenth Amendment affirms the ancient and fundamental rule of citizenship by birth within the territory, in the allegiance and under the protection of the country, including all children here born of resident aliens, with the exceptions or qualifications (as old as the rule itself) of children of foreign sovereigns or their ministers, or born on foreign public ships, or of enemies within and during a hostile occupation of part of our territory, and with the single additional exception of children of members of the Indian tribes owing direct allegiance to their several tribes. The Amendment, in clear words and in manifest intent, includes the children born within the territory of the United States of all other persons, of whatever race or color, domiciled within the United States. Every citizen or subject of another country, while domiciled here, is within the allegiance and the protection, and consequently subject to the jurisdiction, of the United States. . . .

It is true that Chinese persons born in China cannot be naturalized, like other aliens, by proceedings under the naturalization laws. But this is for want of any statute or treaty authorizing or permitting such naturalization, as will appear by tracing the history of the statutes, treaties, and decisions upon that subject—always bearing in mind that statutes enacted by Congress, as well as treaties made by the President and Senate, must yield to the paramount and supreme law of the Constitution. . . .

The Fifteenth Amendment and the Right to Vote

131. *The Fifteenth Amendment*

Proposed February 27, 1869; adopted March 30, 1870.

SECTION 1. The right of citizens of the United States to vote shall not be denied or abridged by the United States or by any State on account of race, color, or previous condition of servitude.

SECTION 2. The Congress shall have power to enforce this article by appropriate legislation.

132. *The Ku Klux Klan and the Fifteenth Amendment*

A. "THE FIFTEENTH AMENDMENT DOES NOT CONFER THE RIGHT OF SUFFRAGE UPON ANYONE."

U.S. v. Reese, 92 U.S. 214 (1876).

WAITE, C.J.: . . . The Fifteenth Amendment does not confer the right of suffrage upon anyone. It prevents the States or the United States, however, from giving preference, in this particular, to one citizen of the United States over another on account of race, etc. Before its adoption, this could be done. . . . Now it cannot. If citizens of one race having certain qualifications are permitted to vote, those of another having the same qualifications must be. . . . It follows that the Amendment has invested the citizen of the United States with a new constitutional right which is within the protecting power of Congress. That right is exemption from discrimination in the exercise of the elective franchise on account of race, color, or previous condition of servitude. . . .

The power of Congress to legislate at all upon the subject of voting at State elections rests upon this Amendment. It cannot be contended that the Amendment confers authority to impose penalties for every wrongful refusal to receive the vote of a qualified elector at State elections. It is only when the wrongful refusal at such an election is on account of race, etc., that Congress can interfere and provide for its punishment. . . .

B. THE KU KLUX KLAN CASE

Ex parte Yarbrough, 110 U.S. 651 (1884).

MILLER, J.: . . . Stripped of its technical verbiage, the offence charged in this indictment is that the defendants conspired to intimidate Berry Saunders, a citizen of African descent, in the exercise of his right to vote for a member of the Congress of the United States, and in the execution of that conspiracy they beat, bruised, wounded and otherwise maltreated him; and in the second count, that they did this on account of his race, color, and previous condition of servitude, by going in disguise and assaulting him on the public highway and on his own premises. . . .

That a government whose essential character is republican, whose executive head and legislative body are both elective, whose most numerous and powerful branch of the legislature is elected by the people directly, has no power by appropriate laws to secure this election from the influence of violence, of corruption. and of fraud, is a proposition so startling as to arrest attention and demand the gravest consideration.

If this government is anything more than a mere aggregation of delegated agents of other States and governments, each of which is superior to the general government, it must have the power to protect the elections on which its existence depends from violence and corruption.

If it has not this power, it is left helpless before the two great natural and historical enemies of all republics, open violence and insidious corruption.

The proposition that it has no such power is supported by the old argument, often heard, often repeated, and in this court never assented to, that when a question of the power of Congress arises the advocate of the power must be able to place his finger on words which expressly grant it. The brief of the counsel before us, though directed to the authority of that body to pass criminal laws, uses the same language. Because there is no *express* power to provide for preventing violence exercised on the voter as a means of controlling his vote, no such law can be enacted. It destroys at one blow, in construing the Constitution of the United States, the doctrine universally applied to all instruments of writing, that what is implied is as much a part of the instrument as what is expressed. This principle, in its application to the Constitution of the United States, more than to almost any other writing, is a necessity, by reason of the inherent inability to put into words all derivative powers,—a difficulty which the instrument itself recognizes by conferring on Congress the authority to pass all laws necessary and proper to carry into execution the powers expressly granted, and all other powers vested in the government or any branch of it by the Constitution. . . .

The States, in prescribing the qualifications of voters for the most numerous branch of their own legislatures, do not do this with reference to the election for members of Congress. Nor can they prescribe the qualification for voters for those *eo nomine*. They define who are to vote for the popular branch of their own legislature, and the Constitution of the United States says the same persons shall vote for members of Congress in that state. It adopts the qualification thus furnished as the qualification of its own electors for members of Congress.

It is not true, therefore, that electors for members of Congress owe their right to vote to the state law, in any sense which makes the exercise of the right to depend exclusively on the law of the State. . . .

In a republican government, like ours, where political power is reposed in representatives of the entire body of the people, chosen at short intervals by popular elections, the temptations to control these elections by violence and by corruption is a constant source of danger.

Such has been the history of all republics, and, though ours has been comparatively free from both these evils in the past, no lover of his country can shut his eyes to the fear of future danger from both sources.

If the recurrence of such acts as these prisoners stand convicted of are too common in one quarter of the country, and give omen of danger from lawless violence, the free use of money in elections, arising from the vast growth of recent wealth in other quarters, presents equal cause for anxiety.

If the government of the United States has within its constitutional domain no authority to provide against these evils, if the very sources of power may be poisoned by corruption or controlled by violence and outrage, without legal restraint, then, indeed, is the country in danger, and its best powers, its highest purposes, the hopes which it inspires, and the love which enshrines it, are at the mercy of the combinations of those who respect no right but brute force on the one hand, and unprincipled corruptionists on the other.

CHAPTER XV

The Waite-Fuller Court and the Industrial Revolution

THE Civil War Amendments did not erect bulwarks of civil liberties protecting individual rights as their sponsors envisioned. Instead, they were gradually developed into formidable legal protections of corporate-property rights against state regulation. A classic protest against such governmental interference is set forth in the Jacobs case (No. 133). A New York court struck down a state law forbidding the manufacture of cigars in tenement houses because it could not "perceive how the cigarmaker is to be improved in his health or morals by forcing him from his home and its hallowed associations and beneficent influences to ply his trade elsewhere." Although Governor Theodore Roosevelt condemned the ruling because it showed that judges "knew nothing whatever of the needs, or the life and labor, of three-fourths of their fellow citizens . . . ," the Jacobs view dominated the bench more and more in the late 19th century. Some protested. A future Supreme Court Justice, for example, foresaw the evils of unregulated *laissez faire* and proclaimed the judicial necessity "of weighing considerations of social advantage" (No. 134).

The key to the rapid industrialization of the postwar period was the development of nationwide transportation facilities. Built with the aid of state and federal legislation and subsidies, the railroads too often ignored the interests of the public. In 1871 Charles Francis Adams, Lincoln's wartime ambassador to England and later a railroad executive, noted that interests controlling the railroads "have declared war, negotiated peace, reduced courts, legislatures, and sovereign states to an unqualified obedience to their will, disturbed trade, agitated the currency, imposed taxes, and boldly setting both law and public opinion at defiance, have freely exercised many other attributes of sovereignty." In the absence of federal legislation, the states were the only governmental agencies to enact regulatory measures. The Granger cases, which tested these statutes, are of historic importance in American constitutional law. Chief Justice Waite upheld state regulation of railroad and storage facilities as a legitimate exercise of the state's police power to protect the public welfare. In the Munn decision (No. 135), involving warehouse storage charges, he ruled that "when private property is affected with a public interest it ceases to be *juris privati* only." Waite agreed that state regulation might be abused, but suggested that "for protection against abuses by legislatures the people must resort to the polls, not the courts." On the same day the Court applied the same rule to railroad rates, observing that the railroads involved were "employed in state as well as interstate commerce, and until Congress acts, the State must be permitted to adopt such rules and regulations as may be necessary for the promotion of the general welfare of the people within its own jurisdiction, even though in so doing those without may be indirectly affected." (*Peik v. Chicago and Northwestern Railway Co.*, 1877).

Ten years later, however, in the Wabash Case the Court reversed its position (No. 136), invalidating an Illinois statute that prohibited "long-and-short haul" rate discriminations on the ground that state regulation violated Congress's exclusive power over interstate commerce. Since the states had been the only regulators of railroads until this time, the decision temporarily killed all regulation of rail transportation, making it imperative that Congress act. Simultaneously, a congressional committee concluded that "the paramount evil chargeable against transportation systems is unjust discrimination between persons, places, commodities, or particular descriptions of traffic." Viewing the Wabash decision as an invitation to act, Congress passed the Interstate Commerce Act, establishing the first permanent regulatory agency in American history. Designed to regulate railroad abuses, the Interstate Commerce Commission was authorized to investigate complaints against the railroads, but enforcement of its rulings was vested in the Courts.

Although the Act specified that all rail charges should be "reasonable and just," these terms were not defined nor was the Commission specifically empowered to fix "just" rates. Moreover, the burden of proof for alleged violations was placed on the Commission; the railroads were not bound by "cease and desist" orders until they were approved by the judiciary. Indeed, Senator Nelson W. Aldrich candidly admitted that the act was "a delusion and a sham . . . an empty menace to great interests, made to answer the clamor of the ignorant and unreasoning."

Whether one agrees with Senator Aldrich's statement or not, judicial review by a court composed largely of ex-corporation lawyers quickly rendered the Commission ineffective as a regulatory body. Between 1887 and 1905 the Supreme Court heard sixteen cases involving the Interstate Commerce Act; in fifteen it ruled in favor of the railroads. The most important of these decisions was the Maximum Freight Rate Case (No. 137), in which the railroads challenged the Commission's authority to fix rates. Although the I. C. C. had never assumed that it had the power to promulgate rate schedules prior to a complaint, for ten years it had followed up its "cease and desist" orders with alternative rates that were "reasonable." Now the Court ruled that the Commission had never possessed this vital power. The final blow came in the same year in the Alabama Midland Railway Case (1897) when the Court nullified for practical purposes the long- and short-haul clause. "By virtue of judicial decisions," the I. C. C. confessed in its annual report of 1897, "we have ceased to be a body for the regulation of interstate carriers . . . The people should no longer look to this commission for a protection which it is powerless to extend." Thus, as Attorney General Richard S. Olney had predicted five years earlier, the act to regulate railroads was transformed judicially into "a sort of barrier between the railroad corporations and the people" (No. 138).

The concentration of economic power, well exemplified by the organization of transcontinental transportation in large railroad systems, grew steadily in the post-Civil War industrial boom. Like the railroads, other gigantic corporations threatened to monopolize the economic life of the nation, and by the 1880's public opinion began to demand effective regulation of the trusts. In his annual message in 1888, President Cleveland warned that "corporations which should be carefully restrained creatures of the law and servants of the people, are fast becoming the people's masters." In that same year, both major parties inserted antimonopoly planks in their national platforms. This widespread opposition led to the Sherman Anti-Trust Act in 1890. Hailed as a victory over "unlawful restraints and monopolies," the measure carefully avoided defining the terms trust, monopoly, conspiracy, combination, or restraint. Moreover, no enforcement machinery was prescribed, apart from instituting suits in federal courts. Commenting on these ambiguities, Mr. Dooley, the shrewd observer created by the humorist Finley Peter Dunne, prophesied that "what looks like a stone-wall to a layman is a triumphal arch to a corporation lawyer." In the first interpretation by the Supreme Court (No. 139), the law was rendered ineffective by narrow construction of its terms. The Knight case held that control of 98 per cent of the nation's sugar refining capacity did not restrain trade and commerce since "commerce succeeds to manufacture, and is not a part of it." In a lone dissent, Justice Harlan protested that under the guise of economic freedom, individual liberty was being subordinated to industrial combinations "so all-pervading that they threaten the integrity of our institutions." But there were no protests from Attorney-General Olney, who virtually admitted sabotaging the antitrust law in his complacent acceptance of business triumph: "You will have observed that the government has been defeated . . . on the trust question. I always supposed it would be, and have taken the responsibility of not prosecuting under a law I believed to be no good."

If Olney was reluctant to use the Sherman Act against business, the Justice Department was not so hesitant in utilizing it against labor unions. In breaking the Pullman strike of 1894, the federal government used two almost equally effective instruments—troops, and an injunction based partially on the Anti-Trust Act. The injunction against the American Railway Union was upheld in a contempt case at the circuit court level (No. 140). This interpretation was challenged by the

Union's president, Eugene V. Debs, who sued out a writ of habeas corpus in the Supreme Court. Although Olney had specifically directed that the Sherman Act should be "strictly enforced against all violators," his argument in *In re Debs* skirted that issue and urged broader grounds to justify governmental interference. For the most part, the Supreme Court followed Olney's reasoning (No. 141).

The year 1895 saw a third major defense of the gospel of wealth by the Supreme Court. Economically, the Income Tax decision (No. 142) was consistent with the Court's construction of a legal bulwark protecting vested rights and corporate property. As recently as 1881 the Court had unanimously upheld the Civil War income tax, ruling that it did not violate the direct tax clauses of the Constitution since these clauses applied only to taxes on land and on persons (*Springer v. U.S.*). When the Wilson-Gorman Tariff Act of 1894 enacted a 2 per cent tax on incomes over $4,000, however, the Court, grown conservative in the years since 1881, struck down the tax provisions as unconstitutional levies and an assault upon capital. The Sixteenth Amendment (Chapter XVIII) was added to the Constitution as a direct, but long deferred, result of this case.

When the Supreme Court was erecting a constitutional defense against national regulation of property, it evolved an interpretation of the due process clause of the Fourteenth Amendment which eventually made it possible to strike down state supervision. In the Slaughterhouse Cases (Chapter XIV), the first interpretation of due process, Justice Miller refused to convert the clause from a guarantee of just procedure to a device for reviewing the substance of state laws. "Such a ruling," he said, "would constitute this Court a perpetual censor upon all legislation of the states." Four years later in *Munn v. Illinois,* the Court again waved aside substantive due process in favor of the police powers of the states. Denouncing this judicial hands-off position in a vigorous dissent, Justice Field asserted that procedural due process did not afford sufficient protection for property rights. The majority's decision, he concluded, was "subversive of the right of private property, heretofore believed to be protected by constitutional guarantees against legislative interference."

Between 1877 and 1890 seven participants in the Slaughterhouse and Munn cases died or resigned from the Supreme Court. During this period Field and his new colleagues brought about a judicial revolution in the interpretation of due process. As early as 1882, Roscoe Conkling, a member of the congressional committee that drafted the Fourteenth Amendment, supplied the Court with a convenient if not altogether reliable argument, asserting that the committee had used the word "person" instead of "citizen" in the due process clause to protect corporations as well as individuals (*San Mateo County v. Southern Pacific Railroad Co.*). Four years later the Court endorsed this position in *Santa Clara County v. Southern Pacific Railroad Company* (No. 143). In the Minnesota Commission Case (1889) the Court completed the judicial about-face, transforming itself, in Justice Miller's words, into a "perpetual censor" of state legislation, and establishing itself as the final arbiter of the reasonableness of railroad rates. The development of substantive due process culminated in *Smyth v. Ames* (No. 144). In voiding a Nebraska intrastate rate law, the Court decided that "reasonable" rates must yield a "fair return" on a "fair evaluation" of the property regulated. The very vagueness of this terminology buttressed the Court's new censorial role, increasing both the scope and the economic importance of judicial review in an industrialized society.

Presages of Future Change

133. *"Governmental interferences disturb the normal adjustments of the social fabric."*

In re Jacobs, 98 New York 98 (1885).

Earl, J.: . . . Generally it is for the legislature to determine what laws and regulations are needed to protect the public health and secure the public comfort and safety, and while its measures are calculated, intended, convenient and appropriate to accomplish these ends, the exercise of its discretion is not subject to review by the courts. But they must have some relation to these ends. Under the mere guise of police regulations, personal rights and private property cannot arbitrarily be invaded, and the determination of the legislature is not final or conclusive. If it passes an act ostensibly for the public health, and thereby destroys or takes away the property of a citizen, or interferes with his personal liberty, then it is for the courts to scrutinize the act and see whether it really relates to and is convenient and appropriate to promote the public health. It matters not that the legislature may in the title to the act, or in its body, declare that it is intended for the improvement of the public health. . . . What possible relation to the health of the occupants of a large tenement-house could cigarmaking in one of its remote rooms have? If the legislature had in mind the protection of the occupants of the tenement-houses, why was the act confined in its operation to the two cities only? It is plain that this is not a health law, and that it has no relation whatever to the public health. . . . Such legislation may invade one class of rights to-day and another to-morrow, and if it can be sanctioned under the Constitution, while far removed in time we will not be far away in practical statesmanship from those ages when governmental prefects supervised the building of houses, the rearing of cattle, the sowing of seed and the reaping of grain, and governmental ordinances regulated the movements and labor of artisans, the rate of wages, the price of food, the diet and clothing of the people, and a large range of other affairs long since in all civilized lands regarded as outside of governmental functions. Such governmental interferences disturb the normal adjustments of the social fabric, and usually derange the delicate and complicated machinery of industry and cause a score of ills while attempting the removal of one.

When a health law is challenged in the courts as unconstitutional on the ground that it arbitrarily interferes with personal liberty and private property without due process of law, the courts must be able to see that it has at least in fact some relation to the public health, that the public health is the end actually aimed at, and that it is appropriate and adapted to that end. This we have not been able to see in this law, and we must, therefore, pronounce it unconstitutional and void. . . .

134. *Oliver Wendell Holmes, "The Path of the Law,"* 1897

Harvard Law Review, 10 (1897), 457-78.

The training of lawyers is a training in logic. The processes of analogy, discrimination, and deduction are those in which they are most at home. The language of judicial decision is mainly the language of logic. And the logical method and form flatter that longing for certainty and for repose which is in every human mind. But certainty generally is illusion, and repose is not the destiny of man. Behind the logical form lies a judgment as to the relative worth and importance of competing legislative grounds, often an inarticulate and unconscious judgment, it is true, and yet the very root and nerve of the whole proceeding. You can give any conclusion a logical form. . . . We do not realize how large a part of our law is open to reconsideration upon a slight change in the habit of the public mind. No concrete proposition is self evident, no matter how ready we may be to accept it, not even Mr. Herbert Spencer's "Every man has a right to do what he wills, provided he interferes not with a like right on the part of his neighbors." . . .

I think that the judges themselves have failed adequately to recognize their duty of weighing considerations of social advantage. The duty is inevitable, and the result of the often proclaimed judicial aversion to deal with such considerations is simply to leave the very ground and foundation of judgments inarticulate, and often unconscious, as I have said. When socialism first began to be talked about, the comfortable classes of the community were a good deal frightened. I suspect that this fear has influenced judicial action both here and in England. . . . I think that something similar has led people who no longer hope to control the legislatures to look to the courts as expounders of the Constitutions, and that in some courts new principles have been discovered outside the bodies of those instruments, which may be generalized into acceptance of the economic doctrines which prevailed about fifty years ago, and a wholesale prohibition of what a tribunal of lawyers does not think about right. I cannot but believe that if the training of lawyers led them habitually to consider more definitely and explicitly the social advantage on which the rule they lay down must be justified, they sometimes would hesitate where now they are confident, and see that really they were taking sides upon debatable and often burning questions.

Government Regulation of Economic Enterprise

THE RAILROADS AND THE REVOLT OF THE GRANGERS

135. *Private Property and Public Regulation*

Munn v. Illinois, 94 U.S. 113 (1877).

WAITE, C.J.: . . . The Constitution contains no definition of the word "deprive," as used in the Fourteenth Amendment. To determine its signification, therefore, it is necessary to ascertain the effect which usage has given it, when employed in the same or a like connection.

While this provision of the amendment is new in the Constitution of the United States, as a limitation upon the powers of the States, it is old as a principle of civilized government. It is found in Magna Charta, and, in substance if not in form, in nearly or quite all the constitutions that have been from time to time adopted by the several States of the Union. By the Fifth Amendment, it was introduced into the Constitution of the United States as a limitation upon the powers of the national government, and by the Fourteenth, as a guarantee against any encroachment upon an acknowledged right of citizenship by the legislatures of the States. . . .

When one becomes a member of society, he necessarily parts with some rights or privileges which, as an individual not affected by his relations to others, he might retain. "A body politic," as aptly defined in the preamble of the constitution of Massachusetts, "is a social compact by which the whole people covenants with each citizen, and each citizen with the whole people, that all shall be governed by certain laws for the common good." This does not confer power upon the whole people to control rights which are purely and exclusively private. . . ; but it does authorize the establishment of laws requiring each citizen to so conduct himself, and so use his own property, as not unnecessarily to injure another. . . . From this source come the police powers, which, as was said by Mr. Chief Justice Taney in the *License Cases* . . . "are nothing more or less than the powers of government inherent in every sovereignty, . . . that is to say, . . . the power to govern men and things." Under these powers the government regulates the conduct of its citizens one towards another, and the manner in which each shall use his own property, when such regulation becomes necessary for the public good. . . .

From this it is apparent that, down to the time of the adoption of the Fourteenth Amendment, it was not supposed that statutes regulating the use, or even the price of the use, of private property necessarily deprived an owner of his property without due process of law. Under some circumstances they may, but not under all. The amendment does not change the law in this particular: it simply prevents the States from doing that which will operate as such a deprivation.

This brings us to inquire as to the principles upon which this power of regulation rests, in order that we may determine what is within and what without its operative effect. Looking, then, to the common law, from whence came the right which the Constitution protects, we find that when private property is "affected with a public interest, it ceases to be *juris privati* only." This was said by Lord Chief Justice Hale more than two hundred years ago, in his treatise *De Portibus Maris,* 1 Harg. Law Tracts, 78, and has been accepted without objection as an essential element in the law of property ever since. Property does become clothed with a public interest when used in a manner to make it of public consequence, and affect the community at large. When, therefore, one devotes his property to a use in which the public has an interest, he, in effect, grants to the public an interest in that use, and must submit to be controlled by the public for the common good, to the extent of the interest he has thus created. He may withdraw his grant by discontinuing the use; but, so long as he maintains the use, he must submit to the control. . . .

Common carriers exercise a sort of public office, and have duties to perform in which the public is interested. . . . Their business is, therefore, "affected with a public interest," within the meaning of the doctrine which Lord Hale has so forcibly stated.

But we need not go further. Enough has already been said to show that, when private property is devoted to a public use, it is subject to public regulation. It remains only to ascertain whether the warehouses of these plaintiffs in error, and the business which is carried on there, come within the operation of this principle. . . .

It must . . . be conceded that it is a business in which the whole public has a direct and positive interest. It presents, therefore, a case for the application of a long-known and well-established principle in social science, and this statute simply extends the law so as to meet this new development of commercial progress. There is no attempt to compel these owners to grant the public an interest in their property, but to decline their obligations, if they use it in this particular manner. . . .

It is insisted, however, that the owner of property is entitled to a reasonable compensation for its use, even though it be clothed with a public interest, and that what is reasonable is a judicial and not a legislative question.

As has already been shown, the practice has been otherwise. In countries where the common law prevails, it has been customary from time immemorial for the legislature to declare what shall be a reasonable compensation under such circumstances, or perhaps more properly speaking, to fix a maximum beyond which any charge made would be unreasonable. Undoubtedly in mere private contracts, relating to matters in which the public has no interest, what is reasonable must be ascertained judicially. But this is because the legislature has no control over such a contract. So, too, in matters which do not affect the public interest, and as to which legislative control may be exercised . . . the courts must determine what is reasonable. The controlling fact is the power to regulate at all. If that exists, the right to establish the maximum charge, as one of the means of regulation, is implied. . . .

136. *Regulation of interstate commerce "should be done by the Congress."*

Wabash, St. Louis and Pacific Railway Company v. Illinois, 118 U.S. 557 (1886).

MILLER, J.: . . . The obvious injustice of such a rule as this, which railroad companies are by heavy penalties compelled to conform to, in regard to commerce among the States, when applied to transportation which includes Illinois in a long line of carriage through several States, shows the value of the constitutional provision which confides the power of regulating interstate commerce to the Congress of the United States, whose enlarged view of the interests of all the States, and of the railroads concerned, better fits it to establish just and equitable rules.

Of the justice or propriety of the principle which lies at the foundation of the Illinois statute it is not the province of this court to speak. As restricted to a transportation which begins and ends within the limits of the State it may be very just and equitable, and it certainly is the province of the state legislature to determine that question. But when it is attempted to apply to transportation through an entire series of States a principle of this kind, and each one of the States shall attempt to establish its own rates of transportation, its own methods to prevent discrimination in rates, or to permit it, the deleterious influence upon the freedom of commerce among the States, and upon the transit of goods through those States, cannot be overestimated. That this species of regulation is one which must be, if established at all, of a general and national character, and cannot be safely and wisely remitted to local rules and local regulations, we think is clear from what has already been said. And if it be a regulation of commerce, as we think we have demonstrated it is, and as the Illinois court concedes it to be, it must be of that national character; and the regulation can only appropriately exist by general rules and principles, which demand that it should be done by the Congress of the United States under the commerce clause of the Constitution.

137. *The Maximum Freight Rate Case: Judicial Emasculation of the I. C. C.*

I. C. C. v. Cincinnati, New Orleans, and Texas Pacific Railway Company, 167 U.S. 479 (1897).

Brewer, J.: . . . Before the passage of the act it was generally believed that there were great abuses in railroad management and railroad transportation, and the grave question which Congress had to consider was how those abuses should be corrected and what control should be taken of the business of such corporations. The present inquiry is limited to the question as to what it determined should be done with reference to the matter of rates. There were three obvious and dissimilar courses open for consideration. Congress might itself prescribe the rates; or it might commit to some subordinate tribunal this duty; or it might leave with the companies the right to fix rates, subject to regulations and restrictions, as well as to that rule which is as old as the existence of common carriers, to wit, that rates must be reasonable. There is nothing in the act fixing rates. Congress did not attempt to exercise that power, and, if we examine the legislative and public history of the day, it is apparent that there was no serious thought of doing so.

The question debated is whether it vested in the Commission the power and the duty to fix rates; and the fact that this is a debatable question, and has been most strenuously and earnestly debated, is very persuasive that it did not. The grant of such a power is never to be implied. The power itself is so vast and comprehensive, so largely affecting the rights of carrier and shipper, as well as indirectly all commercial transactions, the language by which the power is given had been so often used and was so familiar to the legislative mind and is capable of such definite and exact statement, that no just rule of construction would tolerate a grant of such power by mere implication. . . .

It will be perceived that in this case the Interstate Commerce Commission assumed the right to prescribe rates which should control in the future, and this application to the court was for a mandamus to compel the companies to comply with their decision; that is, to abide by their legislative determination as to the maximum rates to be observed in the future. Now, nowhere in the Interstate Commerce Act do we find words giving to the Commission power to "increase or reduce any of the rates"; "to establish rates of charges"; "to make and fix reasonable and just rates of freight and passenger tariffs"; "to make a schedule of reasonable maximum rates of charges"; "to fix tables of maximum charges"; to compel the carrier "to adopt such rate, charge or classification as said commissioners shall declare to be equitable and reasonable." The power, therefore, is not expressly given. . . .

We have, therefore, these considerations presented: First. The power to prescribe a tariff or rates for carriage by a common carrier is a legislative and not an administrative or judicial function, and, having respect to the large amount of property invested in railroads, the various companies engaged therein, the thousands of miles of road, and the millions of tons of freight carried, the varying and diverse conditions attaching to such carriage, is a power of supreme delicacy and importance. Second. That Congress has transferred such a power to any administrative body is not to be presumed or implied from any doubtful and uncertain language. The words and phrases efficacious to make such a delegation of power are well understood, and have been frequently used, and, if Congress had intended to grant such a power to the Interstate Commerce Commission it cannot be doubted that it would have used language open to no misconstruction, but clear and direct. Third. Incorporating into a statute the common law obligation resting upon the carrier to make all its charges reasonable and just, and directing the Commission to execute and enforce the provisions of the act, does not by implication carry to the Commission, or invest it with the power to exercise, the legislative function of prescribing rates which shall control in the future. Fourth. Beyond the inference which irresistibly follows from the omission to grant in express terms to the commission this power of fixing rates is the clear language of section 6, recognizing the right of the carrier to establish rates, to increase or reduce them, and prescribing the conditions upon which such increase or reduction may be made, and requiring, as the only conditions of its action, first, publication; and, second, the filing of the tariff with the Commission. The grant to the Commission of the power to prescribe the form of the schedules, and to direct the place and manner of publication of joint rates, thus specifying the scope and limit of its functions in this respect, strengthens the conclusion that the power to prescribe rates or fix any tariff for the future is not among the powers granted to the Commission. . . .

Our conclusion, then, is that Congress has not conferred upon the Commission the legislative power of prescribing rates either maximum or minimum or absolute. As it did not give the express power to the Commission, it did not intend to secure the same result indirectly by empowering that tribunal to determine what in reference to the past was reasonable and just, whether as maximum, minimum or absolute, and then enable it to obtain from the courts a peremptory order that in the future the railroad companies should follow the rates thus determined to have been in the past reasonable and just. . . .

138. *The I. C. C. Act is "protection against hasty . . . legislation hostile to railroad interests."*

Richard S. Olney to Charles C. Perkins, December 28, 1892, Letterbook, IV, 353-4, Olney Papers (Library of Congress).

My impression would be that, looking at the matter from a railroad point of view exclusively, it would not be a wise thing to undertake to abolish the [Interstate Commerce] Commission. The attempt would not be likely to succeed—if it did not succeed and were made on the ground of the inefficiency and uselessness of the Commission, the result would very probably be giving it the powers it now lacks. The Commission, as its functions have now been limited by the Courts, is, or can be made of great use to the railroads. It satisfies the popular clamor for a government supervision of railroads, at the same time that the supervision is almost entirely nominal. Further, the older such a commission gets to be, the more inclined it will be found to be to take the business and railroad view of things. It thus becomes a sort of barrier between the railroad corporations and the people and a sort of protection against hasty and crude legislation hostile to railroad interests. The Commission costs something, of course. But so long as its powers are advisory merely, for the reasons just stated, it strikes me it is well worth the money. The part of wisdom is not to destroy the Commission, but to utilize it. . . .

MONITORING THE MENACE OF MONOPOLY

139. *"Commerce succeeds to manufacture, and is not a part of it."*

U.S. v. E. C. Knight, 156 U.S. 1 (1895).

FULLER, C.J.: . . . The fundamental question is, whether conceding that the existence of a monopoly in manufacture is established by the evidence, that monopoly can be directly suppressed under the act of Congress in the mode attempted by this bill. . . .

Doubtless the power to control the manufacture of a given thing involves in a certain sense the control of its disposition, but this is a secondary and not the primary sense; and although the exercise of that power may result in bringing the operation of commerce into play, it does not control it, and affects it only incidentally and indirectly. Commerce succeeds to manufacture, and is not a part of it. The power to regulate commerce is the power to prescribe the rule by which commerce shall be governed, and is a power independent of the power to suppress monopoly. But it may operate in repression of monopoly whenever it comes within the rules by which commerce is governed or whenever the transaction is itself a monopoly of commerce.

It is vital that the independence of the commercial power and of the police power, and the delimitation between them, however sometimes perplexing, should always be recognized and observed, for while the one furnishes the strongest bond of union, the other is essential to the autonomy of the States as required by our dual form of government; and acknowledged evils, however grave and urgent they may appear to be, had better be borne, than the risk be run, in the effort to suppress them, of more serious consequences by resort to expedients of even doubtful constitutionality.

It will be perceived how far-reaching the proposition is that the power of dealing with a monopoly directly may be exercised by the general government whenever interstate or international commerce may be ultimately affected. The regulation of commerce applies to the subjects of commerce, and not to matters of internal police. Contracts to buy, sell, or exchange goods to be transported among the several States, the transportation and its instrumentalities, and articles bought, sold, or exchanged for the purposes of such transit among the States, or put in the way of transit, may be regulated, but this is because they form part of interstate trade or commerce. The fact that an article is manufactured for export to another State does not of itself make it an article of interstate commerce, and the intent of the manufacturer does not determine the time when the article or product passes from the control of the State and belongs to commerce. . . .

Contracts, combinations, or conspiracies to control domestic enterprise in manufacture, agriculture, mining production in all its forms, or to raise or lower prices or wages, might unquestionably tend to restrain external as well as domestic trade, but the restraint would be an indirect result, however inevitable and whatever its extent, and such result would not necessarily determine the object of the contract, combination, or conspiracy.

Again, all the authorities agree that in order to vitiate a contract or combination it is not essential that its result should be a complete monopoly; it is sufficient if it really tends to that end and to deprive the public of the advantages which flow from free competition. Slight reflection will show that if the national power extends to all contracts and combinations in manufacture, agriculture, mining, and other productive industries, whose ultimate result may affect external commerce, comparatively little of business operations and affairs would be left for state control.

It was in the light of well-settled principles that the act of July 2, 1890 was framed. Congress did not attempt thereby to assert the power to deal with monopoly directly as such; or to limit and restrict the rights of corporations created by the States or the citizens of the States in the acquisition, control, or disposition of property; or to regulate or prescribe the price or prices at which such property or the products thereof should be sold; or to make criminal the acts of persons in the acquisition and control of property which the States of their residence or creation sanctioned or permitted. Aside from the provisions applicable where Congress might exercise municipal power, what the law struck at was combinations, contracts, and conspiracies to monopolize trade and commerce among the several States or with foreign nations; but the contracts and acts of the defendants related exclusively to the acquisition of the Philadelphia refineries and the business of sugar refining in Pennsylvania, and bore no direct relation to commerce between the States or with foreign nations. The object was manifestly private gain in the manufacture of the commodity, but not through the control of interstate or foreign commerce. It is true that the bill alleged that the products of these refineries were sold and distributed among the several States, and that all the companies were engaged in trade or commerce with the several States and with foreign nations; but this was no more than to say that trade and commerce served manufacture to fulfil its function. . . . There was nothing in the proofs to indicate any intention to put a restraint upon trade or commerce, and the fact, as we have seen, that trade or commerce might be indirectly affected was not enough to entitle complainants to a decree. . . .

140. *Circuit Judge Woods Brings Labor Unions Under the Sherman Act*

U.S. v. Debs et al, 64 Fed. 724 (1894).

WOODS, Circuit Judge: . . . The position of the defendants in respect to this statute, as stated in one of the briefs, is that it "is directed at capital," "at dangers very generally supposed to result from vast aggregations of capital," that "the evil aimed at is one of a contractual character, and not of force and violence." . . . It is said we may gather from the debates in congress, as from any other source, "the history of the evil which the legislation was intended to remedy." Doubtless this is often true; and in this instance it is perhaps apparent that the original measure, as proposed in the senate, "was directed wholly against trusts, and not at organizations of labor in any form." But it also appears that before the bill left the senate its title had been changed, and material additions made to the text; and it is worthy of note that a proviso to the effect that the act should not be construed to apply "to any arrangements, agreements or combinations made between laborers with a view of lessening hours of labor or of increasing their wages, nor to any arrangements, agreements or combinations among persons engaged in agriculture made with the view of enhancing the price of agricultural . . . products" was not adopted. Such an amendment, doubtless, was not necessary in order to exclude agreements and arrangements of the kind mentioned; but the offering of the proposition shows that the possible application of the statute to cases not in the nature of trusts or monopolies, and in which workmen or farmers should be concerned, was not overlooked. But it is more significant that, upon the introduction of the bill into the house, the chairman of the judiciary committee . . . made the following statement: "Now just what contracts, what combinations in the form of trusts, or what conspiracies will be in restraint of trade or commerce, mentioned in the bill, will not be known until the courts have construed and interpreted this provision."

It is therefore the privilege and duty of the court, uncontrolled by considerations drawn from other sources, to find the meaning of the statute in the terms of its provisions, interpreted by the settled rules of construction. That the original design to suppress trusts and monopolies created by contract or combination in the form of trust, which of course would be of a "contractual character" was adhered to, is clear; but it is equally clear that a further and more comprehensive purpose came to be entertained, and was embodied in the final form of the enactment. Combinations are condemned, not only when they take the form of trusts, but in whatever form found, if they be in restraint of trade. That is the effect of the words "or otherwise." . . . Any proposed restraint of trade, though it be in itself innocent, if it is to be accomplished by conspiracy, is unlawful. . . .

I have not failed, I think, to appreciate the just force of the argument to the contrary, of my opinion,—it has sometimes entangled me in doubt,—but my conclusion is clear, that under the act of 1890, the court had jurisdiction of the case presented in the application, and that the injunction granted was not without authority of law, nor for any reason invalid. . . .

141. *The Court exercises "the strong arm of the national government."*

In re Debs, 158 U.S. 564 (1895).

Brewer, J.: . . . As, under the Constitution, power over interstate commerce and the transportation of the mails is vested in the national government, and Congress by virtue of such grant has assumed actual and direct control, it follows that the national government may prevent any unlawful and forcible interference therewith. . . .

The entire strength of the nation may be used to enforce in any part of the land the full and free exercise of all national powers and the security of all rights entrusted by the Constitution to its care. The strong arm of the national government may be put forth to brush away all obstructions to the freedom of interstate commerce or the transportation of the mails. If the emergency arises, the army of the Nation, and all its militia, are at the service of the Nation to compel obedience to its laws. . . .

But . . . is there no other alternative than the use of force on the part of the executive authorities whenever obstructions arise to the freedom of interstate commerce or the transportation of the mails? Is the army the only instrument by which rights of the public can be enforced and the peace of the nation preserved? Grant that any public nuisance may be forcibly abated either at the instance of the authorities, or by any individual suffering private damage therefrom, the existence of this right of forcible abatement is not inconsistent with nor does it destroy the right of appeal in an orderly way to the court for a judicial determination, and an exercise of their powers by writ of injunction and otherwise to accomplish the same result. . . .

The national government, given by the Constitution power to regulate interstate commerce, has by express statute assumed jurisdiction over such commerce when carried upon railroads. It is charged, therefore, with the duty of keeping those highways of interstate commerce free from obstruction, for it has always been recognized as one of the powers and duties of a government to remove obstructions from the highway under its control. . . .

Summing up our conclusions, we hold that the government of the United States is one having jurisdiction over every foot of soil within its territory, and acting directly upon each citizen; that while it is a government of enumerated powers, it has within the limits of those powers all the attributes of sovereignty; that to it is committed power over interstate commerce and the transmission of the mail; that the powers thus conferred upon the national government are not dormant, but have been assumed and put into practical exercise by the legislation of Congress; that in the exercise of those powers it is competent for the nation to remove all obstructions upon highways, natural or artificial, to the passage of interstate commerce or the carrying of the mail; that while it may be competent for the government (through the executive branch and in the use of the entire executive power of the nation) to forcibly remove all such obstructions, it is equally within its competency to appeal to the civil courts for an inquiry and determination as to the existence and character of any alleged obstructions, and if such are found to exist, or theaten to occur, to invoke the powers of these courts to remove or restrain such obstruction; that the jurisdiction of courts to interfere in such matters by injunction is one recognized from ancient times and by indubitable authority; that such jurisdiction is not ousted by the fact that the obstructions are accompanied by or consist of acts in themselves violations of the criminal law; that the proceeding by injunction is of a civil character, and may be enforced by proceedings in contempt; that such proceedings are not in execution of the criminal laws of the land; that the penalty for a violation of injunction is no substitute for and no defense to a prosecution for any criminal offenses committed in the course of such violation; that the complaint filed in this case clearly showed an existing obstruction of artificial highways for the passage of interstate commerce and the transmission of the mail—an obstruction not only temporarily existing, but threatening to continue; that under such complaint the circuit court had power to issue its process of injunction; that it having been issued and served on these defendants, the circuit court had authority to inquire whether its orders had been disobeyed, and when it found that they had been, then to proceed under section 725, Revised Statutes, which grants power "to punish by fine or imprisonment, . . . disobedience, . . . by any party . . . or other person, to any lawful writ, process, order, rule, decree or command," and enter the order of punishment complained of; and, finally, that, the circuit court, having full jurisdiction in the premises, its finding of the fact of disobedience is not open to review on *habeas corpus* in this or any other court. . . .

We enter into no examination of the [Sherman] act of July 2, 1890 . . . upon which the Circuit Court relied mainly to sustain its jurisdiction. It must not be understood from this that we dissent from the conclusions of that court in reference to the scope of the act, but simply that we prefer to rest our judgment on the broader ground which has been discussed in this opinion, believing it of importance that the principles underlying it should be fully stated and affirmed.

The petition for a writ of *habeas corpus* is denied.

THE INCOME TAX AND THE GOSPEL OF WEALTH

142. *The Court Rules that Income Taxes Are an Assault on Capital*

Pollock v. Farmers' Loan and Trust Company 158 U.S. 601 (1895).

FULLER, C.J.: . . . Our previous decision was confined to the consideration of the validity of the tax on the income from real estate, and on the income from municipal bonds. . . .

We are now permitted to broaden the field of inquiry, and to determine to which of the two great classes a tax upon a person's entire income, whether derived from rents or products, or otherwise, of real estate, or from bonds, stocks, or other forms of personal property, belongs; and we are unable to conclude that the enforced subtraction from the yield of all the owner's real or personal property, in the manner prescribed, is so different from a tax on the property itself, that it is not a direct, but an indirect, tax in the meaning of the Constitution. . . .

We know of no reason for holding otherwise than that the words "direct taxes" on the one hand, and "duties, imposts and excises," on the other, were used in the Constitution in their natural and obvious sense. Nor, in arriving at what those terms embrace, do we perceive any ground for enlarging them beyond, or narrowing them within, their natural and obvious import at the time the Constitution was framed and ratified. . . .

The Constitution prohibits any direct tax, unless in proportion to numbers as ascertained by the census, and, in the light of the circumstances to which we have referred, is it not an evasion of that prohibition to hold that a general unapportioned tax, imposed upon all property owners as a body for or in respect of their property, is not direct, in the meaning of the Constitution, because confined to the income therefrom?

Whatever the speculative views of political economists or revenue reformers may be, can it be properly held that the Constitution, taken in its plain and obvious sense, and with due regard to the circumstances attending the formation of the government, authorizes a general unapportioned tax on the products of the farm and the rents of real estate, although imposed merely because of ownership, and with no possible means of escape from payment, as belonging to a totally different class from that which includes the property from whence the income proceeds?

There can be but one answer, unless the constitutional restriction is to be treated as utterly illusory and futile, and the object of its framers defeated. We find it impossible to hold that a fundamental requisition deemed so important as to be enforced by two provisions, one affirmative and one negative, can be refined away by forced distinctions between that which gives value to property and the property itself.

Nor can we perceive any ground why the same reasoning does not apply to capital in personalty held for the purpose of income, or ordinarily yielding income, and to the income therefrom. . . .

Personal property of some kind is of general distribution, and so are incomes, though the taxable range thereof might be narrowed through large exemptions. . . .

Nor are we impressed with the contention that, because in the four instances in which the power of direct taxation has been exercised, Congress did not see fit, for reasons of expediency, to levy a tax on personalty, this amounts to such a practical construction of the Constitution that the power did not exist, that we must regard ourselves bound by it. We should regret to be compelled to hold the powers of the general government thus restricted, and certainly we cannot accede to the idea that the Constitution has become weakened by a particular course of inaction under it. . . .

We have unanimously held in this case that, so far as this law operates on the receipts from municipal bonds, it cannot be sustained, because it is a tax on the power of the States and on their instrumentalities to borrow money, and consequently repugnant to the Constitution. But, if, as contended, the interest, when received, has become merely money in the recipient's pocket, and taxable, as such, without reference to the source from which it came, the question is immaterial whether it could have been originally taxed at all or not. This was admitted by the Attorney General, with characteristic candor; and it follows that if the revenue derived from municipal bonds cannot be taxed, because the source cannot be, the same rule applies to revenue from any other source not subject to the tax, and the lack of power to levy any but an apportioned tax on real and personal property equally exists as to the revenue therefrom.

Admitting that this act taxes the income of property, irrespective of its source, still we cannot doubt that such a tax is necessarily a direct tax in the meaning of the Constitution. . . .

The power to tax real and personal property and the income from both, there being an apportionment, is conceded; that such a tax is a direct tax in the meaning of the Constitution has not been, and, in our judgment, cannot be successfully denied; and yet we are thus invited to hesitate in the enforcement of the mandate of the Constitution, which prohibits Congress from laying a direct tax on the revenue from property of the citizen without regard to state lines, and in such manner that the States cannot intervene by payment in regulation of their own resources, lest a government of delegated powers should be found to be, not less powerful, but less absolute, than the imagination of the advocate had supposed.

We are not here concerned with the question whether an income tax be or be not desirable, nor whether such a tax would enable the government to diminish taxes on consumption and duties on imports, and to enter upon what may be believed to be a reform of its fiscal and commercial system. Questions of that character belong to the controversies of political parties, and cannot be settled by judicial decision. In these cases our province is to determine whether this income tax on the revenue from property does or does not belong to the class of direct taxes. If it does, it is, being unapportioned, in violation of the Constitution, and we must so declare. . . .

Our conclusions may, therefore, be summed up as follows:

First. We adhere to the opinion already announced, that, taxes on real estate being indisputably direct taxes, taxes on the rents or income of real estate are equally direct taxes.

Second. We are of opinion that taxes on personal property, or on the income of personal property, are likewise direct taxes.

Third. The tax imposed by sections twenty-seven to thirty-seven, inclusive, of the act of 1894, so far as it falls on the income of real estate and of personal property, being a direct tax within the meaning of the Constitution, and, therefore, unconstitutional and void because not apportioned according to representation, all those sections, constituting one entire scheme of taxation, are necessarily invalid.

Judicial Development of Due Process as a Limitation on Public Control

THE FOURTEENTH AMENDMENT AND STATE REGULATORY POWER

143. *The Corporation as a Person*

Santa Clara County v. Southern Pacific Railroad Company, 118 U.S. 394 (1886).

One of the points made and discussed at length in the brief of counsel for defendants in error was that "Corporations are persons within the meaning of the Fourteenth Amendment to the Constitution of the United States." Before argument

Mr. Chief Justice Waite said: The Court does not wish to hear argument on the question whether the provision in the Fourteenth Amendment to the Constitution, which forbids a State to deny to any person within its jurisdiction the equal protection of the laws, applies to these corporations. We are all of the opinion that it does.

DUE PROCESS AND RAILROAD RATE MAKING

144. *To be reasonable, rates must yield a "fair return."*

Smyth v. Ames, 169 U.S. 466 (1898).

Harlan, J.: . . . By the Fourteenth Amendment, it is provided that no State shall deprive any person of property without due process of law nor deny to any person within its jurisdiction the equal protection of the laws. That corporations are persons within the meaning of this Amendment is now settled. . . . What amounts to deprivation of property without due process of law or what is a denial of the equal protection of the laws is often difficult to determine, especially where the question relates to the property of a *quasi* public corporation and the extent to which it may be subjected to public control. But this court, speaking by Chief Justice Waite, has said that, while a State has power to fix the charges for railroad companies for the transportation of persons and property within its own jurisdiction, unless restrained by valid contract, or unless what is done amounts to a regulation of foreign or interstate commerce, such power is not without limit; and that, "under pretense of regulating fares, and freights, the state cannot require a railroad corporation to carry persons or property without reward; neither can it do that which in law amounts to a taking of private property for public use without just compensation, or without due process of law." . . .

The plaintiffs contended that a railroad company is entitled to exact such charges for transportation as will enable it, at all times, not only to pay operating expenses, but also to meet the interest regularly accruing upon all its outstanding obligations, and justify a dividend upon all its stock; and that to prohibit it from maintaining rates or charges for transportation adequate to *all* those ends will deprive it of its property without due process of law, and deny to it the equal protection of the laws. This contention . . . should not be passed without examination.

In our opinion, the broad proposition advanced by counsel involves some misconception of the relations between the public and a railroad corporation. It is unsound in that it practically excludes from consideration the fair value of the property used, omits altogether any consideration of the right of the public to be exempt from unreasonable exactions, and makes the interests of the corporation maintaining a public highway the sole test in determining whether the rates established by or for it are such as may be rightfully prescribed as between it and the public. . . .

We hold, however, that the basis of all calculations as to the reasonableness of rates to be charged by a corporation maintaining a highway under legislative sanction must be the fair value of the property being used by it for the convenience of the public. And, in order to ascertain that value, the original cost of construction, the amount expended in permanent improvements, the amount and market value of its bonds and stocks, the present as compared with the original cost of construction, the probable earning capacity of the property, under particular rates prescribed by statute, and the sum required to meet operating expenses, are all matters for consideration, and are to be given such weight as may be just and right in each case. We do not say that there may not be other matters to be regarded in estimating the value of the property. What the company is entitled to ask is a fair return upon the value of that which it employs for the public convenience. On the other hand, what the public is entitled to demand is that no more be exacted from it for the use of a public highway than the services rendered by it are reasonably worth. . . .

CHAPTER XVI

Imperialism and the Constitution

FOLLOWING the Civil War the powers of the federal government expanded not only in the field of domestic economic regulation but also in the field of foreign policy. The spirit of resurgent nationalism, reflected as early as 1867 in the purchase of Alaska, was also expressed by the Supreme Court in decisions implying the existence of inherent sovereign powers in foreign affairs. In *Chae Chan Ping v. U.S.* (1889), the Court asserted that the United States is "one nation, invested with powers which belong to independent nations." Four years later in Fong Yue Ting (1893), the Court, in another Chinese exclusion case, asserted that "the United States are a sovereign and independent nation, and are vested by the Constitution with the entire control of international relations."

The issues in these cases were simple compared with the political and constitutional complexities posed by the acquisition of a colonial empire as a result of "the splendid little war with Spain." The status of continental territories had been defined by the Northwest Ordinance even before the adoption of the Constitution, and the Constitution authorized Congress "to dispose of and make all needful Rules and Regulations respecting the Territory or other Property belonging to the United States." Alaska, the first non-contiguous territory, presented few new problems, and none at all of governing alien peoples. In 1898, however, the United States, by the annexation of the Hawaiian Islands and the conquest of

Puerto Rico and the Philippines, began exercising sovereign authority over millions of alien subjects. Theoretically, the Treaty of Paris solved the problem simply, by providing that "the civil rights and political status of the native inhabitants hereby ceded to the United States shall be determined by Congress." But this provision did not delineate the nature and extent of congressional power; did it mean that Congress could exercise plenary power without extending the liberties guaranteed by the Constitution, or did it mean that Congress was subject to constitutional limitations in dealing with the newly acquired possessions? Two basic problems arose immediately: (1) does annexed territory become an integral part of the United States, and (2) do the constitutional guarantees also apply to the inhabitants of the territories?

In the Insular Cases, the Court wrestled inconclusively with these problems. *DeLima v. Bidwell* (1901) involved an American importer of Puerto Rican sugar who protested against the payment of tariff duties. The Court ruled that Puerto Rico was no longer a foreign nation but a territory of the United States and ordered the refunding of the duties. By this time, however, Congress had passed the Foraker Act, establishing a civil government for Puerto Rico and levying duties equal to 15 per cent of the regular tariff. Since the Constitution requires tariff uniformity, this clearly indicated that Congress did not consider the island a part of the United States. In *Downes v. Bidwell* (No. 145), the Court upheld Congress, ruling that although Puerto Rico was not a foreign nation, neither was it exactly a part of the United States in a domestic sense. Justice Brown, in the majority opinion, held that Puerto Rico "is a territory appurtenant and belonging to the United States, but not a part of the United States." In Justice White's concurring opinion, the majority evolved the new constitutional doctrine of "incorporation" to justify its negative answer to the popular question of the day: "Does the Constitution follow the flag?" Approving the expansion of American territory and the contraction of the Constitution, White ruled that constitutional provisions did not apply in non-contiguous territory until it was incorporated into the United States by Congress. Mr. Dooley, in one of his shrewd comments lampooning the Court, concluded that "no matter whether the constitution follows the flag or not, th' Supreme Court follows th' illiction returns."

The second problem, involving civil and political rights, came before the Court in a series of cases decided between 1903 and 1922. Drawing a legalistic distinction between fundamental liberties and purely procedural rights, the Court concluded that Congress could not deny the fundamental liberties in any territory, incorporated or unincorporated, nor could it deny procedural rights in incorporated territories. But in unincorporated territories, Congress could extend procedural guarantees at its discretion. The chief difficulty with this delineation, however, was the Court's failure to specify what constituted incorporation. Chief Justice Fuller had deplored the lack of constitutional clarity when Justice White first presented the theory of "incorporation." In his dissent in *Downes,* Fuller had denied that once "an organized and settled province of another sovereignty is acquired by the United States, Congress has the power to keep it, like a disembodied shape, in an intermediate state of ambiguous existence for an indefinite period; and, more than that, that after it has been called from that limbo, commerce with it is absolutely subject to the will of Congress, irrespective of constitutional provisions." But a more candid summary of the Court's attitude was expressed in the *Review of Reviews:* "The decision of the Supreme Court means that we are not to be hampered in our serious policies by the ingenious use of logic in the interpretation of an ancient document that was not intended to hamper posterity."

Thus far, at least, the Court has been content to avoid a definition of "incorporation," preferring instead to settle each question separately after considering the specifications and intentions of congressional enactments. The Mankichi case (No. 146) raised the question of whether guarantees of grand jury indictment and jury trial, in the Bill of Rights, extended to Hawaii. The Court decided that since the annexation of Hawaii did not make it an incorporated territory, these formal rights did not apply. In *Dorr v. U.S.*, the Court reached a similar decision for the Philippines, disregarding, as it had in Mankichi, a vigorous dissent by Justice Harlan (No. 147). As for Alaska, the Rassmussen case extended these guarantees, maintaining that Congress had incorporated that territory by the treaty of acquisition and subsequent legislation (No. 148). A similar issue in Puerto Rico was complicated by the passage of the Organic Act of 1917 conferring citizenship on the inhabitants. Balzac, a newspaper editor convicted of criminal libel, contended that this Act incorporated the island, and hence established jury trial. This fact the Court denied (*Balzac v. Puerto Rico*, 1922).

145. *Status of Non-contiguous Territories*

Downes v. Bidwell, 182 U.S. 244 (1901).

BROWN, J.: This case involves the question whether merchandise brought into the port of New York from Porto Rico, since the passage of the Foraker act, is exempt from duty, notwithstanding the third section of that act, which requires the payment of "fifteen per centum of the duties which are required to be levied, collected and paid upon like articles of merchandise imported from foreign countries." . . .

In the case of *De Lima v. Bidwell* just decided, we held that upon the ratification of the treaty of peace with Spain, Porto Rico ceased to be a foreign country, and became a territory of the United States, and that duties were no longer collectible upon merchandise brought from that island. We are now asked to hold that it became a part of the *United States* within that provision of the Constitution which declares that "all duties, imposts and excises shall be uniform throughout the United States." . . . If Porto Rico be a part of the United States, the Foraker act imposing duties upon its products is unconstitutional, not only by reason of a violation of the uniformity clause, but because by section 9 "vessels bound to or from one State" cannot "be obliged to enter, clear or pay duties in another."

The case also involves the broader question whether the revenue clauses of the Constitution extend of their own force to our newly acquired territories. The Constitution itself does not answer the question. Its solution must be found in the nature of the government created by that instrument, in the opinion of its contemporaries, in the practical construction put upon it by Congress and in the decisions of this court. . . .

To sustain the judgment in the case under consideration it by no means becomes necessary to show that none of the articles of the Constitution apply to the Island of Porto Rico. There is a clear distinction between such prohibitions as go to the very root of the power of Congress to act at all, irrespective of time or place, and such as are operative only "throughout the United States" or among the several States.

Thus, when the Constitution declares that "no bill of attainder or *ex post facto* law shall be passed," and that "no title of nobility shall be granted by the United States," it goes to the competency of Congress to pass a bill *of that description*. Perhaps the same remark may apply to the First Amendment. . . . We do not wish, however, to be understood as expressing an opinion how far the bill of rights contained in the first eight amendments is of general and how far of local application.

Upon the other hand, when the Constitution declares that all duties shall be uniform "throughout the United States," it becomes necessary to inquire whether there be any territory over which Congress has jurisdiction which is not a part of the "United States," by which term we understand the *States* whose people *united* to form the Constitution, and such as have since been admitted to the Union upon an equality with them. Not only did the people in adopting the Thirteenth Amendment thus recognize a distinction between the United States and "any place subject to their jurisdiction," but Congress itself, in the Act of March 27, 1804, . . . providing for the proof of public records, applied the provisions of the act, not only to "every court and office within the United States," but to the "courts and offices of the respective territories of the United States and countries subject to the jurisdiction of the United States." . . .

Unless these words are to be rejected as meaningless, we must treat them as a recognition by Congress of the fact that there may be territories subject to the jurisdiction of the United States, which are not *of* the United States. . . .

Indeed, the practical interpretation put by Congress upon the Constitution has been long continued and uniform to the effect that the Constitution is applicable to territories acquired by purchase or conquest only when and so far as Congress shall so direct. . . .

We are also of opinion that the power to acquire territory by treaty implies, not only the power to govern such territory, but to prescribe upon what terms the United States will receive its inhabitants, and what their *status* shall be in what Chief Justice Marshall termed the "American Empire." . . .

It is obvious that in the annexation of outlying and distant possessions grave questions will arise from differences of race, habits, laws and customs of the people, and from differences of soil, climate and production, which may require action on the part of Congress that would be quite unnecessary in the annexation of contiguous territory inhabited only by people of the same race, or by scattered bodies of native Indians.

We suggest, without intending to decide, that there may be a distinction between certain natural rights enforced in the Constitution by prohibitions against interference with them, and what may be termed artificial or remedial rights which are peculiar to our own system of jurisprudence. Of the former class are the rights to one's own religious opinions and to a public expression of them, or, as sometimes said, to worship God according to the dictates of one's own conscience; the right to personal liberty and individual property; to freedom of speech and of the press; to free access to courts of justice, to due process of law, and to an equal protection of the laws; to immunities from unreasonable searches and seizures, as well as cruel and unusual punishments; and to such other immunities as are indispensable to a free government. Of the latter case are the rights to citizenship, to suffrage, *Minor v. Happersett*, . . . and to the particular methods of procedure pointed out in the Constitution, which are peculiar to Anglo-Saxon jurisprudence, and some of which have already been held by the States to be unnecessary to the proper protection of individuals.

Whatever may be finally decided by the American people as to the *status* of these islands and their inhabitants—whether they shall be introduced into the sisterhood of States or be permitted to form independent governments—it does not follow that, in the meantime, awaiting that decision, the people are in the matter of personal rights unprotected by the provisions of our Constitution and subject to the merely arbitrary control of Congress. Even if regarded as aliens, they are entitled under the principles of the Constitution to be protected in life, liberty and property. This has been frequently held by this court in respect to the Chinese, even when aliens, not possessed of the political rights of citizens of the United States. . . . We do not desire, however, to anticipate the difficulties which would naturally arise in this connection, but merely to disclaim any intention to hold that the inhabitants of these territories are subject to an unrestrained power on the part of Congress to deal with them upon the theory that they have no rights which it is bound to respect. . . .

The liberality of Congress in legislating the Constitution into all our contiguous territories has undoubtedly fostered the impression that it went there by its own force, but there is nothing in the Constitution itself, and little in the interpretation put upon it, to confirm that impression. . . . The executive and legislative departments of the government have for more than a century interpreted this silence as precluding the idea that the Constitution attached to these territores as soon as acquired, and unless such interpretation be manifestly contrary to the letter or spirit of the Constitution, it should be followed by the judicial department. . . .

Patriotic and intelligent men may differ widely as to the desirableness of this or that acquisition, but this is solely a political question. We can only consider this aspect of the case so far as to say that no construction of the Constitution should be adopted which would prevent Congress from considering each case upon its merits, unless the language of the instrument imperatively demand it. A false step at this time might be fatal to the development of what Chief Justice Marshall called the American Empire. Choice in some cases, the natural gravitation of small bodies towards large ones in others, the result of a successful war in still others, may bring about conditions which would render the annexation of distant possessions desirable. If those possessions are inhabited by alien races, differing from us in religion, customs, laws, methods of taxation and modes of thought, the administration of government and justice, according to Anglo Saxon principles, may for a time be impossible; and the question at once arises whether large concessions ought not to be made for a time, that, ultimately, our own theories may be carried out, and the blessings of a free government under the Constitution extended to them. We decline to hold that there is anything in the Constitution to forbid such action.

We are therefore of opinion that the Island of Porto Rico is a territory appurtenant and belonging to the United States, but not a part of the United States within the revenue clauses of the Constitution; that the Foraker act is constitutional, so far as it imposes duties upon imports from such island, and that the plaintiff cannot recover back the duties exacted in this case.

146. *Fundamental and Procedural Rights in Unincorporated Territories*

Hawaii v. Mankichi, 190 U.S. 197 (1903)

BROWN, J.: The question involved in this case is an extremely simple one. The difficulty is in fixing upon the principles applicable to its solution. By a joint resolution adopted by Congress, July 7, 1898 . . . and with the consent of the Republic of Hawaii, . . . the Hawaiian Islands and their dependencies were annexed "as a part of the Territory of the United States, and subject to the sovereign dominion thereof," with the following condition: "The municipal legislation of the Hawaiian Islands, not enacted for the fulfillment of the treaties so extinguished, and not inconsistent with this joint resolution *nor contrary to the Constitution of the United States,* nor to any existing treaty of the United States, shall remain in force until the Congress of the United States shall otherwise determine.' . . . Under the conditions named in this resolution, the Hawaiian Islands remained under the name of the "Republic of Hawaii" until June 14, 1900, when they were formally incorporated by act of Congress under the name of the "Territory of Hawaii." . . . By this act the Constitution was formally extended to these islands, Sec. 5, and special provisions made for empanelling grand juries, and for unanimous verdicts of petty juries. Sec. 83.

The question is whether, in continuing the municipal legislation of the islands not contrary to the Constitution of the United States, it was intended to abolish at once the criminal procedure theretofore in force upon the islands, and to substitute immediately, and without new legislation, the common law proceedings by grand and petit jury, which had been held applicable to other organized Territories. . . .

By a law passed in 1847, the number of a jury was fixed at twelve, but a verdict might be rendered upon the agreement of nine jurors. The question involved in this case is whether it was intended that this practice should be instantly changed, and the criminal procedure embodied in the Fifth and Sixth Amendments to the Constitution be adopted as of August 12, 1898, when the Hawaiian flag was hauled down and the American flag hoisted in its place.

If the words of the Newlands resolution, adopting the municipal legislation of Hawaii *not contrary to the Constitution of the United States,* be literally applied, the petitioner is entitled to his discharge, since that instrument expressly requires, Amendment 5, that "no person shall be held to answer for a capital or otherwise infamous crime, unless on a presentment or indictment of a grand jury"; and, Amendment 6, that "in all criminal prosecutions the accused shall enjoy the right to a speedy and public trial by an impartial jury of the State and district wherein the crime shall have been committed." But there is another question underlying this and all other rules for the interpretation of statutes, and that is, What was the intention of the legislative body? . . .

If the negative words of the resolution, "nor contrary to the Constitution of the United States," be construed as imposing upon the islands every provision of a Constitution which must have been unfamiliar to a large number of their inhabitants, and for which no previous preparation had been made, the consequences in this particular connection would be that every criminal in the Hawaiian Islands convicted of an infamous offense between August 12, 1898, and June 14, 1900, when the act organizing the territorial government took effect, must be set at large; and every verdict in a civil case rendered by less than a unanimous jury held for naught. Surely, such a result could not have been within the contemplation of Congress. It is equally manifest that such could not have been the intention of the Republic of Hawaii in surrendering its autonomy. Until then it was an independent nation, exercising all the powers and prerogatives of complete sovereignty. It certainly could not have anticipated that, in dealing with another independent nation, and yielding up its sovereignty, it had denuded itself, by a negative pregnant, of all powers of enforcing its criminal laws according to the methods which had been in vogue for sixty years, and was adopting a new procedure for which it had had no opportunity of making preparation. The legislature of the Republic had just adjourned, not to convene again until some time in 1900, and not actually convening until 1901. The resolution on its face bears evidence of having been intended merely for a temporary purpose, and to give time to the Republic to adapt itself to such form of territorial government as should afterwards be adopted in its organic act. . . .

It is not intended here to decide that the words "nor contrary to the Constitution of the United States" are meaningless. Clearly, they would be operative upon any municipal legislation thereafter adopted, and upon any proceedings thereafter had, when the application of the Constitution would not result in the destruction of existing provisions conducive to the peace and good order of the community. . . . Most, if not all, the privileges and immunities contained in the bill of rights of the Constitution were intended to apply from the moment of annexation; but we place our decision of this case upon the ground that the two rights alleged to be violated in this case are not fundamental in their nature, but concern merely a method of procedure which sixty years of practice had shown to be suited to the conditions of the islands, and well calculated to conserve the rights of their citizens to their lives, their property, and their well being. . . .

147. *Justice Harlan Dissents in the Insular Cases*

Insular Cases, 190 U.S. 197, 195 U.S. 138 (1903-04).

HARLAN, J., dissenting in *Mankichi:* I am of the opinion: 1. That when the annexation of Hawaii was completed, the Constitution—without any declaration to that effect by Congress, and without any power of Congress to prevent it—became the supreme law for that country, and, therefore, it forbade the trial and conviction of the accused for murder otherwise than upon a presentment or indictment of a grand jury, and by the unanimous verdict of a petit jury. 2. That if the legality of such trial and conviction is to be tested alone by the Joint Resolution of 1898, then the law is for the accused, because Congress, by that Resolution, abrogated or forbade the enforcement of any municipal law of Hawaii so far as it authorized a trial for an infamous crime otherwise than in the mode prescribed by the Constitution of the United States; and that any other construction of the Resolution is forbidden by its clear, unambiguous words, and is to make, not to interpret, the law.

HARLAN, J., dissenting in *Dorr:* I do not believe now any more than I did when *Hawaii v. Mankichi* . . . was decided, that the provisions of the Federal Constitution as to grand and petit juries relate to mere methods of procedure and are not fundamental in their nature. In my opinion, guaranties for the protection of life, liberty and property, as embodied in the Constitution, are for the benefit of all, of whatever race or nativity, in the States composing the Union, or in any territory, however acquired, over the inhabitants of which the Government of the United States may exercise the powers conferred upon it by the Constitution.

The Constitution declares that *no* person, except in the land or naval forces, shall be held to answer for a capital or otherwise infamous crime, except on the presentment or indictment of a grand jury; and forbids the conviction, in a criminal prosecution, of any person, for any crime, except on the unanimous verdict of a petit jury composed of twelve persons. Necessarily, that mandate was addressed to every one committing crime punishable by the United States. This court, however, holds that these provisions are not fundamental and may be disregarded in any territory acquired in the manner the Philippine Islands were acquired, although, as heretofore decided by this court, they could not be disregarded in what are commonly called the organized territories of the United States. . . . I cannot assent to this interpretation of the Constitution. It is, I submit, so obviously inconsistent with the Constitution that I cannot regard the judgment of the court otherwise than as an amendment of that instrument by judicial construction. . . . No power exists in the judiciary to suspend the operation of the Constitution in any territory governed, as to its affairs and people, by authority of the United States. . . . It is now adjudged that . . . [the jury trial] provision is not fundamental in respect of a part of the people over whom the United States may exercise full legislative, judicial and executive power. . . . Such a mode of constitutional interpretation plays havoc with the old-fashioned ideas of the fathers, who took care to say that the Constitution was the supreme law—supreme everywhere, at all times, and over all persons who are subject to the authority of the United States. . . .

148. *Fundamental and Procedural Rights in Incorporated Territories*

Rassmussen v. U.S., 197 U.S. 516 (1905).

WHITE, J.: The plaintiff in error was indicted for violating section 127 of the Alaska Code, prohibiting the keeping of a disreputable house and punishing the offense by a fine or imprisonment in the county jail. . . .

When the case was called the court announced "that the cause would be tried before a jury composed of six jurors," in accordance with section 171 of the Code for Alaska adopted by Congress. . . .

At the threshold of the case lies the constitutional question whether . . . the provision of the act of Congress in question was repugnant to the Sixth Amendment to the Constitution of the United States. . . .

The validity of the provision in question is . . . sought to be sustained upon the proposition that the Sixth Amendment to the Constitution did not apply to Congress in legislating for Alaska. And this rests upon two contentions which we proceed separately to consider.

1. *Alaska was not incorporated into the United States, and therefore the Sixth Amendment did not control Congress in legislating for Alaska.* . . .

We are brought, then, to determine whether Alaska has been incorporated into the United States as a part thereof, or is simply held, as the Philippine Islands are held, under the sovereignty of the United States as a possession or dependency. . . .

The treaty concerning Alaska, instead of exhibiting, as did the treaty respecting the Philippine Islands, the determination to reserve the question of the status of the acquired territory for ulterior action by Congress, manifested a contrary intention, since it is therein expressly declared . . . that:

"The inhabitants of the ceded territory shall be admitted to the enjoyment of all the rights, advantages, and immunities of citizens of the United States; and shall be maintained and protected in the free enjoyment of their liberty, property and religion."

This declaration, although somewhat changed in phraseology, is the equivalent, as pointed out in *Downes v. Bidwell,* of the formula employed from the beginning to express the purpose to incorporate acquired territory into the United States, especially in the absence of other provisions showing an intention to the contrary. . . .

It follows, then, from the text of the treaty by which Alaska was acquired, from the action of Congress thereunder, and the reiterated decisions of this court, that the proposition that Alaska is not incorporated into and a part of the United States is devoid of merit, and therefore the doctrine settled as to unincorporated territory is inapposite and lends no support to the contention that Congress in legislating for Alaska had authority to violate the express commands of the Sixth Amendment.

This brings us to the second proposition, which is—

2. *That even if Alaska was incorporated into the United States, as it was not an organized territory, therefore the provisions of the Sixth Amendment were not controlling on Congress when legislating for Alaska.*

We do not stop to demonstrate from original considerations the unsoundness of this contention and its irreconcilable conflict with the essential principles upon which our constitutional system of government rests. Nor do we think it is required to point out the inconsistency which would arise between various provisions of the Constitution if the proposition was admitted, or the extreme extension on the one hand, and the undue limitation on the other, of the powers of Congress which would be occasioned by conceding it. This is said, because, in our opinion, the unsoundness of the proposition is conclusively established by a long line of decisions. . . .

The argument by which the decisive force of the cases just cited is sought to be escaped is that, as when the cases were decided there was legislation of Congress extending the Constitution to the District of Columbia or to the particular territory to which a case may have related, therefore the decisions must be taken to have proceeded alone upon the statutes, and not upon the inherent application of the provisions of the Fifth, Sixth, and Seventh Amendments to the District of Columbia or to an incorporated Territory. And, upon the assumption that the cases are distinguishable from the present one upon the basis just stated, the argument proceeds to insist that the Sixth Amendment does not apply to the Territory of Alaska, because section 1891 of the Revised Statutes only extends the Constitution to the organized Territories, in which, it is urged, Alaska is not embraced.

Whilst the premise as to the existence of legislation declaring the extension of the Constitution to the Territories with which the cases were respectively concerned is well founded, the conclusion drawn from that fact is not justified. Without attempting to examine in detail the opinions in the various cases, in our judgment it clearly results from them that they substantially rested upon the proposition that where territory was a part of the United States the inhabitants thereof were entitled to the guarantees of the Fifth, Sixth and Seventh Amendments, and that the act or acts of Congress purporting to extend the Constitution were considered as declaratory merely of a result which existed independently by the inherent operation of the Constitution. . . .

As it conclusively results from the foregoing considerations that the Sixth Amendment to the Constitution was applicable to Alaska, and as of course, being applicable, it was controlling upon Congress in legislating for Alaska, it follows that the provision of the act of Congress under consideration, depriving persons accused of a misdemeanor in Alaska of a right to trial by a common law jury, was repugnant to the Constitution and void. . . .

CHAPTER XVII

Governmental Efforts to Restore Competition

For nearly fifty years following the Civil War amendments, no basic alterations were made in the form of the federal government. However, constitutional developments of major importance were taking place by the turn of the century. Not the least of these was the revolt against mechanistic concepts of law and the attempt to supplant fixed doctrines with a jurisprudence that combined pragmatic insights and social conscience in dealing with economic and social problems. The shift from the theory that the Constitution belonged to the professional lawyer and the judges to the view that it was everyman's property can be well illustrated by contrasting the remarks of E. J. Phelps, one of the early presidents of the American Bar Association, and Oliver Wendell Holmes, Jr., Theodore Roosevelt's first appointee to the Supreme Court.

In 1879 Phelps declared that the sacred Constitution should not be profaned by public discussion; it should not be "hawked about the country, debated in the newspapers, discussed from the stump, elucidated by pot-house politicians and dunghill editors, or by scholars . . . who have never found leisure for the grace of English grammar or the embellishment of correct spelling." Obviously, the logic of the law could be discovered only by members of bench and bar. To the high priests of the old jurisprudence, the criticism from within the guild by Holmes was heresy. "The life of law," he said as early as 1880, "has not been logic; it has been experience. The felt necessities of the time, the prevalent moral and political theories, intuitions of public policy, avowed or unconscious, even the prejudices which judges share with their fellow-men, have had a good deal more to do than the syllogism in determining the rules by which men should be governed."

By 1900 the problem of interpreting the Constitution in dealing with the complex problems of industrialization was critical. A deep-rooted demand for reform and regulation found a unifying figure in Theodore Roosevelt, who dominated the national scene from 1901 until 1909. Like Holmes, the new President declared that the Constitution "must be interpreted, not as a strait-jacket, not as laying the hand of death upon our development, but as an instrument designed for the life and healthy growth of the Nation." In reasserting national authority, Roosevelt stressed the executive branch of the government as the agency of reform, and utilized executive commissions to curb corporate power. By 1911 the Supreme Court accepted the doctrine of "administrative discretion" and acknowledged that commission rulings had the force of law (*U.S. v. Grimaud*).

A revitalized I. C. C. was one of the first results of the Roosevelt leadership. The Elkins Act of 1903 strengthened the Commission's control over rebates, and the Hepburn Act of 1906 gave authority to fix just and reasonable maximum railroad rates, which were binding on the carriers. No longer did the Commission have to go to court to enforce its order. In two early cases involving the Illinois Central Railroad, the Court first upheld the Commission's fact-finding authority (*Illinois Central v. I. C. C.*, 1907) and later refused to interfere with the Commission's policy-making discretion (*I. C. C. v. Illinois Central* [No. 149]). In 1910 Congress bolstered the Commission's authority by granting it original rate-making power, and the Court approved this delegation in 1914 (*U.S. v. Atchison, Topeka, and Santa Fe*).

With the development of effective federal control of railroad rates, railroad lawyers argued that federal regulation excluded state authority over intrastate rates. In the Minnesota Rate Cases (1913), the Court rejected this contention, asserting that a state might properly act in a field where it did not conflict with federal laws. A year later, in the Shreveport Rate Case (No. 150), Justice Charles Evans Hughes ruled that the Commission's power extended to intrastate rates, arguing that local activity affecting interstate commerce came within the scope of federal power. This "affect" doctrine became a key constitutional device for extending national authority over widely divergent areas of local economic activity.

Perhaps Teddy Roosevelt's most widely remembered sobriquet was that of "Trust Buster." His ambivalence hardly justified this title, as Mr. Dooley incisively pointed out: "Th' trusts, says he [Tiddy] are heejoous monsthers built up by th' inlightened intherprise ov th' men that have done so much to advance progress in our beloved counthry. . . . On wan hand I wud stamp them undher fut; on th' other hand, not so fast." Certainly the Court had moved lethargically enough in the Knight case (Chapter XV). But in two later cases, clearly involving interstate commerce, it had applied the Sherman Act positively. In the Trans-Missouri Freight Association case (1897), the Court ruled that a combination of eighteen competitive railroads which existed to fix rates violated the antitrust law. Rejecting the "rule of reason," it held that whether or not the rates were reasonable, the act applied to any combination in restraint of trade. In the field of manufacture, a unanimous Court partially revitalized the Sherman Act in the Addystone Pipe and Steel Company case (1899), distinguishing it from the Knight case on the ground that in this instance the combination not only manufactured items but also directly controlled prices in interstate commerce.

Roosevelt's reputation as a "Trust Buster" can be measured by his successful attack on the Northern Securities Company, a holding company uniting the Northern Pacific and the Great Northern Railroads. A 5 to 4 Court ruled that the acquisition by a holding company of stock control of competing carriers, even though reasonable, constituted an illegal monopoly (No. 151). In a surprise dissent, Holmes pleaded for the "rule of reason" (No. 152). The next year, however, Holmes wrote a unanimous opinion upholding the government's antitrust prosecution of the "Beef Trust." He first expanded the commerce clause by formulating the "stream of commerce" concept, and then applied the Sherman Act literally to the meat-packers' combination in Chicago (Swift case [No. 153]).

The direct effect of Roosevelt's two major victories was virtually nil. The Beef Trust was dissolved, but managed to reintegrate sufficiently to circumvent the government's injunction in the Swift case, and the Northwestern railroads established an effective community of interest for directing their policies. Although Roosevelt continued to press the prosecution of monopolistic giants, particularly against the unpopular Standard Oil and American Tobacco combines, he popularized a distinction between "good" and "bad" trusts, conceding that the size and power of a consolidation did not necessarily render it illegal. When the Standard Oil and American Tobacco companies were dissolved in 1911, the Supreme Court elevated Roosevelt's ethical distinction to a legal doctrine. This differentiation between "reasonableness" and "unreasonableness" amended the Sherman Act by judicial interpretation (No. 154), thus giving the statute new meaning and less authority. Justice Harlan considered the "rule of reason" nothing more than judicial usurpation (No. 155).

President Woodrow Wilson also opposed the rule. In 1912 the Democratic platform condemned private monopoly as "indefensible and intolerable," and demanded "the enactment of such additional legislation as may be necessary to make it impossible for a private monopoly to exist in the United States." In his acceptance speech, Wilson emphatically endorsed this plank, and called for new laws to meet "conditions which menace our civilization." In 1914 Congress passed an act establishing the Federal Trade Commission, outlawing unfair methods of competition, and authorizing the issuance of "cease and desist" orders. A companion measure, enacted a month later, was specifically designed to strengthen the Sherman Act. The Clayton Anti-Trust Act prohibited a number of abuses of "big business," and specifically exempted labor unions and farmer organizations from its terms.

The latter provision was a direct outgrowth of the Danbury Hatter's Case (*Loewe v. Lawlor* [No. 156]), and the opinion in *Buck Stove Company v. Gompers* (1914). Both cases involved attempts by the American Anti-Boycott Association to outlaw the boycott by bringing it within the purview of the Sherman Act as a conspiracy in restraint of trade. In both, the Court applied the antitrust statute against labor unions. The personal involvement of Samuel Gompers, the president of the American Federation of Labor, in the Buck Stove Case brought home to organized labor the necessity of congressional repeal of "judicial legislation." The Clayton Anti-Trust Act (No. 157), therefore, was hailed as the "Magna Charta" of labor since it limited "government by injunction," and legalized strikes, peaceful picketing, and boycotts. Judicial interpretation, however, subsequently restricted these new guarantees.

Congress and the courts consistently dealt with railroad labor in a separate category because of its intimate connection with interstate commerce. The Erdman Act of 1898, a result of the vicious labor disputes of that decade, stated that railroads could not prevent their employees from joining a union. Ten years later the Court invalidated this Act, upholding the use of "yellow-dog contracts." (*Adair v. U.S.* [*No.* 158]). Important as a leading labor case, the decision was also a landmark in constitutional law; for the first time an act of Congress was ruled unconstitutional for violating the due process clause of the Fifth Amendment. Not until 1917, when the prewar emergency forced the hand of a reluctant Court, was a railroad labor law regulating hours approved by the federal judiciary. To prevent a nation-wide railroad strike on the eve of America's entry into World War I, Congress in 1916 passed the Adamson Act, specifying eight hours as a day's work on interstate railroads. In *Wilson v. New* (No. 159), a bare majority of the Court upheld the establishment of a temporary standard of wages and hours as an emergency measure.

Despite the concentrated efforts of both Republicans and Democrats during the Progressive Era, government regulations designed to restore competition and to improve industrial and labor relations frequently fell short of progressive reform ideals. In his testimony before the United States Commission on Industrial Relations in 1915, Louis D. Brandeis, a leading reformer later appointed to the Supreme Court, painted a Progressive portrait of the American economy which contrasted the dull industrial absolutism of the period to the bright achievements in political democracy (No. 160).

Revival of the Interstate Commerce Commission

149. *The Court May Not Usurp Administrative Functions of the I. C. C.*

I. C. C. v. Illinois Central Railroad Company, 215 U.S. 452 (1910).

WHITE, J.: Whether a duty rested upon the Illinois Central Railroad Company to obey an order made by the Interstate Commerce Commission is the question here to be decided. . . .

In determining whether an order of the

commission shall be suspended or set aside, we must consider, *a,* all relevant questions of constitutional power or right; *b,* all pertinent questions as to whether the administrative order is within the scope of the delegated authority under which it purports to have been made; and, *c,* a proposition which we state independently, although in its essence it may be contained in the previous one, viz., whether, even although the order be in form within the delegated power, nevertheless it must be treated as not embraced therein, because the exertion of authority which is questioned has been manifested in such an unreasonable manner as to cause it, in truth, to be within the elementary rule that the substance, and not the shadow, determines the validity of the exercise of the power. . . . Plain as it is that the powers just stated are of the essence of judicial authority, and which, therefore, may not be curtailed, and whose discharge may not be by us in a proper case avoided, it is equally plain that such perennial powers lend no support whatever to the proposition that we may, under the guise of exerting judicial power, usurp merely administrative functions by setting aside a lawful administrative order upon our conception as to whether the administrative power has been wisely exercised. . . .

In view, however, of the great importance of the questions directly arising for decision, . . . we shall . . . come at once to the propositions of power previously stated.

First. *That the act to regulate commerce has not delegated to the commission authority to regulate the distribution of company fuel cars in times of car shortage as a means of prohibiting unjust preferences or undue discrimination.* . . .

The deduction from the proposition is, as the movement of coal under the conditions stated is not commerce, it is therefore not within the authority delegated to the commission by the act of Congress, as all such acts have relation to the regulation of commerce, and do not, therefore, embrace that which is not commerce. . . .

When the erroneous assumption upon which the proposition must rest is considered, its unsoundness is readily demonstrable. That assumption is this, that commerce in the constitutional sense only embraces shipment in a technical sense, and does not, therefore, extend to carriers engaged in interstate commerce, certainly in so far as so engaged, and the instrumentalities by which such commerce is carried on, a doctrine the unsoundness of which has been apparent ever since the decision in *Gibbons v. Ogden,* . . . and which has not since been open to question. It may not be doubted that the equipment of a railroad company engaged in interstate commerce, included in which are its coal cars, are instruments of such commerce. From this it necessarily follows that such cars are embraced within the governmental power of regulation which extends, in time of car shortage, to compelling a just and equal distribution and the prevention of an unjust and discriminatory one.

The corporation as a carrier engaged in interstate commerce being then, as to its interstate commerce business, subject to the control exerted by the act to regulate commerce, and the instrumentalities employed for the purpose of such commerce, being likewise so subject to control, we are brought to consider the remaining proposition, which is,

Second. *That even if power has been delegated to the commission by the act to regulate commerce, the order whose continued enforcement was enjoined by the court below was beyond the authority delegated by the statute.*

In view of the facts found by the commission as to preferences and discriminations resulting from the failure to count the company fuel cars in the daily distribution in times of car shortage, and in further view of the far-reaching preferences and discriminations alleged in the answer of the commission in this case, and which must be taken as true, as the cause was submitted on bill and answer, it is beyond controversy that the subject with which the order dealt was within the sweeping provisions of §3 of the act to regulate commerce, prohibiting preferences and discriminations. . . .

It follows from what we have said that the court below erred in enjoining the order of the commission, in so far as it related to company fuel cars, and its decree is therefore reversed, and the case remanded for further proceedings in conformity with this opinion.

150. *When intrastate transactions affect interstate commerce, Congress may prescribe the final rule.*

The Shreveport Rate Case, 234 U.S. 342 (1914).

HUGHES, C.J.: These suits were brought in the Commerce Court . . . to set aside an order of the Interstate Commerce Commission, dated March 11, 1912, upon the ground that it exceeded the Commission's authority. . . .

The gravamen of the complaint, said the Interstate Commerce Commission, was that the carriers made rates out of Dallas and other Texas points into eastern Texas which were much lower than those which they extended into Texas from Shreveport. The situation may be briefly described: Shreveport, Louisiana, is about 40 miles from the Texas state line, and 231 miles from Houston, Texas, on the line of the Houston, East & West Texas and Houston and Shreveport Companies . . . ; it is 189 miles from Dallas, Texas, on the line of the Texas & Pacific. Shreveport competes with both cities for the trade of the intervening territory. The rates on these lines from Dallas and Houston, respectively, eastward to intermediate points, in Texas, were much less, according to distance, than from Shreveport westward to the same points. It is undisputed that the difference was substantial, and injuriously affected the commerce of Shreveport. . . .

The Interstate Commerce Commission found that the interstate class rates out of Shreveport to named Texas points were unreasonable, and it established maximum class rates for this traffic. . . .

The point of the objection to the order is that, as the discrimination found by the Commission to be unjust arises out of the relation of intrastate rates, maintained under state authority, to interstate rates that have been upheld as reasonable, its correction was beyond the Commission's power. . . . The invalidity of the order is challenged upon two grounds:

(1.) That Congress is impotent to control the intrastate charges of an interstate carrier even to the extent necessary to prevent injurious discrimination against interstate traffic. . . .

Congress is empowered to regulate,—that is, to provide the law for the government of interstate commerce; to enact 'all appropriate legislation' for its 'protection and advancement' . . . As it is competent for Congress to legislate to these ends, unquestionably it may seek their attainment by requiring that the agencies of interstate commerce shall not be used in such manner as to cripple, retard, or destroy it. The fact that carriers are instruments of intrastate commerce, as well as of interstate commerce, does not derogate from the complete and paramount authority of Congress over the latter, or preclude the Federal power from being exerted to prevent the intrastate operations of such carriers from being made a means of injury to that which has been confided to Federal care. Wherever the interstate and intrastate transactions of carriers are so related that the government of the one involves the control of the other, it is Congress, and not the state, that is entitled to prescribe the final and dominant rule, for otherwise Congress would be denied the exercise of its constitutional authority, and the state, and not the nation, would be supreme within the national field. . . .

It is for Congress to supply the needed correction where the relation between intrastate and interstate rates presents the evil to be corrected, and this it may do completely by reason of its control over the interstate carrier in all matters having such a close and substantial relation to interstate commerce that it is necessary or appropriate to exercise the control for the effective government of that commerce.

It is also clear that, in removing the injurious discriminations against interstate traffic arising from the relation of intrastate to interstate rates, Congress is not bound to reduce the latter below what it may deem to be a proper standard fair to the carrier and to the public. Otherwise, it could prevent the injury to interstate commerce only by the sacrifice of its judgment as to interstate rates. Congress is entitled to maintain its own standard as to these rates, and to forbid any discriminatory action by interstate carriers which will obstruct the freedom of movement of interstate traffic over their lines in accordance with the terms it establishes.

Having this power, Congress could provide for its execution through the aid of a subordinate body; and we conclude that the order of the Commission now in question cannot be held invalid upon the ground that it exceeded the authority which Congress could lawfully confer. . . .

Reinvigoration of the Sherman Act

BEGINNINGS OF EFFECTIVE REGULATION

151. *The Court "Busts" a Trust*

Northern Securities Company v. U.S., 193 U.S. 197 (1904).

HARLAN, J.: . . . The Government charges that if the combination was held not to be in violation of the act of Congress, then all efforts of the National Government to preserve to the people the benefits of free competition among carriers engaged in interstate commerce will be wholly unavailing, and all transcontinental lines, indeed the entire railway systems of the country, may be absorbed, merged and consolidated, thus placing the public at the absolute mercy of the holding corporation. . . .

From the decisions in . . . [previous] cases certain propositions are plainly deducible and embrace the present case. Those propositions are:

That although the act of Congress known as the Anti-Trust Act has no reference to the mere manufacture or production of articles or commodities within the limits of the several States, it does embrace and declare to be illegal every contract, combination or conspiracy, in whatever form, or whatever nature, and whoever may be parties to it, which directly or necessarily operates *in restraint* of trade or commerce *among the several States or with foreign nations;*

That the act is not limited to restraints of interstate and international trade or commerce that are unreasonable in their nature, but embraces *all* direct *restraints* imposed by any combination, conspiracy or monopoly upon such trade or commerce;

That railroad carriers engaged in interstate or international commerce are embraced by the act;

That combinations even among *private* manufacturers or dealers whereby *interstate or international commerce* is restrained are equally embraced by the act;

That Congress has the power to establish *rules* by which *interstate and international* commerce shall be governed, and, by the Anti-Trust Act, has prescribed the rule of free competition among those engaged in such commerce;

That *every* combination or conspiracy which would extinguish competition between otherwise competing railroads engaged in *interstate trade or commerce,* and which would *in that way* restrain *such* trade or commerce, is made illegal by the act;

That the natural effect of competition is to increase commerce, and an agreement whose direct effect is to prevent this play of competition restrains instead of promotes trade and commerce;

That to vitiate a combination, such as the act of Congress condemns, it need not be shown that the combination, in fact, results or will result in a total suppression of trade or in a complete monopoly, but it is only essential to show that by its necessary operation it tends to restrain interstate or international trade or commerce and to deprive the public of the advantages that flow from free competition;

That the constitutional guarantee of liberty of contract does not prevent Congress from prescribing the rule of free competition for those engaged in *interstate and international* commerce; and,

That under its power to regulate commerce among the several States and with foreign nations, Congress had authority to enact the statute in question. . . .

What the Government particularly complains of, indeed, all that it complains of here, is the existence of a combination among the stockholders of competing railroad companies which in violation of the act of Congress restrains interstate and international commerce through the agency of a common corporate trustee designated to act for both companies in repressing free competition between them. . . .

Whether the free operation of the normal laws of competition is a wise and wholesome rule for trade and commerce is an economic question which this court need not consider or determine. Undoubtedly, there are those who think that the general business interests and prosperity of the country will be best promoted if the rule of competition is not applied. But there are others who believe that such a rule is more necessary in these days of enormous wealth than it ever was in any former period of our history. Be all this as it may, Congress has, in effect, recognized the rule of free competition by declaring illegal every combination or conspiracy in restraint of interstate and international commerce. . . .

Guided by these long-established rules of construction, it is manifest that if the Anti-Trust Act is held not to embrace a case such as is now before us, the plain intention of the legislative branch of the Government will be defeated. If Congress has not, by the words used in the act, described this and like cases, it would, we apprehend, be impossible to find words that would describe them. . . .

152. "*Great cases like hard cases make bad law.*"

Northern Securities Company v. U.S., 193 U.S. 197 (1904).

HOLMES, J., dissenting: . . . Great cases like hard cases make bad law. For great cases are called great, not by reason of their real importance in shaping the law of the future, but because of some accident of immediate overwhelming interest which appeals to the feelings and distorts the judgment. These immediate interests exercise a kind of hydraulic pressure which makes what previously was clear seem doubtful, and before which even well settled principles of law will bend. What we have to do in this case is to find the meaning of some not very difficult words. . . .

In my opinion there is no attempt to monopolize, and what, as I have said, in my judgment amounts to the same thing, that there is no combination in restraint of trade, until something is done with the intent to exclude strangers to the combination from competing with it in some part of the business which it carries on.

Unless I am entirely wrong in my understanding of what a "combination in restraint of trade" means, then the same monopoly may be attempted and effected by an individual, and is made equally illegal in that case by §2. . . .

A partnership is not a contract or combination in restraint of trade between the partners unless the well known words are to be given a new meaning invented for the purpose of this act. . . . The law, I repeat, says nothing about competition, and only prevents its suppression by contracts or combinations in restraint of trade, and such contracts or combinations derive their character as restraining trade from other features than the suppression of competition alone. . . . If the restraint on the freedom of the members of a combination caused by their entering into partnership is a restraint of trade, every such combination, as well the small as the great, is within the act. . . .

I am happy to know that only a minority of my brethren adopt an interpretation of the law which in my opinion would make eternal the *bellum omnium contra omnes* and disintegrate society so far as it could into individual atoms. If that were its intent I should regard calling such a law a regulation of commerce as a mere pretense. It would be an attempt to reconstruct society. I am not concerned with the wisdom of such an an attempt, but I believe that Congress was not entrusted by the Constitution with the power to make it and I am deeply persuaded that it has not tried.

153. *The "Stream of Commerce" Doctrine*

Swift and Company v. U.S., 196 U.S. 375 (1905).

HOLMES, J.: . . . Although the combination alleged embraces restraint and monopoly of trade within a single State, its effect upon commerce among the States is not accidental, secondary, remote or merely probable. On the allegations of the bill the latter commerce no less, perhaps even more, than commerce within a single State is an object of attack. . . . Moreover, it is a direct object, it is that for the sake of which the several specific acts and courses of conduct are done and adopted. Therefore the case is not like *United States v. E. C. Knight Co.,* . . . where the subject matter of the combination was manufacture and the direct object monopoly of manufacture within a State. However likely a monopoly of commerce among the States in the article manufactured was to follow from the agreement it was not a necessary consequence nor a primary end. Here the subject matter is sales and the very point of the combination is to restrain and monopolize commerce among the States in respect to such sales. . . .

Commerce among the States is not a technical legal conception, but a practical one, drawn from the course of business. When cattle are sent for sale from a place in one State, with the expectation that they will end their transit, after purchase, in another, and when in effect they do so, with only the interruption necessary to find a purchaser at the stock yards, and when this is a typical, constantly recurring course, the current thus existing is a current of commerce among the States, and the purchase of the cattle is a part and incident of such commerce. What we say is true at least of such a purchase by residents in another State from that of the seller and of the cattle. And we need not trouble ourselves at this time as to whether the statute could be escaped by any arrangement as to the place where the sale in point of law is consummated. . . .

The injunction against taking part in a combination, the effect of which will be a restraint of trade among the States by directing the defendants' agents to refrain from bidding against one another at the sales of live stock, is justified so far as the subject matter is concerned. . . .

TRIUMPH OF THE RULE OF REASON

154. *Amending the Anti-Trust Act by "Judicial Legislation"*

Standard Oil Company v. U.S., 221 U.S. 1 (1911).

WHITE, C.J.: . . . It is certain that only one point of concord between the parties is discernible, which is, that the controversy in every aspect is controlled by a correct conception of the meaning of the first and second sections of the Anti-trust Act. . . . We shall make our investigation under four separate headings: First. The text of the first and second sections of the act originally considered and its meaning in the light of the common law and the law of this country at the time of its adoption. Second. The contentions of the parties concerning the act, and the scope and effect of the decisions of this court upon which they rely. . . .

In view of the common law and the law in this country as to restraint of trade, which we have reviewed, and the illuminating effect which that history must have under the rule to which we have referred, we think it results:

a. That the context manifests that the statute was drawn in the light of the existing practical conception of the law of restraint of trade, because it groups as within that class, not only contracts which were in restraint of trade in the subjective sense, but all contracts or acts which theoretically were attempts to monopolize, yet which in practice had come to be considered as in restraint of trade in a broad sense.

b. That in view of the many new forms of contracts and combinations which were being evolved from existing economic conditions, it was deemed essential by an all-embracing enumeration to make sure that no form of contract or combination by which an undue restraint of interstate or foreign commerce was brought about could save such restraint from condemnation. The statute under this view evidenced the intent not to restrain the right to make and enforce contracts, whether resulting from combination or otherwise, which did not unduly restrain interstate or foreign commerce, but to protect that commerce from being restrained by methods, whether old or new, which would constitute an interference that is an undue restraint.

c. And as the contracts or acts embraced in the provision were not expressly defined, since the enumeration addressed itself simply to classes of acts, those classes being broad enough to embrace every conceivable contract or combination which could be made concerning trade or commerce or the subjects of such commerce, and thus caused any act done by any of the enumerated methods anywhere in the whole field of human activity to be illegal if in restraint, it inevitably follows that the provision necessarily called for the exercise of judgment which required that some standard should be resorted to for the purpose of determining whether the prohibitions contained in the statute had or had not in any given case been violated. Thus not specifying but indubitably contemplating and requiring a standard, it follows that it was intended that the standard of reason which had been applied at the common law and in this country in dealing with subjects of the character embraced by the statute, was intended to be the measure used for the purpose of determining whether in a given case a particular act had or had not brought about the wrong against which the statute provided. . . .

155. *Courts "have no function to declare a public policy, nor to amend legislative enactments."*

Standard Oil Co. v. U.S., 221 U.S. 1 (1911).

HARLAN, J., dissenting in part: . . . In order that my objections to certain parts of the court's opinion may distinctly appear, I must state the circumstances under which Congress passed the Anti-trust Act, and trace the course of judicial decisions as to its meaning and scope. . . .

All who recall the condition of the country in 1890 will remember that there was everywhere, among the people generally, a deep feeling of unrest. The Nation had been rid of human slavery—fortunately, as all now feel—but the conviction was universal that the country was in real danger from another kind of slavery sought to be fastened on the American people, namely, the slavery that would result from aggregations of capital in the hands of a few individuals and corporations controlling, for their own profit and advantage exclusively, the entire business of the country, including the production and sale of the necessaries of life. Such a danger was thought to be then imminent, and all felt that it must be met firmly and by such statutory regulations as would adequately protect the people against oppression and wrong. Congress therefore took up the matter and gave the whole subject the fullest consideration. . . .

Guided by these considerations, and to the end that the people, *so far as interstate commerce* was concerned, might not be dominated by vast combinations and monopolies, having power to advance their own selfish ends, regardless of the general interests and welfare, Congress passed the Anti-trust Act of 1890. . . .

After what has been adjudged, upon full consideration, as to the meaning and the scope of the Anti-trust Act, and in view of the usages of this court when attorneys for litigants have attempted to reopen questions that have been deliberately decided, I confess to no little surprise as to what has occurred in the present case. The court says that the previous cases, above cited, "cannot by any possible conception be treated as authoritative without the certitude that *reason* was resorted to for the purpose of deciding them." . . . It is more than once intimated, if not suggested, that if the Anti-Trust Act is to be construed as prohibiting *every* contract or combination, of whatever nature, which is in fact in restraint of commerce, regardless of the reasonableness or unreasonableness of such restraint, that fact would show that the court had not proceeded, in its decision, according to "the light of reason," but had disregarded the "rule of reason" . . . Now this court is asked to do that which it has distinctly declared it could not and would not do, and has now done what it then said it could not constitutionally do. It has, by mere interpretation, modified the act of Congress, and deprived it of practical value as a defensive measure against the evils to be remedied. . . . In effect, the court says, that it will now, for the first time, bring the discussion under the "light of reason" and apply the "rule of reason" to the questions to be decided. I have the authority of this court for saying that such a course of proceeding on its part would be "judicial legislation." . . .

But my brethren, in their wisdom, have deemed it best to pursue a different course. They have now said to those who condemn our former decisions and who object to all legislative prohibitions of contracts, combinations, and trusts in restraint of interstate commerce, "You may *now* restrain such commerce, provided you are reasonable about it; only take care that the restraint is not undue." . . .

It remains for me to refer, more fully than I have heretofore done, to another, and, in my judgment—if we look to the future—the most important aspect of this case. That aspect concerns the usurpation by the judicial branch of the Government of the functions of the legislative department. . . .

I said at the outset that the action of the court in this case might well alarm thoughtful men who revered the Constitution. I meant by this that many things are intimated and said in the court's opinion which will not be regarded otherwise than as sanctioning an invasion by the judiciary of the constitutional domain of Congress —an attempt by interpretation to soften or modify what some regard as a harsh public policy. This court, let me repeat, solemnly adjudged many years ago that it could not, except by *"judicial legislation"* read words into the Anti-trust Act not put there by Congress, and which, being inserted, give it a meaning which the words of the act, as passed, if properly interpreted, would not justify. The court has decided that it could not thus change a public policy formulated and declared by Congress; that Congress has paramount authority to regulate interstate commerce, and that it alone can change a policy once inaugurated by legislation. The courts have nothing to do with the wisdom or policy of an act of Congress. Their duty is to ascertain the will of Congress, and if the statute embodying the expression of that will is constitutional, the courts must respect it. They have no function to declare a public policy, nor to *amend* legislative enactments. . . . Nevertheless, if I do not misapprehend its opinion, the court has now read into the act of Congress words which are not to be found there, and has thereby done that which it adjudged in 1896 and in 1898 could not be done without violating the Constitution, namely, by interpretation of a statute, changed a public policy declared by the legislative department. . . .

Federal Regulation of Labor

LABOR AS A COMBINATION IN RESTRAINT OF TRADE

156. *The Danbury Hatters Encounter the Sherman Act*

Loewe v. Lawlor, 208 U.S. 274 (1908).

FULLER, C.J.: . . . The combination charged falls within the class of restraints of trade aimed at compelling third parties and strangers involuntarily not to engage in the course of trade except on conditions that the combination imposes; and there is no doubt that . . . "at common law every person has individually, and the public also has collectively, a right to require that the course of trade should be kept free from unreasonable obstruction." But the objection here is to the jurisdiction, because, even conceding that the declaration states a case good at common law, it is contended that it does not state one within the statute. Thus, it is said, that the restraint alleged would operate to entirely destroy plaintiffs' business and thereby include intrastate trade as well; that physical obstruction is not alleged as contemplated; and that defendants are not themselves engaged in interstate trade.

We think none of these objections are tenable, and that they are disposed of by previous decisions of this court. . . .

The [Sherman] act made no distinction between classes. It provided that "every" contract, combination or conspiracy in restraint of trade was illegal. The records of Congress show that several efforts were made to exempt, by legislation, organizations of farmers and laborers from the operation of the act and that all these efforts failed, so that the act remained as we have it before us. . . .

The . . . plaintiffs were manufacturers of hats in Danbury, Connecticut, . . . and were then and there engaged in an interstate trade in some twenty States other than . . . Connecticut; that they were practically dependent upon such interstate trade to consume the product of their factory, only a small percentage of their entire output being consumed in . . . Connecticut; that all the time the alleged combination was formed they were in the process of manufacturing a large number of hats for the purpose of fulfilling engagements then actually made with consignees and wholesale dealers in States other than Connecticut, and that if prevented from carrying on the work of manufacturing these hats they would be unable to complete their engagements.

That defendants were members of a vast combination called the United Hatters of North America, comprising about 9,000 members and including a large number of subordinate unions, and that they were combined with some 1,400,000 others into another association known as The American Federation of Labor. . . ; that defendants were "engaged in a combined scheme and effort to force all manufacturers of fur hats in the United States, including the plaintiffs, against their will and their previous policy of carrying on their business, to organize their workmen in the departments of making and finishing, in each of their factories, into an organization . . . or as the defendants and their confederates term it, to unionize their shops, with the intent thereby to control the employment of labor in and the operation of said factories, and to subject the same to the direction and control of persons, other than the owners of the same, in a manner extremely onerous and distasteful to such owners, and to carry out such scheme, effort and purpose, by restraining and destroying the interstate trade and commerce of such manufacturers, by means of intimidation of and threats made to such manufacturers and their customers in the several States, or boycotting them, their product and their customers, using therefor all the powerful means at their command, . . . until such time as, from the damage and loss of business . . . , the said manufacturers should yield to the said demand to unionize their factories."

That the conspiracy or combination was so far progressed that out of eighty-two manufacturers of this country engaged in the production of fur hats seventy had accepted the terms and acceded to the demand that the shop should be conducted in accordance, so far as conditions of employment were concerned, with the will of the American Federation of Labor; the local union demanded of plaintiffs that they should unionize their shop under peril of being boycotted by this combination, which demand defendants declined to comply with; thereupon the American Federation of Labor, acting through its official organ and through its organizers, declared a boycott. . . .

We think a case within the statute was set up and that the demurrer should have been overruled. . . .

157. *The "Magna Charta" of Labor*

Sections 6 and 20, The Clayton Anti-Trust Act, *U.S. Stat. at L.*, XXXVIII, 731, 738 (October 15, 1914).

SEC. 6. That the labor of a human being is not a commodity or article of commerce. Nothing contained in the anti-trust laws shall be construed to forbid the existence and operation of labor, agricultural, or horticultural organizations, instituted for the purposes of mutual help, and not having capital stock or conducted for profit, or to forbid or restrain individual members of such organizations from lawfully carrying out the legitimate objects thereof; nor shall such organizations, or the members thereof, be held or construed to be illegal combinations or conspiracies in restraint of trade, under the anti-trust laws.

SEC. 20. That no restraining order or injunction shall be granted by any court of the United States, or a judge or the judges thereof, in any case between an employer and employees or between employers and employees, or between employees, or between persons employed and persons seeking employment, involving, or growing out of, a dispute concerning terms or conditions of employment, unless necessary to prevent irreparable injury to property, or to a property right, of the party making the application, for which injury there is no adequate remedy at law, and such property or property right must be described with a particularity in the application, which must be in writing and sworn to by the applicant or by his agent or attorney.

And no such restraining order or injunction shall prohibit any person or persons, whether singly or in concert, from terminating any relation of employment, or from ceasing to perform any work or labor, or from recommending, advising, or persuading others by peaceful means so to do; or from attending at any place where any such person or persons may lawfully be, for the purpose of peacefully obtaining or communicating information, or from peacefully persuading any person to work or to abstain from working; or from ceasing to patronize or to employ any party to such dispute, or from recommending, advising, or persuading others by peaceful and lawful means so to do; or from paying or giving to, or withholding from, any person engaged in such dispute, any strike benefits or other moneys or things of value; or from peaceably assembling in a lawful manner, and for lawful purposes; or from doing any act or thing which might lawfully be done in the absence of such dispute by any party thereto; nor shall any of the acts specified in this paragraph be considered or held to be violations of any law of the United States.

THE FEDERAL GOVERNMENT AND RAILROAD LABOR

158. *The "Yellow-Dog Contract" and Union Membership*

Adair v. U.S., 208 U.S. 161 (1908).

HARLAN, J.: . . . May Congress make it a criminal offense against the United States—as, by the 10th section of the Act of 1898 it does,—for an agent or officer of an interstate carrier, . . . to discharge an employee from service simply because of his membership in a labor organization? . . .

The first inquiry is whether the part of the 10th section of the Act of 1898 upon which the first count of the indictment is based is repugnant to the 5th Amendment of the Constitution, declaring that no person shall be deprived of liberty or property without due process of law. In our opinion that section in the particular mentioned is an invasion of the personal liberty, as well as of the right of property, guaranteed by that Amendment. Such liberty and right embrace the right to make contracts for the purchase of the labor of others, and equally the right to make contracts for the sale of one's own labor; each right, however, being subject to the fundamental condition that no contract, whatever its subject matter, can be sustained which the law, upon reasonable grounds, forbids as inconsistent with the public interest, or as hurtful to the public order, or as detrimental to the common good. . . . It is sufficient in this case to say that, as agent of the railroad company, and, as such, responsible for the conduct of the business of one of its departments, it was the defendant Adair's right—and that right inhered in his personal liberty, and was also a right of property—to serve his employer as best he could, so long as he did nothing that was reasonably forbidden by law as injurious to the public interest. It was the right of the defendant to prescribe the terms upon which the services of Coppage would be accepted, and it was the right of Coppage to become or not, as he chose, an employee of the railroad company upon the terms offered to him. . . .

In every case that comes before this court, therefore, where legislation of this character is concerned, . . . the question necessarily arises: Is this a fair, reasonable, and appropriate exercise of the police power of the state, or is it an unreasonable, unnecessary, and arbitrary interference with the right of the individual to his personal liberty or to enter into those contracts in relation to labor which may seem to him appropriate or necessary for the support of himself and his family? . . .

While . . . the right of liberty and property guaranteed by the Constitution against deprivation without due process of law is subject to such reasonable restraints as the common good or the general welfare may require, it is not within the functions of government . . . to compel any person in the course of his business and against his will, to accept or retain the personal services of another, or to compel any person, against his will, to perform personal services for another. . . .

As the relations and the conduct of the parties towards each other was not controlled by any contract other than a general agreement on one side to accept the services of the employee and a general agreement on the other side to render services to the employer,—no term being fixed for the continuance of the employment,—Congress could not, consistently with the 5th Amendment, make it a crime against the United States to discharge the employee because of his being a member of a labor organization.

But it is suggested that the authority to make it a crime . . . can be referred to the power of Congress to regulate interstate commerce, without regard to any question of personal liberty or right of property arising under the 5th Amendment. This suggestion can have no bearing, in the present discussion unless the statute, in the particular just stated, is, within the meaning of the Constitution, a regulation of commerce among the States. If it be not, then clearly the government cannot invoke the commerce clause of the Constitution as sustaining the indictment against Adair. . . .

Looking alone at the words of the statute for the purpose of ascertaining its scope and effect, and of determining its validity, we hold that there is no such connection between interstate commerce and membership in a labor organization as to authorize Congress to make it a crime against the United States for an agent of an interstate carrier to discharge an employee because of such membership on his part. . . .

It results, on the whole case, that the provision of the statute under which the defendant was convicted must be held to be repugnant to the 5th Amendment and as not embraced by nor within the power of Congress to regulate interstate commerce, but, under the guise of regulating commerce, and as applied to this case, it arbitrarily sanctions an illegal invasion of the personal liberty as well as the right of property of the defendant Adair.

159. *The Court Considers Emergency Wage-and-Hour Legislation*

Wilson v. New, 243 U.S. 332 (1917).

WHITE, C.J.: . . . Did . . . [Congress] have the power in order to prevent the interruption of interstate commerce to exert its will to supply the absence of a wage scale resulting from the disagreement as to wages between the employers and employees and to make its will on that subject controlling for the limited period provided for?

Coming to the general considerations by which both subjects must be controlled, to simplify the analysis for the purpose of considering the question of inherent power, we put the question as to the eight-hour standard entirely out of view on the ground that the authority to permanently establish it is so clearly sustained as to render the subject not disputable. . . .

That the business of common carriers by rail is in a sense a public business because of the interest of society in the continued operation and rightful conduct of such business, and that the public interest begets a public right of regulation to the full extent necessary to secure and protect it, is settled by so many decisions, state and federal, and is illustrated by such a continuous exertion of state and federal legislative power, as to leave no room for question on the subject. It is also equally true that as the right to fix by agreement between the carrier and its employees a standard of wages to control their relations is primarily private, the establishment and giving effect to such agreed-on standard is not subject to be controlled or prevented by public authority. But taking all these propositions as undoubted, if the situation which we have described and with which the act of Congress dealt be taken into view, that is, the dispute between the employers and employees as to a standard of wages, their failure to agree, the resulting absence of such standard, the entire interruption of interstate commerce which was threatened, and the infinite injury to the public interest which was imminent, it would seem inevitably to result that the power to regulate necessarily obtained and was subject to be applied to the extent necessary to provide a remedy for the situation, which included the power to deal with the dispute, to provide by appropriate action for a standard of wages to fill the want of one caused by the failure to exert the private right on the subject, and to give effect by appropriate legislation to the regulations thus adopted. This must be unless it can be said that the right to so regulate as to save and protect the public interest did not apply to a case where the destruction of the public right was imminent as the result of a dispute between the parties and their consequent failure to establish by private agreement the standard of wages which was essential; in other words that the existence of the public right and the public power to preserve it was wholly under the control of the private right to establish a standard by agreement. Nor is it an answer to this view to suggest that the situation was one of emergency and that emergency cannot be made the source of power. . . . The proposition begs the question, since although an emergency may not call into life a power which has never lived, nevertheless emergency may afford a reason for the exertion of a living power already enjoyed. . . .

We are of the opinion that the reasons stated conclusively establish that from the point of view of inherent power the act which is before us was clearly within the legislative power of Congress to adopt, and that in substance and effect it amounted to an exertion of its authority under the circumstances disclosed to compulsorily arbitrate the dispute between the parties by establishing as to the subject matter of that dispute a legislative standard of wages operative and binding as a matter of law upon the parties,—a power none the less efficaciously exerted because exercised by direct legislative act instead of by the enactment of other and appropriate means providing for the bringing about of such result. If it be conceded that the power to enact the statute was in effect the exercise of the right to fix wages where, by reason of the dispute, there had been a failure to fix by agreement, it would simply serve to show the nature and character of the regulation essential to protect the public right and safeguard the movement of interstate commerce, not involving any denial of the authority to adopt it. . . .

A PROGRESSIVE PORTRAIT OF THE INDUSTRIAL SCENE

160. *Louis Brandeis Describes Industrial and Labor Relations*, 1916

U. S. Commission on Industrial Relations, *Final Report and Testimony,* VIII (Sen. Doc. No. 415, 64th Cong., 1st Sess.), 7659-60.

MR. BRANDEIS: My observation leads me to believe that while there are many contributing causes to unrest, that there is one cause which is fundamental. That is the necessary conflict—the contrast between our political liberty and our industrial absolutism. We are as free politically, perhaps, as free as it is possible for us to be. . . .

On the other hand, in dealing with industrial problems the position of the ordinary worker is exactly the reverse. The individual employee has no effective voice or vote. And the main objection, as I see it, to the very large corporation is, that it makes possible—and in many cases makes inevitable—the exercise of industrial absolutism. It is not merely the case of the individual worker against employer which, even if he is a reasonably sized employer, presents a serious situation calling for the interposition of a union to protect the individual. But we have the situation of an employer so potent, so well-organized, with such concentrated forces and with such extraordinary powers of reserve and the ability to endure against strikes and other efforts of a union, that the relatively loosely organized masses of even strong unions are unable to cope with the situation. . . . The result, in the cases of these large corporations, may be to develop a benevolent absolutism, but it is an absolutism all the same; and it is that which makes the great corporation so dangerous. There develops within the State a state so powerful that the ordinary social and industrial forces existing are insufficient to cope with it. . . .

The social justice for which we are striving is an incident of our democracy, not the main end. It is rather the result of democracy—perhaps its finest expression—but it rests upon democracy, which implies the rule by the people. And therefore the end for which we must strive is the attainment of rule by the people, and that involves industrial democracy as well as political democracy.

There must be a division not only of profits, but a division also of responsibilities. The employees must have the opportunity of participating in the decisions as to what shall be their condition and how the business shall be run. They must learn also in sharing that responsibility that they must bear [too] the suffering arising from grave mistakes, just as the employer must. But the right to assist in making the decisions, the right of making their own mistakes, if mistakes there must be, is a privilege which should not be denied to labor. We must insist upon labor sharing the responsibilities for the result of the business. . . .

CHAPTER XVIII

The Police Power and the Progressive Era

ORDINARILY laws protecting the public health, safety, morals, and general welfare of a community are prerogatives of the states. None of these "police powers" is delegated by the Constitution to the federal government. Although Chief Justice Marshall referred to a federal police power as early as 1827 (*Brown v. Maryland, Chapter* VII), his casual use of the phrase did not establish such a power, and throughout the nineteenth century it was generally agreed that this general power was reserved to the states exclusively by the Tenth Amendment. During the Progressive Era, however, Congress began using its commerce, taxing, and postal powers as devices for accomplishing purely social ends. In this indirect manner, Congress has expanded its control over social and economic problems in areas where it formerly had no direct authority.

In an important test case in 1903, the Supreme Court gave judicial sanction to the principle of a federal police power. *Champion v. Ames* (No. 161) upheld a federal act of 1895 prohibiting the distribution of lottery tickets through interstate commerce or the mails. The next year the Court sustained the use of the federal taxing power as an instrument of social control (*McCray v. U.S., 1904*). As a result of these cases, a reform-minded Congress promptly passed new regulatory legislation in areas thus opened to it. Between 1903 and World War I, laws were passed dealing with subjects as diverse as meat inspection and phosphorus matches, narcotics and prostitution. Of major constitutional importance were the cases sustaining the Pure Food and Drug Act of 1906 (*Hipolite Egg Co. v. U.S.*, 1911), the legislation restricting shipment of liquor into dry states (*Clark Distilling Co. v. W. Maryland R.R. Co.*, 1917), and the Mann White Slave Act proscribing the interstate transportation of women for immoral purposes (*Hoke v. U.S.*, [No. 162]). In the latter case, Justice McKenna specifically upheld use of the commerce power "to promote the general welfare, material and moral."

In only one case during this period did the Supreme Court refuse to validate Congress's social measures. Encouraged by the Court's consistent approval of reform legislation based on the commerce power, Congress in 1916 struck at the evil of child labor by excluding from interstate shipment products manufactured by children. When the Court ruled on this law, however, Justice Day, after misquoting the Tenth Amendment, disregarded the ruling in Hoke and reverted to the Knight doctrine that states have the "expressly" reserved power to regulate production and manufacturing (*Hammer v. Dagenhart* [No. 163]). This concept of "dual federalism" was attacked by Justice Holmes who declared that the Child Labor Law was a direct exercise of the commerce power which did "not meddle with anything belonging to the states. They may regulate their internal affairs and their domestic commerce as they like. But when they seek to send their products across the state line they are no longer within their rights." Holmes's dissent indicated that the decision resulted from the difference between the majority's conception of acceptable social policy and Congress's attitude toward "the evil of premature and excessive child labor."

Even before the Supreme Court formulated the doctrine of "dual federalism" as a weapon against federal regulation in areas presumably reserved to the states, it had restricted the police power of the states by using the equally effective principle of substantive due process. The leading refinement of this principle was the evolution of the "liberty of contract" theory. In *Allgeyer v. Louisiana* (No. 164), the Court defined "liberty," as guaranteed by the due process clause of the Fourteenth Amendment, to include the liberty of the individual to enter into contracts without state interference. Although the liberty of contract theory originated in the Allgeyer Insurance case, it became identified chiefly with labor contracts. The Court posited two propositions: (1) an essential equality of bargaining power existed between an individual employee and his employer, and (2) any interference by the state with this equitable arrangement was "unreasonable" and violated the individual's liberty without due process of law. *Coppage v. Kansas* (No. 165) outlawed a state law prohibiting yellow-dog contracts as an illegal restriction upon freedom of contract.

At almost the same time that the Court enunciated the "liberty of contract" theory in *Allgeyer*, it gave the formula a broad enough application to sustain a Utah statute establishing the eight-hour day in the mining industry (*Holden v. Hardy* [No. 166]). Here the Court simply argued that the statute was a legitimate exercise of the state police power to protect the health of workers in a particularly dangerous occupation. Yet the Court, only seven years later, threw out for the first time a state labor statute because it was contrary to the Fourteenth Amendment. Fearful that legislative regulation of labor relations was "on the increase," Justice Peckham rejected the Hardy precedent of 1898 and ruled that the New York statute establishing a sixty-hour week for bakers was not a health law but only "meddlesome interference with the rights of the individual" (*Lochner v. New York* [No. 167]). In one of his more famous statements, Justice Holmes (No. 168) replied that "the Fourteenth Amendment does not enact Mr. Herbert Spencer's Social Statics" or any other social or economic theory. For all practical purposes, however, Peckham's opinion did just that, translating the dominant industrial laissez-faire social theory into constitutional law for nearly three decades.

The severe criticism that greeted the Lochner decision seemed to confirm Holmes's contention that the case was decided "upon an economic theory which a large part of the country does not entertain." As Mayor Gaynor of New York once put it, "There were no journeymen bakers that I know of clamoring for any such liberty." Doubtless such widespread criticism was felt by the majority. During this period the "Brandeis Brief," which presented statistical, historical, sociological, and economic data to support social legislation, was introduced (No. 169), and the Court, seemingly reoriented, upheld in 1908 an Oregon law establishing a ten-hour working day for women (*Muller v. Oregon*). In 1917 it went further, validating a general ten-hour statute (*Bunting v. Oregon*).

Judicial tolerance of legislative experimentation with the state police power seemed to be assured by Justice McKenna's statement in Bunting: "There is a contention made that the law, even regarded as regulating hours of service, is not either necessary or useful for the preservation of the health of employees in mills, factories and manufacturing establishments. The record contains no facts to support the contention and against it is the judgment of the legislature and the Supreme Court of Oregon." A similar attitude had been expressed as early as 1905 in a decision sustaining a compulsory vaccination law in Massachusetts. Rejecting the argument that laws against smallpox contagion violated the due process clause of the Fourteenth Amendment, Justice Harlan pointed out the Massachusetts constitution of 1780 had "laid down as a fundamental principle of the social compact that the whole people covenants with each citizen, and each citizen with the whole people, and that all shall be governed by certain laws for 'the common good'. . . . While this court should guard with firmness every right appertaining to life, liberty or property as secured to the individual by the Supreme Law of the Land, it is of the last importance that it should not invade the domain of local authority except when it is plainly necessary to do so in order to enforce that law" (*Jacobson v. Massachusetts* [No. 170]).

The apparent inconsistency in the due process cases can best be explained by frank recognition of the role played by the individual judge's social and economic philosophy. With the Court's acceptance of the "rule of reason" test, judges pitted their concepts of desirable public policy against those of duly elected legislators, accepting regulations which to them seemed reasonable and rejecting as unreasonable those which did not square with their predilections.

Although constitutional reinterpretation during the Progressive Era made it possible to deal with twentieth-century social and industrial problems, the traditional machinery of formal amendment was also utilized as a method of constitutional change. Such reform objectives as a graduated income tax, direct election of Senators, prohibition, and woman suffrage (No. 171A-D) were achieved by adding four amendments between 1913 and 1920. Another constitutional reflection of Progressivism involved the amendment of state constitutions to provide a greater measure of direct democracy. In 1902 the Oregon Constitution was amended to allow the people of the state the right of direct participation in the legislative process through the initiative and the referendum. In *Pacific States Telephone and Telegraph Co. v. Oregon* (No. 172), the Court maintained a hands-off attitude toward these democratic experiments, dismissing as a political question the contention that these reforms destroyed the republican form of government in Oregon. Not so reluctant as the Court in discussing political questions, President William Howard Taft vetoed the Arizona Admission Act because the constitution of the new state provided for judicial recall (No. 173). Sacrificing progressive reform to pragmatic necessity, Arizona removed the objectional constitutional provision and promptly joined the Union as the forty-eighth state. After admission, Arizona reaffirmed its progressivism by restoring judicial recall through the amendment process.

The Development of the Federal Police Power

161. *Federal Power over Health, Welfare, and Morals*

Champion v. Ames, 188 U.S. 321 (1903).

HARLAN, J.: . . . The Constitution does not define what is to be deemed a legitimate regulation of interstate commerce. In *Gibbons v. Ogden* it was said that the power to regulate such commerce is the power to prescribe the rule by which it is to be governed. But this general observation leaves it to be determined, when the question comes before the court, whether Congress in prescribing a particular rule, has exceeded its power under the Constitution. . . .

We have said that the carrying from State to State of lottery tickets constitutes interstate commerce, and that the regulation of such commerce is within the power of Congress under the Constitution. Are we prepared to say that a provision which is, in effect *a prohibition* of the carriage of such articles from State to State is not a fit or appropriate mode for the *regulation* of that particular kind of commerce? If lottery traffic, *carried on through interstate commerce,* is a matter of which Congress may take cognizance and over which its power may be exerted, can it be possible that it must tolerate the traffic, and simply regulate the manner in which it may be carried on? Or may not Congress, for the protection of the people of all the States, and under the power to regulate interstate commerce, devise such means, within the scope of the Constitution, and not prohibited by it, as will drive that traffic out of commerce among the States? . . .

It must not be forgotten that the power of Congress to regulate commerce among the States is plenary, is complete in itself, and is subject to no limitations except such as may be found in the Constitution. . . .

If it be said that the act of 1895 is inconsistent with the Tenth Amendment, reserving to the States respectively, or to the people, the powers not delegated to the United States, the answer is that the power to regulate commerce among the States has been expressly delegated to Congress. . . .

In legislating upon the subject of the traffic in lottery tickets, as carried on through interstate commerce, Congress only supplemented the action of those States—perhaps all of them—which, for the protection of the public morals, prohibit the drawing of lotteries, as well as the sale or circulation of lottery tickets, within their respective limits. It said, in effect, that it would not permit the declared policy of the States, which sought to protect their people against the mischiefs of the lottery business, to be overthrown or disregarded by the agency of interstate commerce. We should hesitate long before adjudging that an evil of such appalling character, carried on through interstate commerce, cannot be met and crushed by the only power competent to that end. We say competent to that end, because Congress alone has the power to occupy, by legislation, the whole field of interstate commerce. . . .

It is said, however, that if, in order to suppress lotteries carried on through interstate commerce, Congress may exclude lottery tickets from such commerce, that principle leads necessarily to the conclusion that Congress may arbitrarily exclude from commerce among the States any article, commodity, or thing, of whatever kind or nature, or however useful or valuable, which it may choose, no matter with what motive, to declare shall not be carried from one State to another. It will be time enough to consider the constitutionality of such legislation when we must do so. The present case does not require the court to declare the full extent of the power that Congress may exercise in the regulation of commerce among the States. We may, however, repeat, in this connection, what the court has heretofore said, that the power of Congress to regulate commerce among the States, although plenary, cannot be deemed arbitrary, since it is subject to such limitations or restrictions as are prescribed by the Constitution. This power, therefore, may not be exercised so as to infringe rights secured or protected by that instrument. It would not be difficult to imagine legislation that would be justly liable to such an objection as that stated, and be hostile to the objects for the accomplishment of which Congress was invested with the general power to regulate commerce among the several States. But, as often said, the possible abuse of a power is not an argument against its existence. There is probably no governmental power that may not be exerted to the injury of the public. . . .

We decide nothing more in the present case than that lottery tickets are subjects of traffic among those who choose to sell or buy them; that the carriage of such tickets by independent carriers from one State to another is therefore interstate commerce; that under its power to regulate commerce among the several States Congress—subject to the limitations imposed by the Constitution upon the exercise of the powers granted—has plenary authority over such commerce, and may prohibit the carriage of such tickets from State to State; and that legislation to that end, and of that character, is not inconsistent with any limitation or restriction imposed upon the exercise of the powers granted to Congress.

162. *Prostitution and Pure Morals*

Hoke v. U.S., 227 U.S. 308 (1913).

McKENNA, J.: . . . Commerce among the States . . . consists of intercourse and traffic between their citizens, and includes the transportation of persons as well as of property; . . . that is, a person may move or be moved in interstate commerce. And the act under consideration was drawn in view of that possibility. What the act condemns is transportation obtained or aided or transportation induced in interstate commerce for the immoral purposes mentioned. But an objection is made and urged with earnestness. It is said that it is the right and privilege of a person to move between States and that such being the right, another cannot be made guilty of the crime of inducing or assisting or aiding in the exercise of it and "that the motive or intention of the passenger, either before beginning the journey, or during or after completing it, is not a matter of interstate commerce." The contentions confound things important to be distinguished. It urges a right exercised in morality to sustain a right to be exercised in immorality. . . .

Plaintiffs in error admit that the State may control the immoralities of its citizens. Indeed, this is their chief insistence, and they especially condemn the act under review as a subterfuge and an attempt to interfere with the police power of the States to regulate the morals of their citizens and assert that it is in consequence an invasion of the reserved powers of the States. There is unquestionably a control in the States over the morals of their citizens, and, it may be admitted, it extends to making prostitution a crime. It is a control, however, which can be exercised only within the jurisdiction of the States, but there is a domain which the States cannot reach and over which Congress alone has power; and if such power be exerted to control what the States cannot it is an argument for—not against—its legality. Its exertion does not encroach upon the jurisdiction of the States. We have cited examples; others may be adduced. The Pure Food and Drugs Act . . . is a conspicuous instance. In all other instances a clash of national legislation with the power of the States was urged, and in all rejected.

Our dual form of government has its perplexities, State and Nation having different spheres of jurisdiction, . . . but it must be kept in mind that we are one people; and the powers reserved to the States and those conferred on the Nation are adapted to be exercised, whether independently or concurrently, to promote the general welfare, material and moral. This is the effect of the decisions, and surely if the facility of interstate transportation can be taken away from the demoralization of lotteries, the debasement of obscene literature, the contagion of diseased cattle or persons, the impurity of food and drugs, the like facility can be taken away from the systematic enticement to and the enslavement in prostitution and debauchery of women, and, more insistently, of girls.

This is the aim of the law expressed in broad generalization; and motives are made of determining consequences. Motives executed by actions may make it the concern of Government to exert its powers. Right purpose and fair trading need no restrictive regulation, but let them be transgressed and penalties and prohibitions must be applied. We may illustrate again by the Pure Food and Drugs Act. Let an article be debased by adulteration, let it be misrepresented by false branding, and Congress may exercise its prohibitive power. It may be that Congress could not prohibit the manufacture of the article in a State. It may be that Congress could not prohibit in all of its conditions its sale within a State. But Congress may prohibit its transportation between the States, and by that means defeat the motive and evils of its manufacture. . . .

Of course it will be said that women are not articles of merchandise, but this does not affect the analogy of the cases; the substance of the congressional power is the same, only the manner of its exercise must be accommodated to the difference in its objects. It is misleading to say that men and women have rights. Their rights cannot fortify or sanction their wrongs; and if they employ interstate transportation as a facility of their wrongs, it may be forbidden to them. . . .

The principle established by the cases is the simple one, when rid of confusing and distracting considerations, that Congress has power over transportation "among the several States"; that the power is complete in itself, and that Congress, as an incident to it may adopt not only means necessary but convenient to its exercise, and the means may have the quality of police regulations. . . .

163. *Child Labor, the Tenth Amendment, and "Dual Federalism"*

Hammer v. Dagenhart, 247 U.S. 251 (1918).

DAY, J.: . . . It is insisted that adjudged cases in this court establish the doctrine that the power to regulate given to Congress incidentally includes the authority to prohibit the movement of ordinary commodities, and therefore that the subject is not open for discussion. The cases demonstrate the contrary. They rest upon the character of the particular subjects dealt with and the fact that the scope of governmental authority, state or national, possessed over them, is such that the authority to prohibit is, as to them, but the exertion of the power to regulate. . . .

In each of these instances the use of interstate transportation was necessary to the accomplishment of harmful results. In other words, although the power over interstate transportation was to regulate, that could only be accomplished by prohibiting the use of the facilities of interstate commerce to effect the evil intended.

This element is wanting in the present case. The thing intended to be accomplished by this statute is the denial of the facilities of interstate commerce to those manufacturers in the States who employ children within the prohibited ages. The act in its effect does not regulate transportation among the States, but aims to standardize the ages at which children may be employed in mining and manufacturing within the States. The goods shipped are of themselves harmless. The act permits them to be freely shipped after thirty days from the time of their removal from the factory. When offered for shipment, and before transportation begins, the labor of their production is over, and the mere fact that they were intended for interstate commerce transportation does not make their production subject to federal control under the commerce power.

Commerce "consists of intercourse and traffic . . . and includes the transportation of persons and property, as well as the purchase, sale and exchange of commodities." The making of goods and the mining of coal are not commerce, nor does the fact that these things are to be afterwards shipped, or used in interstate commerce, make their production a part thereof. . . .

Over interstate transportation, or its incidents, the regulatory power of Congress is ample, but the production of articles intended for interstate commerce is a matter of local regulation. . . .

If it were otherwise, all manufacture intended for interstate shipment would be brought under federal control to the practical exclusion of the authority of the States, a result certainly not contemplated by the framers of the Constitution when they vested in Congress the authority to regulate commerce among the States. . . .

The grant of power to Congress over the subject of interstate commerce was to enable it to regulate such commerce, and not to give it authority to control the States in their exercise of the police power over local trade and manufacture.

The grant of authority over a purely federal matter was not intended to destroy the local power always existing and carefully reserved to the States in the Tenth Amendment to the Constitution. . . .

That there should be limitations upon the right to employ children in mines and factories in the interest of their own and the public welfare, all will admit. That such employment is generally deemed to require regulation is shown by the fact that the brief of counsel states that every state in the Union has a law upon the subject, limiting the right to thus employ children. In North Carolina, the State wherein is located the factory in which the employment was had in the present case, no child under twelve years of age is permitted to work.

It may be desirable that such laws be uniform, but our federal government is one of enumerated powers. . . .

In interpreting the Constitution it must never be forgotten that the Nation is made up of States to which are entrusted the powers of local government. And to them and to the people the powers not expressly delegated to the National Government are reserved. . . . To sustain this statute would not be in our judgment a recognition of the lawful exertion of congressional authority over interstate commerce, but would sanction an invasion by the federal power of the control of a matter purely local in its character, and over which no authority has been delegated to Congress in conferring the power to regulate commerce among the States. . . .

In our view the necessary effect of this act is, by means of a prohibition against the movement in interstate commerce of ordinary commercial commodities, to regulate the hours of labor of children in factories and mines within the States, a purely state authority. Thus the act in a twofold sense is repugnant to the Constitution. It not only transcends the authority delegated to Congress over commerce, but also exerts a power as to a purely local matter to which the federal authority does not extend. The far-reaching result of upholding the act cannot be more plainly indicated than by pointing out that if Congress can thus regulate matters intrusted to local authority by prohibition of the movement of commodities in interstate commerce, all freedom of commerce will be at an end, and the power of the states over local matters may be eliminated, and thus our system of government be practically destroyed.

For these reasons we hold that this law exceeds the constitutional authority of Congress. It follows that the decree of the district court must be affirmed.

Judicial Interpretation of State Police Power

DUE PROCESS AND LIBERTY OF CONTRACT

164. *"Liberty of Contract" and the Scope of Judicial Authority*

Allgeyer v. Louisiana, 165 U.S. 578 (1897).

PECKHAM, J.: . . . The Supreme Court of Louisiana says that the act of writing within that State, the letter of notification, was an act therein done to effect an insurance on property then in the State, in a marine insurance company which had not complied with its laws, and such act was, therefore, prohibited by the statute. As so construed we think the statute is a violation of the Fourteenth Amendment of the Federal Constitution, in that it deprives the defendants of their liberty without due process of law. The statute which forbids such act does not become due process of law, because it is inconsistent with the provisions of the Constitution of the Union. The liberty mentioned in that amendment means not only the right of the citizen to be free from the more physical restraint of his person, as by incarceration, but the term is deemed to embrace the right of the citizen to be free in the enjoyment of all his faculties; to be free to use them in all lawful ways; to live and work where he will; to earn his livelihood by any lawful calling; to pursue any livelihood or avocation, and for that pur pose to enter into all contracts which may be proper, necessary and essential to his carrying out to a successful conclusion the purposes above mentioned.

It was said by Mr. Justice Bradley, in *Butchers' Union Company v. Crescent City Company* . . . "The right to follow any of the common occupations of life is an inalienable right. It was formulated as such under the phrase 'pursuit of happiness' in the Declaration of Independence. . . . This right is a large ingredient in the civil liberty of the citizen." Again, . . . the learned justice said: "I hold that the liberty of pursuit—the right to follow any of the ordinary callings of life—is one of the privileges of a citizen of the United States." And again, . . . "But if it does not abridge the privileges and immunities of a citizen of the United States to prohibit him from pursuing his chosen calling, and giving to others the exclusive right of pursuing it, it certainly does deprive him (to a certain extent) of his liberty; for it takes from him the freedom of adopting and following the pursuit which he prefers; which, as already intimated, is a material part of the liberty of the citizen." It is true that these remarks were made in regard to questions of monopoly, but they well describe the rights which are covered by the word "liberty" as contained in the Fourteenth Amendment. . . .

The foregoing extracts have been made for the purpose of showing what general definitions have been given in regard to the meaning of the word "liberty" as used in the amendment, but we do not intend to hold that in no such case can the State exercise its police power. When and how far such power may be legitimately exercised with regard to these subjects must be left for determination to each case as it arises.

Has not a citizen of a State, under the

provisions of the Federal Constitution above mentioned, a right to contract outside of the State for insurance on his property—a right of which state legislation cannot deprive him? We are not alluding to acts done within the State by an insurance company or its agents doing business therein, which are in violation of the state statutes. . . . When we speak of the liberty to contract for insurance or to do an act to effectuate such a contract already existing, we refer to and have in mind the facts of this case, where the contract was made outside the State, and as such was a valid and proper contract. The act done within the limits of the State under the circumstances of this case and for the purpose therein mentioned, we hold a proper act, one which the defendants were at liberty to perform and which the state legislature had no right to prevent, at least with reference to the Federal Constitution. To deprive the citizen of such a right as herein described without due process of law is illegal. Such a statute as this in question is not due process of law, because it prohibits an act which under the Federal Constitution the defendants had a right to perform. This does not interfere in any way with the acknowledged right of the State to enact such legislation in the legitimate exercise of its police or other powers as to it may seem proper. In the exercise of such right, however, care must be taken not to infringe upon those other rights of the citizen which are protected by the Federal Constitution.

In the privileges of pursuing an ordinary calling or trade and of acquiring, holding and selling property must be embraced the right to make all proper contracts in relation thereto, and although it may be conceded that this right to contract in relation to persons or property or to do business within the jurisdiction of the State may be regulated and sometimes prohibited when the contracts or business conflict with the policy of the State as contained in its statutes, yet the power does not and cannot extend to prohibiting a citizen from making contracts of the nature involved in this case outside of the limits and jurisdiction of the State, and which are also to be performed outside of such jurisdiction; nor can the State legally prohibit its citizens from doing such an act as writing this letter of notification, even though the property which is the subject of the insurance may at the time when such insurance attaches be within the limits of the State. . . .

165. *Freedom of Contract and Yellow-Dog Contracts*

Coppage v. Kansas, 236 U.S. 1 (1915).

PITNEY, J.: . . . Unless it is to be overruled, . . . [*Adair v. U.S.*] is controlling upon the present controversy; for if Congress is prevented from arbitrary interference with the liberty of contract because of the "due process" provisions of the Fifth Amendment, it is too clear for argument that the States are prevented from the like interference by virtue of the corresponding clause of the Fourteenth Amendment; and hence if it be unconstitutional for Congress to deprive an employer of liberty or property for threatening an employee with loss of employment or discriminating against him because of his membership in a labor organization, it is unconstitutional for a State to similarly punish an employer for requiring his employee, as a condition of securing or retaining employment, to agree not to become or remain a member of such an organization while so employed. . . .

Included in the right of personal liberty and the right of private property—partaking of the nature of each—is the right to make contracts for the acquisition of property. Chief among such contracts is that of personal employment, by which labor and other services are exchanged for money or other forms of property. If this right be struck down or arbitrarily interfered with, there is a substantial impairment of liberty in the long-established constitutional sense. The right is as essential to the laborer as to the capitalist, to the poor as to the rich; for the vast majority or persons have no other honest way to begin to acquire property, save by working for money.

An interference with this liberty so serious as that now under consideration, and so disturbing of equality of right, must be deemed to be arbitrary, unless it be supportable as a reasonable exercise of the police power of the State. But, notwithstanding the strong general presumption in favor of the validity of state laws, we do not think the statute in question, as construed and applied in this case, can be sustained as a legitimate exercise of that power. . . .

As to the interest of the employed, it is said by the Kansas Supreme Court . . . to be a matter of common knowledge that "employees, as a rule, are not financially able to be as independent in making contracts for the sale of their labor as are employers in making a contract of purchase thereof." No doubt, wherever the right of private property exists, there must and will be inequalities of fortune; and thus it naturally happens that parties negotiating about a contract are not equally unhampered by circumstances. This applies to all contracts, and not merely to that between employer and employee. Indeed, a little reflection will show that wherever the right of private property and the right of free contract co-exist, each party when contracting is inevitably more or less influenced by the question whether he has much property, or little, or none; for the contract is made to the very end that each may gain something that he needs or desires more urgently than that which he proposes to give in exchange. And, since it is self-evident that, unless all things are held in common, some persons must have more property than others, it is from the nature of things impossible to uphold freedom of contract and the right of private property without at the same time recognizing as legitimate those inequalities of fortune that are the necessary result of the exercise of those rights. But the Fourteenth Amendment, in declaring that a State shall not "deprive any person of life, liberty, or property without due process of law," gives to each of these an equal sanction; it recognizes "liberty" and "property" as co-existent human rights, and debars the States from any unwarranted interference with either.

And since a State may not strike them down directly, it is clear that it may not do so indirectly, as by declaring in effect that the public good requires the removal of those inequalities that are but the normal and inevitable result of their exercise, and then invoking the police power in order to remove the inequalities, without other object in view. The police power is broad, and not easily defined, but it cannot be given the wide scope that is here asserted for it, without in effect nullifying the constitutional guaranty. . . .

It is said in the opinion of the state court that membership in a labor organization does not necessarily affect a man's duty to his employer; that the employer has no right, by virtue of the relation, "to dominate the life nor to interfere with the liberty of the employee in matters that do not lessen or deteriorate the service"; and that "the statute implies that labor unions are lawful and not inimical to the rights of employers." The same view is presented in the brief of counsel for the State, where it is said that membership in a labor organization is the "personal and private affair" of the employee. To this line of argument it is sufficient to say that it cannot be judicially declared that membership in such an organization has no relation to a member's duty to his employer; and therefore, if freedom of contract is to be preserved, the employer must be left at liberty to decide for himself whether such membership by his employee is consistent with the satisfactory performance of the duties of the employment. . . .

Of course we do not intend to say, nor to intimate, anything inconsistent with the right of individuals to join labor unions, nor do we question the legitimacy of such organizations so long as they conform to the laws of the land as others are required to do. Conceding the full right of the individual to join the union, he has no inherent right to do this and still remain in the employ of one who is unwilling to employ a union man, any more than the same individual has a right to join the union without the consent of the organization. . . .

DUE PROCESS AND REGULATION OF THE HOURS OF LABOR

166. *"The right of contract is . . . subject to certain limitations which the state may lawfully impose."*

Holden v. Hardy, 169 U.S. 366 (1898).

BROWN, J.: This case involves the constitutionality of an act of the legislature of Utah of March 30, 1896, chap. 72, entitled "An Act Regulating the Hours of Employment in Underground Mines and in Smelters and Ore Reduction Works." . . .

The validity of the statute in question is . . . challenged upon the ground of an alleged violation of the Fourteenth Amendment to the Constitution of the United States, in that it abridges the privileges or immunities of citizens of the United States; deprives both the employer and the laborer of his property without due process of law, and denies to them the equal protection of the laws. . . .

While the cardinal principles of justice are immutable, the methods by which justice is administered are subject to constant fluctuation, and the Constitution of the United States, which is necessarily and to a large extent inflexible and exceedingly difficult of amendment, should not be so construed as to deprive the states of the power to so amend their laws as to make them conform to the wishes of the citizens as they may deem best for the public welfare without bringing them into conflict with the supreme law of the land. . . .

This right of contract, however, is itself subject to certain limitations which the state may lawfully impose in the exercise of its police powers. While this power is inherent in all governments, it has doubtless been greatly expanded in its application during the past century, owing to an enormous increase in the number of occupations which are dangerous, or so far detrimental to the health of employees as to demand special precaution for their well-being and protection, or the safety of adjacent property. While this court has held . . . that the police power cannot be put forward as an excuse for oppressive and unjust legislation, it may be lawfully resorted to for the purpose of preserving the public health, safety, or morals, or the abatement of public nuisances, and a large discretion "is necessarily vested in the legislature to determine, not only what the interests of the public require, but what measures are necessary for the protection of such interests." . . .

Upon the principles above stated, we think the act in question may be sustained as a valid exercise of the police power of the State. The enactment does not profess to limit the hours of all workmen, but merely those who are employed in underground mines, or in the smelting, reduction, or refining of ores or metals. These employments when too long pursued the legislature has judged to be detrimental to the health of the employees, and, so long as there are reasonable grounds for believing that this is so, its decision upon this subject cannot be reviewed by the Federal courts.

While the general experience of mankind may justify us in believing that men may engage in ordinary employments more than eight hours per day without injury to their health, it does not follow that labor for the same length of time is innocuous when carried on beneath the surface of the earth, where the operative is deprived of fresh air and sunlight, and is frequently subjected to foul atmosphere and a very high temperature, or to influence of noxious gases, generated by the processes of refining or smelting. . . .

It may not be improper to suggest in this connection that although the prosecution in this case was against the employer of labor, who apparently under the statute is the only one liable, his defence is not so much that his right to contract has been infringed upon, but that the act works a peculiar hardship to his employees, whose right to labor as long as they please is alleged to be thereby violated. The argument would certainly come with better grace and greater cogency from the latter class. But the fact that both parties are of full age and competent to contract does not necessarily deprive the State of the power to interfere where the parties do not stand upon an equality, or where the public health demands that one party to the contract shall be protected against himself. "The State still retains an interest in his welfare, however reckless he may be. The whole is no greater than the sum of all the parts, and when the individual health, safety, and welfare are sacrificed or neglected, the state must suffer."

We have no disposition to criticise the many authorities which hold that state statutes restricting the hours of labor are unconstitutional. Indeed, we are not called upon to express an opinion upon this subject. It is sufficient to say of them that they have no application to cases where the legislature had adjudged that a limitation is necessary for the preservation of the health of employees, and there are reasonable grounds for believing that such determination is supported by the facts. The question in each case is whether the legislature has adopted the statute in exercise of a reasonable discretion, or whether its action be a mere excuse for an unjust discrimination, or the oppression, or spoliation of a particular class. . . .

167. *"Meddlesome interference with the rights of the individual."*

Lochner v. New York, 198 U.S. 45 (1905).

PECKHAM, J.: . . . The State . . . has power to prevent the individual from making certain kinds of contracts, and in regard to them the Federal Constitution offers no protection. If the contract be one which the State, in the legitimate exercise of its police power, has the right to prohibit, it is not prevented from prohibiting it by the Fourteenth Amendment. . . .

This court has recognized the existence and upheld the exercise of the police powers of the States in many cases which might fairly be considered as border ones, and it has, in the course of its determination of questions regarding the asserted invalidity of such statutes, on the ground of their violation of the rights secured by the federal Constitution, been guided by rules of a very liberal nature, the application of which has resulted, in numerous instances, in upholding the validity of state statutes thus assailed. . . .

It must, of course, be conceded that there is a limit to the valid exercise of the police power by the State. There is no dispute concerning this general proposition. Otherwise the Fourteenth Amendment would have no efficacy and the legislatures of the States would have unbounded power, and it would be enough to say that any piece of legislation was enacted to conserve the morals, the health, or the safety of the people; such legislation would be valid, no matter how absolutely without foundation the claim might be. . . . In every case that comes before this court, therefore, where legislation of this character is concerned, and where the protection of the federal Constitution is sought, the question necessarily arises: Is this a fair, reasonable, and appropriate exercise of the police power of the State, or is it an unreasonable, unnecessary, and arbitrary interference with the right of the individual to his personal liberty or to enter into those contracts in relation to labor which may seem to him appropriate or necessary for the support of himself and his family? Of course the liberty of contract relating to labor includes both parties to it. The one has as much right to purchase as the other to sell labor. . . .

The question whether this act is valid as a labor law, pure and simple, may be dismissed in a few words. There is no reasonable ground for interfering with the liberty of person or the right of free contract, by determining the hours of labor, in the occupation of a baker. There is no contention that bakers as a class are not equal in intelligence and capacity to men in other trades or manual occupations, or that they are not able to assert their rights and care for themselves without the protecting arm of the State, interfering with their independence of judgment and of action. They are in no sense wards of the State. Viewed in the light of a purely labor law, with no reference whatever to the question of health, we think that a law like the one before us involves neither the safety, the morals, nor the welfare, of the public, and that the interest of the public is not in the slightest degree affected by such an act. The law must be upheld, if at all, as a law pertaining to the health of the individual engaged in the occupation of a baker. It does not affect any other portion of the public than those who who engaged in that occupation. Clean and wholesome bread does not depend upon whether the baker works but ten hours per day or only sixty hours a week. The limitation of the hours of labor does not come within the police power on that ground.

It is a question of which of two powers or rights shall prevail—the power of the State to legislate or the right of the individual to liberty of person and freedom of contract. The mere assertion that the subject relates, though but in a remote degree, to the public health, does not necessarily render the enactment valid. The act must have a more direct relation, as a means to an end, and the end itself must be appropriate and legitimate, before an act can be held to be valid which interferes with the general right of an individual to be free in his person and in his power to contract in relation to his own labor. . . .

We think the limit of the police power has been reached and passed in this case. . . . Statutes of the nature of that under review, limiting the hours in which grown and intelligent men may labor to earn their living, are mere meddlesome interferences with the rights of the individual. . . .

It is manifest to us that the limitation of the hours of labor as provided for in this section of the statute . . . has no such direct relation to and no such substantial effect upon the health of the employee, as to justify us in regarding the section as really a health law. It seems to us that the real object and purpose were simply to regulate the hours of labor between the master and his employees . . .

in a private business, not dangerous in any degree to morals or in any real and substantial degree, to the health of the employees. Under such circumstances the freedom of master and employee to contract with each other in relation to their employment, and in defining the same, cannot be prohibited or interfered with, without violating the Federal Constitution.

168. *"The Fourteenth Amendment does not enact Spencer's Social Statics."*

Lochner v. New York, 198 U.S. 45 (1905).

Holmes, J., dissenting: . . . This case is decided upon an economic theory which a large part of the country does not entertain. If it were a question whether I agreed with that theory, I should desire to study it further and long before making up my mind. But I do not conceive that to be my duty, because I strongly believe that my agreement or disagreement has nothing to do with the right of a majority to embody their opinions in law. It is settled by various decisions of this court that state constitutions and state laws may regulate life in many ways which we as legislators might think as injudicious or if you like as tyrannical as this, and which equally with this, interfere with the liberty to contract. Sunday laws and usury laws are ancient examples. A more modern one is the prohibition of lotteries. The liberty of the citizen to do as he likes so long as he does not interfere with the liberty of others to do the same, which has been a shibboleth for some well-known writers, is interfered with by school laws, by the post-office, by every state or municipal institution which takes his money for purposes thought desirable, whether he likes it or not. The Fourteenth Amendment does not enact Mr. Herbert Spencer's Social Statics. . . . United States and state statutes and decisions cutting down the liberty to contract by way of combination are familiar to this court. . . . Some of these laws embody convictions or prejudices which judges are likely to share. Some may not. But a constitution is not intended to embody a particular economic theory, whether of paternalism and the organic relation of the citizen to the state or of *laissez faire*. It is made for people of fundamentally differing views, and the accident of our finding certain opinions natural and familiar or novel and even shocking ought not to conclude our judgment upon the question whether statutes embodying them conflict with the Constitution of the United States.

General propositions do not decide concrete cases. The decision will depend on a judgment or intuition more subtle than any articulate major premise. But I think that the proposition just stated, if it is accepted, will carry us far toward the end. Every opinion tends to become a law. I think that the word liberty in the Fourteenth Amendment, is perverted when it is held to prevent the natural outcome of a dominant opinion, unless it can be said that a rational and fair man necessarily would admit that the statute proposed would infringe fundamental principles as they have been understood by the traditions of our people and our law. It does not need research to show that no such sweeping condemnation can be passed upon the statute before us. A reasonable man might think it a proper measure on the score of health. Men whom I certainly could not pronounce unreasonable would uphold it as a first instalment of a general regulation of the hours of work. Whether in the latter aspect it would be open to the charge of inequality I think it unnecessary to discuss.

169. *The "Brandeis Brief" Adds a New Dimension to Legal Argument*

Louis D. Brandeis, Brief for Defendant in Error, *Muller v. Oregon, Transcripts of Records and File Copies of Briefs*, 1907, XXIV (Cases 102-7), Library of the Supreme Court, Washington, D.C.

This case presents the single question whether the Statute of Oregon, . . . which provides that "no female [shall] be employed in any mechanical establishment or factory or laundry" "more than ten hours during any one day," is unconstitutional and void as violating the Fourteenth Amendment of the Federal Constitution.

The decision in this case will, in effect, determine the constitutionality of nearly all the statutes in force in the United States, limiting the hours of labor of adult women. . . .

The facts of common knowledge of which the Court may take judicial notice . . . establish, we submit, conclusively, that there is reasonable ground for holding that to permit women in Oregon to work in a "mechanical establishment, or factory, or laundry" more than ten hours in one day is dangerous to the public health, safety, morals, or welfare. . . .

The leading countries in Europe in which women are largely employed in factory or similar work have found it necessary to take action for the protection of their health and safety and the public welfare, and have enacted laws limiting the hours of labor for adult women. . . .

Twenty States of the Union . . . have [also] enacted laws limiting the hours of labor for adult women. . . .

In the United States, as in foreign countries, there has been a general movement to strengthen and to extend the operation of these laws. In no State has any such law been held unconstitutional, except in Illinois. . . .

I. THE DANGER OF LONG HOURS

A. *Causes*

(1) Physical Differences Between Men and Women. . . .

Report of Select Committee on Shops Early Closing Bill, British House of Commons, 1895.

Dr. Percy Kidd, physician in Brompton and London Hospitals:

The most common effect I have noticed of the long hours is general deterioration of health; very general symptoms which we medically attribute to over-action, and debility of the nervous system; that includes a great deal more than what is called nervous disease, such as indigestion, constipation, a general slackness, and a great many other indefinite symptoms.

Are those symptoms more marked in women than in men?

I think they are much more marked in women. I should say one sees a great many more women of this class than men; but I have seen precisely the same symptoms in men, I should not say in the same proportion, because one has not been able to make anything like a statistical inquiry. There are other symptoms, but I mention those as being the most common. Another symptom especially among women is anemia, bloodlessness or pallor, that I have no doubt is connected with long hours indoors. . . .

Report of the Maine Bureau of Industrial and Labor Statistics, 1888.

Let me quote from Dr. Ely Von der Warker (1875):

Woman is badly constructed for the purposes of standing eight or ten hours upon her feet. I do not intend to bring into evidence the peculiar position and nature of the organs contained in the pelvis, but to call attention to the peculiar construction of the knee and the shallowness of the pelvis, and the delicate nature of the foot as part of a sustaining column. The knee joint of woman is a sexual characteristic. Viewed in front and extended, the joint in but a slight degree interrupts the gradual taper of the thigh into the leg. Viewed in a semi-flexed position, the joint forms a smooth ovate spheriod. The reason of this lies in the smallness of the patella in front, and the narrowness of the articular surfaces of the tibia and femur, and which in man form the lateral prominences, and thus is much more perfect as a sustaining column than that of a woman. The muscles which keep the body fixed upon the thighs in the erect position labor under the disadvantage of shortness of purchase, owing to the short distance, compared to that of men, between the crest of the ilium and the great trochanter of the femur, thus giving to man a much larger purchase in the leverage existing between the trunk and the extremities. Comparatively the foot is less able to sustain weight than that of man, owing to its shortness and the more delicate formation of the tarsus and metatarsus. . . .

Infant Mortality: A Social Problem. George Newman, M.D., *London,* 1906.

The results of fatigue become manifest in various ways, not the least being the occurrence of accidents or of physical breakdown. The former, as is now well recognized, occur most frequently in fatigued workers. For example, since 1900 there has been a steady, though not marked, increase in the number of accidents to women over eighteen years of age in laundries. In 1900 such accidents numbered 131; in 1904, 157. Now it has been shown that whilst the first half of the day yields about the same number of accidents as the second half, more accidents, amounting to nearly double the number, occur between the hours of 11 A.M. and 1 P.M., and between 4 P.M. and 7 P.M. than at any other time of the day. . . .

Relations between Labor and Capital. United States Senate Committee, 1883.

Vol. I. *Testimony of* Robert Howard, *Mule-Spinner in Fall River Cotton Mills.*

I have noticed that the hard, slavish overwork is driving those girls into the saloons, after they leave the mills evenings . . . good, respectable girls, but they come out so tired and so thirsty and so exhausted . . . from working along steadily from hour to hour and breathing the noxious effluvia from the grease and other ingredients used in the mill. . . .

Drinking is most prevalent among working people where the hours of labor are long. . . .

President Roosevelt's Annual Message delivered to the Second Session of the 59th Congress, December 4, 1906.

More and more [of] our people are growing to recognize the fact that the questions which are not merely of industrial but of social importance outweigh all others; and these two questions (labor of women and children) most emphatically come in the category of those which affect in the most far-reaching way the home-life of the nation. . . .

Industrial Conference National Civic Federation, 1902.

The most striking fact about this question of hours of labor seems to be its universality. In virtually every country dominated by Western civilization the daily work-time in mechanical industries is being cut down by successive movements that appear to be as inevitable as the tide, and that have the appearance of steps in the path of human progress. . . . (George Gunton, page 190).

That the time is now ripe for another

general reduction in the daily working time is indicated by the testimony of physicians and the mortality statistics of occupations. . . . (A. J. Weber, Chief Statistician, New York Department of Labor, page 200). . . .

LAUNDRIES

The special prohibition in the Oregon Act of more than ten hours' work in laundries is not an arbitrary discrimination against that trade. Laundrics would probably not be included under the general term of "manufacturing" or "mechanical establishments"; and yet the special dangers of long hours in laundries, as the business is now conducted, present strong reasons for providing a legal limitation of the hours of work in that business. . . .

CONCLUSION

We submit that in view of the facts above set forth and of legislative action extending over a period of more than sixty years in the leading countries in Europe, and in twenty of our States, it cannot be said that the Legislature of Oregon has no reasonable ground for believing that the public health, safety, or welfare did not require a legal limitation on women's work in manufacturing and mechanical establishments and laundries to ten hours in one day.

DUE PROCESS AND PUBLIC HEALTH

170. *Is Smallpox Contagion Guaranteed by the Fourteenth Amendment?*

Jacobson v. Massachusetts, 197 U.S. 11 (1905).

HARLAN, J.: . . . The authority of the State to enact this statute is to be referred to what is commonly called the police power—a power which the State did not surrender when becoming a member of the Union under the Constitution. Although this court has refrained from any attempt to define the limits of that power, yet it has distinctly recognized the authority of a State to enact quarantine laws and "health laws of every description"; indeed, all laws that relate to matters completely within its territory and which do not by their necessary operation affect the people of other States. According to settled principles the police power of a State must be held to embrace, at least, such reasonable regulations established directly by legislative enactment as will protect the public health and the public safety. . . . It is equally true that the State may invest local bodies called into existence for purposes of local administration with authority in some appropriate way to safeguard the public health and the public safety. . . .

The defendant insists that his liberty is invaded when the State subjects him to fine or imprisonment for neglecting or refusing to submit to vaccination; that a compulsory vaccination law is unreasonable, arbitrary and oppressive, and, therefore, hostile to the inherent right of every freeman to care for his own body and health in such way as to him seems best; and that the execution of such a law against one who objects to vaccination, no matter for what reason, is nothing short of an assault upon his person. But the liberty secured by the Constitution of the United States to every person within its jurisdiction does not import an absolute right in each person to be, at all times and in all circumstances, wholly freed from restraint. There are manifold restraints to which every person is necessarily subject for the common good. On any other basis organized society could not exist with safety to its members. Society based on the rule that each one is a law unto himself would soon be confronted with disorder and anarchy. Real liberty for all could not exist under the operation of a principle which recognizes the right of each individual person to use his own, whether in respect of his person or his property, regardless of the injury that may be done to others. . . .

The defendant did not offer to prove that, by reason of his then condition, he was in fact not a fit subject of vaccination. . . .

We are unwilling to hold it to be an element in the liberty secured by the Constitution of the United States that one person, or a minority of persons, residing in any community and enjoying the benefits of its local government, should have the power thus to dominate the majority when supported in their action by the authority of the State. While this court should guard with firmness every right appertaining to life, liberty or property as secured to the individual by the Supreme Law of the Land, it is of the last importance that it should not invade the domain of local authority except when it is plainly necessary to do so in order to enforce that law. The safety and the health of the people of Massachusetts are, in the first instance, for that Commonwealth to guard and protect. . . .

Constitutional Reflections of Progressivism

PROGRESSIVISM AND REFORM AMENDMENTS

171. *Changing the Constitution*

A. THE SIXTEENTH AMENDMENT: INCOME TAX

Proposed July 12, 1909; adopted February 25, 1913.

The Congress shall have power to lay and collect taxes on incomes, from whatever source derived, without apportionment among the several States, and without regard to any census or enumeration.

B. THE SEVENTEENTH AMENDMENT: DIRECT ELECTION OF SENATORS

Proposed May 16, 1912; adopted May 31, 1913.

The Senate of the United States shall be composed of two Senators from each State, elected by the people thereof, for six years; and each Senator shall have one vote. The electors in each State shall have the qualifications requisite for electors of the most numerous branch of the State legislature.

When vacancies happen in the representation of any State in the Senate, the executive authority of such State shall issue writs of election to fill such vacancies: *Provided,* That the legislature of any State may empower the executive thereof to make temporary appointment until the people fill the vacancies by election as the legislature may direct.

This amendment shall not be so construed as to affect the election or term of any Senator chosen before it becomes valid as part of the Constitution.

C. THE EIGHTEENTH AMENDMENT: PROHIBITION

Proposed December 18, 1917; adopted January 29, 1919.

1. After one year from the ratification of this article the manufacture, sale, or transportation of intoxicating liquors within, the importation thereof into, or the exportation thereof from the United States and all territory subject to the jurisdiction thereof for beverage purposes is hereby prohibited.

2. The Congress and the several States shall have concurrent power to enforce this article by appropriate legislation.

3. This article shall be inoperative unless it shall have been ratified as an amendment to the Constitution by the Legislatures of the several States, as provided in the Constitution, within seven years from the date of the submission hereof to the States by the Congress.

D. THE NINETEENTH AMENDMENT: WOMAN SUFFRAGE

Proposed June 4, 1919; adopted August 26, 1920.

1. The right of citizens of the United States to vote shall not be denied or abridged by the United States or by any State on account of sex.

2. Congress shall have power, by appropriate legislation, to enforce the provisions of this article.

THE PREROGATIVES OF STATEHOOD

172. *Direct Democracy and a Republican Form of Government*

Pacific States Telephone and Telegraph Co. v. Oregon, 223 U.S. 118 (1912).

WHITE, C.J.: . . . The assignments of error filed on the allowance of the writ of error are numerous. The entire matters covered by each and all of them in the argument, however, are reduced to six propositions, which really amount to but one, since they are all based upon the single contention that the creation by a State of the power to legislate by the initiative and referendum causes the prior lawful state government to be bereft of its lawful character as the result of the provisions of §4 of Art. IV of the Constitution, that "The United States shall guarantee to every State in this Union, a Republican Form of Government. . . ." This being the basis of all the contentions, the case comes to the single issue whether the enforcement of that provision, because of its political character, is exclusively committed to Congress or is judicial in its character. . . .

Do the provisions of . . . [§4, Art. IV] obliterate the division between judicial authority and legislative power upon which the Constitution rests? In other words, do they authorize the judiciary to substitute its judgment as to a matter purely political for the judgment of Congress on a subject committed to it and thus overthrow the Constitution upon the ground that thereby the guarantee to the States of a government republican in form may be secured, a conception which after all rests upon the assumption that the States are to be guaranteed a government republican in form by destroying the very existence of a government republican in form in the Nation.

We shall not stop to consider the text to point out how absolutely barren it is of support for the contentions sought to be based upon it, since the repugnancy of those contentions to the letter and spirit of that text is so conclusively established by prior decisions of this court as to cause the matter to be absolutely foreclosed. . . .

The court, speaking through Mr. Chief Justice Fuller, in *Taylor v. Beckham*, No. 1, . . said:

"But it is said that the Fourteenth Amendment must be read with §4 of Art. IV, of the Constitution, providing that: 'the United States shall guarantee to every State in this Union a republican form of government. . . .'"

"It was long ago settled that the enforcement of this guarantee belonged to the political department. *Luther v. Borden*. . . . In that case it was held that the question, which of the two opposing governments of Rhode Island, namely, the charter government or the government established by a voluntary convention, was the legitimate one, was a question for the determination of the political department; and when that department had decided, the courts were bound to take notice of the decision and follow it. . . ."

It is indeed a singular misconception of the nature and character of our constitutional system of government to suggest that the settled distinction which the doctrine just stated points out between judicial authority over justiciable controversies and legislative power as to purely political questions tends to destroy the duty of the judiciary in proper cases to enforce the Constitution. The suggestion but results from failing to distinguish between things which are widely different, that is, the legislative duty to determine the political questions involved in deciding whether a state government republican in form exists, and the judicial power and ever-present duty whenever it becomes necessary, in a controversy properly submitted, to enforce and uphold the applicable provisions of the Constitution as to each and every exercise of governmental power. . . .

As the issues presented, in their very essence, are, and have long since by this court been, definitely determined to be political and governmental, and embraced within the scope of the powers conferred upon Congress, and not, therefore, within the reach of judicial power, it follows that the case presented is not within our jurisdiction, and the writ of error must therefore be, and it is, dismissed for want of jurisdiction.

173. *President Taft's Veto of the Arizona Enabling Act, August 22, 1911*

Richardson, ed., *Messages and Papers of the Presidents,* XI, 7636-44.

I return herewith, without my approval, House joint resolution No. 14, "To admit the Territories of New Mexico and Arizona as States into the Union on an equal footing with the original States." . . .

If I sign this joint resolution, I do not see how I can escape responsibility for the judicial recall of the Arizona constitution. . . .

This provision of the Arizona constitution, in its application to county and State judges, seems to me so pernicious in its effect, so destructive of independence in the judiciary, so likely to subject the rights of the individual to the possible tyranny of a popular majority, and, therefore, to be so injurious to the cause of free government, that I must disapprove a constitution containing it. . . .

A government is for the benefit of all the people. . . . Now, as the government is for all the people, and is not solely for a majority of them, the majority in exercising control either directly or through its agents is bound to exercise the power for the benefit of the minority as well as the majority. . . . No honest, clear-headed man, however great a lover of popular government, can deny that the unbridled expression of the majority of a community converted hastily into law or action would sometimes make a government tyrannical and cruel. Constitutions are checks upon the hasty action of the majority. They are the self-imposed restraints of a whole people upon a majority of them to secure sober action and a respect for the rights of the minority, and of the individual in his relation to other individuals, and in his relation to the whole people in their character as a state or government. . . .

By the recall in the Arizona constitution it is proposed to give to the majority power to remove arbitrarily, and without delay, any judge who may have the courage to render an unpopular decision. . . . Could there be a system more ingeniously devised to subject judges to momentary gusts of popular passion than this? We cannot be blind to the fact that often an intelligent and respectable electorate may be so roused upon an issue that it will visit with condemnation the decision of a just judge, though exactly in accord with the law governing the case, merely because it affects unfavorably their contest. . . .

Judicial recall is advocated on the ground that it will bring the judges more into sympathy with the popular will and the progress of ideas among the people. It is said that now judges are out of touch with the movement toward a wider democracy and a greater control of governmental agencies in the interest and for the benefit of the people. The righteous and just course for a judge to pursue is ordinarily fixed by statute or clear principles of law, and the cases in which his judgment may be affected by his political, economic, or social views are infrequent. But even in such cases, judges are not removed from the people's influence. Surround the judiciary with all the safeguards possible, create judges by appointment, make their tenure for life, forbid diminution of salary during their term, and still it is impossible to prevent the influence of popular opinion from coloring judgments in the long run. Judges are men, intelligent, sympathetic men, patriotic men, and in those fields of the law in which the personal equation unavoidably plays a part, there will be found a response to sober popular opinion as it changes to meet the exigency of social, political, and economic changes. Indeed this should be so. Individual instances of a hidebound and retrograde conservatism on the part of courts in decisions which turn on the individual economic or sociological views of the judges may be pointed out; but they are not many, and do not call for radical action. . . .

But it is said that the people of Arizona are to become an independent State when created, and even if we strike out judicial recall now, they can reincorporate it in their constitution after statehood.

To this I would answer that in dealing with the courts, which are the cornerstone of good government, and in which not only the voters, but the nonvoters and nonresidents, have a deep interest as a security for their rights of life, liberty, and property, no matter what the future action of the State may be, it is necessary for the authority which is primarily responsible for its creation to assert in no doubtful tones the necessity for an independent and untrammeled judiciary. . . .

CHAPTER XIX

World War I

EVEN though the United States entered the World War on a note of Wilsonian idealism, the shattering experience of total war ended the era of Progressivism. In shifting to wartime mobilization, however, broad federal powers, which had been utilized to further domestic reforms, were expanded to meet the overwhelming demands of international conflict, accelerating the trend towards national centralization and executive leadership. The extent of federal power and presidential control raised formidable constitutional issues. The Lever Act (No. 174), one of the most important war measures, was a drastic enactment authorizing federal control of the domestic economy, a sphere normally reserved for the states. Only one feature of this law, as subsequently amended, was declared unconstitutional. In *U.S. v. Cohen Grocery* (1921), the Court voided the price-fixing provisions that failed to specify what constituted unjust prices. By concentrating on the detailed phrasing of only one section of the statute, the Court implicitly accepted the broad grant of power. In *Matthew Addy Co. v. U.S.* (1924), the Court also decided a similar case on narrow technical grounds, thus avoiding an adverse decision on a war measure, even though hostilities had ceased nearly six years earlier.

Another example of expanding federal power and increased executive authority was presidential seizure and government operation of the nation's rail network. As early as 1916, an Army Appropriation Act had authorized the President "in time of war . . . to take possession and assume control of any system . . of transportation." After presidential seizure in 1917, Congress passed the Railway Administration Act (1918) providing for government operation of the roads and compensation of their owners. The Court upheld executive seizure in *Northern Pacific Railway Co. v. North Dakota* (No. 175).

Prohibition of the manufacture and sale of alcoholic beverages also extended federal powers. The Selective Service Law of 1917 had forbidden the sale of liquor on military posts or to military personnel in uniform. In 1918 Congress empowered the President to prohibit the sale of liquor near coal mines, munition factories, shipbuilding and other war plants. Ironically, however, complete prohibition was not established until ten days after the signing of the Armistice. In the so-called Wartime Prohibition Cases (1918), Justice Brandeis upheld the act under the federal war power, ruling that the conflict had not been officially terminated.

One of the most sweeping delegations of legislative authority to the executive came in the Overman Act (No. 176), which gave the President almost unlimited power to reorganize federal agencies directing the nation's resources in wartime. The broad scope of the measure aroused bitter opposition, and Senator Frank B. Brandagee caustically proposed that "if any power, constitutional or not, has been inadvertently omitted from this bill, it is hereby granted in full." Passed by a wide margin, the Act never came before the Court for adjudication.

Despite the limitations imposed by the first ten amendments on governmental interference with individual liberties, federal authority was expanded at the expense of traditional civil rights. Although Congress had passed a conscription act during the Civil War, the Court had not reviewed its constitutionality. It was not until 1918 that Chief Justice White ruled in the Selective Draft Law Cases (No. 177) that the power of conscription was implied by the provision authorizing Congress to declare war and to raise and support armies.

The most drastic abrogation of civil liberties during the war came as a result of the Espionage Act (1917) and the Sedition Act (1918). The first measure contained two sections dealing with freedom of speech and of the press. One punished attempts to cause disobedience or insubordination in the armed forces, to obstruct enlistments, or to make false reports intended to obstruct military operations. Postal censorship was established by Title 12 which banned treasonable or seditious material from the mails. Both sections were so loosely phrased as to constitute severe threats to basic freedoms, if interpreted as broadly as other wartime legislation. In *Schenck v. U.S.* (No. 178), Justice Holmes enunciated the "clear and present danger" doctrine as the proper standard by which to measure the extent of freedom of speech. Applying this rule, Holmes ruled that Schenck's antidraft pamphlets constituted an immediate danger to the recruiting service, amounting to a violation of the Espionage Act.

It was the Sedition Act, however, which lent itself most readily to regimentation of speech and press. In the Abrams case (No. 179), the defendants were charged with using "disloyal, scurrilous, and abusive language about the form of government of the United States" and opposing the "cause of the United States" in their denunciation of its expeditionary force to Russia. Two aspects of the case have had continuing significance: (1) in upholding the Sedition statute, the majority established the principle of curtailment of free speech despite the

First Amendment guarantees, and (2) Holmes' eloquent dissent (No. 180) elaborated the "clear and present danger" rule as the leading defense against overzealous enforcement of such a law.

Wartime Economic Controls

CONGRESS ENACTS EMERGENCY LEGISLATION

174. *The National Security and Internal Controls*

Lever Act, *U. S. Stat. at L.*, XL, 276-87 (August 10, 1917).

Be it enacted, That by reason of the existence of a state of war, it is essential to the national security and defense, for the successful prosecution of the war, and for the support and maintenance of the Army and Navy, to assure an adequate supply and equitable distribution, and to facilitate the movement, of foods, feeds, fuel . . . and equipment required for the actual production of foods, feeds, and fuel, hereafter in this Act called necessaries; to prevent, . . . scarcity, monopolization, hoarding, injurious speculation, manipulations . . . and private controls, affecting such supply, . . . and to establish and maintain governmental control of such necessaries during the war. For such purposes the instrumentalities . . . and prohibitions hereinafter set forth are created. The President is authorized to make such regulations and to issue such orders as are essential effectively to carry out the provisions of this Act. . . .

SEC. 14. That whenever the President shall find that an emergency exists requiring stimulation of the production of wheat and that it is essential that the producers of wheat, produced within the United States, shall have the benefits of the guaranty provided for in this section, he is authorized, . . . to determine and fix and to give public notice of what, under specified conditions, is a reasonable guaranteed price for wheat, in order to assure such producers a reasonable profit. The President shall thereupon fix such guaranteed price. . . . Thereupon, the Government of the United States hereby guarantees every producer of wheat produced within the United States, that, upon compliance by him with the regulations prescribed, he shall receive for any wheat produced in reliance upon this guarantee within the period, not exceeding eighteen months, prescribed in the notice, a price not less than the guaranteed price therefor as fixed pursuant to this section. . . . The guaranteed prices for the several standard grades of wheat for the crop of nineteen hundred and eighteen, shall be based upon number one northern spring or its equivalent at not less than $2 per bushel at the principal interior primary markets. This guaranty shall not be dependent upon the action of the President under the first part of this section, but is hereby made absolute and shall be binding until May first, nineteen hundred and nineteen. . . .

For the purpose of making any guaranteed price effective under this section, or whenever he deems it essential . . . the President is authorized also, in his discretion, to purchase any wheat for which a guaranteed price shall be fixed . . . and to hold, transport, or store it, or to sell, dispose of, and deliver the same. . . .

SEC. 15. That from and after thirty days from the date of the approval of this Act no foods, fruits, food materials, or feeds shall be used in the production of distilled spirits for beverage purposes. . . . Nor shall there be imported into the United States any distilled spirits. Whenever the President shall find that limitation, regulation, or prohibition of the use of foods, fruits, food materials, or feeds in the production of malt or vinous liquors for beverage purposes, or that reduction of the alcoholic content of any such malt or vinous liquor, is essential, in order to assure an adequate and continuous supply of food, or that the national security and defense will be subserved thereby, he is authorized, from time to time, to prescribe and give public notice of the extent of the limitation, regulation, prohibition, or reduction so necessitated. . . .

SEC. 16. That the President is authorized and directed to commandeer any or all distilled spirits in bond or in stock at the date of the approval of this Act for redistillation, in so far as such redistillation may be necessary to meet the requirements of the Government in the manufacture of munitions and other military and hospital supplies. . . .

SEC. 24. That the provisions of this Act shall cease to be in effect when the existing state of war between the United States and Germany shall have terminated. . . .

SEC. 25. That the President of the United States shall be, . . . empowered, whenever and wherever in his judgment necessary for the efficient prosecution of the war, to fix the price of coal and coke, wherever and whenever sold . . . to regulate the method of production, sale, shipment, distribution, apportionment, or storage thereof among dealers and consumers. . . .

175. *"The complete character of the war power is not disputable."*

Northern Pacific Railway Co. v. North Dakota, 250 U.S. 135 (1919).

WHITE, C.J.: . . . No elaboration could make clearer than do the Act of Congress of 1916, the proclamation of the President exerting the powers given, and the Act of 1918 dealing with the situation created by the exercise of such authority, that no divided but a complete possession and control were given the United States for all purposes as to the railroads in question. But if it be conceded that despite the absolute clarity of the provisions concerning the control given the United States, and the all-embracing scope of that control, there is room for some doubt, the consideration of the general context completely dispels hesitancy. . . . There is no basis for the contention that the power to make rates and enforce them which was plainly essential to the authority given was not included in it.

Conclusive as are these inferences, they are superfluous, since . . . §10 . . . confers the complete and undivided power to fix rates. The provision is this: "That during the period of Federal control, whenever in his opinion the public interest requires, the President may initiate rates, fares, charges, classifications, regulations, and practices by filing the same with the Interstate Commerce Commission, which . . . rates . . . and practices shall not be suspended by the commission pending final determination." These quoted words are immediately followed by provisions further defining the power of the Commission and its duty in the premises, so as to enable it beyond doubt to consider the situation resulting from the act and to which the rates were to be applied. The unison between that which is inferable and that which is expressed demonstrates the true significance of the statute. . . .

Besides, the presumption in question but denied the power exerted in the adoption of the statute, and displaced by an imaginary the dominant presumption which arose by operation of the Constitution as an inevitable effect of the adoption of the statute, as shown by the following:

(a) The complete and undivided character of the war power of the United States is not disputable. . . . On the face of the statutes it is manifest that they were in terms based upon the war power, since the authority they gave arose only because of the existence of war, and the right to exert such authority was to cease upon the war's termination. To interpret, therefore, the exercise of the power by a presumption of the continuance of a state power limiting and controlling the national authority was but to deny its existence. It was akin to the contention that the supreme right to raise armies and use them in case of war did not extend to directing where and when they should be used. . . .

(b) The elementary principle that under the Constitution the authority of the Government of the United States is paramount when exerted as to subjects concerning which it has the power to control, is indisputable. This being true, it results that although authority to regulate within a given sphere may exist in both the United States and in the States, when the former calls into play constitutional authority within such general sphere the necessary effect of doing so is, that to the extent that any conflict arises the state power is limited, since in case of conflict that which is paramount necessarily controls that which is subordinate.

Again, as the power which was exerted was supreme, to interpret it upon the basis that its exercise must be presumed to be limited was to deny the power itself. Thus, once more it comes to pass that the application of the assumed presumption was in effect but a form of expression by which the power which Congress had exerted was denied. In fact, error arising from indulging in such erroneous presumption permeates every contention. . . .

The confusion produced is . . . aptly illustrated by the rule of interpretation by which it is insisted that the express power to fix rates conferred by the statute was rightly disregarded. Thus, while admitting that the power which was conferred to initiate rates when considered in and of itself included all rates, it is nevertheless said that such power must be presumed to be limited to the only character of rates which under the prior law the Interstate Commerce Commission had the power to consider, that is, interstate rates, because the new rates when initiated were to be acted upon by that body. As, however, the statute in terms gives power to the Interstate Commerce Commission to consider the new rates in the light of the new and unified control which it creates, the error in the contention becomes manifest. . . .

It follows that the judgment below was erroneous. . . .

EXECUTIVE REORGANIZATION OF WARTIME BUREAUCRACY

176. *Congress Delegates Authority to the President as Commander in Chief*

Overman Act, *U. S. Stat. at L.*, XL, 556-7 (May 20, 1918).

Be it enacted . . . That for the national security and defense, for the successful prosecution of the war, for the support and maintenance of the Army and Navy, for the better utilization of resources and industries, and for the more effective exercise and more efficient administration by the President of his powers as Commander in Chief of the land and naval forces the President is hereby authorized to make such redistribution of functions among executive agencies as he may deem necessary, including any functions, duties, and powers hitherto by law conferred upon any executive department, commission, bureau, agency, office, or officer, in such manner as in his judgment shall seem best fitted to carry out the purposes of this Act, and to this end is authorized to make such regulations and to issue such orders as he may deem necessary, which regulations and orders shall be in writing and shall be filed with the head of the department affected and constitute a public record: *Provided*, . . . That the termination of this Act shall not affect any act done or any right or obligation accruing or accrued pursuant to this Act and during the time that this Act is in force: *Provided further*, That the authority by this Act granted shall be exercised only in matters relating to the conduct of the present war.

SEC. 2. That in carrying out the purposes of this Act the President is authorized to utilize, coordinate, or consolidate any executive or administrative commissions, bureaus, agencies, offices, or officers now existing by law, to transfer any duties or powers from one existing department, commission . . . to another, to transfer the personnel thereof or any part of it either by detail or assignment, together with the whole or any part of the records and public property belonging thereto. . . .

SEC. 5. That should the President, in redistributing the functions among the executive agencies as provided in this Act, conclude that any bureau should be abolished and it or their duties and functions conferred upon some other department or bureau or eliminated entirely, he shall report his conclusions to Congress with such recommendations as he may deem proper.

SEC. 6. That all laws or parts of laws conflicting with the provisions of this Act are to the extent of such conflict suspended while this Act is in force. . . .

Personal Controls: Selective Service, and Civil Liberties

177. Constitutionality of Conscription

Selective Draft Law Cases, *Arver v. U.S.*, 245 U.S. 366 (1918).

WHITE, C.J.: . . . The possession of authority to enact the statute must be found in the clauses of the Constitution giving Congress power "to declare war; . . . to raise and support armies, but no appropriation of money to that use shall be for a longer term than two years; . . . to make rules for the government and regulation of the land and naval forces." Article I, §8. And of course the powers conferred by these provisions like all other powers given carry with them as provided by the Constitution the authority "to make all laws which shall be necessary and proper for carrying into execution the foregoing powers." Article I, §8.

As the mind cannot conceive an army without the men to compose it, on the face of the Constitution the objection that it does not give power to provide for such men would seem to be too frivolous for further notice. It is said, however, that since under the Constitution as originally framed state citizenship was primary and United States citizenship but derivative and dependent thereon, therefore the power conferred upon Congress to raise armies was only coterminous with United States citizenship and could not be exerted so as to cause that citizenship to lose its dependent character and dominate state citizenship. But the proposition simply denies to Congress the power to raise armies which the Constitution gives. That power by the very terms of the Constitution, being delegated, is supreme. Article 6. In truth the contention simply assails the wisdom of the framers of the Constitution in conferring authority on Congress and in not retaining it as it was under the Confederation in the several States. Further it is said, the right to provide is not denied by calling for volunteer enlistments, but it does not and cannot include the power to exact enforced military duty by the citizen. This however but challenges the existence of all power, for a governmental power which has no sanction to it and which therefore can only be exercised provided the citizen consents to its exertion is in no substantial sense a power. It is argued, however, that although this is abstractedly true, it is not concretely so because as compelled military service is repugnant to a free government and in conflict with all the great guarantees of the Constitution as to individual liberty, it must be assumed that the authority to raise armies was intended to be limited to the right to call an army into existence counting alone upon the willingness of the citizen to do his duty in time of public need, that is, in time of war. But the premise of this proposition is so devoid of foundation that it leaves not even a shadow of ground upon which to base the conclusion. Let us see if this is not at once demonstrable. It may not be doubted that the very conception of a just government and its duty to the citizen includes the reciprocal obligation of the citizen to render military service in case of need and the right to compel it. . . .

In the Colonies before the separation from England there cannot be the slightest doubt that the right to enforce military service was unquestioned and that practical effect was given to the power in many cases. Indeed the brief of the government contains a list of Colonial acts manifesting the power and its enforcement in more than two hundred cases. And this exact situation existed also after the separation. Under the Articles of Confederation it is true Congress had no such power, as its authority was absolutely limited to making calls upon the States for the military forces needed to create and maintain the army, each State being bound for its quota as called. But it is indisputable that the States in response to the calls made upon them met the situation when they deemed it necessary by directing enforced military service on the part of the citizens. In fact the duty of the citizen to render military service and the power to compel him against his consent to do so was expressly sanctioned by the constitutions of at least nine of the States. . . .

When the Constitution came to be formed it may not be disputed that one of the recognized necessities for its adoption was the want of power in Congress to raise an army and the dependence upon the States for their quotas. In supplying the power it was manifestly intended to give it all and leave none to the States, since besides the delegation to Congress of authority to raise armies the Constitution prohibited the States, without the consent of Congress, from keeping troops in time of peace or engaging in war. Article I, §10. . . .

Thus sanctioned as is the act before us by the text of the Constitution, and by its significance as read in the light of the fundamental principles with which the subject is concerned, by the power recognized and carried into effect in many civilized countries, by the authority and practice of the colonies before the Revolution, of the States under the Confederation and of the Government since the formation of the Constitution, the want of merit in the contentions that the act in the particulars which we have been previously called upon to consider was beyond the constitutional power of Congress, is manifest. . . .

In reviewing the subject we have hitherto considered it as it has been argued from the point of view of the Constitution as it stood prior to the adoption of the Fourteenth Amendment. But to avoid all misapprehension we briefly direct attention to that Amendment for the purpose of pointing out, as has been frequently done in the past, how completely it broadened the national scope of the Government under the Constitution by causing citizenship of the United States to be paramount and dominant instead of being subordinate and derivative, and therefore, operating as it does upon all the powers conferred by the Constitution, leaves no possible support for the contentions made, if their want of merit was otherwise not so clearly made manifest.

It remains only to consider contentions which, while not disputing power, challenge the act because of the repugnancy to the Constitution supposed to result from some of its provisions. First, we are of opinion that the contention that the act is void as a delegation of federal power to state officials because of some of its administrative features is too wanting in merit to require further notice. Second, we think that the contention that the statute is void because vesting administrative officers with legislative discretion has been so completely adversely settled as to require reference only to some of the decided cases. . . . A like conclusion also adversely disposes of a similar claim concerning the conferring of judicial power. . . . And we pass without anything but statement the proposition that an establishment of a religion or an interference with the free exercise thereof repugnant to the First Amendment resulted from the exemption clauses of the act to which we at the outset referred, because we think its unsoundness is too apparent to require us to do more.

Finally, as we are unable to conceive upon what theory the exaction by government from the citizen of the performance of his supreme and noble duty of contributing to the defense of the rights and honor of the nation, as the result of a war declared by the great representative body of the people, can be said to be the imposition of involuntary servitude in violation of the prohibitions of the Thirteenth Amendment, we are constrained to the conclusion that the contention to that effect is refuted by its mere statement.

Affirmed.

178. *The "Clear and Present Danger" Test Qualifies Free Speech*

Schenck v. U.S., 249 U.S. 47 (1919).

HOLMES, J.: . . . According to the testimony Schenck said he was general secretary of the Socialist party and had charge of the Socialist headquarters from which the documents were sent. He identified a book found there as the minutes of the Executive Committee of the party. The book showed a resolution of August 13, 1917, that 15,000 leaflets should be printed on the other side of one of them in use, to be mailed to men who had passed exemption boards, and for distribution. Schenck personally attended to the printing. On August 20, the general secretary's report said, "Obtained new leaflets from printer and started work addressing envelopes" &c.; and there was a resolve that Comrade Schenck be allowed $125 for sending leaflets through the mail. He said that he had about fifteen or sixteen thousand printed. There were files of the circular in question in the inner office which he said were printed on the other side of the one sided circular and were there for distribution. Other copies were proved to have been sent through the mails to drafted men. Without going into confirmatory details that were proved, no reasonable man could doubt that the defendant Schenck was largely instrumental in sending the circulars about. . . .

The document in question upon its first printed side recited the first section of the Thirteenth Amendment, said that the idea embodied in it was violated by the Conscription Act and that a conscript is little better than a convict. In impassioned language it intimated that conscription was despotism in its worse form and a monstrous wrong against humanity in the interest of Wall Street's chosen few. It said, "Do not submit to intimidation," but in form at least confined itself to peaceful measures such as a petition for the repeal of the act. The other and later printed side of the sheet was headed "Assert Your Rights." It stated reasons for alleging that any one violated the Constitution when he refused to recognize "your right to assert your opposition to the draft," and went on "If you do not assert and support your rights, you are helping to deny or disparage rights which it is the solemn duty of all citizens and residents of the United States to retain." It described the arguments on the other side as coming from cunning politicians and a mercenary capitalist press, and even silent consent to the conscription law as helping to support an infamous conspiracy. It denied the power to send our citizens away to foreign shores to shoot up the people of other lands, and added that words could not express the condemnation such cold-blooded ruthlessness deserves, &c., &c., winding up "You must do your share to maintain, support and uphold the rights of the people of this country." Of course the document would not have been sent unless it had been intended to have some effect, and we do not see what effect it could be expected to have upon persons subject to the draft except to influence them to obstruct the carrying of it out. The defendants do not deny that the jury might find against them on this point.

But it is said, suppose that that was the tendency of this circular, it is protected by the First Amendment to the Constitution. . . . We admit that in many places and in ordinary times the defendants in saying all that was said in the circular would have been within their constitutional rights. But the character of every act depends upon the circumstances in which it is done. . . . The most stringent protection of free speech would not protect a man in falsely shouting fire in a theatre and causing a panic. It does not even protect a man from an injunction against uttering words that may have all the effect of force. . . . The question in every case is whether the words used are used in such circumstances and are of such a nature as to create a clear and present danger that they will bring about the substantive evils that Congress has a right to prevent. It is a question of proximity and degree. When a nation is at war many things that might be said in time of peace are such a hindrance to its effort that their utterance will not be endured so long as men fight and that no Court could regard them as protected by any constitutional right. It seems to be admitted that if an actual obstruction of the recruiting service were proved, liability for words that produced that effect might be enforced. The statute of 1917 in §4 punishes conspiracies to obstruct as well as actual obstruction. If the act, (speaking, or circulating a paper,) its tendency and the intent with which it is done are the same, we perceive no ground for saying that success alone warrants making the act a crime. . . .

Judgments affirmed.

179. *Sedition and Speech in World War I*

Abrams v. U.S., 250 U.S. 616 (1919).

Clarke, J.: On a single indictment, containing four counts, the five plaintiffs . . . were convicted of conspiring to violate provisions of the [Sedition] Act . . . of May 16, 1918. . . .

Each of the first three counts charged the defendants with conspiring, when the United States was at war with the Imperial Government of Germany, to unlawfully utter, print, write and publish: In the first count, "disloyal, scurrilous and abusive language about the form of Government of the United States;" in the second count, language "intended to bring the form of Government of the United States into contempt, scorn, contumely and disrepute;" and in the third count, language "intended to incite, provoke and encourage resistance to the United States in said war." The charge in the fourth count was that the defendants conspired "when the United States was at war with the Imperial German Government, . . . unlawfully and wilfully, by utterance, writing, printing and publication, to urge, incite and advocate curtailment of production of things and products, to wit, ordinance and ammunition, necessary and essential to the prosecution of the war." The offenses were charged in the language of the act of Congress.

It was charged in each count of the indictment that it was part of the conspiracy that the defendants would attempt to accomplish their unlawful purpose by printing, writing and distributing in the City of New York many copies of a leaflet or circular, printed in the English language, and of another printed in the Yiddish language, copies of which, properly identified, were attached to the indictment.

All of the five defendants were born in Russia. They were intelligent, had considerable schooling, and at the time they were arrested they had lived in the United States terms varying from five to ten years, but none of them had applied for naturalization. Four of them testified as witnesses in their own behalf and of these, three frankly avowed that they were "rebels," "revolutionists," "anarchists," that they did not believe in government in any form, and they declared that they had no interest whatever in the Government of the United States. The fourth defendant testified that he was a "socialist" and believed in "a proper kind of government, not capitalistic," but in his classification the Government of the United States was "capitalistic."

It was admitted on the trial that the defendants had united to print and distribute the described circulars and that five thousand of them had been printed and distributed about the 22d day of August, 1918. The group had a meeting place in New York City, in rooms rented by defendant Abrams, under an assumed name, and there the subject of printing the circulars was discussed about two weeks before the defendants were arrested. The defendant Abrams, although not a printer, on July 27, 1918, purchased the printing outfit with which the circulars were printed and installed it in a basement room where the work was done at night. The circulars were distributed some by throwing them from a window of a building where one of the defendants was employed and others secretly, in New York City.

The defendants pleaded "not guilty," and the case of the Government consisted in showing the facts we have stated, and in introducing in evidence copies of the two printed circulars attached to the indictment, a sheet entitled "Revolutionists Unite for Action," written by the defendant Lipman, and found on him when he was arrested, and another paper, found at the headquarters of the group, and for which Abrams assumed responsibility.

Thus the conspiracy and the doing of the overt acts charged were largely admitted and were fully established.

On the record thus described it is argued, somewhat faintly, that the acts charged against the defendants were not unlawful because within the protection of that freedom of speech and of the press which is guaranteed by the First Amendment to the Constitution of the United States, and that the entire Espionage Act is unconstitutional because in conflict with that Amendment. . . .

The first of the two articles attached to the indictment is conspicuously headed, "The Hypocrisy of the United States and her Allies." After denouncing President Wilson as a hypocrite and a coward because troops were sent into Russia, it proceeds to assail our Government in general . . .

It will not do to say, as is now argued, that the only intent of these defendants was to prevent injury to the Russian cause. Men must be held to have intended, and to be accountable for, the effects which their acts were likely to produce. Even if their primary purpose and intent was to aid the cause of the Russian Revolution, the plan of action which they adopted necessarily involved, before it could be realized, defeat of the war program of the United States, for the obvious effect of this appeal, if it should become effective, as they hoped it might, would be to persuade persons of character such as those whom they regarded themselves as addressing, not to aid government loans and not to work in ammunition factories, where their work would produce "bullets, bayonets, cannon" and other munitions of war, the use of which would cause the "murder" of Germans and Russians. . . .

That the interpretation we have put upon these articles, circulated in the greatest port of our land, from which great numbers of soldiers were at the time taking ship daily, and in which great quantities of war supplies of every kind were at the time being manufactured for transportation overseas, is not only the fair interpretation of them, but that it is the meaning which their authors consciously intended should be conveyed by them to others is further shown by the additional writings found in the meeting place of the defendant group and on the person of one of them. . . .

These excerpts sufficiently show, that while the immediate occasion for this particular outbreak of lawlessness, on the part of the defendant alien anarchists, may have been resentment caused by our Government sending troops into Russia as a strategic operation against the Germans on the eastern battle front, yet the plain purpose of their propaganda was to excite, at the supreme crisis of the war, disaffection, sedition, riots, and, as they hoped, revolution, in this country for the purpose of embarrassing and if possible defeating the military plans of the Government in Europe. A technical distinction may perhaps be taken between disloyal and abusive language applied to the *form* of our government or language intended to bring the *form* of our government into contempt and disrepute, and language of like character and intended to produce like results directed against the President and Congress, the agencies through which that form of government must function in time of war. But it is not necessary to a decision of this case to consider whether such distinction is vital or merely formal, for the language of these circulars was obviously intended to provoke and to encourage resistance to the United States in the war, as the third count runs, and, the defendants, in terms, plainly urged and advocated a resort to a general strike of workers in ammunition factories for the purpose of curtailing the production of ordnance and munitions necessary and essential to the prosecution of the war as is charged in the fourth count. Thus it is clear not only that some evidence but that much persuasive evidence was before the jury tending to prove that the defendants were guilty as charged in both the third and fourth counts of the indictment and under the long established rule of law hereinbefore stated the judgment of the District Court must be

Affirmed.

180. *"We should be eternally vigilant against attempts to check the expression of opinions."*

Abrams v. U.S., 250 U.S. 616 (1919).

Holmes, J., dissenting: . . . No argument seems to me necessary to show that these pronunciamentos in no way attack the form of government of the United States, or that they do not support either of the first two counts. What little I have to say about the third count may be postponed until I have considered the fourth. With regard to that it seems too plain to be denied that the suggestion to workers in the ammunition factories that they are producing bullets to murder their dearest, and the further advocacy of a general strike, both in the second leaflet, do urge curtailment of production of things necessary to the prosecution of the war within the meaning of the [Sedition] Act. . . . But to make the conduct criminal that statute requires that it should be "with intent by such curtailment to cripple or hinder the United States in the prosecution of the war." It seems to me that no such intent is proved.

I am aware of course that the word intent as vaguely used in ordinary legal discussion means no more than knowledge at the time of the act that the consequences said to be intended will ensue. Even less than that will satisfy the general principle of civil and criminal liability. A man may have to pay damages, may be sent to prison, at common law might be hanged, if at the time of his act he knew facts from which common experience showed that the consequences would follow, whether he individually could foresee them or not. But, when words are used exactly, a deed is not done with intent to produce a consequence unless that consequence is the aim of the deed. It may be obvious, and obvious to the actor, that the consequence will follow, and he may be liable for it even if he regrets it, but he does not do the act with intent to produce it unless the aim to produce it is the proximate motive of the specific act, although there may be some deeper motive behind.

It seems to me that this statute must be taken to use its words in a strict and accurate sense. They would be absurd in any other. A patriot might think that we were wasting money on aeroplanes, or making more cannon of a certain kind than we needed, and might advocate curtailment with success, yet even if it turned out that the curtailment hindered and was thought by other minds to have been obviously likely to hinder the United States in the prosecution of the war, no one would hold such conduct a crime. I admit that my illustration does not answer all that might be said but it is enough to show what I think and to let me pass to a more important aspect of the case. I refer to the First Amendment to the Constitution that Congress shall make no law abridging the freedom of speech. . . .

I do not doubt for a moment that by the same reasoning that would justify punishing persuasion to murder, the United States constitutionally may punish speech that produces or is intended to produce a clear and imminent danger that it will bring about forthwith certain substantive evils that the United States constitutionally may seek to prevent. The power undoubtedly is greater in time of war than in time of peace because war opens dangers that do not exist at other times.

But as against dangers peculiar to war, as against others, the principle of the right to free speech is always the same. It is only the present danger of immediate evil or an intent to bring it about that warrants Congress in setting a limit to the expression of opinion where private rights are not concerned. Congress certainly cannot forbid all effort to change the mind of the country. Now nobody can suppose that the surreptitious publishing of a silly leaflet by an unknown man, without more, would present any immediate danger that its opinions would hinder the success of the government arms or have any appreciable tendency to do so. Publishing those opinions for the very purpose of obstructing however, might indicate a greater danger and at any rate would have the quality of an attempt. So I assume that the second leaflet if published for the purposes alleged in the fourth count might be punishable. But it seems pretty clear to me that nothing less than that would bring these papers within the scope of this law. An actual intent in the sense that I have explained is necessary to constitute an attempt, where a further act of the same individual is required to complete the substantive crime. . . .

I do not see how anyone can find the intent required by the statute in any of the defendants' words. The second leaflet is the only one that affords even a foundation for the charge, and there, without invoking the hatred of German militarism expressed in the former one, it is evident from the beginning to the end that the only object of the paper is to help Russia and stop American intervention there against the popular government—not to impede the United States in the war that it was carrying on. To say that two phrases taken literally might import a suggestion of conduct that would have interference with the war as an indirect and probably undesired effect seems to me by no means enough to show an attempt to produce that effect. . . .

In this case sentences of twenty years imprisonment have been imposed for the publishing of two leaflets that I believe the defendants had as much right to publish as the Government has to publish the Constitution of the United States now vainly invoked by them. Even if I am technically wrong and enough can be squeezed from these poor and puny anonymities to turn the color of legal litmus paper; I will add, even if what I think the necessary intent were shown; the most nominal punishment seems to me all that possibly could be inflicted, unless the defendants are to be made to suffer not for what the indictment alleges but for the creed that they avow—a creed that I believe to be the creed of ignorance and immaturity when honestly held, as I see no reason to doubt that it was held here, but which, although made the subject of examination at the trial, no one has a right even to consider in dealing with the charges before the Court.

Persecution for the expression of opinions seems to me perfectly logical. If you have no doubt of your premises or your power and want a certain result with all your heart you naturally express your wishes in law and sweep away all opposition. To allow opposition by speech seems to indicate that you think the speech impotent, as when a man says that he has squared the circle, or that you do not care whole-heartedly for the result, or that you doubt either your power or your premises. But when men have realized that time has upset many fighting faiths, they may come to believe even more than they believe the very foundations of their own conduct that the ultimate good desired is better reached by free trade in ideas—that the best test of truth is the power of the thought to get itself accepted in the competition of the market, and that truth is the only ground upon which their wishes safely can be carried out. That at any rate is the theory of our Constitution. It is an experiment, as all life is an experiment. Every year if not every day we have to wager our salvation upon some prophecy based upon imperfect knowledge. While that experiment is part of our system I think that we should be eternally vigilant against attempts to check the expression of opinions that we loathe and believe to be fraught with death, unless they so imminently threaten immediate interference with the lawful and pressing purposes of the law that an immediate check is required to save the country. I wholly disagree with the argument of the Government that the First Amendment left the common law as to seditious libel in force. History seems to me against the notion. I had conceived that the United States through many years had shown its repentence for the Sedition Act of 1798, by repaying fines that it imposed. Only the emergency that makes it immediately dangerous to leave the correction of evil counsels to time warrants making any exception to the sweeping command, "Congress shall make no law . . . abridging the freedom of speech." Of course I am speaking only of expressions of opinion and exhortations, which were all that were uttered here, but I regret that I cannot put into more impressive words my belief that in their conviction upon this indictment the defendants were deprived of their rights under the Constitution of the United States.

Mr. Justice Brandeis concurs with the foregoing opinion.

CHAPTER XX

Diverse Trends of the Twenties

PRESIDENT Warren G. Harding's declaration that "what America needs is less government in business and more business in government" heralded a period of "normalcy" which rejected Wilsonian and Progressive idealism in all three branches of government. The solemn averment of Harding's successor, Calvin Coolidge, that "the business of America is business" was an excellent barometer of the climate of opinion of the 1920's. Caught between the new "normalcy" and the expansive constitutional doctrines that had been used to justify wartime measures, the Court tended to vacillate between acquiescence in the constitutional conservatism of the new era and maintenance of the tradition of national supremacy. One of the developments of the 1920's, therefore, was the proclivity of the justices to be consistently inconsistent in defining the scope of national power.

One of the most impressive announcements of national power, for instance, came in 1920 in an unsuspect case involving migratory birds. Interpreting the treaty-making power broadly, Justice Holmes ruled that a treaty, once ratified, could be implemented by legislation that would have been invalid in the absence of the treaty (*Missouri v. Holland* [*No. 181*]). If the subject matter was sufficiently related to the general welfare, and if it was a national interest that could be protected "only by national action in concert with another power," the treaty-making power could be used to expand the regulatory power of Congress. In an era of *laissez faire*, however, Congress made no effort to extend its regulatory power in this, or any other, way.

On the other hand, Congress did utilize its investigatory powers and in *McGrain v. Daugherty* (No. 182) received strong Court support. Following the scandals of the Harding administration, a congressional committee, seeking an explanation for the activities and inactivities of Harry M. Daugherty, ex-Attorney General, subpoenaed his brother who ignored the order. To obtain information necessary for legislation, the Court ruled, Congress may exercise the judicial power of subpoenaing witnesses and punish them for contempt if they fail to appear. Two years later, the Court upheld the right of congressional committees to punish a witness for contempt if he refuses to answer questions (*Barry v. U.S. ex rel Cunningham, 1929*).

The nation's highest tribunal also continued its broad interpretation of the commerce power, expanded the taxing power, and strengthened the President's right to remove appointive officials. Chief Justice William Howard Taft and a unanimous Court upheld the Transportation Act of 1920 and justified federal intervention to alter intrastate rail rates fixed by a state commission, arguing that "the Nation cannot exercise complete effective control over interstate commerce without incidental regulation of intrastate commerce" (*Railroad Commission of Wisconsin v. C. B. & Q. R.R. Co. [No. 183]*). In *Stafford v. Wallace* (1922), Taft also gave new emphasis to the "current of commerce" doctrine enunciated in the Swift case (Chapter XVII). Upholding a federal statute regulating stockyards and meat packing, the Chief Justice indicated that the Court would not invalidate the measure "by a nice and technical inquiry into the non-interstate character of some of its necessary incidents and facilities." Federal taxing power received a similar sanction when, in *Massachusetts v. Mellon* (1923), the Court implied that revenue raised by national taxation could be used for economic and social purposes that were usually within the domain of the states. In a final important area, former President Taft upheld the power of the Chief Executive to remove appointive officers, thus vindicating Andrew Johnson posthumously by ruling unconstitutional that portion of the Tenure of Office Act of 1867 which required the President to obtain Senate approval before removing executive officials appointed by him (*Myers v. U.S., 1926*).

Despite these examples, the Court during the Twenties generally acquiesced in business domination over regulatory commissions and administrative agencies, thus translating contemporary conservatism into constitutional law. As early as 1920, the Court negated the government's attempt to dissolve the United States Steel Corporation (No. 184), which then had the largest capitalization of any American business. Applying the "rule of reason," Justice McKenna denied that the company's monopolistic practices were unlawful; this judicial approval of business amalgamation set in motion an economic movement characteristic of the decade. The period also saw a renewal of the old system of business agreement, which now took the form of price and policy arrangements by trade associations. Originally hostile, the Court soon followed the lead of Secretary of Commerce Herbert Hoover, who was persuading businessmen to standardize their products and adopt codes of fair practice. In 1925, six of the Justices agreed that such activities, rather than fostering commercial restraints, tended "to stabilize trade and industry . . . and to avoid the waste which inevitably attends the unintelligent conduct of economic enterprise" (*Maple Flooring Manufacturers Association v. U.S.* [No. 185]). At the same time, the Court curtailed the Federal Trade Commission's right to define unfair trade practices (*F. T. C. v. Gratz* [No. 186]), and severely restricted its fact-finding authority (*F. T. C. v. Curtis Publishing Co., 1923*).

Despite an apparent inconsistency at the constitutional level, there was something of a pattern of consistency in the economics of the Court's decisions: business ordinarily won and labor usually lost. At the very moment that the Court limited federal regulatory power over business, it utilized federal legislation to protect employers and curtail trade-union practices. In 1921, the anti-injunction provisions of the Clayton Act (Chapter XVII) were virtually emasculated, and the way paved for the renewed use of the federal antitrust laws against unions (*Duplex Printing Press Co. v. Deering* [No. 187]). After a campaign of eleven years, however, a combination of liberal Republicans and Democrats pushed through the Norris-LaGuardia Act (1932) in an attempt to limit the issuance of labor injunctions.

During the decade, the Court struck down a child-labor law for the second time. In reframing that measure, care had been taken to avoid the commerce base proscribed by the Court in *Hammer v. Dagenhart* (Chapter XVIII); instead, the new statute proposed to eliminate the evil by levying a tax upon the profits of firms employing children. Such a use of the taxing power had strong precedents, and only one month after the passage of this measure, the Court sustained a similar prohibitive tax on the sale of narcotics (*U.S. v. Doremus, 1919*). But in *Bailey v. Drexel Furniture Co.* (No. 188), Chief Justice Taft condemned the child-labor law as an illegal use of the taxing power and an interference by Congress with matters reserved to the states by the Tenth Amendment. Thus, the "dual federalism" concept of *Hammer v. Dagenhart* again was employed to curtail national authority. Conceding their failure to achieve their purposes through legislation, the opponents of child labor wrote their desires into an amendment (No. 189), but it was never adopted.

The property-conscious majority of the Court also refused to accept state economic and social controls. Although a militant minority condemned the "use of the Fourteenth Amendment . . . to prevent the making of social experiments that an important part of the community desires, in the insulated chambers afforded by the several states," Justice Sutherland set the tone for the decade by overruling a minimum wage law for women in the District of Columbia (*Adkins v. Children's Hospital* [No. 190]). Despite the fact that similar state laws had previously received judicial sanction in *Bunting v. Oregon* and *Muller v. Oregon* (Chapter XVIII), Sutherland distinguished those precedents on the grounds that they dealt with hours of labor and not minimum wages, and returned to the Lochner concept of "freedom of contract." He condemned wage legislation as economically and socially unsound and a denial of due process of law, maintaining that "the good of society as a whole cannot be better served than by the preservation against arbitrary restraint of the liberties of its constituent members."

Following this precedent, the Court overruled a wide variety of state regulatory laws. Over the strong protests of four of the justices, the majority used both the due process and equal protection clauses of the Fourteenth Amendment to upset an Arizona anti-injunction law (*Truax v. Corrigan, 1921*). Brandeis and Holmes dissented, arguing that the majority would have upheld the legislation as a reasonable legal experiment if the "contemporary conditions, social, industrial and political, of the community to be affected" had been given as much consideration as the legal factors (No. 191).

Typical of the Court's laissez-faire attitude toward public regulation was the sharp curtailment of the scope of the "public interest" doctrine, which had first been set forth in *Munn v. Illinois* (Chapter XV). In *Wolff Packing Co. v. Court of Industrial Relations of Kansas* (No. 192), Chief Justice Taft ruled that a mere declaration by a state legislature that a business is "affected with a public interest" does not justify regulation. Concerning what types of businesses might be regulated, Taft was clear only on public utilities. He included businesses "which though not public at their inception may be said to have risen to be such," but that definition was sufficiently indefinite to require judicial evaluation of cases as they arose. The Court repeatedly struck down state laws that it believed fell outside this category. Again a minority protested. When a New York statute designed to protect the public against theater ticket "scalpers" was ruled out as a violation of the Fourteenth Amendment, Holmes registered an eloquent protest, contending that a legislature "can do whatever it sees fit to do unless it is restrained by some express prohibition in the Constitution of the United States or of the state" (*Tyson v. Banton* [No. 193]).

It was not until the 1930's, however, that the Court acknowledged the unworkability of its standard. In *Nebbia v. New York* (No. 194), Justice Roberts not only reversed the trend of the previous decade, but virtually eliminated the "affection with a public interest" doctrine as a constitutional concept. "There is no closed class or category of businesses affected with a public interest," he stated. "The States' power extends to every regulation of any business reasonably required and appropriate for the public protection."

In an interesting ruling that did not involve economic affairs, the Court of the Twenties took a far more liberal view of state legislative authority. Upholding a Virginia statute permitting sterilization of inmates in institutions for the feebleminded, Holmes ruled that the needs of society superceded the invasion of individual liberty: "We have seen more than once that the public welfare may call upon the best citizens for their lives. It would be strange if it could not call upon those who already sap the strength of the state for . . . lesser sacrifices" (*Buck v. Bell* [No. 195]).

The Maintenance of the Tradition of National Supremacy

EXTENSION OF GOVERNMENTAL AUTHORITY

181. *Is the Treaty Power Limited by the Tenth Amendment?*

Missouri v. Holland, 252 U.S. 416 (1920).

HOLMES, J.: . . . The question raised is the general one whether the treaty and statute are void as an interference with the rights reserved to the States.

To answer this question it is not enough to refer to the Tenth Amendment, reserving the powers not delegated to the United States, because by Article II, §2, the power to make treaties is delegated expressly, and by Article VI treaties made under the authority of the United States, along with the Constitution and laws of the United States made in pursuance thereof, are declared the supreme law of the land. If the treaty is valid there can be no dispute about the validity of the statute under Article I, §8, as a necessary and proper means to execute the powers of the Government. The language of the Constitution as to the supremacy of treaties being general, the question before us is narrowed to an inquiry into the ground upon which the present supposed exception is placed.

It is said that a treaty cannot be valid if it infringes the Constitution, that there are limits, therefore, to the treaty-making power, and that one such limit is that what an act of Congress could not do unaided, in derogation of the powers reserved to the States, a treaty cannot do. An earlier act of Congress that attempted by itself and not in pursuance of a treaty to regulate the killing of migratory birds within the States had been held bad in the District Court. . . . Those decisions were supported by arguments that migratory birds were owned by the States in their sovereign capacity for the benefit of their people, and that under cases like *Geer v. Connecticut,* . . . this control was one that Congress had no power to displace. The same argument is supposed to apply now with equal force.

Whether the two cases cited were decided rightly or not they cannot be accepted as a test of the treaty power. Acts of Congress are the supreme law of the land only when made in pursuance of the Constitution, while treaties are declared to be so when made under the authority of the United States. It is open to question whether the authority of the United States means more than the formal acts prescribed to make the convention. We do not mean to imply that there are no qualifications to the treaty-making power; but they must be ascertained in a different way. It is obvious that there may be matters of the sharpest exigency for the national well being that an act of Congress could not deal with but that a treaty followed by such an act could, and it is not lightly to be assumed that, in matters requiring national action, "a power which must belong to and somewhere reside in every civilized government" is not to be found. *Andrews v. Andrews.* . . . What was said in that case with regard to the powers of the States applies with equal force to the powers of the nation in cases where the States individually are incompetent to act. We are not yet discussing the particular case before us but only are considering the validity of the test proposed. With regard to that we may add that when we are dealing with words that also are a constituent act, like the Constitution of the United States, we must realize that they have called into life a being the development of which could not have been foreseen completely by the most gifted of its begetters. It was enough for them to realize or to hope that they had created an organism; it has taken a century and has cost their successors much sweat and blood to prove that they created a nation. The case before us must be considered in the light of our whole experience and not merely in that of what was said a hundred years ago. The treaty in question does not contravene any prohibitory words to be found in the Constitution. The only question is whether it is forbidden by some invisible radiation from the general terms of the Tenth Amendment. We must consider what this country has become in deciding what that amendment has reserved.

The State as we have intimated founds its claim of exclusive authority upon an assertion of title to migratory birds, an assertion that is embodied in statute. No doubt it is true that as between a State and its inhabitants the State may regulate the killing and sale of such birds, but it does not follow that its authority is exclusive of paramount powers. To put the claim of the State upon title is to lean upon a slender reed. Wild birds are not in the possession of anyone; and possession is the beginning of ownership. The whole foundation of the State's rights is the presence within their jurisdiction of birds that yesterday had not arrived, tomorrow may be in another State and in a week a thousand miles away. If we are to be accurate we cannot put the case of the State upon higher ground than that the treaty deals with creatures that for the moment are within the state borders, that it must be carried out by officers of the United States within the same territory, and that but for the treaty the State would be free to regulate this subject itself. . . .

Here a national interest of very nearly the first magnitude is involved. It can be protected only by national action in concert with that of another power. The subject-matter is only transitorily within the State and has no permanent habitat therein. But for the treaty and the statute there soon might be no birds for any powers to deal with. We see nothing in the Constitution that compels the government to sit by while a food supply is cut off and the protectors of our forests and our crops are destroyed. It is not sufficient to rely upon the States. The reliance is vain, and were it otherwise, the question is whether the United States is forbidden to act. We are of opinion that the treaty and statute must be upheld. . . .

182. *"The power of inquiry . . . is an essential . . . auxiliary to the legislative function."*

McGrain v. Daugherty, 273 U.S. 135 (1927).

VAN DEVANTER, J.: . . . The first of the principal questions . . . is . . . whether the Senate—or the House of Representatives . . . has power, through its own process, to compel a private individual to appear before it or one of its committees and give testimony needed to enable it efficiently to exercise a legislative function belonging to it under the Constitution.

The Constitution provides for a Congress consisting of a Senate and House of Representatives and invests it with "all legislative powers" granted to the United States, and with power "to make all laws which shall be necessary and proper" for carrying into execution these powers and "all other powers" vested by the Constitution in the United States or in any department or officer thereof. . . . But there is no provision expressly investing either house with power to make investigations and exact testimony to the end that it may exercise its legislative function advisedly and effectively. So the question arises whether this power is so far incidental to the legislative function as to be implied.

In actual legislative practice power to secure needed information by such means has long been treated as an attribute of the power to legislate. It was so regarded in the British Parliament and in the Colonial legislatures before the American Revolution; and a like view has prevailed and been carried into effect in both houses of Congress and in most of the state legislatures.

This power was both asserted and exerted by the House of Representatives in 1792, when it appointed a select committee to inquire into the St. Clair expedition and authorized the committee to send for necessary persons, papers and records. Mr. Madison, who had taken an important part in framing the Constitution only five years before, and four of his associates in that work, were members of the House of Representatives at the time, and all voted for the inquiry. . . . Other exertions of the power by the House of Representatives, as also by the Senate, are shown in the citations already made. Among those by the Senate, the inquiry ordered in 1859 respecting the raid by John Brown and his adherents on the armory and arsenal of the United States at Harper's Ferry is of special significance. The resolution directing the inquiry authorized the committee to send for persons and papers, to inquire into the facts pertaining to the raid and the means by which it was organized and supported, and to report what legislation, if any, was necessary to preserve the peace of the country and protect the public property. The resolution was briefly discussed and adopted without opposition. . . .

The state courts quite generally have held that the power to legislate carries with it by necessary implication ample authority to obtain information needed in the rightful exercise of that power, and to employ compulsory process for the purpose. . . .

We have referred to the practice of the two houses of Congress; and we now shall notice some significant congressional enactments. . . . They show very plainly that Congress intended thereby (a) to recognize the power of either house to institute inquiries and exact evidence touching subjects within its jurisdiction and on which it was disposed to act; (b) to recognize that such inquiries may be conducted through committees; (c) to subject defaulting and contumacious witnesses to indictment and punishment in the courts, and thereby to enable either house to exert the power of inquiry "more effectually"; and (d) to open the way for obtaining evidence in such an inquiry, which otherwise could not be obtained, by exempting witnesses required to give evidence therein from criminal and penal prosecutions in respect of matters disclosed by their evidence.

Four decisions of this Court are cited and more or less relied on. . . .

While these cases are not decisive of the question we are considering, they definitely settle two propositions which we recognize as entirely sound and having a bearing on its solution: One, that the two houses of Congress, in their separate relations, possess not only such powers as are expressly granted to them by the Constitution, but such auxiliary powers as are necessary and appropriate to make the express powers effective; and, the other, that neither house is invested with "general" power to inquire into private affairs and compel disclosures, but only with such limited power of inquiry as is shown to exist when the rule of constitutional interpretation just stated is rightly applied. . . .

We are of opinion that the power of inquiry—with process to enforce it—is an essential and appropriate auxiliary to the legislative function. It was so regarded and employed in American legislatures before the Constitution was framed and ratified. Both houses of Congress took this view of it early in their history . . .

We come now to the question whether it sufficiently appears that the purpose for which the witness's testimony was sought was to obtain information in aid of the legislative function. The court below answered the question in the negative, and put its decision largely on this ground. . . .

We are of opinion that the court's ruling on this question was wrong, and that it sufficiently appears, when the proceedings are rightly interpreted, that the object of the investigation and of the effort to secure the witness's testimony was to obtain information for legislative purposes.

It is quite true that the resolution directing the investigation does not in terms avow that it is intended to be in aid of legislation; but it does show that the subject to be investigated was the administration of the Department of Justice—whether its functions were being properly discharged or were being neglected or misdirected, and particularly whether the Attorney General and his assistants were performing or neglecting their duties in respect of the institution and prosecution of proceedings to punish crimes and enforce appropriate remedies against the wrongdoers—specific instances of alleged neglect being recited. Plainly the subject was one on which legislation could be had and would be materially aided by the information which the investigation was calculated to elicit. This becomes manifest when it is reflected that the functions of the Department of Justice, the powers and duties of the Attorney General and the duties of his assistants, are all subject to regulation by congressional legislation, and that the department is maintained and its activities are carried on under such appropriations as in the judgment of Congress are needed from year to year.

The only legitimate object the Senate could have in ordering the investigation was to aid it in legislating; and we think the subject-matter was such that the presumption should be indulged that this was the real object. An express avowal of the object would have been better; but in view of the particular subject-matter was not indispensable. . . .

We conclude that the investigation was ordered for a legitimate object; that the witness wrongfully refused to appear and testify before the committee and was lawfully attached; that the Senate is entitled to have him give testimony pertinent to the inquiry, either at its bar or before the committee; and that the district court erred in discharging him from custody under the attachment. . . .

BROAD CONSTRUCTION OF REGULATORY POWER

183. *The Paramount Power of Congress over Commerce*

Wisconsin Railroad Fares Case, 257 U.S. 563 (1922).

TAFT, C.J.: The Commission's order, interference with which was enjoined by the District Court, effects the removal of the unjust discrimination found to exist against persons in interstate commerce, and against interstate commerce, by fixing a minimum for intrastate passenger fares in Wisconsin at 3.6 cents per mile. . . .

We have two questions to decide.

First. Do the intrastate passenger fares

work undue prejudice against persons in interstate commerce, such as to justify a horizontal increase of them all?

Second. Are these intrastate fares an undue discrimination against interstate commerce as a whole which it is the duty of the Commission to remove? . . .

The order in this case . . . is much wider than the orders made in the proceedings following the *Shreveport* and *Illinois Central Cases*. There, as here, the report of the Commission showed discrimination against persons and localities at border points and the orders were extended to include all rates or fares from all points in the State to border points. But this order is not so restricted. It includes fares between all interior points, although neither may be near the border, and the fares between them may not work a discrimination against interstate travelers at all. Nothing in the precedents cited justifies an order affecting all rates of a general description when it is clear that this would include many rates not within the proper class or reason of the order. . . .

Intrastate rates and the income from them must play a most important part in maintaining an adequate national railway system. Twenty per cent. of the gross freight receipts of the railroads of the country are from intrastate traffic, and fifty per cent. of the passenger receipts. The ratio of the gross intrastate revenue to the interstate revenue is a little less than one to three. If the rates, on which such receipts are based, are to be fixed at a substantially lower level than in interstate traffic, the share which the intrastate traffic will contribute will be proportionately less. . . .

It is objected here, as it was in the Shreveport Case, that orders of the Commission which raise the intrastate rates to a level of the interstate structure violate the specific proviso of the original Interstate Commerce Act . . . that the Commission is not to regulate traffic wholly within a State. To this the same answer must be made as was made in the Shreveport Case, . . . that such orders as to intrastate traffic are merely incidental to the regulation of interstate commerce, and necessary to its efficiency. Effective control of the one must embrace some control over the other, in view of the blending of both in actual operation. The same rails and the same cars carry both. The same men conduct them. Commerce is a unit and does not regard state lines, and while, under the Constitution, interstate and intrastate commerce are ordinarily subject to regulation by different sovereignties, yet when they are so mingled together that the supreme authority, the Nation, cannot exercise complete effective control over interstate commerce without incidental regulation of intrastate commerce, such incidental regulation is not an invasion of state authority or a violation of the proviso. . . .

Congress in its control of its interstate commerce system, is seeking in the Transportation Act to make the system adequate to the needs of the country by securing for it a reasonably compensatory return for all the work it does. The States are seeking to use that same system for intrastate traffic. That entails large duties and expenditures on the interstate commerce which may burden it unless compensation is received for the intrastate business reasonably proportionate to that for the interstate business. Congress as the dominant controller of interstate commerce may, therefore, restrain undue limitations of the earning power of the interstate commerce system in doing state work. The affirmative power of Congress in developing interstate commerce agencies is clear. . . . In such development, it can impose any reasonable condition on a State's use of interstate carriers for intrastate commerce it deems necessary or desirable. This is because of the supremacy of the national power in this field. . . .

Conservatism and Constitutional Law

CORPORATIONS, TRADE ASSOCIATIONS, AND COMPETITION

184. *Judicial Limitations of Regulatory Power*

U.S. v. United States Steel Corporation, 251 U.S. 417 (1920).

McKenna, J.: . . . [In the opinion of two judges in a lower court] testimony did "not show that the corporation in and of itself ever possessed or exerted sufficient power when acting alone to control prices of the products of the industry." Its power was efficient only when in co-operation with its competitors, and hence it concerted with them in the expedients of pools, associations, trade meetings, and finally in a system of dinners inaugurated in 1907 by the president of the company, E. H. Gary, and called "the Gary Dinners." The dinners were congregations of producers and "were nothing but trade meetings," successors of the other means of associated action and control through such action. They were instituted first in "stress of panic," but, their potency being demonstrated, they were afterwards called to control prices "in periods of industrial calm." "They were pools without penalties" and more efficient in stabilizing prices. But it was the further declaration that "when joint action was either refused or withdrawn the Corporation's prices were controlled by competition."

The Corporation, it was said, did not at any time abuse the power or ascendency it possessed. It resorted to none of the brutalities or tyrannies that the cases illustrate of other combinations. It did not secure freight rebates; it did not increase its profits by reducing the wages of its employees—whatever it did was not at the expense of labor; it did not increase its profits by lowering the quality of its products, nor create an artificial scarcity of them; it did not oppress or coerce its competitors—its competition, though vigorous, was fair; it did not undersell its competitors in some localities by reducing its prices there below those maintained elsewhere, or require its customers to enter into contracts limiting their purchases or restricting them in resale prices; it did not obtain customers by secret rebates or departures from its published prices; there was no evidence that it attempted to crush its competitors or drive them out of the market, nor did it take customers from its competitors by unfair means, and in its competition it seemed to make no difference between large and small competitors. Indeed it is said in many ways and illustrated that "instead of relying upon its own power to fix and maintain prices, the corporation, at its very beginning sought and obtained the assistance of others." It combined its power with that of its competitors. It did not have power in and of itself, and the control it exerted was only in and by association with its competitors. Its offense, therefore, such as it was, was not different from theirs and was distinguished from "theirs only in the leadership it assumed in promulgating and perfecting the policy." This leadership it gave up and it had ceased to offend against the law before this suit was brought. It was hence concluded that it should be distinguished from its organizers and that their intent and unsuccessful attempt should not be attributed to it, that it "in and of itself is not now and has never been a monopoly or a combination in restraint of trade," and a decree of dissolution should not be entered against it. . . .

We have seen that the judges of the District Court unanimously concurred in the view that the Corporation did not achieve monopoly, and such is our deduction. . . . Monopoly, therefore, was not achieved, and competitors had to be persuaded by pools, associations, and trade meetings, all of them, it may be, violations of the law. . . . They were scattered through the years from 1901 . . . until 1911, but . . . abandoned nine months before this suit. . . .

What, then, can now be urged against the Corporation? . . .

The company's officers, and, as well, its competitors and customers, testified that its competition was genuine. . . . No practical witness was produced by the Government in opposition. . . . Counsel say, "They [the Corporation is made a plural] called . . . two hundred witnesses out of some forty thousand customers, and they expect with that evidence to overcome the whole train of price movement since the Corporation was formed." . . .

The opinion of an editor of a trade journal is adduced, and that of an author and teacher of economics whose philosophical deductions had, perhaps, fortification from experience as Deputy Commissioner of Corporations and as an employee in the Bureau of Corporations. His deduction was that when prices are constant through a definite period an artificial influence is indicated. . . . It has become an aphorism that there is danger of deception in generalities, and in a case of this importance we should have something surer for judgment than speculation,—something more than a deduction . . . even though the facts it rests on or asserts were not contradicted. . . .

Against it competitors, dealers, and customers of the Corporation testify in multitude that . . . prices . . . varied according to natural conditions. . . .

The Corporation is undoubtedly of impressive size, and it takes an effort of resolution not to be affected by it or to exaggerate its influence. But . . . the law does not make mere size an offense or the existence of unexerted power an offense. . . .

The Steel Corporation by its formation united under one control competing companies, and thus, it is urged, a condition was brought about in violation of the statute. . . .

We have seen whatever there was of wrong intent could not be executed; whatever there was of evil effect was discontinued before this suit was brought; and this, we think, determines the decree.

185. *Trade associations tend "to stabilize trade and industry."*

Maple Flooring Manufacturers Association v. U.S., 268 U.S. 563 (1925).

STONE, J.: . . . In March, 1922, the corporate defendants organized the defendant Maple Flooring Manufacturers Association, but for many years prior to that time and certainly since 1913 a substantial number of the corporate defendants have participated actively in maintaining numerous successive trade associations of the same name, which were predecessors of the present association. . . . The defendants have engaged in many activities to which no exception is taken by the Government and which are admittedly beneficial to the industry and to consumers; such as co-operative advertising and the standardization and improvement of the product. The activities . . . of the present Association of which the Government complains may be summarized as follows:

(1) The computation and distribution among the members of the association of the average cost to association members of all dimensions and grades of flooring.

(2) The compilation and distribution among members of a booklet showing freight rates on flooring from Cadillac, Michigan, to between five and six thousand points of shipment in the United States.

(3) The gathering of statistics which at frequent intervals are supplied by each member of the Association to the Secretary of the Association giving complete information as to the quantity and kind of flooring sold and prices received by the reporting members, and the amount of stock on hand, which information is summarized by the Secretary and transmitted to members without, however, revealing the identity of the members in connection with any specific information thus transmitted.

(4) Meetings at which the representatives of members congregate and discuss the industry and exchange views as to its problems.

We think it might be urged, on the basis of this record that the defendants, by their course of conduct, instead of evidencing the purpose of persistent violators of law, had steadily indicated a purpose to keep within the boundaries of legality as rapidly as those boundaries were marked out by the decisions of courts interpreting the Sherman Act. . . .

It is not, we think, open to question that the dissemination of pertinent information concerning any trade or business tends to stabilize that trade or business and to produce uniformity of price and trade practice. Exchange of price quotations of market commodities tends to produce uniformity of prices in the markets of the world. Knowledge of the supplies of available merchandise tends to prevent over-production and to avoid the economic disturbances produced by business crises resulting from over-production. But the natural effect of the acquisition of wider and more scientific knowledge of business conditions, on the minds of the individuals engaged in commerce, and its consequent effect in stabilizing production and price, can hardly be deemed a restraint of commerce or if so it cannot, we think be said to be an unreasonable restraint, or in any respect unlawful.

It is the consensus of opinion of economists and of many of the most important agencies of Government that the public interest is served by the gathering and dissemination, in the widest possible manner, of information with respect to the production and distribution, cost and prices in actual sales, of market commodities, because the making available of such information tends to stabilize trade and industry, to produce fairer price levels and to avoid the waste which inevitably attends the unintelligent conduct of economic enterprise. Free competition means a free and open market among both buyers and sellers for the sale and distribution of commodities. Competition does not become less free merely because the conduct of commercial operations becomes more intelligent through the free distribution of knowledge of all the essential factors entering into the commercial transaction. . . .

It was not the purpose or the intent of the Sherman Anti-Trust Law to inhibit the intelligent conduct of business operations, nor do we conceive that its purpose was to suppress such influences as might affect the operations of interstate commerce through the application to them of the individual intelligence of those engaged in commerce, enlightened by accurate information as to the essential elements of the economics of a trade or business, however gathered or disseminated. . . .

We decide only that trade associations or combinations of persons or corporations which openly and fairly gather and disseminate information . . . as did these defendants, and who . . . meet and discuss such information and statistics without however reaching or attempting to reach any agreement or any concerted action with respect to prices or restraining competition, do not thereby engage in unlawful restraint of commerce. . . .

JUDICIAL RESTRICTIONS ON FEDERAL ADMINISTRATIVE COMMISSIONS

186. *The Courts, the F. T. C., and Unfair Competition*

F. T. C. v. Gratz, 253 U.S. 421 (1920).

McREYNOLDS, J.: . . . It is unnecessary . . . to discuss conflicting views concerning validity and meaning of the act creating the [Federal Trade] commission and effect of the evidence presented. The judgment below must be affirmed since, in our opinion, the first count of the complaint is wholly insufficient to charge respondents with practicing "unfair methods of competition in commerce" within the fair intendment of those words. We go no further and confine this opinion to the point specified. . . .

The words "unfair method of competition" are not defined by the statute and their exact meaning is in dispute. It is for the courts, not the commission, ultimately to determine as matter of law what they include. They are clearly inapplicable to practices never heretofore regarded as opposed to good morals because characterized by deception, bad faith, fraud or oppression, or as against public policy because of their dangerous tendency unduly to hinder competition or create monopoly. The act was certainly not intended to fetter free and fair competition as commonly understood and practiced by honorable opponents in trade.

Count one alleges . . . that Warren, Jones & Gratz are engaged in selling, either directly to the trade or through their co-respondents, cotton ties . . . and also jute bagging. . . . [Two concerns] are the selling and distributing agents of Warren, Jones & Gratz, and as such sell and distribute their ties and bagging to jobbers and dealers who resell them to retailers, ginners, and farmers. That with the purpose and effect of discouraging and stifling competition in the sale of such bagging all the respondents for more than a year have refused to sell any of such ties unless the purchaser would buy from them a corresponding amount of bagging —six yards with as many ties.

The complaint contains no intimation that Warren, Jones & Gratz did not properly obtain their ties and bagging as merchants usually do; the amount controlled by them is not stated; nor is it alleged that they held a monopoly of either ties or bagging or had ability, purpose or intent to acquire one. So far as appears, acting independently, they undertook to sell their lawfully acquired property in the ordinary course, without deception, misrepresentation, or oppression, and at fair prices, to purchasers willing to take it upon terms openly announced.

Nothing is alleged which would justify the conclusion that the public suffered injury or that competitors had reasonable ground for complaint. All question of monopoly or combination being out of the way, a private merchant, acting with entire good faith, may properly refuse to sell except in conjunction, such closely associated articles as ties and bagging. If real competition is to continue the right of the individual to exercise reasonable discretion in respect of his own business methods must be preserved. . . .

ADULT AND CHILD LABOR

187. *Labor, the Injunction, and the Anti-Trust Acts*

Duplex Printing Press Co. v. Deering, 254 U.S. 443 (1921).

Pitney, J.: . . . That . . . [the] complainant has sustained substantial damage to its interstate trade, and is threatened with further and irreparable loss and damage in the future, is proved by clear and undisputed evidence. Hence the right to an injunction is clear if the threatened loss is due to a violation of the Sherman Act, as amended by the Clayton Act. . . .

The substance of the matters here complained of is an interference with complainant's interstate trade intended to have coercive effect upon complainant, and produced by what is commonly known as a "secondary boycott," that is, a combination not merely to refrain from dealing with complainant, or to advise or by peaceful means persuade complainant's customers to refrain ("primary boycott") but to exercise coercive pressure upon such customers . . . in order to cause them to withhold . . . patronage. . . .

As we shall see, the recognized distinction between a primary and a secondary boycott is material to be considered upon the question of a proper construction of the Clayton Act. . . .

The principal reliance is upon §20. . . . The second paragraph declares that "no *such* restraining order or injunction" shall prohibit certain conduct specified—manifestly still referring to a "case between an employer and employees, . . . involving, or growing out of, a dispute concerning terms or conditions of employment," as designated in the first paragraph. It is very clear that the restriction upon the use of the injunction is in favor only of those concerned as parties to such a dispute as is described. . . .

The majority of the Circuit Court of Appeals appear to have entertained the view that the words "employers and employees," as used in §20, should be treated as referring to "the business class or clan to which the parties ligitant respectively belong;" and that, . . . §20 operated to permit members of the Machinists' Union elsewhere—some 60,000 in number—although standing in no relation of employment under complainant, past, present, or prospective, to make that dispute their own, and proceed to instigate sympathetic strikes, picketing, and boycotting against employers wholly unconnected with complainant's factory, and having relations with complainant only in the way of purchasing its product in the ordinary course of interstate commerce—and this where there was no dispute between such employers and their employees respecting terms or conditions of employment.

We deem this construction altogether inadmissible. . . .

The emphasis placed on the words "lawful" and "lawfully," "peaceful" and "peacefully," and the references to the dispute and the parties to it, strongly rebut a legislative intent to confer a general immunity for conduct violative of the anti-trust laws, or otherwise unlawful. The subject of the boycott is dealt with specifically in the "ceasing to patronize" provision, and by the clear force of the language employed the exemption is limited to pressure exerted upon a "party to such dispute" by means of "peaceful and *lawful*" influence upon neutrals. There is nothing here to justify defendants or the organizations they represent in using either threats or persuasion to bring about strikes or a cessation of work on the part of employees of complainant's customers or prospective customers, or of the trucking company employed by the customers, with the object of compelling such customers to withdraw or refrain from commercial relations with complainant, and of thereby constraining complainant to yield the matter in dispute. To instigate a sympathetic strike in aid of a secondary boycott cannot be deemed "peaceful and lawful" persuasion. . . .

The question whether the bill legalized a secondary boycott . . . was emphatically and unequivocally answered [in the debates in the House] . . . in the negative. The subject . . . was under consideration when the bill was framed, and the section as reported was carefully prepared with the settled purpose of excluding the secondary boycott, and confining boycotting to the parties to the dispute, allowing parties to cease to patronize and to ask others to cease to patronize a party to the dispute; it was the opinion of the committee that it did not legalize the secondary boycott; it was not their purpose to authorize such a boycott; not a member of the committee would vote to do so; clarifying amendment was unnecessary; the section as reported expressed the real purpose so well that it could not be tortured into a meaning authorizing the secondary boycott. . . .

There should be an injunction against defendants and the associations represented by them. . . .

188. *Child Labor and Federal Taxation*

Bailey v. Drexel Furniture Co., 259 U.S. 20 (1922).

TAFT, C.J.: . . . The law is attacked on the ground that it is a regulation of the employment of child labor in the States—an exclusively state function under the Federal Constitution and within the reservations of the Tenth Amendment. It is defended on the ground that it is a mere excise tax levied by the Congress of the United States under its broad power of taxation conferred by §8, Article I, of the federal Constitution. We must construe the law and interpret the intent and meaning of Congress from the language of the act. The words are to be given their ordinary meaning unless the context shows that they are differently used. Does this law impose a tax with only that incidental restraint and regulation which a tax must inevitably involve? Or does it regulate by the use of the so-called tax as a penalty? If a tax, it is clearly an excise. If it were an excise on a commodity or other thing of value we might not be permitted under previous decisions of this court to infer solely from its heavy burden that the act intends a prohibition instead of a tax. But this act is more. It provides a heavy exaction for a departure from a detailed and specified course of conduct in business. That course of business is that employers shall employ in mines and quarries, children of an age greater than sixteen years; in mills and factories, children of an age greater than fourteen years, and shall prevent children of less than sixteen years in mills and factories from working more than eight hours a day or six days in the week. If an employer departs from this prescribed course of business, he is to pay to the Government one-tenth of his entire net income in the business for a full year. The amount is not to be proportioned in any degree to the frequency of the departures, but is to be paid by the employer in full measure whether he employs five hundred children for a year, or employs only one for a day. Moreover, if he does not know the child is within the named age limit, he is not to pay; that is to say, it is only where he knowingly departs from the prescribed course that payment is to be exacted. . . .

In the light of these features of the act, a court must be blind not to see that the so-called tax is imposed to stop the employment of children within the age limits prescribed. Its prohibitory and regulatory effect and purpose are palpable. All others can see and understand this. How can we properly shut our minds to it?

It is the high duty and function of this court in cases regularly brought to its bar to decline to recognize or enforce seeming laws of Congress, dealing with subjects not entrusted to Congress but left or committed by the supreme law of the land to the control of the States. We can not avoid the duty even though it requires us to refuse to give effect to legislation designed to promote the highest good. The good sought in unconstitutional legislation is an insidious feature because it leads citizens and legislators of good purpose to promote it without thought of the serious breach it will make in the ark of our covenant or the harm which will come from breaking down recognized standards. In the maintenance of local self government, on the one hand, and the national power on the other, our country has been able to endure and prosper for near a century and a half.

Out of a proper respect for the acts of a coördinate branch of the Government, this court has gone far to sustain taxing acts as such, even though there has been ground for suspecting from the weight of the tax it was intended to destroy its subject. But, in the act before us, the presumption of validity cannot prevail, because the proof of the contrary is found on the very face of its provisions. Grant the validity of this law, and all that Congress would need to do, hereafter, in seeking to take over to its control any one of the great number of subjects of public interest, jurisdiction of which the States have never parted with, and which are reserved to them by the Tenth Amendment, would be to enact a detailed measure of complete regulation of the subject and enforce it by a so-called tax upon departures from it. To give such magic to the word "tax" would be to break down all constitutional limitation of the powers of Congress and completely wipe out the sovereignty of the States. . . .

For the reasons given, we must hold the Child Labor Tax Law invalid and the judgment of the district court is Affirmed.

189. *Child Labor Amendment, Proposed June 4, 1924*

U. S. Stat. at L., XLIII, 670.

SECTION 1. The Congress shall have power to limit, regulate, and prohibit the labor of persons under eighteen years of age.

SECTION 2. The power of the several States is unimpaired by this Article except that the operation of State laws shall be suspended to the extent necessary to give effect to legislation enacted by the Congress.

The Extent of State Regulation Under the Fourteenth Amendment

THE POLICE POWER AND WORKING CONDITIONS

190. *"Freedom of contract is . . . the general rule and restraint the exception."*

Adkins v. Children's Hospital, 261 U.S. 525 (1923).

SUTHERLAND, J.: . . . The statute now under consideration is attacked upon the ground that it authorizes an unconstitutional interference with the freedom of contract included within the guaranties of the due process clause of the Fifth Amendment. That the right to contract about one's affairs is a part of the liberty of the individual protected by this clause is settled by the decisions of this Court and is no longer open to question. . . . Within this liberty are contracts of employment of labor. In making such contracts, generally speaking, the parties have an equal right to obtain from each other the best terms they can as the result of private bargaining. . . .

There is, of course, no such thing as absolute freedom of contract. It is subject to a great variety of restraints. But freedom of contract is, nevertheless, the general rule and restraint the exception; and the exercise of legislative authority to abridge it can be justified only by the existence of exceptional circumstances. . . .

[The present law] is simply and exclusively a price-fixing law, confined to adult women (for we are not now considering the provisions relating to minors), who are legally as capable of contracting for themselves as men. It forbids two parties having lawful capacity—under penalties as to the employer—to freely contract with one another in respect of the price for which one shall render service to the other in a purely private employment where both are willing, perhaps anxious, to agree, even though the consequence may be to oblige one to surrender a desirable engagement and the other to dispense with the services of a desirable employee. . . .

The standard furnished by the statute for the guidance of the board is so vague as to be impossible of practical application with any reasonable degree of accuracy. What is sufficient to supply the necessary cost of living for a woman worker and maintain her in good health and protect her morals is obviously not a precise or unvarying sum—not even approximately so. The amount will depend upon a variety of circumstances: the individual temperament, habits of thrift, care, ability to buy necessaries intelligently, and whether the woman live alone or with her family. To those who practice economy, a given sum will afford comfort while to those of a contrary habit the same sum will be wholly inadequate. The coöperative economies of the family group are not taken into account though they constitute an important consideration in estimating the cost of living, for it is obvious that the individual expense will be less in the case of a member of a family than in the case of one living alone. The relation between earnings and morals is not capable of standardization. It cannot be shown that well paid women safeguard their morals more carefully than those who are poorly paid. Morality rests upon other considerations than wages; and there is, certainly, no such prevalent connection between the two as to justify a broad attempt to adjust the latter with reference to the former. . . .

The feature of this statute which, perhaps more than any other, puts upon it the stamp of invalidity is that it exacts from the employer an arbitrary payment for a purpose and upon a basis having no causal connection with his business, or the contract or the work the employee engages to do. The declared basis, as already pointed out, is not the value of the service rendered but the extraneous circumstances that the employee needs to get a prescribed sum of money to insure her subsistence, health and morals. The ethical right of every worker, man or woman, to a living wage, may be conceded. One of the declared and important purposes of trade organizations is to secure it. And with that principle and with every legitimate effort to realize it in fact, no one can quarrel, but the fallacy of the proposed method of attaining it is that it assumes that every employer is bound at all events to furnish it. . . .

Finally, it may be said that if, in the interest of the public welfare, the police power may be invoked to justify the fixing of a minimum wage, it may, when the public welfare is thought to require it, be invoked to justify a maximum wage. The power to fix high wages connotes, by like reasoning, the power to fix low wages. If, in the face of the guaranties of the Fifth Amendment, this form of legislation shall be legally justified, the field for the operation of the police power will have been widened to a great and dangerous degree. If, for example, in the opinion of future lawmakers, wages in the building trades shall become so high as to preclude people of ordinary means from building and owning homes, an authority which sustains the minimum wage will be invoked to support a maximum wage for building laborers and artisans, and the same argument which has been here urged to strip the employer of his constitutional liberty of contract in one direction will be utilized to strip the employee of his constitutional liberty of contract in the opposite direction. A wrong decision does not end with itself: it is a precedent, and, with the swing of sentiment, its bad influence may run from one extremity of the arc to the other.

It has been said that legislation of the kind now under review is required in the interest of social justice, for whose ends freedom of contract may lawfully be subjected to restraint. The liberty of the individual to do as he pleases, even in innocent matters, is not absolute. It must frequently yield to the common good, and the line beyond which the power of interference may not be pressed is neither definite nor unalterable but may be made to move, within limits not well defined, with changing need and circumstance. Any attempt to fix a rigid boundary would be unwise and futile. But, nevertheless, there are limits to the power, and when these have been passed, it becomes the plain duty of the courts in the proper exercise of their authority to so declare. To sustain the individual freedom of action contemplated by the Constitution, is not to strike down the common good but to exalt it; for surely the good of society as a whole cannot be better served than by the preservation against arbitrary restraint of the liberties of its constituent members.

It follows from what has been said that the act in question passes the limit prescribed by the Constitution . . .

191. *"The law of property . . . is not appropriate for dealing with the forces beneath social unrest."*

Truax v. Corrigan, 257 U.S. 312 (1921).

BRANDEIS, J., dissenting: . . . Few laws are of universal application. It is of the nature of our law that it has dealt not with man in general, but with him in relationships. That a peculiar relationship of individuals may furnish legal basis for the classification which satisfies the requirement of the Fourteenth Amendment is clear. That the relation of employer and employee affords a constitutional basis for legislation applicable only to persons standing in that relation has been repeatedly held by this court. The questions submitted are whether this statutory prohibition of the remedy by injunction is in itself arbitrary and so unreasonable as to deprive the employer of liberty or property without due process of law;—and whether limitation of this prohibition to controversies involving employment denies him equal protection of the laws.

Whether a law enacted in the exercise of the police power is justly subject to the charge of being unreasonable or arbitrary, can ordinarily be determined only by a consideration of the contemporary conditions, social, industrial and political, of the community to be affected thereby. Resort to such facts is necessary, among other things, in order to appreciate the evils sought to be remedied and the possible effects of the remedy proposed. Nearly all legislation involves a weighing of public needs as against private desires; and likewise a weighing of relative social values. Since government is not an exact science, prevailing public opinion concerning the evils and the remedy is among the important facts deserving consideration; particularly, when the public conviction is both deep-seated and widespread and has been reached after deliberation. What, at any particular time, is the paramount public need is, necessarily, largely a matter of judgment. Hence, in passing upon the validity of a law challenged as being unreasonable, aid may be derived from the experience of other countries and of the several States of our Union in which the common law and its conceptions of liberty and of property prevail. The history of the rules governing contests between employer and employed in the several English-speaking countries illustrates both the susceptibility of such rules to change and the variety of contemporary opinion as to what rules will best serve the public interest. . . .

In England, observance of the rules of the contest has been enforced by the courts almost wholly through the criminal law or through actions at law for compensation. . . . Resort to the injunction has not been frequent and it has played no appreciable part there in the conflict between capital and labor. In America the injunction did not secure recognition as a possible remedy until 1888. When a few years later its use became extensive and conspicuous, the controversy over the remedy overshadowed in bitterness the question of the relative substantive rights of the parties. In the storms of protest against this use many thoughtful lawyers joined. . . .

It was urged that the real motive in seeking the injunction was not ordinarily to prevent property from being injured nor to protect the owner in its use, but to endow property with active, militant power which would make it dominant over men. In other words, that under the guise of protecting property rights, the employer was seeking sovereign power. And many disinterested men, solicitous only for the public welfare, believed that the law of property was not appropriate for dealing with the forces beneath social unrest; that in this vast struggle it was unwise to throw the power of the State on one side or the other according to principles deduced from that law; that the problem of the control and conduct of industry demanded a solution of its own; and that, pending the ascertainment of new principles to govern industry, it was wiser for the State not to interfere in industrial struggles by the issuance of an injunction.

After the constitutionality and the propriety of the use of the injunction in labor disputes was established judicially, those who opposed the practice sought the aid of Congress and state legislatures. . . . These legislative proposals occupied the attention of Congress during every session but one in the twenty years between 1894 and 1914. Reports recommending such legislation were repeatedly made. . . . [In 1914] Congress passed and the President approved the Clayton Act, §20 of which is substantially the same as Paragraph 1464 of the Arizona Civil Code. . . .

The acknowledged legislative discretion exerted in classification, so frequently applied in defining rights, extends equally to the grant of remedies. It is for the legislature to say—within the broad limits of the discretion which it possesses—whether or not the remedy for a wrong shall be both criminal and civil and whether or not it shall be both at law and in equity. . . .

For these reasons, as well as for others . . . , the judgment of the Supreme Court of Arizona should, in my opinion, be affirmed:—first, because in permitting damage to be inflicted by means of boycott and peaceful picketing Arizona did not deprive the plaintiffs of property without due process of law or deny them equal protection of the laws; and secondly, because, if Arizona was constitutionally prohibited from adopting this rule of substantive law, it was still free to restrict the extraordinary remedies of equity where it considered their exercise to be detrimental to the public welfare, since such restriction was not a denial to the employer either of due process or of equal protection of the laws.

SOCIAL LEGISLATION AND THE PUBLIC WELFARE

192. *The Court Narrows the Public Interest Doctrine to Restrict State Regulation*

Wolff Packing Co. v. Court of Industrial Relations of Kansas, 262 U.S. 522 (1923).

Taft, C.J.: . . . The necessary postulate of the Industrial Court Act is that the State, representing the people, is so much interested in their peace, health, and comfort, that it may compel those engaged in the manufacture of food and clothing, and the production of fuel, whether owners or workers, to continue in their business and employment on terms fixed by an agency of the State, if they cannot agree. Under the construction adopted by the State Supreme Court, the act gives the Industrial Court authority to permit the owner or employer to go out of the business if he shows that he can only continue on the terms fixed at such heavy loss that collapse will follow; but this privilege, under the circumstances, is generally illusory. . . . A laborer dissatisfied with his wages is permitted to quit, but he may not agree with his fellows to quit, or combine with others to induce them to quit.

These qualifications do not change the essence of the act. It curtails the right of the employer, on the one hand, and that of the employee, on the other, to contract about his affairs. This is part of the liberty of the individual protected by the guaranty of the due process clause of the Fourteenth Amendment. . . .

It is manifest from an examination of the cases cited . . . that the mere declaration by a legislature that a business is affected with a public interest is not conclusive of the question whether its attempted regulation on that ground is justified. The circumstances of its alleged change from the status of a private business and its freedom from regulation into one in which the public have come to have an interest, are always a subject of judicial inquiry. . . .

It has never been supposed, since the adoption of the Constitution, that the business of the butcher, or the baker, the tailor, the woodchopper, the mining operator, or the miner, was clothed with such a public interest that the price of his product or his wages could be fixed by State regulation. . . .

To say that a business is clothed with a public interest is not to determine what regulation is permissible in view of the private rights of the owner. The extent to which an inn or a cab system may be regulated may differ widely from that allowable as to a railroad or other common carrier. It is not a matter of legislative discretion solely. It depends upon the nature of the business, on the feature which touches the public, and on the abuses reasonably to be feared. To say that business is clothed with a public interest is not to import that the public may take over its entire management and run it at the expense of the owner. The extent to which regulation may reasonably go varies with different kinds of business. The regulation of rates to avoid monopoly, is one thing. The regulation of wages is another. A business may be of such character that only the first is permissible, while another may involve such a possible danger of monopoly on the one hand, and such disaster from stoppage on the other, that both come within the public concern and power of regulation.

If, as, in effect, contended by counsel for the State, the common callings are clothed with a public interest by a mere legislative declaration, which necessarily authorizes full and comprehensive regulation within legislative discretion, there must be a revolution in the relation of government to general business. This will be running the public-interest argument into the ground. . . . It will be impossible to reconcile such result with the freedom of contract and of labor secured by the Fourteenth Amendment.

This brings us to the nature and purpose of the regulation under the Industrial Court Act. The avowed object is continuity of food, clothing, and fuel supply. By §6 reasonable continuity and efficiency of the industries specified are declared to be necessary for the public peace, health, and general welfare, and all are forbidden to hinder, limit, or suspend them. Section 7 gives the Industrial Court power, in case of controversy between employers and workers which may endanger the continuity or efficiency of service, to bring the employer and employee before it, and after hearing and investigation, to fix the terms and conditions between them. The employer is bound by this act to pay the wages fixed; and while the worker is not required to work at the wages fixed, he is forbidden on penalty of fine or imprisonment, to strike against them, and thus is compelled to give up that means of putting himself on an equality with his employer which action in concert with his fellows gives him. . . .

The minutely detailed government supervision, including that of their relations to their employees, to which the railroads of the country have been gradually subjected by Congress through its power over interstate commerce, furnishes no precedent for regulation of the business of the plaintiff, whose classification as public is, at the best, doubtful. It is not too much to say that the ruling in *Wilson v. New* went to the borderline, although it concerned an interstate common carrier in the presence of a nation-wide emergency and the possibility of great disaster. Certainly there is nothing to justify extending the drastic regulation sustained in that exceptional case to the one before us.

We think the Industrial Court Act . . . is in conflict with the Fourteenth Amendment and deprives it [the packing house] of its property and liberty of contract without due process of law.

The judgment of the court below is reversed.

193. *"Government does not go beyond its sphere in attempting to make life livable."*

Tyson v. Banton, 273 U.S. 418 (1927).

HOLMES, J., dissenting: We fear to grant power and are unwilling to recognize it when it exists. The States very generally have stripped jury trials of one of their most important characteristics by forbidding the judges to advise the jury upon the facts, . . . and when legislatures are held to be authorized to do anything considerably affecting public welfare, it is covered by apologetic phrases like the police power, or the statement that the business concerned has been dedicated to a public use. The former expression is convenient, to be sure, to conciliate the mind to something that needs explanation: the fact that the constitutional requirement of compensation when property is taken cannot be pressed to its grammatical extreme; that property rights may be taken for public purposes without pay if you do not take too much; that some play must be allowed to the joints if the machine is to work. But police power often is used in a wide sense to cover and, as I said, to apologize for the general power of the legislature to make a part of the community uncomfortable by a change.

I do not believe in such apologies. I think the proper course is to recognize that a state legislature can do whatever it sees fit to do unless it is restrained by some express prohibition in the Constitution of the United States or of the State, and that courts should be careful not to extend such prohibitions beyond their obvious meaning by reading into them conceptions of public policy that the particular court may happen to entertain. Coming down to the case before us, I think, as I intimated in *Adkins v. Children's Hospital,* . . . that the notion that a business is clothed with a public interest and has been devoted to the public use is little more than a fiction intended to beautify what is disagreeable to the sufferers. The truth seems to me to be that, subject to compensation when compensation is due, the legislature may forbid or restrict any business when it has a sufficient force of public opinion behind it. Lotteries were thought useful adjuncts of the State a century or so ago; now they are believed to be immoral and they have been stopped. Wine has been thought good for man from the time of the Apostles until recent years. But when public opinion changed it did not need the Eighteenth Amendment, notwithstanding the Fourteenth, to enable a State to say that the business should end. . . . What has happened to lotteries and wine might happen to theatres in some moral storm of the future, not because theatres were devoted to a public use, but because people had come to think that way.

But if we are to yield to fashionable conventions, it seems to me that theatres are as much devoted to public use as anything well can be. We have not that respect for art that is one of the glories of France. But to many people the superfluous is the necessary, and it seems to me that government does not go beyond its sphere in attempting to make life livable for them. I am far from saying that I think this particular law a wise and rational provision. That is not my affair. But if the people of the State of New York speaking by their authorized voice say that they want it, I see nothing in the Constitution of the United States to prevent their having their will.

194. *"There is no closed class or category of businesses affected with a public interest."*

Nebbia v. New York, 291 U.S. 502 (1934).

ROBERTS, J.: . . . We are told that because the law essays to control prices it denies due process. Notwithstanding the admitted power to correct existing economic ills by appropriate regulation of business, even though an indirect result may be a restriction of the freedom of contract or a modification of charges for services or the price of commodities, the appellant urges that direct fixation of prices is a type of regulation absolutely forbidden. His position is that the Fourteenth Amendment requires us to hold the challenged statute void for this reason alone. The argument runs that the public control of rates or prices is *per se* unreasonable and unconstitutional, save as applied to businesses affected with a public interest; that a business so affected is one in which property is devoted to an enterprise of a sort which the public itself might appropriately undertake, or one whose owner relies on a public grant or franchise for the right to conduct the business, or in which he is bound to serve all who apply; in short, such as is commonly called a public utility; or a business in its nature a monopoly. The milk industry, it is said, possesses none of these characteristics, and, therefore, not being affected with a public interest, its charges may not be controlled by the state. Upon the soundness of this contention the appellant's case against the statute depends.

We may as well say at once that the dairy industry is not, in the accepted sense of the phrase, a public utility. We think the appellant is also right in asserting that there is in this case no suggestion of any monopoly or monopolistic practice. It goes without saying that those engaged in the business are in no way dependent upon public grants or franchises for the privilege of conducting their activities. But if, as must be conceded, the industry is subject to regulation in the public interest, what constitutional principle bars the state from correcting existing maladjustments by legislation touching prices? We think there is no such principle. The due process clause makes no mention of sales or of prices any more than it speaks of business or contracts or buildings or other incidents of property. The thought seems nevertheless to have persisted that there is something peculiarly sacrosanct about the price one may charge for what he makes or sells, and that, however able to regulate other elements of manufacture or trade, with incidental effect upon price, the state is incapable of directly controlling the price itself. The view was negatived many years ago. *Munn. v. Illinois*. . . .

It is clear that there is no closed class or category of businesses affected with a public interest, and the function of courts in the application of the Fifth and Fourteenth Amendments is to determine in each case whether circumstances vindicate the challenged regulation as a reasonable exertion of governmental authority or condemn it as arbitrary or discriminatory. . . . The phrase "affected with a public interest" can, in the nature of things, mean no more than that an industry, for adequate reason, is subject to control for the public good. In several of the decisions of this court wherein the expressions "affected with a public interest," and "clothed with a public use," have been brought forward as the criteria of the validity of price control, it has been admitted that they are not susceptible of definition and form an unsatisfactory test of the constitutionality of legislation directed at business practices or prices. These decisions must rest, finally, upon the basis that the requirements of due process were not met because the laws were found arbitrary in their operation and effect. But there can be no doubt that upon proper occasion and by appropriate measures the state may regulate a business in any of its aspects, including the prices to be charged for the products or commodities it sells.

So far as the requirement of due process is concerned, and in the absence of other constitutional restriction, a state is free to adopt whatever economic policy may reasonably be deemed to promote public welfare, and to enforce that policy by legislation adapted to its purpose. The courts are without authority either to declare such policy, or, when it is declared by the legislature, to override it. If the laws passed are seen to have a reasonable relation to a proper legislative purpose, and are neither arbitrary nor discriminatory, the requirements of due process are satisfied, and judicial determination to that effect renders a court *functus officio*. . . . And it is equally clear that if the legislative policy be to curb unrestrained and harmful competition by measures which are not arbitrary or discriminatory it does not lie with the courts to determine that the rule is unwise. With the wisdom of the policy adopted, with the adequacy or practicability of the law enacted to forward it, the courts are both incompetent and unauthorized to deal. . . .

Price control, like any other form of regulation, is unconstitutional only if arbitrary, discriminatory, or demonstrably irrelevant to the policy the legislature is free to adopt, and hence an unnecessary and unwarranted interference with individual liberty.

Tested by these considerations we find no basis in the due process clause of the Fourteenth Amendment for condemning the provisions of the Agriculture and Markets Law here drawn into question.

195. *"Three generations of imbeciles are enough."*

Buck v. Bell, 274 U.S. 200 (1927).

Holmes, J.: . . . An Act of Virginia . . . recites that the health of the patient and the welfare of society may be promoted in certain cases by the sterilization of mental defectives, under careful safeguard, &c. . . . ; that the Commonwealth is supporting in various institutions many defective persons who if now discharged would become a menace but if incapable of procreating might be discharged with safety and become self-supporting with benefit to themselves and to society. . . .

We have seen more than once that the public welfare may call upon the best citizens for their lives. It would be strange if it could not call upon those who already sap the strength of the State for these lesser sacrifices, often not felt to be such by those concerned, in order to prevent our being swamped with incompetence. It is better for all the world, if instead of waiting to execute degenerate offspring for crime, or to let them starve for their imbecility, society can prevent those who are manifestly unfit from continuing their kind. The principle that sustains compulsory vaccination is broad enough to cover cutting the Fallopian tubes. . . . Three generations of imbeciles are enough.

But, it is said, however it might be if this reasoning were applied generally, it fails when it is confined to the small number who are in the institutions named and is not applied to the multitudes outside. It is the usual last resort of constitutional arguments to point out shortcomings of this sort. But the answer is that the law does all that is needed when it does all that it can, indicates a policy, applies it to all within the lines, and seeks to bring within the lines all similarly situated so far and so fast as its means allow. . . .

CHAPTER XXI

A New Era in Civil Liberties

IT WAS logical that a Court dedicated to a defense of individualism should not concern itself exclusively with protecting property rights but should also examine constitutional guarantees of personal liberties. One of the most spectacular developments in the latter field was the Supreme Court's broadening of the concept of liberty in the Fourteenth Amendment to include the guarantees of the First Amendment, thus protecting basic civil liberties from state, as well as federal, abridgment. Ever since *Barron v. Baltimore* (Chapter IV), the Bill of Rights had been interpreted as a limitation upon the federal government, but not upon the states. "Neither the Fourteenth Amendment," the Court said in 1922, "nor any other provision of the Constitution of the United States imposes upon the states any restrictions about 'freedom of speech.'" In a remarkable reversal less than three years later, the Court casually cast aside this traditional view and effectively nationalized the First Amendment by reading it into the due process clause of the Fourteenth Amendment. The Gitlow case (No. 196), however, was not an unqualified victory in the field of civil liberties, for by reviving the "bad tendency" test as a measure of permissible free speech, it upheld the state legislative restriction.

In *Whitney v. California*, the Court again ruled that the state statute involved did not unduly restrict freedom of speech, but Justice Brandeis wrote a concurring opinion rejecting the Gitlow test and restating the "clear and present danger" test (No. 197). Another California case challenged the validity of a law forbidding the display of a red flag. Yetta Stromberg was convicted for participating in leading a Communist youth-camp group in the following flag salute: "I pledge allegiance to the workers' red flag and to the cause for which it stands, one aim throughout our lives, freedom for the working class." Chief Justice Hughes struck down the state statute on the ground that it was a denial of the liberty guaranteed by the due process clause of the Fourteenth Amendment (*Stromberg v. California* [*No.* 198]). At the same session, Hughes also invalidated the "Minnesota gag law," ruling that freedom of the press is another of the First Amendment rights protected by the liberty guaranteed by the Fourteenth Amendment (*Near v. Minnesota* [*No.* 199]).

Another aspect of the Court's concern for fundamental freedoms of the individual was revealed in the highly controversial 5 to 4 decision in *Olmstead v. U.S.* (No. 200). Over the vigorous dissents of Brandeis (No. 201) and Holmes, who branded wire tapping "dirty business," Chief Justice Taft ruled that this practice did not constitute an illegal search or seizure. In 1934, however, Congress passed a law stating that "no person not being authorized by the sender shall intercept any communication and divulge or publish the existence, contents, substance . . . of such intercepted communication to any person." Three years later, in *Nardone v. U.S.*, the Court held that evidence obtained in searches violating the statute was inadmissible in a federal prosecution.

The famous "Scottsboro cases" made two major contributions to American constitutional law. In the first (*Powell v. Alabama,* 1932), a majority agreed that seven Negroes convicted of rape and sentenced to death were deprived of life and liberty without due process of law when they were denied assistance of counsel, thus reading the guarantees of the Sixth Amendment into the Fourteenth Amendment. The second Scottsboro case (*Norris v. Alabama* [*No.* 202]) raised the question of the guarantee of a fair and impartial jury. As early as 1880 the Court had ruled that a Negro was denied equal protection of the laws when tried by a jury from which Negroes were excluded by law because of their color (*Strauder v. West Virginia*). At the same time, however, the Court decided that a Negro was not denied due process merely because there were no Negroes on his jury (*Virginia v. Rives*). It was not until fifty-five years later that the Norris case challenged the standard southern practice of not calling Negroes for jury service. Then the Court held that systematic exclusion of Negroes by the state violated the Fourteenth Amendment's mandate of equal protection of the laws.

Another minority group for which the Court showed a measure of solicitude was aliens. In *Truax v. Raich* (1915), the Court invalidated, for denying equal protection, an Arizona law that discriminated against aliens in employment. In *Terrance v. Thompson* (1923), however, the Court differentiated between this right and the right to own land. Further manifestations of the xenophobia of the 1920's were the quota provision in the Immigration Act of 1924 and the decision in *Mahler v. Eby* (1924), which upheld a federal statute facilitating the deportation of undesirable aliens. Chief Justice Taft explained that "the right to expel aliens is a sovereign power, necessary to the safety to the country, and only limited by treaty obligations."

Broadening the Concept of Liberty to Protect Freedom of Expression

196. Nationalization of First Amendment Freedoms

Gitlow v. New York, 268 U.S. 652 (1925).

SANFORD, J.: Benjamin Gitlow was indicted in the supreme court of New York, with three others, for the statutory crime of criminal anarchy. . . .

The indictment was in two counts. The first charged that the defendants had advocated, advised, and taught the duty, necessity, and propriety of overthrowing and overturning organized government by force, violence, and unlawful means, by certain writings therein set forth, entitled, "The Left Wing Manifesto"; the second, that the defendants had printed, published, and knowingly circulated and distributed a certain paper called "The Revolutionary Age," containing the writings set forth in the first count, advocating, advising, and teaching the doctrine that organized government should be overthrown by force, violence, and unlawful means. . . .

There was no evidence of any effect resulting from the publication and circulation of the Manifesto.

No witnesses were offered in behalf of the defendant. . . .

The sole contention here is, essentially, that, as there was no evidence of any concrete result flowing from the publication of the Manifesto, or of circumstances showing the likelihood of such result, the statute as construed and applied by the trial court penalizes the mere utterance, as such, of "doctrine" having no quality of incitement, without regard either to the circumstances of its utterance or to the likelihood of unlawful sequences; and that, as the exercise of the right of free expression with relation to government is only punishable "in circumstances involving likelihood of substantive evil," the statute contravenes the due process clause of the Fourteenth Amendment. The argument in support of this contention rests primarily upon the following propositions: first, that the "liberty" protected by the Fourteenth Amendment includes the liberty of speech and of the press; and second, that while liberty of expression "is not absolute," it may be restrained "only in circumstances where its exercise bears a causal relation with some substantive evil, consummated, attempted, or likely"; and as the statute "takes no account of circumstances," it unduly restrains this liberty, and is therefore unconstitutional.

The precise question presented, and the only question which we can consider under this writ of error, then, is whether the statute, as construed and applied in this case by the state courts, deprived the defendant of his liberty of expression, in violation of the due process clause of the Fourteenth Amendment. . . .

For the present purposes we may and do assume that freedom of speech and of the press—which are protected by the First Amendment from abridgment by Congress—are among the fundamental personal rights and "liberties" protected by the due process clause of the Fourteenth Amendment from impairment by the states. . . .

That a state, in the exercise of its police power, may punish those who abuse this freedom by utterances inimical to the public welfare, tending to corrupt public morals, incite to crime, or disturb the public peace, is not open to question. . . .

And, for yet more imperative reasons, a State may punish utterances endangering the foundations of organized government and threatening its overthrow by unlawful means. These imperil its own existence as a constitutional state. Freedom of speech and press, said Story . . . , does not protect disturbances of the public peace or the attempt to subvert the government. It does not protect publications or teachings which tend to subvert or imperil the government, or to impede or hinder it in the performance of its governmental duties. It does not protect publications prompting the overthrow of government by force; the punishment of those who publish articles which tend to destroy organized society being essential to the security of freedom and the stability of the state. And a State may penalize utterances which openly advocate the overthrow of the representative and constitutional form of government of the United States and the several states, by violence or other unlawful means. In short, this freedom does not deprive a State of the primary and essential right of self-preservation, which, so long as human governments endure, they cannot be denied. . . .

By enacting the present statute the State has determined, through its legislative body, that utterances advocating the overthrow of organized government by force, violence, and unlawful means, are so inimical to the general welfare, and involve such danger of substantive evil, that they may be penalized in the exercise of its police power. That determination must be given great weight. Every presumption is to be indulged in favor of the validity of the statute. . . . That utterances inciting to the overthrow of organized government by unlawful means present a sufficient danger of substantive evil to bring their punishment within the range of legislative discretion is clear. Such utterances, by their very nature, involve danger to the public peace and to the security of the state. They threaten breaches of the peace and ultimate revolution. And the immediate danger is none the less real and substantial because the effect of a given utterance cannot be accurately foreseen. The state cannot reasonably be required to measure the danger from every such utterance in the nice balance of a jeweler's scale. A single revolutionary spark may kindle a fire that, smoldering for a time, may burst into a sweeping and destructive conflagration. It cannot be said that the state is acting arbitrarily or unreasonably when, in the exercise of its judgment as to the measures necessary to protect the public peace and safety, it seeks to extinguish the spark without waiting until it has enkindled the flame or blazed into the conflagration. It cannot reasonably be required to defer the adoption of measures for its own peace and safety until the revolutionary utterances lead to actual disturbances of the public peace or imminent and immediate danger of its own destruction; but it may, in the exercise of its judgment, suppress the threatened danger in its incipiency. . . .

We cannot hold that the present statute is an arbitrary or unreasonable exercise of the police power of the state, unwarrantably infringing the freedom of speech or press; and we must and do sustain its constitutionality.

This being so it may be applied to every utterance—not too trivial to be beneath the notice of the law—which is of such a character and used with such intent and purpose as to bring it within the prohibition of the statute. . . . In other words, when the legislative body has determined generally, in the constitutional exercise of its discretion, that utterances of a certain kind involve such danger of substantive evil that they may be punished, the question whether any specific utterance coming within the prohibited class is likely, in and of itself, to bring about the substantive evil, is not open to consideration. It is sufficient that the statute itself be constitutional, and that the use of the language comes within its prohibition. . . .

197. *"It is the function of speech to free men from the bondage of irrational fears."*

Whitney v. California, 274 U.S. 357 (1927).

BRANDEIS, J., concurring: . . . The right of free speech, the right to teach and the right of assembly are, of course, fundamental rights. . . . These may not be denied or abridged. But, although the rights of free speech and assembly are fundamental, they are not in their nature absolute. Their exercise is subject to restriction, if the particular restriction proposed is required in order to protect the State from destruction or from serious injury, political, economic or moral. That the necessity which is essential to a valid restriction does not exist unless speech would produce, or is intended to produce, a clear and imminent danger of some substantive evil which the State constitutionally may seek to prevent has been settled. . . .

This Court has not yet fixed the standard by which to determine when a danger shall be deemed clear; how remote the danger may be and yet be deemed present; and what degree of evil shall be deemed sufficiently substantial to justify resort to abridgement of free speech and assembly as the means of protection. To reach sound conclusions on these matters, we must bear in mind why a State is, ordinarily, denied the power to prohibit dissemination of social, economic and political doctrine which a vast majority of its citizens believes to be false and fraught with evil consequence.

Those who won our independence believed that the final end of the State was to make men free to develop their faculties; and that in its government the deliberative forces should prevail over the arbitrary. They valued liberty both as an end and as a means. They believed liberty to be the secret of happiness and courage to be the secret of liberty. They believed that freedom to think as you will and to speak as you think are means indispensable to the discovery and spread of political truth; that without free speech and assembly discussion would be futile; that with them, discussion affords ordinarily adequate protection against the dissemination of noxious doctrine; that the greatest menace to freedom is an inert people; that public discussion is a political duty; and that this should be a fundamental principle of the American government. They recognized the risks to which all human institutions are subject. But they knew that order cannot be secured merely through fear of punishment for its infraction; that it is hazardous to discourage thought, hope and imagination; that fear breeds repression; that repression breeds hate; that hate menaces stable government; that the path of safety lies in the opportunity to discuss freely supposed grievances and proposed remedies; and that the fitting remedy for evil counsels is good ones. Believing in the power of reason as applied through public discussion, they eschewed silence coerced by law—the argument of force in its worst form. Recognizing the occasional tyrannies of governing majorities, they amended the Constitution so that free speech and assembly should be guaranteed.

Fear of serious injury cannot alone justify suppression of free speech and assembly. Men feared witches and burnt women. It is the function of speech to free men from the bondage of irrational fears. To justify suppression of free speech there must be reasonable ground to fear that serious evil will result if free speech is practiced. There must be a reasonable ground to believe that the danger apprehended is imminent. There must be reasonable ground to believe that the evil to be prevented is a serious one. Every denunciation of existing law tends in some measure to increase the probability that there will be violation of it. Condonation of a breach enhances the probability. Propagation of the criminal state of mind by teaching syndicalism increases it. Advocacy of law-breaking heightens it still further. But even advocacy of violation, however reprehensible morally, is not a justification for denying free speech where the advocacy falls short of incitement and there is nothing to indicate that advocacy would be immediately acted on. The wide difference between advocacy and incitement, between preparation and attempt, between assembling and conspiracy, must be borne in mind. In order to support a finding of a clear and present danger it must be shown either that immediate serious violence was to be expected or was advocated, or that the past conduct furnished reason to believe that such advocacy was then contemplated.

Those who won our independence by revolution were not cowards. They did not fear political change. They did not exalt order at the cost of liberty. To courageous, self-reliant men, with confidence in the power of free and fearless reasoning applied through the processes of popular government, no danger flowing from speech can be deemed clear and present, unless the incidence of the evil apprehended is so imminent that it may befall before there is an opportunity for full discussion. If there be time to expose through discussion the falsehood and fallacies, to avert the evil by processes of education, the remedy to be applied is more speech, not enforced silence. Only an emergency can justify repression. Such must be the rule if authority is to be reconciled with freedom. Such, in my opinion, is the command of the Constitution. It is therefore always open to Americans to challenge a law abridging free speech and assembly by showing that there was no emergency justifying it.

Moreover, even imminent danger cannot justify resort to prohibition of these functions essential to effective democracy, unless the evil apprehended is relatively serious. Prohibition of free speech and assembly is a measure so stringent that it would be inappropriate as the means for averting a relatively trivial harm to society. A police measure may be unconstitutional merely because the remedy, although effective as means of protection, is unduly harsh or oppressive. . . . Among free men, the deterrents ordinarily to be applied to prevent crime are education and punishment for violations of the law, not abridgment of the rights of free speech and assembly. . . .

Whenever the fundamental rights of free speech and assembly are alleged to have been invaded, it must remain open to a defendant to present the issue whether there actually did exist at the time a clear danger; whether the danger, if any, was imminent; and whether the evil apprehended was one so substantial as to justify the stringent restriction interposed by the legislature. . . .

Whether in 1919, when Miss Whitney did the things complained of, there was in California such clear and present danger of serious evil, might have been made the important issue in the case. She might have required that the issue be determined either by the court or the jury. She claimed below that the statute as applied to her violated the Federal Constitution; but she did not claim that it was void because there was no clear and present danger of serious evil, nor did she request that the existence of these conditions of a valid measure thus restricting the rights of free speech and assembly be passed upon by the court or jury. On the other hand, there was evidence on which the court or jury might have found that such danger existed. I am unable to assent to the suggestion in the opinion of the Court that assembling with a political party, formed to advocate the desirability of a proletarian revolution by mass action at some date necessarily far in the future, is not a right within the protection of the Fourteenth Amendment. . . .

198. *Red Flags, Communism, and "Dangerous Tendency"*

Stromberg v. California, 283 U.S. 359 (1931).

HUGHES, C.J.: . . . It appears that the appellant, a young woman of nineteen, a citizen of the United States by birth, was one of the supervisors of a summer camp for children, between ten and fifteen years of age, in the foothills of the San Bernardina mountains. Appellant led the children in their daily study, teaching them history and economics. "Among other things, the children were taught class consciousness, the solidarity of the workers, and the theory that the workers of the world are of one blood and brothers all." Appellant was a member of the Young Communist League, an international organization affiliated with the Communist Party. The charge against her concerned a daily ceremony at the camp, in which the appellant supervised and directed the children in raising a red flag, "a camp-made reproduction of the flag of Soviet Russia, which was also the flag of the Communist Party in the United States." . . . The stipulation further shows that "a library was maintained at the camp containing a large number of books, papers and pamphlets, including much radical communist propaganda, specimens of which are quoted in the opinion of the state court." These quotations abundantly demonstrated that the books and pamphlets contained incitements to violence and to "armed uprisings," teaching "the indispensability of a desperate, bloody, destructive war as the immediate task of the coming action." . . .

It has been determined that the conception of liberty under the due process clause of the Fourteenth Amendment embraces the right of free speech. . . . The right is not an absolute one, and the State in the exercise of its police power may punish the abuse of this freedom. There is no question but that the State may thus provide for the punishment of those who indulge in utterances which incite to violence and crime and threaten the overthrow of organized government by unlawful means. There is no constitutional immunity for such conduct abhorrent to our institutions. . . .

The question is thus narrowed to that of the validity of the first clause, that is, with respect to the display of the flag "as a sign, symbol or emblem of opposition to organized government," and the construction which the state court has placed upon this clause removes every element of doubt. The state court recognized the indefiniteness and ambiguity of the clause. The court considered that it might be construed as embracing conduct which the State could not constitutionally prohibit. Thus it was said that the clause "might be construed to include the peaceful and orderly opposition to a government as organized and controlled by one political party by those of another political party equally high minded and patriotic, which did not agree with the one in power. It might also be construed to include peaceful and orderly opposition to government by legal means and within constitutional limitations." The maintenance of the opportunity for free political discussion to the end that government may be responsive to the will of the people and that changes may be obtained by lawful means, an opportunity essential to the security of the Republic, is a fundamental principle of our constitutional system. A statute which, upon its face, and as authoritatively construed, is so vague and indefinite as to permit the punishment of the fair use of this opportunity is repugnant to the guarantee of liberty contained in the Fourteenth Amendment. The first clause of the statute being invalid upon its face, the conviction of the appellant, which so far as the record discloses may have rested upon that clause exclusively, must be set aside.

199. *The Court Invalidates the Minnesota "Gag Law"*

Near v. Minnesota, 283 U.S. 697 (1931).

HUGHES, C.J.: . . . This statute for the suppression as a public nuisance of a newspaper or periodical, is unusual, if not unique, and raises questions of grave importance transcending the local interests involved in the particular action. It is no longer open to doubt that the liberty of the press, and of speech, is within the liberty safeguarded by the due process clause of the Fourteenth Amendment from invasion by state action. . . . Liberty of speech, and of the press, is also not an absolute right, and the state may punish its abuse. . . . Liberty, in each of its phases, has its history and connotation and, in the present instance, the inquiry is as to the historic conception of the liberty of the press and whether the statute under review violates the essential attributes of that liberty. . . .

If we cut through mere details of procedure, the operation and effect of the statute in substance is that public authorities may bring the owner or publisher of a newspaper or periodical before a judge upon a charge of conducting a business of publishing scandalous and defamatory matter—in particular that the matter consists of charges against public officers of official dereliction—and unless the owner or publisher is able and disposed to bring competent evidence to satisfy the judge that the charges are true and are published with good motives and for justifiable ends, his newspaper or periodical is suppressed and further publication is made punishable as a contempt. This is of the essence of censorship.

The question is whether a statute authorizing such proceedings in restraint of publication is consistent with the conception of the liberty of the press as historically conceived and guaranteed. In determining the extent of the constitutional protection, it has been generally, if not universally, considered that it is the chief purpose of the guaranty to prevent previous restraints upon publication. The struggle in England, directed against the legislative power of the licenser, resulted in renunciation of the censorship of the press. . . . The liberty deemed to be established was thus described by Blackstone: "The liberty of the press is indeed essential to the nature of a free state; but this consists in laying no *previous* restraints upon publications, and not in freedom from censure for criminal matter when published. . . ."

The criticism upon Blackstone's statement has not been because immunity from previous restraint upon publication has not been regarded as deserving of special emphasis, but chiefly because that immunity cannot be deemed to exhaust the conception of the liberty guaranteed by state and federal constitutions. The point of criticism has been "that the mere exemption from previous restraints cannot be all that is secured by the constitutional provisions"; and that "the liberty of the press might be rendered a mockery and a delusion, and the phrase itself a by-word, if, while every man was at liberty to publish what he pleased, the public authorities might nevertheless punish him for harmless publications." . . . But it is recognized that punishment for the abuse of the liberty accorded to the press is essential to the protection of the public, and that the common law rules that subject the libeler to responsibility for the public offense, as well as for the private injury, are not abolished by the protection extended in our constitutions. . . . In the present case, we have no occasion to inquire as to the permissible scope of subsequent punishment. For whatever wrong the appellant has committed or may commit, by his publications, the state appropriately affords both public and private redress by its libel laws. As has been noted, the statute in question does not deal with punishments; it provides for no punishment, except in case of contempt for violation of the court's order, but for suppression and injunction, that is, for restraint upon publication.

The objection has also been made that the principle as to immunity from previous restraint is stated too broadly, if ever such restraint is deemed to be prohibited. That is undoubtedly true; the protection even as to previous restraint is not absolutely unlimited. But the limitation has been recognized only in exceptional cases: "When a nation is at war many things that might be said in time of peace are such a hindrance to its effort that their utterance will not be endured so long as men fight and that no court could regard them as protected by any constitutional right." *Schenck v. United States*. . . .

The exceptional nature of its limitations places in a strong light the general conception that liberty of the press, historically considered and taken up by the federal Constitution, has meant, principally although not exclusively, immunity from previous restraints or censorship. The conception of the liberty of the press in this country had broadened with the exigencies of the colonial period and with the efforts to secure freedom from oppressive administration. That liberty was especially cherished for the immunity it afforded from previous restraint of the publication of censure of public officers and charges of official misconduct. . . .

The importance of this immunity has not lessened. While reckless assaults upon public men, and efforts to bring obloquy upon those who are endeavoring faithfully to discharge official duties, exert a baleful influence and deserve the severest condemnation in public opinion, it cannot be said that this abuse is greater, and it is believed to be less, than that which characterized the period in which our institutions took shape. Meanwhile, the administration of government has become more complex, the opportunities for malfeasance and corruption have multiplied, crime has grown to most serious proportions, and the danger of its protection by unfaithful officials and of the impairment of the fundamental security of life and property by criminal alliances and official neglect, emphasizes the primary need of a vigilant and courageous press, especially in great cities. The fact that the liberty of the press may be abused by miscreant purveyors of scandal does not make any the less necessary the immunity of the press from previous restraint in dealing with official misconduct. Subsequent punishment for such abuses as may exist is the appropriate remedy, consistent with constitutional privilege. . . .

The statute in question cannot be justified by reason of the fact that the publisher is permitted to show, before injunction issues, that the matter published is true and is published with good motives and for justifiable ends. If such a statute, authorizing suppression and injunction on such a basis, is constitutionally valid, it would be equally permissible for the legislature to provide that at any time the publisher of any newspaper could be brought before a court, or even an administrative officer (as the constitutional protection may not be regarded as resting on mere procedural details) and required to produce proof of the truth of his publication, or of what he intended to publish, and of his motives, or stand enjoined. If this can be done, the legislature may provide machinery for determining in the complete exercise of its discretion what are justifiable ends and restrain publication accordingly. And it would be but a step to a complete system of censorship. The recognition of authority to impose previous restraint upon publication in order to protect the community against the circulation of charges of misconduct, and especially of official misconduct, necessarily would carry with it the admission of the authority of the censor against which the constitutional barrier was erected. The preliminary freedom, by virtue of the very reason for its existence, does not depend, as this Court has said, on proof of truth. . . .

Equally unavailing is the insistence that the statute is designed to prevent the circulation of scandal which tends to disturb the public peace and to provoke assaults and the commission of crime. Charges of reprehensible conduct, and in particular of official malfeasance, unquestionably create a public scandal, but the theory of the constitutional guaranty is that even a more serious public evil would be caused by authority to prevent publication. . . . There is nothing new in the fact that charges of reprehensible conduct may create resentment and the disposition to resort to violent means of redress, but this well-understood tendency did not alter the determination to protect the press against censorship and restraint upon publication. . . . The danger of violent reactions becomes greater with effective organization of defiant groups resenting exposure, and if this consideration warranted legislative interference with the initial freedom of publication, the constitutional protection would be reduced to a mere form of words.

For these reasons we hold the statute, so far as it authorized the proceedings in this action under clause (b) of section one, to be an infringement of the liberty of the press guaranteed by the Fourteenth Amendment. . . .

Due Process and the Rights of Accused

SEARCHES AND SEIZURES

200. *Is Wire Tapping an Illegal Search and Seizure?*

Olmstead v. U.S., 277 U.S. 438 (1928).

TAFT, C.J.: . . . The Fourth Amendment provides: "The right of the people to be secure in their persons, houses, papers, and effects, against unreasonable searches and seizures, shall not be violated. . . ." And the Fifth: "No person . . . shall be compelled in any criminal case to be a witness against himself. . . ."

There is no room in the present case for applying the Fifth Amendment unless the Fourth Amendment was first violated. There was no evidence of compulsion to induce the defendants to talk over their many telephones. They were continually and voluntarily transacting business without knowledge of the interception. Our consideration must be confined to the Fourth Amendment. . . .

The well known historical purpose of the Fourth Amendment, directed against general warrants and writs of assistance, was to prevent the use of governmental force to search a man's house, his person, his papers, and his effects, and to prevent their seizure against his will. . . .

The Amendment itself shows that the search is to be of material things—the person, the house, his papers or his effects. The description of the warrant necessary to make the proceeding lawful is that it must specify the place to be searched and the person or *things* to be seized. . . .

The language of the Amendment can not be extended and expanded to include telephone wires reaching to the whole world from the defendant's house or office. The intervening wires are not part of his house or office, any more than are the highways along which they are stretched. . . .

Congress may, of course, protect the secrecy of telephone messages by making them, when intercepted, inadmissible in evidence in federal criminal trials, by direct legislation, and thus depart from the common law of evidence. But the courts may not adopt such a policy by attributing an enlarged and unusual meaning to the Fourth Amendment. The reasonable view is that one who installs in his house a telephone instrument with connecting wires intends to project his voice to those quite outside, and that the wires beyond his house and messages while passing over them are not within the protection of the Fourth Amendment. Here those who intercepted the projected voices were not in the house of either party to the conversation.

Neither the cases we have cited nor any of the many federal decisions brought to our attention hold the Fourth Amendment to have been violated as against a defendant unless there has been an official search and seizure of his person or such a seizure of his papers or his tangible material effects or an actual physical invasion of his house "or curtilage" for the purpose of making a seizure.

We think, therefore, that the wire-tapping here disclosed did not amount to a search or seizure within the meaning of the Fourth Amendment. . . .

Some of our number . . . have concluded that there is merit in the twofold objection overruled in both courts below that evidence obtained through intercepting of telephone messages by government agents was inadmissible because the mode of obtaining it was unethical and a misdemeanor under the law of Washington. To avoid any misapprehension of our views of that objection, we shall deal with it in both of its phases. . . .

The common law rule is that the admissibility of evidence is not affected by the illegality of the means by which it was obtained. . . .

Nor can we, without the sanction of congressional enactment, subscribe to the suggestion that the courts have a discretion to exclude evidence, the admission of which is not unconstitutional, because unethically secured. This would be at variance with the common law doctrine generally supported by authority. There is no case that sustains, nor any recognized text book that gives color to such a view. Our general experience shows that much evidence has always been receivable although not obtained by conformity to the highest ethics. The history of criminal trials shows numerous cases of prosecutions of oathbound conspiracies for murder, robbery, and other crimes where officers of the law have disguised themselves and joined the organizations, taken the oaths and given themselves every appearance of active members engaged in the promotion of crime for the purpose of securing evidence. Evidence secured by such means has always been received.

A standard which would forbid the reception of evidence if obtained by other than nice ethical conduct by government officials would make society suffer and give criminals greater immunity than has been known heretofore. In the absence of controlling legislation by Congress, those who realize the difficulties in bringing offenders to justice may well deem it wise that the exclusion of evidence should be confined to cases where rights under the Constitution would be violated by admitting it. . . .

201. *"If the Government becomes a law-breaker, it breeds contempt for law."*

Olmstead v. U.S. (1928).

BRANDEIS, J., dissenting: . . . The government makes no attempt to defend the methods employed by its officers. Indeed, it concedes that if wire-tapping can be deemed a search and seizure within the Fourth Amendment, such wire-tapping as was practised in the case at bar was an unreasonable search and seizure, and that the evidence thus obtained was inadmissible. But it relies on the language of the amendment; and it claims that the protection given thereby cannot properly be held to include a telephone conversation. . . .

When the Fourth and Fifth Amendments were adopted, "the form that evil had theretofore taken" had been necessarily simple. Force and violence were then the only means known to man by which a government could directly effect self-incrimination. It could compel the individual to testify—a compulsion effected, if need be, by torture. It could secure possession of his papers and other articles incident to his private life—a seizure effected, if need be, by breaking and entry. Protection against such invasion of "the sanctities of a man's home and the privacies of life" was provided in the Fourth and Fifth Amendments, by specific language. . . . But "time works changes, brings into existence new conditions and purposes." Subtler and more far-reaching means of invading privacy have become available to the government. Discovery and invention have made it possible for the government, by means far more effective than stretching upon the rack, to obtain disclosure in court of what is whispered in the closet. . . .

The progress of science in furnishing the government with means of espionage is not likely to stop with wire-tapping. Ways may some day be developed by which the government, without removing papers from secret drawers, can reproduce them in court, and by which it will be enabled to expose to a jury the most intimate occurrences of the home. Advances in the psychic and related sciences may bring means of exploring unexpressed beliefs, thoughts and emotions. . . . Can it be that the Constitution affords no protection against such invasions of individual security? . . .

Applying to the Fourth and Fifth Amendments the established rule of construction, the defendants' objections to the evidence obtained by a wire-tapping must, in my opinion, be sustained. It is, of course, immaterial where the physical connection with the telephone wires leading into the defendants' premises was made. And it is also immaterial that the intrusion was in aid of law enforcement. Experience should teach us to be most on our guard to protect liberty when the government's purposes are beneficent. Men born to freedom are naturally alert to repel invasion of their liberty by evil-minded rulers. The greatest dangers to liberty lurk in insidious encroachment by men of zeal, well-meaning, but without understanding.

Independently of the constitutional question, I am of opinion that the judgment should be reversed. By the laws of Washington, wire-tapping is a crime. . . . To prove its case, the government was obliged to lay bare the crimes committed by its officers on its behalf. A federal court should not permit such a prosecution to continue. . . .

Decency, security, and liberty alike demand that government officials shall be subjected to the same rules of conduct that are commands to the citizen. In a government of laws, existence of the government will be imperiled if it fails to observe the law scrupulously. Our government is the potent, the omnipresent, teacher. For good or for ill, it teaches the whole people by its example. Crime is contagious. If the government becomes a law-breaker, it breeds contempt for law; it invites every man to become a law unto himself; it invites anarchy. To declare that in the administration of the criminal law the end justifies the means—to declare that the government may commit crimes in order to secure the conviction of a private criminal—would bring terrible retribution. Against that pernicious doctrine this Court should resolutely set its face.

202. *Jury Trial and the Right to Counsel: The Scottsboro Cases*

Norris v. Alabama, 294 U.S. 587 (1935).

HUGHES, C.J.: . . . There is no controversy as to the constitutional principle involved . . . this Court thus stated the principle in *Carter v. Texas* . . . in relation to exclusion from service on grand juries: "Whenever by any action of a state, whether through its legislature, through its courts, or through its executive or administrative officers, all persons of the African race are excluded, solely because of their race or color, from serving as grand jurors in the criminal prosecution of a person of the African race, the equal protection of the laws is denied to him, contrary to the Fourteenth Amendment.["] . . . The principle is equally applicable to a similar exclusion of negroes from service on petit juries. . . . And although the state statute defining the qualifications of jurors may be fair on its face, the constitutional provision affords protection against action of the state through its administrative officers in effecting the prohibited discrimination. . . . The testimony, as the state court said, tended to show that "in a long number of years no negro had been called for jury service in that county." It appeared that no negro had served on any grand or petit jury in that county within the memory of witnesses who had lived there all their lives. Testimony to that effect was given by men whose ages ran from fifty to seventy-six years. Their testimony was uncontradicted. It was supported by the testimony of officials. The clerk of the jury commission and the clerk of the circuit court had never known of a negro serving on a grand jury in Jackson County. The court reporter, who had not missed a session in that county in twenty-four years, and two jury commissioners testified to the same effect. One of the latter, who was a member of the commission which made up the jury roll for the grand jury which found the indictment, testified that he had "never known of a single instance where any negro sat on any grand or petit jury in the entire history of that county."

That testimony in itself made out a *prima facie* case of the denial of the equal protection which the Constitution guarantees. . . . The case thus made was supplemented by direct testimony that specified negroes, thirty or more in number, were qualified for jury service. Among these were negroes who were members of school boards, or trustees, of colored schools, and property owners and householders. It also appeared that negroes from that county had been called for jury service in the federal court. Several of those who were thus described as qualified were witnesses. While there was testimony which cast doubt upon the qualifications of some of the negroes who had been named, and there was also general testimony by the editor of a local newspaper who gave his opinion as to the lack of "sound judgment" of the "good negroes" in Jackson County, we think that the definite testimony as to the actual qualifications of individual negroes, which was not met by any testimony equally direct, showed that there were negroes in Jackson County qualified for jury service. . . .

We are of the opinion that the evidence required a different result from that reached in the state court. We think that the evidence that for a generation or longer no negro had been called for service on any jury in Jackson County, that there were negroes qualified for jury service, that according to the practice of the jury commission their names would normally appear on the preliminary list of male citizens of the requisite age but that no names of negroes were placed on the jury roll, and the testimony with respect to the lack of appropriate consideration of the qualifications of negroes, established the discrimination which the Constitution forbids. The motion to quash the indictment upon that ground should have been granted. . . .

The evidence that for many years no negro had been called for jury service itself tended to show the absence of the names of negroes from the jury rolls, and the state made no effort to prove their presence. . . .

That showing as to the long-continued exclusion of negroes from jury service, and as to the many negroes qualified for that service, could not be met by mere generalities. If, in the presence of such testimony as defendant adduced, the mere general assertions by officials of their performance of duty were to be accepted as an adequate justification for the complete exclusion of negroes from jury service, the constitutional provision—adopted with special reference to their protection—would be but a vain and illusory requirement. . . .

We are concerned only with the federal question which we have discussed, and in view of the denial of the federal right suitably asserted, the judgment must be reversed and the cause remanded for further proceedings not inconsistent with this opinion. . . .

CHAPTER XXII

The New Deal and the Old Supreme Court

To cope with the most disastrous economic emergency which the American people had ever faced, President Franklin D. Roosevelt launched a vigorous New Deal, predicated on the proposition that drastic federal control over banking and finance, labor, manufacturing, and agriculture could be effected within the American constitutional framework. "Our Constitution," the new President declared in his inaugural address, "is so simple, so practical that it is possible always to meet extraordinary needs by changes in emphasis and arrangement without loss of essential form." Unless this view was shared by the Supreme Court, however, New Deal legislation would have to travel a rough road, for never before in the country's history had federal authority over national economic life been asserted as extensively as it was under Roosevelt's leadership.

The fate of the relief, recovery, and reform programs depended in the final analysis on which set of judicial precedents the Supreme Court applied—that which stressed broad commerce and taxing powers to control industry, or that which relied on a definition of federal authority as narrow as the Knight (Chapter XV) and Dagenhart (Chapter XVIII) rules. Unfortunately for the New Deal, the Court of the early 1930's was composed of four justices highly conservative in their economic views and bitterly opposed to any extension of governmental power over the nation's social and economic life. This solid phalanx of Justices Butler, McReynolds, Sutherland, and Van Devanter was frequently joined by either Justice Roberts or Chief Justice Hughes, or both, enabling it to dominate judicial action. Only Justices Brandeis, Cardozo, and Stone consistently displayed a social consciousness and a willingness to experiment with new approaches to pressing economic problems.

During Roosevelt's first term, his administration won but two limited victories in the constitutional warfare. In the "Gold Clause" cases, the Court accepted the Congressional resolution of 1933 which nullified the gold clause in public and private contracts. Although the four conservative justices dissented bitterly—McReynolds, visibly shaken, muttered, "The Constitution is gone!"—these technical decisions established no important precedents for expanded federal power, merely implementing the long-established national authority over monetary matters. In considering a challenge to the constitutionality of the Tennessee Valley Authority, the Court carefully limited its ruling to uphold only the construction of the Wilson Dam and the sale of its surplus power (*Ashwander v. T. V. A.* [*No.* 203]). Because the dam had been built under the National Defense Act, the ruling was based primarily upon the war power and did not deal with the constitutionality of the whole T. V. A. The decision therefore left the door open for a variety of challenges on other grounds by opponents of T. V. A.

These minor victories were more than offset by a stunning series of defeats. Between January, 1935, and May, 1936, twelve major statutes were ruled unconstitutional in decisions which frequently involved a return to nineteenth-century legal concepts, rejected by the Court even during the "normalcy" of the 1920's. The measures invalidated were of such wide application that the principal programs of the early New Deal were sapped of all vitality. Significantly, the first attack was on the National Industrial Recovery Act. This measure provided for federal control of the entire industrial structure of the country through the enforcement of codes of fair practice and procedure. In the "Hot Oil" case (*Panama Refining Co. v. Ryan, 1935*), the Court upset the provision that granted the President power to control interstate oil shipments, on the ground, never stated previously, that such extensive executive authority resulted from an unconstitutional delegation of legislative power. Although Congress hastened to revise the statute to alleviate judicial misgivings, the oil decision was a portent of things to come. Five months later, the Court relied on the same constitutional concept, plus an extremely narrow interpretation of the commerce clause, and invalidated the entire N. I. R. A. in the famous "sick chicken" case (*Schechter Poultry Corporation v. U.S.* [*No.* 204]). Asked to comment on the ruling in a press conference, the President responded bitterly: "We have been relegated to the horse-and-buggy definition of interstate commerce."

In 1936, a series of fateful decisions confirmed the Schechter doctrine and created a constitutional dilemma for the administration. The Agricultural Adjustment Act was the next to fall. Based on the assumption that the farmer's plight was caused by overproduction, the A. A. A. of 1933 provided benefit payments for acreage reduction; the amount paid was to be recovered by the government through a general tax on the processing of the commodity. In *U.S. v. Butler* (No. 205), Justice Roberts, speaking for six of the Justices, overruled the measure as "a scheme for purchasing with Federal Funds submission to Federal Regulation of a subject reserved to the States." The opinion was noteworthy both for Roberts's contention that the Court's work was purely mechanical, and for his deep probing into the meaning of the general welfare clause. He concluded that the federal government possessed the power to tax and appropriate for the general welfare apart from the other enumerated powers of Congress, but then ruled that even this expansive authority could not justify the processing tax since it was not really a tax but a part of an illegal system for regulating agricultural production. In a stinging dissent, Justice Stone berated the inconsistency of the majority's position and warned against a "tortured construction of the Constitution."

Following the death of the N. I. R. A., the government did not again seek to control the nation's economy through one omnibus law. Instead, its programs were carefully limited to specific areas and groups. Typical was the Bituminous Coal Act of 1935, which enjoyed the support of both miners and operators. The measure was intended to control prices and wages and enforce collective bargaining in the "sick" coal industry; it sought constitutional justification in the commerce clause. President Roosevelt requested Congress to pass the bill "despite admitted doubts as to whether the Supreme Court would uphold it." Strengthened by the growing Liberty League and viewing the Supreme Court as a partner, business began a test case against the law the day it was passed. When the case reached the Supreme Court, the conservative majority, consistent with its Schechter ruling, nullified the entire act, reverting to the "direct-indirect" concept of the Knight and Dagenhart cases (*Carter v. Carter Coal Company* [No. 206]). Although many agreed with Justice Cardozo that "a great principle of constitutional law is not susceptible of comprehensive statement in an adjective," the ruling stood as an ominous threat to other recently passed legislation, such as the National Labor Relations Act, the Social Security Act, and the Public Utility Holding Company Act.

Bolstered by a smashing election victory in 1936, President Roosevelt set out to "save the Constitution from the Court and the Court from itself." In February, 1937, a bill was submitted to Congress for reorganizing the federal judiciary. Reminiscent of a measure proposed by Justice McReynolds while Attorney General under Woodrow Wilson, the act's most controversial provision would have increased the membership of the Supreme Court from nine to a maximum of fifteen, if judges reaching the age of seventy refused to retire. Other provisions would have reorganized lower federal courts and modified judicial procedure. The original measure gave no indication of motive, carefully avoiding any suggestion of the desire to alter "reactionary" court decisions, but in a "fireside chat" on March 9, the President left no doubts as to his purposes and goals (No. 207).

The "court-packing" bill precipitated the bitterest domestic controversy of Roosevelt's long Presidency. Attacked as executive usurpation and an attempt to destroy judicial independence, the measure became a political rallying point for Republicans and dissident Democrats, who until that time had been hesitant to launch a head-on attack on the popular Chief Executive. Following heated hearings, the Senate Judiciary Committee in June rejected the proposal in a report which insinuated that the President was trying to subvert American institutions and overturn the Constitution by questionable methods (No. 208).

Although this report deplored any attempt to make the federal judiciary "subservient to the pressures of public opinion of the hour," the Court, unaltered in personnel, had already been responding to such pressures in a series of decisions validating New Deal legislation. The first of these was indicative of the Court's changed attitude. Federal minimum wage legislation had been precluded for years by the Adkins ruling (Chapter XX), and when a New York State minimum wage law was challenged in 1936, the Justices had held, in a 5 to 4 decision (*Morehead v. N.Y. ex rel. Tipaldo*), that such legislation was also beyond the authority of the states. At the height of the judiciary controversy, Justice Roberts reversed his stand of ten months earlier and joined a majority of five, led by Chief Justice Hughes, in upholding a similar minimum wage statute of the State of Washington (*West Coast Hotel Co. v. Parrish* [No. 209]). The opinion specifically overruled the Adkins case, and although Hughes carefully avoided a positive reversal of the New York decision, constitutional lawyers agreed that this was done primarily to save embarrassment; it certainly did not hide the clear implication that the latter was also invalid.

The Parrish decision inaugurated a general reappraisal of New Deal legislation, and Court approval removed the administration's chief cause of concern over the high tribunal. Thus, as a journalist of the day put it, "a switch in time saved nine." Roosevelt had accomplished his original desire to remove the judicial roadblock to his programs. The subsequent defeat of the "court-packing" plan was accepted with reluctance but with a knowledge that a chastened judiciary had now heeded Justice Stone's admonition in his Butler dissent: "For the removal of unwise laws from the statute books, appeal lies not to the courts but to the ballot and to the processes of democratic government."

Judicial Review of National Control over Economic Regulation

203. *The New Deal Wins a Limited Judicial Victory*

Ashwander v. T. V. A., 297 U.S. 288 (1936).

HUGHES, C.J.: . . . The Government's contention is that the Wilson Dam was constructed, and the power plant connected with it was installed, in the exercise by the Congress of its war and commerce powers, that is, for the purposes of national defense and the improvement of navigation. . . .

We may take judicial notice of the international situation at the time the Act of 1916 was passed, and it cannot be successfully disputed that the Wilson Dam and its auxiliary plants, including the hydro-electric power plant, are, and were intended to be, adapted to the purposes of national defense. While the District Court found that there is no intention to use the nitrate plants or the hydro-electric units installed at Wilson Dam for the production of war materials in time of peace, "the maintenance of said properties in operating condition and the assurance of an abundant supply of electric energy in the event of war, constitute national defense assets." This finding has ample support.

The Act of 1916 also had in view "improvements to navigation." Commerce includes navigation. "All America understands, and has uniformly understood," said Chief Justice Marshall in *Gibbons v. Ogden*, . . . "the word 'commerce,' to comprehend navigation." The power to regulate interstate commerce embraces the power to keep the navigable rivers of the United States free from obstructions to navigation and to remove such obstructions when they exist. . . .

The Government acquired full title to the dam site, with all riparian rights. The power of falling water was an inevitable incident of the construction of the dam. That water power came into the exclusive control of the Federal Government. The mechanical energy was convertible into electric energy, and the water power, the right to convert it into electric energy, and the electric energy thus produced, constitute property belonging to the United States. . . .

Authority to dispose of property constitutionally acquired by the United States is expressly granted to the Congress by §3 of Article IV of the Constitution. This section provides:

> The Congress shall have Power to dispose of and make all needful Rules and Regulations respecting the Territory or other Property belonging to the United States; and nothing in this Constitution shall be so construed as to Prejudice any Claims of the United States, or of any particular State.

To the extent that the power of disposition is thus expressly conferred, it is manifest that the Tenth Amendment is not applicable. And the Ninth Amendment (which petitioners also invoke) in insuring the maintenance of the rights retained by the people does not withdraw the rights which are expressly granted to the Federal Government. . . .

As to the mere sale of surplus energy, nothing need be added to what we have said as to the constitutional authority to dispose. The Government could lease or sell and fix the terms. Sales of surplus energy to the Power Company by the Authority continued a practice begun by the Government several years before. The contemplated interchange of energy is a form of disposition and presents no questions which are essentially different from those that are pertinent to sales.

The transmission lines which the Authority undertakes to purchase from the Power Company lead from the Wilson Dam to a large area within about fifty miles of the dam. These lines provide the means of distributing the electric energy, generated at the dam, to a large population. They furnish a method of reaching a market. The alternative method is to sell the surplus energy at the dam, and the market there appears to be limited to one purchaser, the Alabama Power Company, and its affiliated interests. We know of no constitutional ground upon which the Federal Government can be denied the right to seek a wider market. We suppose that in the early days of mining in the West, if the Government had undertaken to operate a silver mine on its domain, it could have acquired the mules or horses and equipment to carry its silver to market. And the transmission lines for electric energy are but a facility for conveying to market that particular sort of property, and the acquisition of these lines raises no different constitutional question, unless in some way there is an invasion of the rights reserved to the State or to the people. We find no basis for concluding that the limited undertaking with the Alabama Power Company amounts to such an invasion. Certainly, the Alabama Power Company has no constitutional right to insist that it shall be the sole purchaser of the energy generated at the Wilson Dam; that the energy shall be sold to it or go to waste.

We limit our decision to the case before us, as we have defined it. The argument is earnestly presented that the Government by virtue of its ownership of the dam and power plant could not establish a steel mill and make and sell steel products, or a factory to manufacture clothing or shoes for the public, and thus attempt to make its ownership of energy, generated at its dam, a means of carrying on competitive commercial enterprises and thus drawing to the Federal Government the conduct and management of business having no relation to the purposes for which the Federal Government was established. The picture is eloquently drawn but we deem it to be irrelevant to the issue here. The Government is not using the water power at the Wilson Dam to establish any industry or business. It is not using the energy generated at the dam to manufacture commodities of any sort for the public. The Government is disposing of the energy itself which simply is the mechanical energy, incidental to falling water at the dam, converted into the electric energy which is susceptible of transmission. The question here is simply as to the acquisition of the transmission lines as a facility for the disposal of that energy. And the Government rightly conceded at the bar, in substance, that it was without constitutional authority to acquire or dispose of such energy except as it comes into being in the operation of works constructed in the exercise of some power delegated to the United States. As we have said, these transmission lines lead directly from the dam, which has been lawfully constructed, and the question of the constitutional right of the Government to acquire or operate local or urban distribution systems is not involved. We express no opinion as to the validity of such an effort, as to the status of any other dam or power development in the Tennessee Valley, whether connected with or apart from the Wilson Dam, or as to the validity of the Tennessee Valley Authority Act or of the claims made in the pronouncements and program of the Authority apart from the questions we have discussed in relation to the particular provisions of the contract of January 4, 1934, affecting the Alabama Power Company.

204. *The N. I. R. A. and the "Sick Chicken" Case*

Schechter Poultry Corporation v. U.S., 295 U.S. 495 (1935).

HUGHES, C.J.: . . . Two preliminary points are stressed by the Government with respect to the appropriate approach to the important questions presented. We are told that the provision of the statute authorizing the adoption of codes must be viewed in the light of the grave national crisis with which Congress was confronted. Undoubtedly, the conditions to which power is addressed are always to be considered when the exercise of power is challenged. Extraordinary conditions may call for extraordinary remedies. But the argument necessarily stops short of an attempt to justify action which lies outside the sphere of constitutional authority. Extraordinary conditions do not create or enlarge constitutional power. The Constitution established a national government with powers deemed to be adequate, as they have proved to be both in war and peace, but these powers of the national government are limited by the constitutional grants. Those who act under these grants are not at liberty to transcend the imposed limits because they believe that more or different power is necessary. Such assertions of extraconstitutional authority were anticipated and precluded by the explicit terms of the Tenth Amendment. . . .

The further point is urged that the national crisis demanded a broad and intensive coöperative effort by those engaged in trade and industry, and that this necessary cooperation was sought to be fostered by permitting them to initiate the adoption of codes. But the statutory plan is not simply one for voluntary effort. It does not seek merely to endow voluntary trade or industrial associations or groups with privileges or immunities. It involves the coercive exercise of the lawmaking power. The codes of fair competition, which the statute attempts to authorize, are codes of laws. If valid, they place all persons within their reach under the obligation of positive law, binding equally those who assent and those who do not assent. Violations of the provisions of the codes are punishable as crimes. . . .

The question of the delegation of legislative power. . . . The Congress is not permitted to abdicate or to transfer to others the essential legislative functions with which it is thus vested. We have repeatedly recognized the necessity of adapting legislation to complex conditions involving a host of details with which the national legislature cannot deal directly. We pointed out in the Panama Company case that the Constitution has never been regarded as denying to Congress the necessary resources of flexibility and practicality, which will enable it to perform its function in laying down policies and establishing standards, while leaving to selected instrumentalities the making of subordinate rules within prescribed limits and the determination of facts to which the policy as declared by the legislature is to apply. But we said that the constant recognition of the necessity and validity of such provisions, and the wide range of administrative authority which has been developed by means of them, cannot be allowed to obscure the limitations of the authority to delegate, if our constitutional system is to be maintained. . . .

Such a sweeping delegation of legislative power [as that in the National Industrial Recovery Act] finds no support in the decisions upon which the Government especially relies. . . .

To summarize and conclude upon this point: Section 3 of the Recovery Act is without precedent. It supplies no standards for any trade, industry or activity. It does not undertake to prescribe rules of conduct to be applied to particular states of fact determined by appropriate administrative procedure. Instead of prescribing rules of conduct, it authorizes the making of codes to prescribe them. For that legislative undertaking, §3 sets up no standards, aside from the statement of the general aims of rehabilitation, correction and expansion described in section one. In view of the scope of that broad declaration, and of the nature of the few restrictions that are imposed, the discretion of the President in approving or prescribing codes, and thus enacting laws for the government of trade and industry throughout the country, is virtually unfettered. We think that the code-making authority thus conferred is an unconstitutional delegation of legislative power. . . .

The question of the application of the provisions of the Live Poultry Code to intrastate transactions. . . . This aspect of the case presents the question whether the particular provisions of the Live Poultry Code, which the defendants were convicted for violating and for having conspired to violate, were within the regulating power of Congress.

These provisions relate to the hours and wages of those employed by defendants in their slaughterhouses in Brooklyn and to the sales there made to retail dealers and butchers.

(1) Were these transactions *"in"* interstate commerce? . . .

The undisputed facts . . . afford no warrant for the argument that the poultry handled by defendants at their slaughterhouse markets was in a *"current"* or *"flow"* of interstate commerce and was thus subject to congressional regulation. The mere fact that there may be a constant flow of commodities into a State does not mean that the flow continues after the property has arrived and has become commingled with the mass of property within the State and is there held solely for local disposition and use. So far as the poultry here in question is concerned, the flow in interstate commerce had ceased. The poultry had come to a permanent rest within the State. It was not held, used, or sold by defendants in relation to any further transactions in interstate commerce and was not destined for transportation to other states. Hence, decisions which deal with a stream of interstate commerce—where goods come to rest within a State temporarily and are later to go forward in interstate commerce—and with the regulations of transactions involved in that practical continuity of movement, are not applicable here. . . .

(2) Did the defendants' transactions directly *"affect"* interstate commerce so as to be subject to federal regulation? The power of Congress extends not only to the regulation of transactions which are part of interstate commerce, but to the protection of that commerce from injury. . . .

In determining how far the federal government may go in controlling intrastate transactions upon the ground that they "affect" interstate commerce, there is a necessary and well-established distinction between direct and indirect effects. The precise line can be drawn only as individual cases arise, but the distinction is clear in principle. . . .

The question of chief importance relates to the provisions of the Code as to the hours and wages of those employed in defendants' slaughterhouse markets. It is plain that these requirements are imposed in order to govern the details of defendants' management of their local business. The persons employed in slaughtering and selling in local trade are not employed in interstate commerce. Their hours and wages have no direct relation to interstate commerce. . . . If the federal government may determine the wages and hours of employees in the internal commerce of a State, because of their relation to cost and prices and their indirect effect upon interstate commerce, it would seem that a similar control might be exerted over other elements of cost, also affecting prices, such as the number of employees, rents, advertising, methods of doing business, etc. All the processes of production and distribution that enter into cost could likewise be controlled. If the cost of doing an intrastate business is in itself the permitted object of federal control, the extent of the regulation of cost would be a question of discretion and not of power.

The Government also makes the point that efforts to enact state legislation establishing high labor standards have been impeded by the belief that unless similar action is taken generally, commerce will be diverted from the States adopting such standards, and that this fear of diversion has led to demands for federal legislation on the subject of wages and hours. The apparent implication is that the federal authority under the commerce clause should be deemed to extend to the establishment of rules to govern wages and hours in intrastate trade and industry generally throughout the country, thus overriding the authority of the States to deal with domestic problems arising from labor conditions in their internal commerce.

It is not the province of the Court to consider the economic advantages or disadvantages of such a centralized system. It is sufficient to say that the Federal Constitution does not provide for it. Our growth and development have called for wide use of the commerce power of the federal government in its control over the expanded activities of interstate commerce, and in protecting that commerce from burdens, interferences, and conspiracies to restrain and monopolize it. But the authority of the federal government may not be pushed to such an extreme as to destroy the distinction, which the commerce clause itself establishes, between commerce "among the several States" and the internal concerns of a State. The same answer must be made to the contention that is based upon the serious economic situation which led to the passage of the Recovery Act,—the fall in prices, the decline in wages and employment, and the curtailment of the market for commodities. Stress is laid upon the great importance of maintaining wage distributions which would provide the necessary stimulus in starting "the cumulative forces making for expanding commercial activity." Without in any way disparaging this motive, it is enough to say that the recuperative efforts of the federal government must be made in a manner consistent with the authority granted by the Constitution.

We are of the opinion that the attempt through the provisions of the Code to fix the hours and wages of employees of defendants in their intrastate business was not a valid exercise of federal power. . . .

205. *The First Triple A and "Coercion by Economic Pressure"*

U.S. v. Butler, 297 U.S. 1 (1936).

ROBERTS, J.: . . . It is inaccurate and misleading to speak of the exaction from processors prescribed by the challenged act as a tax, or to say that as a tax it is subject to no infirmity. A tax, in the general understanding of the term, and as used in the Constitution, signifies an exaction for the support of the Government. The word has never been thought to connote the expropriation of money from one group for the benefit of another. We may concede that the latter sort of imposition is constitutional when imposed to effectuate regulation of a matter in which both groups are interested and in respect of which there is a power of legislative regulation. But manifestly no justification for it can be found unless as an integral part of such regulation. . . .

We conclude that the act is one regulating agricultural production; that the tax is a mere incident of such regulation and that the respondents have standing to challenge the legality of the exaction. . . .

The Government asserts that even if the respondents may question the propriety of the appropriation embodied in the statute their attack must fail because Article I, §8 of the Constitution authorizes the contemplated expenditure of the funds raised by the tax. This contention presents the great and the controlling question in the case. . . .

There should be no misunderstanding as to the function of this court in such a case. It is sometimes said that the court assumes a power to overrule or control the action of the people's representatives. This is a misconception. The Constitution is the supreme law of the land ordained and established by the people. All legislation must conform to the principles it lays down. When an act of Congress is appropriately challenged in the courts as not conforming to the constitutional mandate the judicial branch of the Government has only one duty,—to lay the article of the Constitution which is invoked beside the statute which is challenged and to decide whether the latter squares with the former. All the court does, or can do, is to announce its considered judgment upon the question. The only power it has, if such it may be called, is the power of judgment. This court neither approves nor condemns any legislative policy. Its delicate and difficult office is to ascertain and declare whether the legislation is in accordance with, or in contravention of, the provisions of the Constitution; and, having done that, its duty ends. . . .

Article I, §8, of the Constitution vests sundry powers in the Congress. But two of its clauses have any bearing upon the validity of the statute under review.

The third clause endows the Congress with power "to regulate Commerce . . . among the several States." Despite a reference in its first section to a burden upon, and an obstruction of the normal currents of commerce, the act under review does not purport to regulate transactions in interstate or foreign commerce. Its stated purpose is the control of agricultural production, a purely local activity in an effort to raise the prices paid the farmer. Indeed, the Government does not attempt to uphold the validity of the act on the basis of the commerce clause, which, for the purpose of the present case, may be put aside as irrelevant.

The clause thought to authorize the legislation,—the first,—confers upon the Congress power "to lay and collect Taxes, Duties, Imposts and Excises, to pay the Debts and provide for the common Defence and general Welfare of the United States." . . . The Government asserts that warrant is found in this clause for the adoption of the Agricultural Adjustment Act. The argument is that Congress may appropriate and authorize the spending of moneys for the "general welfare"; that the phrase should be liberally construed to cover anything conducive to national welfare; that decision as to what will promote such welfare rests with Congress alone, and the courts may not review its determination; and finally that the appropriation under attack was in fact for the general welfare of the United States. . . .

Since the foundation of the Nation sharp differences of opinion have persisted as to the true interpretation of the phrase. Madison asserted it amounted to no more than a reference to the other powers enumerated in the subsequent clauses of the same section; that, as the United States is a government of limited and enumerated powers, the grant of power to tax and spend for the general national welfare must be confined to the enumerated legislative fields committed to the Congress. In this view the phrase is mere tautology, for taxation and appropriation are or may be necessary incidents of the exercise of any of the enumerated legislative powers. Hamilton, on the other hand, maintained the clause confers a power separate and distinct from those later enumerated, is not restricted in meaning by the grant of them, and Congress consequently has a substantive power to tax and to appropriate, limited only by the requirement that it shall be exercised to provide for the general welfare of the United States. Each contention has had the support of those whose views are entitled to weight. This court has noticed the question, but has never found it necessary to decide which is the true construction. Mr. Justice Story, in his Commentaries, espouses the Hamiltonian position. . . . While, therefore, the power to tax is not unlimited, its confines are set in the clause which confers it, and not in those of §8 which bestow and define the legislative powers of the Congress. It results that the power of Congress to authorize expenditure of public moneys for public purposes is not limited by the direct grants of legislative power found in the Constitution.

But the adoption of the broader construction leaves the power to spend subject to limitations. . . .

That the qualifying phrase must be given effect all advocates of broad construction admit. Hamilton, in his well known Report on Manufactures, states that the purpose must be "general, and not local." . . .

We are not now required to ascertain the scope of the phrase "general welfare of the United States" or to determine whether an appropriation in aid of agriculture falls within it. Wholly apart from that question, another principle embedded in our Constitution prohibits the enforcement of the Agricultural Adjustment Act. The act invades the reserved rights of the states. It is a statutory plan to regulate and control agricultural production, a matter beyond the powers delegated to the federal government. The tax, the appropriation of the funds raised, and the direction for their disbursement, are but parts of the plan. They are but means to an unconstitutional end. . . .

The power of taxation, which is expressly granted, may, of course, be adopted as a means to carry into operation another power also expressly granted. But resort to the taxing power to effectuate an end which is not legitimate, not within the scope of the Constitution, is obviously inadmissible. . . .

If the taxing power may not be used as the instrument to enforce a regulation of matters of state concern with respect to which the Congress has no authority to interfere, may it, as in the present case, be employed to raise the money necessary to purchase a compliance which the Congress is powerless to command? The Government asserts that whatever might be said against the validity of the plan, if compulsory, it is constitutionally sound because the end is accomplished by voluntary cooperation. There are two sufficient answers to the contention. The regulation is not in fact voluntary. The farmer, of course, may refuse to comply, but the price of such refusal is the loss of benefits. The amount offered is intended to be sufficient to exert pressure on him to agree to the proposed regulation. The power to confer or withhold unlimited benefits is the power to coerce or destroy. If the cotton grower elects not to accept the benefits, he will receive less for his crops; those who receive payments will be able to undersell him. The result may well be financial ruin. . . . The Department of Agriculture has properly described the plan as one to keep a non-cooperating minority in line. This is coercion by economic pressure. The asserted power of choice is illusory. . . .

Congress has no power to enforce its commands on the farmer to the ends sought by the Agricultural Adjustment Act. It must follow that it may not indirectly accomplish those ends by taxing and spending to purchase compliance. The Constitution and the entire plan of our government negative any such use of the power to tax and to spend as the act undertakes to authorize. It does not help to declare that local conditions throughout the nation have created a situation of national concern; for this is but to say that whenever there is a widespread similarity of local conditions, Congress may ignore constitutional limitations upon its own powers and usurp those reserved to the states. If, in lieu of compulsory regulation of subjects within the states' reserved jurisdiction, which is prohibited, the Congress could invoke the taxing and spending power as a means to accomplish the same end, clause 1 of §8 of Article I would become the instrument for total subversion of the governmental powers reserved to the individual states. . . .

206. *Industry and Labor: The Second Phase*

Carter v. Carter Coal Company, 298 U.S. 238 (1936).

SUTHERLAND, J.: . . . The position of the Government, as we understand it, is that the validity of the exaction does not rest upon the taxing power but upon the power of Congress to regulate interstate commerce; and that if the act in respect of the labor and price-fixing provisions be not upheld, the "tax" must fall with them. With that position we agree and confine our consideration accordingly. . . .

Since the validity of the act depends upon whether it is a regulation of interstate commerce, the nature and extent of the power conferred upon Congress by the commerce clause becomes the determinative question in this branch of the case. . . . We first inquire, then—What is commerce? The term, as this court many times has said, is one of extensive import. No all-embracing definition has ever been formulated. The question is to be approached both affirmatively and negatively—that is to say, from the points of view as to what it includes and what it excludes. . . .

That commodities produced or manufactured within a state are intended to be sold or transported outside the state does not render their production or manufacture subject to federal regulation under the commerce clause. . . .

We have seen that the word "commerce" is the equivalent of the phrase "intercourse for the purposes of trade." Plainly, the incidents leading up to and culminating in the mining of coal do not constitute such intercourse. The employment of men, the fixing of their wages, hours of labor and working conditions, the bargaining in respect to these things—whether carried on separately or collectively—each and all constitute intercourse for the purposes of production, not of trade. The latter is a thing apart from the relation of employer and employee, which in all producing occupations is purely local in character. Extraction of coal from the mine is the aim and the completed result of local activities. Commerce in the coal mined is not brought into being by force of these activities, but by negotiations, agreements, and circumstances entirely apart from production. Mining brings the subject matter of commerce into existence. Commerce disposes of it.

A consideration of the foregoing, and of many cases which might be added to those already cited, renders inescapable the conclusion that the effect of the labor provisions of the act, including those in respect of minimum wages wage agreements, collective bargaining, and the Labor Board and its powers, primarily falls upon production and not upon commerce; and confirms the further resulting conclusion that production is a purely local activity. It follows that none of these essential antecedents of production constitutes a transaction in or forms any part of interstate commerce. . . . Everything which moves in interstate commerce has had a local origin. Without local production somewhere, interstate commerce, as now carried on, would practically disappear. Nevertheless, the local character of mining, of manufacturing and of crop growing is a fact, and remains a fact, whatever may be done with the products. . . .

But §1 (the preamble) of the act now under review declares that all production and distribution of bituminous coal "bear upon and directly affect its interstate commerce"; and that regulation thereof is imperative for the protection of such commerce. The contention of the government is that the labor provisions of the act may be sustained in that view.

That the production of every commodity intended for interstate sale and transportation has some effect upon interstate commerce may be, if it has not already been, freely granted; and we are brought to the final and decisive inquiry, whether here that effect is direct, as the "preamble" recites, or indirect. The distinction is not formal, but substantial in the highest degree, as we pointed out in the *Schechter* case. . . .

Whether the effect of a given activity or condition is direct or indirect is not always easy to determine. The word "direct" implies that the activity or condition invoked or blamed shall operate proximately —not mediately, remotely, or collaterally —to produce the effect. It connotes the absence of an efficient intervening agency or condition. And the extent of the effect bears no logical relation to its character. The distinction between a direct and an indirect effect turns, not upon the magnitude of either the cause or the effect, but entirely upon the manner in which the effect has been brought about. If the production by one man of a single ton of coal intended for interstate sale and shipment, and actually so sold and shipped, affects interstate commerce indirectly, the effect does not become direct by multiplying the tonnage, or increasing the number of men employed, or adding to the expense or complexities of the business, or by all combined. It is quite true that rules of law are sometimes qualified by considerations of degree, as the government argues. But the matter of degree has no bearing upon the question here, since that question is not— What is the *extent* of the local activity or condition, or the *extent* of the effect produced upon interstate commerce? but— What is the *relation* between the activity or condition and the effect?

Much stress is put upon the evils which come from the struggle between employers and employees over the matter of wages, working conditions, the right of collective bargaining, etc., and the resulting strikes, curtailment and irregularity of production and effect on prices; and it is insisted that interstate commerce is *greatly* affected thereby. But, in addition to what has just been said, the conclusive answer is that the evils are all local evils over which the federal government has no legislative control. The relation of employer and employee is a local relation. At common law, it is one of the domestic relations. The wages are paid for the doing of local work. Working conditions are obviously local conditions. The employees are not engaged in or about commerce, but exclusively in producing a commodity. And the controversies and evils, which it is the object of the act to regulate and minimize, are local controversies and evils affecting local work undertaken to accomplish that local result. Such effect as they may have upon commerce, however extensive it may be, is secondary and indirect. An increase in the greatness of the effect adds to its importance. It does not alter its character. . . .

The want of power on the part of the federal government is the same whether the wages, hours of service, and working conditions, and the bargaining about them, are related to production before interstate commerce has begun, or to sale and distribution after it has ended. . . .

Wages, hours of labor, and working conditions are to be so adjusted as to effectuate the purposes of the act; and prices are to be so regulated as to *stabilize* wages, working conditions, and hours of labor which have been or are to be fixed under the labor provisions. The two are so woven together as to render the probability plain enough that uniform prices, in the opinion of Congress, could not be fairly fixed or effectively regulated, without also regulating those elements of labor which enter so largely into the cost of production. . . .

The conclusion is unavoidable that the price-fixing provisions of the code are so related to and dependent upon the labor provisions as conditions, considerations or compensations, as to make it clearly probable that the latter being held bad, the former would not have been passed. The fall of the latter, therefore, carries down with it the former. . . .

The price-fixing provisions of the code are thus disposed of without coming to the question of their constitutionality; but neither this disposition of the matter, nor anything we have said, is to be taken as indicating that the court is of opinion that these provisions, if separately enacted, could be sustained. . . .

The Court Crisis of 1936-37

207. *Franklin D. Roosevelt, Radio Address on Judicial Reform, March 9, 1937*

Senate Reports, 75th Cong., 1st Sess., Jan. 5–Aug. 21, 1937, Report No. 711, I, 41-4.

Since the rise of the modern movement for social and economic progress through legislation, the Court has more and more often and more and more boldly asserted a power to veto laws passed by the Congress and State legislatures in complete disregard of this original limitation.

In the last 4 years the sound rule of giving statutes the benefit of all reasonable doubt has been cast aside. The Court has been acting not as a judicial body, but as a policy-making body.

When the Congress has sought to stabilize national agriculture, to improve the conditions of labor, to safeguard business against unfair competition, to protect our national resources, and in many other ways to serve our clearly national needs, the majority of the Court has been assuming the power to pass on the wisdom of these acts of the Congress—and to approve or disapprove the public policy written into these laws.

That is not only my accusation. It is the accusation of most distinguished Justices of the present Supreme Court. I have not the time to quote to you all the language used by dissenting Justices in many of these cases. But in the case holding the Railroad Retirement Act unconstitutional, for instance, Chief Justice Hughes said in a dissenting opinion that the majority opinion was "a departure from sound principles," and placed "an unwarranted limitation upon the commerce clause." And three other Justices agree with him.

In the case holding the A. A. A. unconstitutional, Justice Stone said of the majority opinion that it was a "tortured construction of the Constitution." And two other Justices agreed with him.

In the case holding the New York Minimum Wage Law unconstitutional, Justice Stone said that the majority were actually reading into the Constitution their own "personal economic predilections," and that if the legislative power is not left free to choose the methods of solving the problems of poverty, subsistence, and health of large numbers in the community, then "government is to be rendered impotent." And two other Justices agreed with him.

In the face of these dissenting opinions, there is no basis for the claim made by some members of the Court that something in the Constitution has compelled them regretfully to thwart the will of the people.

In the face of such dissenting opinions, it is perfectly clear that as Chief Justice Hughes has said, "We are under a Constitution, but the Constitution is what the judges say it is."

The Court in addition to the proper

use of its judicial functions has improperly set itself up as a third House of the Congress—a super-legislature, as one of the Justices has called it—reading into the Constitution words and implications which are not there, and which were never intended to be there.

We have, therefore, reached the point as a Nation where we must take action to save the Constitution from the Court and the Court from itself. We must find a way to take an appeal from the Supreme Court to the Constitution itself. We want a Supreme Court which will do justice under the Constitution—not over it. In our courts we want a government of laws and not of men.

I want—as all Americans want—an independent judiciary as proposed by the framers of the Constitution. That means a Supreme Court that will enforce the Constitution as written—that will refuse to amend the Constitution by the arbitrary exercise of judicial power—amendment by judicial say-so. It does not mean a judiciary so independent that it can deny the existence of facts universally recognized.

How, then, could we proceed to perform the mandate given us? It was said in last year's Democratic platform, "If these problems cannot be effectively solved within the Constitution, we shall seek such clarifying amendment as will assure the power to enact those laws, adequately to regulate commerce, protect public health and safety, and safeguard economic security." In other words, we said we would seek an amendment only if every other possible means by legislation were to fail. . . .

Whenever a judge or justice of any Federal court has reached the age of 70 and does not avail himself of the opportunity to retire on a pension, a new member shall be appointed by the President then in office, with the approval, as required by the Constitution, of the Senate of the United States.

That plan has two chief purposes: By bringing into the judicial system a steady and continuing stream of new and younger blood, I hope, first, to make the administration of all Federal justice speedier and therefore less costly; secondly, to bring to the decision of social and economic problems younger men who have had personal experience and contact with modern facts and circumstances under which average men have to live and work. This plan will save our National Constitution from hardening of the judicial arteries. . . .

Those opposing this plan have sought to arouse prejudice and fear by crying that I am seeking to "pack" the Supreme Court and that a baneful precedent will be established.

What do they mean by the words "packing the Court?"

Let me answer this question with a bluntness that will end all honest misunderstanding of my purposes.

If by that phrase "packing the Court" it is charged that I wish to place on the bench spineless puppets who would disregard the law and would decide specific cases as I wished them to be decided, I make this answer: That no President fit for his office would appoint, and no Senate of honorable men fit for their office would confirm, that kind of appointees to the Supreme Court.

But if by that phrase the charge is made that I would appoint and the Senate would confirm Justices worthy to sit beside present members of the Court who understand those modern conditions; that I will appoint Justices who will not undertake to override the judgment of the Congress on legislative policy; that I will appoint Justices who will act as Justices and not as legislators—if the appointment of such Justices can be called "packing the Courts"—then I say that I, and with me the vast majority of the American people, favor doing just that thing—now. . . .

Like all lawyers, like all Americans, I regret the necessity of this controversy. But the welfare of the United States, and indeed of the Constitution itself, is what we all must think about first. Our difficulty with the Court today rises not from the Court as an institution but from human beings within it. But we cannot yield our constitutional destiny to the personal judgment of a few men who, being fearful of the future, would deny us the necessary means of dealing with the present.

This plan of mine is no attack on the Court; it seeks to restore the Court to its rightful and historic place in our system of constitutional government and to have it resume its high task of building anew on the Constitution "a system of living law." . . .

208. *Adverse Report of the Senate Judiciary Committee, 1937*

Senate Reports, 75th Cong., 1st Sess., Jan. 5–Aug. 21, 1937, Report No. 711, I, 1-23 *passim*.

The effect of this bill is not to provide for an increase in the number of Justices composing the Supreme Court. The effect is to provide a forced retirement or, failing in this, to take from the Justices affected a free exercise of their independent judgment. . . .

Let us, for the purpose of the argument, grant that the Court has been wrong, wrong not only in that it has rendered mistaken opinions but wrong in the far more serious sense that it has substituted its will for the congressional will in the matter of legislation. May we nevertheless safely punish the Court?

Today it may be the Court which is charged with forgetting its constitutional duties. Tomorrow it may be the Congress. The next day it may be the Executive. If we yield to temptation now to lay the lash upon the Court, we are only teaching others how to apply it to ourselves and to the people when the occasion seems to warrant. Manifestly, if we may force the hand of the Court to secure our interpretation of the Constitution, then some succeeding Congress may repeat the process to secure another and a different interpretation and one which may not sound so pleasant in our ears as that for which we now contend.

There is a remedy for usurpation or other judicial wrongdoing. If this bill be supported by the toilers of this country upon the ground that they want a Court which will sustain legislation limiting hours and providing minimum wages, they must remember that the procedure employed in the bill could be used in another administration to lengthen hours and to decrease wages. If farmers want agricultural relief and favor this bill upon the ground that it gives them a Court which will sustain legislation in their favor, they must remember that the procedure employed might some day be used to deprive them of every vestige of a farm relief.

When members of the Court usurp legislative powers or attempt to exercise political power, they lay themselves open to the charge of having lapsed from that "good behavior" which determines the period of their official life. But, if you say, the process of impeachment is difficult and uncertain, the answer is, the people made it so when they framed the Constitution. It is not for us, the servants of the people, the instruments of the Constitution, to find a more easy way to do that which our masters made difficult.

But, if the fault of the judges is not so grievous as to warrant impeachment, if their offense is merely that they have grown old, and we feel, therefore, that there should be a "constant infusion of new blood," then obviously the way to achieve that result is by constitutional amendment fixing definite terms for the members of the judiciary or making mandatory their retirement at a given age. Such a provision would indeed provide for the constant infusion of new blood, not only now but at all times in the future. The plan before us is but a temporary expedient which operates once and then never again, leaving the Court as permanently expanded to become once more a court of old men, gradually year by year falling behind the times. . . .

We are told that a reactionary oligarchy defies the will of the majority, that this is a bill to "unpack" the Court and give effect to the desires of the majority; that is to say, a bill to increase the number of Justices for the express purpose of neutralizing the views of some of the present members. In justification we are told, but without authority, by those who would rationalize this program, that Congress was given the power to determine the size of the Court so that the legislative branch would be able to impose its will upon the judiciary. This amounts to nothing more than the declaration that when the Court stands in the way of a legislative enactment, the Congress may reverse the ruling by enlarging the Court. When such a principle is adopted, our constitutional system is overthrown! . . .

Even if every charge brought against the so-called "reactionary" members of this Court be true, it is far better that we await orderly but inevitable change of personnel than that we impatiently overwhelm them with new members. Exhibiting this restraint, thus demonstrating our faith in the American system, we shall set an example that will protect the independent American judiciary from attack as long as this Government stands. . . .

True it is, that courts like Congresses, should take account of the advancing strides of civilization. True it is that the law, being a progressive science, must be pronounced progressively and liberally; but the milestones of liberal progress are made to be noted and counted with caution rather than merely to be encountered and passed. Progress is not a mad mob march; rather, it is a steady, invincible stride. . . .

If, under the "hydraulic pressure" of our present need for economic justice, we destroy the system under which our people have progressed to a higher degree of justice and prosperity than that ever enjoyed by any other people in all the history of the human race, then we shall destroy not only all opportunity for further advance but everything we have thus far achieved. . . .

Even if the case were far worse than it is alleged to be, it would still be no argument in favor of this bill to say that the courts and some judges have abused their power. The courts are not perfect, nor are the judges. The Congress is not perfect, nor are Senators and Representatives. The Executive is not perfect. These branches of government and the offices under them are filled by human beings who for the most part strive to live up to the dignity and idealism of a system that was designed to achieve the greatest possible measure of justice and freedom for all the people. We shall destroy the system when we reduce it to the imperfect standards of the men who operate it. We shall strengthen it and ourselves, we shall make justice and liberty for all men more certain when, by patience and self-restraint, we maintain it on the high plane on which it was conceived.

Inconvenience and even delay in the enactment of legislation is not a heavy price to pay for our system. Constitutional democracy moves forward with certainty rather than with speed. The safety and the permanence of the progressive march of our civilization are far more important to us and to those who are to come after us than the enactment now of any particular law. The Constitution of the United States provides ample opportunity for the expression of popular will to bring about such reforms and changes as the people may deem essential to their present and future welfare. It is the people's charter of the powers granted those who govern them. . . .

SUMMARY

We recommend the rejection of this bill as a needless, futile, and utterly dangerous abandonment of constitutional principle.

It was presented to the Congress in a most intricate form and for reasons that obscured its real purpose.

It would not banish age from the bench nor abolish divided decisions.

It would not affect the power of any court to hold laws unconstitutional nor withdraw from any judge the authority to issue injunctions.

It would not reduce the expense of litigation nor speed the decision of cases.

It is a proposal without precedent and without justification.

It would subjugate the courts to the will of Congress and the President and thereby destroy the independence of the judiciary, the only certain shield of individual rights.

It contains the germ of a system of centralized administration of law that would enable an executive so minded to send his judges into every judicial district in the land to sit in judgment on controversies between the Government and the citizen.

It points the way to the evasion of the Constitution and establishes the method whereby the people may be deprived of their right to pass upon all amendments of the fundamental law.

It stands now before the country, acknowledged by its proponents as a plan to force judicial interpretation of the Constitution, a proposal that violates every sacred tradition of American democracy.

Under the form of the Constitution it seeks to do that which is unconstitutional.

Its ultimate operation would be to make this Government one of men rather than one of law, and its practical operation would be to make the Constitution what the executive or legislative branches of the Government choose to say it is—an interpretation to be changed with each change of administration.

It is a measure which should be so emphatically rejected that its parallel will never again be presented to the free representatives of the free people of America.

209. *The Court Reverses Itself on Minimum Wage Legislation*

West Coast Hotel Co. v. Parrish, 300 U.S. 379 (1937).

HUGHES, C.J.: This case presents the question of the constitutional validity of the minimum wage law of the State of Washington.

The Act, entitled "Minimum Wages for Women," authorizes the fixing of minimum wages for women and minors. . . .

The appellant conducts a hotel. The appellee Elsie Parrish was employed as a chambermaid and (with her husband) brought this suit to recover the difference between the wages paid her and the minimum wage fixed pursuant to the state law. The minimum wage was $14.50 per week of 48 hours. The appellant challenged the act as repugnant to the due process clause of the Fourteenth Amendment of the Constitution of the United States. . . .

The appellant relies upon the decision of this Court in *Adkins v. Children's Hospital*, . . . which held invalid the District of Columbia Minimum Wage Act which was attacked under the due process clause of the Fifth Amendment. . . .

We think that the question which was not deemed to be open in the *Morehead* case is open and is necessarily presented here. The Supreme Court of Washington has upheld the minimum wage statute of that State. It has decided that the statute is a reasonable exercise of the police power of the State. In reaching that conclusion the state court has invoked principles long established by this Court in the application of the Fourteenth Amendment. The state court has refused to regard the decision in the *Adkins* case as determininative and has pointed to our decisions both before and since that case as justifying its position. We are of the opinion that this ruling of the state court demands on our part a reexamination of the *Adkins* case. The importance of the question, in which many States having similar laws are concerned, the close division by which the decision in the *Adkins* case was reached, and the economic conditions which have supervened, and in the light of which the reasonableness of the exercise of the protective power of the State must be considered, make it not only appropriate, but we think imperative, that in deciding the present case the subject should receive fresh consideration. . . .

The principle which must control our decision is not in doubt. The constitutional provision invoked is the due process clause of the Fourteenth Amendment governing the States, as the due process clause invoked in the *Adkins* case governed Congress. In each case the violation alleged by those attacking minimum wage regulation for women is deprivation of freedom of contract. What is this freedom? The Constitution does not speak of freedom of contract. It speaks of liberty and prohibits the deprivation of liberty without due process of law. In prohibiting that deprivation the Constitution does not recognize an absolute and uncontrollable liberty. Liberty in each of its phases has its history and connotation. But the liberty safeguarded is liberty in a social organization which requires the protection of law against the evils which menace the health, safety, morals and welfare of the people. Liberty under the Constitution is thus necessarily subject to the restraints of due process, and regulation which is reasonble in relation to its subject and is adopted in the interests of the community is due process. . . .

The minimum wage to be paid under the Washington statute is fixed after full consideration by representatives of employers, employees and the public. It may be assumed that the minimum wage is fixed in consideration of the services that are performed in the particular occupations under normal conditions. Provision is made for special licenses at less wages in the case of women who are incapable of full service. The statement of Mr. Justice Holmes in the *Adkins* case is pertinent: . . . . [Holmes is then cited to the effect that the law does not coerce specific payments or employment, but like any police law, establishes a minimum standard which, if not adhered to, will warrant federal action.]

What can be closer to the public interest than the health of women and their protection from unscrupulous and overreaching employers? And if the protection of women is a legitimate end of the exercise of state power, how can it be said that the requirement of the payment of a minimum wage fairly fixed in order to meet the very necessities of existence is not an admissible means to that end? The legislature of the State was clearly entitled to consider the situation of women in employment, the fact that they are in the class receiving the least pay, that their bargaining power is relatively weak, and that they are the ready victims of those who would take advantage of their necessitous circumstances. The legislature was entitled to adopt measures to reduce the evils of the "sweating system," the exploiting of workers at wages so low as to be insufficient to meet the bare cost of living thus making their very helplessness the occasion of a most injurious competition. The legislature had the right to consider that its minimum wage requirements would be an important aid in carrying out its policy of protection. The adoption of similar requirements by many States evidences a deep-seated conviction both as to the presence of the evil and as to the means adapted to check it. Legislative response to that conviction cannot be regarded as arbitrary or capricious and that is all we have to decide. Even if the wisdom of the policy be regarded as debatable and its effects uncertain, still the legislature is entitled to its judgment.

There is an additional and compelling consideration which recent economic experience has brought into a strong light. The exploitation of a class of workers who are in an unequal position with respect to bargaining power and are thus relatively defenceless against the denial of a living wage is not only detrimental to their health and well being but casts a direct burden for their support upon the community. What these workers lose in wages the taxpayers are called upon to pay. The bare cost of living must be met. We may take judicial notice of the unparalleled demands for relief which arose during the recent period of depression and still continue to an alarming extent despite the degree of economic recovery which has been achieved. It is unnecessary to cite official statistics to establish what is of common knowledge through the length and breadth of the land. While in the instant case no factual brief has been presented, there is no reason to doubt that the State of Washington has encountered the same social problem that is present elsewhere. The community is not bound to provide what is in effect a subsidy for unconscionable employers. The community may direct its law-making power to correct the abuse which springs from their selfish disregard of the public interest. . . .

CHAPTER XXIII

The Revolution in Constitutional Law

IF EVER the platitude about losing the battle and winning the war applied to constitutional controversies, it did in 1936-37. After the initial concession toward expanded state authority in the Parrish case (Chapter XXII), the new majority proceeded to broaden the permissible areas of federal regulation so extensively that a "Constitutional Revolution, Ltd.," in the words of Professor Edward S. Corwin, was the result.

During the 168 days that Congress devoted to Roosevelt's reorganization proposal, the Court applied its newly discovered nationalism to uphold extensive labor-management regulations, unemployment and old-age benefits under the Social Security Act, mortgage moratoriums, agricultural controls, and a wide variety of similiar federal measures. The case which broke the log jam of narrow precedents was *N. L. R. B. v. Jones & Laughlin Steel Corporation* (No. 210), decided early in April, 1937. In upholding the National Labor Relations Act, Chief Justice Hughes not only validated the most favorable law that American labor had ever won, but so broadened the interpretation of what constituted interstate commerce that the main doubt in later cases became not so much what was included under the controlling power of the national government as what was not. Of necessity, the decision repudiated the rulings in the Schechter and Carter cases, although not without the bitter protests of Justices Butler, McReynolds, Sutherland, and Van Devanter. Hughes also sanctioned a broad jurisdiction for the National Labor

Relations Board and consistently upheld the Board's authority, even when the local production being supervised had only the remotest effect upon interstate commerce (*N. L. R. B. v. Fainblatt*, 1939).

The Court also broadened its interpretation of the federal taxing power. The Social Security Act of 1935 had been passed in answer to demands for national assistance to protect individuals against the hazards of sickness, old age, and unemployment. Its constitutional base was Congress's broad power to tax for the general welfare. In *Stewart Machine Co. v. Davis* (1937), Justice Cardozo upheld the tax that the measure imposed upon employers and ruled that the program of conditional Federal grants-in-aid was not illegal coercion of the states. In *Helvering et al. v. Davis* (No. 211), he upheld the old-age tax and benefit provisions of the act, while setting forth a strongly nationalistic theory of taxing power, based, ironically, upon Roberts's opinion in *U.S. v. Butler*.

These commerce and taxing decisions were handed down before any change in Court membership. By the middle of 1937, older justices began retiring and within three years, five of the judges were Roosevelt appointees. This "Roosevelt Court" continued to sustain New Deal measures and also reinterpreted broadly a variety of older statutes. Typical were laws dealing with labor activities. For many years the Sherman and Clayton Anti-Trust Acts had been used as restraints on labor unions. In a 1940 case involving sit-down strikers in a Philadelphia hosiery plant, Justice Stone sharply curtailed this application (*Apex Hosiery Co. v. Leader* [*No. 212*]). Previously it had been necessary, in order to establish the liability of unions under the measures, to prove only that there existed an intent to restrain interstate commerce, coupled with a direct and substantial restraint. But now Stone ruled that it had to be shown that the union's activities had the effect of suppressing a free competitive market, either by monopolizing the supply, controlling the prices, or discriminating between would-be purchasers. Similarly, in a case involving the Norris-LaGuardia Act of 1932 (*U.S. v. Hutcheson* [*No. 213*]), the Court ruled that within the Act's definition of a permissible labor dispute, a union might strike, picket, and engage in all the other acts specifically enumerated in section 20 of the Clayton Act without fear of injunction, damage suit, or prosecution, as far as the antitrust laws were concerned. Thus, the Hutcheson and Apex decisions seemed virtually to remove union activity from the threat of liability under the antitrust laws. In *Phelps Dodge v. N. L. R. B.*, decided in 1941, the Court struck at "yellow-dog contracts," ruling that an employer was engaging in an unfair labor practice by refusing to hire workmen because of their labor-union affiliations.

Federal wage and hour legislation also received judicial sanction in 1941 in a decision with important constitutional implications (*U.S. v. Darby* [*No. 214*]). Relying upon Holmes's dissent in *Hammer v. Dagenhart*, Justice Stone specifically overruled that precedent and returned to the *McCulloch v. Maryland* principle that the enumerated powers of the national government can be implemented by Congress through whatever necessary and proper means Congress may determine. In the commerce field, this doctrine meant a return to the *Gibbons v. Ogden* principle: when intrastate activities are so commingled with or related to interstate commerce as to demand uniform regulation, the commerce clause applies. Justice Jackson went even further. In upholding the validity of the wheat-marketing provisions of the 1938 A. A. A.—the Court had earlier sustained the general provisions of the measure in *Mulford v. Smith,* 1939—Jackson threw out all distinctions such as "direct" and "indirect," "production" and "commerce," and emphasized the economic effect upon interstate commerce as the true test of whether local activities could be regulated by Congress under the commerce power (*Wickard v. Filburn* [No. 215]). The ruling left doubt as to whether there was any limit to the commerce power as a tool for federal regulation, a view confirmed by Justice Murphy's 1945 statement that "the commerce power is as broad as the economic needs of the nation." Thus nearly forty years of constitutional strictures on federal authority under the commerce clause seemed at an end. Implementing its new interpretation of the commerce clause, the Court upheld federal authority over the coal and natural gas industries, navigable streams, and public utilities.

The new constitutional nationalism which characterized the Roosevelt Court did not necessarily imply that state power was curtailed. On the contrary, state governments collected and spent more money, employed more people, and engaged in more activities than ever before in their history, evolving a remarkable adjustment of federal-state authority in an era of expanding governmental power. The Roosevelt Court reversed the long-standing practice of intergovernmental tax immunity and upheld a state income tax levied on a federal employee (*Graves v. New York ex rel. O'Keefe* [No. 216]). In succeeding cases, the Court also looked with general favor on a variety of new types of state taxation. Moreover, permissible areas of state police power were expanded when the Court took a long step backward toward the old Cooley doctrine of "selective exclusiveness" (see Chapter IX). In the same vein, *Swift v. Tyson,* which for a century had permitted the federal courts to disregard decisions of the state courts on matters of state law, was formally overruled in 1938 (*Erie Railroad v. Tompkins*).

The 1930's also saw new approaches to major constitutional problems involving the legislative and executive departments of the government. The Twentieth Amendment eliminated the "lame duck" session of Congress (No. 217A), and the Twenty-first ended the "noble experiment" with prohibition (No. 217B). Two important decisions illustrate the contradictory attitudes of the "old court" toward Presidential authority. In 1935, *Humphrey's Executor* (*Rathbun*) *v. U.S.* (No. 218) sharply curtailed the Chief Executive's power to remove appointive officers vested with judicial and legislative powers (in this case a member of an independent regulatory commission), thus modifying Taft's decision in the Myers case (see Introduction to Chapter XX). In 1936, however, Justice Sutherland ruled that the President, by virtue of the inherent authority of his office, possessed "plenary and exclusive power" over all international affairs, and that this power did not require an act of Congress as a basis for its exercise (*U.S. v. Curtiss-Wright Export Corporation* [No. 219]). Sutherland also ruled (*U.S. v. Belmont,* 1937) that executive agreements on foreign issues have the same legal effect as treaties. Since these can be negotiated independently, they further strengthen the President's position in the handling of foreign affairs. Although this procedure had early critics, it was President Roosevelt's wartime usages, particularly at Yalta, which aroused the most opposition, culminating in a postwar effort to curb presidential authority by the amendment process (Chapter XXVI).

The New Deal and the Court's New Attitude

210. *The Court Reconsiders Federal Regulation of Industrial and Labor Relations*

N. L. R. B. v. Jones & Laughlin Steel Corporation, 301 U.S. 1 (1937).

HUGHES, C.J.: . . . *The scope of the Act.*—The Act is challenged in its entirety as an attempt to regulate all industry, thus invading the reserved powers of the States over their local concerns. It is asserted that the references in the Act to interstate and foreign commerce are colorable at best; that the Act is not a true regulation of such commerce or of matters which directly affect it but on the contrary has the fundamental object of placing under the compulsory supervision of the federal government all industrial labor relations within the nation. The argument seeks support in the broad words of the preamble and in the sweep of the provisions of the Act, and it is further insisted that its legislative history shows an essential universal purpose in the light of which its scope cannot be limited by either construction or by the application of the separability clause.

If this conception of terms, intent and consequent inseparability were sound, the Act would necessarily fall by reason of the limitation upon the federal power which inheres in the constitutional grant, as well as because of the explicit reservation of the Tenth Amendment. *Schechter Corporation v. United States.* . . . The authority of the federal government may not be pushed to such an extreme as to destroy the distinction, which the commerce clause itself establishes, between commerce "among the several States" and the internal concerns of a State. That distinction between what is national and what is local in the activities of commerce is vital to the maintenance of our federal system. . . .

But we are not at liberty to deny effect to specific provisions, which Congress has constitutional power to enact, by superimposing upon them inferences from general legislative declarations of an ambiguous character, even if found in the same statute. The cardinal principle of statutory construction is to save and not to destroy. We have repeatedly held that as between two possible interpretations of a statute, by one of which it would be unconstitutional and by the other valid, our plain duty is to adopt that which will save the act. Even to avoid a serious doubt the rule is the same. . . .

We think it clear that the National Labor Relations Act may be construed so as to operate within the sphere of constitutional authority. The jurisdiction conferred upon the Board, and invoked in this instance, is found in §10 (a), which provides:

> Sec. 10 (a). The Board is empowered, as hereinafter provided, to prevent any person from engaging in any unfair labor practice (listed in section 8) affecting commerce.

The critical words of this provision, prescribing the limits of the Board's authority in dealing with the labor practices, are "affecting commerce." The Act specifically defines the "commerce" to which it refers (§2 (6)). . . .

There can be no question that the commerce thus contemplated by the Act (aside from that within a Territory or the District of Columbia) is interstate and foreign commerce in the constitutional sense. The Act also defines the term "affecting commerce" (§2 (7)). . . .

This definition is one of exclusion as well as inclusion. The grant of authority to the Board does not purport to extend to the relationship between all industrial employees and employers. Its terms do not impose collective bargaining upon all industry regardless of effects upon interstate or foreign commerce. It purports to reach only what may be deemed to burden or obstruct that commerce and, thus qualified, it must be construed as contemplating the exercise of control within constitutional bounds. It is a familiar principle that acts which directly burden or obstruct interstate or foreign commerce, or its free flow, are within the reach of the congressional power. Acts having that effect are not rendered immune because they grow out of labor disputes. . . . It is the effect upon commerce, not the source of the injury, which is the criterion. . . . Whether or not particular action does affect commerce in such a close and intimate fashion as to be subject to federal control, and hence to lie within the authority conferred upon the Board, is left by the statute to be determined as individual cases arise. We are thus to inquire whether in the instant case the constitutional boundary has been passed. . . .

The application of the Act to employees engaged in production.—The principle involved.—Respondent says that whatever may be said of employees engaged in interstate commerce, the industrial relations and activities in the manufacturing department of respondent's enterprise are not subject to federal regulation. The argument rests upon the proposition that manufacturing in itself is not commerce. . . .

The Government distinguishes these cases. The various parts of respondent's enterprise are described as interdependent and as thus involving "a great movement of iron ore, coal and limestone along well-defined paths to the steel mills, thence through them, and thence in the form of steel products into the consuming centers of the country—a definite and well-understood course of business." It is urged that these activities constitute a "stream" or "flow" of commerce, of which the Aliquippa manufacturing plant is the focal point, and that industrial strife at that point would cripple the entire movement. Reference is made to our decision sustaining the Packers and Stockyards Act. . . . The Court found that the stockyards were but a "throat" through which the current of commerce flowed and the transactions which there occurred could not be separated from that movement. . . .

Respondent contends that the instant case presents material distinctions. . . .

We do not find it necessary to determine whether these features of defendant's business dispose of the asserted analogy to the "stream of commerce" cases. The congressional authority to protect interstate commerce from burdens and obstructions is not limited to transactions which can be deemed to be an essential part of a "flow" of interstate or foreign commerce. Burdens and obstructions may be due to injurious action springing from other sources. The fundamental principle is that the power to regulate commerce is the power to enact "all appropriate legislation" for "its protection and advancement" . . . ; to adopt measures "to promote its growth and insure its safety" . . . ; "to foster, protect, control and restrain." . . . That power is plenary and may be exerted to protect interstate commerce "no matter what the source of the dangers which threaten it." . . . Although activities may be intrastate in character when separately considered, if they have such a close and substantial relation to interstate commerce that their control is essential or appropriate to protect that commerce from burdens and obstructions, Congress cannot be denied the power to exercise that control. . . . Undoubtedly the scope of this power must be considered in the light of our dual system of government and may not be extended so as to embrace effects upon interstate commerce so indirect and remote that to embrace them, in view of our complex society, would effectually obliterate the distinction between what is national and what is local and create a completely centralized government. . . . The question is necessarily one of degree. . . .

It is thus apparent that the fact that the employees here concerned were engaged in production is not determinative. The question remains as to the effect upon interstate commerce of the labor practice involved. . . .

Effects of the unfair labor practice in respondent's enterprise.—Giving full weight to respondent's contention with respect to a break in the complete continuity of the "stream of commerce" by reason of respondent's manufacturing operations, the fact remains that the stoppage of those operations by industrial strife would have a most serious effect upon interstate commerce. In view of respondent's far-flung activities, it is idle to say that the effect would be indirect or remote. It is obvious that it would be immediate and might be catastrophic. We are asked to shut our eyes to the plainest facts of our national life and to deal with the question of direct and indirect effects in an intellectual vacuum. Because there may be but indirect and remote effects upon interstate commerce in connection with a host of local enterprises throughout the country, it does not follow that other industrial activities do not have such a close and intimate relation to interstate commerce as to make the presence of industrial strife a matter of the most urgent national concern. When industries organize themselves on a national scale, making their relation to interstate commerce the dominant factor in their activities, how can it be maintained that their industrial labor relations constitute a forbidden field into which Congress may not enter when it is necessary to protect interstate commerce from the paralyzing consequences of industrial war? We have often said that interstate commerce itself is a practical conception. It is equally true that interferences with that commerce must be appraised by a judgment that does not ignore actual experience. . . .

Our conclusion is that the order of the Board was within its competency and that the Act is valid as here applied. . . .

211. *Promoting the General Welfare through Social Security*

Helvering et al. v. Davis, 301 U.S. 619 (1937).

CARDOZO, J.: The Social Security Act . . . is challenged once again. . . .

In this case Titles VIII and II are the subject of attack. Title VIII. . . . lays a special income tax upon employees to be deducted from their wages and paid by the employers. Title II provides for the payment of Old Age Benefits, and supplies the motive and occasion, in the view of the assailants of the statute, for the levy of the taxes imposed by Title VIII. . . .

The [district] court held that Title II was void as an invasion of powers reserved by the Tenth Amendment to the states or to the people, and that Title II in collapsing carried Title VIII along with it. . . .

The scheme of benefits created by the provisions of Title II is not in contravention of the limitations of the Tenth Amendment.

Congress may spend money in aid of the "general welfare." Constitution, Art. I, section 8; *United States v. Butler* . . . ; *Steward Machine Co. v. Davis*. . . . There have been great statesmen in our history who have stood for other views. We will not resurrect the contest. It is now settled by decision. *United States v. Butler.* . . . The conception of the spending power advocated by Hamilton and strongly reinforced by Story has prevailed over that of Madison, which has not been lacking in adherents. Yet difficulties are left when the power is conceded. The line must still be drawn between one welfare and another, between particular and general. Where this shall be placed cannot be known through a formula in advance of the event. There is a middle ground or certainly a penumbra in which discretion is at large. The discretion, however, is not confided to the courts. The discretion belongs to Congress, unless the choice is clearly wrong, a display of arbitrary power, not an exercise of judgment. This is now familiar law. "When such a contention comes here we naturally require a showing that by no reasonable possibility can the challenged legislation fall within the wide range of discretion permitted to the Congress." *United States v. Butler.* . . . Nor is the concept of the general welfare static. Needs that were narrow or parochial a century ago may be interwoven in our day with the well-being of the nation. What is critical or urgent changes with the times.

The purge of nation-wide calamity that began in 1929 has taught us many lessons. Not the least is the solidarity of interests that may once have seemed to be divided. Unemployment spreads from state to state, the hinterland now settled that in pioneer days gave an avenue of escape. . . . Spreading from State to State, unemployment is an ill not particular but general, which may be checked, if Congress so determines, by the resources of the Nation. If this can have been doubtful until now, our ruling today in the case of the *Steward Machine Co.* . . . has set the doubt at rest. But the ill is all one or at least not greatly different whether men are thrown out of work because there is no longer work to do or because the disabilities of age make them incapable of doing it. Rescue becomes necessary irrespective of the cause. The hope behind this statute is to save men and women from the rigors of the poor house as well as from the haunting fear that such a lot awaits them when journey's end is near. . . .

A recent study of the Social Security Board informs us that "one-fifth of the aged in the United States were receiving old-age assistance, emergency relief, institutional care, employment under the works program, or some other form of aid from public or private funds; two-fifths to one-half were dependent on friends and relatives, one-eighth had some income from earnings; and possibly one-sixth had some savings or property. Approximately three out of four persons 65 or over were probably dependent wholly or partially on others for support." We summarize in the margin the results of other studies by state and national commissions. They point the same way.

The problem is plainly national in area and dimensions. Moreover, laws of the separate states cannot deal with it effectively. Congress, at least, had a basis for that belief. States and local governments are often lacking in the resources that are necessary to finance an adequate program of security for the aged. This is brought out with a wealth of illustration in recent studies of the problem. Apart from the failure of resources, states and local governments are at times reluctant to increase so heavily the burden of taxation to be borne by their residents for fear of placing themselves in a position of economic disadvantage as compared with neighbors or competitors. We have seen this in our study of the problem of unemployment compensation. *Steward Machine Co. v. Davis.* . . . A system of old age pensions has special dangers of its own, if put in force in one state and rejected in another. The existence of such a system is a bait to the needy and dependent elsewhere, encouraging them to migrate and seek a haven of repose. Only a power that is national can serve the interests of all.

Whether wisdom or unwisdom resides

in the scheme of benefits set forth in Title II, it is not for us to say. The answer to such inquiries must come from Congress, not the courts. Our concern here, as often, is with power, not with wisdom. Counsel for respondent has recalled to us the virtues of self-reliance and frugality. There is a possibility, he says, that aid from a paternal government may sap those sturdy virtues and breed a race of weaklings. If Massachusetts so believes and shapes her laws in that conviction, must her breed of sons be changed, he asks, because some other philosophy of government finds favor in the halls of Congress? But the answer is not doubtful. One might ask with equal reason whether the system of protective tariffs is to be set aside at will in one state or another whenever local policy prefers the rule of *laissez faire*. The issue is a closed one. It was fought out long ago. When money is spent to promote the general welfare, the concept of welfare or the opposite is shaped by Congress, not the states. So the concept be not arbitrary, the locality must yield. Constitution, Art. VI, Par. 2.

The New Deal and the Roosevelt Court

212. *The Reassessment of Labor Under the Sherman Act*

Apex Hosiery Co. v. Leader, 310 U.S. 469 (1940).

STONE, J.: . . . Only a single question is presented by the record for our decision, whether the evidence . . . whose verity must be taken to be established by the jury's verdict, establishes a restraint of trade or commerce which the Sherman Act condemns. . . .

The Sherman Act admittedly does not condemn all combinations and conspiracies which interrupt interstate transportation . . .

This Court has never applied the Act to laborers or to others as a means of policing interstate transportation, and so the question to which we must address ourselves is whether a conspiracy of strikers in a labor dispute to stop the operation of the employer's factory in order to enforce their demands against the employer is the kind of restraint of trade or commerce at which the Act is aimed, even though a natural and probable consequence of their acts and the only effect on trade or commerce was to prevent substantial shipments interstate by the employer.

A point strongly urged in behalf of respondents in brief and argument before us is that Congress intended to exclude labor organizations and their activities wholly from the operation of the Sherman Act. To this the short answer must be made that for the thirty-two years which have elapsed since the decision in *Loewe v. Lawlor* . . . this Court, in its efforts to determine the true meaning and application of the Sherman Act has repeatedly held that the words of the act, "Every contract, combination . . . or conspiracy in restraint of trade or commerce" do embrace to some extent and in some circumstances labor unions and their activities; and that during that period Congress, although often asked to do so, has passed no act purporting to exclude labor unions wholly from the operation of the Act. On the contrary Congress has repeatedly enacted laws restricting or purporting to curtail the application of the Act to labor organizations and their activities, thus recognizing that to some extent not defined they remain subject to it. . . .

While we must regard the question whether labor unions are to some extent and in some circumstances subject to the Act as settled in the affirmative, it is equally plain that this Court has never thought the Act to apply to all labor union activities affecting interstate commerce. . . .

The question remains whether the effect of the combination or conspiracy among respondents was a restraint of trade within the meaning of the Sherman Act. This is not a case of a labor organization being used by combinations of those engaged in an industry as the means or instrument for suppressing competition or fixing prices. . . . Here it is plain that the combination or conspiracy did not have as its purpose restraint upon competition in the market for petitioner's product. Its object was to compel petitioner to accede to the union demands and an effect of it, in consequence of the strikers' tortious acts, was the prevention of the removal of petitioner's product for interstate shipment. So far as appears the delay of these shipments was not intended to have and had no effect on prices of hosiery in the market. . . .

Since the enactment of the declaration in §6 of the Clayton Act . . . , it would seem plain that restraints on the sale of the employee's services to the employer, however much they curtail the competition among employees, are not in themselves combinations or conspiracies in restraint of trade or commerce under the Sherman Act.

Strikes or agreements not to work, entered into by laborers to compel employers to yield to their demands, may restrict to some extent the power of employers who are parties to the dispute to compete in the market with those not subject to such demands. But under the doctrine applied to non-labor cases, the mere fact of such restrictions on competition does not in itself bring the parties to the agreement within the condemnation of the Sherman Act. . . .

These cases show that activities of labor organizations not immunized by the Clayton Act are not necessarily violations of the Sherman Act. Underlying and implicit in all of them is recognition that the Sherman Act was not enacted to police interstate transportation, or to afford a remedy for wrongs, which are actionable under state law, and result from combinations and conspiracies which fall short, both in their purpose and effect, of any form of market control of a commodity, such as to "monopolize the supply, control its price, or discriminate between its would-be purchasers. . . ." We do not hold that conspiracies to obstruct or prevent transportation in interstate commerce can in no circumstances be violations of the Sherman Act. Apart from the Clayton Act it makes no distinction between labor and non-labor cases. . . .

If, without such effects on the market, we were to hold that a local factory strike, stopping production and shipment of its product interstate, violates the Sherman law, practically every strike in modern industry would be brought within the jurisdiction of the federal courts, under the Sherman Act to remedy local law violations. The Act was plainly not intended to reach such a result, its language does not require it, and the course of our decision precludes it. The maintenance in our federal system of a proper distribution between state and national governments of police authority and of remedies private and public for public wrongs is of far-reaching importance. An intention to disturb the balance is not lightly to be imputed to Congress. The Sherman Act is concerned with the character of the prohibited restraints effected by violence and those achieved by peaceful but oftentimes quite as effective means. Restraints not within the Act, when achieved by peaceful means, are not brought within its sweep merely because, without other differences, they are attended by violence. . . .

213. *The Norris–LaGuardia Act, Unions, and Federal Antitrust Legislation*

U.S. v. Hutcheson, 312 U.S. 219 (1941).

FRANKFURTER, J.: Whether the use of conventional, peaceful activities by a union in controversy with a rival union over certain jobs is a violation of the Sherman Act . . . is the question. . . .

Whether trade union conduct constitutes a violation of the Sherman Law is to be determined only by reading the Sherman Law and §20 of the Clayton Act and the Norris-LaGuardia Act as a harmonizing text of outlawry of labor conduct. . . .

There is nothing remotely within the terms of §20 that differentiates between trade union conduct directed against an employer because of a controversy arising in the relation between employer and employee, as such, and conduct similarly directed but ultimately due to an internecine struggle between two unions seeking the favor of the same employer. Such strife between competing unions has been an obdurate conflict in the evolution of so-called craft unionism and has undoubtedly been one of the potent forces in the modern development of industrial unions. These conflicts have intensified industrial tension but there is not the slightest warrant for saying that Congress has made §20 applicable to trade union conduct resulting from them. . . .

It is at once apparent that the acts with which the defendants are charged are the kind of acts protected by §20 of the Clayton Act. The refusal of the Carpenters to work for Anheuser-Busch or on construction work being done for it and its adjoining tenant, and the peaceful attempt to get members of other unions similarly to refuse to work, are plainly within the free scope accorded to workers by §20 for "terminating any relation of employment," or "ceasing to perform any work or labor," or "recommending, advising, or persuading others by peaceful means so to do." The picketing of Anheuser-Busch premises with signs to indicate that Anheuser-Busch was unfair to organized labor, a familiar practice in these situations, comes within the language "attending at any place where any such person or persons may lawfully be, for the purpose of peacefully obtaining or communicating information, or from peacefully persuading any person to work or to abstain from working." Finally, the recommendation to union members and their friends not to buy or use the product of Anheuser-Busch is explicitly covered by "ceasing to patronize . . . any party to such dispute, or from recommending, advising, or persuading others by peaceful and lawful means so to do."

Clearly, then, the facts here charged constitute lawful conduct under the Clayton Act unless the defendants cannot invoke that Act because outsiders to the immediate dispute also shared in the conduct. But we need not determine whether the conduct is legal within the restrictions which *Duplex Co. v. Deering* gave to the immunities of §20 of the Clayton Act. Congress in the Norris-LaGuardia Act has expressed the public policy of the United States and defined its conception of a "labor dispute" in terms that no longer leave room for doubt. . . .

The relation of the Norris-LaGuardia

Act to the Clayton Act is not that of a tightly drawn amendment to a technically phrased tax provision. The underlying aim of the Norris-LaGuardia Act was to restore the broad purpose which Congress thought it had formulated in the Clayton Act but which was frustrated, so Congress believed, by unduly restrictive judicial construction. . . .

The Norris-LaGuardia Act reasserted the original purpose of the Clayton Act by infusing into it the immunized trade union activities as redefined by the later Act. In this light §20 removes all such allowable conduct from the taint of being a "violation of any law of the United States," including the Sherman Law. . . .

214. *"It is within the legislative power to fix maximum hours" and minimum wages.*

U.S. v. Darby, 312 U.S. 100 (1941).

STONE, C.J.: The two principal questions raised by the record in this case are, *first*, whether Congress has constitutional power to prohibit the shipment in interstate commerce of lumber manufactured by employees whose wages are less than a prescribed minimum or whose weekly hours of labor at that wage are greater than a prescribed maximum, and, *second*, whether it has power to prohibit the employment of workmen in the production of goods "for interstate commerce" at other than prescribed wages and hours. . . .

While manufacture is not of itself interstate commerce, the shipment of manufactured goods interstate is such commerce and the prohibition of such shipment by Congress is indubitably a regulation of the commerce. The power to regulate commerce is the power "to prescribe the rule by which commerce is governed." *Gibbons v. Ogden*. . . . It extends not only to those regulations which aid, foster and protect the commerce, but embraces those which prohibit it. . . . It is conceded that the power of Congress to prohibit transportation in interstate commerce includes noxious articles, . . . stolen articles, . . . kidnapped persons, . . . and articles such as intoxicating liquor or convict made goods, traffic in which is forbidden or restricted by the laws of the state of destination. . . .

But it is said that the present prohibition falls within the scope of none of these categories; that while the prohibition is nominally a regulation of the commerce its motive or purpose is regulation of wages and hours of persons engaged in manufacture, the control of which has been reserved to the states and upon which Georgia and some of the states of destination have placed no restriction; that the effect of the present statute is not to exclude the prescribed articles from interstate commerce in aid of state regulation as in *Kentucky Whip & Collar Co. v. Illinois Central Railroad Co.* . . . but instead, under the guise of a regulation of interstate commerce, it undertakes to regulate wages and hours within the state contrary to the policy of the state which has elected to leave them unregulated.

The power of Congress over interstate commerce "is complete in itself, may be exercised to its utmost extent, and acknowledges no limitations other than are prescribed in the Constitution." . . . That power can neither be enlarged nor diminished by the exercise or non-exercise of state power. . . . Congress, following its own conception of public policy concerning the restrictions which may appropriately be imposed on interstate commerce, is free to exclude from the commerce articles whose use in the states for which they are destined it may conceive to be injurious to the public health, morals or welfare, even though the state has not sought to regulate their use. . . .

Such regulation is not a forbidden invasion of state power merely because either its motive or its consequence is to restrict the use of articles of commerce within the states of destination; and is not prohibited unless by other constitutional provisions. It is no objection to the assertion of the power to regulate interstate commerce that its exercise is attended by the same incidents which attend the exercise of the police power of the states. . . .

The motive and purpose of the present regulation are plainly to make effective the Congressional conception of public policy that interstate commerce should not be made the instrument of competition in the distribution of goods produced under substandard labor conditions, which competition is injurious to the commerce and to the states from and to which the commerce flows. The motive and purpose of a regulation of interstate commerce are matters for the legislative judgment upon the exercise of which the Constitution places no restriction and over which the courts are given no control. . . . Whatever their motive and purpose, regulations of commerce which do not infringe some constitutional prohibition are within the plenary power conferred on Congress by the Commerce Clause. Subject only to that limitation, presently to be considered, we conclude that the prohibition of the shipment interstate of goods produced under the forbidden substandard labor conditions is within the constitutional authority of Congress.

In the more than a century which has elapsed since the decision of *Gibbons v. Ogden,* these principles of constitutional interpretation have been so long and repeatedly recognized by this Court as applicable to the Commerce Clause, that there would be little occasion for repeating them now were it not for the decision of this Court twenty-two years ago in *Hammer v. Dagenhart.* . . . In that case it was held by a bare majority of the Court over the powerful and now classic dissent of Mr. Justice Holmes setting forth the fundamental issues involved, that Congress was without power to exclude the products of child labor from interstate commerce. The reasoning and conclusion of the Court's opinion there cannot be reconciled with the conclusion which we have reached, that the power of Congress under the Commerce Clause is plenary to exclude any article from interstate commerce subject only to the specific prohibitions of the Constitution.

Hammer v. Dagenhart has not been followed. The distinction on which the decision was rested that Congressional power to prohibit interstate commerce is limited to articles which in themselves have some harmful or deleterious property—a distinction which was novel when made and unsupported by any provision of the Constitution—has long since been abandoned. . . .

The conclusion is inescapable that *Hammer v. Dagenhart,* was a departure from the principles which have prevailed in the interpretation of the commerce clause both before and since the decision and that such vitality, as a precedent, as it then had has long since been exhausted. It should be and now is overruled.

Validity of the wage and hour requirements. Section 15(a) (2) and §§6 and 7 require employers to conform to the wage and hour provisions with respect to all employees engaged in the production of goods for interstate commerce. As appellee's employees are not alleged to be "engaged in interstate commerce" the validity of the prohibition turns on the question whether the employment, under other than the prescribed labor standards, of employees engaged in the production of goods for interstate commerce is so related to the commerce and so affects it as to be within the reach of the power of Congress to regulate it. . . .

Congress, having by the present Act adopted the policy of excluding from interstate commerce all goods produced for the commerce which do not conform to the specified labor standards, it may choose the means reasonably adapted to the attainment of the permitted end, even though they involve control of intrastate activities. . . . A familiar like exercise of power is the regulation of intrastate transactions which are so commingled with or related to interstate commerce that all must be regulated if the interstate commerce is to be effectively controlled. . . .

So far as *Carter v. Carter Coal Co.* . . . is inconsistent with this conclusion, its doctrine is limited in principle by the decisions under the Sherman Act and the National Labor Relations Act, which we have cited and which we follow. . . .

Our conclusion is unaffected by the Tenth Amendment. . . . The amendment states but a truism that all is retained which has not been surrendered. There is nothing in the history of its adoption to suggest that it was more than declaratory of the relationship between the national and state governments as it had been established by the Constitution before the amendment or that its purpose was other than to allay fears that the new national government might seek to exercise powers not granted, and that the states might not be able to exercise fully their reserved powers. . . .

The Act is sufficiently definite to meet constitutional demands. One who employs persons, without conforming to the prescribed wage and hour conditions, to work on goods which he ships or expects to ship across state lines, is warned that he may be subject to the criminal penalties of the Act. No more is required. . . .

215. *The New Interpretation of Legislation on Agriculture*

Wickard v. Filburn, 317 U.S. 111 (1942).

JACKSON, J.: . . . Appellee says that this is a regulation of production and consumption of wheat. Such activities are, he urges, beyond the reach of Congressional power under the Commerce Clause, since they are local in character, and their effects upon interstate commerce are at most "indirect." In answer the Government argues that the statute regulates neither production nor consumption, but only marketing; and, in the alternative, that if the Act does go beyond the regulation of marketing it is sustainable as a "necessary and proper" implementation of the power of Congress over interstate commerce.

The Government's concern lest the Act be held to be a regulation of production or consumption, rather than of marketing, is attributable to a few dicta and decisions of this Court which might be understood to lay it down that activities such as "production," "manufacturing," and "mining" are strictly "local" and, except in special circumstances which are not present here, cannot be regulated under the commerce power because their effects upon interstate commerce are, as matter of law, only "indirect." Even today, when this power has been held to have great latitude, there is no decision of this Court that such activities may be regulated where no part of the product is intended for interstate commerce or intermingled with the subjects thereof. We believe that a review of the course of decision under the Commerce Clause will make plain, however, that questions of the power of Congress are not to be decided by reference to any formula which would give controlling force to nomenclature such as "production" and "indirect" and foreclose consideration of the actual effects of the activity in question upon interstate commerce. . . .

The Court's recognition of the relevance of the economic effects in the application of the Commerce Clause . . . has made the mechanical application of legal formulas no longer feasible. Once an economic measure of the reach of the power granted to Congress in the Commerce Clause is accepted, questions of federal power cannot be decided simply by finding the activity in question to be "production," nor can consideration of its economic effects be foreclosed by calling them "indirect. . . ."

Whether the subject of the regulation in question was "production," "consumption," or "marketing" is, therefore, not material for purposes of deciding the question of federal power before us. That an activity is of local character may help in a doubtful case to determine whether Congress intended to reach it. The same consideration might help in determining whether in the absence of Congressional action it would be permissible for the state to exert its power on the subject matter, even though in so doing it to some degree affected interstate commerce. But even if appellee's activity be local and though it may not be regarded as commerce, it may still, whatever its nature, be reached by Congress if it exerts a substantial economic effect on interstate commerce, and this irrespective of whether such effect is what might at some earlier time have been defined as "direct" or "indirect." . . .

The effect of consumption of home-grown wheat on interstate commerce is due to the fact that it constitutes the most variable factor in the disappearance of the wheat crop. Consumption on the farm where grown appears to vary in an amount greater than 20 per cent of average production. The total amount of wheat consumed as food varies but relatively little, and use as seed is relatively constant. . . .

It is well established by decisions of this Court that the power to regulate commerce includes the power to regulate the prices at which commodities in that commerce are dealt in and practices affecting such prices. One of the primary purposes of the Act in question was to increase the market price of wheat, and to that end to limit the volume thereof that could affect the market. It can hardly be denied that a factor of such volume and variability as home-consumed wheat would have a substantial influence on price and market conditions. This may arise because being in marketable condition such wheat overhangs the market and, if induced by rising prices, tends to flow into the market and check price increases. But if we assume that it is never marketed, it supplies a need of the man who grew it which would otherwise be reflected by purchases in the open market. Home-grown wheat in this sense competes with wheat in commerce. The stimulation of commerce is a use of the regulatory function quite as definitely as prohibitions or restrictions thereon. This record leaves us in no doubt that Congress may properly have considered that wheat consumed on the farm where grown, if wholly outside the scheme of regulation, would have a substantial effect in defeating and obstructing its purpose to stimulate trade therein at increased prices.

It is said, however, that this Act, forcing some farmers into the market to buy what they could provide for themselves, is an unfair promotion of the markets and prices of specializing wheat growers. It is of the essence of regulation that it lays a restraining hand on the self-interest of the regulated and that advantages from the regulation commonly fall to others. The conflicts of economic interest between the regulated and those who advantage by it are wisely left under our system to resolution by the Congress under its more flexible and responsible legislative process. Such conflicts rarely lend themselves to judicial determination. And with the wisdom, workability, or fairness, of the plan of regulation we have nothing to do. . . .

216. *Intergovernmental Tax Immunity*

Graves v. New York ex rel. O'Keefe, 306 U.S. 466 (1939).

STONE, J.: . . . The single question with which we are now concerned is whether the tax laid by the state upon the salary of respondent, employed by a corporate instrumentality of the federal government, imposes an unconstitutional burden upon that government. . . .

Congress has declared . . . that the Home Owners' Loan Corporation is an instrumentality of the United States and that its bonds are exempt, as to principal and interest, from federal and state taxation, except surtaxes, estate, inheritance and gift taxes. The corporation itself, "including its franchise, its capital, reserves and surplus, and its loans and income," is likewise exempted from taxation; its real property is subject to tax to the same extent as other real property. But Congress has given no intimation of any purpose either to grant or withhold immunity from state taxation of the salary of the corporation's employees, and the Congressional intention is not to be gathered from the statute by implication. . . .

It is true that the silence of Congress, when it has authority to speak, may sometimes give rise to an implication as to the Congressional purpose. The nature and extent of that implication depend upon the nature of the Congressional power and the effect of its exercise. But there is little scope for the application of that doctrine to the tax immunity of governmental instrumentalities. The constitutional immunity of either government from taxation by the other, where Congress is silent, has its source in an implied restriction upon the powers of the taxing government. So far as the implication rests upon the purpose to avoid interference with the functions of the taxed government or the imposition upon it of the economic burden of the tax, it is plain that there is no basis for implying a purpose of Congress to exempt the federal government or its agencies from tax burdens which are unsubstantial or which courts are unable to discern. Silence of Congress implies immunity no more than does the silence of the Constitution. It follows that when exemption from state taxation is claimed on the ground that the federal government is burdened by the tax, and Congress has disclosed no intention with respect to the claimed immunity, it is in order to consider the nature and effect of the alleged burden, and if it appears that there is no ground for implying a constitutional immunity, there is equally a want of any ground for assuming any purpose on the part of Congress to create an immunity.

The present tax is a non-discriminatory tax on income applied to salaries at a specified rate. It is not in form or substance a tax upon the Home Owners' Loan Corporation or its property or income, nor is it paid by the corporation or the government from their funds. It is laid upon income which becomes the property of the taxpayer when received as compensation for his services; and the tax laid upon the privilege of receiving it is paid from his private funds and not from the funds of the government, either directly or indirectly. The theory, which once won a qualified approval, that a tax on income is legally or economically a tax on its source, is no longer tenable, . . . and the only possible basis for implying a constitutional immunity from state income tax of the salary of an employee of the national government or of a governmental agency is that the economic burden of the tax is in some way passed on so as to impose a burden on the national government tantamount to an interference by one government with the other in the performance of its functions. . . .

Assuming, as we do, that the Home

Owners' Loan Corporation is clothed with the same immunity from state taxation as the government itself, we cannot say that the present tax on the income of its employees lays any unconstitutional burden upon it. All the reasons for refusing to imply a constitutional prohibition of federal income taxation of salaries of state employees, stated at length in the Gerhardt case, are of equal force when immunity is claimed from state income tax on salaries paid by the national government or its agencies. In this respect we perceive no basis for a difference in result whether the taxed income be salary or some other form of compensation, or whether the taxpayer be an employee or an officer of either a state or the national government, or of its instrumentalities. In no case is there basis for the assumption that any such tangible or certain economic burden is imposed on the government concerned as would justify a court's declaring that the taxpayer is clothed with the implied constitutional tax immunity of the government by which he is employed. That assumption, made in *Collector v. Day*, . . . and in *New York ex rel. Rogers v. Graves*, . . . is contrary to the reasoning and to the conclusions reached in the *Gerhardt* case. . . . In their light the assumption can no longer be made. *Collector v. Day*, . . . and *New York ex rel. Rogers v. Graves*, . . . are overruled so far as they recognize an implied constitutional immunity from income taxation of the salaries of officers or employees of the national or a state government or their instrumentalities.

So much of the burden of a non-discriminatory general tax upon the incomes of employees of a government, state or national, as may be passed on economically to that government, through the effect of the tax on the price level of labor or materials, is but the normal incident of the organization within the same territory of two governments, each possessing the taxing power. The burden, so far as it can be said to exist or to affect the government in any indirect or incidental way, is one which the Constitution presupposes, and hence it cannot rightly be deemed to be within an implied restriction upon the taxing power of the national and state governments which the Constitution has expressly granted to one and has confirmed to the other. The immunity is not one to be implied from the Constitution, because if allowed it would impose to an inadmissible extent a restriction on the taxing power which the Constitution has reserved to the state governments.

Shifting Areas of National Authority

THE AMENDING PROCESS

217. *"Lame Ducks" and Liquor*

A. THE TWENTIETH AMENDMENT

Proposed March 2, 1932; adopted February 6, 1933.

SECTION 1. The terms of the President and Vice-President shall end at noon on the twentieth day of January, and the terms of Senators and Representatives at noon on the third day of January of the years in which such terms would have ended if this article had not been ratified; and the terms of their successors shall then begin.

SECTION 2. The Congress shall assemble at least once in every year, and such meeting shall begin at noon on the third day of January, unless they shall by law appoint a different day.

SECTION 3. If, at the time fixed for the beginning of the term of the President the President-elect shall have died, the Vice-President-elect shall become President. If a President shall not have been chosen before the time fixed for the beginning of his term, or if the President-elect shall have failed to qualify, then the Vice-President-elect shall act as President until a President shall have qualified; and the Congress may by law provide for the case wherein neither a President-elect nor a Vice-President-elect shall have qualified, declaring who shall then act as President, or the manner in which one who is to act shall be selected, and such person shall act accordingly until a President or Vice-President shall have qualified.

SECTION 4. The Congress may by law provide for the case of the death of any of the persons from whom the House of Representatives may choose a President whenever the right of choice shall have devolved upon them, and for the case of the death of any of the persons from whom the Senate may choose a Vice-President whenever the right of choice shall have devolved upon them.

SECTION 5. Sections 1 and 2 shall take effect on the Fifteenth day of October following the ratification of this article.

SECTION 6. This article shall be inoperative unless it shall have been ratified as an amendment to the Constitution by the legislatures of three-fourths of the several states within seven years from the date of its submission.

B. THE TWENTY-FIRST AMENDMENT

Proposed February 20, 1933; adopted December 5, 1933.

SECTION 1. The eighteenth article of amendment to the Constitution of the United States is hereby repealed.

SECTION 2. The transportation or importation into any state, territory, or possession of the United States for delivery or use therein of intoxicating liquors, in violation of the laws thereof, is hereby prohibited.

SECTION 3. This article shall be inoperative unless it shall have been ratified as an amendment to the Constitution by conventions in the several states, as provided in the Constitution, within seven years from the date of the submission hereof to the states by the Congress.

THE REMOVAL POWER OF THE PRESIDENT

218. *"Illimitable power of removal is not possessed by the President."*

Humphrey's Executor (Rathbun) v. U.S., 295 U.S. 602 (1935).

SUTHERLAND, J.: . . . "Do the provisions of §1 of the Federal Trade Commission Act, stating that 'any commissioner may be removed by the President for inefficiency, neglect of duty or malfeasance in office,' restrict or limit the power of the President to remove a commissioner except upon one or more of the causes named?

"If the foregoing question is answered in the affirmative, then—

"2. If the power of the President to remove a commissioner is restricted or limited as shown by the foregoing interrogatory and the answer made thereto, is such a restriction or limitation valid under the Constitution of the United States?" . . .

The commission is to be nonpartisan; and it must, from the very nature of its duties, act with entire impartiality. It is charged with the enforcement of no policy except the policy of the law. Its duties are neither political nor executive, but predominantly quasi-legislative. Like the Interstate Commerce Commission, its members are called upon to exercise the trained judgment of a body of experts "appointed by law and informed by experience." . . .

The legislative reports in both houses of Congress clearly reflect the view that a fixed term was necessary to the effective and fair administration of the law. . . .

The debates in both houses demonstrate that the prevailing view was that the commission was not to be "subject to anybody in the government but only to the people of the United States," free from "political domination or control," or the "probability or possibility of such a thing," to be "separate and apart from any existing department of the government—not subject to the orders of the President." . . .

Thus the language of the act, the legislative reports and the general purposes of the legislation as reflected by the debates, all combine to demonstrate the congressional intent to create a body of experts who shall gain experience by length of service—a body which shall be independent of executive authority, *except in its selection,* and free to exercise its judgment without the leave or hindrance of any other official or any department of the government. To the accomplishment of these purposes it is clear that Congress was of opinion that length and certainty of tenure would vitally contribute. And to hold that, nevertheless, the members of the commission continue in office at the mere will of the President, might be to thwart, in large measure, the very ends which Congress sought to realize by definitely fixing the term of office.

We conclude that the intent of the act is to limit the executive power of removal to the causes enumerated, the existence of none of which is claimed here; and we pass to the second question.

Second. To support its contention that the removal provision of §1, as we have just construed it, is an unconstitutional interference with the executive powers of the President, the government's chief reliance is *Myers v. U.S.* . . . Nevertheless, the narrow point actually decided was only that the President had power to remove a postmaster of the first class, without the advice and consent of the Senate, as required by act of Congress. . . .

The office of postmaster is so essentially unlike the office now involved that the decision in the Myers case cannot be accepted as controlling our decision here. A postmaster is an executive officer restricted to the performance of executive functions. He is charged with no duty at all related to either the legislative or judicial power. . . . The necessary reach of the decision goes far enough to include all purely executive officers. It goes no farther; much less does it include an officer who occupies no place in the executive department and who exercises no part of the executive power vested by the Constitution in the President.

The Federal Trade Commission is an administrative body created by Congress to carry into effect legislative policies emlimited. In this vast external realm, with the legislative standard therein prescribed, and to perform other specified duties as a legislative or as a judicial aid. Such a body cannot in any proper sense be characterized as an arm or an eye of the executive. Its duties are performed without executive leave and, in the contemplation of the statute, must be free from executive control. . . .

We think it plain under the Constitution that illimitable power of removal is not possessed by the President in respect of officers of the character of those just named. The authority of Congress, in creating quasi-legislative or quasi-judicial agencies, to require them to act in discharge of their duties independently of executive control, cannot well be doubted; and that authority includes, as an appropriate incident, power to fix the period during which they shall continue, and to forbid their removal except for cause in the meantime. For it is quite evident that one who holds his office only during the pleasure of another cannot be depended upon to maintain an attitude of independence against the latter's will.

The fundamental necessity of maintaining each of the three general departments of government entirely free from the control or coercive influence, direct or indirect, of either of the others, has often been stressed and is hardly open to serious question. So much is implied in the very fact of the separation of the powers of these departments by the Constitution, and in the rule which recognizes their essential coequality. The sound application of a principle that makes one master in his own house precludes him from imposing his control in the house of another who is master there. . . .

Whether the power of the President to remove an officer shall prevail over the authority of Congress to condition the power by fixing a definite term and precluding a removal except for cause will depend upon the character of the office; the Myers decision, affirming the power of the President alone to make the removal, is confined to purely executive officers; and as to officers of the kind here under consideration, we hold that no removal can be made during the prescribed term for which the officer is appointed, except for one or more of the causes named in the applicable statute.

To the extent that, between the decision in the Myers case, which sustains the unrestrictable power of the President to remove purely executive officers, and our present decision that such power does not extend to an office such as that here involved, there shall remain a field of doubt, we leave such cases as may fall within it for future consideration and determination as they arise.

THE TREATY POWER AND EXECUTIVE AGREEMENTS

219. *The President's Plenary Power over International Affairs*

U.S. v. Curtiss-Wright Export Corporation, 299 U.S. 304 (1936).

SUTHERLAND, J.: . . . *First.* It is contended that by the Joint Resolution, the going into effect and continued operation of the resolution was conditioned (a) upon the President's judgment as to its beneficial effect upon the reestablishment of peace between the countries engaged in armed conflict in the Chaco; (b) upon the making of a proclamation, which was left to his unfettered discretion, thus constituting an attempted substitution of the President's will for that of Congress; (c) upon the making of a proclamation putting an end to the operation of the resolution, which again was left to the President's unfettered discretion; and (d) further, that the extent of its operation in particular cases was subject to limitation and exception by the President, controlled by no standard. In each of these particulars, appellees urge that Congress abdicated its essential functions and delegated them to the Executive.

Whether, if the Joint Resolution had related solely to internal affairs it would be open to the challenge that it constituted an unlawful delegation of legislative power to the Executive, we find it unnecessary to determine. The whole aim of the resolution is to affect a situation entirely external to the United States, and falling within the category of foreign affairs. The determination which we are called to make, therefore, is whether the Joint Resolution, as applied to that situation, is vulnerable to attack under the rule that forbids a delegation of the law-making power. In other words, assuming (but not deciding) that the challenged delegation, if it were confined to internal affairs, would be invalid, may it nevertheless be sustained on the ground that its exclusive aim is to afford a remedy for a hurtful condition within foreign territory?

It will contribute to the elucidation of the question if we first consider the differences between the powers of the federal government in respect of foreign or external affairs and those in respect of domestic or internal affairs. That there are differences between them, and that these differences are fundamental, may not be doubted.

The two classes of powers are different, both in respect of their origin and their nature. The broad statement that the federal government can exercise no powers except those specifically enumerated in the Constitution, and such implied powers as are necessary and proper to carry into effect the enumerated powers, is categorically true only in respect of our internal affairs. In that field, the primary purpose of the Constitution was to carve from the general mass of legislative powers *then possessed by the states* such portions as it was thought desirable to vest in the federal government, leaving those not included in the enumeration still in the States. *Carter v. Carter Coal Co.* . . . That this doctrine applies only to powers which the states had, is self evident. And since the states severally never possessed international powers, such powers could not have been carved from the mass of state powers but obviously were transmitted to the United States from some other source. . . . [There follows a detailed discussion of the historical sources of the federal government's exclusive power over foreign relations.]

It results that the investment of the federal government with the powers of external sovereignty did not depend upon the affirmative grants of the Constitution. The powers to declare and wage war, to conclude peace, to make treaties, to maintain diplomatic relations with other sovereignties, if they had never been mentioned in the Constitution, would have vested in the federal government as necessary concomitants of nationality. Neither the Constitution nor the laws passed in pursuance of it have any force in foreign territory unless in respect of our own citizens . . . ; and operations of the nation in such territory must be governed by treaties, international understandings and compacts, and the principles of international law. As a member of the family of nations, the right and power of the United States in that field are equal to the right and power of the other members of the international family. Otherwise, the United States is not completely sovereign. . . .

Not only, as we have shown, is the federal power over external affairs in origin and essential character different from that over internal affairs, but participation in the exercise of the power is significantly limited. In this vast external realm, with its important, complicated, delicate and manifold problems, the President alone has the power to speak or listen as a representative of the nation. He *makes* treaties with the advice and consent of the Senate; but he alone negotiates. Into the field of negotiation the Senate cannot intrude; and Congress itself is powerless to invade it. . . .

It is important to bear in mind that we are here dealing not alone with an authority vested in the President by an exertion of legislative power, but with such an authority plus the very delicate, plenary and exclusive power of the President as the sole organ of the federal government in the field of international relations—a power which does not require as a basis for its exercise an act of Congress, but which, of course, like every other governmental power, must be exercised in subordination to the applicable provisions of the Constitution. It is quite apparent that if, in the maintenance of our international relations, embarrassment—perhaps serious embarrassment—is to be avoided and success for our aims achieved, congressional legislation which is to be made effective through negotiation and inquiry within the international field must often accord to the President a degree of discretion and freedom from statutory restriction which would not be admissible were domestic affairs alone involved. Moreover he, not Congress, has the better opportunity of knowing the conditions which prevail in foreign countries, and especially is this true in time of war. He has his confidential sources of information. He has his agents in the form of diplomatic, consular and other officials. Secrecy in respect of information gathered by them may be highly necessary, and the premature disclosure of it productive of harmful results. Indeed, so clearly is this true that the first President refused to accede to a request to lay before the House of Representatives the instructions, correspondence and documents relating to the negotiation of the Jay Treaty. . . .

In the light of the foregoing observations, it is evident that this court should not be in haste to apply a general rule which will have the effect of condemning legislation like that under review as constituting an unlawful delegation of legislative power. The principles which justify such legislation find overwhelming support in the unbroken legislative practice which has prevailed almost from the inception of the national government to the present day. . . .

The result of holding that the joint resolution here under attack is void and unenforceable as constituting an unlawful delegation of legislative power would be to stamp this multitude of comparable acts and resolutions as likewise invalid. And while this court may not, and should not, hesitate to declare acts of Congress, however many times repeated, to be unconstitutional if beyond all rational doubt it finds them to be so, an impressive array of legislation such as we have just set forth, enacted by nearly every Congress from the beginning of our national existence to the present day, must be given unusual weight in the process of reaching a correct determination of the problem. A legislative practice such as we have here, evidenced not by only occasional instances, but marked by the movement of a steady stream for a century and a half of time, goes a long way in the direction of proving the presence of unassailable ground for the constitutionality of the practice, to be found in the origin and history of the power involved, or in its nature or in both combined. . . .

The uniform, long-continued and undisputed legislative practice just disclosed rests upon an admissible view of the Constitution which, even if the practice found far less support in principle than we think it does, we should not feel at liberty at this late day to disturb. . . .

CHAPTER XXIV

The Roosevelt Court and Civil Liberties

FULLY as important as the Roosevelt Court's expansion of governmental authority in the economic realm were the restraints imposed on federal and state power in order to protect civil liberty. In the late 1930's and early 1940's, judicial supervision of civil liberties created a body of constitutional law unique in the annals of American history. The chief constitutional basis for this rapid development of new safeguards was the expanded concept of basic liberties guaranteed by the Fourteenth Amendment, begun in the Gitlow case in 1925 and strengthened in the Stromberg and Near decisions in 1931 (Chapter XXI).

By 1937 various First and Sixth Amendment guarantees had been held to comprise part of the "liberty" that the Fourteenth Amendment forbids the states to abridge without due process of law. However, the question of whether all the guarantees of the first eight amendments were applicable to the states still needed settlement. In *Palko v. Connecticut* (No. 220), the Court set forth a standard reminiscent of the distinction in the Insular Cases (Chapter XVI). Employing selective natural law principles, Justice Cardozo drew a line between those rights "implicit in the concept of ordered liberty," such as the First Amendment freedoms of speech, assembly, press, and religion, and rights merely procedural or remedial, and he ruled in the immediate case that the Fourteenth Amendment did not include the double jeopardy provision of the Fifth Amendment. Although the decision clearly avoided making all the guarantees of the Bill of Rights applicable to the states, it opened the door for judicial development of a wide variety of constitutional rights, creating a new area of substantive due process in the field of civil liberties at almost the same moment that the Court rejected this concept in the area of economic and social legislation.

The expansion was especially noteworthy in its relation to First Amendment freedoms. In the field of freedom of the press, it made possible a notable ruling against indirect censorship by the Huey Long government in Louisiana (*Grosjean v. American Press Company* [No. 221]). For a unanimous Court, Justice Sutherland announced that "the states are precluded from abridging the freedom of speech or of the press by force of the due process clause of the Fourteenth Amendment." In *DeJonge v. Oregon* (No. 222), freedom of assembly was held to be a Fourteenth Amendment liberty protected from state encroachment. Chief Justice Hughes therefore voided the conviction of a Communist who had been prosecuted under a state criminal syndicalism law for having spoken at a peaceable public meeting. Although the majority could not agree about which clause of the Fourteenth Amendment applied, they did invalidate Jersey City's restrictions on public meetings in *Hague v. C. I. O.* (1939). Some of the justices thought that Boss Hague's machine had abridged the privileges and immunities of United States citizens, but Justice Stone, who wrote the opinion, held to the more conventional view that the municipal ordinance deprived persons of their liberty without due process of law.

In other speech and press cases, the Court revived the Holmes-Brandeis "clear and present danger" rule as a standard by which to measure state denial of due process. In upholding the legality of speeches and printed material disseminated by a Negro Communist organizer, the Court rejected the Gitlow "bad tendency" test, pointing out that the Georgia syndicalist statute against incitement to insurrection "has not made membership in the Communist Party unlawful by reason of its supposed dangerous tendency even in the remote future" (*Herndon v. Lowry*, 1937). Begining in 1941, the Court also applied the "clear and present danger" rule in voiding, as a denial of due process, contempts of court by publication (*Bridges v. California*, 1941; *Pennekamp v. Florida*, 1946). At the same time, the Court made it clear that freedom of the press does not exempt newspapers from government regulation of their business activities and labor relations (*Associated Press v. U.S.*, 1945).

In expanding the area of protected speech, the Roosevelt Court in 1940 brought peaceful picketing in labor disputes under the liberty guarantees of the Fourteenth Amendment. As early as 1937, Justice Brandeis had linked picketing to speech (*Senn v. Tile Layers Protective Union*), and *Thornhill v. Alabama* (No. 223) elevated that dictum to ruling law. In striking down an antipicketing statute, the Court said: "The dissemination of information concerning the facts of a labor dispute must be regarded as within that area of free discussion that is guaranteed by the Constitution." The public display of placards by pickets was interpreted as a legitimate exercise of free speech. Later decisions indicated that picketing accompanied by violence or intimidation does not enjoy the same protection.

Another important labor union case invalidated a Texas statute requiring union organizers to register with city authorities before soliciting union memberships (*Thomas v. Collins* [No. 224]). "Lawful public assemblies, involving no element of grave and immediate danger to an interest the state is entitled to protect," Justice Rutledge observed for a 5 to 4 majority, "are not instruments of harm which require previous identification of the speaker." In both Thornhill and Thomas, the "clear and present danger" doctrine was invoked, but it was used to void state statutes rather than test their applicability. In the Thomas case, moreover, the Court combined this doctrine with its "preferred position" theory, asserting that the "indispensable democratic freedoms secured by the First Amendment" are so basic that any attempt to restrict them "must be justified by clear public interest, threatened not doubtfully or remotely, but by clear and present danger."

The solicitude of the Roosevelt Court for civil liberties resulted in a rash of cases dealing with state and local ordinances directed at the militant techniques of an unorthodox religious group, the Jehovah Witnesses. In their legal fight against restrictions on their liberty, the Witnesses brought nearly two dozen cases to the Court which clarified broad areas of constitutional law relating to the First Amendment freedoms of religion, assembly, speech, and press. In the first of this series, *Lovell v. Griffin* (1938), a unanimous Court struck down a Georgia city ordinance forbidding the distribution of pamphlets, handbills, and other literature without prior permission from the city manager. Such a rule subjected the press to "license and censorship" and constituted a denial of due process of law. In *Cantwell v. Connecticut* (1940), the Court invalidated, as a "censorship of religion" that denied due process, a statute requiring a permit for all solicitors for religious or charitable causes. Although both of these opinions were unanimous, the Court split sharply in *Jones v. Opelika* (1942), upholding a nondiscriminatory tax on peddling or canvassing which placed no special burden on those selling religious books. When Justice Rutledge replaced Justice Byrnes in 1943, a new 5 to 4 majority reversed the Opelika decision, interpreting door-to-door book sales by Witnesses as a religious rather than a commercial venture (*Murdock v. Pennsylvania* [No. 225]). This tax immunity for vendors of religious books was made complete in *Follett v. McCormick* (1944).

Other claims by the Witnesses have not received judicial blessing. The Court sustained the conviction of a Witness who created a breach of the peace by using libelous and "fighting words," held that Witnesses who allow children to sell religious literature violate state child labor laws, and upheld a fee to cover the cost of extra police for parade duty, even though the procession was a religious one. But the most spectacular reversal for the Witnesses came in the compulsory flag-salute case in 1940. In *Minersville School District v. Gobitis,* Justice Frankfurter sustained a Pennsylvania statute that directed the expulsion of children who refused to salute the flag in school ceremonies. Abandoning the "clear and present danger" test, the majority ruled that such a law did not restrict freedom of religion unconstitutionally. But a change of Court personnel and strong misgivings on the part of some of the majority made it possible for the Court to overrule Gobitis in *West Virginia State Board v. Barnette.* Stressing that the refusal to salute did not interfere with the rights of other individuals, Justice Jackson made an eloquent defense of nonconformity in all areas (No. 226). Frankfurter reaffirmed his original position in an equally brilliant plea for judicial acknowledgment of the competence of legislatures to deal with questions of local educational policy.

Despite the Court's reluctance to apply all the procedural rights of the first eight amendments to the states, the justices did develop many limitations on state criminal procedure. Although the elements of a fair and decent trial have been spelled out piecemeal, the Court has been consistent in proscribing actual brutality and flagrant intimidation to secure confessions. In 1940, Justice Black, speaking for a unanimous Court, wrote a dramatic decision that struck at more subtle means of pressure in invalidating a conviction of four Negroes obtained by ceaseless "grilling" by state officials (*Chambers v. Florida* [No. 227]). During the same period, the McNabb case set down a rule to guide federal courts in deciding on the admissibility of confessions, whether obtained by coercion or not. In this case a confession to murder was secured without coercion, but before the prisoner was arraigned; the Court stated flatly that "a confession is inadmissible if made during illegal detention due to a failure promptly to carry a prisoner before a committing magistrate, whether or not the 'confession is the result of torture, physical or psychological.'" On the other hand, the Court, in its consideration of the rights of accused persons, retreated from its earlier ruling (*Powell v. Alabama*, 1932) that the absence of adequate counsel deprived a person of life or liberty without due process of law. For a decade it was presumed that this first Scottsboro case had nailed down the right to counsel in criminal trials as one of the due process requirements. But in *Betts v. Brady* (1942) the majority ruled that in noncapital cases the right was not a fundamental one, since a number of state constitutions did not recognize it, nor was it required by common law. Protest against this ruling was strong, both on and off the bench; to many it seemed to tilt "the scales against the safeguarding of one of the most precious rights of man" (No. 228).

Federal protection of the rights of accused persons, of militant minority religious sects, and of labor was paralleled by an almost revolutionary reversal of the status of the Negro in American constitutional law. The attitude of the nation's highest tribunal always has been of supreme importance in determining the legal position of the Negro, for court consent has been necessary to legalize his subordinate status. For the Negro, the suffrage issue has been a key consideration, and the Court generally has nullified state legislation clearly inconsistent with the Fifteenth Amendment. In 1915 the "grandfather clause" was outlawed as a violation of that provision (*Guinn v. U.S.*). In 1916 Oklahoma replaced this law with a more subtle code that effectively disfranchised Negroes. Not until 1939 did this law come up for decision, and the Roosevelt Court promptly canceled it, observing that the Fifteenth Amendment "nullifies sophisticated as well as simple-minded modes of discrimination" (*Lane v. Wilson*).

The white primary question first received judicial interpretation in 1927, when a Texas law excluding Negroes from participating in primaries was struck down as an infringement of the Fourteenth Amendment (*Nixon v. Herndon*). Disfranchisement was then achieved when the Democratic Party in Texas, without legislative assistance, organized as a "private club," restricted its membership to whites, and thus barred Negroes from party primary elections. The "old Court" upheld this device in 1935 on the grounds that the political party was a private and not a governmental body, and private persons or groups could not violate the Fourteenth Amendment (*Grovey v. Townsend*). In 1941, however, a case came before the Roosevelt Court involving the failure of state officials, acting under "color" of state law, to count primary election ballots properly (*U.S. v. Classic, 1941*). Justice Stone ruled that the federal government could guarantee the right to vote in a primary in a one-party state where the primary was obviously an integral step in the election of members of Congress. The opinion did not mention the Grovey precedent, but the two were clearly in conflict and three years later the Court formally overruled Grovey and outlawed the Texas ruse as a violation of the Fifteenth Amendment (*Smith v. Allwright* [No. 229]). "Constitutional rights would be of little value," said Justice Rutledge, "if they could be thus indirectly denied." The Smith case did not end Southern efforts to disfranchise the Negro (Chapter XXVIII, No. 270) but the impressive growth of Negro voting in every Southern state indicates the gradual improvement of the political status of the Negro.

The judicial attack on discrimination by the Roosevelt Court also led to the first serious reconsideration of the "separate but equal" doctrine in 1938. The University of Missouri Law School had refused to admit a Negro student even though there were no separate or equal facilities in the state. This, said Chief Justice Hughes, was a violation of the equal protection clause of the Fourteenth Amendment. Carefully avoiding explicit conflict with the Plessy doctrine, Hughes insisted only that equality meant what it said: "The admissibility of laws separating the races . . . rests wholly upon the equality of the privileges which the laws give to the separated groups within the State" (*Missouri ex rel. Gaines v. Canada* [No. 230]). Subsequent cases applied the same principle to transportation facilities (*Mitchell v. U.S., 1941; Morgan v. Virginia, 1945*), and the whole series of rulings posed a threat to the entire legal pattern of segregation in the South.

To its contribution to the constitutional doctrine of liberty the Roosevelt Court also added a unique footnote. Instances of legislative punishment have been rare in American history, but in 1946 the liberty-minded justices had an opportunity to rule on this almost unprecedented issue. To strike at three executive officials who had been attacked by the House UnAmerican Activities Committee, Congress, through a rider to an appropriations bill, had cut off their salaries and thus forced their removal from the federal payroll. When the trio sued for their back salaries, Justice Black branded the congressional action illegal as a bill of attainder (*U.S. v. Lovett, Watson, and Dodd* [No. 231]), ruling an act of Congress unconstitutional in one of the few occasions since the "Court-packing" fight.

The Scope and Theory of Federal Protection

220. *Freedoms "implicit in the concept of ordered liberty."*

Palko v. Connecticut, 302 U.S. 319 (1937).

CARDOZO, J.: . . . The argument for appellant is that whatever is forbidden by the Fifth Amendment is forbidden by the Fourteenth also. The Fifth Amendment, which is not directed to the states, but solely to the federal government, creates immunity from double jeopardy. No person shall be "subject for the same offense to be twice put in jeopardy of life or limb." The Fourteenth Amendment ordains, "nor shall any State deprive any person of life, liberty, or property, without due process of law." To retry a defendant, though under one indictment and only one, subjects him, it is said, to double jeopardy in violation of the Fifth Amendment, if the prosecution is one on behalf of the United States. From this the consequence is said to follow that there is a denial of life or liberty without due process of law, if the prosecution is one on behalf of the people of a state. . . .

This thesis is even broader. Whatever would be a violation of the original Bill of Rights (Amendments 1 to 8) if done by the federal government is now equally unlawful by force of the Fourteenth Amendment if done by a state. There is no such general rule.

The Fifth Amendment provides, among other things, that no person shall be held to answer for a capital or otherwise infamous crime unless on presentment or indictment of a grand jury. This Court has held that, in prosecutions by a state, presentment or indictment by a grand jury may give way to informations at the instance of a public officer. *Hurtado v. California*. . . . The Fifth Amendment provides also that no person shall be compelled in any criminal case to be a witness against himself. This Court has said that, in prosecutions by a state, the exemption will fail if the state elects to end it. *Twining v. New Jersey*. . . . The Sixth Amendment calls for a jury trial in criminal cases and the Seventh for a jury trial in civil cases at common law where the value in controversy shall exceed twenty dollars. This Court has ruled that consistently with those amendments trial by jury may be modified by a state or abolished altogether. . . .

On the other hand, the due process clause of the Fourteenth Amendment may make it unlawful for a state to abridge by its statutes the freedom of speech which the First Amendment safeguards against encroachment by the Congress . . . or the like freedom of the press . . . or the free exercise of religion . . . or the right of peaceable assembly, without which speech would be unduly trammeled . . . or the right of one accused of crime to the benefit of counsel. . . . In these and other situations immunities that are valid as against the federal government by force of the specific pledges of particular amendments have been found to be implicit in the concept of ordered liberty, and thus, through the Fourteenth Amendment, become valid as against the states.

The line of division may seem to be wavering and broken if there is a hasty catalogue of the cases on the one side and the other. Reflection and analysis will induce a different view. There emerges the perception of a rationalizing principle which gives to discrete instances a proper order and coherence. The right to trial by jury and the immunity from prosecution except as the result of an indictment may have value and importance. Even so, they are not of the very essence of a scheme of ordered liberty. To abolish them is not to violate a "principle of justice so rooted in the traditions and conscience of our people as to be ranked as fundamental." . . . Few would be so narrow or provincial as to maintain that a fair and enlightened system of justice would be impossible without them. What is true of jury trials and indictments is true also, as the cases show, of the immunity from compulsory self-incrimination. . . . This too might be lost, and justice still be done. Indeed, today as in the past there are students of our penal system who look upon the immunity as a mischief rather than a benefit, and who would limit its scope or destroy it altogether. . . . The exclusion of these immunities and privileges from the privileges and immunities protected against the action of the states has not been arbitrary or casual. It has been dictated by a study and appreciation of the meaning, the essential implications, of liberty itself.

We reach a different plane of social and moral values when we pass to the privileges and immunities that have been taken over from the earlier articles of the federal Bill of Rights and brought within the Fourteenth Amendment by a process of absorption. These in their origin were effective against the federal government alone. If the Fourteenth Amendment has absorbed them, the process of absorption has had its source in the belief that neither liberty nor justice would exist if they were sacrificed. . . . This is true, for illustration, of freedom of thought and speech. Of that freedom one may say that it is the matrix, the indispensable condition, of nearly every other form of freedom. With rare aberrations a pervasive recognition of that truth can be traced in our history, political and legal. So it has come about that the domain of liberty, withdrawn by the Fourteenth Amendment from encroachment by the states, has been enlarged by latter-day judgments to include liberty of the mind as well as liberty of action. . . .

Our survey of the cases serves, we think, to justify the statement that the dividing line between them, if not unfaltering throughout its course, has been true for the most part to a unifying principle. On which side of the line the case made out by the appellant has appropriate location must be the next inquiry and the final one. Is that kind of double jeopardy to which the statute has subjected him a hardship so acute and shocking that our polity will not endure it? Does it violate those "fundamental principles of liberty and justice which lie at the base of all our civil and political institutions?" . . . The answer surely must be "no." . . . The state is not attempting to wear the accused out by a multitude of cases with accumulated trials. It asks no more than this, that the case against him shall go on until there shall be a trial free from the corrosion of substantial legal error. . . . This is not cruelty at all, nor even vexation in any immoderate degree. If the trial had been infected with error adverse to the accused, there might have been review at his instance, and as often as necessary to purge the vicious taint. A reciprocal privilege, subject at all times to the discretion of the presiding judge . . . , has now been granted to the state. There is here no seismic innovation. The edifice of justice stands, in its symmetry, to many, greater than before.

Freedom Under the First Amendment

FREEDOM OF SPEECH, PRESS, AND ASSEMBLY

221. *Informed Public Opinion Restrains Misgovernment*

Grosjean v. American Press Company, 297 U.S. 233 (1936).

SUTHERLAND, J.: This suit was brought by appellees, nine publishers of newspapers in the State of Louisiana, to enjoin the enforcement against them of the Provisions of . . . [an act] of Louisiana as follows:

"That every person, firm, association, or corporation, domestic or foreign, engaged in the business of selling, or making any charge for, advertising or for advertisements, whether printed or published, or to be printed or published, in any newspaper, magazine, periodical or publication whatever having a circulation of more than 20,000 copies per week, or displayed and exhibited, or to be displayed and exhibited by means of moving pictures, in the State of Louisiana, shall, in addition to all other taxes and licenses levied and assessed in this State, pay a license tax for the privilege of engaging in such business in this State of two per cent. of the gross receipts of such business." . . .

The validity of the act is assailed as violating the Federal Constitution in two particulars—(1) that it abridges the freedom of the press in contravention of the due process clause contained in §1 of the Fourteenth Amendment; (2) that it denies appellees the equal protection of the laws in contravention of the same Amendment. . . .

1. The first point presents a question of the utmost gravity and importance; for, if well made, it goes to the heart of the natural right of the members of an organized society, united for their common good, to impart and acquire information about their common interests. The First Amendment to the Federal Constitution . . . is not a restraint upon the powers of the states, [but] the states are precluded from abridging the freedom of speech or of the press by force of the due process clause of the Fourteenth Amendment. . . .

That freedom of speech and of the press are rights of the same fundamental character, safeguarded by the due process of law clause of the Fourteenth Amendment against abridgement by state legislation, has likewise been settled by a series of decisions of this Court beginning with *Gitlow v. New York* . . . and ending with *Near v. Minnesota.* . . . The word "liberty" contained in that amendment embraces not only the right of a person to be free from physical restraint, but the right to be free in the enjoyment of all his faculties as well. . . .

The tax imposed is designated a "license tax for the privilege of engaging in such business"—that is to say, the business of selling, or making any charge for, advertising. As applied to appellees, it is a tax of two per cent. on the gross receipts derived from advertisements. . . . It thus operates as a restraint in a double sense. First, its effect is to curtail the amount of revenue realized from advertising, and, second, its direct tendency is to restrict circulation. This is plain enough when we consider that, if it were increased to a high degree, as it could be if valid, it well might result in destroying both advertising and circulation.

A determination of the question whether the tax is valid in respect of the point now under review, requires an examination of the history and circumstances which antedated and attended the adoption of the abridgement clause of the First Amendment, since that clause expresses one of those "fundamental principles of liberty and justice which lie at the base of all our civil and political institutions," and, as such, is embodied in the concept "due process of law," and, therefore, protected against hostile state invasion by the due process clause of the Fourteenth Amendment. . . .

It is impossible to concede that by the words "freedom of the press" the framers of the amendment intended to adopt merely the narrow view then reflected by the law of England that such freedom consisted only in immunity from previous censorship; for this abuse had then permanently disappeared from English practice. It is equally impossible to believe that it was not intended to bring within the reach of these words such modes of restraint as were embodied in the two forms of taxation already described. . . .

This court had occasion in *Near v. Minnesota* . . . to discuss at some length the subject in its general aspect. . . . Liberty of the press within the meaning of the constitutional provision, it was broadly said, meant "principally although not exclusively, immunity from previous restraints or [from] censorship."

Judge Cooley has laid down the test to be applied—"The evils to be prevented were not the censorship of the press merely, but any action of the government by means of which it might prevent such free and general discussion of public matters as seems absolutely essential to prepare the people for an intelligent exercise of their rights as citizens." . . .

It is not intended by anything we have said to suggest that the owners of newspapers are immune from any of the ordinary forms of taxation for support of the government. But this is not an ordinary form of tax, but one single in kind, with a long history of hostile misuse against the freedom of the press.

The predominant purpose of the grant of immunity here invoked was to preserve an untrammeled press as a vital source of public information. The newspapers, magazines and other journals of the country, it is safe to say, have shed and continue to shed, more light on the public and business affairs of the nation than any other instrumentality of publicity; and since informed public opinion is the most potent of all restraints upon misgovernment, the suppression or abridgement of the publicity afforded by a free press cannot be regarded otherwise than with grave concern. The tax here involved is bad not because it takes money from the pockets of the appellees. If that were all, a wholly different question would be presented. It is bad because, in the light of its history and of its present setting, it is seen to be a deliberate and calculated device in the guise of a tax to limit the circulation of information to which the public is entitled in virtue of the constitutional guaranties. A free press stands as one of the great interpreters between the government and the people. To allow it to be fettered is to fetter ourselves. . . .

222. *"Peaceable assembly for lawful discussion cannot be made a crime."*

DeJonge v. Oregon, 299 U.S. 353 (1937).

HUGHES, C.J.: . . . Appellant moved for a direction of acquittal, contending that the statute as applied to him, for merely assisting at a meeting called by the Communist party at which nothing unlawful was done or advocated, violated the due process clause of the Fourteenth Amendment of the Constitution of the United States. . . . Having limited the charge to defendant's participation in a meeting called by the Communist party, the State Court sustained the conviction upon that basis regardless of what was said or done at the meeting. . . .

The broad reach of the statute as thus applied is plain. While defendant was a member of the Communist party, that membership was not necessary to conviction on such a charge. A like fate might have attended any speaker, although not a member who "assisted in the conduct" of the meeting. However innocuous the object of the meeting, however lawful the subjects and tenor of the addresses, however reasonable and timely the discussion, all those assisting in the conduct of the meeting would be subject to imprisonment as felons if the meeting were held by the Communist party. . . .

Thus if the Communist party had called a public meeting in Portland to discuss the tariff, or the foreign policy of the government, or taxation, or relief, or candidacies for the offices of President, members of Congress, Governor or State legislators, every speaker who assisted in the conduct of the meeting would be equally guilty with the defendant in this case, upon the charge as here defined and sustained. . . .

While the States are entitled to protect themselves from the abuse of the privileges of our institutions through an attempted substitution of force and violence in the place of peaceful political action in order to effect revolutionary changes in government, none of our decisions go to the length of sustaining such a curtailment of the right of free speech and assembly as the Oregon statute demands in its present application.

Freedom of speech and of the press are fundamental rights which are safeguarded by the due process clause of the Fourteenth Amendment of the Federal Constitution. The right of peaceable assembly is a right cognate to those of free speech and free press and is equally fundamental. . . .

The First Amendment of the Federal Constitution expressly guarantees that right against abridgment by Congress. But explicit mention there does not argue exclusion elsewhere. For the right is one that cannot be denied without violating those fundamental principles of liberty and justice which lie at the base of all civil and political institutions, principles which the Fourteenth Amendment embodies in the general terms of its due process clause.

These rights may be abused by using speech or press or assembly in order to incite to violence and crime. The people, through their Legislatures, may protect themselves against that abuse. But the legislative intervention can find constitutional justification only by dealing with the abuse. The rights themselves must not be curtailed.

The greater the importance of safeguarding the community from incitements to the overthrow of our institutions by force and violence, the more imperative is the need to preserve inviolate the constitutional rights of free speech, free press and free assembly in order to maintain the opportunity for free political discussion, to the end that government may be responsive to the will of the people and that changes, if desired, may be obtained by peaceful means. Therein lies the security of the republic, the very foundation of constitutional government.

It follows from these considerations that, consistently with the Federal Constitution, peaceable assembly for lawful discussion cannot be made a crime. The holding of meetings for peaceable political action cannot be proscribed. Those who assist in the conduct of such meetings cannot be branded as criminals on that score. The question, if the rights of free speech and peaceable assembly are to be preserved, is not as to the auspices under which the meeting is held, but as to its purpose; not as to the relations of the speakers, but whether their utterances transcend the bounds of the freedom of speech which the Constitution protects.

If the persons assemblying have committed crimes elsewhere, if they have formed or are engaged in a conspiracy against the public peace and order, they may be prosecuted for their conspiracy or other violation of valid laws.

But it is a different matter when the State, instead of prosecuting them for such offenses, seizes upon mere participation in a peaceable assembly and a lawful public discussion as the basis for a criminal charge.

We are not called upon to review the findings of the State court as to the objectives of the Communist party. Notwithstanding those objectives, the defendant still enjoyed his personal right of free speech and to take part in a peaceable assembly having a lawful purpose, although called by that party. The defendant was none the less entitled to discuss the public issues of the day and thus in a lawful manner, without incitement to violence or crime, to seek redress of alleged grievances. That was of the essence of his guaranteed personal liberty.

We hold that the Oregon statute as applied to the particular charge as defined by the State court is repugnant to the due process clause of the Fourteenth Amendment.

FREEDOM OF SPEECH, AND LABOR RELATIONS

223. *Is Picketing Speech?*

Thornhill v. Alabama, 310 U.S. 88 (1940).

MURPHY, J.: . . . The freedom of speech and of the press, which are secured by the First Amendment against abridgment by the United States, are among the fundamental personal rights and liberties which are secured to all persons by the Fourteenth Amendment against abridgment by a State.

The safeguarding of these rights to the ends that men may speak as they think on matters vital to them and that falsehoods may be exposed through the processes of education and discussion is essential to free government. Those who won our independence had confidence in the power of free and fearless reasoning and communication of ideas to discover and spread political and economic truth. Noxious doctrines in those fields may be refuted and their evil averted by the courageous exercise of the right of free discussion. Abridgment of freedom of speech and of the press, however, impairs those opportunities for public education that are essential to effective exercise of the power of correcting error through the processes of popular government. . . . Mere legislative preference for one rather than another means for combatting substantive evils, therefore, may well prove an inadequate foundation on which to rest regulations which are aimed at or in their operation diminish the effective exercise of rights so necessary to the maintenance of democratic institutions. It is imperative that, when the effective exercise of these rights is claimed to be abridged, the courts should "weigh the circumstances" and "appraise the substantiality of the reasons advanced" in support of the challenged regulations. . . .

Proof of an abuse of power in the particular case has never been deemed a requisite for attack on the constitutionality of a statute purporting to license the dissemination of ideas. . . . The cases when interpreted in the light of their facts indicate that the rule is not based upon any assumption that application for the license would be refused or would result in the imposition of other unlawful regulations. Rather it derives from an appreciation of the character of the evil inherent in a licensing system. The power of the licensor against which John Milton directed his assault by his "Appeal for the Liberty of Unlicensed Printing" is pernicious not merely by reason of the censure of particular comments but by reason of the threat to censure comments on matters of public concern. It is not merely the sporadic abuse of power by the censor but the pervasive threat inherent in its very existence that constitutes the danger to freedom of discussion. See *Near v. Minnesota*. . . . A like threat is inherent in a penal statute, like that in question here, which does not aim specifically at evils within the allowable area of state control but, on the contrary, sweeps within its ambit other activities that in ordinary circumstances constitute an exercise of freedom of speech or of the press. The existence of such a statute, which readily lends itself to harsh and discriminatory enforcement by local prosecuting officials, against particular groups deemed to merit their displeasure, results in a continuous and pervasive restraint on all freedom of discussion that might reasonably be regarded as within its purview. It is not any less effective or, if the restraint is not permissible, less pernicious than the restraint on freedom of discussion imposed by the threat of censorship. An accused, after arrest and conviction under such a statute, does not have to sustain the burden of demonstrating that the State could not constitutionally have written a different and specific statute covering his activities as disclosed by the charge and the evidence introduced against him. . . . Where regulations of the liberty of free discussion are concerned, there are special reasons for observing the rule that it is the statute, and not the accusation or the evidence under it, which prescribes the limits of permissible conduct and warns against transgression. . . .

The Alabama statute has been applied by the state courts so as to prohibit a single individual from walking slowly and peacefully back and forth on the public sidewalk in front of the premises of an employer, without speaking to anyone, carrying a sign or placard on a staff above his head stating only the fact that the employer did not employ union men affiliated with the American Federation of Labor; the purpose of the described activity was concededly to advise customers and prospective customers of the relationship existing between the employer and its employees and thereby to induce such customers not to patronize the employer. . . . The statute as thus authoritatively construed and applied leaves room for no exceptions based upon either the number of persons engaged in the proscribed activity, the peaceful character of their demeanor, the nature of their dispute with an employer, or the restrained character and the accurateness of the terminology used in notifying the public of the facts of the dispute. . . .

In sum, whatever the means used to publicize the facts of a labor dispute, whether by printed sign, by pamphlet, by word of mouth or otherwise, all such activity without exception is within the inclusive prohibition of the statute so long as it occurs in the vicinity of the scene of the dispute. . . .

We think that §3448 is invalid on its face.

The freedom of speech and of the press guaranteed by the Constitution embraces at the least the liberty to discuss publicly and truthfully all matters of public concern without previous restraint or fear of subsequent punishment. . . .

Free discussion concerning the conditions in industry and the causes of labor disputes appears to us indispensable to the effective and intelligent use of the processes of popular government to shape the destiny of modern industrial society. . . .

The range of activities proscribed by §3448, whether characterized as picketing or loitering or otherwise, embraces nearly every practicable, effective means whereby those interested—including the employees directly affected—may enlighten the public on the nature and causes of a labor dispute. The safeguarding of these means is essential to the securing of an informed and educated public opinion with respect to a matter which is of public concern. It may be that effective exercise of the means of advancing public knowledge may persuade some of those reached to refrain from entering into advantageous relations with the business establishment which is the scene of the dispute. Every expression of opinion on matters that are important has the potentiality of inducing action in the interests of one rather than another group in society. But the group in power at any moment may not impose penal sanctions on peaceful and truthful discussion of matters of public interest merely on a showing that others may thereby be persuaded to take action inconsistent with its interests. Abridgment of the liberty of such discussion can be justified only where the clear danger of substantive evils arises under circumstances affording no opportunity to test the merits of ideas by competition for acceptance in the market of public opinion. We hold that the danger of injury to an industrial concern is neither so serious nor so imminent as to justify the sweeping proscription of freedom of discussion embodied in §3448. . . .

224. *The Right of Workmen to Discuss Their Affairs*

Thomas v. Collins, 323 U.S. 516 (1944).

RUTLEDGE, J.: . . . The case confronts us again with the duty our system places on this Court to say where the individual's freedom ends and the State's power begins. Choice on that border, now as always delicate, is perhaps more so where the usual presumption supporting legislation is balanced by the preferred place given in our scheme to the great, the indispensable democratic freedoms secured by the First Amendment. . . .

That the State has power to regulate labor unions with a view to protecting the public interest is, as the Texas court said, hardly to be doubted. They cannot claim special immunity from regulation. Such regulation however, whether aimed at fraud or other abuses, must not trespass upon the domain set apart for free speech and free assembly. . . . The right thus to discuss, and inform people concerning, the advantages and disadvantages of unions and joining them is protected not only as part of free speech, but as part of free assembly. . . .

These rights of assembly and discussion are protected by the First Amendment. Whatever would restrict them, without sufficient occasion, would infringe its safeguards. The occasion was clearly protected. The speech was an essential part of the occasion, unless all meaning and purpose were to be taken from it. And the invitations, both general and particular, were parts of the speech, inseparable incidents of the occasion and of all that was said or done.

That there was restriction upon Thomas' right to speak and the rights of the workers to hear what he had to say, there can be no doubt. The threat of the restraining order, backed by the power of contempt, and of arrest for crime, hung over every word. . . .

No speaker, in such circumstances, safely could assume that anything he might say upon the general subject would not be understood by some as an invitation. In short, the supposedly clear-cut distinction between discussion, laudation, general advocacy, and solicitation puts the speaker in these circumstances wholly at the mercy of the varied understanding of his hearers and consequently of whatever inference may be drawn as to his intent and meaning.

Such a distinction offers no security for free discussion. In these conditions it blankets with uncertainty whatever may be said. It compels the speaker to hedge and trim. He must take care in every word to create no impression that he means, in advocating unionism's most central principle, namely, that workingmen should unite for collective bargaining, to urge those present to do so. The vice is not merely that invitation, in the circumstances shown here, is speech. It is also that its prohibition forbids or restrains discussion which is not or may not be invitation. The sharp line cannot be drawn surely or securely. The effort to observe it could not be free speech, free press, or free assembly, in any sense of free advocacy of principle or cause. The restriction's effect, as applied, in a very practical sense was to prohibit Thomas not only to solicit members and memberships, but also to speak in advocacy of the cause of trade unionism in Texas, without having first procured the card. Thomas knew this and faced the alternatives it presented. When served with the order he had three choices: (1) to stand on his right and speak freely; (2) to quit, refusing entirely to speak; (3) to trim, and even thus to risk the penalty. He chose the first alternative. We think he was within his rights in doing so.

The assembly was entirely peaceable, and had no other than a wholly lawful purpose. The statements forbidden were not in themselves unlawful, had no tendency to incite to unlawful action, involved no element of clear and present, grave and immediate danger to the public welfare. Moreover, the State has shown no justification for placing restrictions on the use of the word "solicit." We have here nothing comparable to the case where use of the word "fire" in a crowded theater creates a clear and present danger which the State may undertake to avoid or against which it may protect. *Schenck v. United States*. . . . We cannot say that "solicit" in this setting is such a dangerous word. So far as free speech alone is concerned, there can be no ban or restriction or burden placed on the use of such a word except on showing of exceptional circumstances where the public safety, morality or health is involved or some other substantial interest of the community is at stake.

If therefore use of the word or language equivalent in meaning was illegal here, it was so only because the statute and the order forbade the particular speaker to utter it. When legislation or its application can confine labor leaders on such occasions to innocuous and abstract discussion of the virtues of trade unions and so becloud even this with doubt, uncertainty and the risk of penalty, freedom of speech for them will be at an end. A restriction so destructive of the right of public discussion, without greater or more imminent danger to the public interest than existed in this case, is incompatible with the freedoms secured by the First Amendment. . . .

Apart from its "business practice" theory, the State contends that Section 5 is not inconsistent with freedom of speech and assembly, since this is merely a previous identification requirement which, according to the State court's decision, gives the Secretary of State only "ministerial, not discretionary" authority.

How far the State can require previous identification by one who undertakes to exercise the rights secured by the First Amendment has been largely undetermined. . . .

As a matter of principle a requirement of registration in order to make a public speech would seem generally incompatible with an exercise of the rights of free speech and free assembly. Lawful public assemblies, involving no element of grave and immediate danger to an interest the state is entitled to protect, are not instruments of harm which require previous identification of the speakers. And the right either of workmen or of unions under these conditions to assemble and discuss their own affairs is as fully protected by the Constitution as the right of businessmen, farmers, educators, political party members or others to assemble and discuss their affairs and to enlist the support of others.

We think the controlling principle is stated in *DeJonge v. Oregon*. . . . In that case this Court held that "consistently with the Federal Constitution, peaceable assembly for lawful discussion cannot be made a crime." . . .

If the exercise of the rights of free speech and free assembly cannot be made a crime, we do not think this can be accomplished by the device of requiring previous registration as a condition for exercising them and making such a condition the foundation for restraining in advance their exercise and for imposing a penalty for violating such a restraining order. So long as no more is involved than exercise of the rights of free speech and free assembly, it is immune to such a restriction. If one who solicits support for the cause of labor may be required to register as a condition to the exercise of his right to make a public speech, so may he who seeks to rally support for any social, business, religious or political cause. We think a requirement that one must register before he undertakes to make a public speech to enlist support for a lawful movement is quite incompatible with the requirements of the First Amendment.

Once the speaker goes further, however, and engages in conduct which amounts to more than the right of free discussion comprehends, as when he undertakes the collection of funds or securing subscriptions, he enters a realm where a reasonable registration or identification requirement may be imposed. In that context such solicitation would be quite different from the solicitation involved here. . . .

As we think the requirement of registration, in the present circumstances, was in itself an invalid restriction, we have no occasion to consider whether the restraint as imposed goes beyond merely requiring previous identification or registration. . . .

The restraint is not small when it is considered what was restrained. The right is a national right, federally guaranteed. There is some modicum of freedom of thought, speech and assembly which all citizens of the Republic may exercise throughout its length and breadth, which no State, nor all together, nor the Nation itself, can prohibit, restrain or impede. If the restraint were smaller than it is, it is from petty tyrannies that large ones take root and grow. This fact can be no more plain than when they are imposed on the most basic rights of all. Seedlings planted in that soil grow great and, growing, break down the foundations of liberty. . . .

RELIGION AND SPEECH

225. *Preaching, Pamphlet Peddling, and Privacy*

Murdock v. Pennsylvania, 319 U.S. 105 (1943).

Douglas, J.: . . . The First Amendment, which the Fourteenth makes applicable to the states, declares that "Congress shall make no law respecting an establishment of religion, or prohibiting the free exercise thereof; or abridging the freedom of speech, or of the press. . . ." It could hardly be denied that a tax laid specifically on the exercise of those freedoms would be unconstitutional. Yet the license tax imposed by this ordinance is, in substance, just that.

Petitioners spread their interpretations of the Bible and their religious beliefs largely through the hand distribution of literature by full or part time workers. They claim to follow the example of Paul, teaching "publickly, and from house to house." Acts 20:20. . . .

The hand distribution of religious tracts is an age-old form of missionary evangelism—as old as the history of printing presses. It has been a potent force in various religious movements down through the years. This form of evangelism is utilized today on a large scale by various religious sects whose colporteurs carry the Gospel to thousands upon thousands of homes and seek through personal visitations to win adherents to their faith. It is more than preaching; it is more than distribution of religious literature. It is a combination of both. Its purpose is as evangelical as the revival meeting. This form of religious activity occupies the same high estate under the First Amendment as do worship in the churches and preaching from the pulpits. It has the same claim to protection as the more orthodox and conventional exercises of religion. It also has the same claim as the others to the guarantees of freedom of speech and freedom of the press. . . .

We are concerned, however, in these cases merely with one narrow issue. . . . The cases present a single issue—the constitutionality of an ordinance which as construed and applied requires religious colporteurs to pay a license tax as a condition to the pursuit of their activities.

The alleged justification for the exaction of this license tax is the fact that the religious literature is distributed with a solicitation of funds. . . . But the mere fact that the religious literature is "sold" by itinerant preachers rather than "donated" does not transform evangelism into a commercial enterprise. If it did, then the passing of the collection plate in church would make the church service a commercial project. The constitutional rights of those spreading their religious beliefs through the spoken and printed word are not to be gauged by standards governing retailers or wholesalers of books. The right to use the press for expressing one's views is not to be measured by the protection afforded commercial handbills. It should be remembered that the pamphlets of Thomas Paine were not distributed free of charge. It is plain that a religious organization needs funds to remain a going concern. But an itinerant evangelist, however misguided or intolerant he may be, does not become a mere book agent by selling the Bible or religious tracts to help defray his expenses or to sustain him. Freedom of speech, freedom of the press, freedom of religion are available to all, not merely to those who can pay their own way. As we have said, the problem of drawing the line between a purely commercial activity and a religious one will at times be difficult. On this record it plainly cannot be said that petitioners were engaged in a commercial rather than a religious venture. It is a distortion of the facts of record to describe their activities as the occupation of selling books and pamphlets. . . .

We do not mean to say that religious groups and the press are free from all financial burdens of government. See *Grosjean v. American Press Co.* . . . We have here something quite different, for example, from a tax on the income of one who engages in religious activities or a tax on property used or employed in connection with those activities. It is one thing to impose a tax on the income or property of a preacher. It is quite another thing to exact a tax from him for the privilege of delivering a sermon. The tax imposed by the City of Jeannette is a flat license tax, the payment of which is a condition of the exercise of these constitutional privileges. The power to tax the exercise of a privilege is the power to control or suppress its enjoyment. *Magnano Co. v. Hamilton.* . . . Those who can tax the exercise of this religious practice can make its exercise so costly as to deprive it of the resources necessary for its maintenance. Those who can tax the privilege of engaging in this form of missionary evangelism can close its doors to all those who do not have a full purse. Spreading religious beliefs in this ancient and honorable manner would thus be denied the needy. Those who can deprive religious groups of their colporteurs can take from them a part of the vital power of the press which has survived from the Reformation.

It is contended, however, that the fact that the license tax can suppress or control this activity is unimportant if it does not do so. But that is to disregard the nature of this tax. It is a license tax—a flat tax imposed on the exercise of a privilege granted by the Bill of Rights. A state may not impose a charge for the enjoyment of a right granted by the Federal Constitution. . . .

226. *Conformity and Liberty: The Flag Salute Cases*

West Virginia State Board v. Barnette, 319 U.S. 624 (1943).

JACKSON, J.: . . . Appellees, citizens of the United States and of West Virginia, brought suit in the United States District Court for themselves and others similarly situated asking its injunction to restrain enforcement of these laws and regulations against Jehovah's Witnesses. The Witnesses are an unincorporated body teaching that the obligation imposed by law of God is superior to that of laws enacted by temporal government. Their religious beliefs include a literal version of Exodus, Chapter 20, verses 4 and 5, which says: "Thou shalt not make unto thee any graven image, or any likeness of anything that is in heaven above, or that is in the earth beneath, or that is in the water under the earth; thou shalt not bow down thyself to them, nor serve them." They consider that the Flag is an "image" within this command. For this reason they refuse to salute it. . . .

This case calls upon us to reconsider a precedent decision, as the Court throughout its history often has been required to do. Before turning to the Gobitis case, however, it is desirable to notice certain characteristics by which this controversy is distinguished.

The freedom asserted by these appellees does not bring them into collision with rights asserted by any other individual. It is such conflicts which most frequently require intervention of the State to determine where the rights of one end and those of another begin. But the refusal of these persons to participate in the ceremony does not interfere with or deny rights of others to do so. Nor is there any question in this case that their behavior is peaceable and orderly. The sole conflict is between authority and rights of the individual. The State asserts power to condition access to public education on making a prescribed sign and profession and at the same time to coerce attendance by punishing both parent and child. The latter stand on a right of self-determination in matters that touch individual opinion and personal attitude.

As the present Chief Justice said in dissent in the Gobitis case, the State may "require teaching by instruction and study of all in our history and in the structure and organization of our government, including the guaranties of civil liberty, which tend to inspire patriotism and love of country." Here, however, we are dealing with a compulsion of students to declare a belief. They are not merely made acquainted with the flag salute so that they may be informed as to what it is or even what it means. The issue here is whether this slow and easily neglected route to aroused loyalties constitutionally may be short-cut by substituting a compulsory salute and slogan. . . .

There is no doubt that, in connection with the pledges, the flag salute is a form of utterance. Symbolism is a primitive but effective way of communicating ideas. The use of an emblem or flag to symbolize some system, idea, institution, or personality, is a short cut from mind to mind. . . .

It is also to be noted that the compulsory flag salute and pledge requires affirmation of a belief and an attitude of mind. It is not clear whether the regulation contemplates that pupils forego any contrary convictions of their own and become unwilling converts to the prescribed ceremony or whether it will be acceptable if they simulate assent by words without belief and by a gesture barren of meaning. It is now a commonplace that censorship or suppression of expression of opinion is tolerated by our Constitution only when the expression presents a clear and present danger of action of a kind the State is empowered to prevent and punish. It would seem that involuntary affirmation could be commanded only on even more immediate and urgent grounds than silence. But here the power of compulsion is invoked without any allegation that remaining passive during a flag salute ritual creates a clear and present danger that would justify an effort even to muffle expression. To sustain the compulsory flag salute we are required to say that a Bill of Rights which guards the individual's right to speak his own mind, left it open to public authorities to compel him to utter what is not in his mind.

Whether the First Amendment to the Constitution will permit officials to order observance of ritual of this nature does not depend upon whether as a voluntary exercise we would think it to be good, bad or merely innocuous. . . .

Nor does the issue as we see it turn on one's possession of particular religious views or the sincerity with which they are held. While religion supplies appellees' motive for enduring the discomforts of making the issue in this case, many citizens who do not share these religious views hold such a compulsory rite to infringe constitutional liberty of the individual. It is not necessary to inquire whether non-conformist beliefs will exempt from the duty to salute unless we first find power to make the salute a legal duty.

The Gobitis decision, however, *assumed*, as did the argument in that case and in this, that power exists in the State to impose the flag salute discipline upon school children in general. The Court only examined and rejected a claim based on religious beliefs of immunity from an unquestioned general rule. The question which underlies the flag salute controversy is whether such a ceremony so touching matters of opinion and political attitude may be imposed upon the individual by official authority under powers committed to any political organization under our Constitution. . . .

In weighing arguments of the parties

it is important to distinguish between the due process clause of the Fourteenth Amendment as an instrument for transmitting the principles of the First Amendment and those cases in which it is applied for its own sake. The test of legislation which collides with the Fourteenth Amendment, because it also collides with the principles of the First, is much more definite than the test when only the Fourteenth is involved. Much of the vagueness of the due process clause disappears when the specific prohibitions of the First become its standard. The right of a State to regulate, for example, a public utility may well include, so far as the due process test is concerned, power to impose all of the restrictions which a legislature may have a "rational basis" for adopting. But freedoms of speech and of press, of assembly, and of worship may not be infringed on such slender grounds. They are susceptible of restriction only to prevent grave and immediate danger to interests which the State may lawfully protect. It is important to note that while it is the Fourteenth Amendment which bears directly upon the State it is the more specific limiting principles of the First Amendment that finally govern this case.

Nor does our duty to apply the Bill of Rights to assertions of official authority depend upon our possession of marked competence in the field where the invasion of rights occurs. True, the task of translating the majestic generalities of the Bill of Rights, conceived as part of the pattern of liberal government in the eighteenth century, into concrete restraints on officials dealing with the problems of the twentieth century, is one to disturb self-confidence. These principles grew in soil which also produced a philosophy that the individual was the center of society, that his liberty was attainable through mere absence of governmental restraints, and that government should be entrusted with few controls and only the mildest supervision over men's affairs. We must transplant these rights to a soil in which the laissez-faire concept or principle of non-interference has withered at least as to economic affairs, and social advancements are increasingly sought through closer integration of society and through expanded and strengthened governmental controls. These changed conditions often deprive precedents of reliability and cast us more than we would choose upon our own judgment. But we act in these matters not by authority of our competence but by force of our commissions. We cannot, because of modest estimates of our competence in such specialties as public education, withhold the judgment that history authenticates as the function of this Court when liberty is infringed. . . .

The case is made difficult not because the principles of its decision are obscure but because the flag involved is our own. Nevertheless, we apply the limitations of the Constitution with no fear that freedom to be intellectually and spiritually diverse or even contrary will disintegrate the social organization. To believe that patriotism will not flourish if patriotic ceremonies are voluntary and spontaneous instead of a compulsory routine is to make an unflattering estimate of the appeal of our institutions to free minds. We can have intellectual individualism and the rich cultural diversities that we owe to exceptional minds only at the price of occasional eccentricity and abnormal attitudes. When they are so harmless to others or to the State as those we deal with here, the price is not too great. But freedom to differ is not limited to things that do not matter much. That would be a mere shadow of freedom. The test of its substance is the right to differ as to things that touch the heart of the existing order.

If there is any fixed star in our constitutional constellation, it is that no official, high or petty, can prescribe what shall be orthodox in politics, nationalism, religion, or other matters of opinion or force citizens to confess by word or act their faith therein. If there are any circumstances which permit an exception, they do not now occur to us.

We think the action of the local authorities in compelling the flag salute and pledge transcends constitutional limitations on their power and invades the sphere of intellect and spirit which it is the purpose of the First Amendment . . . to reserve from all official control. . . .

Procedural Safeguards of Civil Rights

227. *Forced Confessions*

Chambers v. Florida, 309 U.S. 227 (1940).

BLACK, J.: . . . The grave question . . . presented is whether proceedings in which confessions were utilized, and which culminated in sentences of death upon four young negro men in the state of Florida, failed to afford the safeguard of that due process of law guaranteed by the Fourteenth Amendment. . . .

After one week's constant denial of all guilt, petitioners "broke."

Just before sunrise, the state officials got something "worthwhile" from petitioners which the state's attorney would "want"; again he was called; he came; in the presence of those who had carried on and witnessed the all night questioning, he caused his questions and petitioners' answers to be stenographically reported. These are the confessions utilized by the state to obtain the judgments upon which petitioners were sentenced to death. . . . When Chambers was tried, his conviction rested upon his confession and testimony of the other three confessors. The convict guard and the sheriff "were in the court room sitting down in a seat." And from arrest until sentenced to death, petitioners were never—either in jail or in court—wholly removed from the constant observation, influence, custody and control of those whose persistent pressure brought about the sunrise confessions. . . .

The scope and operation of the Fourteenth Amendment have been fruitful sources of controversy in our constitutional history. However, in view of its historical setting and the wrongs which called it into being, the due process provision of the Fourteenth Amendment—just as that in the Fifth—has led few to doubt that it was intended to guarantee procedural standards adequate and appropriate, then and thereafter, to protect, at all times, people charged with or suspected of crime by those holding positions of power and authority. . . .

The determination to preserve an accused's right to procedural due process sprang in large part from knowledge of the historical truth that the rights and liberties of people accused of crime could not be safely entrusted to secret inquisitorial processes. The testimony of centuries, in governments of varying kinds over populations of different races and beliefs, stood as proof that physical and mental torture and coercion had brought about the tragically unjust sacrifices of some who were the noblest and most useful of their generations. The rack, the thumbscrew, the wheel, solitary confinement, protracted questioning and cross questioning, and other ingenious forms of entrapment of the helpless or unpopular had left their wake of mutilated bodies and shattered minds along the way to the cross, the guillotine, the stake and the hangman's noose. And they who have suffered most from secret and dictatorial proceedings have almost always been the poor, the ignorant, the numerically weak, the friendless, and the powerless.

This requirement—of conforming to fundamental standards of procedure in criminal trials—was made operative against the states by the Fourteenth Amendment. . . . To permit human lives to be forfeited upon confessions thus obtained would make of the constitutional requirement of due process of law a meaningless symbol. . . .

We are not impressed by the argument that law enforcement methods such as those under review are necessary to uphold our laws. The Constitution proscribes such lawless means irrespective of the end. And this argument flouts the basic principle that all people must stand on an equality before the bar of justice in every American court. Today, as in ages past. we are not without tragic proof that the exalted power of some governments to punish manufactured crime dictatorially is the handmaid of tyranny. Under our constitutional system, courts stand against any winds that blow as havens of refuge for those who might otherwise suffer because they are helpless, weak, outnumbered, or because they are non-conforming victims of prejudice and public excitement. Due process of law, preserved for all by our Constitution, commands that no such practice as that disclosed by this record shall send any accused to his death. No higher duty, no more solemn responsibility, rests upon this Court, than that of translating into living law and maintaining this constitutional shield deliberately planned and inscribed for the benefit of every human being subject to our Constitution—of whatever race, creed or persuasion.

228. *The Right to Counsel*

Benjamin V. Cohen and Erwin N. Griswold to *The New York Times,* July 29, 1942; published August 2, 1942, 6E.

The important facts in *Betts v. Brady* were simple and undisputed. Betts, a farm hand, was indicted for robbery, [and] the maximum penalty . . . under the laws of Maryland is twenty years' imprisonment. Having no funds, the accused requested the court to appoint counsel for him. The trial judge refused, asserting that it was not the practice in Carroll County, Md. to appoint counsel for indigent defendants save in prosecutions for murder and rape. . . .

Most Americans—lawyers and laymen alike—before the [Supreme Court's] decision in *Betts v. Brady* would have thought that the right of the accused to counsel in a serious criminal case was unquestionably a part of our own Bill of Rights. Certainly the majority of the Supreme Court which rendered the decision . . . would not wish their decision to be used to discredit the significance of that right and the importance of its observance.

Yet at a critical period in world history, *Betts v. Brady* dangerously tilts the scales against the safeguarding of one of the most precious rights of man. For in a free world no man should be condemned to penal servitude for years without having the right of counsel to defend him. The right to counsel, for the poor as well as the rich, is an indispensable safeguard of freedom and justice under law.

Suffrage and Segregation

229. *The "White Primary" Outlawed*

Smith v. Allwright, 321 U.S. 649 (1944).

Reed, J.: . . . Texas is free to conduct her elections and limit her electorate as she may deem wise, save only as her action may be affected by the prohibitions of the United States Constitution or in conflict with powers delegated to and exercised by the National Government. The Fourteenth Amendment forbids a State from making or enforcing any law which abridges the privileges or immunities of citizens of the United States and the Fifteenth Amendment specifically interdicts any denial or abridgement by a State of the right of citizens to vote on account of color. Respondents appeared in the District Court and the Circuit Court of Appeals and defended on the ground that the Democratic party of Texas is a voluntary organization with members banded together for the purpose of selecting individuals of the group representing the common political beliefs as candidates in the general election. As such a voluntary organization, it was claimed, the Democratic party is free to select its own membership and limit to whites participation in the party primary. Such action, the answer asserted, does not violate the Fourteenth, Fifteenth or Seventeenth Amendment as officers of government cannot be chosen at primaries and the Amendments are applicable only to general elections where governmental officers are actually elected. Primaries, it is said, are political party affairs, handled by party, not governmental, officers. . . .

Since *Grovey v. Townsend* and prior to the present suit, no case from Texas involving primary elections has been before this Court. We did decide, however, *United States v. Classic*. . . . The fusing by the Classic case of the primary and general elections into a single instrumentality for choice of officers has a definite bearing on the permissibility under the Constitution of excluding Negroes from primaries. . . . Classic bears upon *Grovey v. Townsend* not because exclusion of Negroes from primaries is any more or less state action by reason of the unitary character of the electoral process but because the recognition of the place of the primary in the electoral scheme makes clear that state delegation to a party of the power to fix the qualifications of primary elections is delegation of a state function that may make the party's action the action of the State. When *Grovey v. Townsend* was written, the Court looked upon the denial of a vote in a primary, as a mere refusal by a party of party membership. As the Louisiana statutes for holding primaries are similar to those of Texas, our ruling in Classic as to the unitary character of the electoral process calls for a reexamination as to whether or not the exclusion of Negroes from a Texas party primary was state action. . . .

It may now be taken as a postulate that the right to vote in such a primary for the nomination of candidates without discrimination by the State, like the right to vote in a general election, is a right secured by the Constitution. By the terms of the Fifteenth Amendment that right may not be abridged by any State on account of race. Under our Constitution the great privilege of the ballot may not be denied a man by the State because of his color.

We are thus brought to an examination of the qualifications for Democratic primary electors in Texas, to determine whether state action or private action has excluded Negroes from participation. . . . [The Court then summarizes Texas statutes regulating primaries.]

We think that this statutory system for the selection of party nominees for inclusion on the general election ballot makes the party which is required to follow these legislative directions an agency of the State in so far as it determines the participants in a primary election. The party takes its character as a state agency from the duties imposed upon it by state statutes; the duties do not become matters of private law because they are performed by a political party. The plan of the Texas primary follows substantially that of Louisiana, with the exception that in Louisiana the State pays the cost of the primary while Texas assesses the cost against candidates. In numerous instances, the Texas statutes fix or limit the fees to be charged. Whether paid directly by the State or through state requirements, it is state action which compels. When primaries become a part of the machinery for choosing officials, state and national, as they have here, the same tests to determine the character of discrimination or abridgement should be applied to the primary as are applied to the general election. If the State requires a certain electoral procedure, prescribes a general election ballot made up of party nominees so chosen and limits the choice of the electorate in general elections for state offices, practically speaking, to those whose names appear on such a ballot, it endorses, adopts and enforces the discrimination against Negroes, practiced by a party entrusted by Texas law with the determination of the qualifications of participants in the primary. This is state action within the meaning of the Fifteenth Amendment.

The United States is a constitutional democracy. Its organic law grants to all citizens a right to participate in the choice of elected officials without restriction by any State because of race. This grant to the people of the opportunity for choice is not to be nullified by a State through casting its electoral process in a form which permits a private organization to practice racial discrimination in the election. Constitutional rights would be of little value if they could be thus indirectly denied.

The privilege of membership in a party may be, as this Court said in *Grovey v. Townsend*, . . . no concern of a State. But when, as here, that privilege is also the essential qualification for voting in a primary to select nominees for a general election, the State makes the action of the party the action of the State. . . . Here we are applying, contrary to the recent decision in *Grovey v. Townsend*, the well-established principle of the Fifteenth Amendment, forbidding the abridgement by a State of a citizen's right to vote. *Grovey v. Townsend* is overruled.

230. *"Equality" in the "Separate but Equal" Doctrine*

Missouri ex rel. Gaines v. Canada, 305 U.S. 337 (1938).

HUGHES, C.J.: . . . Petitioner is a citizen of Missouri. In August, 1935, he was graduated with the degree of Bachelor of Arts at the Lincoln University, an institution maintained by the State of Missouri for the higher education of negroes. That University has no law school. Upon the filing of his application for admission to the law school of the University of Missouri, the registrar advised him to communicate with the president of Lincoln University and the latter directed petitioner's attention to §9622 of the Revised Statutes of Missouri. . . .

Petitioner was advised to apply to the State Superintendent of Schools for aid under that statute. . . . It appears that there are schools of law in connection with the state universities of four adjacent States, Kansas, Nebraska, Iowa, and Illinois, where nonresident negroes are admitted. . . .

While there is no express constitutional provision requiring that the white and negro races be separated for the purpose of higher education, the state court on a comprehensive review of the state statutes held that it was intended to separate the white and negro races for that purpose also. Referring in particular to Lincoln University, the court deemed it to be clear "that the Legislature intended to bring the Lincoln University up to the standard of the University of Missouri, and give to the whites and negroes an equal opportunity for higher education—the whites at the University of Missouri, and the negroes at Lincoln University." Further, the court concluded that the provisions of §9622 . . . to the effect that negro residents "may attend the university of any adjacent State with their tuition paid, pending the full development of Lincoln University," made it evident "that the Legislature did not intend that negroes and whites should attend the same university in this State." In that view it necessarily followed that the curators of the University of Missouri acted in accordance with the policy of the State in denying petitioner admission to its School of Law upon the sole ground of his race.

In answering petitioner's contention that this discrimination constituted a denial of his constitutional right, the state court has fully recognized the obligation of the State to provide negroes with advantages for higher education substantially equal to the advantages afforded to white students. The State has sought to fulfill that obligation by furnishing equal facilities in separate schools, a method the validity of which has been sustained by our decisions. . . .

The state court stresses the advantages that are afforded by the schools of the adjacent States . . . which admit non-resident negroes. . . . Petitioner insists that for one intending to practice in Missouri there are special advantages in attending a law school there, both in relation to the opportunities for the particular study of Missouri law and for the observation of the local courts, and also in view of the prestige of the Missouri law school among the citizens of the State, his prospective clients. Proceeding with its examination of relative advantages, the state court found that the difference in distances to be traveled afforded no substantial ground of complaint and that there was an adequate appropriation to meet the full tuition fees which petitioner would have to pay.

We think that these matters are beside the point. The basic consideration is not as to what sort of opportunities other States provide, or whether they are as good as those in Missouri, but as to what opportunities Missouri itself furnishes to white students and denies to negroes solely upon the ground of color. The admissibility of laws separating the races in the enjoyment of privileges afforded by the State rests wholly upon the equality of the privileges which the laws give to the separated groups within the State. The question here is not of a duty of the State to supply legal training, or of the quality of the training which it does supply, but of its duty when it provides such training to furnish it to the residents of the State upon the basis of an equality of right. By the operation of the laws of Missouri a privilege has been created for white law students which is denied to negroes by reason of their race. The white resident is afforded legal education within the State; the negro resident having the same qualifications is refused it there and must go outside the State to obtain it. That is a denial of the equality of legal right to the enjoyment of the privilege which the State has set up, and the provision for the payment of tuition fees in another State does not remove the discrimination. . . .

In the instant case, the state court did note that petitioner had not applied to the management of Lincoln University for legal training. But, as we have said, the state court did not rule that it would have been the duty of the curators to grant such an application, but on the contrary took the view, as we understand it, that the curators were entitled under the state law to refuse such an application and in its stead to provide for petitioner's tuition in an adjacent State. That conclusion presented the federal question as to the constitutional adequacy of such a provision while equal opportunity for legal training within the State was not furnished, and this federal question the state court entertained and passed upon. We must conclude that in so doing the court denied the federal right which petitioner set up and the question as to the correctness of that decision is before us. We are of the opinion that the ruling was in error, and that petitioner was entitled to be admitted to the law school of the State University in the absence of other and proper provision for his legal training within the State. . . .

Legislative Punishment

231. *Legislative Trials and Bills of Attainder*

U.S. v. Lovett, Watson, and Dodd, 328 U.S. 303 (1946).

BLACK, J.: . . . We hold that the purpose of §304 was not merely to cut off respondents' compensation through regular disbursing channels but permanently to bar them from government service, and that the issue of whether it is constitutional is justiciable. The Section's language as well as the circumstances of its passage which we have just described show that no mere question of compensation procedure or of appropriations was involved, but that it was designed to force the employing agencies to discharge respondents and to bar their being hired by any other governmental agency. . . . Any other interpretation of the section would completely frustrate the purpose of all who sponsored §304, which clearly was to "purge" the then existing and all future lists of government employees of those whom Congress deemed guilty of "subversive activities" and therefore "unfit" to hold a federal job. What was challenged, therefore, is a statute which, because of what Congress thought to be their political beliefs, prohibited respondents from ever engaging in any government work, except as jurors or soldiers. . . .

We hold that §304 falls precisely within the category of Congressional actions which the Constitution barred by providing that "No Bill of Attainder or Ex Post Facto Law shall be passed." . . . [Neither *Cummings v. Missouri* nor *Ex parte* Garland have] ever been overruled. They stand for the proposition that legislative acts, no matter what their form, that apply either to named individuals or to easily ascertainable members of a group in such a way as to inflict punishment on them without a judicial trial are bills of attainder prohibited by the Constitution.

Adherence to this principle requires invalidation of §304. We do adhere to it.

Section 304 was designed to apply to particular individuals. Just as the statute in the two cases mentioned it "operates as a legislative decree of perpetual exclusion" from a chosen vocation. . . . This permanent proscription from any opportunity to serve the Government is punishment, and of a most severe type. It is a type of punishment which Congress has only invoked for special types of odious and dangerous crimes, such as treason, . . . acceptance of bribes by members of Congress, . . . or by other government officials. . . ; and interference with elections by Army and Navy officers. . . .

Section 304, thus, clearly accomplishes the punishment of named individuals without a judicial trial. The fact that the punishment is inflicted through the instrumentality of an Act specifically cutting off the pay of certain named individuals found guilty of disloyalty, makes it no less galling or effective than if it had been done by an Act which designated the conduct as criminal. . . . The effect was to inflict punishment without the safeguards of a judicial trial and "determined by no previous law or fixed rule." The Constitution declares that that cannot be done either by a State or by the United States.

Those who wrote our Constitution well knew the danger inherent in special legislative acts which take away the life, liberty, or property of particular named persons because the legislature thinks them guilty of conduct which deserves punishment. They intended to safeguard the people of this country from punishment without trial by duly constituted courts. . . . Our ancestors had ample reason to know that legislative trials and punishments were too dangerous to liberty to exist in the nation of free men they envisioned. And so they proscribed bills of attainder. Section 304 is one. Much as we regret to declare that an Act of Congress violates the Constitution, we have no alternative here. . . .

CHAPTER XXV

Total War and the Constitution

The effort to extend democratic guarantees at home was soon overshadowed by the growing antidemocratic threats abroad. For the third time in less than a century, war created the problem of adapting constitutional processes to cataclysmic national emergency. Precedents set in World War I smoothed the way for prompt mobilization. Indeed, the First War Powers Act of December, 1941, virtually re-enacted the provisions of the Overman Act of 1918 (Chapter XIX). Moreover, the frequent resort to the doctrine of emergency powers during the depression years accustomed Congress, the courts, and the people to acquiesce in plenary executive authority. Like Lincoln and Wilson, Roosevelt often exercised Presidential prerogative prior to congressional approval. Such was the case in the establishment of the Office of Price Administration, the most powerful independent administrative agency in World War II. In April, 1941, long before Congress granted price-fixing powers, the O. P. A. was created by executive order. The crisis of Pearl Harbor brought statutory approval early in 1942, when Congress delegated to this agency virtually unlimited legislative authority over the national economy.

In *Yakus v. U.S.* (No. 232), the Emergency Price Control Act was attacked as an unconstitutional delegation of legislative power without adequate standards for determining "fair and equitable" price ceilings. Following the peacetime rule formulated in a fair labor standards case in 1941 (*Opp Cotton Mills v. Adminis-*

trator), Chief Justice Stone strongly defended broad delegation of discretionary authority. The question of enforcement of administrative orders also reached the Court in 1944 at a critical moment of the war effort. In *Steuart & Bros. v. Bowles*, an O. P. A. order penalizing an oil distributor for violating the rationing system was upheld as a necessary implication of the Second War Powers Act of 1942, even though the O. P. A. order was alleged to be punishment without proper judicial process.

Just as Congress controlled consumer prices during the wartime emergency, so, too, did it move to protect the public from profiteering on government contracts. To curb excessive profits, Congress passed the Renegotiation Act authorizing the reopening of contracts when evidence indicated that the government was being "gouged." The question of the establishment of a sufficient standard for defining excessive profits was raised in *Lichter v. U.S.* (No. 233). Emphasizing "the compelling necessity for the immediate production" of war goods at reasonable prices, Justice Burton upheld the measure as a policy necessary to prosecute "total global warfare."

Wartime curbs on economic activity were accompanied by similar restrictions on individual liberties. Interestingly enough, one of the early questions related not to the protection of the rights of American citizens but to that of enemy military personnel. In 1942 eight Nazi saboteurs sneaked ashore in New York and Florida from a German submarine. Promptly seized by the F. B. I., the Germans were tried by a special military commission. In a spectacular move, the prisoners challenged the military trial and appealed to the Supreme Court for writs of habeas corpus. Although the Court upheld the military proceedings (*Ex parte* Quirin, 1942), the fact that it would consider whether these persons were protected by basic constitutional provisions suggested that the Court would weigh carefully any governmental invasion of individual rights. As Chief Justice Stone stated, "the court's duty . . . in time of war as well as in time of peace [is] to preserve unimpaired the constitutional safeguards of civil liberty." In an important postwar case (*In re* Yamashita [No. 234]), the Court again reviewed the conduct of military trials of enemy personnel. Although some have contended that the Court's willingness to examine the prisoner's protest against summary military conviction alone constituted an important safeguard to civil liberty, others have condemned the failure to adhere to fundamental procedural guarantees.

Of much greater constitutional consequence was the question of military control of American civilians. Only hours after bombs fell on Pearl Harbor, the governor of Hawaii, acting in conformity with the Hawaiian Organic Act of 1900, placed the territory under martial law, and surrendered governing authority to the army. Until 1944 military tribunals replaced civilian courts in the administration of criminal justice. Not until 1946 was there a successful challenge to summary military trials. In a case involving the conviction of a civilian shipfitter for brawling with Marine sentries (*Duncan v. Kahanamoku* [No. 235]), the Court ruled that the Hawaiian Organic Act "was not intended to authorize the supplanting of courts by military tribunals."

World War II also afforded the Supreme Court the first opportunity in the nation's history to define the meaning of the treason clause in the Constitution. The two leading treason trials were an aftermath to the case of the Nazi saboteurs. In *Cramer v. U.S.* (1945), the Court insisted on a narrow definition of treason, and ruled that Cramer's consorting with the saboteurs did not constitute an "overt act" clearly manifesting treasonable intentions. In *Haupt v. U.S.* (No. 236), however, the Supreme Court, for the first time in its history, upheld a treason conviction. Although the case was quite similar to Cramer's, the Court modified its restrictive interpretation of "overt acts," and made possible the subsequent prosecution of several American citizens for giving aid and comfort to the enemy in time of war.

The most drastic invasion of the rights of citizens by the federal government in American history occurred when President Roosevelt issued an executive order in February, 1942, later reinforced by congressional enactment, authorizing exclusion of "any or all persons" from areas designated by local military commanders. Aimed at the Japanese-Americans on the West coast, this program established detention camps into which 112,000 uprooted Japanese were herded. Cases challenging such summary treatment soon reached the Supreme Court, and in 1943 the Justices upheld a military curfew regulation, but avoided consideration of the constitutionality of American detention camps (*Hirabayashi v. U.S.*). This important issue came before the Court the next year in *Korematsu v. U.S.* (No. 237). Once again the Court side-stepped the basic issue, concentrating instead on the legality of the military evacuation program. Although the majority argued that exclusion was based on military necessity rather than racial prejudice, Justice Murphy found that the removal order was justified "upon questionable racial and sociological grounds" which were "utterly revolting to a free people." At the same time, however, the Court ruled that a person whose loyalty had been established could not be detained in relocation camps (*Ex parte* Endo, 1944).

Unlike World War I, restrictions on freedom of expression were few. In only one case was the Supreme Court confronted with a prosecution under the original Espionage Act of 1917. Without specifically overruling Schenck (Chapter XIX), a 5 to 4 majority upheld a citizen's right to express himself "either by temperate reasoning or by immoderate and vicious invective" (*Hartzel v. U.S.* [1944]), even during wartime. An interesting question in time of war was raised in *Girouard v. U.S.* (1946). In the prosperous and peaceful 1920's, a female pacifist had been denied citizenship because she refused to swear that she would bear arms in the country's defense (*Schwimmer v. U.S.*, 1929). During World War II, however, Girouard, a Seventh Day Adventist, was admitted to citizenship, even though he expressed a similar view. Attempts to cancel citizenship papers on the ground that they had been obtained spuriously were also rejected by the high tribunal in two important wartime decisions (*Schneiderman v. U.S.*, 1943, and *Baumgartner v. U.S.*, 1944).

Wartime Economic Regulation

232. *The Power to Fix Consumer Prices*

Yakus v. U.S., 321 U.S. 414 (1944).

STONE, C.J.: . . . That Congress has constitutional authority to prescribe commodity prices as a war emergency measure, and that the Act was adopted by Congress in the exercise of that power, are not questioned here, and need not now be considered save as they have a bearing on the procedural features of the Act later to be considered, which are challenged on constitutional grounds.

Congress enacted the Emergency Price Control Act in pursuance of a defined policy and required that the prices fixed by the Administrator should further that policy and conform to standards prescribed by the Act. The boundaries of the field of the Administrator's permissible action are marked by the statute. . . . It is enough to satisfy the statutory requirements that the Administrator finds that the prices fixed will tend to achieve that objective and will conform to those standards, and that the courts in an appropriate proceeding can see that substantial basis for those findings is not wanting.

The Act is thus an exercise by Congress of its legislative power. In it Congress has stated the legislative objective, has prescribed the method of achieving that objective—maximum price fixing—, and has laid down standards to guide the administrative determination of both the occasions for the exercise of the price-fixing power, and the particular prices to be established. . . .

The Constitution as a continuously operative charter of government does not demand the impossible or the impracticable. It does not require that Congress find for itself every fact upon which it desires to base legislative action or that it make for itself detailed determinations which it has declared to be prerequisite to the application of the legislative policy to particular facts and circumstances impossible for Congress itself properly to investigate. The essentials of the legislative function are the determination of the legislative policy and its formulation and promulgation as a defined and binding rule of conduct—here the rule, with penal sanctions, that prices shall not be greater than those fixed by maximum price regulations which conform to standards and will tend to further the policy which Congress has established. These essentials are preserved when Congress has specified the basic conditions of fact upon whose existence or occurrence, ascertained from relevant data by a designated administrative agency, it directs that its statutory command shall be effective. It is no objection that the determination of facts and the inferences to be drawn from them in the light of the statutory standards and declaration of policy call for the exercise of judgment, and for the formulation of subsidiary administrative policy within the prescribed statutory framework. . . .

Nor does the doctrine of separation of powers deny to Congress power to direct that an administrative officer properly designated for that purpose have ample latitude within which he is to ascertain the conditions which Congress has made prerequisite to the operation of its legislative command. Acting within its constitutional power to fix prices it is for Congress to say whether the data on the basis of which prices are to be fixed are to be confined within a narrow or a broad range. In either case the only concern of courts is to ascertain whether the will of Congress has been obeyed. This depends not upon the breadth of the definition of the facts or conditions which the administrative officer is to find but upon the determination whether the definition sufficiently marks the field within which the Administrator is to act so that it may be known whether he has kept within it in compliance with the legislative will. . . .

The standards prescribed by the present Act, with the aid of the "statement of considerations" required to be made by the Administrator, are sufficiently definite and precise to enable Congress, the courts and the public to ascertain whether the Administrator, in fixing the designated prices, had conformed to those standards. Compare *Hirabayashi v. United States*. . . . Hence we are unable to find in them an unauthorized delegation of legislative power. The authority to fix prices only when prices have risen or threaten to rise to an extent or in a manner inconsistent with the purpose of the Act to prevent inflation is not broader than the authority to fix maximum prices when deemed necessary to protect consumers against unreasonably high prices, sustained in *Sunshine Anthracite Coal Co. v. Adkins* . . . or the authority to take possession of and operate telegraph lines whenever deemed necessary for the national security or defense, upheld in *Dakota Cent. Tel. Co. v. South Dakota* . . . or the authority to suspend tariff provisions upon finding that the duties imposed by a foreign state are "reciprocally unequal and unreasonable," held valid in *Field v. Clark*. . . .

Congress, in . . . authorizing consideration by the district court of the validity of the Act alone, gave clear indication that the validity of the Administrator's regulations or orders should not be subject to attack in criminal prosecutions for their violation, at least before their invalidity had been adjudicated by recourse to the protest procedure prescribed by the statute. Such we conclude is the correct construction of the Act. . . .

Our decisions leave no doubt that when justified by compelling public interest the legislature may authorize summary action subject to later judicial review of its validity. . . . Measured by these standards we find no denial of due process under the circumstances in which this Act was adopted and must be applied, in its denial of any judicial stay pending determination of a regulation's validity. . . .

233. *Congressional Control of Prices Paid by the Government*

Lichter v. U.S., 334 U.S. 742 (1948).

BURTON, J.: . . . On the basis of (a) the nature of the particular constitutional powers being employed, (b) the current administrative practice later incorporated into the Act and (c) the adequacy of the statutory term "excessive profits" as used in this context, we hold that the authority granted was a lawful delegation of administrative authority and not an unconstitutional delegation of legislative power.

(a) *A constitutional power implies a power of delegation of authority under it sufficient to effect its purposes.*—This power is especially significant in connection with constitutional war powers under which the exercise of broad discretion as to methods to be employed may be essential to an effective use of its war powers by Congress. The degree to which Congress must specify its policies and standards in order that the administrative authority granted may not be an unconstitutional delegation of its own legislative power is not capable of precise definition. In peace or in war it is essential that the Constitution be scrupulously obeyed, and particularly that the respective branches of the Government keep within the powers assigned to each by the Constitution. On the other hand, it is of the highest importance that the fundamental purposes of the Constitution be kept in mind and given effect in order that, through the Constitution, the people of the United States may in time of war as in peace bring to the support of those purposes the full force of their united action. . . .

In 1942, in the early stages of total global warfare, the exercise of a war power such as the power "To raise and support Armies . . ." and "To provide and maintain a Navy . . . ," called for the production by us of war goods in unprecedented volume with the utmost speed, combined with flexibility of control over the product and with a high degree of initiative on the part of the producers. Faced with the need to exercise that power, the question was whether it was beyond the constitutional power of Congress to delegate to the high officials named therein the discretion contained in the original Renegotiation Act of April 28, 1942, and the amendments of October 21, 1942. We believe that the administrative authority there granted was well within the constitutional war powers then being put to their predestined uses.

(b) *The administrative practices developed under the Renegotiation Act demonstrated the definitive adequacy of the term "excessive profits" as used in the Act.*— The administrative practices currently developed under the Act in interpreting the term "excessive profits" appear to have come well within the scope of the congressional policy. We have referred above to the War Department Directive of August 10, 1942, and to the Joint Departmental Statement of March 31, 1943, both of which were placed before appropriate Congressional Committees. These clearly stated practices are evidence of a current correct understanding of the congressional intent. This appears from the fact that the congressional action of October 21, 1942, made effective as of April 28, 1942, was taken in the light of the above-mentioned directive and without restricting its effect. . . .

(c) *The statutory term "excessive profits" in its context, was a sufficient expression of legislative policy and standards to render it constitutional.*—The fact that this term later was further defined both by administrative action and by statutory amendment indicates the probable desirability of such added definition, but it does not demonstrate that such further definition was a constitutional necessity essential to the validity of the original exercise by Congress of its war powers in initiating a new solution of an unprecedented problem. The fact that the congressional definition confirmed the administrative practice which already was in effect under the original statutory language tends to show that a statutory definition was not necessary in order to give effect to the congressional intent. . . .

It is not necessary that Congress supply administrative officials with a specific formula for their guidance in a field where flexibility and the adaptation of the congressional policy to infinitely variable conditions constitute the essence of the program. . . . Standards prescribed by Congress are to be read in the light of the conditions to which they are to be applied. . . . The purpose of the Renegotiation Act and its factual background establish a sufficient meaning for "excessive profits" as those words are used in practice. . . .

Wartime Civil Liberties

MILITARY TRIALS OF ENEMY MILITARY PERSONNEL

234. *Judicial Review of Decisions of Military Tribunals*

In re Yamashita, 327 U.S. 1 (1946).

STONE, C.J.: . . . Petitioner argues, as ground for the writ of habeas corpus, that Article 25 of the Articles of War prohibited the reception in evidence by the commission of depositions on behalf of the prosecution in a capital case, and that Article 38 prohibited the reception of hearsay and of opinion evidence.

We think that neither Article 25 nor Article 38 is applicable to the trial of an enemy combatant by a military commission for violations of the law of war. Article 2 of the Articles of War enumerates "the persons . . . subject to these articles," who are denominated, for purposes of the Articles, as "persons subject to military law." In general, the persons so enumerated are members of our own Army and of the personnel accompanying the Army. Enemy combatants are not included among them. Articles 12, 13, and 14, before the adoption of Article 15 in 1916, made all "persons subject to military law" amenable to trial by courts-martial for any offense made punishable by the Articles of War. Article 12 makes triable by general court-martial "any other person who by the law of war is subject to trial by military tribunals." Since Article 2, in its 1916 form, includes some persons who, by the law of war, were, prior to 1916, triable by military commission, it was feared by the proponents of the 1916 legislation that in the absence of a saving provision, the authority given by Articles 12, 13 and 14 to try such persons before courts-martial might be construed to deprive the non-statutory military commission of a portion of what was considered to be its traditional jurisdiction. To avoid this, and to preserve that jurisdiction intact, Article 15 was added to the Articles. It declared that "The provisions of these articles conferring jurisdiction upon courts-martial shall not be construed as depriving military commissions . . . of concurrent jurisdiction in respect of offenders or offenses that . . . by the law of war may be triable by such military commissions."

By thus recognizing military commissions in order to preserve their traditional jurisdiction over enemy combatants unimpaired by the Articles, Congress gave sanction, as we held in *Ex parte Quirin*, to any use of the military commission contemplated by the common law of war. But it did not thereby make subject to the Articles of War persons other than those defined by Article 2 as being subject to the Articles, nor did it confer the benefits of the Articles upon such persons. The Articles recognized but one kind of military commission, not two. But they sanctioned the use of that one for the trial of two classes of persons, to one of which the Articles do, and to the other of which they do not, apply in such trials. Being of this latter class, petitioner cannot claim the benefits of the Articles, which are applicable only to the members of the other class. Petitioner, an enemy combatant, is therefore not a person made subject to the Articles of War by Article 2, and the military commission before which he was tried, though sanctioned, and its jurisdiction saved, by Article 15, was not convened by virtue of the Articles of War, but pursuant to the common law of war. It follows that the Articles of War, including Articles 25 and 38, were not applicable to petitioner's trial and imposed no restrictions upon the procedure to be followed. The Articles left the control over the procedure in such a case where it had previously been, with the military command. . . .

We cannot say that the commission, in admitting evidence to which objection is now made, violated any act of Congress, treaty or military command defining the commission's authority. For reasons already stated we hold that the commission's rulings on evidence and on the mode of conducting these proceedings against petitioner are not reviewable by the courts, but only by the reviewing military authorities. From this viewpoint it is unnecessary to consider what, in other situations, the Fifth Amendment might require, and as to that no intimation one way or the other is to be implied. Nothing we have said is to be taken as indicating any opinion on the question of the wisdom of considering such evidence, or whether the action of a military tribunal in admitting evidence, which Congress or controlling military command has directed to be excluded, may be drawn in question by petition for habeas corpus or prohibition. . . .

It thus appears that the order convening the commission was a lawful order, that the commission was lawfully constituted, that petitioner was charged with violation of the law of war, and that the commission had authority to proceed with the trial, and in doing so did not violate any military, statutory, or constitutional command. We have considered, but find it unnecessary to discuss, other contentions which we find to be without merit. We therefore conclude that the detention of the petitioner for trial and his detention upon his conviction, subject to the prescribed review by the military authorities, were lawful, and that the petition for certiorari, and leave to file in this Court petitions for writs of habeas corpus and prohibition should be, and they are *Denied.*

MILITARY TRIALS OF AMERICAN CITIZENS

235. *"Civil liberty and . . . martial law cannot endure together."*

Duncan v. Kahanamoku, 327 U.S. 304 (1946).

BLACK, J.: . . . Did the Organic Act during the period of martial law give the armed forces power to supplant all civilian laws and to substitute military for judicial trials under the conditions that existed in Hawaii at the time these petitioners were tried? The relevant conditions, for our purposes, were the same when both petitioners were tried. The answer to the question depends on a correct interpretation of the Act. . . . Both the language of the Organic Act and its legislative history fail to indicate that the scope of "martial law" in Hawaii includes the supplanting of courts by military tribunals, [so] we must look to other sources in order to interpret that term. We think the answer may be found in the birth, development and growth of our governmental institutions up to the time Congress passed the Organic Act. Have the principles and practices developed during the birth and growth of our political institutions been such as to persuade us that Congress intended that loyal civilians in loyal territory should have their daily conduct governed by military orders substituted for criminal laws, and that such civilians should be tried and punished by military tribunals? Let us examine what those principles and practices have been, with respect to the position of civilian government and the courts and compare that with the standing of military tribunals throughout our history.

People of many ages and countries have feared and unflinchingly opposed the kind of subordination of executive, legislative and judicial authorities to complete military rule which according to the government Congress has authorized here. In this country that fear has become part of our cultural and political institutions. The story of that development is well known and we see no need to retell it all. . . .

Courts and their procedural safeguards are indispensable to our system of government. They were set up by our founders to protect the liberties they valued. . . . Our system of government clearly is the antithesis of total military rule and the founders of this country are not likely to have contemplated complete military dominance within the limits of a Territory made part of this country and not recently taken from an enemy. They were opposed to governments that placed in the hands of one man the power to make, interpret and enforce the laws. Their philosophy has been the people's throughout our history. For that reason we have maintained legislatures chosen by citizens or their representatives and courts and juries to try those who violate legislative enactments. We have always been especially concerned about the potential evils of summary criminal trials and have guarded against them by provisions embodied in the Constitution itself. See *Ex parte Milligan*. . . . Legislatures and courts are not merely cherished American institutions; they are indispensable to our Government.

Military tribunals have no such standing. . . . Congress prior to the time of the enactment of the Organic Act had only once authorized the supplanting of the courts by military tribunals. Legislation to that effect was enacted immediately after the South's unsuccessful attempt to secede from the Union. In so far as that legislation applied to the Southern States after the war was at an end it was challenged by a series of Presidential vetoes as vigorous as any in the country's history. And in order to prevent this Court from passing on the constitutionality of this legislation Congress found it necessary to curtail our appellate jurisdiction. Indeed, prior to the Organic Act, the only time this Court had ever discussed the supplanting of courts by military tribunals in a situation other than that involving the establishment of a military government over recently occupied enemy territory, it had emphatically declared that "civil liberty and this kind of martial law cannot endure together; the antagonism is irreconcilable; and, in the conflict, one or the other must perish." *Ex parte Milligan*. . . .

We believe that when Congress passed the Hawaiian Organic Act and authorized the establishment of "martial law" it had in mind and did not wish to exceed the boundaries between military and civilian power, in which our people have always believed, which responsible military and executive officers had heeded, and which had become part of our political philosophy and institutions prior to the time Congress passed the Organic Act. The phrase "martial law" as employed in that Act, therefore, while intended to authorize the military to act vigorously for the maintenance of an orderly civil government and for the defense of the island against actual or threatened rebellion or invasion, was not intended to authorize the supplanting of courts by military tribunals. Yet the government seeks to justify the punishment of both White and Duncan on the ground of such supposed Congressional authorization. We hold that both petitioners are now entitled to be released from custody.

TREASON

236. *Enemy Sabotage and Treason*

Haupt v. U.S., 330 U.S. 631 (1947).

Jackson, J.: . . . Petitioner is the father of Herbert Haupt, one of the eight saboteurs convicted by a military tribunal. . . . Sheltering his son, assisting him in getting a job, and in acquiring an automobile, all alleged to be with knowledge of the son's mission, involved defendant in the treason charge. . . .

It is urged that the conviction cannot be sustained because there is no sufficient proof of adherence to the enemy, the acts of aid and comfort being natural acts of aid for defendant's own son. Certainly that relationship is a fact for the jury to weigh along with others, and they were correctly instructed that if they found that defendants' intention was not to injure the United States but merely to aid his son "as an individual, as distinguished from assisting him in his purposes, if such existed, of aiding the German Reich, or of injuring the United States, the defendant must be found not guilty." The defendant can complain of no error in such a submission. It was for the jury to weigh the evidence that the acts proceeded from parental solicitude against the evidence of adherence to the German cause. It is argued that Haupt merely had the misfortune to sire a traitor and all he did was to act as an indulgent father toward a disloyal son. In view however of the evidence of defendant's own statements that after the war he intended to return to Germany, that the United States was going to be defeated, that he would never permit his boy to join the American Army, that he would kill his son before he would send him to fight Germany, and others to the same effect, the jury apparently concluded that the son had the misfortune of being a chip off the old block—a tree inclined as the twig had been bent—metaphors which express the common sense observation that parents are as likely to influence the character of their children as are children to shape that of their parents. Such arguments are for the jury to decide. . . .

Haupt has been twice tried and twice found guilty. The law of treason makes, and properly makes, conviction difficult but not impossible. His acts aided an enemy of the United States toward accomplishing his mission of sabotage. The mission was frustrated but defendant did his best to make it succeed. His overt acts were proved in compliance with the hard test of the Constitution, are hardly denied, and the proof leaves no reasonable doubt of the guilt.

THE JAPANESE MINORITY AND EMERGENCY DETENTION

237. *Forced Exclusion, Racism, and Concentration Camps*

Korematsu v. U.S., 323 U.S. 214 (1944).

Black, J.: . . . The petitioner, an American citizen of Japanese descent, was convicted in a federal district court for remaining in San Leandro, California, a "Military Area," contrary to Civilian Exclusion Order No. 34 of the Commanding General of the Western Command, U.S. Army, which directed that after May 9,

1942, all persons of Japanese ancestry should be excluded from that area. No question was raised as to petitioner's loyalty to the United States. . . .

It should be noted, to begin with, that all legal restrictions which curtail the civil rights of a single racial group are immediately suspect. That is not to say that all such restrictions are unconstitutional. It is to say that courts must subject them to the most rigid scrutiny. Pressing public necessity may sometimes justify the existence of such restrictions; racial antagonism never can. . . .

In the light of the principles we announced in the *Hirabayashi* case, we are unable to conclude that it was beyond the war power of Congress and the Executive to exclude those of Japanese ancestry from the West Coast war area at the time they did. True, exclusion from the area in which one's home is located is a far greater deprivation than constant confinement to the home from 8 p.m. to 6 a.m. Nothing short of apprehension by the proper military authorities of the gravest imminent danger to the public safety can constitutionally justify either. But exclusion from a threatened area, no less than curfew, has a definite and close relationship to the prevention of espionage and sabotage. The military authorities, charged with the primary responsibility of defending our shores, concluded that curfew provided inadequate protection and ordered exclusion. They did so, as pointed out in our *Hirabayashi* opinion, in accordance with Congressional authority to the military to say who should, and who should not, remain in the threatened areas.

In this case the petitioner challenges the assumptions upon which we rested our conclusions in the *Hirabayashi* case. He also urges that by May 1942, when Order No. 34 was promulgated, all danger of Japanese invasion of the West Coast had disappeared. After careful consideration of these contentions we are compelled to reject them. . . .

Like curfew, exclusion of those of Japanese origin was deemed necessary because of the presence of an unascertained number of disloyal members of the group, most of whom we have no doubt were loyal to this country. It was because we could not reject the finding of the military authorities that it was impossible to bring about an immediate segregation of the disloyal from the loyal that we sustained the validity of the curfew order as applying to the whole group. In the instant case, temporary exclusion of the entire group was rested by the military on the same ground. The judgment that exclusion of the whole group was for the same reason a military imperative answers the contention that the exclusion was in the nature of group punishment based on antagonism to those of Japanese origin. That there were members of the group who retained loyalties to Japan has been confirmed by investigations made subsequent to the exclusion. Approximately five thousand American citizens of Japanese ancestry refused to swear unqualified allegiance to the United States and to renounce allegiance to the Japanese Emperor, and several thousand evacuees requested repatriation to Japan.

We uphold the exclusion order as of the time it was made and when the petitioner violated it. . . . In doing so, we are not unmindful of the hardships imposed by it upon a large group of American citizens. . . . But hardships are part of war, and war is an aggregation of hardships. All citizens alike, both in and out of uniform, feel the impact of war in greater or lesser measure. Citizenship has its responsibilities as well as its privileges, and in time of war the burden is always heavier. Compulsory exclusion of large groups of citizens from their homes, except under circumstances of direst emergency and peril, is inconsistent with our basic governmental institutions. But when under conditions of modern warfare our shores are threatened by hostile forces, the power to protect must be commensurate with the threatened danger. . . .

It is now argued that the validity of the exclusion order cannot be considered apart from the orders requiring him, after departure from the area, to report and to remain in an assembly or relocation center. The contention is that we must treat these separate orders as one and inseparable; that, for this reason, if detention in the assembly or relocation center would have illegally deprived the petitioner of his liberty, the exclusion order and his conviction under it cannot stand.

We are thus being asked to pass at this time upon the whole subsequent detention program in both assembly and relocation centers, although the only issues framed at the trial related to petitioner's remaining in the prohibited area in violation of the exclusion order. Had petitioner here left the prohibited area and gone to an assembly center we cannot say either as a matter of fact or law that his presence in that center would have resulted in his detention in a relocation center. Some who did report to the assembly center were not sent to relocation centers, but were released upon condition that they remain outside the prohibited zone until the military orders were modified or lifted. This illustrates that they pose different problems and may be governed by different principles. The lawfulness of one does not necessarily determine the lawfulness of the others. This is made clear when we analyze the requirements of the separate provisions of the separate orders. These separate requirements were that those of Japanese ancestry (1) depart from the area; (2) report to and temporarily remain in an assembly center; (3) go under military control to a relocation center there to remain for an indeterminate period until released conditionally or unconditionally by the military authorities. Each of these requirements, it will be noted, imposed distinct duties in connection with the separate steps in a complete evacuation program. Had Congress directly incorporated into one Act the language of these separate orders, and provided sanctions for their violations, disobedience of any one would have constituted a separate offense. . . . There is no reason why violations of these orders, insofar as they were promulgated pursuant to Congressional enactment, should not be treated as separate offenses.

The *Endo* case . . . graphically illustrates the difference between the validity of an order to exclude and the validity of a detention order after exclusion has been effected.

Since the petitioner has not been convicted of failing to report or to remain in an assembly or relocation center, we cannot in this case determine the validity of those separate provisions of the order. It is sufficient here for us to pass upon the order which petitioner violated. To do more would be to go beyond the issues raised, and to decide momentous questions not contained within the framework of the pleadings or the evidence in this case. It will be time enough to decide the serious constitutional issues which petitioner seeks to raise when an assembly or relocation order is applied or is certain to be applied to him, and we have its terms before us. . . .

It is said that we are dealing here with the case of imprisonment of a citizen in a concentration camp solely because of his ancestry, without evidence or inquiry concerning his loyalty and good disposition towards the United States. Our task would be simple, our duty clear, were this a case involving the imprisonment of a loyal citizen in a concentration camp because of racial prejudice. Regardless of the true nature of the assembly and relocation centers—and we deem it unjustifiable to call them concentration camps with all the ugly connotations that term implies—we are dealing specifically with nothing but an exclusion order. To cast this case into outlines of racial prejudice, without reference to the real military dangers which were presented, merely confuses the issue. . . .

CHAPTER XXVI

Postwar Constitutional Trends

JUST as Congress had authorized governmental reorganization during wartime by reinstating the Overman Act in 1942, it decided in 1945 that the transition to peace necessitated broad governmental changes in the interest of efficient operation. Congress therefore created a bipartisan Commission on Organization of the Executive Branch of the Government, headed by ex-President Herbert Hoover. The Commission's recommendations when presented, however, involved administrative rather than constitutional alterations, but the Twenty-second Amendment (No. 238A), reflecting another aspect of Congress' concern with the American Presidency, clarified a historic constitutional question; and national stress produced by the incapacitating illness of President Eisenhower, along with the absence of a Vice President following Lyndon Johnson's initial succession for the assassinated John F. Kennedy led, by 1967, to an amendment setting forth new procedures to deal with such exigencies. (No. 238B)

Despite the postwar desire to shake off wartime economic controls, the federal government promptly passed the Employment Act of 1946 (No. 239), which established a new concept of the relation of the government to the national economy. Designed to promote maximum employment, production, and purchasing power, the act signalized the government's acceptance of a continuing responsibility for the economic well-being of the nation. This concern was also indicated when Congress enacted the Housing and Rent Act of 1947, continuing the provisions of the wartime Price Control Act. The legislation raised this important question: Does the war power continue after the shooting has ceased? In *Woods v. Miller* (No. 240), the Supreme Court, not without some soul-searching, answered in the affirmative.

Another manifestation of governmental control over the economy was increased restraints on organized labor. Despite the Norris-LaGuardia Act's protection against labor injunctions, fines of $3,500,000 against the United Mine Workers and $10,000 against John L. Lewis were sustained by the Supreme Court for contempt of a court order requiring the miners to continue working in the government-held pits until a contract could be negotiated (*U.S. v. United Mine Workers*, 1947). Although the fine was later reduced to $700,000, the decision indicated a changing attitude toward labor. Indeed, the Republican capture of Congress in 1946 foreshadowed the drastic revision of labor legislation for the first time since the passage of the Wagner Act. The enactment of the Taft-Hartley Act (1947) over President Truman's veto opened a new chapter in the history of labor-management relations in the United States. Unlike New Deal legislation, the measure sought to eliminate an alleged bias in favor of unions by arming management with new rights and by limiting long-established trade union practices such as the closed shop. With growing charges of scandal and extortion, especially against such unions as the Teamsters, Congress was induced by the late 1950's to enact a further compulsory housecleaning measure, the Landrum-Griffin Labor Management Reporting and Disclosures Act. This restricted secondary boycotts, called for precise controls over union elections, demanded strict reporting of a union's financial transactions, outlawed extortion picketing, authorized state jurisdiction over labor disputes not handled by the N. L. R. B., and modified union security provisions for certain national unions. In the interim, a number of states also enacted various antilabor laws. In the Lincoln Federal decision (No. 241), the Court upheld state laws forbidding closed-shop contracts and rejected the union's attempt to utilize management's ancient defense against governmental regulation—"liberty of contract." On the other hand, the Warren Court in May 1956 struck down eighteen states' "right-to-work" laws—laws banning union shops—as they applied to railroad workers, on the ground that states had no right to regulate or interfere with labor conduct in interstate commerce when that conduct was already controlled by federal law (*Railway Employee's Dept. v. Hanson*, 1956).

Antitrust policy in the postwar years varied greatly with the philosophy of high administration leaders, especially Justice Department personnel. Congress opened the door to more rigid enforcement of vital Section 7 of the Clayton Act through a significant amendment, the Celler-Kefauver Act of 1950, extending proscriptions against mergers far beyond limiting the simple acquisition of controlling stock in a competitive corporation. The Supreme Court in 1957 made clear that both stock and asset acquisitions were covered by the section. The Kennedy administration, while initially showing interest in using the battery of antitrust statutes, backed away sharply after its acrimonious showdown with big steel, and seemed to feel thereafter that a favorable business climate demanded new caution. But during the years 1963–65, stirred by a new aggressiveness among Justice Department officials, the Supreme Court handed down eight major antitrust decisions, whose scope was so sweeping that in mid-1965 Attorney General Katzenbach assured worried business leaders that the Department planned a breathing spell before pushing the strictures to their limits. Anthony Lewis summarized the trend cogently in the *New York Times* in late 1964, indicating that the department's determination to "prevent any movements toward significant new economic concentration by merger" gives "any executive of a large business . . . plenty to think about as he contemplates the Clayton Act of today" (No. 242). And such activities did not stop with business. The Court also made it clear (*U. M. W. v. Pennington,* 1965) that labor unions forfeited their exemption from the antitrust strictures in agreeing with one set of employers to impose excessive wage scales on their competitors, as a device for eliminating competition.

The highly activist Court altered its policy in connection with "fair trade" laws. In 1951 it had struck at such legislation in *Schwegman Brothers v. Calvert,* but Congress promptly enacted the McGuire Act in 1952, exempting state-approved fair trading from the federal antitrust laws. When that statute was challenged in 1964, the Court held that "whether it is good policy to permit such laws is a matter for Congress to decide. Where the statutory language and the legislative history clearly indicate the purpose of Congress, that purpose must be upheld" (*Hudson Distributors v. Lilly,* 1964).

The line between public regulation and governmental operation of private business was clearly drawn in *Youngstown Sheet and Tube Co. v. Sawyer* (No. 243), one of the most important postwar constitutional decisions. During the Korean conflict, President Truman authorized Secretary of Commerce Sawyer to seize and operate steel mills to ensure production of vital defense materials. The executive order was not based on any statutory authority, but only on the ground that the threatened strike created a national emergency. When the companies sought an injunction against the government, the federal spokesman argued that seizure was based upon Article II of the Constitution, "and whatever inherent, implied or residual powers may flow therefrom." In argument before the Supreme Court, government counsel stressed the concept of an expanded Presidential prerogative during national emergencies. In a 6 to 3 decision featuring a sharp dissent by Chief Justice Vinson, the majority dealt decisive blows to the dual doctrines of the president's emergency power and his inherent power in domestic affairs.

Another persistent postwar issue involved tidelands oil. In 1947 the Court ruled that the United States had dominion over the resources of the soil under the marginal sea adjoining California (No. 244). That state had maintained that it was entitled, by virtue of the conventional "equal footing" clause in the act admitting it to the Union, to the rights enjoyed by the original states and that those states owned such offshore areas. The Court concluded that such ownership had not been established at the time of the Constitution, and that the interests of sovereignty favored national dominion. Three years later the Court rejected a similar contention by Texas. But following the victorious Eisenhower campaign of 1952, in which the Republicans had courted the South and West with promises of offshore riches, Congress passed the Submerged Lands Act of 1953, vesting in the states the ownership of lands beneath the marginal sea adjacent to the respective states. The Supreme Court subsequently denied leave to file complaints challenging the statute. In 1965, however, the Court once again limited state jurisdiction to areas within three geographical miles of the coastline and excluded further areas which California claimed as being within her "historic state boundaries" (*U.S. v. California*, 1965).

Postwar constitutional problems in the international field stemmed from America's participation in the United Nations and involvement in the cold war. Conscious of its new international responsibilities, the United States took a leading part in the establishment of the United Nations. To assist in the maintenance of peace through collective security—by force if necessary—the United States accepted military commitments which raised fundamental constitutional questions of effective international security action and Congressional control of the war-making power. These issues became crucial as international friction intensified. The United States, for the first time in its history, joined a peacetime defensive alliance, the North Atlantic Treaty Organization. Article 5 of the Treaty pledged the United States, along with other signatories, to automatic intervention in case any member suffered armed attack. It posed this thorny question: Does such a commitment upset the traditional balance between the executive and legislative branches in questions of war and peace? With the invasion of South Korea by Communist forces, presidential discretion rather than Congressional action provided a dramatic answer. President Truman, on June 25, 1950, without a formal declaration of war and without consulting Congress, ordered United States air and sea forces "to give the Korean Government troops cover and support," and ordered the Seventh Fleet to prevent any attack on Formosa. This pronouncement quickly involved the United States in large-scale warfare in Korea. The Korean conflict did not attain actual war status because Congress never declared war. Although Congress backed the President's policy with appropriations, there were challenges leveled both against Truman's unilateral action and his bypassing of Congress (No. 245).

Since the President had based his move on treaty obligations to the United Nations, a logical point of attack was the treaty-making power of the federal government and the broad implications of that power inherent in Holmes' decision in *Missouri v. Holland* (Chapter XX). Attention had been focused on this power as early as 1948 when the United Nations Charter was cited by four members of the Supreme Court as a yardstick with which to measure the constitutionality of a state statute (*Oyama v. California*). The leader in the movement to curb the treaty-making authority was Senator John W. Bricker of Ohio, who first introduced an amendment to that effect in 1952. Congress defeated both the Bricker Amendment (No. 246) in 1954 and a revision in 1956, thus quieting once again a historical controversy going back to George Washington.

Yet constitutional problems stemming from America's treaty commitments proliferated and intensified. This was especially true as American service personnel spanned the globe and problems concerning their rights cropped up with increasing frequency, again giving rise to the old issue of whether the Constitution follows the flag. In 1950 Congress set up a Uniform Code of Military Justice to make not only service personnel but also their civilian dependents subject to court martial for crimes committed abroad. The Court, worried about granting the military powers not hitherto thought consistent with the Constitution, first reluctantly acquiesced. It then reversed itself, insisting that constitutional safeguards apply to United States government action against any citizen abroad. "We should not break faith with this nation's tradition of keeping military power subservient to civilian authority," wrote Justice Black, in a case involving military trial of a civilian wife for a capital offense (*Reid v. Covert, 1957*). In 1960 the Court extended the rule by holding that Congress lacked the power to authorize military trials of any civilian for any offense (*Kinsella v. U.S., ex rel Singleton*), thus throwing back to that body the necessity for establishing civilian courts in which the constitutional rights of civilians, especially jury trial, would be guaranteed. A similar concern for individual rights led the Justices in 1964 to rule unconstitutional an act of Congress that deprived naturalized Americans of their citizenship on the basis of residence abroad, insisting that "the rights of citizenship of the native-born and of the naturalized person are of the same dignity and are coextensive" (*Schneider v. Rusk*).

Constitutional Change and the Executive

238. *Permissible Length of Service, and Presidential Disability*

A. THE TWENTY-SECOND AMENDMENT: TWO-TERM TENURE OF OFFICE

Proposed March 24, 1947; adopted February 26, 1951.

SECTION 1. No person shall be elected to the office of the President more than twice, and no person who has held the office of President, or acted as President, for more than two years of a term to which some other person was elected President shall be elected to the office of the President more than once. But this article shall not apply to any person holding the office of President when this article was proposed by the Congress, and shall not prevent any person who may be holding the office of President, or acting as President, during the term within which this article becomes operative from holding the office of President or acting as President during the remainder of such term.

SECTION 2. This article shall be inoperative unless it shall have been ratified as an amendment to the Constitution by the legislatures of three-fourths of the several states within seven years from the date of its submission to the states by the Congress.

B. THE TWENTY-FIFTH AMENDMENT: PROCEDURE DURING PRESIDENTIAL INCAPACITY

Proposed July 7, 1965; adopted February 11, 1967.

SECTION 1. In case of the removal of the President from office or of his death or resignation, the Vice President shall become President.

SEC. 2. Whenever there is a vacancy in the office of the Vice President, the President shall nominate a Vice President who shall take office upon confirmation by a majority vote of both Houses of Congress.

SEC. 3. Whenever the President transmits to the President pro tempore of the Senate and the Speaker of the House of Representatives his written declaration that he is unable to discharge the powers and duties of his office, and until he transmits to them a written declaration to the contrary, such powers and duties shall be discharged by the Vice President as Acting President.

SEC. 4. Whenever the Vice President and a majority of either the principal officers of the executive departments or of such other body as Congress may by law provide, transmit to the President pro tempore of the Senate and the Speaker of the House of Representatives their written declaration that the President is unable to discharge the powers and duties of his office, the Vice President shall immediately assume the powers and duties of the office as Acting President.

Thereafter, when the President transmits to the President pro tempore of the Senate and the Speaker of the House of Representatives his written declaration that no inability exists, he shall resume the powers and duties of his office unless the Vice President and a majority of either the principal officers of the executive department or of such other body as Congress may by law provide, transmit within four days to the President pro tempore of the Senate and the Speaker of the House of Representatives their written declaration that the President is unable to discharge the powers and duties of his office. Thereupon Congress shall decide the issue, assembling within forty-eight hours for that purpose if not in session. If the Congress, within twenty-one days after receipt of the latter written declaration, or, if Congress is not in session, within twenty-one days after Congress is required to assemble, determines by two-thirds vote of both Houses that the President is unable to discharge the powers and duties of his office, the Vice President shall continue to discharge the same as Acting President; otherwise, the President shall resume the powers and duties of his office.

Postwar Regulation of the Economy

THE EXTENT OF FEDERAL AUTHORITY OVER THE NATION'S ECONOMY

239. *The Employment Act of 1946*

U. S. Stat. at L., LX, 23–6.

DECLARATION OF POLICY

SEC. 2. The Congress hereby declares that it is the continuing policy and responsibility of the Federal Government to use all practical means consistent with its needs and obligations and other essential considerations of national policy, with the assistance and cooperation of industry, agriculture, labor, and State and local governments, to coordinate and utilize all its plans, functions, and resources for the purpose of creating and maintaining, in a manner calculated to foster and promote free competitive enterprise and the general welfare, conditions under which there will be afforded useful employment opportunities, including self-employment, for those able, willing, and seeking to work, and to promote maximum employment, production, and purchasing power.

ECONOMIC REPORT OF THE PRESIDENT

SEC. 3. (a) The President shall transmit to the Congress within sixty days after the beginning of each regular session (commencing with the year 1947) an economic report (hereinafter called the "Economic Report") setting forth (1) the levels of employment, production, and purchasing power obtaining in the United States and such levels needed to carry out the policy declared in section 2; (2) current and foreseeable trends in the levels of employment, production, and purchasing power; (3) a review of the economic program of the Federal Government and a review of economic conditions affecting employment in the United States or any considerable portion thereof during the preceding year and of their effect upon employment, production, and purchasing power; and (4) a program for carrying out the policy declared in section 2, together with such recommendations for legislation as he may deem necessary or desirable. . . .

COUNCIL OF ECONOMIC ADVISERS TO THE PRESIDENT

SEC. 4. (a) There is hereby created in the Executive Office of the President a Council of Economic Advisers (hereinafter called the "Council"). The Council shall be composed of three members who shall be appointed by the President, by and with the advice and consent of the Senate, and each of whom shall be a person who, as a result of his training, experience, and attainments, is exceptionally qualified to analyze and interpret economic developments, to appraise programs and activities of the Government in the light of the policy declared in section 2, and to formulate and recommend national economic policy to promote employment, production, and purchasing power under free competitive enterprise. . . .

(c) It shall be the duty and function of the Council—(1) to assist and advise the President in the preparation of the Economic Report; (2) to gather timely and authoritative information concerning economic developments and economic trends, both current and prospective, to analyze and interpret such information in the light of the policy declared in section 2 for the purpose of determining whether such developments and trends are interfering, or are likely to interfere, with the achievement of such policy, and to compile and submit to the President studies relating to such developments and trends; (3) to appraise the various programs and activities of the Federal Government in the light of the policy declared in section 2 for the purpose of determining the extent to which such programs and activities are contributing, and the extent to which they are not contributing, to the achievement of such policy, and to make recommendations to the President with respect thereto; (4) to develop and recommend to the President national economic policies to foster and promote free competitive enterprise, to avoid economic fluctuations or to diminish the effects thereof, and to maintain employment, production, and purchasing power. . . .

240. *Rent Control: Does the War Power Continue After the Fighting is Over?*

Woods v. Miller, 333 U.S. 138 (1948).

DOUGLAS, J.: . . . The case is here on a direct appeal . . . from a judgment of the District Court holding unconstitutional Title II of the Housing and Rent Act of 1947. . . .

The Act became effective on July 1, 1947, and the following day the appellee demanded of its tenants increases of 40% and 60% for rental accommodations in the Cleveland Defense-Rental Area, an admitted violation of the act and regulations adopted pursuant thereto. . . .

The District Court was of the view that the authority of Congress to regulate rents by virtue of the war power . . . ended with the Presidential Proclamation terminating hostilities on December 31, 1946, since that proclamation inaugurated "peace-in-fact" though it did not mark termination of the war. It also concluded that, even if the war power continues, Congress did not act under it because it did not say so, and only if Congress says so, or enacts provisions so implying, can it be held that Congress intended to exercise such power. That Congress did not so intend, said the District Court, follows from the provision that the Housing Expediter can end controls in any area without regard to the official termination of the war, and from the fact that the preceding federal rent control laws (which were concededly exercises of the war power) were neither amended nor extended. The District Court expressed the further view that rent control is not within the war power because "the emergency created by housing shortage came into existence long before the war." . . .

We conclude, in the first place, that the war power sustains this legislation. The Court said in *Hamilton v. Kentucky Distilleries Co.,* . . . that the war power includes the power "to remedy the evils which have arisen from its rise and progress" and continues for the duration of that emergency. Whatever may be the consequences when war is officially terminated, the war power does not necessarily end with the cessation of hostilities. . . .

The constitutional validity of the present legislation follows *a fortiori* from such cases. The legislative history of the present Act makes abundantly clear that there has not yet been eliminated the deficit in housing which in considerable measure was caused by the heavy demobilization of veterans and by the cessation or reduction in residential construction during the period of hostilities due to the allocation of building materials to military projects. Since the war effort contributed heavily to that deficit, Congress has the power even after the cessation of hostilities to act to control the forces that a short supply of the needed article created. If that were not true, the Necessary and Proper Clause, . . . would be drastically limited in its application to the several war powers. The Court has declined to follow that course in the past. . . . We decline to take it today. The result would be paralyzing. It would render Congress powerless to remedy conditions the creation of which necessarily followed from the mobilization of men and materials for successful prosecution of the war. So to read the Constitution would be to make it self-defeating.

We recognize the force of the argument that the effects of war under modern conditions may be felt in the economy for years and years, and that if the war power can be used in days of peace to treat all the wounds which war inflicts on our society, it may not only swallow up all other powers of Congress but largely obliterate the Ninth and Tenth Amendments as well. There are no such implications in today's decision. We deal here with the consequences of a housing deficit greatly intensified during the period of hostilities by the war effort. Any power, of course, can be abused. But we cannot assume that Congress is not alert to its constitutional responsibilities. And the question whether the war power has been properly employed in cases such as this is open to judicial inquiry. . . .

The question of the constitutionality of action taken by Congress does not depend on recitals of the power which it undertakes to exercise. Here it is plain from the legislative history that Congress was invoking its war power to cope with a current condition of which the war was a direct and immediate cause. Its judgment on that score is entitled to the respect granted like legislation enacted pursuant to the police power. . . .

POSTWAR LABOR PROBLEMS AND FEDERAL JURISDICTION

241. *Opening the Gates of the Closed Shop*

Lincoln Federal Labor Union v. Northwestern Iron & Metal Co., 335 U.S. 525 (1949).

BLACK, J.: . . . It is contended that these state laws abridge the freedom of speech and the opportunities of unions and their members "peaceably to assemble, and to petition the Government for a redress of grievances." Under the state policy adopted by these laws, employers must, other considerations being equal, give equal opportunities for remunerative work to union and non-union members without discrimination against either. In order to achieve this objective of equal opportunity for the two groups, employers are forbidden to make contracts which would obligate them to hire or keep none but union members. Nothing in the language of the laws indicates a purpose to prohibit speech, assembly, or petition. Precisely what these state laws do is to forbid employers acting alone or in concert with labor organizations deliberately to restrict employment to none but union members. . . .

We deem it unnecessary to elaborate the numerous reasons for our rejection of this contention of appellants. Nor need we appraise or analyze with particularity the rather startling ideas suggested to support some of the premises on which appellants' conclusions rest. There cannot be wrung from a constitutional right of workers to assemble to discuss improvement of their own working standards, a further constitutional right to drive from remunerative employment all other persons who will not or cannot participate in union assemblies. The constitutional right of workers to assemble, to discuss and formulate plans for furthering their own self-interest in jobs cannot be construed as a constitutional guarantee that none shall get and hold jobs except those who will join in the assembly or will agree to abide by the assembly's plans. For where conduct affects the interests of other individuals and the general public, the legality of that conduct must be measured by whether the conduct conforms to valid law, even though the conduct is engaged in pursuant to plans of an assembly. . . .

It is contended that these state laws deprive appellants of their liberty without due process of law in violation of the Fourteenth Amendment. Appellants argue that the laws are specifically designed to deprive all persons within the two states of "liberty" (1) to refuse to hire or retain any person in employment because he is or is not a union member, and (2) to make a contract or agreement to engage in such employment discrimination against union or non-union members. . . .

Many cases are cited by appellants in which this Court has said that in some instances the due process clause protects the liberty of persons to make contracts. But none of these cases, even those according the broadest constitutional protection to the making of contracts, ever went so far as to indicate that the due process clause bars a state from prohibiting contracts to engage in conduct banned by a valid state law. So here, if the provisions in the state laws against employer discrimination are valid it follows that the contract prohibition or of some valid federal law. . . . to the decisive question under the due process contention, which is: Does the due process clause forbid a state to pass laws clearly designed to safeguard the opportunity of non-union workers to get and hold jobs, free from discrimination against them because they are non-union workers?

There was a period in which labor union members who wanted to get and hold jobs were the victims of widespread employer discrimination practices. Contracts between employers and their employees were used by employers to accomplish this anti-union employment discrimination. Before hiring workers, employers required them to sign agreements stating that the workers were not and would not become labor union members. Such anti-union practices were so obnoxious to workers that they gave these required agreements the name of "yellow dog contracts." This hostility of workers also prompted passage of state and federal laws to ban employer discrimination against union members and to outlaw yellow dog contracts. . . . [There follows a discussion of the Allgeyer, Lochner, Adair, and Coppage cases.]

This Court, beginning at least as early as 1934, when the *Nebbia* case was decided, has steadily rejected the due process philosophy enunciated in the *Adair-Coppage* line of cases. In doing so it has consciously returned closer and closer to the earlier constitutional principle that states have power to legislate against what are found to be injurious practices in their internal commercial and business affairs, so long as their laws do not run afoul of some specific federal constitutional prohibition, or of some valid federal law. . . . Under this constitutional doctrine the due process clause is no longer to be so broadly construed that the Congress and state legislatures are put in a strait jacket when they attempt to suppress business and industrial conditions which they regard as offensive to the public welfare.

Appellants now ask us to return, at least in part, to the due process philosophy that has been deliberately discarded. Claiming that the Federal Constitution itself affords protection for union members against discrimination, they nevertheless assert that the same Constitution forbids a state from providing the same protection for non-union members. Just as we have held that the due process clause erects no obstacle to block legislative protection of union members, we now hold that legislative protection can be afforded non-union workers.

BIG GOVERNMENT AND BIG BUSINESS

242. *The Recurrent Trust Problem*

Anthony Lewis, "Clayton Antitrust Law 50 Years Old and Strong," *New York Times*, October 25, 1964, III, 1. © 1964 by the *New York Times* Company. Reprinted by permission.

Fifty years ago last week President Woodrow Wilson signed into law a bill whose short title said its purpose was "to supplement existing laws against unlawful restraints and monopolies." It was the Clayton Act, second of this country's basic anti-trust statutes . . . [which] dealt with such subjects as price discrimination and tie-in agreements. It made embezzlement of corporation funds in interstate commerce a Federal crime. It prohibited railroads from buying supplies from companies in which their directors had a substantial interest.

But the section of the act that turned out to have the real bite in the long run—the one that is on businessmen's minds today—was the anti-merger provisions. This is Section 7.

Curiously, Section 7 was virtually a dead letter for many years. It was weakened by interpretations holding that it applied only to acquisitions of another company's stock, not its assets, and only where the result might be to lesson direct competition between the acquiring and acquired corporations. In 1950, in the Celler-Kefauver Act, Congress removed these doubts. It made clear that both stock and asset acquisitions were covered (The Supreme Court held in 1957, in the duPont-General Motors case, that the statute had always covered both). And Congress in the 1950 amendment demonstrated the intention to deal not only with horizontal mergers between competitors. Also covered were vertical acquisitions—of a supplier—or customer—and conglomerate mergers, between makers of differing products. Section 7 as it stands condemns any merger whose effect, "in any line of commerce in any section of the country . . . may be substantially to lessen competition, or to tend to create a monopoly." As always, it is up to the courts to give meaning to those vague words in concrete cases. A rundown of just a few recent cases demonstrates why business planners today are bound to have Section 7 on their minds.

Just two months ago an agreement by the Chrysler Corporation to acquire Mack Trucks, Inc., smashed on the rocks of the Clayton Act's anti-merger proviso. Chrysler contended that the deal would enable it to compete more effectively with bigger makers of heavy-duty trucks. But Federal District Judge Reyner J. Wortendyke, Jr. of New Jersey said the merger would stop planned Chrysler expansion of its own truck efforts and eliminate an independent competitor. Judge Wortendyke temporarily enjoined the merger and Chrysler and Mack then called it off. Few doubted that the judge was correctly reading the Supreme Court's recent opinions, for their trend has unmistakably been to deal strictly with mergers.

Last June 22, the Supreme Court for the first time held that Section 7 applied to joint ventures—agreements by competing companies to set up a joint corporation for certain purposes. On the same day the court upset a decision that a merger of glass and metal container manufacturers could not be anti-competitive. On April 6, the court applied in stringent terms to a Lexington, Kentucky bank merger the Prohibition in Section 1 of the Sherman Act against combinations in restraint of trade. In that case, Justice William O. Douglas said any horizontal merger of companies that were "major competitive factors" in a market violated the Sherman Act. Thus the court seemed to take a broad view of the anti-merger effects of both anti-trust statutes.

One moral spun out of the recent cases is that the largest American companies can no longer safely expand by merger. Under Justice Department attack the Humble Oil and Refining Company thus gave up its attempt to acquire the Western facilities of the Tidewater Oil Company. Humble had only a tiny share of the West Coast market, but its national economic power was so great that the department felt any acquisition would hurt competition.

Another point that has been emphasized in recent opinions is that actual proof of injury need not be shown. It is enough to prove a tendency—economic concentration "in its incipiency," as Chief Justice Earl Warren put it in 1962. Beyond that, the thrust is toward simplifying standards of proof generally—toward eliminating the mounds of economic data that characterize anti-trust trials. Justice Byron R. White said last June: "Where a merger is of such a size as to be inherently suspect, elaborate proof of market structure, market behavior, and probably anti-competitive effects may be dispensed with in view of Section 7's design to prevent undue concentration."

The importance of merger policing by the Justice Department lies partly in the fact that it is so difficult to reach situations where concentration is already a fact. It has been years since a large-scale attack on monopolization was brought successfully under Section 2 of the Sherman Act. The department is determined to prevent any movements toward significant new economic concentration by merger. It will use both Section 7 and the Sherman Act's Section 1, as expounded in the Lexington bank case last April, toward that end.

Mr. Orrick, the anti-trust chief, has . . . raised the interesting possibility of using Section 7 more and more vigorously to attack long-past mergers by companies that are now giants. He did so last May in a speech celebrating the forthcoming anniversary of the Clayton Act. "Surely the pervasively negative impact which undue concentration has on our economic, political, and social life justifies using all legal tools available," Mr. Orrick said. "Although we are planning no broad-gauge inquiry into past (merger) transactions, in appropriate hard-core cases of economic concentration we will give serious consideration to its (Section 7's) use. Where anti-competitive overconcentration exists, Congress has made it my duty to act to maintain the free competitive economy so vital to our national welfare."

It is clear that any executive of a large business has plenty to think about as he contemplates the Clayton Act today.

243. *The Steel Seizure Case*

Youngstown Sheet and Tube Co. v. Sawyer, 343 U.S. 579 (1952).

Black, J.: We are asked to decide whether the President was acting within his constitutional power when he issued an order directing the Secretary of Commerce to take possession of and operate most of the Nation's steel mills. The mill owners argue that the President's order amounts to lawmaking, a legislative function which the Constitution has expressly confided to the Congress and not the President. The Government's position is that the order was made on findings of the President that his action was necessary to avert a national catastrophe which would inevitably result from a stoppage of steel production, and that in meeting this grave emergency the

President was acting within the aggregate of his constitutional powers as the Nation's Chief Executive and the Commander in Chief of the Armed Forces of the United States. The issue emerges here from the following series of events:

In the latter part of 1951, a dispute arose between the steel companies and their employees over terms and conditions that should be included in new collective bargaining agreements. Long-continued conferences failed to resolve the dispute. On December 18, 1951, the employees' representative, United Steelworkers of America, C.I.O, gave notice of an intention to strike when the existing bargaining agreements expired on December 31. The Federal Mediation and Conciliation Service then intervened in an effort to get labor and management to agree. This failing, the President on December 22, 1951, referred the dispute to the Federal Wage Stabilization Board to investigate and make recommendations for fair and equitable terms of settlement. This Board's report resulted in no settlement. On April 4, 1952, the Union gave notice of a nation-wide strike called to begin at 12:01 A.M., April 9. The indispensability of steel as a component of substantially all weapons and other war materials led the President to believe that the proposed work stoppage would immediately jeopardize our national defense and that governmental seizure of the steel mills was necessary in order to assure the continued availability of steel. Reciting these considerations for his action, the President, a few hours before the strike was to begin, issued Executive Order 10340 . . . The order directed the Secretary of Commerce to take possession of most of the steel mills and keep them running. The Secrtary immediately issued his own possessory orders, calling upon the presidents of the various seized companies to serve as operating managers for the United States. They were directed to carry on their activities in accordance with regulations and directions of the Secretary. The next morning the President sent a message to Congress reporting his action. . . . Twelve days later he sent a second message. . . . Congress has taken no action.

Obeying the Secretary's orders under protest, the companies brought proceedings against him in the District Court. . . . The District Court was asked to declare the orders of the President and the Secretary invalid and to issue preliminary and permanent injunctions restraining their enforcement. Opposing the motion for preliminary injunction, the United States asserted that a strike disrupting steel production for even a brief period would so endanger the well-being and safety of the Nation that the President had "inherent power" to do what he had done —power "supported by the Constitution, by historical precedent, and by court decisions." . . . Holding against the Government on all points, the District Court on April 30 issued a preliminary injunction restraining the Secretary from "continuing the seizure and possession of the plants . . . and from acting under the purported authority of Executive Order No. 10340." . . . On the same day the Court of Appeals stayed the District Court's injunction. . . . Deeming it best that the issues raised be promptly decided by this Court, we granted certiorari on May 3 and set the cause for argument on May 12. . . .

The President's power, if any, to issue the order must stem either from an act of Congress or from the Constitution itself. There is no statute that expressly authorizes the President to take possession of property as he did here. Nor is there any act of Congress to which our attention has been directed from which such a power can fairly be implied. Indeed, we do not understand the Government to rely on statutory authorization for this seizure. There are two statutes which do authorize the President to take both personal and real property under certain conditions. However, the Government admits that these conditions were not met and that the President's order was not rooted in either of the statutes. . . .

Moreover, the use of the seizure technique to solve labor disputes in order to prevent work stoppages was not only unauthorized by any congressional enactment; prior to this controversy, Congress had refused to adopt that method of settling labor disputes. When the Taft-Hartley Act was under consideration in 1947, Congress rejected an amendment which would have authorized such governmental seizures in cases of emergency. Apparently it was thought that the technique of seizure, like that of compulsory arbitration, would interfere with the process of collecive bargaining. Consequently, the plan Congress adopted in that Act did not provide for seizure under any circumstances. Instead, the plan sought to bring about settlements by use of the customary devices of mediation, conciliation, investigation by boards of inquiry, and public reports. In some instances temporary injunctions were authorized to provide cooling-off periods. All this failing, unions were left free to strike after a secret vote by employees as to whether they wished to accept their employers' final settlement offer.

It is clear that if the President had authority to issue the order he did, it must be found in some provisions of the Constitution. And it is not claimed that express constitutional language grants this power to the President. The contention is that presidential power should be implied from the aggregate of his powers under the Constitution. Particular reliance is placed on provisions in Article II which say that "The executive Power shall be vested in a President . . ."; that "he shall take Care that the Laws be faithfully executed"; and that he "shall be Commander in Chief of the Army and Navy of the United States."

The order cannot properly be sustained as an exercise of the President's military power as Commander in Chief of the Armed Forces. The Government attempts to do so by citing a number of cases upholding broad powers in military commanders engaged in day-to-day fighting in a theater of war. Such cases need not concern us here. Even though "theater of war" be an expanding concept, we cannot with faithfulness to our constitutional system hold that the Commander in Chief of the Armed Forces has the ultimate power as such to take possession of private property in order to keep labor disputes from stopping production. This is a job for the Nation's lawmakers, not for its military authorities.

Nor can the seizure order be sustained because of the several constitutional provisions that grant executive power to the President. In the framework of our Constitution, the President's power to see that the laws are faithfully executed refutes the idea that he is to be a lawmaker. The Constitution limits his functions in the lawmaking process to the recommending of laws he thinks wise and the vetoing of laws he thinks bad. And the Constitution is neither silent nor equivocal about who shall make laws which the President is to execute. The first section of the first article says that "All legislative Powers herein granted shall be vested in a Congress of the United States. . . ." After granting many powers to the Congress, Article I goes on to provide that Congress may "make all Laws which shall be necessary and proper for carrying into Execution the foregoing Powers and all other Powers vested by this Constitution in the Government of the United States, or in any Department or Officer thereof."

The President's order does not direct that a congressional policy be executed in a manner prescribed by Congress—it directs that a presidential policy be executed in a manner prescribed by the President. The preamble of the order itself, like that of many statutes, sets out reasons why the President believes certain policies should be adopted, proclaims these policies as rules of conduct to be followed, and again, like a statute, authorizes a government official to promulgate additional rules and regulations consistent with the policy proclaimed and needed to carry that policy into execution. The power of Congress to adopt such public policies as those proclaimed by the order is beyond question. It can authorize the taking of private property for public use. It can make laws regulating the relationships between employers and employees, prescribing rules designed to settle labor disputes, and fixing wages and working conditions in certain fields of our economy. The Constitution did not subject this lawmaking power of Congress to presidential or military supervision or control. . . .

The Founders of this Nation entrusted the law-making power to the Congress alone in both good and bad times. It would do no good to recall the historical events, the fears of power and the hopes for freedom that lay behind their choice. Such a review would but confirm our holding that this seizure order cannot stand.

THE TIDELANDS AND FEDERAL-STATE RELATIONS

244. *The federal government has "paramount rights."*

U.S. v. California, 332 U.S. 19 (1947).

BLACK, J.: . . . The point of difference is as to who owns, or has paramount rights in and power over several thousand square miles of land under the ocean off the coast of California. The difference involves the conflicting claims of federal and state officials as to which government, state or federal, has a superior right to take or authorize the taking of the vast quantities of oil and gas underneath that land, much of which has already been and more of which is about to be, taken by or under authority of the state. Such concrete conflicts as these constitute a controversy in the classic legal sense, and are the very kind of differences which can only be settled by agreement, arbitration, force, or judicial action. . . .

The crucial question on the merits is not merely who owns the bare legal title to the lands under the marginal sea. The United States here asserts rights in two capacities transcending those of a mere property owner. In one capacity it asserts the right and responsibility to exercise whatever power and dominion are necessary to protect this country against dangers to the security and tranquility of its people incident to the fact that the Unied States is located immediately adjacent to the ocean. The Government also appears in its capacity as a member of the family of nations. In that capacity it is responsible for conducting United States relations with other nations. It asserts that proper exercise of these constitutional responsibilities requires that it have power, unencumbered by state commitments, always to determine what agreements will be made concerning the control and use of the marginal sea and the land under it. . . . In the light of the foregoing, our question is whether the state or the Federal Government has the paramount right and power to determine in the first instance when, how, and by what agencies, foreign or domestic, the oil and other resources of the soil of the marginal sea, known or hereafter discovered, may be exploited. . . . [There follows a discussion of the accretion by the federal government of domination over the three-mile belt.]

Not only has acquisition, as it were, of the three-mile belt, been accomplished by the national Government, but protection and control of it has been and is a function of national external sovereignty. . . . The three-mile rule is but a recognition of the necessity that a government next to the sea must be able to protect itself from dangers incident to its location. It must have powers of dominion and regulation in the interest of its revenues, its health, and the security of its people from wars waged on or too near its coasts. And insofar as the nation asserts its rights under international law, whatever of value may be discovered in the seas next to its shores and within its protective belt, will most naturally be appropriated for its use. But whatever any nation does in the open sea, which detracts from its common usefulness to nations, or which another nation may charge detracts from it, is a question for consideration among nations as such, and not their separate governmental units. What this Government does, or even what the states do, anywhere in the ocean, is a subject upon which the nation may enter into and assume treaty or similar international obligations. . . . The very oil about which the state and nation here contend might well become the subject of international dispute and settlement.

The ocean, even its three-mile belt, is thus of vital consequence to the nation in its desire to engage in commerce and to live in peace with the world; it also becomes of crucial importance should it ever again become impossible to preserve that peace. And as peace and world commerce are the paramount responsibilities of the nation, rather than an individual state, so, if wars come, they must be fought by the nation. . . . The state is not equipped in our constitutional system with the powers or the facilities for exercising the responsibilities which would be concomitant with the dominion which it seeks. Conceding that the state has been authorized to exercise local police power functions in the part of the marginal belt within its declared boundaries, these do not detract from the Federal Government's paramount rights in and power over this area. . . .

We decide for the reasons we have stated that California is not the owner of the three-mile marginal belt along its coast, and that the Federal Government rather than the state has paramount rights in and power over that belt, an incident to which is full dominion over the resources of the soil under that water area, including oil. . . .

The Cold War and Constitutional Problems

245. *Presidential Power to Commit American Forces in Foreign Areas*

Arthur Sears Henning, Editorial in *Washington Times-Herald,* July 3, 1950; *Congressional Record,* Vol. 96, Pt. 16, p. 4901.

One of the most sensational aspects of American intervention in the Korean War is President Truman's demonstration of the use of the United Nations to bypass the United States Congress as the sole repository under the Constitution of the prerogative to declare war.

While the undertaking to defend South

Korea from invasion by the Russian puppet republic of North Korea has received almost unanimous support in Congress, Mr. Truman's procedure for calling American armed power into action is being widely questioned as to its legality and also as to the implications of the precedent in the future.

There are misgivings and apprehensions that the United Nations will come in time to supersede Congress not only in the matter of declaring war but in the matter of legislation generally.

Mr. Truman in invoking the authority of the United Nations instead of the authority of Congress to make war, has shown how a dictator could operate to flout Congress and carry into effect a Socialist program, such as the welfare state or police state, or even impose on the country a completely totalitarian form of government. All he would need would be the approval of the United Nations which the United States is bound by treaty to carry out.

In the Korean venture, Mr. Truman wanted to make it a United Nations war, not a United States war, for the wider international support that might be obtained. There was ground for United Nations action, for the South Korean Republic was set up by the United Nations and justifiably could claim United Nations protection.

In addition, Mr. Truman wanted to avoid asking Congress for a declaration of war on any other authority for employing American Armed Forces in Korea. Such a request, he thought, would only provoke division and result in at least several days' delay before an enabling resolution could be adopted.

So Mr. Truman decided to ignore Congress. The news of the Reds' attack on South Korea reached Mr. Truman the night of June 24. He decided that the United States should enter the war. At 3 A.M. June 25, Mr. Truman, through an American U.N. delegate, asked Secretary General Lie to convene a special meeting of the United Nations Security Council that day. That was done. By 6 P.M. Sunday, June 25, the council had adopted an American resolution declaring the Korean aggression a breach of the peace, calling for immediate cessation of hostilities, and asking all member nations to render every assistance to execute this mandate.

Acting under the color of that authority, though it was not in accord with the act of Congress requiring congressional approval of the use of American forces by the United Nations, Mr. Truman ordered United States air and naval units to Korea. The next day, June 26, the President warned those responsible for the act of aggression that the United States takes a very serious view of the invasion.

On June 27, Mr. Truman emphasized his by-passing of Congress by calling members of its Foreign Affairs and Armed Services Committees to the White House and reading to them his announcement that military forces were being sent to Korea and Formosa and military aid would be furnished to the Philippines and Indochina. He asked no advice. He merely stated an accomplished fact under the aegis, not of Congress, but of the United Nations.

The theory that the authority of the United Nations under which Mr. Truman acted overrides the authority of Congress is based on the contention that in adhering to the Charter of the United Nations the United States bound itself to support United Nations acts, whether approved or disapproved by Congress. The United Nations Charter is a treaty and under our Constitution a treaty, no less than the Constitution and the laws, is the supreme law of the land.

246. *The Bricker Amendment and the Treaty-making Power*

A. 1954 VERSION

Senate Report No. 412, 82nd Congress, 2nd Session.

SECTION 1. A provision of a treaty which conflicts with this Constitution shall not be of any force or effect.

SECTION 2. A treaty shall become effective as internal law in the United States only through legislation which would be valid in the absence of a treaty.

SECTION 3. Congress shall have power to regulate all executive and other agreements with any foreign power or international organization. All such agreements shall be subject to the limitations imposed on treaties by this article.

B. 1956 VERSION

A provision of a treaty or other international agreement which conflicts with any provision of this Constitution shall not be of any force and effect.

CHAPTER XXVII

The "Preferred" Freedoms in a Postwar World

THE spirit of millenarianism which pervaded the thinking of Americans as World War II ground to its conclusion was highlighted by the challenging opportunity to establish civil liberties for all citizens. This ambitious objective was shared by many leaders in high office, and particularly by President Truman. In 1946, he established the President's Committee on Civil Rights, affirming that "the preservation of civil rights, guaranteed by the Constitution, is essential to domestic tranquility, national security, the general welfare, and the continued existence of our free institutions." The Committee's report in 1947 was a further extension of the radically new approach instigated by Frank Murphy as Attorney General in the late 1930's, stressing the federal government's commitment to assist Americans to attain the wide spectrum of fundamental freedoms guaranteed by the Bill of Rights. The federal government now was obligated not only to be a shield in protecting the citizen against those who would endanger his rights; it would be a sword to cut away potential legal snares before the citizen became trapped in them. Or in the Committee's words, the federal government now had a duty to act as a "friendly vigilant defender of the rights and equalities of all Americans" (No. 247).

Although charting a high-minded course, the report was not self-enforcing. With Congress soon coming under conservative leadership and the executive branch unable to implement the report by striking down legal strictures, the responsibility for implementation quickly fell to the courts. The more activist judges welcomed this development, but the advocates of judicial self-restraint were apprehensive. Disputes were inevitable, for the Roosevelt Court, although it had elevated problems of civil liberties to new heights of judicial concern, had not succeeded in building a coherent constitutional theory out of its diverse rulings. Moreover, the divergent views frequently had equally valid legal precedent. To create further difficulties, the Court received its new assignment almost simultaneously with the outbreak of the cold war, and the new national concern for security was sufficiently exaggerated to create a poor climate for extending individual freedom beyond old limits. Nonetheless, the Court wielded the new governmental sword with a firm and resolute hand, although trimming occasionally on security issues, particularly when Communists were involved.

Although the Court had previously wrestled with the free exercise provision of the religion clause in the First Amendment, it had had little opportunity to define the more vital establishment of religion clause until the postwar period. Operating with the traditional interpretation that the amendment erects a "wall of separation" between church and state, the Court now set out to define more precisely what that wall separated. Starting in 1947 with the Everson case, the Court decided that the wall was not breached when local authorities in New Jersey used tax revenue to support bus transportation for students to parochial schools. However, it was breached, the Court ruled in the McCollum case of the following year, when public-school classrooms were used for the religious instruction conducted by denominational teachers during regular school time. The protest which the ruling aroused may have convinced the Court to rethink the released time issue, for when a case arose in 1952 (No. 248) the Court sanctioned religious instruction during school hours, again by denominational teachers, if such instruction were conducted outside public-school buildings.

Yet more sensitive problems were to arise in this area. With the Warren Court's growing, self-professed concern for the individual, it was predictable that members of religious minorities would challenge official religious exercises in the public schools. In a highly assailed and much misunderstood ruling in 1962 (*Engle v. Vitale*), the Court was asked to consider a compulsory prayer, composed and imposed by the New York State Regents. Its negative ruling not only raised the wall higher, but also led other citizens to successfully challenge compulsory recitation of the Lord's Prayer and Bible reading in the classroom (No. 249). If a new judicial rule emerged from such widely divergent actions, it was one which drew a sharp line between "pupil welfare" and religious indoctrination. The state, the Court seemed to be saying, could extend public revenue and other support to assist children in gaining an education, even in religious schools. But the state should not support, even indirectly, any practice which constituted in any way public endorsement of religious indoctrination.

One other religious issue required drawing of different kinds of lines. Sunday closing laws, and "blue laws" generally, had an ancient history in America, yet they worked a serious hardship upon religious minorities who did not celebrate Sunday as the Sabbath and who wished to conduct business then. Yet despite the bitter protest of Douglas, Brennen, and Stewart, Chief Justice Warren upheld such laws as not imposing sufficiently damaging strictures to constitute an unwarranted burden on religion (*McGowan v. Maryland, et al.*, 1961).

The First Amendment guarantees of freedom of speech, press, and assembly also produced a wide range of judicial reinterpretation, as the Court brought under its aegis more and more of the problems of life in a pluralistic, industrial society. Pure free speech could not avoid becoming involved with the tensions of the times. In a non-Communist case in 1949, the Court upheld the right of a violently anti-Semitic, racist disciple of the American fascist Gerald L. K. Smith to speak, even though his utterance produced violent response from peripheral listeners (*Terminiello v. Chicago*). But with the Korean War, the growing shrillness of Senator Joseph McCarthy, and mounting national apprehensions, the Justices acquiesced in the arrest of a leftist college student for extreme statements, including a call for Negroes to "rise up in arms and fight for their rights" (No. 250).

Libel as an aspect of free speech also came in for significant modern reinterpretation. Against the bitter protest of libertarians such as Black and Douglas, the Court in 1952 upheld an Illinois group-libel law as a reasonable extension of the law of libelous utterances which are not within "the area of constitutionally protected speech" (No. 251). Thus malicious indictments of religious or minority groups could be punished without fear of First Amendment violation. By contrast, however, the Court of the 1960's restricted individual libel to historically new confines when, during the height of racial tension in Alabama, the *New York Times* carried a paid advertisement sharply critical of Southern law-enforcement officials. When the police commissioner of Montgomery brought civil libel action against the *Times* and others, a jury awarded him $500,000 damages. In reviewing the case, the Supreme Court entered an area of the common law usually interpreted only by state courts and held that the constitutional protection of speech and press prohibits a public official from recovering damages in a libel suit against critics of his official conduct unless actual malice is proved. Speaking of "a profound national commitment to the principle that debate on public issues should be uninhibited, robust, and wide-open," the Court observed that critical comment "may well include vehement, caustic, and sometimes unpleasantly sharp attacks on government and public officials" (No. 252). And in a subsequent case, the Court applied the *Times* principle to what was acknowledged as willful and malicious libel of judges in Louisiana, thereby completing the elimination of the ancient concept of seditious libel from American law (*Garrison v. Louisiana*, 1964).

Censorship was another First Amendment area which drew modern reassessment. The Court, by bringing movie censorship, as well as book censorship, under the First Amendment in 1948 (*U.S. v. Paramount Pictures*), wrapped both with freedom of the press guarantees, and from then on handled both largely under the same type of rule. In *Burstyn v. Wilson*, in 1952, the Court unanimously struck down state censorship of motion pictures, but left open the possibility that if a meaningful standard could be developed as a guideline to a picture-maker, then it might be willing to take a more sanguine view of public regulation. Similarly in *Butler v. Michigan*, in 1957, the Warren Court reversed a conviction under a Michigan statute which banned books containing obscene, immoral, or lewd language for their potentially harmful influence upon youths. "The incidence of this enactment," Justice Frankfurter ruled, "is to reduce the adult population of Michigan to reading what is fit for children" (No. 253). This statement implied, however, that the state standard was meaningless.

Apparently impatient that legislative bodies had not established workable standards, the Court set forth its own rule in the Roth and Alberts cases later in 1957, arguing that neither books nor movies were censorable unless "utterly without redeeming social importance." The Court upheld these convictions for obscenity and suggested that such censorable material might be judged by the test of "whether to the average person, applying contemporary community standards, the dominant theme of the material taken as a whole appeals to prurient interest" (No. 254). Subsequent cases indicated the standard, while seemingly clear and precise, would be applied flexibly given the individual elements in each case and situation. Thus the Court expanded the criteria required for an obscenity conviction to a clear knowledge on the part of a bookseller of the contents of his merchandise before he could be justly accused of "pandering" (*Smith v. California*, 1959). In 1964, it added the qualification that material which appealed to prurient interest could not be defined as obscene unless it were also "patently offensive to current community standards of decency" (*Manual Enterprises v. Day*). Further, it held as relevant consideration of the way the material was advertised. In this regard, the Court took a different look at "pandering" in light of the Roth rule and decided that evidence that a publisher deliberately represented his publications as erotically arousing, and commercially exploited them as erotica solely for the sake of prurient appeal, clearly warranted his conviction, even though the material might in other contexts have warranted First Amendment protection (*Ginzberg v. U.S.*, 1966).

The same flexibility was present in movie censorship, with the Court ruling invalid, in a unanimous decision, a ban by the Regents of the University of the State of New York on a film which they maintained set forth wrong ideas (in this case, adultery) as "desirable, accepted, and proper forms of behavior" (*Kingsley International Picture Corp. v. N.Y. Regents*, 1959). But it sustained a Chicago city ordinance requiring that films be submitted to city officials who must grant permission to show them, on the grounds that this was not an arbitrary and unwarranted example of prior restraint in violation of the First Amendment (*Times Film Co. v. Chicago*, 1961).

Libertarians on the bench objected to the Roth rule from the outset (No. 255) and were even unhappy with its subsequent modification in 1964 (*Jacobellis v. Ohio*), when the Court redefined the "contemporary community" as being the national community, thereby making more difficult the injection of local sentiments into its positive application. They were somewhat more pleased in 1965—though still denouncing any censorship as a violation of freedom of speech—when the Court unanimously tightened procedural safeguards, establishing the principle of speedy court review of any ban imposed by a censor (*Freedman v. Maryland*). Even so, Justices Douglas and Black wrote a brief concurring opinion, stating that they favored an end to all types of censorship in order to "give full literal meaning to the command of the First Amendment."

In the years since World War II the Court has also been forced to reassess the relationship of First Amendment freedoms to other forms of business and economic activity. In *Giboney v. Empire Storage and Ice Co.*, decided during the hostile atmosphere of Taft-Hartley enactment, it retreated sharply from the Thornhill doctrine (Chapter XXIV) by balancing the speech element in picketing against other social values (No. 256). And in two subsequent cases involving the stormy Teamsters Union (*I. B. T. v. Hanke*, 1950, and *I. B. T. v. Vogt*, 1957) it moved away from considering picketing as a "preferred" constitutional right protected by the free speech guarantees of the First Amendment and recognized an almost unlimited right in the several states to regulate the practice for whatever rational purpose they wished. The Court, on the other hand, clearly extended the *Thomas v. Collins* rule (Chapter XXIV), underwriting the ability of union organizers to solicit membership, even in the face of a city ordinance to the contrary (*Staub v. Baxley*, 1958). And in two divergent cases, one involving union-shop agreements (*International Assn. of Machinists v. Street*, 1961), the other, membership in the integrated Wisconsin Bar Association (*Lathrop v. Donohue*, 1961), the Court assessed the right of an individual member of a formal body to dissent from formal positions of the body.

Finally, the First Amendment was invoked in a novel way to overrule Connecticut's 80-year-old law forbidding the use of contraceptives or the dispensation of information regarding their use. "The First Amendment has a penumbra where privacy is protected from government restriction," wrote Justice Douglas, stating that such protection had been afforded to individuals acting in a variety of political and social ways. "Would we allow the police to search the sacred precincts of marital bedrooms for telltale evidence of the use of contraceptives? The very idea is repulsive to the notions of privacy surrounding the marriage relationship. The right of privacy which presses for recognition here is a legitimate one" (No. 257).

The Elusive Goal: To Secure These Rights

247. *"A friendly, vigilant defender of the rights and equalities of all Americans."*

To Secure These Rights: The Report of the President's Committee on Civil Rights (Washington, 1947), 4–10.

The central theme in our American heritage is the importance of the individual person. From the earliest moment of our history we have believed that every human being has an essential dignity and integrity which must be respected and safeguarded. Moreover, we believe that the welfare of the individual is the final goal of group life. Our American heritage further teaches that to be secure in the rights he wishes for himself, each man must be willing to respect the rights of other men. This is the conscious recognition of a basic moral principle: that all men are created equal as well as free. Stemming from this principle is the obligation to build social institutions that will guarantee equality of opportunity to all men. Without this equality freedom becomes an illusion. Thus the only aristocracy that is consistent with the free way of life is an aristocracy of talent and achievement. The grounds on which our society accords respect, influence, or reward to each of its citizens must be limited to the quality of his personal character and his social contribution.

This concept of equality which is so vital a part of the American heritage knows no kinship with notions of human uniformity or regimentation. We abhor the totalitarian arrogance which makes one man say that he will respect another man as his equal only if he has "*my* race, *my* religion, *my* political views, *my* social position." In our land men are equal, but they are free to be different. From these very differences among our people has come the great human and national strength of America. . . .

The men who founded our Republic, as those who have built any constitutional democracy, faced the task of reconciling personal liberty and group authority, or of establishing an equilibrium between them. In a democratic state we recognize that the common interests of the people must be managed by laws and procedures established by majority rule. But a democratic majority, left unrestrained, may be as ruthless and tyrannical as were the earlier absolute monarchs. Seeing this clearly, and fearing it greatly, our forefathers built a constitutional system in which valued personal liberties, carefully enumerated in a Bill of Rights, were placed beyond the reach of popular majorities. Thus the people permanently denied the federal government power to interfere with certain personal rights and freedoms.

Freedom, however, as we now use the term, means even more than the traditional "freedoms" listed in our Bill of Rights—important as they are. Freedom has come to mean the right of a man to manage his own affairs as he sees fit up to the point where what he does interferes with the equal rights of others in the community to manage their affairs—or up to the point where he begins to injure the welfare of the whole group. It is clear that in modern democratic society a man's freedom in this broader sense is not and cannot be absolute—nor does it exist in a vacuum—but instead is hedged about by the competing rights of others and the demands of the social welfare. In this context it is government which must referee the clashes which arise among the freedoms of citizens, and protect each citizen in the enjoyment of the maximum freedom to which he is entitled.

There is no essential conflict between freedom and government. Bills of rights restrain government from abridging individual civil liberties, while government itself by sound legislative policies protects citizens against the aggressions of others seeking to push their freedoms too far. Thus in the words of the Declaration of Independence: "Man is endowed by his Creator with certain inalienable rights. Among these are life, liberty, and the pursuit of happiness. To secure these rights, *governments are instituted among men.*"

The rights essential to the citizen in a free society can be described in different words and in varying orders. The three great rights of the Declaration of Independence have just been mentioned. Another noble statement is made in the Bill of Rights of our Constitution. A more recent formulation is found in the Four Freedoms.

Four basic rights have seemed important to this Committee and have influenced its labors. We believe that each of these rights is essential to the well-being of the individual and to the progress of society.

The Right to Safety and Security of the Person

Freedom can exist only where the citizen is assured that his person is secure against bondage, lawless violence, and arbitrary arrest and punishment. Freedom from slavery in all its forms is clearly necessary if all men are to have equal opportunity to use their talents and to lead worthwhile lives. Moreover, to be free, men must be subject to discipline by society only for commission of offenses clearly defined by law and only after trial by due process of law. Where the administration of justice is discriminatory, no man can be sure of security. . . .

The Right to Equality of Opportunity

It is not enough that full and equal membership in society entitles the individual to an equal voice in the control of his government; it must also give him the right to enjoy the benefits of society and to contribute to its progress. The opportunity of each individual to obtain useful employment, and to have access to services in the fields of education, housing, health, recreation, and transportation, whether available free or at a price, must be provided with complete disregard for race, color, creed, and national origin. Without this equality of opportunity the individual is deprived of the chance to develop his potentialities and to share the fruits of society. The group also suffers through the loss of the contributions which might have been made by persons excluded from the main channels of social and economic activity.

THE HERITAGE AND THE REALITY

Our American heritage of freedom and equality has given us prestige among the nations of the world and a strong feeling of national pride at home. There is much reason for that pride. But pride is no substitute for steady and honest performance, and the record shows that at varying times in American history the gulf between ideals and practice has been wide. We have had human slavery. We have had religious persecution. We have had mob rule. We still have their ideological remnants in the unwarrantable "pride and prejudice" of some of our people and practices. . . . But we have seen nothing to shake our conviction that the civil rights of the American people—all of them—can be strengthened quickly and effectively by the normal processes of democratic, constitutional government. That strengthening, we believe, will make our daily life more and more consonant with the spirit of the American heritage of freedom. But it will require as much courage, as much imagination, as much perseverance as anything which we have ever done together. . . .

The Right to Citizenship and its Privileges

. . . Because the right to participate in the political process is customarily limited to citizens there can be no denial of access to citizenship based upon race, color, creed or national origin. . . .

To deny qualified citizens the right to vote while others exercise it is to do violence to the principle of freedom and equality. Without the right to vote, the individual loses his voice in the group effort and is subjected to rule by a body from which he has been excluded. Likewise, the right of the individual to vote is important to the group itself. Democracy assumes that the majority is more likely as a general rule to make decisions which are wise and desirable from the point of view of the interests of the whole society than is any minority. Every time a qualified person is denied a voice in public affairs, one of the components of a potential majority is lost, and the formation of a sound public policy is endangered.

To the citizen in a democracy, freedom is a precious possession. Accordingly, all able-bodied citizens must enjoy the right to serve the nation and the cause of freedom in time of war. . . . In particular, any discrimination which, while imposing an obligation, prevents members of minority groups from rendering full military service in defense of their country is for them a peculiarly humiliating badge of inferiority. The nation also suffers a loss of manpower and is unable to marshal maximum strength at a moment when such strength is most needed.

The Right to Freedom of Conscience and Expression

In a free society there is faith in the ability of the people to make sound, rational judgments. But such judgments are possible only where the people have access to all relevant facts and to all prevailing interpretations of the facts. How can such judgments be formed on a sound basis if arguments, viewpoints, or opinions are arbitrarily suppressed? How can the concept of the marketplace of thought in which truth ultimately prevails retain its validity if the thought of certain individuals is denied the right of circulation? . . .

Our forefathers fought bloody wars and suffered torture and death for the right to worship God according to the varied dictates of conscience. Complete religious liberty has been accepted as an unquestioned personal freedom since our Bill of Rights was adopted. We have insisted only that religious freedom may not be pleaded as an excuse for criminal or clearly antisocial conduct. . . .

The First Freedom

RELIGION AND PUBLIC SUPPORTED EDUCATION

248. "Released Time" Programs of Religious Instruction

Zorach v. Clauson, 343 U.S. 306 (1952).

DOUGLAS, J.: New York City has a program which permits its public schools to release students during the school day so that they may leave the school buildings and school grounds and go to religious centers for religious instruction or devotional exercises. A student is released on written request of his parents. Those not released stay in the classrooms. The churches make weekly reports to the schools, sending a list of children who have been released from public school but who have not reported for religious instruction.

This "released time" program involves neither religious instruction in public school classrooms nor the expenditure of public funds. All costs, including the application blanks, are paid by the religious organizations. The case is therefore unlike *Illinois ex rel. McCollum v. Board of Education* . . . which involved a "released time" program from Illinois. In that case the classrooms were turned over to religious instructors. We accordingly held that the program violated the First Amendment which (by reason of the Fourteenth Amendment) prohibits the states from establishing religion or prohibiting its free exercise.

Appellants, who are taxpayers and residents of New York City and whose children attend its public schools, challenge the present law, contending it is in essence not different from the one involved in the McCollum Case. Their argument, stated elaborately in various ways, reduces itself to this: the weight and influence of the school is put behind a program for religious instruction; public school teachers police it, keeping tab on students who are released; the classroom activities come to a halt while the students who are released for religious instruction are on leave; the school is a crutch on which the churches are leaning for support in their religious training; without the cooperation of the schools this "released time" program, like the one in the McCollum Case, would be futile and ineffective. . . .

The briefs and arguments are replete with data bearing on the merits of this type of "released time" program. . . . Those matters are of no concern here, since our problem reduces itself to whether New York by this system has either prohibited the "free exercise" of religion or has made a law "respecting an establishment of religion" within the meaning of the First Amendment.

It takes obtuse reasoning to inject any issue of the "free exercise" of religion into the present case. No one is forced to go to the religious classroom and no religious exercise or instruction is brought to the classrooms of the public schools. A student need not take religious instruction. He is left to his own desires as to the manner or time of his religious devotions, if any. . . .

Moreover, apart from that claim of coercion, we do not see how New York by this type of "released time" program has made a law respecting an establishment of religion within the meaning of the First Amendment. There is much talk of the separation of Church and State in the history of the Bill of Rights and in the decisions clustering around the First Amendment. . . . There cannot be the slightest doubt that the First Amendment reflects the philosophy that Church and State should be separated. And so far as interference with the "free exercise" of religion and an "establishment" of religion are concerned, the separation must be complete and unequivocal. The First Amendment within the scope of its coverage permits no exception; the prohibition is absolute. The First Amendment, however, does not say that in every and all respects there shall be a separation of Church and State. Rather, it studiously defines the manner, the specific ways, in which there shall be no concert or union or dependency one on the other. That is the common sense of the matter. Otherwise, the state and religion would be aliens to each other—hostile, suspicious, and even unfriendly. Churches could not be required to pay even property taxes. Municipalities would not be permitted to render police or fire protection to religious groups. Policemen who helped parishioners into their places of worship would violate the Constitution. Prayers in our legislative halls; the appeals to the Almighty in the messages of the Chief Executive; the proclamations making Thanksgiving Day a holiday; "so help me God" in our courtroom oaths—these and all other references to the Almighty that run through our laws, our public rituals, our ceremonies would be flouting the First Amendment. A fastidious atheist or agnostic could even object to the supplication with which the Court opens each session: "God save the United States and this Honorable Court."

We would have to press the concept of separation of Church and State to these extremes to condemn the present law on constitutional grounds. . . .

We are a religious people whose institutions presuppose a Supreme Being. We guarantee the freedom to worship as one chooses. We make room for as wide a variety of beliefs and creeds as the spiritual needs of man deem necessary. We sponsor an attitude on the part of government that shows no partiality to any one group and that lets each flourish according to the zeal of its adherents and the appeal of its dogma. When the state encourages religious instruction or cooperates with religious authorities by adjusting the schedule of public events to sectarian needs, it follows the best of our traditions. For it then respects the religious nature of our people and accommodates the public service to their spiritual needs. To hold that it may not would be to find in the Constitution a requirement that the government show a callous indifference to religious groups. That would be preferring those who believe in no religion over those who do believe. . . .

In the McCollum Case the classrooms were used for religious instruction and the force of the public school was used to promote that instruction. Here, as we have said, the public schools do no more than accommodate their schedules to a program of outside religious instruction. We follow the McCollum Case. But we cannot expand it to cover the present released time program unless separation of Church and State means that public institutions can make no adjustments of their schedules to accommodate the religious needs of the people. We cannot read into the Bill of Rights such a philosophy of hostility to religion.

Affirmed.

249. *The Neutrality of the State in Religion*

Abington School District v. Schempp; Murray v. Curlett, 374 U.S. 203 (1963).

Clark, J.: Once again we are called upon to consider the scope of the provisions of the First Amendment to the United States Constitution which declares that "Congress shall make no law respecting an establishment of religion or prohibiting the free exercise thereof. . . ." These companion cases present the issues in the context of state action requiring that schools begin each day with readings from the Bible. While raising the basic questions under slightly different factual situations, the cases permit of joint treatment. In light of the history of the First Amendment and of our cases interpreting and applying its requirements, we hold that the practices at issue and the laws requiring them are unconstitutional under the Establishment Clause, as applied to the states through the Fourteenth Amendment. . . .

This Court has decisively settled that the First Amendment's mandate that "Congress shall make no law respecting an establishment of religion, or prohibiting the free exercise thereof" has been made wholly applicable to the states by the Fourteenth Amendment. . . . In a series of cases since *Cantwell* the Court has repeatedly reaffirmed that doctrine, and we do so now. . . .

This Court has rejected unequivocally the contention that the establishment clause forbids only governmental preference of one religion over another. Almost 20 years ago in *Everson* . . . the Court said that "neither a state nor the Federal government can set up a church. Neither can pass laws which aid one religion, or prefer one religion over another." . . . Further, Mr. Justice Rutledge, joined by Justices Frankfurter, Jackson and Burton, declared:

> The [First] Amendment's purpose was not to strike merely at the official establishment of a single sect, creed or religion, outlawing only a formal relation such as had prevailed in England and some of the Colonies. Necessarily it was to uproot all such relationships. But the object was broader than separating church and state in this narrow sense. It was to create a complete and permanent separation of the spheres of religious activity and civil authority by comprehensively

forbidding every form of public aid or support for religion. . . .

The same conclusion has been firmly maintained ever since that time . . . and we reaffirm it now. . . .

In *Engel v. Vitale,* only last year, these principles were so universally recognized that the Court without the citation of a single case and over the sole dissent of Mr. Justice Stewart reaffirmed them. The Court found the 22-word prayer used in "New York's program of daily classroom invocation of God's blessings as prescribed in the Regents' prayer . . . [to be] a religious activity." . . . It held that "it is no part of the business of government to compose official prayers for any group of the American people to recite as a part of a religious program carried on by the government. . . . The Court found that the "first and most immediate purpose [of the Establishment Clause] rested on a belief that a union of government and religion tends to destroy government and to degrade religion." . . . When government, the Court said, allies itself with one particular form of religion, the inevitable result is that it incurs "the hatred, disrespect and even contempt of those who held contrary beliefs."

. . . The wholesome "neutrality" of which this Court's cases speak thus stems from a recognition of the teachings of history that powerful sects or groups might bring about a fusion of governmental and religious functions or a concert or dependency of one upon the other to the end that official support of the State or Federal Government would be placed behind the tenets of one or of all orthodoxies. This the Establishment Clause prohibits. . . .

Applying the Establishment Clause principles to the cases at bar we find that the States are requiring the selection and reading at the opening of the school day of verses from the Holy Bible and the recitation of the Lord's Prayer by the students in unison. These exercises are prescribed as part of the curricular activities of students who are required by law to attend school. They are held in the school buildings under the supervision and with the participation of teachers employed in those schools. None of these factors, other than compulsory school attendance, was present in the program upheld in *Zorach v. Clauson.*

The conclusion follows that in both cases the laws require religious exercises and such exercises are being conducted in direct violation of the rights of the appellees and petitioners. Nor are these required exercises mitigated by the fact that individual students may absent themselves upon parental request, for that fact furnishes no defense to a claim of unconstitutionality under the Establishment Clause. . . . Further, it is no defense to urge that the religious practices here may be relatively minor encroachments on the First Amendment. The breach of neutrality that is today a trickling stream may all too soon become a raging torrent and, in the words of Madison, "it is proper to take alarm at the first experiment on our liberties."

. . . It is insisted that unless these religious exercises are permitted a "religion of secularism" is established in the schools. We agree of course that the State may not establish a "religion of secularism" in the sense of affirmatively opposing or showing hostility to religion, thus "preferring those who believe in no religion over those who do believe." . . . We do not agree, however, that this decision in any sense has that effect. In addition, it might well be said that one's education is not complete without a study of comparative religion or the history of religion and its relationship to the advancement of civilization. It certainly may be said that the Bible is worthy of study for its literary and historic qualities. Nothing we have said here indicates that such study of the Bible or of religion, when presented objectively as part of a secular program of education, may not be effected consistent with the First Amendment. But the exercises here do not fall into those categories. They are religious exercises, required by the States in violation of the command of the First Amendment that the Government maintain strict neutrality, neither aiding nor opposing religion.

Finally, we cannot accept that the concept of neutrality, which does not permit a State to require a religious exercise even with the consent of the majority of those affected, collides with the majority's right to free exercise of religion. While the Free Exercise Clause clearly prohibits the use of state action to deny the rights of free exercise to anyone, it has never meant that a majority could use the machinery of the State to practice its beliefs. Such a contention was effectively answered by Mr. Justice Jackson for the Court in *West Virginia Board of Education v. Barnette* . . . :

> The very purpose of a Bill of Rights was to withdraw certain subjects from the vicissitudes of political controversy, to place them beyond the reach of majorities and officials and to establish them as legal principles to be applied by the courts. One's right to . . . freedom of worship . . . and other fundamental rights may not be submitted to vote; they depend on the outcome of no elections.

The place of religion in our society is an exalted one, achieved through a long tradition of reliance on the home, the church and the inviolable citadel of the individual heart and mind. We have come to recognize through bitter experience that it is not within the power of government to invade that citadel, whether its purpose or effect be to aid or oppose, to advance or retard. In the relationship between man and religion, the State is firmly committed to a position of neutrality. . . .

THE PERMISSIBLE LIMITS OF SPEECH AND PRESS FREEDOM

250. *The Soapbox and the Public Interest*

Feiner v. New York, 340 U.S. 315 (1951).

VINSON, C.J.: Petitioner was convicted of the offense of disorderly conduct, a misdemeanor under the New York penal laws . . . [but claims] that the conviction is in violation of the right of free speech under the Fourteenth Amendment. . . .

On the evening of March 8, 1949, petitioner Irving Feiner was addressing an open-air meeting [on a street corner] in the City of Syracuse . . . the police received a telephone complaint concerning the meeting, and two officers were detailed to investigate. One of these officers went to the scene immediately, the other arriving some twelve minutes later. They found a crowd of about seventy-five or eighty people, both Negro and white, filling the sidewalk and spreading out into the street. Petitioner, standing on a large wooden box on the sidewalk, was addressing the crowd through a loud-speaker system attached to an automobile. Although the purpose of his speech was to urge his listeners to attend a meeting to be held that night in the Syracuse Hotel, in its course he was making derogatory remarks concerning President Truman, the American Legion, the Mayor of Syracuse, and other local political officials.

The police officers made no effort to interfere with petitioner's speech, but were first concerned with the effect of the crowd on both pedestrian and vehicular traffic. They observed the situation from the opposite side of the street, noting that some pedestrians were forced to walk in the street to avoid the crowd. Since traffic was passing at the time, the officers attempted to get the people listening to petitioner back on the sidewalk. The crowd was restless and there was some pushing, shoving and milling around. One of the officers telephoned the police station from a nearby store, and then both policemen crossed the street and mingled with the crowd without any intention of arresting the speaker.

At this time, petitioner was speaking in a "loud, high-pitched voice." He gave the impression that he was endeavoring to arouse the Negro people against the whites, urging that they rise up in arms and fight for equal rights. The statements before such a mixed audience "stirred up a little excitement." Some of the onlookers made remarks to the police about their inability to handle the crowd and at least one threatened violence if the police did not act. There were others who appeared to be favoring petitioner's arguments. Because of the feeling that existed in the crowd both for and against the speaker, the officers finally "stepped in to prevent it from resulting in a fight." One of the officers approached the petitioner, not for the purpose of arresting him, but to get him to break up the crowd. He asked petitioner to get down off the box, but the latter refused to accede to his request and continued talking. The officer waited for a minute and then demanded that he cease talking. Although the officer had thus twice requested petitioner to stop over the course of several minutes, petitioner not only ignored him but continued talking. During all this time, the crowd was pressing closer around petitioner and the officer. Finally, the officer told petitioner he was under arrest and ordered him to get down from the box, reaching up to grab him. Petitioner stepped down, announcing over the microphone that "the law has arrived, and I suppose they will take over now." In all, the officer had asked petitioner to get down off the box three times over a space of four or five minutes. Petitioner had been speaking for over a half hour.

On these facts, petitioner was specifically charged with violation of § 722 of the Penal Law of New York . . . particularly Paragraph C . . . "By ignoring and refusing to heed and obey reasonable police orders issued at the time and place mentioned in the Information to regulate and control said crowd and to prevent a breach or breaches of the peace and to prevent injury to pedestrians attempting to use said walk, and being forced into the highway adjacent to the place in question, and prevent injury to the public generally."

We are not faced here with blind condonation by a state court of arbitrary police action. Petitioner was accorded a full, fair trial. The trial judge heard testimony supporting and contradicting the judgment of the police officers that a clear danger of disorder was threatened. After weighing this contradictory evidence, the trial judge reached the conclusion that the police officers were justified in taking action to prevent a breach of the peace. The exercise of the police officers' proper discretionary power to prevent a breach of the peace was thus approved by the trial court and later by two courts on review. The courts below recognized petitioner's right to hold a street meeting at this locality, to make use of loud-speaking equipment in giving his speech, and to make derogatory remarks concerning public officials and the American Legion. They found that the officers in making the arrest were motivated solely by a proper concern for the preservation of order and protection of the general welfare, and that there was no evidence which could lend color to a claim that the acts of the police were a cover for suppression of petitioner's views and opinions. Petitioner was thus neither arrested nor convicted for the making or the content of his speech. Rather, it was the reaction which it actually engendered.

The language of *Cantwell v. Connecticut* . . . is appropriate here:

> The offense known as breach of the peace embraces a great variety of conduct destroying or menacing pub-

lic order and tranquility. It includes not only violent acts but acts and words likely to produce violence in others. No one would have the hardihood to suggest that the principle of freedom of speech sanctions incitement to riot or that religious liberty connotes the privilege to exhort others to physical attack upon those belonging to another sect. When clear and present danger of riot, disorder, interference with traffic upon the public streets, or other immediate threat to public safety, peace, or order appears, the power of the State to prevent or punish is obvious.

The findings of New York courts as to the condition of the crowd and the refusal of petitioner to obey the police requests, supported as they are by the record of this case, are persuasive that the conviction of petitioner for violation of public peace, order and authority does not exceed the bounds of proper state police action. This Court respects, as it must, the interest of the community in maintaining peace and order on its streets.

We cannot say that the preservation of that interest here encroaches on the constitutional rights of this petitioner.

We are well aware that the ordinary murmurings and objections of a hostile audience cannot be allowed to silence a speaker, and are also mindful of the possible danger of giving overzealous police officials complete discretion to break up otherwise lawful public meetings. "A State may not unduly suppress free communication of views, religious or other, under the guise of conserving desirable conditions." *Cantwell v. Connecticut, supra.* But we are not faced here with such a situation. It is one thing to say that the police cannot be used as an instrument for the suppression of unpopular views, and another to say that, when as here, the speaker passes the bounds of argument or persuasion and undertakes incitement to riot, they are powerless to prevent a breach of the peace. Nor in this case can we condemn the considered judgment of three New York courts approving the means which the police, faced with a crisis, used in the exercise of their power and duty to preserve peace and order. The findings of the state courts as to the existing situation and the imminence of greater disorder coupled with petitioner's deliberate defiance of the police officers convince us that we should not reverse this conviction in the name of free speech.

Affirmed.

251. *Race Hatred and Group Libel*

Beauharnais v. Illinois, 343 U.S. 250 (1952).

FRANKFURTER, J.: . . . The testimony at the trial was substantially undisputed. From it the jury could find that Beauharnais was president of the White Circle League; that, at a meeting on January 6, 1950, he passed out bundles of the lithographs in question, together with other literature, to volunteers for distribution on downtown Chicago street corners the following day; . . . and that the leaflets were in fact distributed . . . in accordance with his plan and instructions. The court, together with other charges on burden of proof and the like, told the jury "if you find . . . that the defendant, Joseph Beauharnais, did . . . manufacture, sell, or offer for sale, advertise or publish, present or exhibit in any public place the lithograph . . . then you are to find the defendant guilty. . . ." He refused to charge the jury, as requested by the defendant, that in order to convict they must find "that the article complained of was likely to produce a clear and present danger of a serious substantive evil that rises far above public inconvenience, annoyance or unrest." Upon this evidence and these instructions, the jury brought in the conviction here for review.

The statute before us is not a catchall enactment left at large by the State court which applied it. . . . It is a law specifically directed at a defined evil, its language drawing from history and practice in Illinois and in more than a score of other jurisdictions a meaning confirmed by the Supreme Court of that State in upholding this conviction. We do not, therefore, parse the statute as grammarians or treat it as an abstract exercise in lexicography. We read it in the animating context of well-defined usage. . . .

The Illinois Supreme Court tells us that §224a "is a form of criminal libel law." . . . The defendant, the trial court and the Supreme Court consistently treated it as such. The defendant offered evidence tending to prove the truth of parts of the utterance, and the courts below considered and disposed of this offer in terms of ordinary criminal libel precedents. Section 224a does not deal with the defense of truth, but by the Illinois Constitution, . . . "in all trials for libel, both civil and criminal, the truth, when published with good motives and for justifiable ends, shall be a sufficient defense." . . . Similarly, the action of the trial court in deciding as a matter of law the libelous character of the utterance, leaving to the jury only the question of publication, follows the settled rule in prosecutions for libel in Illinois and other States. Moreover, the Supreme Court's characterization of the words prohibited by the statute as those "liable to cause violence and disorder" paraphrases the traditional justification for punishing libels criminally, namely their "tendency to cause breach of the peace." . . .

No one will gainsay that it is libelous falsely to charge another with being a rapist, robber, carrier of knives and guns, user of marijuana. The precise question before us, then, is whether the protection of "liberty" in the Due Process Clause of the Fourteenth Amendment prevents a State from punishing such libels—as criminal libel has been defined, limited and constitutionally recognized time out of mind—directed at designated collectivities and flagrantly disseminated. There is even authority, however dubious, that such utterances were also crimes at common law. It is certainly clear that some American jurisdictions have sanctioned their punishment under ordinary criminal libel statutes. We cannot say, however, that the question is concluded by history and practice. But if an utterance directed at an individual may be the object of criminal sanctions, we cannot deny to a State power to punish the same utterance directed at a defined group, unless we can say that this is a wilful and purposeless restriction unrelated to the peace and well-being of the State.

Illinois did not have to look beyond her own borders or wait the tragic experience of the last three decades to conclude that wilful purveyors of falsehood concerning racial and religious groups promote strife and tend powerfully to obstruct the manifold adjustments required for free, ordered life in a metropolitan, polyglot community. From the murder of the abolitionist Lovejoy in 1837 to the Cicero riots of 1951, Illinois has been the scene of exacerbated tension between races, often flaring into violence and destruction. In many of these outbreaks, utterances of the character here in question, so the Illinois legislature could conclude, played a significant part. The law was passed on June 29, 1917, at a time when the State was struggling to assimilate vast numbers of new inhabitants, as yet concentrated in discrete racial or national or religious groups—foreign-born brought to it by the crest of the great wave of immigration, and Negroes attracted by jobs in war plants and the allurements of northern cities. Nine years earlier, in the very city where the legislature sat, what is said to be the first northern race riot had cost the lives of six people, left hundreds of Negroes homeless and shocked citizens into action far beyond the borders of the State. Less than a month before the bill was enacted, East St. Louis had seen a day's rioting, prelude to an outbreak, only four days after the bill became law, so bloody that it led to Congressional investigation. A series of bombings had begun which was to culminate two years later in the awful race riot which held Chicago in its grip for seven days in the summer of 1919. Nor has tension and violence between the groups defined in the statute been limited in Illinois to clashes between whites and Negroes.

In the face of this history and its frequent obligato of extreme racial and religious propaganda, we would deny experience to say that the Illinois legislature was without reason in seeking ways to curb false or malicious defamation of racial and religious groups, made in public places and by means calculated to have a powerful emotional impact on those to whom it was presented. "There are limits to the exercise of these liberties [of speech and of the press]. The danger in these times from the coercive activities of those who in the delusion of racial or religious conceit would incite violence and breaches of the peace in order to deprive others of their equal right to the exercise of their liberties, is emphasized by events familiar to all. These and other transgressions of those limits the States appropriately may punish." This was the conclusion, again of a unanimous Court, in 1940. *Cantwell v. Connecticut*. . . .

It may be argued, and weightily, that this legislation will not help matters; that tension and on occasion violence between racial and religious groups must be traced to causes more deeply embedded in our society than the rantings of modern know-nothings. Only those lacking responsible humility will have a confident solution for problems as intractable as the frictions attributable to differences of race, color or religion. This being so, it would be out of bounds for the judiciary to deny the legislature a choice of policy, provided it is not unrelated to the problem and not forbidden by some explicit limitation on the State's power. That the legislative remedy might not in practice mitigate the evil, or might itself raise new problems, would only manifest once more the paradox of reform. It is the price paid for the trial-and-error inherent in legislative efforts to deal with obstinate social issues. . . . Certainly the Due Process Clause does not require the legislature to be in the vanguard of science—especially sciences as young as human ecology and cultural anthropology. . . .

Libelous utterances, not being within the area of constitutionally protected speech, it is unnecessary, either for us or for the State courts, to consider the issues behind the phrase "clear and present danger." Certainly no one would contend that obscene speech, for example, may be punished only upon a showing of such circumstances. Libel, as we have seen, is in the same class.

We find no warrant in the Constitution for denying to Illinois the power to pass the law here under attack. But it bears repeating—although it should not—that our finding that the law is not constitutionally objectionable carries no implication of approval of the wisdom of the legislation or of its efficacy. These questions may raise doubts in our minds as well as in others. It is not for us, however, to make the legislative judgment. We are not at liberty to erect those doubts into fundamental law.

Affirmed.

252. *"Debate on public issues should be uninhibited, robust, and wide-open."*

New York Times Company v. Sullivan, 376 U.S. 255 (1964).

BRENNAN, J.: We are required for the first time in this case to determine the extent to which the constitutional protections for speech and press limit a State's power to award damages in a libel action brought by a public official against critics of his official conduct.

Respondent L. B. Sullivan is one of the three elected Commissioners of the City of Montgomery, Alabama. He testified that he was "Commissioner of Public Affairs and the duties are supervision of the Police Department, Fire Department, Department of Cemetery, and Department of Scales." He brought this civil libel action against the four individual petitioners, who are Negroes and Alabama clergymen, and against petitioner the New York Times Company, a New York corporation which publishes the *New York Times*, a daily newspaper. A jury in the Circuit Court of Montgomery County awarded him damages of $500,000, the full amount claimed, against all the petitioners, and the Supreme Court of Alabama affirmed. . . .

Respondent's complaint alleged that he had been libeled by statements in a full-page advertisement that was carried in the *New York Times* on March 29, 1960. . . . The advertisement was signed at the bottom of the page by the "Committee to Defend Martin Luther King and the Struggle for Freedom in the South," and the officers of the Committee were listed.

Of the 10 paragraphs of text in the advertisement, the third and a portion of the sixth were the basis of respondent's claim of libel. They read as follows:

THIRD PARAGRAPH:

In Montgomery, Alabama, after students sang "My Country, 'Tis of Thee" on the State Capitol steps, their leaders were expelled from school, and truckloads of police armed with shotguns and tear-gas ringed the Alabama State College Campus. When the entire student body protested to state authorities by refusing to re-register, their dining hall was padlocked in an attempt to starve them into submission.

SIXTH PARAGRAPH:

Again and again the Southern violators have answered Dr. King's peaceful protests with intimidation and violence. They have bombed his home almost killing his wife and child. They have assaulted his person. They have arrested him seven times —for "speeding," "loitering" and similar "offenses." And now they have charged him with "perjury"—a *felony* under which they would imprison him for *ten years*. . . .

Although neither of these statements mentions respondent by name, he contended that the word "police" in the third paragraph referred to him as the Montgomery Commissioner who supervised the Police Department, so that he was being accused of "ringing" the campus with police. He further claimed that the paragraph would be read as imputing to the police, and hence to him, the padlocking of the dining hall in order to starve the students into submission. As to the sixth paragraph, he contended that since arrests are ordinarily made by the police, the statement "They have arrested [Dr. King] seven times" would be read as referring to him; he further contended that the "They" who did the arresting would be equated with the "They" who committed the other described acts and with the "Southern violators." . . .

It is uncontroverted that some of the statements contained in the two paragraphs were not accurate descriptions of events which occurred in Montgomery. Although Negro students staged a demonstration on the State Capitol steps, they sang the National Anthem and not "My Country, 'Tis of Thee." Although nine students were expelled by the State Board of Education, this was not for leading the demonstration at the Capitol, but for demanding service at a lunch counter in the Montgomery County Courthouse on another day. . . . The campus dining hall was not padlocked on any occasion, and the only students who may have been barred from eating there were the few who had neither signed a preregistration application nor requested temporary meal tickets. Although the police were deployed near the campus in large numbers on three occasions, they did not at any time "ring" the campus, and they were not called to the campus in connection with the demonstration on the State Capitol steps, as the third paragraph implied. . . .

On the premise that the charges in the sixth paragraph could be read as referring to him, respondent was allowed to prove that he had not participated in the events described. Although Dr. King's home had in fact been bombed twice when his wife and child were there, both of these occasions antedated respondent's tenure as Commissioner, and the police were not only not implicated in the bombings, but had made every effort to apprehend those who were. Three of Dr. King's four arrests took place before respondent became Commissioner. Although Dr. King had in fact been indicted (he was subsequently acquitted) on two counts of perjury, each of which carried a possible five-year sentence, respondent had nothing to do with procuring the indictment.

Respondent made no effort to prove that he suffered actual pecuniary loss as a result of the alleged libel. . . .

The cost of the advertisement was approximately $4800, and it was published by the *Times* upon an order from a New York advertising agency acting for the signatory Committee. The agency submitted the advertisement with a letter from A. Philip Randolph, Chairman of the Committee, certifying that the persons whose names appeared on the advertisement had given their permission. . . . The manager of the Advertising Acceptability Department testified that he had approved the advertisement for publication because he knew nothing to cause him to believe that anything in it was false, and because it bore the endorsement of "a number of people who are well known and whose reputation" he "had no reason to question." Neither he nor anyone else at the *Times* made an effort to confirm the accuracy of the advertisement, either by checking it against recent *Times* news stories relating to some of the described events or by some other means.

Alabama law denies a public officer recovery of punitive damages in a libel action brought on account of a publication concerning his official conduct unless he first makes a written demand for a public retraction and the defendant fails or refuses to comply. . . . Respondent served such a demand upon each of the petitioners. None of the individual petitioners responded to the demand, primarily because each took the position that he had not authorized the use of his name on the advertisement and therefore had not published the statements that respondent alleged to have libeled him. The *Times* did not publish a retraction in response to the demand, but wrote respondent a letter stating, among other things, that "we . . . are somewhat puzzled as to how you think the statements in any way reflect on you," and "you might, if you desire, let us know in what respect you claim that the statements in the advertisement reflect on you." Respondent filed this suit a few days later without answering the letter. The *Times* did, however, subsequently publish a retraction of the advertisement upon the demand of Governor John Patterson of Alabama, who asserted that the publication charged him with "grave misconduct and . . . improper actions and omissions as Governor of Alabama and Ex-Officio Chairman of the State Board of Education of Alabama." When asked to explain why there had been a retraction for the Governor but not for respondent, the Secretary of the *Times* testified: "We did that because we didn't want anything that was published by the *Times* to be a reflection on the State of Alabama and the Governor was, as far as we could see, the embodiment of the State of Alabama and the proper representative of the State and, furthermore, we had by that time learned more of the actual facts which the ad purported to recite and, finally, the ad did refer to the action of the State authorities and the Board of Education presumably of which the Governor is ex-officio chairman. . . ." On the other hand, he testified that he did not think that "any of the language in there referred to Mr. Sullivan."

The trial judge submitted the case to the jury under instructions that the statements in the advertisement were "libelous *per se*" and were not privileged, so that petitioners might be held liable if the jury found that they had published the advertisement and that the statements were made "of and concerning" respondent. The jury was instructed that, because the statements were libelous *per se*, "the law . . . implies legal injury from the bare fact of publication itself," "falsity and malice are presumed," "general damages need not be alleged or proved but are presumed," and "punitive damages may be awarded by the jury even though the amount of actual damages is neither found nor shown." . . . The judge rejected petitioners' contention that his rulings abridged the freedoms of speech and of the press that are guaranteed by the First and Fourteenth Amendments.

In affirming the judgment, the Supreme Court of Alabama sustained the trial judge's rulings and instructions in all respects. . . . It rejected petitioners' constitutional contentions with the brief statements that "The First Amendment of the U.S. Constitution does not protect libelous publications" and "The Fourteenth Amendment is directed against State action and not private action." . . .

Because of the importance of the constitutional issues involved, we granted the separate petitions for certiorari of the individual petitioners and of the *Times*. . . . We reverse the judgment. We hold that the rule of law applied by the Alabama courts is constitutionally deficient for failure to provide the safeguards for freedom of speech and of the press that are required by the First and Fourteenth Amendments in a libel action brought by a public official against critics of his official conduct. We further hold that under the proper safeguards the evidence presented in this case is constitutionally insufficient to support the judgment for respondent.

The . . . contention . . . that the constitutional guarantees of freedom of speech and of the press are inapplicable here, at least so far as the *Times* is concerned, because the allegedly libelous statements were published as part of a paid, "commercial" advertisement . . . is wholly misplaced. . . . The publication here was not a "commercial" advertisement in the sense in which the words were used in *Valentine v. Christensen* [a handbill soliciting business]. It communicated information, expressed opinion, recited grievances, protested claimed abuses, and sought financial support on behalf of a movement whose existence and objective are matters of the highest public interest and concern. . . . That the *Times* was paid for publishing the advertisement is . . immaterial. . . . Any other conclusion would discourage newspapers from carrying "editorial advertisements" of this type, and so might shut off an important outlet for the promulgation of information and ideas by persons who do not themselves have access to publishing facilities—who wish to exercise their freedom of speech even though they are not members of the press. The effect would be to shackle the First Amendment in its attempt to secure "the widest possible dissemination of information from diverse and antagonistic sources" (*Associated Press v. U.S.*). To avoid placing such a handicap upon the freedom of expression, we hold that if the allegedly libelous statements would otherwise be constitutionally protected from the present judgment, they do not forfeit that protection because they were published in the form of a paid advertisement.

Under Alabama law as applied in this case a publication is "libelous *per se*" if the words "tend to injure a person. . . in his reputation" or to "bring [him] into public contempt"; the trial court stated that the standard was met if the words are such as to "injure him in his public office, or impute misconduct to him in his office, or want of official integrity, or want of fidelity to a public trust. . . ." The jury must find that the words were published "of and concerning" the plaintiff, but where the plaintiff is a public official his place in the governmental hierarchy is sufficient evidence to support a finding that his reputation has been affected by statements that reflect upon the agency of which he is in charge. Once "libel per se" has been established, the defendant has no defense as to stated facts unless he can persuade the jury that they were true in all their particulars. . . . His privilege of "fair comment" for expressions of opinion depends on the truth of the facts upon which the comment is based. . . . Unless he can discharge the burden of proving truth, general damages are presumed, and may be awarded without proof of pecuniary injury. A showing of actual malice is apparently a prerequisite to recovery of punitive damages, and the defendant may in any event forestall these by a retraction meeting the statutory requirements. Good motives and belief in truth do not negate an inference of malice, but are relevant only in mitigation of punitive damages if the jury chooses to accord them weight. . . .

The question before us is whether this rule of liability, as applied to an action brought by a public official against critics of his official conduct, abridges the freedom of speech and of the press that is guaranteed by the First and Fourteenth Amendments.

Respondent relies heavily, as did the Alabama courts, on statements of this Court to the effect that the Constitution does not protect libelous publications. Those statements do not foreclose our inquiry here. . . . In deciding the question now, we are compelled by neither precedent nor policy to give any more weight to the epithet "libel" than we have to other "mere labels" of state law. . . . Like "insurrection," contempt, advocacy of unlawful acts, breach of the peace, obscenity, solicitation of legal business, and the various other formulae for the repression of expression that have been challenged in this Court, libel can claim no talismanic immunity from constitutional limitations. It must be measured by standards that satisfy the First Amendment.

The general proposition that freedom of expression upon public questions is secured by the First Amendment has long been settled by our decisions. The constitutional safeguard, we have said, "was fashioned to assure the unfettered interchange of ideas for the bringing about of political and social changes desired by the people." . . . "The maintenance of the opportunity for free political discussion to the end that government may be responsive to the will of the people and that changes may be obtained by lawful means, an opportunity essential to the security of the Republic, is a fundamental principle of our constitutional system." . . . "[I]t is a prized American privilege to speak one's mind, although not always with perfect good taste, on all public institutions," . . . and this opportunity is to be afforded for "vigorous advocacy" no less than "abstract discussion." . . .

Thus we consider this case against the background of a profound national commitment to the principle that debate on public issues should be uninhibited, robust, and wide-open, and that it may well include vehement, caustic, and sometimes unpleasantly sharp attacks on government and public officials. . . . The present advertisement, as an expression of grievance and protest on one of the major public issues of our time, would seem clearly to qualify for the constitutional protection. The question is whether it forfeits that protection by the falsity of some of its factual statements and by its alleged defamation of respondent.

Authoritative interpretations of the First Amendment guarantees have consistently refused to recognize an exception for any test of truth—whether administered by judges, juries, or administrative officials—and especially not one that puts the burden of proving truth on the speaker. . . . The constitutional protection does not turn upon "the truth, popularity, or social utility of the ideas and beliefs which are offered." . . . As Madison said, "Some degree of abuse is inseparable from the proper use of every thing; and in no instance is this more true than in that of the press." . . . That erroneous statement is inevitable in free debate, and that it must be protected if the freedoms of expression are to have the "breathing space" that they "need . . . to survive," . . . was also recognized by the Court of Appeals for the District of Columbia Circuit in *Sweeney v. Patterson*. . . . Judge Edgerton spoke for a unanimous court which affirmed the dismissal of a Congressman's libel suit based upon a newspaper article charging him with anti-Semitism in opposing a judicial appointment. He said:

> Cases which impose liability for erroneous reports of the political conduct of officials reflect the obsolete doctrine that the governed must not criticize their governors. . . . The interest of the public here outweighs the interest of appellant or any other individual. The protection of the public requires not merely discussion, but information. Political conduct and views which some respectable people approve, and others condemn, are constantly imputed to Congressmen. Errors of fact, particularly in regard to a man's mental states and processes, are inevitable. . . . Whatever is added to the field of libel is taken from the field of free debate.

Injury to official reputation affords no more warrant for repressing speech that would otherwise be free than does factual error. Where judicial officers are involved, this Court has held that concern for the dignity and reputation of the courts does not justify the punishment as criminal contempt of criticism of the judge or his decision. . . . This is true even though the utterance contains "half-truths" and "misinformation." . . . Such repression can be justified, if at all, only by a clear and present danger of the obstruction of justice. . . . If judges are to be treated as "men of fortitude, able to thrive in a hardy climate," . . . surely the same must be true of other government officials, such as elected city commissioners. Criticism of their official conduct does not lose its constitutional protection merely because it is effective criticism and hence diminishes their official reputations.

If neither factual error nor defamatory content suffices to remove the constitutional shield from criticism of official conduct, the combination of the two elements is no less inadequate. This is the lesson to be drawn from the great controversy over the Sedition Act of 1798 . . . which first crystallized a national awareness of the central meaning of the First Amendment. See Levy, *Legacy of Suppression* (1960); Smith, *Freedom's Fetters* (1956). That statute made it a crime, punishable by a $5,000 fine and five years in prison, "if any person shall write, print, utter or publish . . . any false, scandalous and malicious writing or writings against the government of the United States, or either house of the Congress . . . , or the President . . . , with the intent to defame . . . or to bring them or either of them, into contempt or disrepute; or to excite against them, or either or any of them, the hatred of the good people of the United States." The Act allowed the defendant the defense of truth, and provided that the jury were to be judges both of the law and the facts. Despite these qualifications, the Act was vigorously condemned as unconstitutional in an attack joined in by Jefferson and Madison. . . .

Although the Sedition Act was never tested in this Court, the attack upon its validity has carried the day in the court of history. Fines levied in its prosecution were repaid by Act of Congress on the ground that it was unconstitutional. . . . Jefferson, as President, pardoned those who had been convicted and sentenced under the Act and remitted their fines, stating: "I discharged every person under punishment or prosecution under the Sedition Law because I considered, and now consider, that law to be a nullity as absolute and palpable as if Congress had ordered us to fall down and worship a golden image." . . . The invalidity of the Act has also been assumed by Justices of this Court. . . . These views reflect a broad consensus that the Act, because of the restraint it imposed upon criticism of government and public officials, was inconsistent with the First Amendment.

There is no force in respondent's argument that the constitutional limitations implicit in the history of the Sedition Act apply only to Congress and not to the States. It is true that the First Amendment was originally addressed only to action by the Federal Government, and that Jefferson, for one, while denying the power of Congress "to controul the freedom of the press," recognized such a power in the States. . . . But this distinction was eliminated with the adoption of the Fourteenth Amendment and the application to the States of the First Amendment's restrictions. . . .

What a State may not constitutionally bring about by means of a criminal statute is likewise beyond the reach of its civil law of libel. The fear of damage awards under a rule such as that invoked by the Alabama courts here may be markedly more inhibiting than the fear of prosecution under a criminal statute. . . . Alabama, for example, has a criminal libel law which . . . allows as punishment upon conviction a fine not exeeding $500 and a prison sentence of six months. . . . Presumably a person charged with violation of this statute enjoys ordinary criminal-law safeguards such as the requirements of an indictment and of proof beyond a reasonable doubt. These safeguards are not available to the defendant in a civil action. The judgment awarded in this case—without the need for any proof of actual pecuniary loss—was one thousand times greater than the maximum fine provided by the Alabama criminal statute, and one hundred times greater than that provided by the Sedition Act. And since there is no double-jeopardy limitation applicable to civil lawsuits, this is not the only judgment that may be awarded against petitioners for the same publication. Whether or not a newspaper can survive a succession of such judgments, the pall of fear and timidity imposed upon those who would give voice to public criticism is an atmosphere in which the First Amendment freedoms cannot survive. Plainly the Alabama law of civil libel is "a form of regulation that creates hazards to protected freedoms markedly greater than those that attend reliance upon the criminal law." . . .

The state rule of law is not saved by its allowance of the defense of truth. A defense for erroneous statements honestly made is no less essential here than was the requirement of proof of guilty knowledge which, in *Smith v. California* . . . we held indispensable to a valid conviction of a bookseller for possessing obscene writings for sale. . . . A rule compelling the critic of official conduct to guarantee the truth of all his factual assertions—and to do so on pain of libel judgments virtually unlimited in amount—leads to a comparable "self-censorship." . . . Under such a rule, would-be critics of official conduct may be deterred from voicing their criticism, even though it is believed to be true and even though it is in fact true, because of doubt whether it can be proved in court or fear of the expense of having to do so. They tend to make only statements which "steer far wider of the unlawful zone." . . . The rule thus dampens the vigor and limits the variety of public debate. It is inconsistent with the First and Fourteenth Amendments.

The constitutional guarantees require, we think, a federal rule that prohibits a public official from recovering damages for a defamatory falsehood relating to his official conduct unless he proves that the statement was made with "actual malice" —that is, with knowledge that it was false or with reckless disregard of whether it was false or not. . . .

Such a privilege for criticism of official conduct is appropriately analogous to the protection accorded a public official when *he* is sued for libel by a private citizen. . . . The States accord the same immunity to statements of their highest officers, although some differentiate their lesser officials and qualify the privilege they enjoy. But all hold that all officials are protected unless actual malice can be proved. The reason for the official privilege is said to be that the threat of damage suits would otherwise "inhibit the fearless, vigorous, and effective administration of policies of government" and "dampen the ardor of all but the most resolute, or the most irresponsible, in the unflinching discharge of their duties." . . . Analogous considerations support the privilege for the citizen-critic of government. It is as much his duty to criticize as it is the official's duty to administer. . . . As Madison said, . . . "the censorial power is in the people over the Government, and not in the Government over the people." It would give public servants an unjustified preference over the public they serve, if critics of official conduct did not have a fair equivalent of the immunity granted to the officials themselves.

We conclude that such a privilege is required by the First and Fourteenth Amendments. . . .

While Alabama law apparently requires proof of actual malice for an award of punitive damages, where general damages are concerned malice is "presumed." Such a presumption is inconsistent with the federal rule. . . . This court's duty is not limited to the elaboration of constitutional principles; we must also in proper cases review the evidence to make certain that those principles have been constitutionally applied. This is such a case, particularly since the question is one of alleged trespass across "the line between speech unconditionally guaranteed and speech which may legitimately be regulated." . . .

We must "make an independent examination of the whole record," . . . so as to assure ourselves that the judgment does not constitute a forbidden intrusion on the field of the free expression.

Applying these standards, we consider that the proof presented to show actual malice lacks the convincing clarity which the constitutional standard demands, and hence that it would not constitutionally sustain the judgment for respondent under the proper rule of law. The case of the individual petitioners requires little discussion. Even assuming that they could constitutionally be found to have authorized the use of their names on the advertisement, there was no evidence whatever that they were aware of any erroneous statements or were in any way reckless in that regard. The judgment against them is thus without constitutional support.

As to the *Times*, we similarly conclude that the facts do not support a finding of actual malice. The statement by the *Times*' Secretary that, apart from the padlocking allegation, he thought the advertisement was "substantially correct," affords no constitutional warrant for the Alabama Supreme Court's conclusion that it was a "cavalier ignoring of the falsity of the advertisement [from which] the jury could not have but been impressed with the bad faith of the *Times*, and its maliciousness inferable therefrom." The statement does not indicate malice at the time of the publication; even if the advertisement was not "substantially correct"—although respondent's own proofs tend to show that it was—that opinion was at least a reasonable one, and there was no evidence to impeach the witness' good faith in holding it. The *Times*' failure to retract upon respondent's demand, although it later retracted upon the demand of Governor Patterson, is likewise not adequate evidence of malice for constitutional purposes. Whether or not a failure to retract may ever constitute such evidence, there are two reasons why it does not here. *First*, the letter written by the *Times* reflected a reasonable doubt on its part as to whether the advertisement could reasonably be taken to refer to respondent at all. *Second*, it was not a final refusal, since it asked for an explanation on this point—a request that respondent chose to ignore. Nor does the retraction upon the demand of the Governor supply the necessary proof. It may be doubted that a failure to retract which is not itself evidence of malice can retroactively become such by virtue of a retraction subsequently made to another party. But in any event that did not happen here, since the explanation given by the *Times*' Secretary for the distinction drawn between respondent and the Governor was a reasonable one, the good faith of which was not impeached.

Finally, there is evidence that the *Times* published the advertisement without checking its accuracy against the news stories in the *Times*' own files. The mere presence of the stories in the files does not, of course, establish that the *Times* "knew" the advertisement was false, since the state of mind required for actual malice would have to be brought home to the persons in the *Times*' organization having responsibility for the publication of the advertisement. With respect to the failure of those persons to make the check, the record shows that they relied upon their knowledge of the good reputation of many of those whose names were listed as sponsors of the advertisement, and upon the letter from A. Philip Randolph, known to them as a responsible individual, certifying that the use of the names was authorized. There was testimony that the persons handling the advertisement saw nothing in it that would render it unacceptable under the *Times*' policy of rejecting advertisements containing "attacks of a personal character"; their failure to reject it on this ground was not unreasonable. We think the evidence against the *Times* supports at most a finding of negligence in failing to discover the misstatements, and is constitutionally insufficient to show the recklessness that is required for a finding of actual malice. . . .

The judgment of the Supreme Court of Alabama is reversed and the case is remanded to that court for further proceedings not inconsistent with this opinion.

Reversed and remanded.

MOVIE AND BOOK CENSORSHIP: THE QUEST FOR A STANDARD

253. *Obscene Literature and the Right to Read*

Butler v. Michigan, 77 S. Ct. 524 (1957).

FRANKFURTER, J.: . . . Appellant was charged with . . . selling to a police officer what the trial judge characterized as "a book containing obscene, immoral, lewd, lascivious language, or descriptions, tending to incite minors to violent or depraved or immoral acts, manifestly tending to corruption of the morals of youth." Appellant moved to dismiss the proceeding on the claim that application of §343 unduly restricted freedom of speech as protected by the Due Process Clause of the Fourteenth Amendment in that the statute (1) prohibited distribution of a book to the general public on the basis of the undesirable influence it may have upon youth; (2) damned a book and proscribed its sale merely because of some isolated passages that appeared objectionable when divorced from the book as a whole; and (3) failed to provide a sufficiently definite standard of guilt. After hearing the evidence, the trial judge denied the motion, and, in an oral opinion, held that ". . . the defendant is guilty because he sold a book in the City of Detroit containing this language [the passages deemed offensive], and also because the Court feels that even viewing the book as a whole, it [the objectionable language] was not necessary to the proper development of the theme of the book nor of the conflict expressed therein." Appellant was fined $100. . . .

Appellant's argument here took a wide sweep. We need not follow him. Thus, it is unnecessary to dissect the remarks of the trial judge in order to determine whether he construed §343 to ban the distribution of books merely because certain of their passages, when viewed in isolation, were deemed objectionable. Likewise, we are free to put aside the claim that the Michigan law falls within the doctrine whereby a New York obscenity statute was found invalid in *Winters v. . . . New York*. . . .

It is clear on the record that appellant was convicted because Michigan . . . made it an offense for him to make available for the general reading public (and he in fact sold to a police officer) a book that the trial judge found to have a potentially deleterious influence upon youth. The State insists that, by thus quarantining the general reading public against books not too rugged for grown men and women in order to shield juvenile innocence, it is exercising its power to promote the general welfare. Surely, this is to burn the house to roast the pig. Indeed, the Solicitor General of Michigan has, with characteristic candor, advised the Court that Michigan has a statute specifically designed to protect its children against obscene matter "tending to the corruption of the morals of youth." But the appellant was not convicted for violating this statute.

We have before us legislation not reasonably restricted to the evil with which it is said to deal. The incidence of this enactment is to reduce the adult population of Michigan to reading only what is fit for children. It thereby arbitrarily curtails one of those liberties of the individual, now enshrined in the Due Process Clause of the Fourteenth Amendment, that history has attested as the indispensable conditions for the maintenance and progress of a free society. We are constrained to reverse this conviction.

254. *Obscenity, Immorality, and Prurient Interest*

Roth v. U.S.; Alberts v. California, 354 U.S. 476 (1957).

BRENNAN, J.: . . . The Constitutionality of a criminal obscenity statute is the question in each of these cases. In *Roth,* the primary constitutional question is whether the federal obscenity statute violates the provision of the First Amendment that "Congress shall make no law . . . abridging the freedom of speech, or of the press. . . ." In *Alberts,* the primary constitutional question is whether the obscenity provisions of the California Penal Code invade the freedoms of speech and press as they may be incorporated in the liberty protected from state action by the Due Process Clause of the Fourteenth Amendment. . . .

Roth conducted a business in New York in the publication and sale of books, photographs and magazines. He used circulars and advertising matter to solicit sales. He was convicted by a jury in the District Court for the Southern District of New York upon 4 counts of a 26-count indictment charging him with mailing obscene circulars and advertising, and an obscene book, in violation of the federal obscenity statute.

Alberts conducted a mail-order business from Los Angeles. He was convicted by the Judge of the Municipal Court of the Beverly Hills Judicial District (having waived a jury trial) under a misdemeanor complaint which charged him with lewdly keeping for sale obscene and indecent books, and with writing, composing and publishing an obscene advertisement of them, in violation of the California Penal Code. . . .

The dispositive question is whether obscenity is utterance within the area of protected speech and press. Although this is the first time the question has been squarely presented to this Court, either under the First Amendment or under the Fourteenth Amendment, expressions found in numerous opinions indicate that this Court has always assumed that obscenity is not protected by the freedoms of speech and press. . . .

The protection given speech and press was fashioned to assure unfettered interchange of ideas for the bringing about of political and social changes desired by the people. . . .

All ideas having even the slightest redeeming social importance—unorthodox ideas, controversial ideas, even ideas hateful to the prevailing climate of opinion—have the full protection of the guaranties, unless excludable because they encroach upon the limited area of more important interests. But implicit in the history of the First Amendment is the rejection of obscenity as utterly without redeeming social importance. This rejection for that reason is mirrored in the universal judgment that obscenity should be restrained, reflected in the international agreement of over 50 nations, in the obscenity laws of all of the 48 States, and in the 20 obscenity laws enacted by the Congress from 1842 to 1956. This is the same judgment expressed by this Court in *Chaplinsky v. New Hampshire,* . . .

". . . There are certain well-defined and narrowly limited classes of speech, the prevention and punishment of which have never been thought to raise any Constitutional problem. These include the lewd and obscene. . . . It has been well observed that such utterances are no essential part of any exposition of ideas, and are of such slight social value as a step to truth that any benefit that may be derived from them is clearly outweighed by the social interest in order and morality." . . . We hold that obscenity is not within the area of constitutionally protected speech or press.

It is strenuously urged that these obscenity statutes offend the constitutional guaranties because they punish incitation to impure sexual *thoughts,* not shown to be related to any overt antisocial conduct which is or may be incited in the persons stimulated to such *thoughts.* In *Roth,* the trial judge instructed the jury: "The words 'obscene, lewd and lascivious' as used in the law, signify that form of immorality which has relation to sexual impurity and has a tendency to excite lustful *thoughts.*" (Emphasis added.) In *Alberts,* the trial judge applied the test . . . whether the material has "a substantial tendency to deprave or corrupt its readers by inciting lascivious *thoughts* or arousing lustful desires." (Emphasis added.) It is insisted that the constitutional guaranties are violated because convictions may be held without proof either that obscene material will perceptibly create a clear and present danger of anti-social conduct, or will probably induce its recipients to such conduct. But, in light of our holding that obscenity is not protected speech, the complete answer to this argument is in the holding of this Court in *Beauharnais v. Illinois* . . . :

> Libelous utterances not being within the area of constitutionally protected speech, it is unnecessary, either for us or for the State courts, to consider the issues behind the phrase "clear and present danger." Certainly no one would contend that obscene speech, for example, may be punished only upon a showing of such circumstances. Libel, as we have seen, is in the same class.

However, sex and obscenity are not synonymous. Obscene material is material which deals with sex in a manner appealing to prurient interest. The portrayal of sex, e.g., in art, literature and scientific works, is not itself sufficient reason to deny material the constitutional protection of freedom of speech and press. Sex, a great and mysterious motive force in human life, has indisputably been a subject of absorbing interest to mankind through the ages: it is one of the vital problems of human interest and public concern. . . .

The fundamental freedoms of speech and press have contributed greatly to the development and well-being of our free society and are indispensable to its continued growth. Ceaseless vigilance is the watchword to prevent their erosion by Congress or by the States. The door barring federal and state intrusion into this area cannot be left ajar; it must be kept tightly closed and opened only the slightest crack necessary to prevent encroachment upon more important interests. It is therefore vital that the standards for judging obscenity safeguard the protection of freedom of speech and press for material which does not treat sex in a manner appealing to prurient interest.

The early leading standard of obscenity allowed material to be judged merely by the effect of an isolated excerpt upon particularly susceptible persons. *Regina v. Hicklin,* [1868]. . . . Some American courts adopted this standard but later decisions have rejected it and substituted this test: whether to the average person, applying contemporary community standards, the dominant theme of the material taken as a whole appeals to prurient interest. The *Hicklin* test, judging obscenity by the effect of isolated passages upon the most susceptible persons, might well encompass material legitimately treating with sex, and so it must be rejected as unconstitutionally restrictive of the freedoms of speech and press. On the other hand, the substituted standard provides safeguards adequate to withstand the charge of constitutional infirmity.

Both trial courts below sufficiently followed the proper standard. Both courts used the proper definition of obscenity. . . .

255. *Punishment for Thoughts Provoked*

Roth v. U.S.; Alberts v. California, 354 U.S. 476 (1957).

DOUGLAS, J., dissenting: When we sustain these convictions, we make the legality of a publication turn on the purity of thought which a book or tract instills in the mind of the reader. I do not think we can approve that standard and be faithful to the command of the First Amendment which by its terms is a restraint on Congress and which by the Fourteenth is a restraint on the States.

In the *Roth* case the trial judge charged the jury that the statutory words "obscene, lewd and lascivious" describe "that form of immorality which has relation to sexual impurity and has a tendency to excite lustful thoughts." He stated that the term "filthy" in the statute pertaining "to that sort of treatment of sexual matters in such a vulgar and indecent way, so that it tends to arouse a feeling of disgust and revulsion." He went on to say that the material "must be calculated to corrupt and debauch the minds and morals" of "the average person in the community" not those of any particular class. "You judge the circulars, pictures and publications which have been put in evidence by present-day standards of the community. You may ask yourselves does it offend the common conscience of the community by present-day standards."

The trial judge who, sitting without a jury, heard the *Alberts* case and the appellate court that sustained the judgment of conviction, . . . held that a book is obscene "if it has a substantial tendency to deprave or corrupt its readers by inciting lascivious thoughts or arousing lustful desire."

By these standards punishment is inflicted for thoughts provoked, not for overt acts nor anti-social conduct. This test cannot be squared with our decisions under the First Amendment. Even the ill-starred *Dennis* case conceded that speech to be punishable must have some relation to action which could be penalized by government. *Dennis v. United States*. . . .

The tests by which these convictions were obtained require only the arousing of sexual thoughts. Yet the arousing of sexual thoughts and desires happens every day in normal life in dozens of ways. Nearly 30 years ago a questionnaire sent to college and normal school women graduates asked what things were most stimulating sexually. Of 409 replies, 9 said "music"; 18 said "pictures"; 29 said "dancing"; 40 said "drama"; 95 said "books"; and 218 said "man." Alpert, Judicial Censorship of Obscene Literature, 52 Harv. L. Rev. 40, 73. . . .

If we were certain that impurity of sexual thoughts impelled to action, we would be on less dangerous ground in punishing the distributors of this sex literature. But it is by no means clear that obscene literature, as so defined, is a significant factor in influencing substantial deviations from the community standards. . . .

The absence of dependable information on the effect of obscene literature on human conduct should make us wary. It should put us on the side of protecting society's interest in literature, except and unless it can be said that the particular publication has an impact on action that the government can control. . . .

I assume there is nothing in the Constitution which forbids Congress from using its power over the mails to proscribe *conduct* on the grounds of good morals. No one would suggest that the First Amendment permits nudity in public places, adultery, and other phases of sexual misconduct. . . .

. . . Government should be concerned with anti-social conduct, not with utterances. Thus if the First Amendment guarantee of freedom of speech and press is to mean anything in this field, it must allow protests even against the moral code that the standard of the day sets for the community. In other words, literature should not be suppressed merely because it offends the moral code of the censor.

The legality of a publication in this country should never be allowed to turn either on the purity of thought which it instills in the mind of the reader or on the degree to which it offends the community conscience. By either test the role of the censor is exalted, and society's values in literary freedom are sacrificed. . . .

I do not think that the problem can be resolved by the Court's statement that "obscenity is not expression protected by the First Amendment." With the exception of *Beauharnais v. Illinois*, . . . none of our cases have resolved problems of free speech and free press by placing any form of expression beyond the pale of the absolute prohibition of the First Amendment. Unlike the law of libel, wrongfully relied on in *Beauharnais*, there is no special historical evidence that literature dealing with sex was intended to be treated in a special manner by those who drafted the First Amendment. In fact, the first reported court decision in this country involving obscene literature was in 1921. . . . I reject too the implication that problems of freedom of speech and of the press are to be resolved by weighing against the values of free expression, the judgment of the Court that a particular form of that expression has "no redeeming social importance." The First Amendment, its prohibition in terms absolute, was designed to preclude courts as well as legislatures from weighing the values of speech against silence. The First Amendment puts free speech in the preferred position.

Freedom of expression can be suppressed if, and to the extent that, it is so closely brigaded with illegal action as to be an inseparable part of it. . . . As a people, we cannot afford to relax that standard. For the test that suppresses a cheap tract today can suppress a literary gem tomorrow. All it need do is to incite a lascivious thought or arouse a lustful desire. The list of books that judges or juries can place in that category is endless.

I would give the broad sweep of the First Amendment full support. I have the same confidence in the ability of our people to reject noxious literature as I have in their capacity to sort out the true from the false in theology, economics, politics, or any other field.

THE VARYING FORMS OF FREE EXPRESSION

256. *The Retreat from the Thornhill Doctrine*

Giboney v. Empire Storage & Ice Co., 336 U.S. 490 (1949).

BLACK, J.: . . . It is contended that the injunction against picketing adjacent to Empire's place of business is an unconstitutional abridgment of free speech because the picketers were attempting peacefully to publicize truthful facts about a labor dispute. See *Thornhill v. Alabama*. . . . But the record here does not permit this publicizing to be treated in isolation. For according to the pleadings, the evidence, the findings, and the argument of the appellants, the sole immediate object of the publicizing adjacent to the premises of Empire, as well as the other activities of the appellants and their allies, was to compel Empire to agree to stop selling ice to nonunion peddlers. Thus all of appellants' activities—their powerful transportation combinations, their patrolling, their formation of a picket line warning union men not to cross at peril of their union membership, their publicizing—constituted a single and integrated course of conduct, which was in violation of Missouri's valid law. In this situation, the injunction did no more than enjoin an offense against Missouri law, a felony.

It rarely has been suggested that the constitutional freedom for speech and press extends its immunity to speech or writing used as an integral part of conduct in violation of a valid criminal statute. We reject the contention now. Nothing that was said or decided in any of the cases relied on by appellants calls for a different holding.

Neither *Thornhill v. Alabama*, nor *Carlson v. California* . . . supports the contention that conduct otherwise unlawful is always immune from state regulations because an integral part of that conduct is carried on by display of placards by peaceful picketers. In both these cases this Court struck down statutes which banned all dissemination of information by people adjacent to certain premises, pointing out that the statutes were so broad that they could not only be utilized to punish conduct plainly illegal but could also be applied to ban all truthful publications of the facts of a labor controversy. But in the Thornhill opinion, . . . the Court was careful to point out that it was within the province of states "to set the limits of permissible contest open to industrial combatants." . . .

After emphasizing state power over industrial conflicts, the Court in the Thornhill opinion went on to say . . . that states may not "in dealing with the evils arising from industrial disputes . . . impair the effective exercise of the right to discuss freely industrial relations. . . ." This statement must be considered in its context. It was directed toward a sweeping state prohibition which this Court found to embrace "nearly every practicable, effective means whereby those interested—including the employees directly affected—may enlighten the public on the nature and causes of a labor dispute." That the general statement of the limitation of a state's power to impair free speech was not intended to apply to the fact situation presented here is further indicated by the cases cited with approval in note 21 of the Thornhill opinion. . . .

We think the circumstances here and the reasons advanced by the Missouri courts justify restraint of the picketing which was done in violation of Missouri's valid law for the sole immediate purpose of continuing a violation of law. In holding this, we are mindful of the essential importance to our society of a vigilant protection of freedom of speech and press. . . . States cannot consistently with our Constitution abridge those freedoms to obviate slight inconveniences or annoyances. . . . But placards used as an essential and inseparable part of a grave offense against an important public law cannot immunize that unlawful conduct from state control. . . .

It is clear that appellants were doing more than exercising a right of free speech or press. . . . They were exercising their economic power together with that of their allies to compel Empire to abide by union rather than by state regulation of trade. . . .

257. *"Various guarantees create zones of privacy."*

Griswold v. Connecticut, 381 U.S. 479 (1965).

DOUGLAS, J.: . . . We do not sit as a super-legislature to determine the wisdom, need, and propriety of laws that touch economic problems, business affairs, or social conditions. This law, however, operates directly on an intimate relation of husband and wife and their physician's role in one aspect of that relation.

The association of people is not mentioned in the Constitution nor in the Bill of Rights. The right to educate a child in a school of the parents' choice—whether public or private or parochial—is also not mentioned. Nor is the right to study any particular subject or any foreign language. Yet the First Amendment has been construed to include certain of those rights. . . .

In *NAACP v. Alabama,* we protected the "freedom to associate and privacy in one's association," noting that freedom of association was a peripheral First Amendment right. Disclosure of membership lists of a constitutionally valid association, we held, was invalid "as entailing the likelihood of a substantial restraint upon the exercise by petitioner's members of their right to freedom of association." In other words, the First Amendment has a penumbra where privacy is protected from govermental intrusion. . . .

Various guarantees create zones of privacy. The right of association contained in the penumbra of the First Amendment is one, as we have seen. The Third Amendment in its prohibition against the quartering of soldiers "in any house" in time of peace without the consent of the owner is another facet of that privacy. The Fourth Amendment explicitly affirms the "right of the people to be secure in their persons, houses, papers, and effects, against unreasonable searches and seizures." The Fifth Amendment in its Self-Incrimination Clause enables the citizen to create a zone of privacy which government may not force him to surrender to his detriment. The Ninth Amendment provides: "The enumeration in the Constitution, of certain rights, shall not be construed to deny or disparage others retained by the people."

The Fourth and Fifth Amendments were described in *Boyd v. United States* . . . as protection against all governmental invasions "of the sanctity of a man's home and the privacies of life." We recently referred in *Mapp v. Ohio* to the Fourth Amendment as creating a "right to privacy, no less important than any other right carefully and particularly reserved to the people." . . . These cases bear witness that the right of privacy which presses for recognition here is a legitimate one.

The present case, then, concerns a relationship lying within the zone of privacy created by several fundamental constitutional guarantees. And it concerns a law which, in forbidding the *use* of contraceptives rather than regulating their manufacture or sale, seeks to achieve its goals by means having a maximum destructive impact upon that relationship. Such a law cannot stand in light of the familiar principle, so often applied by this Court, that a "governmental purpose to control or prevent activities constitutionally subject to state regulation may not be achieved by means which sweep unnecessarily broadly and thereby invade the area of protected freedoms" (*NAACP v. Alabama*). . . . Would we allow the police to search the sacred precincts of marital bedrooms for telltale signs of the use of contraceptives? The very idea is repulsive to the notions of privacy surrounding the marriage relationship.

We deal with a right of privacy older than the Bill of Rights—older than our political parties, older than our school system. Marriage is a coming together for better or for worse, hopefully enduring, and intimate to the degree of being sacred. It is an association that promotes a way of life, not causes; a harmony in living, not political faiths; a bilateral loyalty, not commercial or social projects. Yet it is an association for as noble a purpose as any involved in our prior decisions.

CHAPTER XXVIII

Liberty, Loyalty, and Security

ONE of the chronic and ongoing controversies of the post-World War II years involves the constitutional status of domestic Communists. Did American citizens who subscribed to the principles of the Communist Party or who took part in its councils, or in any way participated in its activities or in furthering its ambitions, surrender their basic rights by so doing? The answer seemed to depend largely upon the tensions and pressures of the times: the courts tilted the scales toward sharp restriction of those rights when events increased anti-Communist hysteria, and tilted the balance back toward individual freedom when tension slackened.

The basic anti-Communist measure in the postwar years was the Smith Act of 1940 (No. 258) which had been passed, significantly, during the brief period of Nazi-Communist collaboration, when fears of such cooperation ran high. Misnamed the Alien Registration Act, the Smith Act was actually the first peacetime alien and sedition legislation since the Federalist laws of 1798 (Vol. I, No. 41). Following Hitler's attack on Russia and America's wartime collaboration with the then highly cooperative Communists, the Smith Act slid into the background and went largely unenforced. But cold war tensions rejuvenated the cries for control of domestice Communists, and by the late 1940's, the Justice Department was moving, under the Smith Act, to jail party leaders on charges of conspiracy and of advocating the overthrow of the government.

Congress adopted additional anti-Communist legislation in the cold war period. It required, in the Taft-Hartley Act of 1947, that labor union officials, in order to use the facilities of the National Labor Relations Board, sign affidavits denying not only membership in the Communist Party but also Communist beliefs. Three years later, despite a resounding veto by President Truman stressing its anticivil liberties nature, Congress enacted a sweeping Internal Security Act. The measure established a Subversive Activities Control Board, required registration of Communist organizations, strengthened espionage laws, provided for the detention of potential spies in national emergencies, and amended laws relating to immigrants, deportation, and naturalization. By 1954 delays and appeals had prevented the registration of any groups with the S. A. C. B., and Congress augmented the restrictive legislation with a somewhat contradictory Communist Control Act, outlawing the Communist Party although not making membership in it a crime.

Interpretation of all this legislation clearly fell to the Supreme Court, which had to walk the tightrope of respecting the wishes of Congress and the administration with regard to its enforcement, without permitting it to become so destructive of the individual rights of Communists that it would strike at the basic rights of other Americans. This proved particularly difficult for the Justices, given, on one hand, their public commitment to the special protection of "preferred freedoms" such as speech and press and, on the other, the fact that their actions in Communist cases were inevitably monitored by super-patriots.

Security clearly dominated early decisions. A bellwether was *American Communication Association v. Douds* (No. 259), in which Chief Justice Vinson sustained the non-Communist oath provisions of the Taft-Hartley Act. Conceding that "Congress had undeniably discouraged the lawful exercise of political freedom" by demanding oaths relating to personal beliefs, he weighed this abridgment of free speech against the government's power to regulate commerce and upheld the oath as a commercial regulation rather than as a speech restriction. In balancing "the power of constitutional government to survive" against the "clear and present danger" test, the Chief Justice warned that the "Court's interpretations of the Constitution [should not] be reduced to the status of mathematical formulas." This ruling paved the way for the highly restrictive decision of a year later, *Dennis v. U.S.*, which upheld the constitutionality of the Smith Act and the conviction under it of ten Communist Party officials. Even though the Chief Justice paid lip service to the "clear and present danger" rule, first formulated by Justice Holmes in *Schenck v. U.S.* (No. 178), he labeled it a "verbalization" denoting an "indeterminate standard" and redefined it to mean "sufficient and probable" danger, thus adopting the ruling which Judge Learned Hand had set forth in the U.S. Circuit Court of Appeals. Chief Justice Vinson's remarkable reinterpretation read the time element out of "clear and present," eliminating the necessity for demonstrating any imminent danger and making speech punishable in proportion to the gravity of the evil advocated. It also argued that the fact that a conspiracy existed created sufficient danger of potential action, if and when possible, to warrant forestalling evils it might foment (No. 260). Justice Black, in an eloquent dissent, rejected this return to the seventeenth-century test of criminality in advocacy cases and expressed hope that "in calmer times when present pressures, passions and fears subside, this, or some later Court will restore the First Amendment liberties to the high preferred place where they belong in a free society."

Those times came surprisingly soon. Senator McCarthy's disastrous embroilment with the army and his subsequent death, the election of General Eisenhower to the Presidency and the establishment of a partial "normalcy," the termination of the Korean War, and de-Stalinization in Russia all created a freer climate for the Court, now under new leadership and with sharply changed personnel. Thus Justice John Marshall Harlan, III, in the 1957 case of *Yates v. U.S.* (No. 261) held that the Smith Act could not be constitutionally applied to advocacy of the mere abstract doctrine of violent overthrow of the government, but could be applied only to the advocacy of action to that end. The decision made successful prosecutions under the Smith Act highly difficult by requiring a heavy burden of proof to show incitement to illegal action. Many convictions were reversed on appeal, while other cases were reluctantly dismissed by the Department of Justice.

The Smith Act did not become a dead letter, however. In 1961, in *Scales v. U.S.*, the Court upheld by a 5 to 4 margin a conviction, under the membership clause, of a Communist whose activities, the majority contended, were sufficient to demonstrate unwarranted advocacy of concrete and dangerous action, "by one having guilty knowledge and intent." The ruling was carefully qualified, however, and emphasized the necessity for showing not only "knowing" membership but deliberate and punishable action to implement it. The point was underlined by a companion ruling, decided the same day by a unanimous court, which reversed a membership conviction in a case where such membership was not accompanied by adequate evidence of illegal advocacy of violent overthow (*Noto v. U.S.*). The effect of the Noto case, which rested upon the ruling in the Yates case, was to make conviction under the act for membership fully as difficult as for advocacy.

Judicial interpretation of the many and varied restrictions of the 1950 Internal Security Act, or McCarran Act, followed a different pattern. The government's long campaign to force the Communist Party to register under Title I of the measure culminated in 1961 when the Court sustained the constitutionality of that section (*Communist Party v. S. A. C. B.*). In 1965, however, Justice Brennan struck down orders issued by the S. A. C. B. requiring individual party members to register, holding that this was a violation of the Fifth Amendment's guarantee against compulsory self-incrimination (*Albertson v. S. A. C. B.*). When the State Department, in the late 1950's, denied passports to Communists under a loose interpretation of other provisions of the measure, the Court held that Congress had not authorized the Secretary of State to withhold a passport if the applicant refused to file a statement about party membership. "The right to travel," Justice Douglas wrote for the majority, "was a part of the 'liberty' of which the citizen cannot be deprived without due process of law under the Fifth Amendment" (*Kent v. Dulles*, 1958). Subsequently, the Department issued new passport regulations on the basis of the Court's 1961 S. A. C. B. ruling. Then in *Aptheker v. Secretary of State* (1964), the Court considered the constitutionality of the legislative grant of power in the Subversive Activities Control Act of 1950 to refuse passports to Communists, ruling it unconstitutional on its face as a denial of the broad freedom to travel. This right, the

Court made clear, applied to Communists seeking to travel for a "wholly innocent purpose." Subsequent problems, however, indicated that the area would require further and more precise definition.

The security question also raised problems concerning the government's relationship with its own employees. When cold war winds fanned flames of apprehension regarding "Communists in government," President Truman moved quickly to provide for careful screening of all governmental workers. The policy completed the reversal of the government's historic assumption regarding the loyalty of its employees. For 150 years (1789–1939), the American people had required only that government servants take an oath to support and defend the federal Constitution. As early as 1938, when the House Un-American Activities Committee was established, and promptly launched a sensational hunt for Communists, radicals, Fascists, "crackpots," and "internationalists" on the federal payroll, doubts were cast on the policy. In 1938, Congress passed Section 9A of the Hatch Act, making it unlawful for any government employee "to have membership in any political party or organization which advocates the overthrow of our constitutional form of government." Beginning in 1941, Congressional appropriation bills included riders stipulating that funds might not be used to pay any person who advocated or was a member of an association which advocated forcible overthrow of the government. With the approval of President Roosevelt, the Civil Service Commission in 1942 began issuing regulations providing for dismissal of any employee if there was a "reasonable doubt" as to his loyalty to the government.

President Truman's Executive Order No. 9835 (No. 262), issued in March 1947, established a comprehensive federal loyalty-security program, for screening both current employees and future applicants for government service. This was only a month after the Court seemed to approve loyalty proceedings by refusing to review the case of a federal officer dismissed on an adverse loyalty finding by the Civil Service Commission (*Freidman v. Schwellenbach*). The Eisenhower administration went a step further. Substituting "security" for "loyalty," Executive Order No. 10450 repealed the Truman order and abolished the line between loyalty and security risk cases. Although retaining "subversive activities or associations" as grounds for removal, it also included acts of indiscretion, or "any behavior, activities, or associations which tend to show that the individual is not trustworthy." Thus, gossips, heavy drinkers, and other undesirables were barred, along with subversives.

Despite wide-scale public criticism of the loyalty and security-risk program for violations of the due process, bill of attainder, and First Amendment provisions, the Court was cautious in attacking it as a whole. However, it has questioned certain of its sections and procedures. In *Joint Anti-Fascist Refugee Committee v. McGrath* (1951), the majority held that the Attorney General's list of subversive organizations, compiled without prior notice and hearing, violated due process. The ruling did not abolish the list or the loyalty program, but it did ensure that hearings precede listing. On the same day, the Court divided evenly in *Bailey v. Richardson* and thus sustained a loyalty board order barring Miss Bailey from government employment for disloyalty on the basis of accusations made by persons who were never revealed to her or to the board. Although the Court did not write an opinion in the case, Justices Jackson, Black, and Douglas discussed it adversely in their concurring opinions in *McGrath* and maintained that "the entire loyalty program grossly deprives government employees of the benefits of constitutional safeguards."

In cases in 1955 (*Peters v. Hobby*) and 1956 (*Cole v. Young*), the Court questioned the discharge of employees, although for highly cautious and narrow procedural grounds. In the Young ruling, Justice Harlan rejected summary procedures in nonsensitive jobs, maintaining that the Eisenhower order should apply only to those in "sensitive" positions involving possible "internal subversion and foreign aggression." And by the latter years of the decade, particularly as public questioning of such summary measures mounted and organizations from the League of Women Voters to the Association of the Bar of the City of New York (No. 263) proposed sharply modified and more responsible alternatives, the Court began a careful evaluation of loyalty-security regulations. In 1959, Chief Justice Warren denied the Defense Department the authority to refuse a vaguely proscribed private employee a security clearance without affording him a fair hearing and the opportunity to confront his accusers. "I am shocked at the government's resort to faceless informers," wrote Warren. "This Court decries a security program which is in conflict with our long accepted notions of fair procedure" (*Greene v. McElroy*). By 1960, when President Eisenhower issued an executive order setting up a new industrial security program, he included vastly improved safeguards, including hearings and confrontation for anyone dealing with classified information, civilian or governmental. This seemed to mark the advent of relaxation of overzealous and frequently annoying and antagonizing security techniques.

Through the same period, many state leaders and local bodies, public and private, felt compelled to enter the loyalty-security arena. Local un-American activities committees, "little Smith Acts," and loyalty oaths for local and state employees were the result. Again, the courts moved cautiously, gearing their handling of cases challenging such local action to the pressures of the times. In the Gerende, Garner, and Adler cases in the early 1950's, the Court initially sustained loyalty oath requirements for candidates for public office, city employees, and public school teachers, respectively. However, in *Wieman v. Updegraff* (No. 264) the Court, indicating that such oaths must be reasonable and should not be ambiguous dragnets designed to punish any citizen with nonconformist ideas, revoked a retroactive Oklahoma loyalty oath statute barring teachers for mere membership in proscribed organizations. Justice Clark, speaking for a unanimous Court, declared that "there can be no dispute about the consequences visited upon a person excluded from public employment on disloyalty grounds." "In the view of the community," Clark wrote, "the stain is a deep one; indeed it has become a badge of infamy." Four years later Clark held that fair play had been denied a teacher who was summarily dismissed for having invoked the privilege against self-incrimination to avoid answering inquiries as to his conduct before a Congressional committee (*Slochower v. Bd. of Higher Education*, 1956). The Court also struck at local actions denying applicants admission to state bars in New Mexico and California on the basis of their alleged radical affiliations (*Schware v. New Mexico Bd. of Bar Examiners, 1957; Konigsberg v. State Bar of California, 1957*). In one of the few Warren Court decisions to deal with jurisdictional rather than procedural questions relating to civil liberties, the majority invalidated a Pennsylvania sedition statute, in the Steve Nelson case. It ruled that the federal government's entry into the loyalty-security field through the Smith and McCarran Acts and the Communist Control Act of 1954 preempted it for federal authority to the exclusion of parallel state legislation and activity (No. 265).

Reaction against these rulings was sharp and several Congressmen introduced legislation designed to countermand them. The Court subsequently backed away from its earlier loyalty-security rulings. In 1960 it upheld the dismissal of two Los Angeles social workers in a situation almost identical with that in the Slochower case (*Nelson v. L.A. County*), and in 1961 reversed its previous California bar admission ruling (*Konigsberg v. State Bar of California*). It insisted in 1959 that its action in the Nelson case was not meant to preclude state activity in the loyalty area, but rather that it simply had sought to proscribe "a race between federal and state prosecutors to the courthouse door" (*Uphaus v. Wyman, 1959*).

As the 1960's progressed, however, times seemed to calm sufficiently to warrant a renewed look at local loyalty programs. In the matter of loyalty oaths, the Court has rather consistently protected political freedom, voiding for vagueness and violation of due process a Florida statute which required state and local public employees to swear that they had never lent their "aid, support, advice, counsel, or influence to the Communist Party" and subjected them to discharge for refusal (No. 266), throwing out two Washington oath statutes, one for teachers and one for all state employees, including teachers, required as a condition of employment (*Baggett v. Bullitt, 1963*), and voiding Arizona's loyalty oath in 1966. In the latter ruling, Justice Douglas assailed the principle of guilt by association, and again, as in *Scales* and *Aptheker*, emphasized that punishment should be confined to clear demonstration that people were guilty not just of belonging to a proscribed organization, but of specific intent to further its illegal aims (*Elfbrandt v. Russel, 1966*). It thus encouraged test cases in other states to strike down or revise oaths of similar vagueness and ambiguity.

Security and Liberty: The Problem of Native Communists

LEGISLATIVE RESTRICTIONS ON FREEDOM OF EXPRESSION

258. *The Peacetime Alien and Sedition Act of 1940*

The Alien Registration Act (Smith Act), *U. S. Stat. at L.*, LIV, 670 (1940).

An Act to prohibit certain subversive activities; to amend certain provisions of law with respect to the admission and deportation of aliens; to require the fingerprinting and registration of aliens; and for other purposes.

TITLE I

SECTION 1. (a) It shall be unlawful for any person, with intent to interfere with, impair, or influence the loyalty, morale, or discipline of the military or naval forces of the United States—

(1) to advise, counsel, urge, or in any manner cause insubordination, disloyalty, mutiny, or refusal of duty by any member of the military or naval forces of the United States; or

(2) to distribute any written or printed matter which advises, counsels, or urges insubordination, disloyalty, mutiny, or refusal of duty by any member of the military or naval forces of the United States. . . .

SEC. 2. (a) It shall be unlawful for any person—

(1) to knowingly or willfully advocate, abet, advise, or teach the duty, necessity, desirability, or propriety of overthrowing or destroying any government in the United States by force or violence, or by the assassination of any officer of any such government;

(2) with the intent to cause the overthrow or destruction of any government in the United States, to print, publish, edit, issue, circulate, sell, distribute, or publicly display any written or printed matter advocating, advising, or teaching the duty, necessity, desirability, or propriety of overthrowing or destroying any government in the United States by force or violence;

(3) to organize or help to organize any society, group, or assembly of persons who teach, advocate, or encourage the overthrow or destruction of any government in the United States by force or violence; or to be or become a member of, or affiliate with, any such society, group, or assembly of persons, knowing the purposes thereof. . . .

259. *The Non-Communist Oath in the Taft-Hartley Law*

American Communications Assn. v. Douds, 339 U.S. 382 (1950).

VINSON, C.J.: These cases present for decision the constitutionality of §9(h) of the National Labor Relations Act, as amended by the Labor Management Relations Act, 1947. This section, commonly referred to as the non-Communist affidavit provision, reads as follows: "No investigation shall be made by the [National Labor Relations] Board of any question affecting commerce concerning the representation of employees, raised by a labor organization . . . , no petition . . . shall be entertained and no complaint shall be issued pursuant to a charge made by a labor organization . . . , unless there is on file with the Board an affidavit executed contemporaneously or within the preceding twelve-month period by each officer of such labor organization and the officers of any national or international labor organization of which it is an affiliate or constituent unit that he is not a member of the Communist Party or affiliated with such party, and that he does not believe in, and is not a member of or supports any organization that believes in or teaches, the overthrow of the United States Government by force or by any illegal or unconstitutional methods. . . ."

The constitutional justification for the National Labor Relations Act was the power of Congress to protect interstate commerce by removing obstructions to the free flow of commerce. . . .

One such obstruction, which it was the purpose of §9(h) of the Act to remove, was the so-called "political strike." Substantial amounts of evidence were presented to various committees of Congress . . . that Communist leaders of labor unions had in the past and would continue in the future to subordinate legitimate trade union objectives to obstructive strikes when dictated by Party leaders, often in support of the policies of a foreign government. . . .

There can be no doubt that Congress may, under its constitutional power to regulate commerce among the several States, attempt to prevent political strikes and other kinds of direct action designed to burden and interrupt the free flow of commerce. We think it is clear, in addition, that the remedy provided by §9(h) bears reasonable relation to the evil which the statute was designed to reach. Congress could rationally find that the Communist Party is not like other political parties in its utilization of positions of union leadership as means by which to bring about strikes and other obstructions of commerce for purposes of political advantage, and that many persons who believe in overthrow of the Government by force and violence are also likely to resort to such tactics when, as officers, they formulate union policy.

The fact that the statute identifies persons by their political affiliations and beliefs, which are circumstances ordinarily irrelevant to permissible subjects of government action, does not lead to the conclusion that such circumstances are never relevant. . . . But the more difficult problem here arises because, in drawing lines on the basis of beliefs and political affiliations, though it may be granted that the proscriptions of the statute bear a reasonable relation to the apprehended evil, Congress has undeniably discouraged the lawful exercise of political freedoms as well. . . . By exerting pressures on unions to deny office to Communists and others identified therein, §9(h) undoubtedly lessens the threat to interstate commerce, but it has the further necessary effect of discouraging the exercise of political rights protected by the First Amendment. Men who hold union offices often have little choice but to renounce Communism or give up their offices. Unions which wish to do so are discouraged from electing Communists to office. . . .

The unions contend that once it is determined that this is a free speech case, the "clear and present danger" test must apply. . . . But they disagree as to how it should be applied. Appellant in No. 10 would require that joining the Communist Party or the expression of belief in overthrow of the Government by force be shown to be a clear and present danger of some substantive evil, since those are the doctrines affected by the statute. Petitioner in No. 13, on the other hand, would require a showing that political strikes, the substantive evil involved, are a clear and present danger to the security of the Nation or threaten widespread industrial unrest.

This confusion suggests that the attempt to apply the term, "clear and present danger," as a mechanical test in every case touching First Amendment freedoms, without regard to the context of its application, mistakes the form in which an idea was cast for the substance of the idea. . . . Although the First Amendment provides that Congress shall make no law abridging the freedom of speech, press or assembly, it has long been established that those freedoms themselves are dependent upon the power of constitutional government to survive. If it is to survive it must have power to protect itself against unlawful conduct and, under some circumstances, against incitements to commit unlawful acts. Freedom of speech thus does not comprehend the right to speak on any subject at any time. The important question that came to this Court immediately after the First World War was not whether, but how far, the First Amendment permits the suppression of speech which advocates conduct inimical to the public welfare. Some thought speech having a reasonable tendency to lead to such conduct might be punished. Justice Holmes and Brandeis took a different view. They thought that the greater danger to a democracy lies in the suppression of public discussion; that ideas and doctrines thought harmful or dangerous are best fought with words. Only, therefore, when force is very likely to follow an utterance before there is a chance for counter-argument to have effect may that utterance be punished or prevented. . . .

But the question with which we are here faced is not the same one that Justices Holmes and Brandeis found convenient to consider in terms of clear and present danger. Government's interest here is not in preventing the dissemination of Communist doctrine or the holding of particular beliefs because it is feared that unlawful action will result therefrom if free speech is practiced. Its interest is in protecting the free flow of commerce from what Congress considers to be substantial evils of conduct that are not the products of speech at all. Section 9(h), in other words, does not interfere with speech because Congress fears the consequences of speech; it regulates harmful conduct which Congress has determined is carried on by persons who may be identified by their political affiliations and beliefs. . . . [It] is designed to protect the public not against what Communists and others identified therein advocate or believe, but against what Congress has concluded they have done and are likely to do again. . . .

When particular conduct is regulated in the interest of public order, and the regulation results in an indirect, conditional, partial abridgment of speech, the duty of the courts is to determine which of these two conflicting interests demands the greater protection under the particular circumstances presented. . . .

In essence, the problem is one of weighing the probable effects of the statute upon the free exercise of the right of speech and assembly against the congressional determination that political strikes are evils of conduct which cause substantial harm to interstate commerce and that Communists and others identified by §9(h) pose continuing threats to that public interest when in positions of union leadership. . . .

The "reasons advanced in support of the regulation" are of considerable weight, as even the opponents of §9(h) agreed. . . . It should be emphasized that Congress, not the courts, is primarily charged with determination of the need for regulation of activities affecting interstate commerce. This Court must, if such regulation unduly infringes personal freedoms, declare the statute invalid under the First Amendment's command that the opportunities for free public discussion be maintained. But insofar as the problem is one of drawing inferences concerning the need for regulation of particular forms of conduct from conflicting evidence, this Court is in no position to substitute its judgment as to the necessity or desirability of the statute for that of Congress. . . .

What of the effects of §9(h) upon the rights of speech and assembly of those proscribed by its terms? The statute does not prevent or punish by criminal sanctions the making of a speech, the affiliation with any organization, or the holding of any belief. But as we have noted, the fact that no direct restraint or punishment is imposed upon speech or assembly does not determine the free speech question. Under some circumstances, indirect "discouragements" undoubtedly have the same coercive effect upon the exercise of First Amendment rights as imprisonment, fines, injunctions or taxes. . . . The "discouragements" of §9(h) proceed, not against the groups or beliefs identified therein, but only against the combination of those affiliations or beliefs with occupancy of a position of great power over the economy of the country. Congress has concluded that substantial harm, in the form of direct, positive action, may be expected from that combination. In this legislation, Congress did not restrain the activities of the Communist Party as a political organization; nor did it attempt to stifle beliefs. . . . Section 9(h) touches only a relative handful of persons, leaving the great majority of persons of the identified affiliations and beliefs completely free from restraint. And it leaves those few who are affected free to maintain their affiliations and beliefs subject only to possible loss of positions which Congress has concluded are being abused to the injury of the public by members of the described groups. . . .

It is contended that the principle that statutes touching First Amendment freedoms must be narrowly drawn dictates that a statute aimed at political strikes should make the calling of such strikes unlawful but should not attempt to bring about the removal of union officers, with its attendant effect upon First Amendment rights. We think, however, that the legislative judgment that interstate commerce must be protected from a continuing threat of such strikes is a permissible one in this case. The fact that the injury to interstate commerce would be an accomplished fact before any sanctions could be applied, the possibility that a large number of such strikes might be called at a time of external or internal crisis, and the practical difficulties which would be encountered in detecting illegal activities of this kind are factors which are persuasive that Congress should not be powerless to remove the threat, not limited to punishing the act. . . .

Previous discussion has considered the constitutional questions raised by §9(h) as they apply alike to members of the Communist Party and affiliated organizations and to persons who believe in overthrow of the Government by force. The breadth of the provision concerning belief in overthrow of the Government by force would raise additional questions, however, if it were read very literally to include all persons who might, under any conceivable circumstances, subscribe to that belief.

But we see no reason to construe the statute so broadly. . . . The congressional purpose is . . . served if we construe the clause, "that he does not believe in . . . the overthrow of the United States Government by force or by any illegal or unconstitutional methods," to apply to persons and organizations who believe in violent overthrow of the Government as it presently exists under the Constitution as an objective, not merely a prophecy. . . .

As thus construed, we think that the "belief" provision of the oath presents no different problem from that present in that part of the section having to do with membership in the Communist Party. Of course we agree that one may not be imprisoned or executed because he holds particular beliefs. But to attack the straw man of "thought control" is to ignore the fact that the sole effect of the statute upon one who believes in overthrow of the Government by force and violence—and does not deny his belief—is that he may be forced to relinquish his position as a union leader. That fact was crucial in our discussion of the statute as it related to membership in the Communist Party. . . .

SEDITION, SUBVERSION, AND SUPPRESSION: THE INTERPRETATION OF THE SMITH ACT

260. *The Redefinition of the "Clear and Present Danger" Test*

Dennis v. U.S., 341 U.S. 494 (1951).

VINSON, C.J.: . . . The obvious purpose of the statute [the Smith Act] is to protect existing Government, not from change by peaceable, lawful and constitutional means, but from change by violence, revolution and terrorism. That it is within the *power* of the Congress to protect the Government of the United States from armed rebellion is a proposition which requires little discussion. Whatever theoretical merit there may be to the argument that there is a "right" to rebellion against dictatorial governments is without force where the existing structure of the government provides for peaceful and orderly change. We reject any principle of governmental helplessness in the face of preparation for revolution, which principle, carried to its logical conclusion, must lead to anarchy. No one could conceive that it is not within the power of Congress to prohibit acts intended to overthrow the Government by force and violence. The question with which we are concerned here is not whether Congress has such *power,* but whether the *means* which it has employed conflict with the First and Fifth Amendments to the Constitution.

One of the bases for the contention that the means which Congress has employed are invalid takes the form of an attack on the face of the statute on the grounds that by its terms it prohibits academic discussion of the merits of Marxism-Leninism, that it stifles ideas and is contrary to all concepts of a free speech and a free press. . . .

The very language of the Smith Act negates the interpretation which petitioners would have us impose on that Act. It is directed at advocacy, not discussion. Thus, the trial judge properly charged the jury that they could not convict if they found that petitioners did "no more than pursue peaceful studies and discussions or teaching and advocacy in the realm of ideas." He further charged that it was not unlawful "to conduct in an American college and university a course explaining the philosophical theories set forth in the books which have been placed in evidence." Such a charge is in strict accord with the statutory language, and illustrates the meaning to be placed on those words. Congress did not intend to eradicate the free discussion of political theories, to destroy the traditional rights of Americans to discuss and evaluate ideas without fear of governmental sanction. Rather Congress was concerned with the very kind of activity in which the evidence showed these petitioners engaged.

But although the statute is not directed at the hypothetical cases which petitioners have conjured, its application in this case has resulted in convictions for the teaching and advocacy of the overthrow of the Government by force and violence, which, even though coupled with the intent to accomplish that overthrow, contains an element of speech. For this reason, we must pay special heed to the demands of the First Amendment marking out the boundaries of speech.

We pointed out in Douds . . . that the basis of the First Amendment is the hypothesis that speech can rebut speech, propaganda will answer propaganda, free debate of ideas will result in the wisest governmental policies. It is for this reason that this Court has recognized the inherent value of free discourse. An analysis of the leading cases in this Court which have involved direct limitations on speech, however, will demonstrate that both the majority of the Court and the dissenters in particular cases have recognized that this is not an unlimited, unqualified right, but that the societal value of speech must, on occasion, be subordinated to other values and considerations. . . .

[The Chief Justice discussed several cases decided in 1919–1920, and stressed the "clear and present danger" test enunciated in Schenck.]

The rule we deduce from these cases is that where an offense is specified by a statute in nonspeech or nonpress terms, a conviction relying upon speech or press as evidence of violation may be sustained only when the speech or publication created a "clear and present danger" of attempting or accomplishing the prohibited crime, *e.g.*, interference with enlistment. The dissents, we repeat, in emphasizing the value of speech, were addressed to the argument of the sufficiency of the evidence. . . .

[The Chief Justice then discussed dissents by Justices Holmes and Brandeis in Gitlow and Whitney, when the "clear and present danger" test was not applied.]

Although no case subsequent to Whitney and Gitlow has expressly overruled the majority opinions in those cases, there is little doubt that subsequent opinions have inclined toward the Holmes-Brandeis rationale. . . . But . . . neither Justice Holmes nor Justice Brandeis ever envisioned that a shorthand phrase should be crystallized into a rigid rule to be applied inflexibly without regard to the circumstances of each case. Speech is not an absolute, above and beyond control by the legislature when its judgment, subject to review here, is that certain kinds of speech are so undesirable as to warrant criminal sanction. Nothing is more certain in modern society than the principle that there are no absolutes, that a name, a phrase, a standard has meaning only when associated with the considerations which gave birth to the nomenclature. See *American Communications Assn. v. Douds* . . . To those who would paralyze our Government in the face of impending threat by encasing it in a semantic strait jacket we must reply that all concepts are relative.

In this case we are squarely presented with the application of the "clear and present danger" test, and must decide what that phrase imports. We first note that many of the cases in which this Court has reversed convictions by use of this or similar tests have been based on the fact that the interest which the State was attempting to protect was itself too insubstantial to warrant restriction of speech. . . . Overthrow of the Government by force and violence is certainly a substantial enough interest for the Government to limit speech. Indeed, this is the ultimate value of any society, for if a society cannot protect its very structure from armed internal attack, it must follow that no subordinate value can be protected. If, then, this interest may be protected, the literal problem which is presented is what has been meant by the use of the phrase "clear and present danger" of the utterances bringing about the evil within the power of Congress to punish.

Obviously, the words cannot mean that before the Government may act, it must wait until the *putsch* is about to be executed, the plans have been laid and the signal is awaited. If Government is aware that a group aiming at its overthrow is attempting to indoctrinate its members and to commit them to a course whereby they will strike when the leaders feel the circumstances permit, action by the Government is required. The argument that there is no need for Government to concern itself, for Government is strong, it possesses ample powers to put down a rebellion, it may defeat the revolution with ease needs no answer. For that is not the question. Certainly an attempt to overthrow the Government by force, even though doomed from the outset because of inadequate numbers or power of the revolutionists, is a sufficient evil for Congress to prevent. The damage which such attempts create both physically and politically to a nation makes it impossible to measure the validity in terms of the probability of success, or the immediacy of a successful attempt. In the instant case the trial judge charged the jury that they could not convict unless they found that petitioners intended to overthrow the Government "as speedily as circumstances would permit." This does not mean, and could not properly mean, that they would not strike until there was certainty of success. What was meant was that the revolutionists would strike when they thought the time was ripe. We must therefore reject the contention that success or probability of success is the criterion.

The situation with which Justices Holmes and Brandeis were concerned in Gitlow was a comparatively isolated event bearing little relation in their minds to any substantial threat to the safety of the community. . . . They were not confronted with any situation comparable to the instant one—the development of an apparatus designed and dedicated to the overthrow of the Government, in the context of world crisis after crisis.

Chief Judge Learned Hand, writing for the majority below, interpreted the phrase as follows: "In each case [courts] must ask whether the gravity of the 'evil,' discounted by its improbability, justifies such invasion of free speech as is necessary to avoid the danger." . . . We adopt this statement of the rule. As articulated by Chief Judge Hand, it is as succinct and inclusive as any other we might devise at this time. It takes into consideration those factors which we deem relevant, and relates their significances. More we cannot expect from words.

Likewise, we are in accord with the court below, which affirmed the trial court's finding that the requisite danger existed. The mere fact that from the period 1945 to 1948 petitioners' activities did not result in an attempt to overthrow the Government by force and violence is of course no answer to the fact that there was a group that was ready to make the attempt. The formation by petitioners of such a highly organized conspiracy, with rigidly disciplined members subject to call when the leaders, these petitioners, felt that the time had come for action, coupled with the inflammable nature of world conditions, similar uprisings in other countries, and the touch-and-go nature of our relations with countries with whom petitioners were in the very least ideologically attuned, convince us that their convictions were justified on this score. And this analysis disposes of the contention that a conspiracy to advocate, as distinguished from the advocacy itself, cannot be constitutionally restrained, because it comprises only the preparation. It is the existence of the conspiracy which creates the danger. . . . If the ingredients of the reaction are present, we cannot bind the Government to wait until the catalyst is added. . . .

We agree that the standard as defined is

not a neat, mathematical formulary. Like all verbalizations it is subject to criticism on the score of indefiniteness. But petitioners themselves contend that the verbalization, "clear and present danger," is the proper standard. We see no difference from the standpoint of vagueness, whether the standard of "clear and present danger" is one contained *in haec verba* within the statute, or whether it is the judicial measure of constitutional applicability. We have shown the indeterminate standard the phrase necessarily connotes. We do not think we have rendered that standard any more indefinite by our attempt to sum up the factors which are included within its scope. We think it well serves to indicate to those who would advocate constitutionally prohibited conduct that there is a line beyond which they may not go—a line, which they, in full knowledge of what they intend and the circumstances in which their activity takes place, will well appreciate and understand. . . .

We hold that §§2(a) (1), 2(a) (3) and 3 of the Smith Act, do not inherently, or as construed or applied in the instant case, violate the First Amendment and other provisions of the Bill of Rights, or the First and Fifth Amendments because of indefiniteness. Petitioners intended to overthrow the Government of the United States as speedily as the circumstances would permit. Their conspiracy to organize the Communist Party and to teach and advocate the overthrow of the Government of the United States by force and violence created a "clear and present danger" of an attempt to overthrow the Government by force and violence. They were properly and constitutionally convicted for violation of the Smith Act. The judgments of conviction are affirmed.

261. *The Limits of Organizing and Advocating*

Yates v. U.S., 354 U.S. 298 (1957).

HARLAN, J.: . . . The conspiracy is alleged to have originated in 1940 and continued down to the date of the indictment in 1951. The indictment charged that in carrying out the conspiracy the defendants and their co-conspirators would (a) become members and officers of the Communist Party, with knowledge of its unlawful purposes, and assume leadership in carrying out its policies and activities; (b) cause to be organized units of the Party in California and elsewhere; (c) write and publish, in the "Daily Worker" and other Party organs, articles on the proscribed advocacy and teaching; (d) conduct schools for the indoctrination of Party members in such advocacy and teaching, and (e) recruit new Party members, particularly from among persons employed in the key industries of the nation. Twenty-three overt acts in furtherance of the conspiracy were alleged. . . . [After a detailed analysis of the term "Organize," the opinion continued] we conclude . . . that since the Communist Party came into being in 1945, and indictment was not returned until 1951, the three-year statute of limitations had run on the "organizing" charge, and required the withdrawal of that part of the indictment from the jury's consideration. . . .

. . . We are thus faced with the question whether the Smith Act prohibits advocacy and teaching of forcible overthrow as an abstract principle, divorced from any effort to instigate action to that end, so long as such advocacy or teaching is engaged in with evil intent. We hold that it does not.

The distinction between advocacy of abstract doctrine and advocacy directed at promoting unlawful action is one that has been consistently recognized in the opinions of this Court. . . . This distinction was heavily underscored in *Gitlow v. New*

York, . . . in which the statute involved was nearly identical with the one now before us.

. . . The legislative history of the Smith Act and related bills shows beyond all question that Congress was aware of the distinction between the advocacy or teaching of abstract doctrine and the advocacy or teaching of action, and that it did not intend to disregard it. The statute was aimed at the advocacy and teaching of concrete action for the forcible overthrow of the Government, and not of principles divorced from action. . . .

In failing to distinguish between advocacy of forcible overthrow as an abstract doctrine and advocacy of action to that end, the District Court appears to have been led astray by the holding in *Dennis* that advocacy of violent action to be taken at some future time was enough. It seems to have considered that, since "inciting" speech is usually thought of as calculated to induce immediate action, and since *Dennis* held advocacy of action for future overthrow sufficient, this meant that advocacy, irrespective of its tendency to generate action, is punishable, provided only that it is uttered with a specific intent to accomplish overthrow. In other words, the District Court apparently thought that *Dennis* obliterated the traditional dividing line between advocacy of abstract doctrine and advocacy of action.

As one of the concurring opinions in *Dennis* put it: "Throughout our decisions there has recurred a distinction between the statement of an idea which may prompt its hearers to take unlawful action, and advocacy that such action be taken." . . . There is nothing in *Dennis* which makes that historic distinction obsolete. . . .

In light of the foregoing we are unable to regard the District Court's charge upon this aspect of the case as adequate. The jury was never told that the Smith Act does not denounce advocacy in the sense of preaching abstractly the forcible overthrow of the Government. We think that the trial court's statement that the proscribed advocacy must include the "urging," "necessity," and "duty" of forcible overthrow, and not merely its "desirability" and "propriety," may not be regarded as a sufficient substitute for charging that the Smith Act reaches only advocacy of action for the overthrow of government by force and violence. The essential distinction is that those to whom the advocacy is addressed must be urged to *do* something, now or in the future, rather than merely to *believe* in something. . . .

We recognize that distinctions between advocacy or teaching of abstract doctrines, with evil intent, and that which is directed to stirring people to action, are often subtle and difficult to grasp, for in a broad sense, as Mr. Justice Holmes said in his dissenting opinion in Citlow, supra: "Every idea is an incitement." But the very subtlety of these distinctions required the most clear and explicit instructions with reference to them, for they concerned an issue which went to the very heart of the charges against these petitioners. The need for precise and understandable instructions on this issue is further emphasized by the equivocal character of the evidence in this record. . . . Instances of speech that could be considered to amount to "advocacy of action" are so few and far between as to be almost completely overshadowed by the hundreds of instances in the record in which overthrow, if mentioned at all, occurs in the course of doctrinal disputation so remote from action as to be almost wholly lacking in probative value. Vague references to "revolutionary" or "militant" action of an unspecified character, which are found in the evidence, might in addition be given too great weight by the jury in the absence of more precise instructions. Particularly in light of this record, we must regard the trial court's charge in this respect as furnishing wholly inadequate guidance to the jury on this central point in the case. We cannot allow a conviction to stand on such "an equivocal direction to the jury on a basic issue." . . .

THE FEDERAL GOVERNMENT'S CONTROL OVER ITS EMPLOYEES

262. *The Federal Loyalty Program, March 21, 1947*

Executive Order 9835, *Federal Register*, XII, 1935–9 (March 25, 1947).

WHEREAS each employee of the Government of the United States is endowed with a measure of trusteeship over the democratic processes which are the heart and sinew of the United States; and

WHEREAS, it is of vital importance that persons employed in the Federal service be of complete and unswerving loyalty to the United States; and

WHEREAS, although the loyalty of by far the overwhelming majority of all Government employees is beyond question, the presence within the Government service of any disloyal or subversive person constitutes a threat to our democratic processes; and

WHEREAS maximum protection must be afforded the United States against infiltration of disloyal persons into the ranks of its employees, and equal protection from unfounded accusations of disloyalty must be afforded the loyal employees of the Government:

NOW, THEREFORE . . . it is hereby, in the interest of the internal management of the Government, ordered as follows:

PART I. INVESTIGATION OF APPLICANTS

1. There shall be a loyalty investigation of every person entering the civilian employment of any department or agency of the executive branch of the Federal Government. . . .

3. An investigation shall be made of all applicants at all available pertinent sources of information and shall include reference to:

A. Federal Bureau of Investigation files.
B. Civil Service Commission files.
C. Military and Naval Intelligence files.
D. The files of any other appropriate government investigative or intelligence agency.
E. House Committee on Un-American Activities files.
F. Local law-enforcement files at the place of residence and employment of the applicant, including municipal, county and State law-enforcement files.
G. Schools and colleges attended by applicant.
H. Former employers of applicant.
I. References given by applicant.
J. Any other appropriate source.

4. Whenever derogatory information with respect to loyalty of an applicant is revealed, a full field investigation shall be conducted. . . .

PART IV. SECURITY MEASURES IN INVESTIGATIONS

1. . . . An investigative agency shall make available . . . all investigative material and information collected by the investigative agency concerning any employee or prospective employee. . . .

2. . . . However, the investigative agency may refuse to disclose the names of confidential informants, provided it furnishes sufficient information about such informants on the basis of which the requesting department or agency can make an adequate evaluation of the information furnished by them, and provided it advises the requesting department or agency in writing that it is essential to the protection of the informants or to the investigation of other cases that the identity of the informants not be revealed. Investigative agencies shall not use this discretion to decline to reveal sources of information where such action is not essential. . . .

PART V. STANDARDS

1. The standard for the refusal of employment or the removal from employment in an executive department or agency on grounds relating to loyalty shall be that, on all the evidence, reasonable grounds exist for belief that the person involved is disloyal to the Government of the United States.

2. Activities and associations of an applicant or employee which may be considered in connection with the determination of disloyalty may include one or more of the following:

A. Sabotage, espionage, or attempts or preparations therefor, knowingly associating with spies or saboteurs;

B. Treason or sedition or advocacy thereof;

C. Advocacy of revolution or force or violence to alter the constitutional form of Government of the United States;

D. Intentional, unauthorized disclosure to any person, under circumstances which may indicate disloyalty to the United States, of documents or information of a confidential or non-public character obtained by the person making the disclosure as a result of his employment by the Government of the United States;

E. Performing or attempting to perform his duties, or otherwise acting, so as to serve the interests of another government in preference to the interests of the United States.

F. Membership in, affiliation with or sympathetic association with any foreign or domestic organization, association, movement, group or combination of persons, designated by the Attorney General as totalitarian, Fascist, Communist, or subversive, or as having adopted a policy of advocating or approving the commission of acts of force or violence to deny other persons their rights under the Constitution of the United States, or as seeking to alter the form of Government of the United States by unconstitutional means. . . .

263. *Proposals for a New "Federal Personnel Security System"*

Report of the Special Committee on the Federal Loyalty-Security Program of the Association of the Bar of the City of New York (New York, 1956), 137–88 *passim*. Reprinted by permission of the Association of the Bar of the City of New York Fund, Inc.

A. COORDINATION AND SUPERVISION

1. The Director of Personnel and Information Security

[1] The Office of Director of Personnel and Information Security should be established in the Executive Office of the President.

[2] The Director should be appointed by the President subject to confirmation by the Senate and serve at the pleasure of the President.

[3] It should be the primary responsibility of the Director to conduct a continuous review of and supervision over:

(a) The personnel security programs, in order to assure efficiency, uniformity and fairness of administration, consonant with the interests of national security.

(b) The classification of information, so that only such information shall be classified as the interest of national security actually require.

[4] In the performance of his responsibility the Director should make recommendations to the President which, when

embodied in regulations prepared by the Director and approved by the President, would be binding upon the departments and agencies concerned.

B. SCOPE

2. Scope of Personal Security

[1] Clearance under the personnel security programs should be required for all sensitive positions and for no others.

[2] The head of each department or agency should designate as sensitive only those positions within his department or agency the occupant of which would

(a) have access to material classified as secret or top-secret in the interests of national security, or,

(b) have a policy-making function which bears a substantial relation to national security.

[3] The President, on recommendation of the Director, should specify criteria in accordance with which the head of each department or agency should classify positions.

3. Classification of Information

The Director should continuously review and, after consultation with the agencies involved, make recommendations to the President concerning the standards and criteria and methods to be used in the classification of information and in its declassification when secrecy is no longer important to the interests of national security. These recommendations, when approved by the President, would be binding upon the departments and agencies concerned.

C. STANDARDS AND CRITERIA

4. Standard for Personnel Security

[1] The personnel security standard for all sensitive positions should be stated as follows:

The personnel security standard shall be whether or not in the interest of the United States the employment or retention in employment of the individual is advisable. In applying this standard a balanced judgment shall be reached after giving due weight to all the evidence, both derogatory and favorable, to the nature of the position, and to the value of the individual to the public service.

5. The Employee's Associations

A person's associations with organizations or individuals may properly be considered in determining his security suitability. But a conclusion against his security suitability on the ground of such associations should not be reached without adequate basis for determining that he shares, is susceptible to, or is influenced by, the actions or views of such organizations or individuals.

6. The Attorney General's List

[1] The Attorney General's list of subversive organizations should be abolished, unless it can be and is modified and revised in the following respects:

(a) The list should not include any organization which has been defunct more than ten years. (Information as to such organizations, however, would be available under the procedures set forth in paragraph [2] of this recommendation.)

(b) The list should give information as to the period and the general nature of the subversive activity of each organization listed.

(c) The list should be kept up to date by periodical supplements eliminating organizations which have been defunct over ten years and adding new organizations found to be subversive since the last publication.

(d) The list should include only those organizations which have been given notice and an opportunity to be heard in conformity with the requirements of due process of law.

(e) The list should contain a statement that mere membership in any of the organizations listed is not in itself to be construed as establishing the subversive character of a member unless membership has been made illegal by statute.

[2] The Department of Justice should upon request make available to security personnel and boards relevant information in its files concerning all organizations, whether defunct or not, the character of which may be pertinent in a pending inquiry. Such information may be taken into consideration in the inquiry together with all other evidence presented.

D. PERSONNEL

7. *Security Personnel*

Personnel engaged in security matters should be individuals whose qualities and standing will inspire confidence in the fair, wise and courageous administration of the programs. To this end the Director should establish training courses for security personnel. The training should include intensive and thorough instruction in

(a) the nature of Communism and the techniques of Communist espionage and infiltration in the United States and in other countries;

(b) the political history of the United States and of the world, especially in this century;

(c) constitutional and legal principles; and

(d) the relative reliability of various kinds of evidence.

E. PROCEDURE[1]

8. *Central Screening Board*

[1] A central screening board should be created in the Civil Service Commission. This board should have the responsibility, except as set forth in paragraph [3] below, of determining whether or not security charges should be filed against any person covered by a security program, whether a Federal or a private employee.

[2] The central screening board should act in panels of not less than three members. At least one member of each panel should be a lawyer, and at least one member should be a person whose only government employment is his work on the board.

[3] Subject to further action by the Director, the Atomic Energy Commission and the Department of Defense should continue their present methods of screening to determine whether or not security charges should be filed, unless they wish to utilize the services of the central screening board. The Director should determine whether any other department or agency may establish or maintain its own screening board.

9. *Screening Procedure*

[1] Screening boards should afford the employee an opportunity for an informal conference with the board or its representatives to answer adverse security information.

[2] When a screening board determines that charges should be filed, it should prepare a specific statement of charges. If a person charged contends that charges are not specific enough to enable him to prepare his defense, the board should, in the exercise of reasonable discretion within the limits of security requirements, determine what additional information shall be furnished him. . . .

[4] Every employee against whom a security question is raised should be entitled

[1] Such highly secret investigative agencies as the Central Intelligence Agency and the Federal Bureau of Investigation would not fall within these recommendations except as the President may determine upon the advice of the Director.

to have an attorney advise and aid him. . . .

10. Treatment of Charged Employees Pending Disposition of Charges

Pending the final disposition of charges against Federal employees or employees of private employers:

[1] The pay of suspended employees should continue.

[2] Employees under charges, if not retained in the positions held when charges are filed, should be transferred without loss of pay to nonsensitive positions instead of being suspended, whenever this is practicable and consistent with the interests of national security.

11. Hearing Boards

[1] Every charged employee, other than a probationary employee, should be entitled to a hearing before a hearing board of three members to be appointed by the head of the charging agency. One member but not more than one member of the hearing board should be an employee of the charging agency, at least one member should be a lawyer, and at least one member should come from outside the government service. In the alternative, a hearing board may be composed entirely of persons outside the government service but in such case also one member should be a lawyer. . . .

12. Hearing Procedure

[1] The charging agency should be entitled to have an attorney present at the hearing. . . .

[3] Every charged employee should be entitled to have an attorney present at the hearing to represent him. The attorney should have the right to offer evidence and cross-examine witnesses.

[4] Hearing boards should prepare written findings of fact and conclusions. These should be furnished to the charged employee for his use with only such deletions as are required in the interests of national security.

[5] The charged employee should be furnished a copy of the transcript of the hearing for his use in the proceedings.

[6] The security hearing should not be public.

13. Appearance of Witnesses and Confrontation

[1] Except as provided below, screening boards and hearing boards should have the power in their discretion to subpoena government witnesses and witnesses for employees and to permit the submission of evidence by depositions, interrogatories, affidavits, letters, and other written statements. . . .

[3] It should be the policy of the government to permit the employee to cross-examine adverse witnesses before a hearing board when the hearing board believes this important for the development of the facts, unless the disclosure of the identity of the witness or requiring him to submit to cross-examination would be injurious to national security. . . .

[5] As to all other witnesses, including casual informants, and with due consideration of the national security and fairness to the employee

(a) the screening board should determine whether it desires a witness to appear before it for interview, and

(b) the hearing board should determine whether the witness should be produced for cross-examination, or whether because of special circumstances he should be interrogated by the board without the employee being present, or whether his evidence should be given to the board in other ways, such as by an affidavit or a signed statement. So far as consistent with the requirements of national security, a hearing board should make available to the employee the substance of all evidence it takes into consideration which was given by any witness whom the employee has not been permitted to cross-examine.

[6] In determining the probative effect of information given by informants who are not made available for cross-examination by the charged employee, under the exceptions contained in paragraphs [4] and [5] above, screening and hearing boards as well as appeal boards and agency heads should always take into account the lack of opportunity for cross-examination. . . .

15. Final Determination

The head of the charging agency should have the power to make the final security determination. . . .

The States and the Security Issue

THE CONSTITUTIONALITY OF STATE LOYALTY LAWS

264. *Innocent Membership and Arbitrary Power*

Wieman v. Updegraff, 344 U.S. 183 (1952).

CLARK, J.: This is an appeal from a decision of the Supreme Court of Oklahoma upholding the validity of a loyalty oath prescribed by Oklahoma statute for all state officers and employees. . . . Appellants, employed by the state as members of the faculty and staff of Oklahoma Agricultural and Mechanical College, failed within the thirty days permitted, to take the oath required by the Act. . . .The appellants . . . attacked the validity of the Act on the grounds, among others, that it was a bill of attainder; an *ex post facto* law; impaired the obligation of their contracts with the State and violated the Due Process Clause of the Fourteenth Amendment. They also sought a mandatory injunction directing the state officers to pay their salaries regardless of their failure to take the oath. Their objections centered largely on the following clauses of the oath:

> . . . That I am not affiliated directly or indirectly . . . with any foreign political agency, party organization or Government, or with any agency, party, organization, association, or group whatever which has been officially determined by the United States Attorney General or other authorized agency of the United States to be a communist front or subversive organization; . . . [and] that within the five (5) years immediately preceding the taking of this oath . . . I have not been a member of . . . [such] agency. . . .

The purpose of the Act, we are told, "was to make loyalty a qualification to hold public office or be employed by the State." . . . During periods of international stress, the extent of legislation with such objectives accentuates our traditional concern about the relation of government to the individual in a free society. The perennial problem of defining that relationship becomes acute when disloyalty is screened by ideological patterns and techniques of disguise that make it difficult to identify. Democratic government is not powerless to meet this threat, but it must do so without infringing the freedoms that are the ultimate values of all democratic living. In the adoption of such means as it believes effective, the legislature is therefore confronted with the problem of balancing its interest in national security with the often conflicting constitutional rights of the individual.

In a series of cases coming here in recent years, we have had occasion to consider legislation aimed at safeguarding the public service from disloyalty. *Garner v. Board of Public Works* . . . (1951); *Adler v. Board of Education* . . . (1952); *Gerende* . . . (1951). . . . It is in the context of these decisions that we determine the validity of the oath before us.

Garner involved a Los Angeles ordinance requiring all city employees to swear that they did not advocate the overthrow of the government by unlawful means or belong to organizations with such objectives. . . . One of the attacks made on the oath in that case was that it violated due process because its negation was not limited to organizations known by the employee to be within the prescribed class. This argument was rejected because we felt justified in assuming that *scienter* was implicit in each clause of the oath.

Adler also indicated the importance of determining whether a rule of exclusion based on association applies to innocent as well as knowing activity. New York had sought to bar from employment in the public schools persons who advocate, or belong to organizations which advocate, the overthrow of the government by unlawful means. The Feinberg Law directed the New York Board of Regents to make a listing, after notice and hearing, of organizations of the type described . . . The Regents provided by regulation that membership in a listed organization should be prima facie evidence of disqualification for office in the New York public schools. In upholding this legislation, we expressly noted that the New York courts had construed the statute to require knowledge of organizational purposes before the regulation could apply. . . .

The oath in Gerende was required of candidates for public office who sought places on a Maryland ballot. On oral argument in that case, the Maryland Attorney General assured us that he would advise the proper state authorities to accept, as complying with the statute, an affidavit stating that the affiant was not engaged in an attempt to overthrow the government by force or violence or knowingly a member of an organization engaged in such an attempt. Because we read an earlier Maryland Court of Appeals' decision as interpreting the statute so that such an affidavit would satisfy its requirements, we affirmed on the basis of this assurance.

We assumed in Garner, that if our interpretation of the oath as containing an implicit *scienter* requirement was correct, Los Angeles would give the petitioners who had refused to sign the oath an opportunity to take it as interpreted and resume their employment. But here, with our decision in Garner before it, the Oklahoma Supreme Court refused to extend to appellants an opportunity to take the oath. In addition, a petition for rehearing which urged that failure to permit appellants to take the oath as interpreted deprived them of due process was denied. This must be viewed as a holding that knowledge is not a factor under the Oklahoma statute. We are thus brought to the question touched on in Garner, Adler, and Gerende: whether the due process clause permits a state in attempting to bar disloyal individuals from its employ, to exclude persons solely on the basis of organizational membership, regardless of their knowledge concerning the organizations to which they had belonged. For, under the statute before us, the fact of membership alone disqualifies. If the rule be expressed as a presumption of disloyalty, it is a conclusive one.

. . .

But membership may be innocent. A

state servant may have joined a proscribed organization unaware of its activities and purposes. In recent years, many completely loyal persons have severed organizational ties after learning for the first time of the character of groups to which they had belonged. . . . At the time of affiliation, a group itself may be innocent, only later coming under the influence of those who would turn it toward illegitimate ends. Conversely, an organization formerly subversive and therefore designated as such may have subsequently freed itself from the influences which originally led to its listing.

There can be no dispute about the consequences visited upon a person excluded from public employment on disloyalty grounds. In the view of the community, the stain is a deep one; indeed, it has become a badge of infamy. Especially is this so in time of cold war and hot emotions when "each man begins to eye his neighbor as a possible enemy." Yet under the Oklahoma Act, the fact of association alone determines disloyalty and disqualification; it matters not whether association existed innocently or knowingly. To thus inhibit individual freedom of movement is to stifle the flow of democratic expression and controversy at one of its chief sources. We hold that the distinction observed between the case at bar and Garner, Adler, and Gerende is decisive. Indiscriminate classification of innocent with knowing activity must fall as an assertion of arbitrary power. The oath offends due process. . . .

Reversed.

265. *Federal Versus State Control of Sedition*

Commonwealth of Pennsylvania v. Nelson, 350 U.S. 497 (1956)

WARREN, C.J.: The respondent Steve Nelson, an acknowledged member of the Communist party, was convicted . . . of a violation of the Pennsylvania Sedition Act and sentenced to imprisonment for twenty years and to a fine of $10,000 and to costs of prosecution in the sum of $13,000. . . . The Supreme Court of Pennsylvania, recognizing but not reaching many alleged serious trial errors and conduct of the trial court infringing upon respondent's right to due process of law, decided the case on the narrow issue of supersession of the state law by the Federal Smith Act. . . .

The precise holding of the court, and all that is before us for review, is that the Smith Act of 1940, as amended in 1948, which prohibits the knowing advocacy of the overthrow of the Government of the United States by force and violence, supersedes the enforceability of the Pennsylvania Sedition Act which proscribes the same conduct. . . .

It should be said at the outset that the decision in this case does not affect the right of states to enforce their sedition laws at times when the Federal Government has not occupied the field and is not protecting the entire country from seditious conduct. The distinction between the two situations was clearly recognized by the court below. Nor does it limit the jurisdiction of the states where the Constitution and Congress have specifically given them concurrent jurisdiction. . . . Neither does it limit the right of the state to protect itself at any time against sabotage or attempted violence of all kinds. Nor does it prevent the state from prosecuting where the same act constitutes both a Federal offense and a state offense under the police power. . . .

Where, as in the instant case, Congress has not stated specifically whether a Federal statute has occupied a field in which the states are otherwise free to legislate, different criteria have furnished touchstones for decision. . . . In this case, we think that each of several tests of supersession is met.

First, "The scheme of Federal regulation [is] so pervasive as to make reasonable the inference that Congress left no room for the states to supplement it." . . . The Congress determined in 1940 that it was necessary for it to re-enter the field of antisubversive legislation, which had been abandoned by it in 1921. In that year it enacted the Smith Act which proscribes advocacy of the overthrow of any government—federal, state or local—by force and violence and organization of and knowing membership in a group which so advocates. Conspiracy to commit any of these acts is punishable under the general criminal conspiracy provisions in 18 U. S. C. §371. The Internal Security Act of 1950 is aimed more directly at Communist organizations. It distinguishes between "Communist-action organizations" and "Communist-front organizations," requiring such organizations to register and file annual reports with the Attorney General, giving complete details as to their officers and funds. Members of Communist-action organizations who have not been registered by their organization must register as individuals. . . . The Communist Control Act of 1954 declares "that the Communist party of the United States, although purportedly a political party is in fact an instrumentality of a conspiracy to overthrow the Government of the United States" and that "its role as the agency of a hostile foreign power renders its existence a clear, present and continuing danger to the security of the United States." . . .

We examine these Acts only to determine the Congressional plan. . . . Taken as a whole they evince a Congressional plan which makes it reasonable to determine that no room has been left for the states to supplement it. Therefore a state sedition statute is superseded regardless of whether it purports to supplement the federal law. . . .

Second, the federal statutes "touch a field in which the Federal interest is so dominant that the Federal system [must] be assumed to preclude enforcement of state laws on the same subject." . . . Congress has devised an all-embracing program for resistance to the various forms of totalitarian aggression. . . . It accordingly proscribed sedition against all government in the nation—national, state and local. . . . Congress having thus treated seditious conduct as a matter of vital national concern, it is in no sense a local enforcement problem. . . .

Third, enforcement of state sedition acts presents a serious danger of conflict with the administration of the federal program. Since 1939, in order to avoid a hampering of uniform enforcement of its program by sporadic local prosecutions, the Federal Government has urged local authorities not to intervene in such matters, but to turn over to the federal authorities immediately and unevaluated all information concerning subversive activities. The President made such a request on Sept. 6, 1939, when he placed the Federal Bureau of Investigation in charge of investigation in this field. . . .

Since we find that Congress has occupied the field to the exclusion of parallel state legislation, that the dominant interest of the Federal Government precludes state intervention and that administration of state Acts would conflict with the operation of the Federal plan, we are convinced that the decision of the Supreme Court of Pennsylvania is unassailable.

266. *Loyalty Oaths and the Vice of Unconstitutional Vagueness*

Cramp v. Board of Public Instruction, 368 U.S. 278 (1961).

STEWART, J.: . . . The issue to be decided is whether a State can constitutionally compel those in its service to swear that they have never "knowingly lent their aid, support, advice, counsel, or influence to the Communist Party." More precisely, can Florida consistently with the Due Process Clause of the Fourteenth Amendment force an employee either to take such an oath, at the risk of subsequent prosecution for perjury, or face immediate dismissal from public service?

The provision of the oath here in question, it is to be noted, says nothing of advocacy of violent overthrow of state or federal government. It says nothing of membership or affiliation with the Communist Party, past or present. The provision is completely lacking in these or any other terms susceptible of objective measurement. Those who take this oath must swear, rather, that they have not in the unending past ever knowingly lent their "aid," or "support," or "advice," or "counsel" or "influence" to the Communist Party. What do these phrases mean? In the not too distant past Communist Party candidates appeared regularly and legally on the ballot in many state and local elections. Elsewhere the Communist Party has on occasion endorsed or supported candidates nominated by others. Could one who had ever cast his vote for such a candidate safely subscribe to this legislative oath? Could a lawyer who had ever represented the Communist Party or its members swear with either confidence or honesty that he had never knowingly lent his "counsel" to the Party? Could a journalist who had ever defended the constitutional rights of the Communist Party conscientiously take an oath that he had never lent the Party his "support?" Indeed, could anyone honestly subscribe to this oath who had ever supported any cause with contemporaneous knowledge that the Communist Party also supported it?

The very absurdity of these possibilities brings into focus the extraordinary ambiguity of the statutory language. With such vagaries in mind, it is not unrealistic to suggest that the compulsion of this oath provision might weigh most heavily upon those whose conscientious scruples were the most sensitive. While it is perhaps fanciful to suppose that a perjury prosecution would ever be instituted for past conduct of the kind suggested, it requires no strain of the imagination to envision the possibility of prosecution for other types of equally guiltless knowing behaviour. It would be blinking reality not to acknowledge that there are some among us always ready to affix a Communist label upon those whose ideas they violently oppose. And experience teaches that prosecutors too are human.

We think this case demonstrably falls within the compass of those decisions of the Court which hold that ". . . a statute which either forbids or requires the doing of an act in terms so vague that men of common intelligence must necessarily guess at its meaning and differ as to its application, violates the first essential of due process of law. . . ."

CHAPTER XXIX

The Nationalization of Procedural Rights

JUST as sensitive Americans sought to bring some harmony between ideals and practice in the areas of racial equality and voting rights, many tried to do the same in the field of procedural guarantees, especially in criminal procedure. The motivation seemed twofold. With greater governmental intervention in the daily lives of all citizens, many felt the Constitution should be more literally interpreted so as to act as a greater bulwark against arbitrariness in the general use of power by public officials. More dramatically and specifically, the often shocking techniques used by police and sheriffs to suppress various aspects of the civil rights movement focused attention on the need to tighten up the individual's protection in arrest, arraignment, and trial procedures. Once again, therefore, it fell to the courts to reconcile practice with high-minded theory and ideals, and, as it turned out, to garner new brick-bats. Often its critics were also the loudest critics of big government and the most vigorous self-proclaimed defenders of pure constitutionalism, who charged it with exaggerated concern for the rights of the citizen involved with the law. Some even went so far as to charge the Court with encouraging crime by coddling criminals. For these citizens, it seemed, the effectiveness of what often amounted to virtual police-state methods outweighed any consideration that ancient and honorable due process of law was being flouted and denied.

In contrast to its internal division over First Amendment problems, the Court has been fairly unified on procedural safeguards. Even such an advanced advocate of judicial self-restraint as Justice Frankfurter could support active judicial protection in the procedural area. "The history of American freedom," wrote the Justice, "is in no small measure the history of procedure." Such a view complemented that of activist Justice Douglas, who pointed out: "It is not without significance that most of the provisions of the Bill of Rights are procedural. It is procedure that spells much of the difference between rule by law and rule by whim or caprice. Steadfast adherence to strict procedural safeguards is our main assurance that there will be equal justice under law."

Although there is no question that the standards of fairness and decency guaranteed by the Fourth through the Eighth Amendments of the Bill of Rights apply in federal prosecutions, there has long been controversy as to which of these standards are essential enough to due process of law to be binding upon the states under the Fourteenth Amendment. On this issue the postwar Court has remained divided. In *Adamson v. California* (1947), the majority outlined its doctrine of selective "incorporation" (No. 267), citing as the *reductio ad absurdum* of full "incorporation" the Seventh Amendment's guarantee of a jury in any civil case where more than twenty dollars was at stake. On the other hand, Justice Black did not waiver from his commitment to the position that all of the procedural guarantees should be incorporated into the Fourteenth Amendment, just as the substantive rights of the First Amendment have been. To leave such a process to the collective whims of a majority of the Judges on a virtual case-to-case basis continued to strike Black as placing too heavy a reliance upon the "evanescent standards of the majority's philosophy." This flexible guide gave the Court power "periodically to expand and contract constitutional standards to conform to the Court's conception of what at a particular time constitutes 'civilized decency' and 'fundamental liberty and justice'" (No. 268).

In rereading Amendments Four through Nine with concern for their applicability to modern problems, the Court has stressed the federal government's responsibility to maintain high standards in matters ranging from search and seizure through right to counsel, voluntary confessions, double jeopardy, and self-incrimination. Yet even here the Court has been anxious to strike a reasonable balance. In the area of search and seizure, for example, while normally insisting upon a rigid adherence to high standards in obtaining a warrant and proceeding with every caution, it has still acknowledged that other factors can be important and that in determining whether a search is "unreasonable," relevant considerations include the nature of the offense, the danger of the suspect's fleeing, the evidence available prior to the search, and the likelihood of otherwise obtaining the property or papers for which the search was made (No. 269). Although continuing to view modern technological devices for gathering evidence as potentially dangerous infringements on individual privacy, it has not been unaware of their potential usefulness in fighting crime and generally making law enforcement more speedy and efficient (*Lopez v. U.S.*, 1963).

Yet the problem of determining the extent to which the federal government should become the "perpetual censor" of the states, in this area, continued to be a sticky one. Since "selective incorporation" was apparently to be the approach, rule-of-thumb standards had to be applied. Here the Court began with a felt obligation to decide state appeals primarily by determining whether fundamental standards of decency had been observed. In *Wolf v. Colorado* (1949), the Court said that "the security of one's privacy against arbitrary intrusion by the police . . . is basic to a free society . . . and as such is enforceable against the states through the Due Process Clause." But it refused to rule that a state must exclude evidence secured by an admittedly unreasonable search and seizure; although the state violated the Constitution in seizing evidence illegally, the state courts could decide on its admissibility. For the next dozen years the Court usually interpreted the "fairness" rule as a warning of its being prepared to strike at unwarranted state practices. Presumably the federal government's positive actions would induce the states to behave similarly. For example, the Court's ruling in *Mallory v. U.S.* (1957) emphasized that anyone under federal arrest must be taken "without unnecessary delay" before a United States commissioner for instruction on his right to silence and counsel, and that admissions obtained during an excessive delay must be excluded. In *Mapp v. Ohio* (1961), however, the Court overruled the Wolf decision, holding that "all evidence obtained by searches and seizures in violation of the Constitution is . . . inadmissible in a state court." The decision seemed to go beyond the fair trial rule; indeed, it represented a giant step forward in setting up positive judicial standards in the general area of state criminal justice (No. 270).

Such application created almost as many problems as it solved, and law enforcement officials raised loud protest (No. 271). It meant that the states would be under surveillance both in the way their officers conducted searches and seizures (*Ker v. California,* 1963) and in the way even "reasonably" seized material could be used in the state courts (*Pugach v. Dollinger,* 1961). Similarly, in overruling *Betts v. Brady,* the Court stated that the Sixth Amendment guarantees were applicable to the states, holding in the headline-making 1963 case of *Gideon v. Wainwright* that failure of a state to appoint counsel in a noncapital criminal case deprived the defendant of due process under the Fourteenth Amendment.

But the right to counsel issue did not stop there. In mid-1964, the Court invalidated the admissions obtained during preindictment interrogation of a murder suspect, when the record showed that the Illinois police and prosecuting attorney had given him no explicit advice of his constitutional right to remain silent and had barred his retained counsel (*Escobedo v. Illinois*). Confessions were now to be scrutinized with care even though officials maintained they were voluntary, with proscribed "third-degree" methods to include many other factors besides simple physical or psychological coercion. The ruling, however, still did not spell out the precise pretrial and prearraignment standards to which the Warren Court expected state and local authorities to adhere. But in the Miranda case in 1966 (No. 272) the Court took this step in a landmark ruling, which further aroused the ire of police and of many average Americans alarmed at the growing crime rate and fearful that the loopholes the decision seemed to afford would return clearly guilty criminals to the streets.

With regard to trial itself, the Court in a sense moved forward against denials of due process by going back to an old federal rule. Guarantees of the Fourth and Fifth Amendments had long been treated by the Supreme Court as closely allied. In a leading case on the Fourth Amendment (*Boyd v. U.S.,* 1886), Justice Bradley observed that "The Fourth and Fifth Amendments run almost into each other" when a law requires the compulsory production of incriminating evidence. The Fifth Amendment, he said, forbids "any forcible and compulsory extortion of a man's own testimony or of his private papers to be used as evidence to convict him of crime or to forfeit his goods." In the Mapp case, the Court held that the Fifth Amendment privilege against self-incrimination implemented the Fourth Amendment's command against unreasonable searches and seizures, and that the "two guarantees of personal security conjoined in the Fourteenth to make the exclusionary rule obligatory upon the States." They thus returned, after years of attrition, to the Boyd rule and extended it to the states. In *Malloy v. Hogan* in 1964, the Court took the next logical step, overruling *Adamson v. California*. Mr. Justice Brennan wrote for the Court: "We hold today that the Fifth Amendment's exception from compulsory self-incrimination is also protected by the Fourteenth Amendment against the States," thus incorporating the self-incrimination privilege independently of search-and-seizure. The next step in extending that historic constitutional right was to rule that a state violated the liberties of a witness when it used in support of its prosecution testimony obtained or extracted by the national government, and conversely, that the risk of exposure to subsequent federal prosecution supported the withholding of testimony solicited by a state. (No. 273). Further, in *Griffin v. California* in 1965, the Court ruled that state judges violated the right against self-incrimination in commenting upon a defendant's failure to testify in his own defense.

Other Bill of Rights guarantees incorporated against state infringement in the Court's new zeal for "perpetuating the principles of humanity and civil liberty" included the Sixth Amendment's guarantee of the right of an accused to confront the witness against him (*Pointer v. Texas,* 1965) and the Eighth Amendment's protection against cruel and unusual punishment (*Robinson v. California,* 1962). But even though portions of the Fourth, Fifth, and Sixth Amendments of the Bill of Rights have been made applicable to the states through the Fourteenth Amendment, the process has remained selective. Although both federal and state jurisdictions have respected the double-jeopardy provisions of the Fifth Amendment, the Court, despite protest by an aroused minority, continued to hold that where the same act is an offense against both the state and the federal government, its prosecution and punishment by both governments is not double jeopardy. Recently the issue reached the judges in a celebrated case in which the federal government, after failing to convict a defendant in a federal court of robbing a federally insured bank in Illinois, induced state authorities to institute a second prosecution and assisted them by gathering evidence and supplying witnesses to convict the accused of the same robbery (*Bartkus v. Illinois,* 1959).

The federal government, while insisting that many of these rights be handled very sensitively at the state level, found itself being criticized because certain of its officials or representatives were not always as careful with such rights. This was particularly true of members of grand juries and Congressional investigating committees who, uninhibited by the automatic protections afforded a citizen in a court of law, tended to abuse their power and, often, the rights of citizens. The resultant tendency of witnesses to invoke the self-incrimination provision of the Fifth

Amendment, while often instinctive, nonetheless grew unpopular by its excessive use. Court test thus became inevitable. In the Blau case (No. 274), Justice Black ruled that admission of membership or leadership in the Communist Party created more than a "mere imaginary possibility" of prosecution under the Smith Act (Chapter XXVII); the Court therefore upheld the right to plead the Fifth Amendment. And in *Adams v. Maryland* (1954) it went a step further, forbidding the use of testimony given before a Congressional committee "in any criminal proceeding in any court," in this instance a state court seeking prosecution based upon evidence so revealed.

The decision aroused Congressional "red hunters," especially Senators Joseph McCarthy and Pat McCarran, who felt that it was the function of a committee to expose, just as it was the function of some other agency, ideally state courts, to prosecute. But they were even more aroused over the fact that unlike courts and administrative agencies, Congressional committees could not coerce witnesses to testify by promising immunity. Consequently, Congress passed a new Immunity Act in 1954, making it possible to force witnesses to testify on matters of national security by granting them immunity from immediate prosecution on the testimony. Sponsors of the act claimed that the measure fully safeguarded witnesses. Others disagreed, pointing to the many severe noncriminal penalties which might be applied to them. Yet the Court in *Ullman v. U.S.* (1956) upheld conviction under the statute, maintaining that such considerations were irrelevant and that the statute fell clearly within the proper meaning of the Fifth Amendment. When "immunity displaces the danger" of prosecution, the majority ruled, constitutional rights are preserved (No. 275). Justice Douglas, in his dissent, disagreed sharply. "One protective function of the Fifth Amendment is at once removed when the guaranty against self-incrimination is qualified in the manner it is today," wrote the Justice. "The privilege of silence is exchanged for a partial, undefined, vague immunity. It means that Congress has granted far less than it has taken away. . . ." (No. 276).

Other abuses of committee power also brought Court test. The Court had turned aside the charge that committee questioning should be confined to matters which had some obvious relationship with future Congressional legislation (*Barsky v. U.S.*, 1948). Now, it took preliminary steps in 1953, in a case involving the House Committee on Lobbying Activities, to restrict committee questioning to those subjects for which the committee had been created (*U.S. v. Rumely*). And with the death of Senator Joseph McCarthy and the calming of anti-Communist hysteria, it sharply rebuked the chronically offending House Un-American Activities Committee in the highly controversial Watkins case, in 1957 (No. 277). "No inquiry is an end in itself," wrote Chief Justice Warren. "It must be related to and in furtherance of a legitimate task of the Congress. Investigations conducted solely for the personal aggrandizement of the investigators or to 'punish' those investigated are indefensible." Yet HUAC had a shrill and powerful constituency, and when, two years later, a witness sought to invoke the Watkins rule, the Court recanted, seeming thereby to renew the Committee's license to investigate freely and with little inhibition (*Barenblatt v. U.S.*, 1959). Subsequent rulings (*Deutch v. U.S.*, 1961; *Russell v. U.S.*, 1962), however, showed the Court's readiness to block overt abuse of Committee power, if not to challenge it directly.

One other judicial entry into the government's loyalty-related procedures brought national controversy and eventual Congressional action. The distress of sensitive citizens had grown as the government, in seeking prosecutions, had relied more and more upon often dubious evidence in F. B. I. files and on the use of paid informants with access to such evidence, while the accused had no such access. Was this not a denial of the Sixth Amendment guarantee of the right of the accused to be confronted with the witnesses against him? In the Jencks case (1957), the Court held that where a witness for the government had reported to the F. B. I., the F. B. I. must open his reports to the defendant in order that he might show discrepancies between the reports and the witnesses' oral testimony. "Justice," said the Court, "requires no less." Congress, asserting its power to control the rules of procedure in the federal courts, promptly moved to limit by law the effect of the decision, requiring the trial judge to pass on the question of whether the reports are relevant to the case for the defense, where the defendant and the government cannot agree. But even such limited privilege is absent from Congressional committee procedures. A person has no right to confront a witness who gives evidence against him before a Congressional committee. Although often criticized as unjust, this rule is defended on the grounds that committee investigations aid the purposes of Congress and are not trials of accused persons.

The Current Status of Procedural Safeguards of Individual Rights

GENERAL THEORY

267. *Interpreting the Due Process Clause of the Fourteenth Amendment*

Adamson v. California, 332 U.S. 46 (1947).

Reed, J.: We shall assume, but without any intention thereby of ruling upon the issue, that permission by law to the court, counsel and jury to comment upon and consider the failure of defendant "to explain or to deny by his testimony any evidence or facts in the case against him" would infringe defendant's privilege against self-incrimination under the Fifth Amendment if this were a trial in a court of the United States under a similar law. Such an assumption does not determine appellant's rights under the Fourteenth Amendment. It is settled law that the clause of the Fifth Amendment, protecting a person against being compelled to be a witness against himself, is not made effective by the Fourteenth Amendment as a protection against state action on the ground that freedom from testimonial compulsion is a right of national citizenship, or because it is a personal privilege or immunity secured by the Federal Constitution as one of the rights of man that are listed in the Bill of Rights.

The reasoning that leads to those conclusions starts with the unquestioned premise that the Bill of Rights, when adopted, was for the protection of the individual against the federal government and its provisions were inapplicable to similar actions done by the states. . . . With the adoption of the Fourteenth Amendment, it was suggested that the dual citizenship recognized by its first sentence, secured for citizens federal protection for their elemental privileges and immunities of state citizenship. The Slaughterhouse Cases decided . . . that these rights, as privileges and immunities of state citizenship, remained under the sole protection of the state governments. This Court . . . has approved this determination. . . . The power to free defendants in state trials from self-incrimination was specifically determined to be beyond the scope of the privileges and immunities clause of the Fourteenth Amendment in *Twining v. New Jersey*. . . . After declaring that state and national citizenship coexist in the same person, the Fourteenth Amendment forbids a state from abridging the privileges and immunities of citizens of the United States. As a matter of words, this leaves a state free to abridge, within the limits of the due process clause, the privileges and immunities flowing from state citizenship. . . . It accords with the constitutional doctrine of federalism by leaving to the states the responsibility of dealing with the privileges and immunities of their citizens except those inherent in national citizenship. . . . We reaffirm the conclusion of the Twining and Palko Cases that protection against self-incrimination is not a privilege or immunity of national citizenship.

Appellant secondly contends that if the privilege against self-incrimination is not a right protected by the privileges and immunities clause of the Fourteenth Amendment against state action, this privilege, to its full scope under the Fifth Amendment, inheres in the right to a fair trial. A right to a fair trial is a right admittedly protected by the due process clause of the Fourteenth Amendment. Therefore, appellant argues, the due process clause of the Fourteenth Amendment protects his privilege against self-incrimination. The due process clause of the Fourteenth Amendment, however, does not draw all the rights of the federal Bill of Rights under its protection. That contention was made and rejected in *Palko v. Connecticut*. . . . Nothing has been called to our attention to show that either the framers of the Fourteenth Amendment or the states that adopted it intended its due process clause to draw within its scope the earlier amendments to the Constitution. Palko held that such provisions of the Bill of Rights as were "implicit in the concept of ordered liberty," . . . became secure from state interference by the clause. But it held nothing more.

Specifically, the due process clause does not protect, by virtue of its mere existence, the accused's freedom from giving testimony by compulsion in state trials that is secured to him against federal interference by the Fifth Amendment. . . . For a state to require testimony from an accused is not necessarily a breach of a state's obligation to give a fair trial. Therefore, we must examine the effect of the California law applied in this trial to see whether the comment on failure to testify violates the protection against state action that the due process clause does grant to an accused. The due process clause forbids compulsion to testify by fear of hurt, torture or exhaustion. It forbids any other type of coercion that falls within the scope of due process. California follows Anglo-American legal tradition in excusing defendants in criminal prosecutions from compulsory testimony. . . . That is a matter of legal policy and not because of the requirements of due process under the Fourteenth Amendment. So our inquiry is directed, not at the broad question of the constitutionality of compulsory testimony from the accused under the due process clause, but to the constitutionality of the provision of the California law that permits comment upon his failure to testify. . . .

However sound may be the legislative conclusion that an accused should not be compelled in any criminal case to be a witness against himself, we see no reason why comment should not be made upon his silence. . . .

We are of the view . . . that a state may control such a situation in accordance with its own ideas of the most efficient administration of criminal justice. . . .

268. *"Extend to all the complete protection of the Bill of Rights."*

Adamson v. California, 332 U.S. 46 (1947).

BLACK, J., dissenting: . . . This decision reasserts a constitutional theory spelled out in *Twining v. New Jersey,* . . . that this Court is endowed by the Constitution with boundless power under "natural law" periodically to expand and contract constitutional standards to conform to the Court's conception of what at a particular time constitutes "civilized decency" and "fundamental liberty and justice." Invoking this Twining rule, the Court concludes that although comment upon testimony in a federal court would violate the Fifth Amendment, identical comment in a state court does not violate today's fashion in civilized decency and fundamentals and is therefore not prohibited by the Federal Constitution as amended. . . .

But I would not reaffirm the Twining decision. I think that decision and the "natural law" theory of the Constitution upon which it relies degrade the constitutional safeguards of the Bill of Rights and simultaneously appropriate for this Court a broad power which we are not authorized by the Constitution to exercise. . . .

The first ten amendments were proposed and adopted largely because of fear that Government might unduly interfere with prized individual liberties. The people wanted and demanded a Bill of Rights written into their Constitution. The amendments embodying the Bill of Rights were intended to curb all branches of the Federal Government in the fields touched by the amendments—Legislative, Executive, and Judicial. The Fifth, Sixth, and Eighth Amendments were pointedly aimed at confining exercise of power by courts and judges within precise boundaries, particularly in the procedure used for the trial of criminal cases. . . . For the fears of arbitrary court action sprang largely from the past use of courts in the imposition of criminal punishments to suppress speech, press, and religion. . . .

But these limitations were not expressly imposed upon state court action. In 1833, *Barron v. Baltimore.* . . . specifically held inapplicable to the states that provision of the Fifth Amendment which declares: "nor shall private property be taken for public use, without just compensation." In deciding the particular point raised, the Court there said that it could not hold that the first eight amendments applied to the states. This was the controlling constitutional rule when the Fourteenth Amendment was proposed in 1866.

My study of the historical events that culminated in the Fourteenth Amendment, and the expressions of those who sponsored and favored, as well as those who opposed, its submission and passage, persuades me that one of the chief objects that the provisions of the Amendment's first section, separately, and as a whole, were intended to accomplish was to make the Bill of Rights applicable to the states. With full knowledge of the import of the Barron decision, the framers and backers of the Fourteenth Amendment proclaimed its purpose to be to overturn the constitutional rule that case had announced. This historical purpose has never received full consideration or exposition in any opinion of this Court interpreting the Amendment. . . .

Whether this Court ever will, or whether it now should, in the light of past decisions, give full effect to what the Amendment was intended to accomplish is not necessarily essential to a decision here. However that may be, our prior decisions, including Twining, do not prevent our carrying out that purpose, at least to the extent of making applicable to the states, not a mere part, as the Court has, but the full protection of the Fifth Amendment's provision against compelling evidence from an accused to convict him of crime. And I further contend that the "natural law" formula which the Court uses to reach its conclusion in this case should be abandoned as an incongruous excrescence on our Constitution. I believe that formula to be itself a violation of our Constitution, in that it subtly conveys to courts, at the expense of legislatures, ultimate power over public policies in fields where no specific provision of the Constitution limits legislative power. . . .

For under the Twining formula, which includes non-regard for the first eight amendments, what are "fundamental rights" and in accord with "canons of decency," as the Court said in Twining, and today reaffirms, is to be independently "ascertained from time to time by judicial action . . ." "what is due process of law depends on circumstances." . . . Thus the power of legislatures became what this Court would declare it to be at a particular time independently of the specific guarantees of the Bill of Rights such as the right to freedom of speech, religion and assembly, the right to just compensation for property taken for a public purpose, the right to jury trial or the right to be secure against unreasonable searches and seizures. . . .

I cannot consider the Bill of Rights to be an outworn 18th Century "strait jacket" as the Twining opinion did. Its provisions may be thought outdated abstractions by some. And it is true that they were designed to meet ancient evils. But they are the same kind of human evils that have emerged from century to century wherever excessive power is sought by the few at the expense of the many. In my judgment the people of no nation can lose their liberty so long as a Bill of Rights like ours survives and its basic purposes are conscientiously interpreted, enforced and respected so as to afford continuous protection against old, as well as new, devices and practices which might thwart those purposes. I fear to see the consequences of the Court's practice of substituting its own concepts of decency and fundamental justice for the language of the Bill of Rights as its point of departure in interpreting and enforcing that Bill of Rights. If the choice must be between the selective process of the Palko decision applying some of the Bill of Rights to the States, or the Twining rule applying none of them, I would choose the Palko selective process. But rather than accept either of these choices, I would follow what I believe was the original purpose of the Fourteenth Amendment—to extend to all the people of the nation the complete protection of the Bill of Rights. . . .

SEARCH AND SEIZURE AND MATERIALS SECURED THEREBY

269. *Are the Fourth Amendment Guarantees Second-class Rights?*

U.S. v. Rabinowitz, 339 U.S. 56 (1950).

MINTON, J.: . . . The question presented here is the reasonableness of a search without a search warrant of a place of business consisting of a one-room office, incident to a valid arrest. . . . The officers . . . arrested the respondent, and over his objection searched the desk, safe, and file cabinets in the office for about an hour and a half. They found and seized 573 stamps, on which it was later determined that overprints had been forged. . . .

Were the 573 stamps, the fruits of this search, admissible in evidence? If legally obtained, these stamps were competent evidence to show intent under the first count of the indictment, and they were the very things the possession of which was the crime charged in the second count. . . .

What is a reasonable search is not to be determined by any fixed formula. The Constitution does not define what are "unreasonable" searches and, regrettably, in our discipline we have no ready litmus-paper test. The recurring questions of the reasonableness of searches must find resolution in the facts and circumstances of each case. . . . Reasonableness is in the first instance for the District Court to determine. We think the District Court's conclusion that here the search and seizure were reasonable should be sustained because: (1) the search and seizure were incident to a valid arrest; (2) the place of the search was a business room to which the public, including the officers, was invited; (3) the room was small and under the immediate and complete control of respondent; (4) the search did not extend beyond the room used for unlawful purposes; (5) the possession of the forged and altered stamps was a crime, just as it is a crime to possess burglars' tools, lottery tickets or counterfeit money.

Assuming that the officers had time to procure a search warrant, were they bound to do so? We think not, because the search was otherwise reasonable, as previously concluded. In a recent opinion, *Trupiano v. United States*, . . . this Court first enunciated the requirement that search warrants must be procured when "practicable" in a case of search incident to arrest. . . .

A rule of thumb requiring that a search warrant always be procured whenever practicable may be appealing from the vantage point of easy administration. But we cannot agree that this requirement should be crystallized into a *sine qua non* to the reasonableness of a search. It is fallacious to judge events retrospectively and thus to determine, considering the time element alone, that there was time to procure a search warrant. Whether there was time may well be dependent upon considerations other than the ticking off of minutes or hours. The judgment of the officers as to when to close the trap on a criminal committing a crime in their presence or who they have reasonable cause to believe is committing a felony is not determined solely upon whether there was time to procure a search warrant. Some flexibility will be accorded law officers engaged in daily battle with criminals for whose restraint criminal laws are essential.

It is appropriate to note that the Constitution does not say that the right of the people to be secure in their persons should not be violated without a search warrant if it is practicable for the officers to procure one. The mandate of the Fourth Amendment is that the people shall be secure against *unreasonable* searches. It is not disputed that there may be reasonable searches, incident to an arrest, without a search warrant. Upon acceptance of this established rule that some authority to search follows from lawfully taking the person into custody, it becomes apparent that such searches turn upon the reasonableness under all the circumstances and not upon the practicability of procuring a search warrant, for the warrant is not required. To the extent that *Trupiano v. United States* . . . requires a search warrant solely upon the basis of the practicability of procuring it rather than upon the reasonableness of the search after a lawful arrest, that case is overruled. The relevant test is not whether it is reasonable to procure a search warrant, but whether the search was reasonable. That criterion in turn depends upon the facts and circumstances—the total atmosphere of the case. It is a sufficient precaution that law officers must justify their conduct before courts which have always been, and must be jealous of the individual's right of privacy within the broad sweep of the Fourth Amendment. . . .

270. *Improperly Seized Evidence and the Exclusionary Rule*

Mapp v. Ohio, 367 U.S. 643 (1961).

CLARK, J.: . . . On May 23, 1957, three Cleveland police officers arrived at appellant's residence in that city pursuant to information that "a person [was] hiding out in the home who was wanted for questioning in connection with a recent bombing, and that there was a large amount of policy paraphernalia being hidden in the home." Miss Mapp and her daughter by a former marriage lived on the top floor of the two-family dwelling. Upon their arrival at that house, the officers knocked on the door and demanded entrance but appellant, after telephoning her attorney, refused to admit them without a search warrant. They advised their headquarters of the situation and undertook a surveillance of the house.

The officers again sought entrance some three hours later when four or more additional officers arrived on the scene. When Miss Mapp did not come to the door immediately, at least one of the several doors to the house was forcibly opened and the policemen gained admittance. Meanwhile Miss Mapp's attorney arrived, but the officers, having secured their own entry, and continuing in their defiance of the law, would permit him neither to see Miss Mapp nor to enter the house. It appears that Miss Mapp was halfway down the stairs from the upper floor to the front door when the officers, in this highhanded manner, broke into the hall. She demanded to see the search warrant. A paper, claimed to be a warrant, was held up by one of the officers. She grabbed the "warrant" and placed it in her bosom. A struggle ensued in which the officers recovered the piece of paper and as a result of which they handcuffed appellant because she had been "belligerent" in resisting their official rescue of the "warrant" from her person. Running roughshod over appellant, a policeman "grabbed" her, "twisted [her] hand," and she "yelled [and] pleaded with him" because "it was hurting." Appellant, in handcuffs, was then forcibly taken upstairs to her bedroom where the officers searched a dresser, a chest of drawers, a closet and some suitcases. They also looked into a photo album and through personal papers belonging to the appellant. The search spread to the rest of the second floor including the child's bedroom, the living room, the kitchen and a dinette. The basement of the building and a trunk found therein were also searched. The obscene materials for possession of which she was ultimately convicted were discovered in the course of that widespread search.

At the trial no search warrant was produced by the prosecution, nor was the failure to produce one explained or accounted for. At best, "there is, in the record, considerable doubt as to whether there ever was any warrant for the search of defendant's home." . . .

The State says that even if the search were made without authority, or otherwise unreasonably, it is not prevented from using the unconstitutionally seized evidence at trial, citing *Wolf v. Colorado,* . . . in which this Court did indeed hold "that in a prosecution in a State court for a State crime the Fourteenth Amendment does not forbid the admission of evidence obtained by an unreasonable search and seizure." . . .

. . . [but] this Court, in *Wolf* . . . , discussed the effect of the Fourth Amendment upon the States through the operation of the Due Process Clause of the Fourteenth Amendment. It said:

> [W]e have no hesitation in saying that were a State affirmatively to sanction such police incursion into privacy it would run counter to the guaranty of the Fourteenth Amendment. . . .

Nevertheless, after declaring that the "security of one's privacy against arbitrary intrusion by the police" is "implicit in the 'concept of ordered liberty' and as such enforceable against the States through the Due Process Clause," cf. *Palko v. Connecticut,* . . . and announcing that it "stoutly adhere[d]" to the *Weeks* decision, the Court decided that the *Weeks* exclusionary rule would not then be imposed upon the States as "an essential ingredient of the right." . . .

Today we once again examine *Wolf's* constitutional documentation of the right to privacy free from unreasonable state intrusion, and, after its dozen years on our books, are led by it to close the only courtroom door remaining open to evidence secured by official lawlessness in flagrant abuse of that basic right, reserved to all persons as a specific guaranty against that very same unlawful conduct. We hold that all evidence obtained by searches and seizures in violation of the Constitution is, by that same authority, inadmissible in a state court.

IV.

Since the Fourth Amendment's right of privacy has been declared enforceable against the States through the Due Process Clause of the Fourteenth, it is enforceable against them by the same sanction of exclusion as is used against the Federal Government. Were it otherwise, then . . . without that rule the freedom from state invasions of privacy would be so ephemeral and so neatly severed from its conceptual nexus with the freedom from all brutish means of coercing evidence as not to merit this Court's high regard as a freedom "implicit in the concept of ordered liberty." At the time that the Court held in *Wolf* that the Amendment was applicable to the States through the Due Process Clause, the cases of this Court, as we have seen, had steadfastly held that as to federal officers the Fourth Amendment included the exclusion of the evidence seized in violation of its provisions. . . . [T]he admission of the new constitutional right by *Wolf* could not consistently tolerate denial of its most important constitutional privilege, namely, the exclusion of the evidence which an accused had been forced to give by reason of the unlawful seizure. To hold otherwise is to grant the right but in reality to withhold its privilege and enjoyment. Only last year the Court itself recognized that the purpose of the exclusionary rule "is to deter—to compel respect for the constitutional guaranty in the only effectively available way—by removing the incentive to disregard it. . . ."

Indeed, we are aware of no restraint, similar to that rejected today, conditioning the enforcement of any other basic constitutional right. The right to privacy, no less important than any other right carefully and particularly reserved to the people, would stand in marked contrast to all other rights declared as "basic to a free society." . . . The Court has not hesitated to enforce as strictly against the States as it does against the Federal Government the rights of free speech and of a free press, the rights to notice and to a fair, public trial, including, as it does, the right not to be convicted by use of a coerced confession, however logically relevant it be, and without regard to its reliability. . . . We find that, as to the Federal Government, the Fourth and Fifth Amendments and, as to the States, the freedom from unconscionable invasions of privacy and the freedom from convictions based upon coerced confessions do enjoy an "intimate relation" in their perpetuation of "principles of humanity and civil liberty (secured) . . . only after years of struggle. . . ."

Moreover, our holding that the exclusionary rule is an essential part of both the Fourth and Fourteenth Amendments is not only the logical dictate of prior cases, but it also makes very good sense. There is no war between the Constitution and common sense. Presently, a federal prosecutor may make no use of evidence illegally seized, but a State's attorney across the street may, although he supposedly is operating under the enforceable prohibitions of the same Amendment. Thus the State, by admitting evidence unlawfully seized, serves to encourage disobedience to the Federal Constitution which it is bound to uphold. . . . In nonexclusionary States, federal officers, being human, were by it invited to and did, as our cases indicate, step across the street to the State's attorney with their unconstitutionally seized evidence. Prosecution on the basis of that evidence was then had in a state court in utter disregard of the enforceable Fourth Amendment. If the fruits of an unconstitutional search had been inadmissible in both state and federal courts, this inducement to evasion would have been sooner eliminated. . . .

Federal-state cooperation in the solution of crime under constitutional standards will be promoted, if only by recognition of their now mutual obligation to respect the same fundamental criteria in their approaches. "However much in a particular case insistence upon such rules may appear as a technicality that inures to the benefit of a guilty person, the history of the criminal law proves that tolerance of shortcut methods in law enforcement impairs its enduring effectiveness." . . . Denying shortcuts to only one of two cooperating law enforcement agencies tends naturally to breed legitimate suspicion of "working arrangements" whose results are equally tainted. . . .

The ignoble shortcut to conviction left open to the State tends to destroy the entire system of constitutional restraints on which the liberties of the people rest. Having once recognized that the right to privacy embodied in the Fourth Amendment is enforceable against the States, and that the right to be secure against rude invasions of privacy by state officers is, therefore, constitutional in origin, we can no longer permit that right to remain an empty promise. Because it is enforceable in the same manner and to like effect as other basic rights secured by the Due Process Clause, we can no longer permit it to be revocable at the whim of any police officer who, in the name of law enforcement itself, chooses to suspend its enjoyment. Our decision, founded on reason and truth, gives to the individual no more than that which the Constitution guarantees him, to the police officer no less than that to which honest law enforcement is entitled, and to the courts, that judicial integrity so necessary in the true administration of justice.

271. *Los Angeles Police Chief W. H. Parker on* Mapp and Mallory

Reprinted from *U.S. News & World Report,* published at Washington, April 20, 1964, 70–71. Copyright 1964 U.S. News & World Report, Inc.

Q. Is it getting harder for police to find and arrest a criminal?

A. Yes. The difficulty that we face is in search and seizure of evidence that might lead us to the solution of a case.

Q. How is that?

A. For a recent example: Two of our men were shot to death in a large store in Los Angeles when questioning a couple—a man and woman—who had aroused suspicion when they tried to cash a check. I think this exemplifies the difference in our problem today, as compared to 10 years ago.

Under past situations, our detectives would have immediately ascertained if there was any evidence in the possession of these people, then taken the couple into custody. But because of the "exclusionary evidence" rule, which requires that there must be probable cause for an arrest before the evidence is searched for and seized, these officers refrained from search. This gave the suspects an opportunity to shoot the officers. So because of their reticence to conduct the search, they both died.

Q. Is the "exclusionary evidence" rule a California law?

A. Yes. It goes back to 1955. But I have very good reason to believe that its adoption was prompted by a U. S. Supreme Court decision in which State courts were admonished to re-examine their position in relation to the "exclusionary evidence" rule of the federal courts.

Our State Supreme Court feared that, if it did not take some action, the Federal Government would impose its will upon the State. This fear was certainly justified, because about two and a half years ago the Supreme Court of the United States, in an Ohio case, imposed the federal "exclusionary evidence" rule upon all the courts of all the States in the United States, and did so under the guise of due process of law.

Q. So it is now more difficult for a police officer to arrest a criminal—

A. That's right. Now, one of the things the U. S. Supreme Court did, in imposing its rule upon the State courts, is to raise the question: What constitutes "probable cause" for an arrest? This question is yet unanswered, which means that our police officers, attempting to cope with the crime problem, are at sea as to precisely when they do have "probable cause" for a valid arrest.

Now, this begets something else in turn—both on the court level and in police operations. The lower courts, not wishing to be reversed, are tending to protect the criminal's rights—bluntly—at the expense of protecting society's rights. And the police officer is inclined to be more conservative about any action that might be overruled by the courts.

So, all the way down the line, the tendency is to debilitate the administration of criminal justice at great expense to the general community.

. . . Q. Is it your feeling, then, that much of this general trend is originating with decisions of the Supreme Court?

A. Yes. May I give you an example? In the Mallory rule, limiting the elapsed time between a suspect's arrest and his arraignment in federal courts. I believe the direct quote out of the Supreme Court's decision is that the "police should not be given an opportunity in which to extract a confession."

Now, this all sounds very noble. It indicates that this rule will, in some way, prevent the police from using the rack and the screw in attempting to extort admissions of guilt from people who may be innocent. But what it actually means is that, as a general rule, confessions obtained before arraignment will not be admitted into evidence, even though valid and even though they may be the difference between success or failure in administering criminal justice.

We may throw out a thousand valid confessions with the hope that in doing so we may strike off some confession that was not properly obtained. This is a very expensive way to operate.

The States probably will get the Mallory rule, too, some day—if present trends continue. In fact, in a recent 5-to-4 decision by the U. S. Supreme Court, we barely escaped having the Mallory rule applied to California courts.

Q. What is the effect of all this on crime? Are criminals more free to operate than in the past?

A. Yes, indeed. Our criminals are at large to a far greater extent than they normally would have been under our previous methods of operation. They're committing far more crime than they normally would have, because they have the opportunity to engage in a greater amount of criminal activity.

Result is, we find ourselves overworked because of the additional crimes that are reported to us. The courts find themselves somewhat overworked because, with this great volume of crime, we are prosecuting far more people than we were. So, instead of fostering obedience to law on the theory that a human being will respond to kindness, we find that the criminal element has accepted leniency as sort of a license to continue its criminal activity. . . .

THE RIGHT TO COUNSEL AND CUSTODIAL INTERROGATION

272. *"It is not admissible to do a great right by doing a little wrong."*

Miranda v. Arizona, 384 U.S. 436 (1966).

WARREN, C.J.: The cases before us raise questions which go to the roots of our concepts of American criminal jurisprudence: the restraints society must observe consistent with the Federal Constitution in prosecuting individuals for crime. More specifically, we deal with the admissibility of statements obtained from an individual who is subjected to custodial police interrogation and the necessity for procedures which assure that the individual is accorded his privilege under the Fifth Amendment to the Constitution not to be compelled to incriminate himself. . . .

We start here, as we did in *Escobedo,* with the premise that our holding is not an innovation in our jurisprudence, but is an application of principles long recognized and applied in other settings. We have undertaken a thorough re-examination of the *Escobedo* decision and the principles it announced, and we reaffirm it. That case was but an explication of basic rights that are enshrined in our Constitution—that "No person . . . shall be compelled in any criminal case to be a witness against himself," and that "the accused shall . . . have the Assistance of Counsel"—rights which were put in jeopardy in that case through official overbearing. . . .

Our holding . . . briefly stated is this: the prosecution may not use statements, whether exculpatory or inculpatory, stemming from custodial interrogation of the defendant unless it demonstrates the use of procedural safeguards effective to secure the privilege against self-incrimination. By custodial interrogation, we mean questioning initiated by law enforcement officers after a person has been taken into custody or otherwise deprived of his freedom of action in any significant way. As for the procedural safeguards to be employed, unless other fully effective means are devised to inform accused persons of their right of silence and to assure a continuous opportunity to exercise it, the following measures are required. Prior to any questioning, the person must be warned that he has a right to remain silent, that any statement he does make may be used as evidence against him, and that he has a right to the presence of an attorney, either retained or appointed. The defendant may waive effectuation of these rights, provided the waiver is made voluntarily, knowingly and intelligently. If, however, he indicates in any manner and at any stage of the process that he wishes to consult with an attorney before speaking there can be no questioning. Likewise, if the individual is alone and indicates in any manner that he does not wish to be interrogated, the police may not question him. The mere fact that he may have answered some questions or volunteered some statements on his own does not deprive him of the right to refrain from answering any further inquiries until he has consulted with an attorney and thereafter consents to be questioned.

The constitutional issue we decide in each of these cases is the admissibility of statements obtained from a defendant questioned while in custody and deprived of his freedom of action. . . . They all share salient features—incommunicado interrogation of individuals in a police-dominated atmosphere, resulting in self-incriminating statements without full warnings of constitutional rights. . . .

The 1961 Commission on Civil Rights found much evidence to indicate that "some policemen still resort to physical force to obtain confessions." . . . Unless a proper limitation upon custodial interrogation is achieved—such as these decisions will advance—there can be no assurance that practices of this nature will be eradicated in the foreseeable future. The conclusion of the Wickersham Commission Report, made over 30 years ago, is still pertinent:

> To the contention that the third degree is necessary to get the facts, the reporters aptly reply in the language of the present Lord Chancellor of England (Lord Sankey): "It is not admissible to do a great right by doing a little wrong. . . . It is not sufficient to do justice by obtaining a proper result by irregular or improper means." Not only does the use of the third degree involve a flagrant violation of law by the officers of the law, but it involves also the dangers of false confessions, and it tends to make police and prosecutors less zealous in the search for objective evidence. As the New York prosecutor quoted in the report said, "It is a short cut and makes the police lazy and unenterprising." Or, as another official quoted remarked: "If you use your fists, you are not so likely to use your wits." We agree with the conclusion expressed in the report, that "The third degree brutalizes the police, hardens the prisoner against society, and lowers the esteem in which the administration of justice is held by the public."

. . . The modern practice of in-custody interrogation is psychologically rather than physically oriented [but] this Court has recognized that coercion can be mental as well as physical, and that the blood of the accused is not the only hallmark of an unconstitutional inquisition. . . .

In none of these cases did the officers undertake to afford appropriate safeguards at the outset of the interrogation to insure that the statements were truly the product of free choice. It is obvious that such an interrogation environment is created for no purpose other than to subjugate the individual to the will of his examiner. This atmosphere carries its own badge of intimidation. To be sure this is not physical intimidation, but it is equally destructive of human dignity. The current practice of incommunicado interrogation is at odds with one of our Nation's most cherished principles—that the individual may not be compelled to incriminate himself. Unless adequate protective devices are employed to dispel the compulsion inherent in custodial surroundings, no statement obtained from the defendant can truly be the product of his free choice.

From the foregoing, we can readily perceive an intimate connection between the privilege against self-incrimination and police custodial questioning. . . .

The question in these cases is whether the privilege is fully applicable during a period of custodial interrogation. In this Court, the privilege has consistently been accorded a liberal construction. . . . We are satisfied that all the principles embodied in the privilege apply to informal compulsion exerted by law-enforcement officers during in-custody questioning. An individual swept from familiar surroundings into police custody, surrounded by antagonistic forces, and subjected to the techniques of persuasion described above cannot be otherwise than under compulsion to speak. As a practical matter, the compulsion to speak in the isolated setting of the police station may well be greater than in courts or other official investigations, where there are often impartial observers to guard against intimidation or trickery. . . .

A different phase of the *Escobedo* decision was significant in its attention to the absence of counsel during the questioning. There, as in the cases today, we sought a protective device to dispel the compelling atmosphere of the interrogation. In *Escobedo*, however, the police did not relieve the defendant of the anxieties which they had created in the interrogation rooms. Rather, they denied his request for the assistance of counsel. . . . This heightened his dilemma, and made his later statements the product of this compulsion. The denial of the defendant's request for his attorney thus undermined his ability to exercise the privilege—to remain silent if he chose or to speak without any intimidation, blatant or subtle. The presence of counsel, in all the cases before us today, would be the adequate protective device necessary to make the process of police interrogation conform to the dictates of the privilege. His presence would insure that statements made in the government-established atmosphere are not the product of compulsion. . . .

Today, then, there can be no doubt that the Fifth Amendment privilege is available outside of criminal court proceedings and serves to protect persons in all settings in which their freedom of action is curtailed from being compelled to incriminate themselves. We have concluded that without proper safeguards the process of in-custody interrogation of persons suspected or accused of crime contains inherently compelling pressures which work to undermine the individual's will to resist and to compel him to speak where he would not otherwise do so freely. In order to combat these pressures and to permit a full opportunity to exercise the privilege against self-incrimination, the accused must be adequately and effectively apprised of his rights and the exercise of those rights must be fully honored.

The principles announced today deal with the protection which must be given to the privilege against self-incrimination when the individual is first subjected to police interrogation while in custody at the station or otherwise deprived of his freedom of action in any way. It is at this point that our adversary system of criminal proceedings commences, distinguishing itself at the outset from the inquisitorial system recognized in some countries. Under the system of warnings we delineate today or under any other system which may be devised and found effective, the safeguards to be erected about the privilege must come into play at this point.

Our decision is not intended to hamper the traditional function of police officers in investigating crime. See *Escobedo v. Illinois*, . . . When an individual is in custody on probable cause, the police may, of course, seek out evidence in the field to be used at trial against him. Such investigation may include inquiry of persons not under restraint. General on-the-scene questioning as to facts surrounding a crime or other general questioning of citizens in the fact-finding process is not affected by our holding. It is an act of responsible citizenship for individuals to give whatever information they may have to aid in law enforcement. In such situations the compelling atmosphere inherent in the process of in-custody interrogation is not necessarily present.

In dealing with statements obtained through interrogation, we do not purport to find all confessions inadmissible. Confessions remain a proper element in law enforcement. Any statement given freely and voluntarily without any compelling influences is, of course, admissible in evidence. The fundamental import of the privilege while an individual is in custody is not whether he is allowed to talk to the police without the benefit of warnings and counsel, but whether he can be interrogated. There is no requirement that police stop a person who enters a police station and states that he wishes to confess to a crime, or a person who calls the police to offer a confession or any other statement he desires to make. Volunteered statements of any kind are not barred by the Fifth Amendment and their admissibility is not affected by our holding today.

To summarize, we hold that when an individual is taken into custody or otherwise deprived of his freedom by the authorities and is subjected to questioning, the privilege against self-incrimination is jeopardized. Procedural safeguards must be employed to protect the privilege, and unless other fully effective means are adopted to notify the person of his right of silence and to assure that the exercise of the right will be scrupulously honored, the following measures are required. He must be warned prior to any questioning that he has the right to remain silent, that anything he says can be used against him in a court of law, that he has the right to the presence of an attorney, and that if he cannot afford an attorney one will be appointed for him prior to any questioning if he so desires. Opportunity to exercise these rights must be afforded to him throughout the interrogation. After such warnings have been given, and such opportunity afforded him, the individual may knowingly and intelligently waive these rights and agree to answer questions or make a statement. But unless and until such warnings and waiver are demonstrated by the prosecution at trial, no evidence obtained as a result of interrogation can be used against him.

THE LIMITS OF FIFTH AMENDMENT GUARANTEES

273. *Compulsory Self-Incrimination and Cooperative Federalism*

Murphy v. New York Harbor Waterfront Commission, 378 U.S. 52 (1964).

GOLDBERG, J.: We have held today that the Fifth Amendment privilege against self-incrimination must be deemed fully applicable to the States through the Fourteenth Amendment. *Malloy v. Hogan*. . . . This case presents a related issue: whether one jurisdiction within our federal structure may compel a witness, whom it has immunized from prosecution under its laws, to give testimony which might then be used to convict him of a crime against another such jurisdiction.

Petitioners were subpoenaed to testify at a hearing conducted by the Waterfront Commission of New York Harbor concerning a work stoppage at the Hoboken, New Jersey, piers. After refusing to respond to certain questions about the stoppage on the ground that the answers might tend to incriminate them, petitioners were granted immunity from prosecution under the laws of New Jersey and New York. Notwithstanding this grant of immunity, they still refused to respond to the questions on the ground that the answers might tend to incriminate them under *federal* law, to which the grant of immunity did not purport to extend. Petitioners were thereupon held in civil and criminal contempt of court. The New Jersey Supreme Court reversed the criminal contempt conviction on procedural grounds but . . . affirmed the civil contempt judgments on the merits. The court held that a State may constitutionally compel a witness to give testimony which might be used in a federal prosecution against him. . . .

Since a grant of immunity is valid only if it is coextensive with the scope of the privilege against self-incrimination . . . we must now decide the fundamental constitutional question of whether, absent an immunity provision, one jurisdiction in our federal structure may compel a witness to give testimony which might incriminate him under the laws of another jurisdiction. The answer to this question must depend . . . on whether such an application of the privilege promotes or defeats its policies and purposes.

The privilege against self-incrimination "registers an important advance in the development of our liberty—'one of the great landmarks in man's struggle to make himself civilized.'" *Ullmann v. United States.* . . . It reflects many of our fundamental values and most noble aspirations: our unwillingness to subject those suspected of crime to the cruel trilemma of self-accusation, perjury or contempt; our preference for an accusatorial rather than an inquisitorial system of criminal justice; our fear that self-incriminating statements will be elicited by inhumane treatment and abuses; our sense of fair play which dictates "a fair state-individual balance by requiring the government to leave the individual alone until good cause is shown for disturbing him and by requiring the government in its contest with the individual to shoulder the entire load," 8 Wigmore, Evidence (McNaughton rev., 1961), . . . our respect for the inviolability of the human personality and of the right of each individual "to a private enclave where he may lead a private life," *United States v. Grunewald,* . . . ; our distrust of self-deprecatory statements; and our realization that the privilege, while sometimes "a shelter to the guilty," is often "a protection to the innocent." *Quinn v. United States.* . . .

Most, if not all, of these policies and purposes are defeated when a witness "can he whipsawed into incriminating himself under both state and federal law even though" the constitutional privilege against self-incrimination is applicable to each. This has become especially true in our age of "cooperative federalism," where the federal and state governments are waging a united front against many types of criminal activity.

Respondent contends, however, that we should adhere to the "established rule" that the constitutional privilege against self-incrimination does not protect a witness in one jurisdiction against being compelled to give testimony which could be used to convict him in another jurisdiction. This "rule" has three decisional facets: *United States v. Murdock* held that the Federal Government could compel a witness to give testimony which might incriminate him under State law; *Knapp v. Schweitzer,* held that a State could compel a witness to give testimony which might incriminate him under federal law; and *Feldman v. U.S.*, held that testimony thus compelled by a State could be introduced into evidence in the federal courts.

Our decision today in *Malloy v. Hogan, supra,* necessitates a reconsideration of this rule. Our review of the pertinent cases in this Court and of their English antecedents reveals that *Murdock* did not adequately consider the relevant authorities and has been significantly weakened by subsequent decisions of this Court, and, further, that the legal premises underlying *Feldman* and *Knapp* have since been rejected. . . .

In light of the history, policies, and purposes of the privilege against self-incrimination, we now accept as correct the construction given the privilege by the English courts and by Chief Justice Marshall and Justice Holmes. See *U.S. v. The Saline Bank of Virginia; Ballmann v. Fagin.* We reject as unsupported by history or policy—the deviation from that construction only recently adopted by this Court in *United States v. Murdock,* and *Feldman v. United States, supra.* We hold that the constitutional privilege against self-incrimination protects a state witness against incrimination under federal as well as state law and a federal witness against incrimination under state as well as federal law.

We must now decide what effect this holding has on existing state immunity legislation. In *Counselman v. Hitchcock,* . . . this Court considered a federal statute which provided that no "evidence obtained from a party or witness by means of a judicial proceeding . . . shall be given in evidence, or in any manner used against him . . . in any Court of the United States. . . ." Notwithstanding this statute, appellant, claiming his privilege against self-incrimination, refused to answer certain questions before a federal grand jury. The Court said "that legislation cannot abridge a constitutional privilege, and that it cannot replace or supply one, at least unless it is so broad as to have the same extent in scope and effect." *Id.,* . . . Applying this principle to the facts of that case, the Court upheld appellant's refusal to answer on the ground that the statute: "could not, and would not, prevent the use of his testimony to search out other testimony to be used in evidence against him or his property, in a criminal proceeding in such court . . . ," *id.,* . . . that it: "could not prevent the obtaining and the use of witnesses and evidence which should be attributable directly to the testimony he might give under compulsion, and on which he might be convicted, when otherwise, and if he had refused to answer, he could not possibly have been convicted . . . ," *ibid.,* and that it: "affords no protection against that use of compelled testimony which consists in gaining therefrom a knowledge of the details of a crime, and of sources of information which may supply other means of convicting the witness or party." . . .

Applying the holding of that case to our holdings today that the privilege against self-incrimination protects a state witness against federal prosecution, . . . and that "the same standards must determine whether [a witness'] silence in either a federal or state proceeding is justified," *Malloy v. Hogan, ante,* at—, we hold the constitutional rule to be that a state witness may not be compelled to give testimony which may be incriminating under federal law unless the compelled testimony and its fruits cannot be used in any manner by federal officials in connection with a criminal prosecution against him. We conclude, moreover, that in order to implement this constitutional rule and accommodate the interests of the State and Federal Governments in investigating and prosecuting crime, the Federal Government must be prohibited from making any such use of compelled testimony and its fruits. This exclusionary rule, while permitting the States to secure information necessary for effective law enforcement, leaves the witness and the Federal Government in substantially the same position as if the witness had claimed his privilege in the absence of a state grant of immunity.

It follows that petitioners here may now be compelled to answer the questions propounded to them. At the time they refused to answer, however, petitioners had a reasonable fear, based on this Court's decision in *Feldman v. United States,* . . . that the federal authorities might use the answers against them in connection with a federal prosecution. We have now overruled *Feldman* and held that the Federal Government may make no such use of the answers. Fairness dictates that petitioners should now be afforded an opportunity, in light of this development, to answer the questions. . . . Accordingly, the judgment of the New Jersey courts ordering petitioners to answer the questions may remain undisturbed. But the judgment of contempt is vacated and the cause remanded to the New Jersey Supreme Court for proceedings not inconsistent with this opinion.

Legislative Investigations and Procedural Rights

CONGRESSIONAL COMMITTEES AND THE RIGHTS OF WITNESSES

274. *Refusal to Testify Under the Fifth Amendment*

Blau v. U.S., 340 U.S. 159 (1950).

BLACK, J.: In response to a subpoena, petitioner appeared as a witness before the United States District Court Grand Jury at Denver, Colorado. There she was asked several questions concerning the Communist Party of Colorado and her employment by it. Petitioner refused to answer these questions on the ground that the answers might tend to incriminate her. She was then taken before the district judge where the questions were again propounded and where she again claimed her constitutional privilege against self-incrimination and refused to testify. The district judge found petitioner guilty of contempt of court and sentenced her to imprisonment for one year. . . .

At the time petitioner was called before the grand jury, the Smith Act was on the statute books making it a crime among other things to advocate knowingly the desirability of overthrow of the Government by force or violence; to organize or help to organize any society or group which teaches, advocates or encourages such overthrow of the Government; to be or become a member of such a group with knowledge of its purposes. These provisions made future prosecution of petitioner far more than "a mere imaginary possibility . . ."; she reasonably could fear that criminal charges might be brought against her if she admitted employment by the Communist Party or intimate knowledge of its workings. Whether such admissions by themselves would support a conviction under a criminal statute is immaterial. Answers to the questions asked by the grand jury would have furnished a link in the chain of evidence needed in a prosecution of petitioner for violation of . . . the Smith Act. Prior decisions of this Court have clearly established that under such circumstances, the Constitution gives a witness the privilege of remaining silent. The attempt by the courts below to compel petitioners to testify runs counter to the Fifth Amendment as it has been interpreted from the beginning. . . .

Reversed.

275. *The Nature of True Immunity*

Ullman v. U.S., 350 U.S. 422 (1956).

FRANKFURTER, J.: On November 10, 1954, the United States Attorney for the Southern District of New York filed an application under the Immunity Act of 1954 . . . for an order requiring petitioner to testify before a grand jury. The Immunity Act, in its pertinent portions, provides:

"(c) Whenever in the judgment of a United States Attorney the testimony of any witness, or the production of books, papers, or other evidence by any witness, in any case or proceeding before any grand jury or court of the United States involving any interference with or endangering of, or any plans or attempts to interfere with or endanger, the national security or defense of the United States by treason, sabotage, espionage, sedition, seditious conspiracy, violations of the Internal Security Act of 1950 . . . the Atomic Energy Act of 1946 . . . sections of the Immigration and Nationality Act . . . and conspiracies involving any of the foregoing, is necessary to the public interest, he, upon the approval of the Attorney General, shall make application to the court that the witness shall be instructed to testify or produce evidence subject to the provisions of this section, and upon order of the court such witness shall not be excused from testifying or from producing books, papers, or other evidence on the ground that the testimony or evidence required of him may tend to incriminate him or subject him to a penalty or forfeiture. But no such witness shall be prosecuted or subjected to any penalty or forfeiture for or on account of any transaction, matter, or thing concerning which he is compelled, after having claimed his privilege against self-incrimination, to testify or produce evidence, nor shall testimony so compelled be used as evidence in any criminal proceeding (except prosecution described in subsection (d) hereof) against him in any court.

"(d) No witness shall be exempt under the provision of this section from prosecution for perjury or contempt committed while giving testimony or producing evidence under compulsion as provided in this section." . . .

Four major questions are raised by this appeal: Is the immunity provided by the Act sufficiently broad to displace the protection afforded by the privilege against self-incrimination? Assuming that the statutory requirements are met, does the Act give the district judge discretion to deny an application for an order requiring a witness to answer relevant questions put by the grand jury, and, if so, is the court thereby required to exercise a function that is not an exercise of "judicial Power"? Did Congress provide immunity from state prosecution for crime, and, if so, is it empowered to do so? Does the Fifth Amendment prohibit compulsion of what would otherwise be self-incriminating testimony no matter what the scope of the immunity statute?

It is relevant to define explicitly the spirit in which the Fifth Amendment's privilege against self-incrimination should be approached. . . .

Too many, even those who should be better advised, view this privilege as a shelter for wrong doers. They too readily assume that those who invoke it are either guilty of crime or commit perjury in claiming the privilege. Such a view does scant honor to the patriots who sponsored the Bill of Rights as a condition to acceptance of the Constitution by the ratifying States. The Founders of the Nation were not naive or disregardful of the interests of justice. . . .

No doubt the constitutional privilege may, on occasion, save a guilty man from his just deserts. It was aimed at a more far-reaching evil—a recurrence of the Inquisition and the Star Chamber, even if not in their stark brutality. Prevention of the greater evil was deemed of more importance than occurrence of the lesser evil. Having had much experience with a tendency in human nature to abuse power, the Founders sought to close the doors against like future abuses by law-enforcing agencies.

As no constitutional guarantee enjoys preference, so none should suffer subordination or deletion. . . . To view a particular provision of the Bill of Rights with disfavor inevitably results in a constricted application of it. This is to disrespect the Constitution.

It is in this spirit of strict, not lax, observance of the constitutional protection of the individual that we approach the claims made by petitioner in this case. The attack on the Immunity Act as violating the Fifth Amendment is not a new one. Sixty years ago this Court considered, in *Brown v. Walker*, the constitutionality of a similar Act. . . .

Petitioner, however, attempts to distinguish *Brown v. Walker* [arguing] that this case is different . . . because the impact of the disabilities imposed by federal and state authorities and the public in general—such as loss of job, expulsion from labor unions, state registration and investigation statutes, passport eligibility, and general public opprobrium—is so oppressive that the statute does not give him true immunity. . . . But as this Court has often held, the immunity granted need only remove those sanctions which generate the fear justifying invocation of the privilege: "The interdiction of the Fifth Amendment operates only where a witness is asked to incriminate himself—in other words, to give testimony which may possibly expose him to a criminal charge. But if the criminality has already been taken away, the Amendment ceases to apply." *Hale v. Henkel*. . . . Here, since the Immunity Act protects a witness who is compelled to answer to the extent of his constitutional immunity, he has of course, when a particular sanction is sought to be imposed against him, the right to claim that it is criminal in nature. . . . [The Court here holds that the district court had no discretion to deny the request for an order to testify merely because it thought the public interest would be best served by such denial. Hence there was no exercise of nonjudicial power.]

Petitioner further argues that the immunity is not constitutionally sufficient so long as a witness is subject to the very real possibility of state prosecution. He urges that the statute does not, and constitutionally could not, grant such immunity. The immunity portion of the statute contains two parts. The first prohibits prosecutions and is worded virtually in the terms of the 1893 Act. The second makes explicit that the compelled testimony shall not be used against the witness in any proceeding in any court. Such a clause was construed in *Adams v. Maryland* . . . to apply to state courts. In *Brown v. Walker*, it was urged that the prohibition against prosecution did not grant protection against prosecution in the state courts. First finding that Congress could constitutionally provide such immunity, the Court then interpreted the statute:

> The act in question contains no suggestion that it is to be applied only to the Federal courts. It declares broadly that "no person shall be excused from attending and testifying . . . before the Interstate Commerce Commission . . . on the ground . . . that the testimony . . . required of him may tend to criminate him," etc. "But no person shall

> be prosecuted or subjected to any penalty or forfeiture for or on account of any transaction, matter or thing concerning which he may testify," etc. It is not that he shall not be prosecuted for or on account of any *crime* concerning which he may testify, which might possibly be urged to apply only to crimes under the Federal law and not to crimes, such as the passing of counterfeit money, etc., which are also cognizable under state laws; but the immunity extends to any *transaction, matter or thing* concerning which he may testify, which clearly indicates that the immunity is intended to be general, and to be applicable whenever and in whatever court such prosecution may be had.

The Report of the Committee on the Judiciary of the House of Representatives supports the broad interpretation of the Act before us:

> Even though the power of Congress to prohibit a subsequent State prosecution is doubtful, such a constitutional question should not prevent the enactment of the recommended bill. The language of the amendment . . . is sufficiently broad to ban a subsequent State prosecution if it be determined that the Congress has the constitutional power to do so. In addition, the amendment recommended provides the additional protection—as set forth in the Adams case, by outlawing the subsequent use of the compelled testimony in any criminal proceeding—State or Federal.
>
> By the use of these two distinct concepts, the committee believes that the fullest protection that can be afforded the witness will be achieved.

Petitioner questions the constitutional power of Congress to grant immunity from state prosecution. Congressional abolition of state power to punish crimes committed in violation of state law presents a more drastic exercise of congressional power than that which we considered in Adams. In that case, only the use of the compelled testimony, not prosecution itself, was prohibited. Here the State is forbidden to prosecute. But it cannot be contested that Congress has power to provide for national defense and the complementary power "To make all Laws which shall be necessary and proper for carrying into Execution the foregoing Powers, and all other Powers vested by this Constitution in the Government of the United States, or in any Department or Officer thereof." U.S. Const., Art. I, §8, cl. 18. The Immunity Act is concerned with the national security. It reflects a congressional policy to increase the possibility of more complete and open disclosure by removal of fear of state prosecution. We cannot say that Congress' paramount authority in safeguarding national security does not justify the restriction it has placed on the exercise of state power for the more effective exercise of conceded federal power. . . .

Petitioner also urges that if *Brown v. Walker* is found nondistinguishable and controlling, then that case should be reconsidered and overruled. He also urges upon us a "return" to a literal reading of the Fifth Amendment. . . .

We are not dealing here with one of the vague, undefinable, admonitory provisions of the Constitution whose scope is inevitably addressed to changing circumstances. The privilege against self-incrimination is a specific provision of which it is peculiarly true that "a page of history is worth a volume of logic." . . . For the history of the privilege establishes not only that it is not to be interpreted literally, but also that its sole concern is, as its name indicates, with the danger to a witness forced to give testimony leading to the infliction of "penalties affixed to the criminal acts . . ." *Boyd v. U.S.* . . . We leave *Boyd* . . . unqualified, as it was left unqualified in *Brown v. Walker*. Immunity displaces the danger. Once the reason for the privilege ceases, the privilege ceases. . . .

276. "The Constitution places the right of silence beyond the reach of government . . ."

Ullman v. U.S., 350 U.S. 422 (1956).

DOUGLAS, J., dissenting: I would reverse the judgment of conviction. I would base the reversal on *Boyd v. United States*, . . . , or, in the alternative, I would overrule the five-to-four decision of *Brown v. Walker*, . . .

First, as to the Boyd case. There are numerous disabilities created by federal law that attach to a person who is a Communist. These disabilities include ineligibility for employment in the Federal Government and in defense facilities, disqualification for a passport, the risk of internment, the risk of loss of employment as a longshoreman—to mention only a few. These disabilities imposed by federal law are forfeitures within the meaning of our cases and as much protected by the Fifth Amendment as criminal prosecution itself. But there is no indication that the Immunity Act . . . grants protection against those disabilities. The majority will not say that it does. I think, indeed, that it must be read as granting only partial, not complete, immunity for the matter disclosed under compulsion. Yet . . . an immunity statute to be valid must "supply a complete protection from all the perils against which the constitutional prohibition was designed to guard. . . ."

Boyd v. United States . . . involved a proceeding to establish a forfeiture of goods alleged to have been fraudulently imported without payment of duties. The claimants resisted an order requiring the production of an invoice to be used against them in the forfeiture proceedings. The Court in an opinion by Mr. Justice Bradley sustained the defense of the Fifth Amendment. The Court said, "A witness, as well as a party, is protected by the law from being compelled to give evidence that tends to criminate him, or to subject his property to forfeiture." . . .

The forfeiture of property on compelled testimony is no more abhorrent than the forfeiture of rights of citizenship. Any forfeiture of rights as a result of compelled testimony is at war with the Fifth Amendment.

The Court apparently distinguishes the Boyd case on the ground that the forfeiture of property was a penalty affixed to a criminal act. The loss of a job and the ineligibility for a passport are also penalties affixed to a criminal act. . . . If there was a penalty suffered in the Boyd case, there are penalties suffered here. Both are hitched to criminal acts. And the Constitution places the property rights involved in the Boyd case no higher than the rights of citizenship involved here. . . .

We should apply the principle of the Boyd case to the present one and hold that since there is not protection in the Immunity Act against loss of rights of citizenship, the immunity granted is less than the protection afforded by the Constitution. . . .

Second, as to *Brown v. Walker*. The difficulty I have with that decision and with the majority of the Court in the present case is that they add an important qualification to the Fifth Amendment. The guaranty is that no person "shall be compelled in any criminal case to be a witness against himself." The majority does not enforce that guaranty as written but qualifies it; and the qualification apparently reads, "but only if criminal conviction might result." Wisely or not, the Fifth Amendment protects against the compulsory self-accusation of crime without exception or qualification. . . .

. . . The forced disclosure may open up vast new vistas for the prosecutor with leads to numerous accusations not within the purview of the question and answer.

What related offenses may be disclosed by leads furnished by the confession? How remote need the offense be before the immunity ceases to protect it? How much litigation will it take to determine it? What will be the reaction of the highest court when the facts of the case reach it?

. . . One protective function of the Fifth Amendment is at once removed when the guaranty against self-incrimination is qualified in the manner it is today.

. . . The privilege of silence is exchanged for a partial, undefined, vague immunity. It means that Congress has granted far less than it has taken away. . . . The guarantee against self-incrimination contained in the Fifth Amendment is not only a protection against conviction and prosecution but a safeguard of conscience and human dignity and freedom of expression as well. My view is that the Framers put it beyond the power of Congress to *compel* anyone to confess his crimes. The evil to be guarded against was partly self-accusation under legal compulsion. But that was only a part of the evil. The conscience and dignity of man were also involved. So too was his right to freedom of expression guaranteed by the First Amendment. The Framers, therefore, created the federally protected right of silence and decreed that the law could not be used to pry open one's lips and make him a witness against himself.

. . . The Fifth amendment was designed to protect the accused against infamy as well as against prosecution. . . . Loss of office, loss of dignity, loss of face were feudal forms of punishment. Infamy was historically considered to be punishment as effective as fine and imprisonment. . . .

There is great infamy involved in the present case, apart from the loss of rights of citizenship under federal law. . . . The disclosure that a person is a Communist practically excommunicates him from society. School boards will not hire him. . . . A lawyer risks exclusion from the bar . . . ; a doctor, the revocation of his license to practice. . . . If an actor, he is on a black list. . . . And he will be able to find no employment in our society except at the lowest level, if at all. . . .

It is no answer to say that a witness who exercises his Fifth Amendment right of silence and stands mute may bring himself into disrepute. If so, that is the price he pays for exercising the right of silence granted by the Fifth Amendment. The critical point is that the Constitution places the right of silence beyond the reach of government. When public opinion casts a person into the outer darkness, as happens today when a person is exposed as a Communist, the government brings infamy on the head of the witness when it compels disclosure. That is precisely what the Fifth Amendment prohibits. . . .

277. *Congressional Power to Expose for the Sake of Exposure*

Watkins v. U.S., 354 U.S. 178 (1957).

Warren, C.J.: Petitioner appeared as a witness in compliance with a subpoena issued by a Subcommittee of the Committee on Un-American Activities of the House of Representatives. . . . The character of petitioner's testimony can perhaps best be summarized by the Government's own appraisal in its brief:

A more complete and candid statement of his past political associations and activities (treating the Communist Party for present purposes as a mere political party) can hardly be imagined. Petitioner certainly was not attempting to conceal or withhold from the Committee his own past political associations, predilections, and preferences. Furthermore, petitioner told the Committee that he was entirely willing to identify for the Committee, and answer any questions it might have concerning, "those persons whom I knew to be members of the Communist Party," provided that, "to [his] best knowledge and belief," they still were members of the Party. . . .

I do not believe that any law in this country requires me to testify about persons who may in the past have been Communist Party members or otherwise engaged in Communist Party activity but who to my best knowledge and belief have long since removed themselves from the Communist movement.

I do not believe that such questions are relevant to the work of this committee nor do I believe that this committee has the right to undertake the public exposure of persons because of their past activities. I may be wrong, and the committee may have this power, but until and unless a court of law so holds and directs me to answer, I most firmly refuse to discuss the political activities of my past associates.

We start with several basic premises on which there is general agreement. The power of the Congress to conduct investigations is inherent in the legislative process. That power is broad. It encompasses inquiries concerning the administration of existing laws as well as proposed or possibly needed statutes. It includes surveys of defects in our social, economic or political system for the purpose of enabling the Congress to remedy them. It comprehends probes into departments of the Federal Government to expose corruption, inefficiency or waste. But broad as is this power of inquiry, it is not unlimited. There is no general authority to expose the private affairs of individuals without justification in terms of the functions of the Congress. This was freely conceded by the Solicitor General in his argument of this case. . . .

It is unquestionably the duty of all citizens to cooperate with the Congress in its efforts to obtain the facts needed for intelligent legislative action. It is their unremitting obligation to respond to subpoenas, to respect the dignity of the Congress and its committees and to testify fully with respect to matters within the province of proper investigation. This, of course, assumes that the constitutional rights of witnesses will be respected by the Congress as they are in a court of justice. The Bill of Rights is applicable to investigations as to all forms of governmental action. Witnesses cannot be compelled to give evidence against themselves. They cannot be subjected to unreasonable search and seizure. Nor can the First Amendment freedoms of speech, press, religion, or political belief and association be abridged. . . .

In the decade following World War II, there appeared a new kind of congressional inquiry unknown in prior periods of American history. Principally this was the result of the various investigations into the threat of subversion of the United States Government, but other subjects of congressional interest also contributed to the changed scene. This new phase of legislative inquiry involved a broad-scale intrusion into the lives and affairs of private citizens. It brought before the courts novel questions of the appropriate limits of congressional inquiry. Prior cases . . . had defined the scope of investigative power in terms of the inherent limitations of the sources of that power. In the more recent cases, the emphasis shifted to problems of accommodating the interest of the Government with the rights and privileges of individuals. The central theme was the application of the Bill of Rights as a restraint upon the assertion of governmental power in this form. . . .

Abuses of the investigative process may imperceptibly lead to abridgment of protected freedoms. The mere summoning of a witness and compelling him to testify, against his will, about his beliefs, expressions or associations is a meaure of governmental interference. And when those forced revelations concern matters that are unorthodox, unpopular, or even hateful to the general public, the reaction in the life of the witness may be disastrous. This effect is even more harsh when it is past beliefs, expressions or associations that are disclosed and judged by current standards rather than those contemporary with the matters exposed. Nor does the witness alone suffer the consequences. Those who are identified by witnesses and thereby placed in the same glare of publicity are equally subject to public stigma, scorn and obloquy. Beyond that, there is more subtle and immeasurable effect upon those who tend to adhere to the most orthodox and uncontroversial views and associations in order to avoid a similar fate at some future time. That this impact is partly the result of non-governmental activity by private persons cannot relieve the investigators of their responsibility for initiating the reaction.

The Court recognized the restraints of the Bill of Rights upon Congressional investigations in *U.S. v. Rumely* . . . where the Court construed narrowly the resolution describing the Committee's authority. It was concluded that when First Amendment rights are threatened, the delegation of power to the committee must be clearly revealed in its character. . . .

We have no doubt that there is no congressional power to expose for the sake of exposure. The public is, of course, entitled to be informed concerning the workings of its government. That cannot be inflated into a general power to expose where the predominant result can only be an invasion of the private rights of individuals. But a solution to our problem is not to be found in testing the motives of committee members for this purpose. Such is not our function. Their motives alone would not vitiate an investigation which had been instituted by a House of Congress if that assembly's legislative purpose is being served.

. . . It is the responsibility of the Congress, in the first instance, to insure that compulsory process is used only in furtherance of a legislative purpose. That requires that the instructions to an investigating committee spell out that group's jurisdiction and purpose with sufficient particularity. Those instructions are embodied in the authorizing resolution. That document is the committee's charter. Broadly drafted and loosely worded, however, such resolutions can leave tremendous latitude to the discretion of the investigators. The more vague the committee's charter is, the greater becomes the possibility that the committee's specific actions are not in conformity with the will of the parent House of Congress.

The authorizing resolution of the Un-American Activities Committee was adopted in 1938 when a select committee, under the chairmanship of Representative Dies, was created. Several years later, the Committee was made a standing organ of the House with the same mandate. It defines the Committee's authority as follows:

> The Committee on Un-American Activities, as a whole or by subcommittee, is authorized to make from time to time investigations of (i) the extent, character, and objects of un-American propaganda activities in the United States, (ii) the diffusion within the United States of subversive and un-American propaganda that is instigated from foreign countries or of a domestic origin and attacks the principle of the form of government as guaranteed by our Constitution, and (iii) all other questions in relation thereto that would aid Congress in any necessary remedial legislation.

It would be difficult to imagine a less explicit authorizing resolution. Who can define the meaning of "un-American"? What is that single, solitary "principle of the form of government as guaranteed by our Constitution"? There is no need to dwell upon the language, however. At one time, perhaps, the resolution might have been read narrowly to confine the Committee to the subject of propaganda. The events that have transpired in the fifteen years before the interrogation of petitioner make such a construction impossible at this date. . . .

The members of the Committee have clearly demonstrated that they did not feel themselves restricted in any way to propaganda in the narrow sense of the word. Unquestionably the Committee conceived of its task in the grand view of its name. Un-American activities were its target, no matter how or where manifested. . . .

Combining the language of the resolution with the construction it has been given, it is evident that the preliminary control of the Committee exercised by the House of Representatives is slight or nonexistent. No one could reasonably deduce from the charter the kind of investigation that the Committee was directed to make. As a result, we are asked to engage in a process of retroactive rationalization. Looking backward from the events that transpired, we are asked to uphold the Committee's actions unless it appears that they were clearly not authorized by the charter. As a corollary to this inverse approach, the Government urges that we must view the matter hospitably to the power of the Congress—that if there is any legislative purpose which might have been furthered by the kind of disclosure sought, the witness must be punished for withholding it. No doubt every reasonable indulgence of legality must be accorded to the actions of a coordinate branch of our Government. But such deference cannot yield to an unnecessary and unreasonable dissipation of precious constitutional freedoms.

The Government contends that the public interest at the core of the investigations of the Un-American Activities Committee is the need by the Congress to be informed of efforts to overthrow the Government by force and violence, so that adequate legislative safeguards can be erected. From this core, however, the Committee can radiate outward infinitely to any topic thought to be related in some way to armed insurrection. The outer reaches of this domain are known only by the content of "un-American activities." Remoteness of subject can be aggravated by a probe for a depth of detail even farther removed from any basis of legislative action. A third dimension is added when the investigators turn their attention to the past to collect minutiae on remote topics, on the hypothesis that the past may reflect upon the present.

It is, of course, not the function of this Court to prescribe rigid rules for the Congress to follow in drafting resolutions establishing investigating committees. That is a matter peculiarly within the realm of the legislature, and its decisions will be accepted by the courts up to the point where their own duty to enforce the constitutionally protected rights of individuals is affected.

. . . Plainly these committees are restricted to the missions delegated to them, i.e., to acquire certain data to be used by the House, or the Senate in coping with a problem that falls within its legislative sphere. No witness can be compelled to make disclosures on matters outside that area. This is a jurisdictional concept of pertinency drawn from the nature of a congressional committee's source of authority. It is not wholly different from nor unrelated to the element of pertinency embodied in the criminal statute under which petitioner was prosecuted. When the definition of jurisdictional pertinency is as uncertain and wavering as in the case of the Un-American Activities Committee, it becomes extremely difficult for the Committee to limit its inquiries to statutory pertinency.

In fulfillment of their obligation under this statute, the courts must accord to the defendants every right which is guaranteed to defendants in all other criminal cases. Among these is the right to have available, through a sufficiently precise statute, information revealing the standard of criminality before the commission of the alleged offense. Applied to persons prosecuted under § 192, this raises a special problem in that the statute defines the crime as refusal to answer "any question pertinent to the question under inquiry." Part of the standard of criminality, therefore, is the pertinency of the questions propounded to the witness.

The problem attains proportion when viewed from the standpoint of the witness who appears before a congressional committee. He must decide at the time the questions are propounded whether or not to answer. . . .

It is obvious that a person compelled to make this choice is entitled to have knowledge of the subject to which the interrogation is deemed pertinent. That knowledge must be available with the same degree of explicitness and clarity that the Due Process Clause requires in the expression of any element of a criminal offense. The "vice of vagueness" must be avoided here as in all other crimes. There are several sources that can outline the "question under inquiry" in such a way that the rules against vagueness are satisfied. The authorizing resolution, the remarks of the chairman or members of the committee, or even the nature of the proceedings themselves might sometimes make the topic clear. This case demonstrates, however, that these sources often leave the matter in grave doubt.

The statement of the Committee Chairman in this case, in response to petitioner's protest, was woefully inadequate to convey sufficient information as to the pertinency of the questions to the subject under inquiry. Petitioner was thus not accorded a fair opportunity to determine whether he was within his rights in refusing to answer, and his conviction is necessarily invalid under the Due Process Clause of the Fifth Amendment.

. . . The conclusions which we have reached in this case will not prevent the Congress, through its committees, from obtaining any information it needs for the proper fulfillment of its role in our scheme of government. The legislature is free to determine the kinds of data that should be collected. It is only those investigations that are conducted by use of compulsory process that give rise to a need to protect the rights of individuals against illegal encroachment. That protection can be readily achieved through procedures which prevent the separation of power from responsibility and which provide the constitutional requisites of fairness for witnesses. A measure of added care on the part of the House and the Senate in authorizing the use of compulsory process and by their committees in exercising that power would suffice. That is a small price to pay if it serves to uphold the principles of limited, constitutional government without constricting the power of the Congress to inform itself.

CHAPTER XXX

The Revolution in Civil Rights

THE American Negro in the post-World War II period looked hopefully to a new day when the rights with which he was theoretically born, but which he had never fully enjoyed, might be realized. His hopes and ambitions were shared by many white Americans in positions of authority. Not only was the color line being broken in such limited areas as major-league baseball and the armed services, but the executive branch was accepting fully the principle of equality of opportunity, as indicated by its endorsement of the report of the President's Committee on Civil Rights (Chap. XXVIII, No. 247). Yet such declarations, no matter how earnestly and sincerely issued and endorsed, had little meaning without concrete implementation—removing the legal restrictions and barriers, formal and informal, which held the Negro in second-class citizenship. Such action was possible only through the legislative and judicial branches. And with Congress and most state legislatures in the late forties and early fifties neither willing nor able to take appropriate action in this area, the task fell clearly to the courts. In some respects this was appropriate, since many of the constitutional strictures were the result of judicial interpretation sustaining state segregation under the "separate but equal" rule and watering down the supposed guarantees of equality of the Fourteenth and Fifteenth Amendments. These interpretations had made possible the complex patterns of segregation which bound the Negro in everything from education and employment to housing, transportation, and access to public facilities.

Shortly before World War II, the Supreme Court started the process of narrowing the scope of the *Plessy v. Ferguson*, "separate but equal" doctrine. In the late 1940's the federal government took new steps against local segregation practices in the areas of housing and transportation. In the former, the Court struck at private agreements in land deeds binding owners not to sell or lease their property to Negroes. Without striking down the covenants themselves, it ruled that their enforcement in state courts would constitute "state action" and therefore violate the equal protection guarantees of the Fifth and Fourteenth Amendments (*Hurd. Hodge*, 1948; *Shelley v. Kraemer* [No. 278]). This rule was strengthened in 1953 when the Court held that a racially restrictive agreement could not be enforced by a suit for damages against a white covenanter who broke the contract (*Barrows v. Jackson*).

In transportation, the Court insisted—in what was becoming a consistent pattern—that if separate facilities were imposed they must be literally equal, not just "substantially" equal. Here the Court was able to use a federal statute to bolster its case, holding that a railroad's allocation of dining-car seats on a segregated basis interfered with equal access of passengers to facilities in violation of the Interstate Commerce Act, which forbids interstate carriers "to subject any particular person . . . to any undue or unreasonable prejudice or disadvantage in any respect whatsoever" (*Henderson v. U.S.*, 1950). In the ruling, the Court came close to reversing the half-century-old Plessy rule in favor of the proposition that separate facilities, no matter how equal, were incompatible with the Constitution. It was clearly moving in this direction, as indicated by its rulings in the same period in the field of education.

Indeed, the sharpest advances on the civil rights frontier were made in a landmark series of school desegregation cases which culminated in the abolition of the "separate but equal" ruling in public education. The Court had begun cautiously in the Gaines case in 1938 (Chapter XXIV, Introduction) to move against the more flagrant examples of inequality rationalized through the "separate but equal" phrase. A series of cases between 1948 and 1950 continued this trend. In a *per curiam* ruling in *Sipuel v. University of Oklahoma* (1948), it held that qualified Negroes must be admitted to the state law school or be furnished an equivalent education in Oklahoma. When a Negro graduate student was admitted to the University of Oklahoma, he was segregated, sitting in a separate row for Negroes in classrooms, reading at a separate table in the library, and eating at a separate table in the cafeteria. A unanimous Court held that the equal protection clause of the Fourteenth Amendment assured the Negro student the same treatment by the state as other students (*McLaurin v. Oklahoma State Regents*, 1950).

On the same day, the Court again achieved unanimity in an even more important case, which made it evident that it would be almost impossible for a state to comply with the "separate but equal" formula in the field of higher education. Although *Sweatt v. Painter* (1950) left that doctrine intact, the Court concluded that separate Negro law schools in Texas were unequal and made it clear that this shortcoming was itself the result of segregation. The Court failed to "reach petitioner's contention that *Plessy v. Ferguson* should be reexamined in the light of contemporary knowledge respecting the purposes of the Fourteenth Amendment and the effects of racial segregation," but such a near miss virtually invited cases raising that very point.

In the five public-school cases brought before the Court in 1952, the constitutional issue of segregation could no longer be evaded. Few cases have been more carefully considered. The Court scheduled the cases for argument in 1952 and after deliberating six months, ordered reargument in 1953. Briefs were presented in the fall of 1953 and on May 17, 1954. A unanimous Supreme Court, speaking through its new Chief Justice Earl Warren, declared that "in the field of public education the doctrine of 'separate but equal' has no place" (*Brown v. Board of Education of Topeka* [No. 279]). Domestically, the unanimous decision was probably the most consequential judicial event of the twentieth century; internationally, it was important enough to be beamed around the world on the Voice of America as an indication that the nation, now the "leader of the Free World," was setting new examples of freedom and equality at home. At the same time, however, the Court postponed the formulation of methods of implementing this historic decision, again scheduling additional argument. A year later, the Court ordered "a prompt and reasonable start toward full compliance" with its antisegregation ruling, and left to the federal district courts the duty of supervising desegregation. Although the Court realistically recognized that this process would take time, it stressed the necessity for "all deliberate speed" (*Brown v. Board of Education, 1955*).

A large segment of southern leadership promptly dug in its heels and set out to oppose judicial policy fully and resolutely. Virginia and several other states resurrected the doctrine of interposition (Chapter IV) and Georgia threatened nullification (Chapters VII and XI). Both moves were interesting exercises in constitutional dialectics, apparently without meaning, however, except as delaying tactics. The most considered statement of constitutional theory underlying the segregationist position was the declaration on integration made by ninety-six southern Congressmen on March 11, 1956 (No. 280). Federal response to such abstract defiance was notably lacking. A group of distinguished leaders of the American bar in mid-1956 did denounce the attacks on the Supreme Court as "reckless in their abuse, . . . heedless of the value of judicial review and . . . dangerous in fomenting disrespect for our highest law." And the executive branch, responsible for implementing and enforcing the Constitution, was distressingly inactive when concrete challenge arose. When a Negro, Autherine Lucy, attempted unsuccessfully to enroll at the University of Alabama in 1956, federal authorities maintained a hands-off policy, and as late as August 1958, Walter Lippmann wrote: "There is no policy for carrying out integration. There is not only no policy, there is no program, no guidance, no rules on how to proceed. For the federal government, which has the duty of realizing the principle, has abstained from working out ways and means for realizing it."

The use of state troops to prevent the Federal Court-ordered integration of Central High School in Little Rock, Arkansas, in 1958, eventually forced the Eisenhower administration into action. Confronted with open state defiance of federal authority, the President reluctantly intervened, dispatching several companies of the United States Army to Little Rock under Section 333, Title 10, of the United

States Code, which authorized the suppression of insurrection and unlawful combinations hindering the execution of either state or federal law. Negroes thus attended school under military protection. The Little Rock School Board then obtained from a District Court judge a two-and-a-half-year suspension of the integration program because of "conditions of chaos, bedlam, and turmoil." Meeting in an extraordinary session in August for the express purpose of resolving the Little Rock controversy, the Supreme Court ruled against this delay. It emphasized the seriousness of state nullification in an opinion which listed each justice separately as author, an unprecedented practice and one not utilized since. In their formal opinion, handed down in September, the unanimous court issued to the states a solemn admonition against further defiance of the supreme law of the land as interpreted by the Court in the Brown case. "No state legislator or executive or judicial officer can war against the Constitution without violating his undertaking to support it." If he could, the Court said, quoting John Marshall, "the Constitution itself becomes a solemn mockery" (No. 281). The principle was reenforced by Congress through Title I of the 1960 Civil Rights Act, which made it a federal crime to obstruct or interfere with a federal court order, or to attempt to do so by threats or force.

Yet southern segregationists had just begun to fight. Virginia, under a program of "massive resistance," made it possible for counties to close their public schools. The legislature repealed the compulsory attendance laws and enacted a statute authorizing tuition grants for parents who wished to transfer their children from integrated public schools to private segregated ones. In the long run, however, this proved to be only another temporary and unsuccessful stall. In May 1964, the Supreme Court ordered Prince Edward County to reopen its public schools, maintaining unanimously that the Constitution did not permit the abolition of public schools in one county of a state while they remained open in others. But Justice Black went one step further in his resounding denunciation of further challenges to the Court's integration policy. Hinting that the pace of desegregation generally would have to pick up ("There has been entirely too much deliberation and not enough speed"), he stated categorically that "the time for more 'deliberate speed' has run out, and that phrase can no longer justify denying . . . schoolchildren their constitutional rights" to an equal education (No. 282). Although the ruling did not prevent diehard segregationists from continuing to contrive obstructionist schemes, it made it clear that the Court expected complete school desegregation immediately and that it stood by to nullify local actions to frustrate it. The enactment of the Civil Rights Act of 1964 (Title VI) seemed to indicate, however, that the process of securing school desegregation might be moved from the federal courts to federal administrative agencies, particularly to the Office of Education. In April 1965, that office issued regulations requiring a "good-faith substantial start" toward desegregation by school districts receiving federal funds. Whether the impact of federal funds or the size of the staff of the Office of Education is large enough to insure speedy compliance remains to be seen.

The integration of other types of tax-supported or licensed public facilities moved with considerably more dispatch than school desegregation. Following the Brown ruling in 1954, the Court had, in *Gayle v. Browder* (1956), explicitly overruled *Plessy v. Ferguson.* It clearly indicated that it would not only sustain enforced integration in interstate trains and buses and in public waiting rooms serving interstate travelers, but that it stood ready to order the end of Jim Crow laws in intrastate commerce (in this instance Montgomery, Alabama, buses), as well. By the early 1960's, often without writing formal opinions, the Court had also ordered integration in public parks and amphitheaters in those parks, public housing, public beaches, municipal golf courses and swimming pools, a leased courthouse cafeteria, seats in a courtroom, and public playgrounds; and had ruled that a statute prohibiting "mixed" athletic contests was void. Finally, in *Watson v. Memphis* (1963), the Court unanimously ruled that the "all deliberate speed" formula used in the school cases did not apply to public recreational facilities. "The basic guarantees of our Constitution," said Justice Goldberg's opinion, "are warrants for the here and now. . . ." In addition, the Court has cleared away Jim Crow restrictions imposed upon those using private facilities while traveling and dining, where those private facilities had some clear relation to interstate commerce. In so doing, it utilized both the commerce and equal protection clauses (*Burton v. Wilmington Parkway*, 1960; *Bailey v. Patterson*, 1962).

The legal integration of private facilities without a clear commerce connection, however, posed a considerably more complex problem. While many merchants, southern as well as northern, welcomed Negro patronage in a variety of stores and commercial facilities, many did not. Legal difficulties arose in coercing some citizens to use their property in ways they did not wish, especially since the Court had consistently maintained that it was essential to show that "state action" deprived the citizen of his rights, before such action could be proscribed. The sit-in movement of the early 1960's forced the issue into both national headlines and the courts. Many merchants and tradesmen had, for years, fallen back on local ordinances requiring segregation in private facilities as grounds for their refusal to integrate. Maintaining that their hands were tied by such ordinances, they argued that they could surely not be expected to break the law. Some even maintained that it was not for them to say whether segregated facilities were right or wrong since they were not the keepers of the community's morals.

In ruling such ordinances unconstitutional in 1963 (*Peterson v. Greenville* [No. 283]), the Supreme Court untied the hands of private citizens, ruling that they must ignore local segregation ordinances, which were unconstitutional since they violated the equal protection clause of the Fourteenth Amendment. The Court even went further, saying that private businessmen could not turn to other kinds of laws such as trespass ordinances and disorderly conduct statutes to evict people requesting service. The ruling, while not forcing integration of private facilities, at least put strong moral pressure upon their owners to make them available, voluntarily, to all would-be patrons.

Action by Congress provided the next legal element in this area. The Public Accommodations section of the 1964 Civil Rights Act (No. 284) provided the legislation to expedite making such facilities available. Although the law was carefully drawn so as to apply to a variety of limited private facilities, it generally required that service of any sizable number of the general public obligated service without discrimination. The Attorney General of the United States was also given authority to file public accommodations suits when he believed there was resistance to the measure. By late 1964, this Title had been upheld unanimously by the Supreme Court as a valid exercise of Congressional power under the Commerce Clause as applied to a motel in Atlanta and a restaurant in Birmingham, both of which had refused to serve Negroes (*Heart of Atlanta Motel v. U.S.; Katzenbach v. McClung*).

The Court also indicated its resoluteness in supporting the integration principle in a number of other disparate areas. In *Eubanks v. Louisiana* in 1958, it reaffirmed its condemnation of trials of Negroes by juries from which other Negroes had been deliberately excluded because of their race. In a series of cases involving the N. A. A. C. P. and other civil rights organizations, both national and local, it struck hard at a variety of local assaults upon them, ranging from attempts to drive the groups out of states to assaults upon their membership or glancing attacks, both personal and financial, upon their supporters, (*N. A. A. C. P. v. Alabama, 1958; Bates v. Little Rock, 1960; Shelton v. Tucker, 1960*). In 1963, it declared that a state's traditional right to regulate the conduct of lawyers could not be used to deny civil rights attorneys their freedom of speech to contact Negroes who might need legal counsel in civil rights cases (*N. A. A. C. P. v. Button*). Later in the same year, it also protected as freedom of speech, assembly, and the right of petition, the right of Negroes to march and demonstrate in orderly fashion, to protest discrimination and segregation practices (No. 285).

Such a right was not absolute, however. As Negro militancy tended to create more and more violence, mounting problems for law enforcement, and public concern and frequent hostility, the Court opened its 1966–67 term on a note of qualification. Speaking rather startlingly through Justice Black, normally its most advanced libertarian in the free speech area, it upheld the arrest of civil rights demonstrators marching on a jail where colleagues were held, sustaining a Florida law designed specifically to encourage curtailment of "malicious and mischievous" defiance of the state's general trespass statute (*Adderley v. Florida, 1966*). Finding no indication that the law was being used for any reason other than to insure jail security, Black considered such a use legitimate, even if free expression might, in the process, be curtailed. To four dissenters, such a rule was ominous and an invitation to use trespass and other comparable laws as a "blunderbuss to suppress civil rights." Only future application of the rule will indicate the extent of restrictiveness, something that Black, at least, could not see as inevitable.

Thus by the 1960's, a process which had begun with the enunciation of high principles by the executive and legislative branches—with the courts lonesomely mounting the firing line to carry them through—had been fully joined by all three branches of the government. Numerous states followed suit through solicitous legislation ranging from fair employment statutes to equal accommodations and other antidiscrimination laws.

Segregation in Housing

278. *Restrictive Covenants*

Shelley v. Kraemer, 334 U.S. 1 (1948).

VINSON, C.J.: . . . These cases present for our consideration questions relating to the validity of court enforcement of private agreements, generally described as restrictive covenants, which have as their purpose the exclusion of persons of designated race or color from the ownership or occupancy of real property. Basic constitutional issues of obvious importance have been raised. . . .

Petitioners urge that they have been denied the equal protection of the laws, deprived of property without due process of law, and have been denied privileges and immunities of citizens of the United States. . . .

It is well, at the outset, to scrutinize the terms of the restrictive agreements involved in these cases. . . . The covenant declares that no part of the affected property shall be "occupied by any person not of the Caucasian race, it being intended hereby to restrict the use of said property . . . against the occupancy as owners or tenants of any portion of said property for resident or other purpose by people of the Negro or Mongolian Race." . . .

It cannot be doubted that among the civil rights intended to be protected from discriminatory state action by the Fourteenth Amendment are the rights to acquire, enjoy, own and dispose of property. Equality in the enjoyment of property rights was regarded by the framers of that Amendment as an essential pre-condition to the realization of other basic civil rights and liberties which the Amendment was intended to guarantee. . . .

It is . . . clear that restrictions on the right of occupancy of the sort sought to be created by the private agreements in these cases could not be squared with the requirements of the Fourteenth Amendment if imposed by state statute or local ordinance. We do not understand respondents to urge the contrary. . . .

But the present cases, unlike those just discussed, do not involve action by state legislatures or city councils. Here the particular patterns of discrimination and the areas in which the restrictions are to operate, are determined, in the first instance, by the terms of agreements among private individuals. Participation of the State consists in the enforcement of the restrictions so defined. The crucial issue with which we are here confronted is whether this distinction removes these cases from the operation of the prohibitory provisions of the Fourteenth Amendment.

Since the decision of this Court in the Civil Rights Cases . . . (1883), the principle has become firmly embedded in our constitutional law that the action inhibited by the first section of the Fourteenth Amendment is only such action as may fairly be said to be that of the States. That Amendment erects no shield against merely private conduct, however discriminatory or wrongful.

We conclude, therefore, that the restrictive agreements standing alone cannot be regarded as a violation of any rights guaranteed to petitioners by the Fourteenth Amendment. So long as the purposes of those agreements are effectuated by voluntary adherence to their terms, it would appear clear that there has been no action by the State and the provisions of the Amendment have not been violated. . . .

But here there was more. These are cases in which the purposes of the agreements were secured only by judicial enforcement by state courts of the restrictive terms of the agreements. The respondents urge that judicial enforcement of private agreement does not amount to state action; or, in any event, the participation of the States is so attenuated in character as not to amount to state action within the meaning of the Fourteenth Amendment. Finally, it is suggested, even if the States in these cases may be deemed to have acted in the constitutional sense, their action did not deprive petitioners of rights guaranteed by the Fourteenth Amendment. We move to a consideration of these matters. . . .

The short of the matter is that from the time of the adoption of the Fourteenth Amendment until the present, it has been the consistent ruling of this Court that the action of the States to which the Amendment has reference includes action of state courts and state judicial officials. Although, in construing the terms of the Fourteenth Amendment, differences have from time to time been expressed as to whether particular types of state action may be said to offend the Amendment's prohibitory provisions, it has never been suggested that state court action is immunized from the operation of those provisions simply because the act is that of the judicial branch of the state government.

Against this background of judicial construction, extending over a period of some three-quarters of a century, we are called upon to consider whether enforcement by state courts of the restrictive agreements in these cases may be deemed to be the acts of those States; and, if so, whether that action has denied these petitioners the equal protection of the laws which the Amendment was intended to insure. . . .

These are not cases, as has been suggested, in which the States have merely abstained from action, leaving private individuals free to impose such discriminations as they see fit. Rather, these are cases in which the States have made available to such individuals the full coercive power of government to deny to petitioners, on the grounds of race or color, the enjoyment of property rights in premises which petitioners are willing and financially able to acquire and which the grantors are willing to sell. The difference between judicial enforcement and nonenforcement of the restrictive covenants is the difference to petitioners between being denied rights of property available to other members of the community and being accorded full enjoyment of those rights on an equal footing. . . .

We hold that in granting judicial enforcement of the restrictive agreements in these cases, the States have denied petitioners the equal protection of the laws and that, therefore, the action of the state courts cannot stand. . . .

The Struggle for Integrated Education

279. *The Court Discards the "Separate but Equal" Doctrine*

Brown v. Board of Education of Topeka, 347 U.S. 483 (1954).

WARREN, C.J.: These cases come to us from the States of Kansas, South Carolina, Virginia, and Delaware. They are premised on different facts and different local conditions, but a common legal question justifies their consideration together in this consolidated opinion.

In each of the cases, minors of the Negro race, through their legal representatives, seek the aid of the courts in obtaining admission to the public schools of their community on a nonsegregated basis. In each instance, they had been denied admission to schools attended by white children under laws requiring or permitting segregation according to race. This segregation was alleged to deprive the plaintiffs of the equal protection of the laws under the Fourteenth Amendment. In each of the cases other than the Delaware case, a three-judge federal district court denied relief to the plaintiffs on the so-called "separate but equal" doctrine announced by this Court in *Plessy v. Ferguson*. . . . Under that doctrine, equality of treatment is accorded when the races are provided substantially equal facilities, even though these facilities be separate. In the Delaware case, the Supreme Court of Delaware adhered to the doctrine, but ordered that the plaintiffs be admitted to the white schools because of their superiority to the Negro schools.

The plaintiffs contend that segregated public schools are not "equal" and cannot be made "equal," and that hence they are deprived of the equal protection of the laws. Because of the obvious importance of the question presented, the Court took jurisdiction. Argument was heard in the 1952 Term, and reargument was heard this Term on certain questions propounded by the Court.

Reargument was largely devoted to the circumstances surrounding the adoption of the Fourteenth Amendment in 1868. It covered exhaustively consideration of the Amendment in Congress, ratification by the states, then existing practices in racial segregation, and the views of proponents and opponents of the Amendment. This discussion and our own investigation convince us that, although these sources cast some light, it is not enough to resolve the problem with which we are faced. At best, they are inconclusive. The most avid proponents of the post-War Amendments undoubtedly intended them to remove all legal distinctions among "all persons born r naturalized in the United States." Their opponents, just as certainly, were antagonistic to both the letter and the spirit of the Amendments and wished them to have the most limited effect. What others in Congress and the state legislature had in mind cannot be determined with any degree of certainty.

An additional reason for the inconclusive nature of the Amendment's history, with respect to segregated schools, is the status of public education at that time. In the South, the movement toward free common schools, supported by general taxation, had not yet taken hold. Education of white children was largely in the hands of private groups. Education of Negroes was almost nonexistent, and practically all of the race were illiterate. In fact, any education of Negroes was forbidden by law in some states. Today, in contrast, many Negroes have achieved outstanding success in the arts and sciences as well as in the business and professional world. It is true that public education had already advanced further in the North, but the effect of the Amendment on Northern States was generally ignored in the congressional debates. Even in the North, the conditions of public education did not approximate those existing today. The curriculum was usually rudimentary; ungraded schools were common in rural areas; the school term was but three months a year in many states; and compulsory school attendance was virtually unknown. As a consequence, it is not surprising that there should be so little in the history of the Fourteenth Amendment relating to its intended effect on public education.

In the first cases in this Court construing the Fourteenth Amendment, decided shortly after its adoption, the Court interpreted it as proscribing all state-imposed discriminations against the Negro race. The doctrine of "separate but equal" did not make its appearance in this Court until 1896 in the case of *Plessy v. Ferguson* . . . involving not education but transportation. American courts have since labored with the doctrine for over half a century. In this Court, there have been six cases involving the "separate but equal" doctrine in the field of public education. In *Cumming v. County Board of Education* . . . [1899], and *Gong Lum v. Rice* . . . [1927], the validity of the doctrine itself was not challenged. In more recent cases, all on the graduate school level, inequality was found in that specific benefits enjoyed by white students were denied to Negro students of the same educational qualifications. . . . [*Gaines, Sipuel, Sweatt, McLaurin.*] In none of these cases was it necessary to reexamine the doctrine to grant relief to the Negro plaintiff. And in *Sweatt v. Painter* . . . , the Court expressly reserved decision on the question whether *Plessy v. Ferguson* should be held inapplicable to public education.

In the instant cases, that question is directly presented. Here, unlike *Sweatt v. Painter,* there are findings below that the Negro and white schools involved have been equalized, or are being equalized, with respect to buildings, curricula, qualifications and salaries of teachers, and other "tangible" factors. Our decision, therefore, cannot turn on merely a comparison of these tangible factors in the Negro and white schools involved in each of the cases. We must look instead to the effect of segregation itself on public education.

In approaching this problem, we cannot turn the clock back to 1868 when the Amendment was adopted, or even to 1896 when *Plessy v. Ferguson* was written. We must consider public education in the light of its full development and its present place in American life throughout the Nation. Only in this way can it be determined if segregation in public schools deprives these plaintiffs of the equal protection of the laws.

Today, education is perhaps the most important function of state and local governments. Compulsory school attendance laws and the great expenditures for education both demonstrate our recognition of the importance of education to our democratic society. It is required in the performance of our most basic public responsibilities, even service in the armed forces. It is the very foundation of good citizenship. Today it is a principal instrument in awakening the child to cultural values, in preparing him for later professional training, and in helping him to adjust normally to his environment. In these days, it is doubtful that any child may reasonably be expected to succeed in life if he is denied the opportunity of an education. Such an opportunity, where the state has undertaken to provide it, is a right which must be made available to all on equal terms.

We come then to the question presented: Does segregation of children in public schools solely on the basis of race, even though the physical facilities and other "tangible" factors may be equal, deprive the children of the minority group of equal educational opportunities? We believe that it does.

In *Sweatt v. Painter,* . . . in finding that a segregated law school for Negroes could not provide them equal educational opportunities, this Court relied in large part on "those qualities which are incapable of objective measurement but which make for greatness in a law school." In *McLaurin v. Oklahoma State Regents,* . . . the Court, in requiring that a Negro admitted to a white graduate school be treated like all other students, again resorted to intangible considerations: ". . . his ability to study, to engage in discussions and exchange views with other students, and, in general, to learn his profession." Such considerations apply with added force to children in grade and high schools. To separate them from others of similar age and qualifications solely because of their race generates a feeling of inferiority as to their status in the community that may affect their hearts and minds in a way unlikely ever to be undone. The effect of this separation on their educational opportunities was well stated by a finding in the Kansas case by a court which nevertheless felt compelled to rule against the Negro plaintiffs:

> Segregation of white and colored children in public schools has a detrimental effect upon the colored children. The impact is greater when it has the sanction of the law; for the policy of separating the races is usually interpreted as denoting the inferiority of the Negro group. A sense of inferiority affects the motivation of a child to learn. Segregation with the sanction of law, therefore, has a tendency to retard the educational and mental development of Negro children and to deprive them of some of the benefits they would receive in a racially integrated school system.

Whatever may have been the extent of psychological knowledge at the time of *Plessy v. Ferguson,* this finding is amply supported by modern authority. Any language in *Plessy v. Ferguson* contrary to this finding is rejected.

We conclude that in the field of public education the doctrine of "separate but equal" has no place. Separate educational facilities are inherently unequal. Therefore, we hold that the plaintiffs and others similarly situated for whom the actions have been brought are, by reason of the segregation complained of, deprived of the equal protection of the laws guaranteed by the Fourteenth Amendment. This disposition makes unnecessary any discussion whether such segregation also violates the Due Process Clause of the Fourteenth Amendment.

Because these are class actions, because of the wide applicability of this decision, and because of the great variety of local conditions, the formulation of decrees in these cases presents problems of considerable complexity. On reargument the consideration of appropriate relief was necessarily subordinated to the primary question—the constitutionality of segregation in public education. We have now announced that such segregation is a denial of the equal protection of the laws. In order that we may have the full assistance of the parties in formulating decrees, the cases will be restored to the docket, and the parties are requested to present further argument on Questions 4 and 5 previously propounded by the Court for the reargument this Term. The Attorney General of the United States is again invited to participate. The Attorneys General of the states requiring or permitting segregation in public education will also be permitted to appear as *amici curiae* upon request to do so by September 15, 1954, and submission of briefs by October 1, 1954.

It is so ordered.

280. *Declaration on Integration by Ninety-six Southern Congressmen*

The New York Times, March 12, 1956.

We regard the decision of the Supreme Court in the school cases as clear abuse of judicial power. It climaxes a trend in the Federal judiciary undertaking to legislate, in derogation of the authority of Congress, and to encroach upon the reserved rights of the states and the people.

The original Constitution does not mention education. Neither does the Fourteenth Amendment nor any other amendment. The debates preceding the submission of the Fourteenth Amendment clearly show that there was no intent that it should affect the systems of education maintained by the states.

The very Congress which proposed the amendment subsequently provided for segregated schools in the District of Columbia.

When the amendment was adopted in 1868, there were thirty-seven states of the Union. Every one of the twenty-six states that had any substantial racial differences among its people either approved the operation of segregated schools already in existence or subsequently established such schools by action of the same law-making body which considered the Fourteenth Amendment.

As admitted by the Supreme Court in the public school case (*Brown v. Board of Education*), the doctrine of separate but equal schools "apparently originated in *Roberts v. City of Boston* (1849), upholding school segregation against attack as being violative of a state constitutional guarantee of equality." This constitutional doctrine began in the North—not in the South—and it was followed not only in Massachusetts but in Connecticut, New York, Illinois, Indiana, Michigan, Minnesota, New Jersey, Ohio, Pennsylvania and other northern states until they, exercising their rights as states through the constitutional processes of local self-government, changed their school systems.

In the case of *Plessy v. Ferguson* in 1896 the Supreme Court expressly declared that under the Fourteenth Amendment no person was denied any of his rights if the states provided separate but equal public facilities. This decision has been followed in many other cases. It is notable that the Supreme Court, speaking through Chief Justice Taft, a former President of the United States, unanimously declared in 1927 in *Lum v. Rice* that the "separate but equal" principle is ". . . within the discretion of the state in regulating its public schools and does not conflict with the Fourteenth Amendment."

This interpretation, restated time and again, became a part of the life of the people of many of the states and confirmed their habits, customs, traditions and way of life. It is founded on elemental humanity and common sense, for parents should not be deprived by Government of the right to direct the lives and education of their own children.

Though there has been no constitutional amendment or act of Congress changing this established legal principle almost a century old, the Supreme Court of the United States, with no legal basis for such action, undertook to exercise their naked judicial power and substituted their personal political and social ideas for the established law of the land.

This unwarranted exercise of power by the court, contrary to the Constitution, is creating chaos and confusion in the states principally affected. It is destroying the amicable relations between the white and Negro races that have been created through ninety years of patient effort by the good people of both races. It has planted hatred and suspicion where there has been heretofore friendship and understanding.

Without regard to the consent of the governed, outside agitators are theatening immediate and revolutionary changes in our public school systems. If done, this is certain to destroy the system of public education in some of the states.

With the gravest concern for the explosive and dangerous condition created by this decision and inflamed by outside meddlers:

We reaffirm our reliance on the Constitution as the fundamental law of the land.

We decry the Supreme Court's encroachments on rights reserved to the states and to the people, contrary to established law and to the Constitution.

We commend the motives of those states which have declared the intention to resist forced integration by any lawful means.

We appeal to the states and people who are not directly affected by these decisions to consider the constitutional principles involved against the time when they too, on issues vital to them, may be the victims of judicial encroachment.

Even though we constitute a minority in the present Congress, we have full faith that a majority of the American people believe in the dual system of government which has enabled us to achieve our greatness and will in time demand that the reserved rights of the states and of the people be made secure against judicial usurpation.

We pledge ourselves to use all lawful means to bring about a reversal of this decision which is contrary to the Constitution and to prevent the use of force in its implementation.

In this trying period, as we all seek to right this wrong, we appeal to our people not to be provoked by the agitators and troublemakers invading our states and to scrupulously refrain from disorder and lawless acts.

281. *Does Violent Local Defiance Warrant Suspension of Legitimate Federal Programs?*

Cooper v. Aaron, 358 U.S. 1 (1958).

Opinion of the Court by THE CHIEF JUSTICE, MR. JUSTICE BLACK, MR. JUSTICE FRANKFURTER, MR. JUSTICE DOUGLAS, MR. JUSTICE BURTON, MR. JUSTICE CLARK, MR. JUSTICE HARLAN, MR. JUSTICE BRENNAN, and MR. JUSTICE WHITTAKER:

. . . On February 20, 1958, the School Board and the Superintendent of Schools filed a petition in the District Court seeking a postponement of their program of desegregation. Their position in essence was that because of extreme hostility, which they stated had been engendered largely by the official attitudes and actions of the Governor and the Legislature, the maintenance of a sound educational program at Central High School, with the Negro students in attendance, would be impossible. The Board therefore proposed that the Negro students already admitted to the school be withdrawn and sent to segregated schools, and that all further steps to carry out the Board's desegregation program be postponed for a period later suggested by the Board to be two and one-half years. . . .

One may well sympathize with the position of the Board in the face of the frustrating conditions which have confronted it, but, regardless of the Board's good faith, the actions of the other state agencies responsible for those conditions compel us to reject the Board's legal position. . . .

The constitutional rights of respondents are not to be sacrificed or yielded to the violence and disorder which have followed upon the actions of the Governor and Legislature. . . .

. . . the constitutional rights of children not to be discriminated against in school admission on grounds of race or color declared by this Court in the Brown case can neither be nullified openly and directly by state legislators or state executive or judicial officers, nor nullified indirectly by them through evasive schemes for segregation whether attempted "ingeniously or ingenuously." *Smith v. Texas.*

What has been said, in the light of the facts developed, is enough to dispose of the case. However, we should answer the premise of the actions of the Governor and Legislature that they are not bound by our holding in the Brown case. It is necessary only to recall some basic constitutional propositions which are settled doctrine.

Article VI of the Constitution makes the Constitution the "supreme Law of the Land." In 1803, Chief Justice Marshall, speaking for a unanimous Court, referring to the Constitution as "the fundamental and paramount law of the nation," declared in the notable case of *Marbury v. Madison* that "It is emphatically the province and duty of the judicial department to say what the law is." This decision declared the basic principle that the federal judiciary is supreme in the exposition of the law of the Constitution, and that principle has ever since been respected by this

Court and the country as a permanent and indispensable feature of our constitutional system. It follows that the interpretation of the Fourteenth Amendment enunciated by this Court in the Brown case is the supreme law of the land . . .

No state legislator or executive or judicial officer can war against the Constitution without violating his undertaking to support it . . .

It is, of course, quite true that the responsibility for public education is primarily the concern of the states, but it is equally true that such responsibilities, like all other state activity, must be exercised consistently with federal constitutional requirements as they apply to state action. The Constitution created a government dedicated to equal justice under law. The Fourteenth Amendment embodied and emphasized that ideal. State support of segregated schools through any arrangement, management, funds, or property cannot be squared with the Amendment's command that no state shall deny to any person within its jurisdiction the equal protection of the laws. The right of a student not to be segregated on racial grounds in schools so maintained is indeed so fundamental and pervasive that it is embraced in the concept of due process of law. *Bolling v. Sharpe*, . . . The basic decision in Brown was unanimously reached by this Court only after the case had been briefed and twice argued and the issue had been given the most serious consideration. Since the first Brown opinion three new Justices have come to the Court. They are at one with the Justices still on the Court who participated in that basic decision as to its correctness, and that decision is now unanimously reaffirmed. The principles announced in that decision and the obedience of the states to them, according to the command of the Constitution, are indispensable for the protection of the freedoms guaranteed by our fundamental charter for all of us. Our constitutional ideal of equal justice under law is thus made a living truth.

282. *"The time for mere 'deliberate speed' has run out. . . ."*

Griffin v. School Board of Prince Edward County, 377 U.S. 218 (1964).

BLACK, J.: . . . the Supreme Court of Appeals of Virginia upheld as valid under state law the closing of the Prince Edward County public schools, the state and county tuition grants for children who attend private schools, and the county's tax concessions for those who make contributions to private schools. The same opinion also held that each county had "an option to operate or not to operate public schools." We accept this case as a definitive and authoritative holding of Virginia law, binding on us, but we cannot accept the Virginia court's further holding, based largely on the Court of Appeals' opinion in this case, that closing the country's public schools under the circumstances of the case did not deny the colored school children of Prince Edward County equal protection of the laws guaranteed by the Federal Constitution.

Since 1959, all Virginia counties have had the benefits of public schools but one: Prince Edward. . . . Virginia law, as here applied, unquestionably treats the school children of Prince Edward differently from the way it treats the school children of all other Virginia counties. Prince Edward children must go to a private school or none at all; all other Virginia children can go to public schools. Closing Prince Edward's schools bears more heavily on Negro children in Prince Edward County since white children there have accredited private schools which they can attend, while colored children until very recently have had no available private schools, and even the school they now attend is a temporary expedient. Apart from this expedient, the result is that Prince Edward County school children, if they go to school in their own county, must go to racially segregated schools which, although designated as private, are beneficiaries of county and state support.

A State, of course, has a wide discretion in deciding whether laws shall operate statewide or shall operate only in certain counties, the legislature "having in mind the needs and desires of each." *Salsburg v. Maryland,* . . . A State may wish to suggest, as Maryland did in *Salsburg,* that there are reasons why one county ought not to be treated like another. . . . But the record in the present case could not be clearer that Prince Edward's public schools were closed and private schools operated in their place with state and county assistance, for one reason, and one reason only: to ensure, through measures taken by the county and the State, that white and colored children in Prince Edward County would not, under any circumstances, go to the same school. Whatever nonracial grounds might support a State's allowing a county to abandon public schools, the object must be a constitutional one, and grounds of race and opposition to desegregation do not qualify as constitutional. . . .

The District Court held that "the public schools of Prince Edward County may not be closed to avoid the effect of the law of the land as interpreted by the Supreme Court, while the Commonwealth of Virginia permits other public schools to remain open at the expense of the taxpayers." . . . At the same time the court gave notice that it would . . . consider an order to accomplish this purpose if the public schools were not reopened by September 7, 1962. That day has long passed, and the schools are still closed. On remand, therefore, the court may find it necessary to consider further such an order. An order of this kind is within the court's power if required to assure these petitioners that their constitutional rights will no longer be denied them. The time for mere "deliberate speed" has run out, and that phrase can no longer justify denying these Prince Edward County school children their constitutional rights to an education equal to that afforded by the public schools in the other parts of Virginia. . . .

The Obligation to Serve All the Public

283. *State Action and Private Choice*

Peterson v. City of Greenville, 373 U.S. 244 (1963).

WARREN, C.J.: The petitioners were convicted in the Recorder's Court of the City of Greenville, South Carolina, for violating the trespass statute of that State. . . . [They] are Negro boys and girls who, on August 9, 1960, entered the S. H. Kress store in Greenville and seated themselves at the lunch counter for the purpose, as they testified, of being served. When the Kress manager observed the petitioners sitting at the counter, he "had one of [his] . . . employees call the Police Department and turn the lights off and state the lunch counter was closed." A captain of police and two other officers responded by proceeding to the store in a patrol car where they were met by other policemen and two state agents who had preceded them there. In the presence of the police and the state agents, the manager "announced that the lunch counter was being closed and would everyone leave" the area. The petitioners, who had been sitting at the counter for five minutes, remained seated and were promptly arrested. The boys were searched, and both boys and girls were taken to police headquarters.

The manager of the store did not request the police to arrest petitioners; he asked them to leave because integrated service was "contrary to local customs" of segregation at lunch counters and in violation of the following Greenville City ordinance requiring separation of the races in restaurants:

> It shall be unlawful for any person owning, managing or controlling any hotel, restaurant, cafe, eating house, boarding-house or similar establishment to furnish meals to white persons and colored persons in the same room, or at the same table, or at the same counter; provided, however, that meals may be served to white persons and colored persons in the same room where separate facilities are furnished. Separate facilities shall be interpreted to mean:
>
> (a) Separate eating utensils and separate dishes for the serving of food, all of which shall be distinctly marked by some appropriate color scheme or otherwise;
>
> (b) Separate tables, counters or booths;
>
> (c) A distance of at least thirty-five feet shall be maintained between the area where white and colored persons are served;
>
> (d) The area referred to in subsection (c) above shall not be vacant but shall be occupied by the usual display counters and merchandise found in a business concern of a similar nature;
>
> (e) A separate facility shall be maintained and used for the cleaning of eating utensils and dishes furnished the two races. Code of Greenville, 1953, as amended in 1958.

The manager and the police conceded that the petitioners were clean, well dressed, unoffensive in conduct, and that they sat quietly at the counter which was designed to accommodate 59 persons. The manager described his establishment as a national chain store of 15 or 20 departments, selling over 10,000 items. He stated that the general public was invited to do business at the store and that the patronage of Negroes was solicited in all departments of the store other than the lunch counter.

Petitioners . . . assert that they have been deprived of the equal protection of the laws secured to them against state action by the Fourteenth Amendment. . . .

The evidence in this case establishes beyond doubt that the Kress management's decision to exclude petitioners from the lunch counter was made because they were Negroes. It cannot be disputed that under our decisions "private conduct abridging individual rights does no violence to the Equal Protection Clause unless to some significant extent the State in any of its manifestations has been found to have become involved in it." . . .

It cannot be denied that here the City of Greenville, an agency of the State, has provided by its ordinance that the decision as to whether a restaurant facility is to be operated on a desegregated basis is to be reserved to it. When the State has commanded a particular result, it has saved to itself the power to determine that result and thereby "to a significant extent" has "become involved" in it, and, in fact, has removed that decision from the sphere of private choice. It has thus effectively determined that a person owning, managing or controlling an eating place is left with no choice of his own but must segregate his white and Negro patrons. The Kress management, in deciding to exclude Negroes, did precisely what the city law required.

Consequently these convictions cannot stand, even assuming, as respondent contends, that the manager would have acted as he did independently of the existence of the ordinance. The State will not be heard to make this contention in support of the convictions. For the convictions had the effect, which the State cannot deny, of enforcing the ordinance passed by the City of Greenville, the agency of the State. When a state agency passes a law compelling persons to discriminate against other persons because of race, and the State's criminal processes are employed in a way which enforces the discrimination mandated by that law, such a palpable violation of the Fourteenth Amendment cannot be saved by attempting to separate the mental urges of the discriminators.

Reversed.

284. *The Civil Rights Act of 1964*

U.S. Commission on Civil Rights, *Civil Rights Digest* (Special Bulletin—August, 1964).

Title II: PUBLIC ACCOMMODATIONS

Discrimination on the basis of race, color, religion, or national origin is specifically forbidden in the following places of public accommodation:

(*a*) hotels and motels, restaurants, lunch counters, movie houses, gasoline stations, theaters and stadiums;

(*b*) any other establishment which offers its services to patrons of the covered establishment; for example,

—a barbershop or tavern located in a hotel, or

—a department store in which there is a restaurant: so long as the covered facilities either affect interstate commerce in their operations, or are supported in their discriminatory practices by State action.

In addition, discrimination is forbidden in any other place of public accommodation that is required to segregate by State or local laws.

If there are no State or local laws requiring segregation, the Federal law does not cover:

(*a*) barbershops, beauty parlors and other service establishments unless they are located in a hotel and offer these services to hotel guests;

(*b*) retail stores that do not serve food, or places of recreation (except as listed above) which do not serve food;

(*c*) lodging houses, hotels or similar places which take temporary guests if they have fewer than six rooms for rent in a building occupied by the owner.

Places that are actually owned and operated as private clubs are exempted from coverage of this title except to the extent that they offer their facilities to patrons of a covered establishment, such as a country club that customarily allows guests of a hotel to use its golf course.

No person may intimidate, threaten or coerce anyone for the purpose of interfering with the rights created by this title. . . .

The provisions of this title may be enforced in two ways:

1. By individual action in a civil suit filed by the persons discriminated against, or

2. By Government action in a civil suit filed by the Attorney General.

In public accommodations suits filed by individuals:

—the court hearing the suit may appoint a lawyer for the person bringing the complaint and exempt the complainant from the payment of certain costs;

—the court may permit the Attorney General to enter the case;

—if there is a State law or local ordinance that prohibits discrimininination, the complaint must first be taken to the State or local authorities, allowing them thirty days to begin a proceeding before suit can be filed in a Federal court;

—once the case is in court, the court can postpone action until the State or local proceeding is completed;

—if there are no State or local antidiscrimination provisions, the court may refer the matter to the Community Relations Service (see Title X) so that it may seek to secure voluntary compliance within no more than 120 days.

The Attorney General may file a public accommodations suit when he believes that there is a pattern or practice of resistance. As in Title I voting suits, he may request a three-judge court for this action.

In public accommodations suits brought either by individuals or the Attorney General, the court may issue temporary or permanent injunctions or restraining orders against those found to be violating the law. A person or persons failing to obey such court decrees may be punished by contempt proceedings under the jury trials provision of the law (see Title XI).

Title III: PUBLIC FACILITIES

The Attorney General is authorized to bring a civil suit to compel desegregation of any publicly owned or operated facility whenever he receives a written complaint of discrimination. He must believe that the complaint merits action and must certify that the individual or individuals making the complaint are themselves unable to take the necessary legal action. State or municipally owned or operated parks, libraries and hospitals are among the facilities covered.

285. *"The Fourteenth Amendment does not permit a State to make criminal the peaceful expression of unpopular views."*

Edwards v. South Carolina, 372 U.S. 229 (1963).

STEWART, J.: . . . The circumstances in this case reflect an exercise of these basic constitutional rights in their most pristine and classic form. The petitioners felt aggrieved by laws of South Carolina which allegedly "prohibited Negro privileges in this State." They peaceably assembled at the site of the State Government and there peaceably expressed their grievances "to the citizens of South Carolina, along with the Legislative Bodies of South Carolina." Not until they were told by police officials that they must disperse on pain of arrest did they do more. Even then, they but sang patriotic and religious songs after one of their leaders had delivered a "religious harangue." There was no violence or threat of violence on their part, or on the part of any member of the crowd watching them. Police protection was "ample." . . .

We do not review in this case criminal convictions resulting from the evenhanded application of a precise and narrowly drawn regulatory statute evincing a legislative judgment that certain specific conduct be limited or proscribed. If, for example, the petitioners had been convicted upon evidence that they had violated a law regulating traffic, or had disobeyed a law reasonably limiting the periods during which the State House grounds were open to the public, this would be a different case. These petitioners were convicted of an offense so generalized as to be, in the words of the South Carolina Supreme Court, "not susceptible of exact definition." And they were convicted upon evidence which showed no more than that the opinions which they were peaceably expressing were sufficiently opposed to the views of the majority of the community to attract a crowd and necessitate police protection.

The Fourteenth Amendment does not permit a State to make criminal the peaceful expression of unpopular views. "[A] function of free speech under our system of government is to invite dispute. It may indeed best serve its high purpose when it induces a condition of unrest, creates dissatisfaction with conditions as they are, or even stirs people to anger. Speech is often provocative and challenging. It may strike at prejudices and preconceptions and have profound unsettling effects as it presses for acceptance of an idea. That is why freedom of speech . . . is . . . protected against censorship or punishment, unless shown likely to produce a clear and present danger of a serious substantive evil that rises far above public inconvenience, annoyance, or unrest. . . . There is no room under our Constitution for a more restrictive view. For the alternative would lead to standardization of ideas either by legislatures, courts, or dominant political or community groups." *Terminiello v. Chicago.* As in the Terminiello case, the courts of South Carolina have defined a criminal offense so as to permit conviction of the petitioners if their speech "stirred people to anger, invited public dispute, or brought about a condition of unrest." A conviction resting on any of those grounds may not stand.

CHAPTER XXXI

The Franchise: Expansion and Reorientation

The ability of the electorate to make its wishes felt through the franchise has been at the core of the democratic system. Yet the right to vote, from the beginning of American history, has been qualified by a variety of factors, ranging from age, sex, and residence, through color, and controlled through regulations ranging from the poll tax and literacy tests to the actions of registrars and ballot counters. Congress left to the states the question of the way votes would count. Thus Congressional districts were to be set up along the skeletal guidelines afforded by Article I, Section 2 of the Constitution, but with broad discretion in their establishment. Similarly, the structure of state legislatures was considered a local issue, and if inequities arose which resulted in public demands for correction, redress lay in the political process. Indeed, as early as 1849 in *Luther v. Borden,* the Supreme Court maintained that issues arising in this area constituted "political questions" for which there was no clear judicial relief. The Fifteenth Amendment, as interpreted by the Courts in the late nineteenth century, altered the situation very little.

But by the 1940's, concern over violation of the right to vote and to have that vote counted fairly was forcing the Court to rethink its position. It was prepared to rule devices such as the Grandfather Clause and the White Primary unconstitutional infringements upon this right and in violation of the guarantees of the Fifteenth Amendment (see Chapter XXIV). And it was at least willing to take cases on the question of reapportionment. In *Colegrove v. Green* in 1946, although the Court dismissed a challenge to Illinois' unequal Congressional districts on the traditional "political question" grounds, four of the seven participating Justices treated apportionment as a justiciable matter, thus leaving the door open for later challenges.

In the postwar years the voting issue intensified. Not only did the clamor increase for the elimination of practices disfranchising eligible Negroes, but with the rapid growth of urban and suburban areas, the frank refusal by rurally dominated legislatures to give their inhabitants political power commensurate with their new populations brought demands for reapportionment. Yet much as with the postwar integration situation, the most direct avenue for immediate relief was the courts. The Justices here moved cautiously, however. Although they had no trouble striking down further southern attempts to disfranchise Negroes through none too subtle local preprimary arrangements (*Terry v. Adams* [No. 286]), they were still highly cautious in tampering with state prerogatives in the districting area, ruling in *South v. Peters* in 1950 (No. 287), for example, that a state's geographical distribution of electoral strength was still a political question. Again, however, a minority voice was heard. Justice Douglas, in a dramatic dissent, denounced the Georgia county-unit system as a device "as deeply rooted in discrimination as the practice which keeps a man from the voting booth because of his race, creed, or color," and suggested strongly that such watering down of the power of the citizen's ballot constituted a denial of his equal protection under the law (No. 288).

In 1957, the courts were joined in this area by Congress. Concerned that no judicial ruling could by itself undermine the practices of discrimination still prevalent at southern polls, Congress passed the first of a series of Civil Rights Acts, setting up a Civil Rights Commission to investigate complaints that the right to vote was being denied to persons for reasons of race and color, and giving it authority to hold public and private hearings on voting discrimination (No. 289). In addition, the measure made it a federal crime to intimidate persons or prevent them from voting in general or primary elections for federal offices, authorizing the Attorney General to seek an injunction when an individual was deprived or about to be deprived of his right to vote. The measure was defied in a number of ways by southerners, and a Georgia federal district court promptly ruled the injunction section unconstitutional. Supreme Court response was quick and decisive, with the Justices not only reversing the Georgia ruling and by implication sustaining fully the constitutionality of the measure (*U.S. v. Raines, 1960*) but also ordering Louisiana authorities to restore the names of nearly 1,400 Negro voters who had been arbitrarily removed from parish registration rolls (*U.S. v. Thomas, 1960*).

Southerners in certain areas, fearing that impediments to the actual casting of Negro votes would be eliminated eventually, attempted new ways to manipulate the Negro vote so as to destroy its impact. In Alabama, this resulted in a 1957 law gerrymandering the city of Tuskegee, home of the famed Negro college, Tuskegee Institute. But by 1960, the Court and Congress seemed to be working in tandem. In that year Congress enacted the second Civil Rights Act authorizing the appointment by federal courts of voter-referees to monitor situations in which disfranchisement seemed forthcoming, and requiring that voting records and registration papers for all federal elections, including primaries, be preserved for twenty-two months, thus attempting to prevent their further destruction by southerners set on defying investigations by the Civil Rights Commission. The Court struck down the Alabama gerrymandering law in a case brought by the chairman of the Division of Social Science of the Tuskegee Institute (*Gomillion v. Lightfoot* [No. 290]). In this decision, the Court carefully differentiated the Alabama case from *Colegrove v. Green,* observing that the issue was not one of diluting the strength of the vote through discriminatory apportionment of Congressional districts, but of affirmative state legislation depriving citizens of their votes on the basis of race, a bald violation of the Fifteenth Amendment. And the implications of the ruling were clear—state legislative districting action did not lie wholly outside judicial control. In addition, Justice Whittaker, in a brief concurring opinion, expressed his view that this issue, and, by implication, other comparable issues was clearly a question of equal protection, coming under the Fourteenth Amendment. The ruling was thus a tacit invitation for citizens to challenge other unequal districting arrangements as direct violations of their rights.

Baker v. Carr, the first of the historic reapportionment cases in 1962, was revolutionary in that it altered the traditional, federal hands-off policy toward districting and apportionment, but it was not wholly unexpected. In holding that urban Tennessee voters were denied equal protection of the laws by an apportionment system which debased their votes—the population disparities between some rural and urban areas exceeded a 22-to-1 ratio—and which the legislature had refused to change for sixty years, despite state constitutional provisions requiring regular ten-year readjustment, Justice Brennan stressed that the Court's decision was the next logical step beyond the Gomillion ruling. But while emphasizing the fact that the exhaustion of other remedies by the aggrieved parties had made the situation a justiciable cause of action, he remanded the case to the Tennessee district court with instructions to hear and decide the apportionment issue on its merits. Thus, in some ways parallel with *Brown v. Board of Education,* the Court turned the task of implementation over to federal district courts and by implication made such courts the avenues for revolution in the area of the franchise. The executive branch of the federal government indicated that it would support reapportionment under court direction when the Solicitor General filed an *amicus curiae* brief in the Tennessee case on behalf of the national government. After the Court announced its opinion, President Kennedy urged the states to rush reapportionment.

The reapportionment ruling had an almost instant impact throughout the nation. Within a short time, actions arose in thirty-nine of the fifty states challenging other local malapportionment practices. In 1963 the Court ruled that Georgia's county-unit system as applied to primary elections for United States Senator and state-wide officers denied underrepresented voters equal protection guaranteed by the Fourteenth Amendment (*Gray v. Sanders*). "The conception of political equality from the Declaration of Independence, to Lincoln's Gettysburg Address, to the Fifteenth, Seventeenth, and Nineteenth Amendments can mean only one thing," wrote a triumphant Justice Douglas for the Court, "one person, one vote." Early the following year, this principle was applied to representation in the federal House of Representatives, with the Court holding that Article I, Section 2 of the federal Constitution, which provides that Representatives in Congress be chosen "by the People of the several States," meant "that nearly as is practicable one man's vote in a congressional election is to be worth as much as another's" (*Wesberry v. Sanders*, 1964).

Hostility to the Court's rulings, strong on a number of fronts, crystallized with the next judicial move. In June 1964, in *Reynolds v. Sims* (No. 292) the Justices broadened the doctrine of *Baker v. Carr* by telescoping the imprecise elements of equality (the "equal protection of the laws" of the Fourteenth Amendment) into the slogan, "one person one vote," and made the doctrine applicable to both houses of state legislatures. In one of several companion cases (*Lucas v. Colorado*), it showed how far it was prepared to go in establishing the principle, rejecting a Senate reapportionment plan based on other than equitable population factors, which the voters of Colorado had approved through popular referendum by a nearly 2 to 1 majority. Angry voices in Congress responded sharply to both rulings, and many national leaders echoed Justice Harlan's strong protest in his Sims dissent, attacking the theory that "every major social ill in the country can find its cure in some 'constitutional principle.' " A number of assaults on the Court followed, along with proposals for delaying the implementation of the rulings or leaving it up to the current state legislatures. Senator Everett Dirksen of Illinois went further, proposing a constitutional amendment and eventually a constitutional convention to override the Sims and Lucas rulings, making it possible for the people of a state, through a referendum, to use 'factors other than population in apportioning one house of a bi-cameral legislature."

Pro-reapportionment elements promptly fought back, arguing especially that the vagueness of "other factors" would allow discrimination against Negroes and other minorities, and generally endorsing Chief Justice Warren's contention that "neither history alone, nor economic or other sorts of group interests, are permissible factors in attempting to justify disparities from population-based representation. Citizens, not history or economic interests, cast votes . . . people, not land or trees or pastures vote." Such citizens were apprehensive of delaying tactics since they saw in them the creation of the ironical situation, as one senator put it, of having "the rotten boroughs decide whether they should continue to be rotten." Rather, they saw nothing unreasonable in the Reynolds timetable, which urged that action be taken as soon as reasonably possible to alter legally challenged systems and that, lacking strong reasons, no further state elections should be conducted under invalid plans. And the general, if not always enthusiastic, acquiescence of practically all of the states indicated that continued hard-core defiance was unlikely.

On the Congressional front, a different type of action had been taking place. In 1961, the Twenty-third Amendment was added to the Constitution (No. 293A), extending long overdue voting rights to citizens of the District of Columbia, and in 1964 the Amendment process was also utilized to outlaw the poll tax in federal elections (No. 293B). More significantly, the Civil Rights Act of 1964 included a further set of provisions on election procedures, especially as they applied to registration requirements. The Court had ruled in *Lassiter v. Northampton Election Board* in 1959 that a state literacy test when impartially administered was allowable and not a violation of the Fifteenth Amendment, although Justice Douglas had been quick to admit that such a test, although fair on its face, might "be employed to perpetuate that discrimination which the amendment was designed to uproot." To meet growing complaints of just such discrimination, the 1964 Act not only provided uniform national standards for state registrars in qualifying voters, but required that only written literacy tests could be used as a qualification for voting and that the tests and answers must be available upon request.

But more was still needed. Addressing a joint session of Congress on March 15, 1965, President Lyndon B. Johnson stated: "Every American citizen must have an equal right to vote. There is no reason which can excuse the denial of that right. There is no duty which weighs more heavily on us than the duty we have to ensure that right." Yet the President was quick to point out that "every device of which human ingenuity is capable has been used to deny this right." He stressed that "experience has clearly shown that the existing process of law cannot overcome systematic and ingenious discrimination. No law that we now have on the books . . . can ensure the right to vote when local officials are determined to deny it."

The Voting Rights Act of 1965, which Mr. Johnson called for in his message, was enacted on August 6, 1965. Its provisions were sharp, clear, and drastic. The measure empowered the Attorney General to send federal registrars to any county he suspected of practicing discrimination. This was to include those with voting-qualification tests which clearly impeded registration and, more explicitly, those where 50 percent or more of the voting age population had failed to register or vote in 1964. The measure also instructed him to file suits to abolish poll taxes in state and local elections and suspended literacy tests as prerequisites to voting. This new law, which the administration began immediately to implement, was the most promising yet enacted in the voting rights area, particularly, as Alexander Bickel wrote at the time, since it "made an end run around the judicial process, and confronted recalcitrant Southern officials with the real locus of continuously effective federal power, which is the executive, rather than the judiciary." The immediate challenges to its constitutionality were quickly answered by the Supreme Court, with Chief Justice Warren, in early March 1966, sustaining fully the challenged sections and, by indirection, the inherent policy and philosophy of the measure (*South Carolina v. Katzenbach* [No. 294]).

Thus, a century and a quarter after England had struck down her "rotten borough" system in the Great Reform Bill of 1832, and nearly a century after the adoption of the Fifteenth Amendment, the American voting system was finally brought into harmony with the general principles and ideals of representative government. Leaders hoped this would induce the best educated, best informed electorate in the world to participate more fully, intelligently, and meaningfully in the democratic process.

Suffrage and Racial Discrimination

286. *The Case of the Texas Jaybirds*

Terry v. Adams, 345 U.S. 461 (1953).

BLACK, J.: . . . In *Smith v. Allwright* . . . (1944), we held that rules of the Democratic Party of Texas excluding Negroes from voting in the party's primaries violated the Fifteenth Amendment. While no state law directed such exclusion, our decision pointed out that many party activities were subject to considerable statutory control. This case raises questions concerning the constitutional power of a Texas county political organization called the Jaybird Democratic Association or Jaybird Party to exclude Negroes from its primaries on racial grounds. The Jaybirds deny that their racial exclusions violate the Fifteenth Amendment. They contend that the Amendment applies only to elections or primaries held under state regulation, that their association is not regulated by the state at all, and that it is not a political party but a self-governing voluntary club. . . .

There was evidence that:

The Jaybird Association or Party was organized in 1889. Its membership was then and always has been limited to white people; they are automatically members if their names appear on the official list of county voters. It has been run like other political parties with an executive committee named from the county's voting precincts. . . . While there is no legal compulsion on successful Jaybird candidates to enter Democratic primaries they have nearly always done so and with few exceptions since 1889 have run and won without opposition in the Democratic primaries and the general elections that followed. Thus the party has been the dominant political group in the county since organization, having endorsed every county-wide official elected since 1889.

It is apparent that Jaybird activities follow a plan purposefully designed to exclude Negroes from voting and at the same time to escape the Fifteenth Amendment's command that the right of citizens to vote shall neither be denied nor abridged on account of race. These were the admitted party purposes according to the following testimony of the Jaybird's president:

> Q. . . . One of the purposes of your organization is for the specific purpose of excluding Negroes from voting, isn't it?
>
> A. Yes. . . .
>
> Q. I will ask you, that is the reason you hold your election in May rather than in June or July, isn't it?
>
> A. Yes.
>
> Q. Because if you held it in July you would have to abide by the statutes and the law by letting them vote?
>
> A. They do vote in July. . . .
>
> Q. . . . My question is that you hold yours in May so you won't have to let them vote, don't you?
>
> A. Yes. . . .
>
> Q. That is the whole policy of your Association?
>
> A. Yes.
>
> Q. And that is its purpose?
>
> A. Yes.

The District Court found that the Jaybird Association was a political organization or party; that the majority of white voters generally abide by the results of its primaries and support in the Democratic primaries the persons endorsed by the Jaybird primaries; and that the chief object of the Association has always been to deny Negroes any voice or part in the election of Fort Bend County officials.

The facts and findings bring this case squarely within the reasoning and holding of the Court of Appeals for the Fourth Circuit in its two recent decisions about excluding Negroes from Democratic primaries in South Carolina. . . . South Carolina had repealed every trace of statutory or constitutional control of the Democratic primaries. It did this in the hope that thereafter the Democratic Party or Democratic "Clubs" of South Carolina would be free to continue discriminatory practices against Negroes as voters. The contention there was that the Democratic "Clubs" were mere private groups; the contention here is that the Jaybird Association is a mere private group. The Court of Appeals in invalidating the South Carolina practices answered these formalistic arguments by holding that no election machinery could be sustained if its purpose or effect was to deny Negroes on account of their race an effective voice in the governmental affairs of their country, state, or community. In doing so the Court relied on the principle announced in *Smith v. Allwright*, . . . that the constitutional right to be free from racial discrimination in voting ". . . is not to be nullified by a state through casting its electoral process in a form which permits a private organization to practice racial discrimination in the election." . . .

It is significant that precisely the same qualifications as those prescribed by Texas entitling electors to vote at county-operated primaries are adopted as the sole qualifications entitling electors to vote at the county-wide Jaybird primaries with a single proviso—Negroes are excluded. Everyone concedes that such a proviso in the county-operated primaries would be unconstitutional. The Jaybird Party thus brings into being and holds precisely the kind of election that the Fifteenth Amendment seeks to prevent. When it produces the equivalent of the prohibited election, the damage has been done. . . .

The Jaybird primary has become an integral part, indeed the only effective part, of the elective process that determines who shall rule and govern in the county. The effect of the whole procedure, Jaybird primary plus Democratic primary plus general election, is to do precisely that which the Fifteenth Amendment forbids—strip Negroes of every vestige of influence in selecting the officials who control the local county matters that intimately touch the daily lives of citizens. . . .

We affirm the District Court's holding that the combined Jaybird-Democratic-general election machinery has deprived these petitioners of their right to vote on account of their race and color. . . .

Apportionment and Discrimination

287. *The County-Unit System and Inequality of Representation*

Per curiam opinion, *South v. Peters,* 339 U.S. 276 (1950).

The Georgia statute which appellants attack as violative of the Fourteenth and Seventeenth Amendments provides that county unit votes shall determine the outcome of a primary election. Each county from six for the eight most populous coun- is allotted a number of unit votes, ranging ties, to two for most of the counties. The candidate who receives the highest popular vote in the county is awarded the appropriate number of unit votes. Appellants, residents of the most populous county in the state, contend that their votes and those of all other voters in that county have on the average but one-tenth the weight of those in the other counties. Urging that this amounts to an unconstitutional discrimination against them, appellants brought this suit to restrain adherence to the statute in the forthcoming Democratic Party primary for United States Senator, Governor and other state offices.

The court below dismissed appellants' petition. . . . We affirm. Federal courts consistently refuse to exercise their equity powers in cases posing political issues arising from a state's geographical distribution of electoral strength among its political subdivisions. See *MacDougall v. Green* . . . (1948); *Colegrove v. Green* . . . (1946). . . .

288. *The County-Unit System and Racial Discrimination*

South v. Peters, 339 U.S. 276 (1950).

DOUGLAS, J., dissenting: I suppose that if a State reduced the vote of Negroes, Catholics, or Jews so that each got only one-tenth of a vote, we would strike the law down. The right to vote in a primary was held in *Nixon v. Herndon* . . . to be covered by the Equal Protection Clause of the Fourteenth Amendment. And where, as in Georgia, a party primary election is an integral part of the state election machinery, the right to vote in it is protected by the Fifteenth Amendment. *Smith v. Allwright*. . . . Under both Amendments discriminations based on race, creed or color fall beyond the pale.

Yet there is evidence in this case showing that Georgia's County Unit System of consolidating votes in primary elections makes an equally invidious discrimination. Under this primary law the nomination does not go to the candidate who gets the majority or plurality of votes. Votes are counted county by county. The winner in each county gets a designated number of votes—six in the most populous counties, four in the next most populous, two in each of the rest.

Plaintiffs are registered voters in Georgia's most populous county—Fulton County. They complain that their votes will be counted so as drastically to reduce their voting strength.

They show that a vote in one county will be worth over 120 times each of their votes. They show that in 45 counties a vote will be given twenty times the weight of each of theirs. They show that on a statewide average each vote outside Fulton County will have over 11 times the weight of each vote of the plaintiffs.

Population figures show that there is a heavy Negro population in the large cities. There is testimony in the record that only in those areas have Negroes been able to vote in important numbers. Yet the County Unit System heavily disenfranchises that urban Negro population. The County Unit System has indeed been called the "last loophole" around our decisions holding that there must be no discrimination because of race in primary as well as in general elections.

The racial angle of the case only emphasizes the bite of the decision which sustains the County Unit System of voting. The discrimination against citizens in the more populous counties of Georgia is plain. Because they are city folks their voting power is only an eleventh or a hundred and twentieth of the voting power of other citizens. I can see no way to save that classification under the Equal Protection Clause. The creation by law of favored groups of citizens and the grant to them of preferred political rights is the worst of all discriminations under a democratic system of government. . . .

Congress Enters the Voting Arena

289. *The First Civil Rights Law Since Reconstruction*

The Civil Rights Act of 1957. *U.S. Stat. at L.,* LXXI, 634 (1957).

An act to provide means of further securing and protecting the civil rights of persons within the jurisdiction of the United States.

Part I—Establishment of the Commission on Civil Rights

Sec. 101. (a) There is created in the executive branch of the Government a Commission on Civil Rights (hereinafter called the "commission").

(b) The commission shall be composed of six members who shall be appointed by the President by and with the advice and consent of the Senate. Not more than three of the members shall at any one time be of the same political party. . . .

Duties of the Commission

Sec. 104 (a). The commission shall—

(1) Investigate allegations in writing under oath or affirmation that certain citizens of the United States are being deprived of their right to vote and have that vote counted by reason of their color, race, religion or national origin; which writing, under oath or affirmation, shall set forth the facts upon which such belief or beliefs are based.

(2) Study and collect information concerning legal developments constituting a denial of equal protection of the laws under the Constitution; and

(3) Appraise the laws and policies of the Federal Government with respect to equal protection of the laws under the Constitution.

(b) The commission shall submit interim reports to the President (3) and to the Congress at such times as either the commission or the President shall deem desirable and shall submit to the President (4) and to the Congress a final and comprehensive report of its activities, findings, and recommendations not later than two years from the date of the enactment of this act.

(c) Sixty days after the submission of its final report and recommendations the commission shall cease to exist.

Part IV—To Provide Means of Further Securing and Protecting the Right to Vote

Sec. 131. (c) Add, immediately following the present text, (13) four new subsections to read as follows:

(b) No person, whether acting under color of law or otherwise, shall intimidate, threaten, coerce or attempt to intimidate, threaten or coerce any other person for the purpose of interfering with the right of such other person to vote or to vote as he may choose, or of causing such other person to vote for, or not to vote for, any candidate for the office of President, Vice President, Presidential elector, member of the Senate or member of the House of Representatives, delegates or commissioners from the territories or possessions, at any general, special, or primary election held solely or in part for the purpose of selecting or electing any such candidate.

(c) Whenever any person has engaged or there are reasonable grounds to believe that any person is about to engage in any act or practice which would deprive any other person of any right or privilege secured by subsection (a) or (b), the Attorney General may institute for the United States, or in the name of the United States, a civil action or other proper proceeding for preventive relief, including an application for a permanent or temporary injunction, restraining order, or other order. In any proceeding hereunder the United States shall be liable for costs the same as a private person.

(d) The district courts of the United States shall have jurisdiction of proceedings instituted pursuant to this section and shall exercise the same without regard to whether the party aggrieved shall have exhausted any administrative or other remedies that may be provided by law.

(e) (14) Any person cited for an alleged contempt under this act shall be allowed to make his full defense by counsel learned in the law; and the court before which he is cited or tried, or some judge thereof, shall immediately, upon his request, assign to him such counsel, not exceeding two, as he may desire, who shall have free access to him at all reasonable hours. He shall be allowed, in his defense to make any proof that he can produce by lawful witnesses, and shall have the like process of the court to compel his witnesses to appear at his trial or hearing, as is usually granted to compel witnesses to appear on behalf of the prosecution. If such person shall be found by the court to be financially unable to provide for such counsel, it shall be the duty of the court to provide such counsel.

State Districting Action and Judicial Control

290. *State Authority Versus Federally Protected Rights*

Gomillion v. Lightfoot, 364 U.S. 339 (1960).

FRANKFURTER, J.: This litigation challenges the validity, under the United States Constitution of Local Act. N. 140, passed by the Legislature of Alabama in 1957, redefining the boundaries of the city of Tuskegee. . . . Petitioners' claim is that enforcement of the statute, which alters the shape of Tuskegee from a square to an uncouth twenty-eight-sided figure, will constitute a discrimination against them in violation of the Due Process and Equal Protection Clauses of the Fourteenth Amendment to the Constitution and will deny them the right to vote in defiance of the Fifteenth Amendment. . . .

The essential inevitable effect of this redefinition of Tuskegee's boundaries is to remove from the city all save only 4 or 5 of its 400 Negro voters while not removing a single white voter or resident. The result of the act is to deprive the Negro petitioners discriminatorily of the benefits of residence in Tuskegee, including *inter alia,* the right to vote in municipal elections.

These allegations, if proven, would abundantly establish that Act 140 was not an ordinary geographic redistricting measure even within familiar abuses of gerrymandering. If these allegations upon a trial remained uncontradicted or unqualified, the conclusion would be irresistible, tantamount for all practical purposes to a mathematical demonstration, that the legislation is solely concerned with segregating white and colored voters by fencing Negro citizens out of town so as to deprive them of their pre-existing municipal vote.

It is difficult to appreciate what stands in the way of adjudging a statute having this inevitable effect invalid in light of the principles by which this Court must judge, and uniformly has judged, statutes that, howsoever speciously defined, obviously discriminate against colored citizens. "The [Fifteenth] Amendment nullifies sophisticated as well as simple-minded modes of discrimination." *Lane v. Wilson.* . . .

A statute which is alleged to have

worked unconstitutional deprivations of petitioners' rights is not immune to attack simply because the mechanism employed by the legislature is a redefinition of municipal boundaries. According to the allegations here made, the Alabama Legislature has not merely redrawn the Tuskegee city limits with incidental inconvenience to the petitioners; it is more accurate to say that it has deprived the petitioners of the municipal franchise and consequent rights and to that end it has incidentally changed the city's boundaries. While in form this is merely an act redefining metes and bounds, if the allegations are established, the inescapable human effect of this essay in geometry and geography is to despoil colored citizens, and only colored citizens, of their theretofore enjoyed voting rights. . . .

When a state exercises power wholly within the domain of state interest, it is insulated from federal judicial review. But such insulation is not carried over when state power is used as an instrument for circumventing a federally protected right. This principle has had many applications. It has long been recognized in cases which have prohibited a state from exploiting a power acknowledged to be absolute in an isolated context to justify the imposition of an "unconstitutional condition." What the Court has said in those cases is equally applicable here, viz., that "Acts generally lawful may become unlawful when done to accomplish an unlawful end, . . . and a constitutional power cannot be used by way of condition to attain an unconstitutional result." . . . For these reasons, the principal conclusions of the District Court and the Court of Appeals are clearly erroneous and the decision below must be reversed.

291. *The Court Enters The "Political Thicket" of Reapportionment*

***Baker v. Carr*, 369 U.S., 186 (1962).**

Brennan, J.: . . . It is . . . alleged that "because of the population changes since 1900, and the failure of the legislature to reapportion itself since 1901," the 1901 statute became "unconstitutional and obsolete." Appellants also argue that, because of the composition of the legislature effected by the 1901 apportionment act, redress in the form of a state constitutional amendment to change the entire mechanism for reapportioning, or any other change short of that, is difficult or impossible. The complaint concludes that "these plaintiffs and others similarly situated, are denied the equal protection of the laws accorded them by the Fourteenth Amendment to the Constitution of the United States by virtue of the debasement of their votes." They seek a declaration that the 1901 statute is unconstitutional and an injunction restraining the appellees from acting to conduct any further elections under it. They also pray that unless and until the General Assembly enacts a valid reapportionment, the District Court should either decree a reapportionment by mathematical application of the Tennessee constitutional formulae to the most recent Federal Census figures, or direct the appellees to conduct legislative elections, primary and general, at large. . . .

Because we deal with this case on appeal from an order of dismissal granted on appellees' motions, precise identification of the issues presently confronting us demands clear exposition of the grounds upon which the District Court rested in dismissing the case. . . .

The District Court's dismissal order . . . rested . . . upon lack of subject-matter jurisdiction and lack of a justiciable cause of action without attempting to distinguish between these grounds. . . . It made clear that its dismissal reflected a view not of doubt that violation of constitutional rights was alleged, but of a court's impotence to correct that violation:

> With the plaintiffs' argument that the legislature of Tennessee is guilty of a clear violation of the state constitution and of the rights of the plaintiffs the Court entirely agrees. It also agrees that the evil is a serious one which should be corrected without further delay. But even so the remedy in this situation clearly does not lie with the courts. It has long been recognized and is accepted doctrine that there are indeed some rights guaranteed by the Constitution for the violation of which the courts cannot give redress.

In light of the District Court's treatment of the case, we hold today only (a) that the court possessed jurisdiction of the subject matter; (b) that a justiciable cause of action is stated upon which appellants would be entitled to appropriate relief; and (c) because appellees raise the issue before this Court, that the appellants have standing to challenge the Tennessee apportionment statutes. Beyond noting that we have no cause at this stage to doubt the District Court will be able to fashion relief if violations of constitutional rights are found, it is improper now to consider what remedy would be most appropriate if appellants prevail at the trial.

The District Court was uncertain whether our cases withholding federal judicial relief rested upon a lack of federal jurisdiction or upon the inappropriateness of the subject matter for judicial consideration—what we have designated "nonjusticiability." The distinction between the two grounds is significant. In the instance of nonjusticiability, consideration of the cause is not wholly immediately foreclosed; rather, the Court's inquiry necessarily proceeds to the point of deciding whether the duty asserted can be judicially identified and its breach judicially determined, and whether protection for the right asserted can be judicially molded. In the instance of lack of jurisdiction the cause either does not "arise under" the Federal Constitution, laws or treaties (or fall within one of the other enumerated categories of Art. III. Sec. 2), or is not a "case or controversy" within the meaning of that section; or the cause is not one described by any jurisdictional statute. Our conclusion . . . that this cause presents no nonjusticiable "political question" settles the only possible doubt that it is a case or controversy. . . . We hold . . . that the matter set forth in the complaint does arise under the Constitution. . . .

In holding that the subject matter of this suit was not justiciable, the District Court relied on *Colegrove v. Green* . . . and subsequent . . . cases . . . We understand the District Court to have read the cited cases as compelling the conclusion that since the appellants sought to have a legislative apportionment held unconstitutional, their suit presented a "political question" and was therefore nonjusticiable. We hold that this challenge to an apportionment presents no nonjusticiable "political question." The cited cases do not hold the contrary.

Of course the mere fact that the suit seeks protection of a political right does not mean it presents a political question. Such an objection "is little more than a play upon words." . . . Rather, it is argued that apportionment cases, whatever the actual wording of the complaint, can involve no federal constitutional right except one resting on the guaranty of a republican form of government, and that complaints based on that clause have been held to present political questions which are nonjusticiable.

We hold that the claim pleaded here neither rests upon nor implicates the Guaranty Clause and that its justiciability is therefore not foreclosed by our decisions of cases involving that clause. The District Court misinterpreted *Colegrove v. Green* and other decisions of this Court on which it relied. Appellants' claim that they are being denied equal protection is justiciable, and if "discrimination is sufficiently shown, the right to relief under the equal protection clause is not diminished by the fact that the discrimination relates to political rights." *Snowden v. Hughes*. . . . To show why we reject the argument based on the Guaranty Clause . . . we deem it necessary first to consider the contours of the "political question" doctrines.

Our discussion . . . requires review of a number of political question cases, in order to expose the attributes of the doctrine. . . . That review reveals that in the Guaranty Clause cases and in the other "political question" cases, it is the relationship between the judiciary and the coordinate branches of the Federal Government, and not the federal judiciary's relationship to the States, which gives rise to the "political question." . . .

The nonjusticiability of a political question is primarily a function of the separation of powers. . . . Prominent on the surface of any case held to involve a political question is found a textually demonstrable constitutional commitment of the issue to a coordinate political department; or a lack of judicially discoverable and manageable standards for resolving it; or the impossibility of deciding without an initial policy determination of a kind clearly for nonjudicial discretion; or the impossibility of a court's undertaking independent resolution without expressing lack of the respect due coordinate branches of government; or an unusual need for unquestioning adherence to a political decision already made; or the potentiality of embarrassment from multifarious pronouncements by various departments on one question.

Unless one of these formulations is inextricable from the case at bar, there should be no dismissal for nonjusticiability on the ground of a political question's presence. The doctrine of which we treat is one of "political questions," not one of "political cases." The courts cannot reject as "no law suit" a bona fide controversy as to whether some action denominated "political" exceeds constitutional authority. . . .

But it is argued that this case shares the characteristics of decisions that constitute a category not yet considered, cases concerning the Constitution's guaranty, in Art. IV, Sec. 4, of a republican form of government. . . . [There follows a discussion of *Luther v. Borden* and other cases in which the republican form of government provision was ruled judicially unenforceable.]

We come, finally, to the ultimate inquiry whether our precedents as to what constitutes a nonjusticiable "political question" bring the case before us under the umbrella of that doctrine. A natural beginning is to note whether any of the common characteristics which we have been able to identity and label descriptively are present. We find none. The question here is the consistency of state action with the Federal Constitution. We have no question decided, or to be decided by a political branch of government coequal with this Court. Nor do we risk embarrassment of our government abroad, or grave disturbance at home if we take issue with Tennessee as to the constitutionality of her action here challenged. Nor need the appellants, in order to succeed in this action, ask the Court to enter upon policy determinations for which judicially manageable standards are lacking. Judicial standards under the Equal Protection Clause are well developed and familiar, and it has been open to courts since the enactment of the Fourteenth Amendment to determine, if on the particular facts they must, that a discrimination reflects *no* policy, but simply arbitrary and capricious action. . . .

We conclude that the nonjusticiability of claims resting on the Guaranty Clause which arises from their embodiment of questions that were thought "political," can have no bearing upon the justiciability of the equal protection claim presented in this case. . . . We emphasize that it is the involvement in Guaranty Clause claims of the elements thought to define "political questions," and no other feature, which could render them nonjusticiable. Specifically, we have said that such claims are not held nonjusticiable because they touch matters of state governmental organization. . . . Only last Term, in *Gomillion v. Lightfoot* . . . we applied the Fifteenth Amendment to strike down a redrafting of municipal boundaries which effected a discriminatory impairment of voting rights, in the face of what a majority of the Court of Appeals thought to be a sweeping commitment to state legislatures of the power to draw and redraw such boundaries. . . .

We conclude that the complaint's allegations of a denial of equal protection present a justiciable constitutional cause of action upon which appellants are entitled to a trial and a decision. The right asserted is within the reach of judicial protection under the Fourteenth Amendment.

The judgment of the District Court is reversed and the cause is remanded for further proceedings consistent with this opinion.

292. *"Legislators represent people, not trees or acres."*

Reynolds v. Sims, 377 U.S. 533 (1964).

WARREN, C.J.: . . . A predominant consideration in determining whether a State's legislative apportionment scheme constitutes an invidious discrimination violative of rights asserted under the Equal Protection Clause is that the rights allegedly impaired are individual and personal in nature. . . .

Legislators represent people, not trees or acres. Legislators are elected by voters, not farms or cities or economic interests. As long as ours is a representative form of government, and our legislatures are those instruments of government elected directly by and directly representative of the people, the right to elect legislators in a free and unimpaired fashion is a bedrock of our political system. . . . Weighing the votes of citizens differently, by any method or means, merely because of where they happen to reside, hardly seems justifiable. One must be ever aware that the Constitution forbids "sophisticated as well as simple-minded modes of discrimination" *Lane v. Wilson.*

. . . . As we stated in *Wesberry v. Sanders:*

> We do not believe that the Framers of the Constitution intended to permit the same vote-diluting discrimination to be accomplished through the device of districts containing widely varied numbers of inhabitants. To say that a vote is worth more in one district than in another would . . . run counter to our fundamental ideas of democratic government.

Logically, in a society ostensibly grounded on representative government, it would seem reasonable that a majority of the people of a State could elect a majority of that State's legislators. To conclude differently, and to sanction minority control of state legislative bodies, would appear to deny majority rights in a way that far surpasses any possible denial of minority rights that might otherwise be thought to result. Since legislatures are responsible for enacting laws by which all citizens are to be governed, they should be bodies which are collectively responsive to the popular will. . . . Our constitutional system amply provides for the protection of minorities by means other than giving them majority control of state legislatures. And the democratic ideas of equality and majority rule, which have served this Nation so well in the past, are hardly of any less significance for the present and the future. . . . Population is, of necessity, the starting point for consideration and the controlling criterion for judgment in legislative apportionment controversies. A citizen, a qualified voter, is no more nor no less so because he lives in the city or on the farm. This is the clear and strong command of our Constitution's Equal Protection Clause. This is an essential part of the concept of a government of laws and not men. This is at the heart of Lincoln's vision of "government of the people, by the people, [and] for the people." The Equal Protection Clause demands no less than substantially equal state legislative representation for all citizens, of all places as well as of all races. . . .

Much has been written since our decision in *Baker v. Carr* about the applicability of the so-called federal analogy to state legislative apportionment arrangements. After considering the matter, the court below concluded that no conceivable analogy could be drawn between the federal scheme and the apportionment of seats in the Alabama Legislature under the proposed constitutional amendment. We agree with the District Court, and find the federal analogy inapposite and irrelevant to state legislative districting schemes. Attempted reliance on the federal analogy appears often to be little more than after-the-fact rationalization offered in defense of maladjusted state apportionment arrangements. . . .

Political subdivisions of States—counties, cities or whatever—never were and never have been considered as sovereign entities. Rather, they have been traditionally regarded as subordinate governmental instrumentalities created by the State to assist in the carrying out of state governmental functions. As stated by the Court in *Hunter v. City of Pittsburgh*. . . . these governmental units are "created as convenient agencies for exercising such of the governmental powers of the State as may be entrusted to them," and the "number, nature and duration of the powers conferred upon [them] . . . and the territory over which they shall be exercised rests in the absolute discretion of the State." The relationship of the States to the Federal Government could hardly be less analogous. . . .

Since we find the so-called federal analogy inapposite to a consideration of the constitutional validity of state legislative apportionment schemes, we necessarily hold that the Equal Protection Clause requires both houses of a state legislature to be apportioned on a population basis. The right of a citizen to equal representation and to have his vote weighted equally with those of all other citizens in the election of members of one house of a bicameral state legislature would amount to little if States could effectively submerge the equal-population principle in the apportionment of seats in the other house. If such a scheme were permissible, an individual citizen's ability to exercise an effective voice in the only instrument of state government directly representative of the people might be almost as effectively thwarted as if neither house were apportioned on a population basis. Deadlock between the two bodies might result in compromise and concession on some issues. But in all too many cases the more probable result would be frustration of the majority will through minority veto in the house not apportioned on a population basis. . . .

By holding that as a federal constitutional requisite both houses of a state legislature must be apportioned on a population basis, we mean that the Equal Protection Clause requires that a State make an honest and good faith effort to construct districts, in both houses of its legislature, as nearly of equal population as is practicable. We realize that it is a practical impossibility to arrange legislative districts so that each one has an identical number of residents, or citizens, or voters. Mathematical exactness or precision is hardly a workable constitutional requirement. . . . Somewhat more flexibility may therefore be constitutionally permissible with respect to state legislative apportionment than in congressional districting. Lower courts can and assuredly will work out more concrete and specific standards for evaluating state legislative apportionment schemes in the context of actual litigation. For the present, we deem it expedient not to attempt to spell out any precise constitutional tests. What is marginally permissible in one State may be unsatisfactory in another, depending on the particular circumstances of the case. Developing a body of doctrine on a case-by-case basis appears to us to provide the most satisfactory means of arriving at detailed constitutional requirements in the area of state legislative apportionment. . . .

That the Equal Protection Clause requires that both houses of a state legislature be apportioned on a population basis does not mean that States cannot adopt some reasonable plan for periodic revision of their apportionment schemes. Decennial reapportionment appears to be a rational approach to readjustment of legislative representation in order to take into account population shifts and growth. . . . While we do not intend to indicate that decennial reapportionment is a constitutional requisite, compliance with such an approach would clearly meet the minimal requirements for maintaining a reasonably current scheme of legislative representation. And we do not mean to intimate that more frequent reapportionment would not be constitutionally permissible or practicably desirable. But if reapportionment were accomplished with less frequency, it would assuredly be constitutionally suspect. . . .

Broadening the Franchise Through Amendment

293. *Home Rule and the Poll Tax*

A. THE TWENTY-THIRD AMENDMENT: THE FRANCHISE IN THE DISTRICT OF COLUMBIA

Proposed June 16, 1960; adopted March 29, 1961.

SECTION 1. The District constituting the seat of Government of the United States shall appoint in such manner as the Congress may direct:

A number of electors of President and Vice President equal to the whole number of Senators and Representatives in Congress to which the District would be entitled if it were a State, but in no event more than the least populous State; they shall be in addition to those appointed by the States, but they shall be considered, for the purposes of the election of President and Vice President, to be electors appointed by a State; and they shall meet in the District and perform such duties as provided by the twelfth article of amendment.

SECTION 2. The Congress shall have power to enforce this article by appropriate legislation.

B. THE TWENTY-FOURTH AMENDMENT: THE POLL TAX IN NATIONAL ELECTIONS

Proposed March 28, 1962; adopted January 24, 1964.

SECTION 1. The right of citizens of the United States to vote in any primary or other election for President or Vice President, for electors for President or Vice President, or for Senator or Representative in Congress, shall not be denied or abridged by the United States or any State by reason of failure to pay any poll tax or other tax.

SECTION 2. The Congress shall have power to enforce this article by appropriate legislation.

294. *"Congress has full remedial powers to effectuate the constitutional prohibition against racial discrimination in voting."*

South Carolina v. Katzenbach, 383 U.S. 301 (1966).

WARREN, C.J.: . . . The Voting Rights Act of 1965 reflects Congress' firm intention to rid the country of racial discrimination in voting. The heart of the Act is a complex scheme of stringent remedies aimed at areas where voting discrimination has been most flagrant. Section 4 (a)—(d) lays down a formula defining the States and political subdivisions to which these new remedies apply. The first of the remedies, contained in §4 (a), is the suspension of literacy tests and similar voting qualifications for a period of five years from the last occurrence of substantial voting discrimination. Section 5 prescribes a second remedy, the suspension of all new voting regulations pending review by federal authorities to determine whether their use would perpetuate voting discrimination. The third remedy, covered in §§6 (b), 7, 9, and 13 (a), is the assignment of federal examiners by the Attorney General to list qualified applicants who are thereafter entitled to vote in all elections.

Other provisions of the Act prescribe subsidiary cures for persistent voting discrimination. Section 8 authorizes the appointment of federal poll-watchers in places to which federal examiners have already been assigned. Section 10 (d) excuses those made eligible to vote in sections of the country covered by §4 (b) of the Act from paying accumulated past poll taxes for state and local elections. Section 12 (e) provides for balloting by persons denied access to the polls in areas where federal examiners have been appointed.

The remaining remedial portions of the Act are aimed at voting discrimination in any area of the country where it may occur. Section 2 broadly prohibits the use of voting rules to abridge exercise of the franchise on racial grounds. Sections 3, 6 (a), and 13 (b) strengthen existing procedures for attacking voting discrimination by means of litigation. Section 4 (e) excuses citizens educated in American schools conducted in a foreign language from passing English-language literacy tests. Section 10 (a)—(c) facilitates constitutional litigation challenging the imposition of all poll taxes for state and local elections. Sections 11 and 12 (a)—(d) authorize civil and criminal sanctions against interference with the exercise of rights guaranteed by the Act.

At the outset, we emphasize that only some of the many portions of the Act are properly before us. . . . These provisions of the Voting Rights Act of 1965 are challenged on the fundamental ground that they exceed the powers of Congress and encroach on an area reserved to the States by the Constitution. . . . The ground rules for resolving this question are clear. The language and purpose of the Fifteenth Amendment, the prior decisions construing its several provisions, and the general doctrines of constitutional interpretation all point to one fundamental principle. As against the reserved powers of the States, Congress may use any rational means to effectuate the constitutional prohibition of racial discrimination in voting. . . .

Section 1 of the Fifteenth Amendment . . . has always been treated as self-executing and has repeatedly been construed, without further legislative specification, to invalidate state voting qualifications or procedures which are discriminatory on their face or in fact or in practice. . . . These decisions have been rendered with full respect for the general rule . . . that States "have broad powers to determine the conditions under which the right of suffrage may be exercised." The gist of the matter is that the Fifteenth Amendment supersedes contrary exertions of state power. "When a State exercises power wholly within the domain of state interest, it is insulated from federal judicial review. But such insulation is not carried over when state power is used as an instrument for circumventing a federally protected right." (*Gomillion v. Lightfoot*). . . .

South Carolina contends that the cases cited above are precedents only for the authority of the judiciary to strike down state statutes and procedures—that to allow an exercise of this authority by Congress would be to rob the courts of their rightful constitutional role. On the contrary, Sec. 2 of the Fifteenth Amendment expressly declares that "Congress shall have the power to enforce this article by appropriate legislation." . . . [Thus] Congress has full remedial powers to effectuate the constitutional prohibition against racial discrimination in voting.

Congress has repeatedly exercised these powers in the past, and its enactments have repeatedly been upheld. For recent examples, see the Civil Rights Act of 1957 [and 1960] . . . [Congress] exercised its authority under the Fifteenth Amendment in an inventive manner when it enacted the Voting Rights Act of 1965. First: The measure prescribes remedies for voting discrimination which go into effect without any need for prior adjudication. This was clearly a legitimate response to the problem. . . . Congress had found that case-by-case litigation was inadequate to combat widespread and persistent discrimination in voting, because of the inordinate amount of time and energy required to overcome the obstructionist tactics invariably encountered in these lawsuits. After enduring nearly a century of systematic resistance to the Fifteenth Amendment, Congress might well decide to shift the advantage of time and inertia from the perpetrators of the evil to its victims. The question remains, of course, whether the specific remedies prescribed in the Act were an appropriate means of combatting the evil, and to this question we shall presently address ourselves.

Second: The Act intentionally confines these remedies to a small number of States and political subdivisions which in most instances were familiar to Congress by name. This, too, was a permissible method of dealing with the problem. Congress had learned that substantial voting discrimination presently occurs in certain sections of the country, and it knew no way of accurately forecasting whether the evil might spread elsewhere in the future. In acceptable legislative fashion, Congress chose to limit its attention to the geographic areas where immediate action seemed necessary. . . . The doctrine of the equality of States, invoked by South Carolina, does not bar this approach, for that doctrine applies only to the terms upon which States are admitted to the Union, and not to the remedies for local evils which have subsequently appeared. . . .

The areas . . . for which there was evidence of actual voting discrimination share two characteristics incorporated by Congress into the coverage formula: the use of tests and devices for voter registration, and a voting rate in the 1964 presidential election at least 12 points below the national average. Tests and devices are relevant to voting discrimination because of their long history as a tool for perpetrating the evil; a low voting rate is pertinent for the obvious reason that widespread disenfranchisement must inevitably affect the number of actual voters. Accordingly, the coverage formula is rational in both practice and theory. . . .

We now arrive at consideration of the specific remedies prescribed by the Act for areas included within the coverage formula. South Carolina assails the temporary suspension of existing voting qualifications, reciting the rule laid down by *Lassiter v. Northampton County Bd. of Elections* . . . that literacy tests and related devices are not in themselves contrary to the Fifteenth Amendment. In that very case, however, the Court went on to say, "Of course a literacy test, fair on its face, may be employed to perpetuate that discrimination which the Fifteenth Amendment was designed to uproot." . . . The record shows that in most of the States covered by the Act, including South Carolina, various tests and devices have been instituted with the purpose of disenfranchising Negroes, have been framed in such a way as to facilitate this aim, and have been administered in a discriminatory fashion for many years. Under these circumstances, the Fifteenth Amendment has clearly been violated.

The Act suspends literacy tests and similar devices for a period of five years from the last occurrence of substantial voting discrimination. This was a legitimate response to the problem, for which there is ample precedent in Fifteenth Amendment cases. . . . Underlying the response was the feeling that States and political subdivisions which had been allowing white illiterates to vote for years could not sincerely complain about "dilution" of their electorates through the registration of Negro illiterates. Congress knew that continuance of the tests and devices in use at the present time, no matter how fairly administered in the future, would freeze the effect of past discrimination in favor of unqualified white registrants. Congress permissibly rejected the alternative of requiring a complete re-registration of all voters, believing that this would be too harsh on many whites who had enjoyed the franchise for their entire adult lives.

The Act suspends new voting regulations pending scrutiny by federal authorities to determine whether their use would violate the Fifteenth Amendment. This may have been an uncommon exercise of congressional power, as South Carolina contends, but the Court has recognized that exceptional conditions can justify legislative measures not otherwise appropriate. . . . Congress knew that some of the States covered by Sec. 4 (b) of the Act had resorted to the extraordinary strategem of contriving new rules of various kinds for the sole purpose of perpetuating voting discrimination in the face of adverse federal decrees. Congress had reason to suppose that these States might try similar maneuvers in the future, in order to evade the remedies for voting discrimination contained in the Act itself. Under the compulsion of these unique circumstances, Congress responded in a permissibly decisive manner. . . .

The Act authorizes the appointment of federal examiners to list qualified applicants who are thereafter entitled to vote, subject to an expeditious challenge procedure. This was clearly an appropriate response to the problem, closely related to remedies authorized in prior cases. In many of the political subdivisions covered by §4 (b) of the Act, voting officials have persistently employed a variety of procedural tactics to deny Negroes the franchise, often in direct defiance or evasion of federal decrees. Congress realized that merely to suspend voting rules which have been misused or are subject to misuse might leave this localized evil undisturbed. As for the briskness of the challenge procedure, Congress knew that in some of the areas affected, challenges had been persistently employed to harass registered Negroes. It chose to forestall this abuse, at the same time providing alternative ways for removing persons listed through error or fraud. . . .

In recognition of the fact that there were political subdivisions covered by §4 (b) of the Act in which the appointment of federal examiners might be unnecessary, Congress assigned the Attorney General the task of determining the localities to which examiners should be sent. There is no warrant for the claim, asserted by Georgia as *amicus curiae*, that the Attorney General is free to use this power in an arbitrary fashion, without regard for the purposes of the Act. Section 6 (b) sets adequate standards to guide the exercise of his discretion, by directing him to calculate the registration ratio of non-whites to whites, and to weigh evidence of good-faith efforts to avoid possible voting discrimination. At the same time, the special termination procedures of §13 (a) provide indirect judicial review for the political subdivisions affected, assuring the withdrawal of federal examiners from areas where they are clearly not needed. . . .

After enduring nearly a century of widespread resistance to the Fifteenth Amendment, Congress has marshalled an array of potent weapons against the evil, with authority in the Attorney General to employ them effectively. Many of the areas directly affected by this development have indicated their willingness to abide by any restraints legitimately imposed upon them. We here hold that the portions of the Voting Rights Act properly before us are a valid means for carrying out the commands of the Fifteenth Amendment. Hopefully, millions of non-white Americans will now be able to participate for the first time on an equal basis in the government under which they live. We may finally look forward to the day when truly "the right of citizens of the United States to vote shall not be denied or abridged by the United States or by any State on account of race, color, or previous condition of servitude."

Epilogue

Liberty Under Law

Editorial on the occasion of the first meeting of the Supreme Court under Chief Justice Earl Warren, *New York Times,* October 5, 1953.

LIBERTY under the law is one of the noblest of human concepts. But how much liberty and how much law?

If nine men, or five men out of nine, had to give the final answer, we could well despair, just as we might well despair if the perpetuation of this republic depended on the election or re-election every four years of a supreme genius as President. But the nine men, however detached, however scrupulously impartial, are part of the world in which they live and move. We do not vote for them or against them, and would not want to, but all honest thought has some influence upon them. They are, at their best, America thinking, just as the President, a general, a manufacturer, a labor leader, a professional man, may be America acting. We may well feel a sense of reverence as the Court walks in—not solely for nine men brought to this place in part by chance as well as by achievement and ability, but for the function they perform. They are a substitute for force—the best yet invented.

The Court resumes. When its entrance is announced we can arise with alacrity, for here in this room, where orders are sometimes given that no other power can contravene, is a symbol of our civilization and our freedom.